SOFTSTAT '89

SOFTSTAT '89

Fortschritte der Statistik-Software 2

5. Konferenz über die wissenschaftliche Anwendung
von Statistik-Software, Heidelberg, 1989

Herausgegeben von
F. Faulbaum, R. Haux und K.-H. Jöckel

169 Abbildungen, 62 Tabellen

Gustav Fischer Verlag · Stuttgart · New York · 1990

Anschriften der Herausgeber:

Dr. Frank Faulbaum
Zentrum für Umfragen, Methoden
und Analysen (ZUMA) e.V.
Postfach 12 21 55, D-6800 Mannheim 1

Prof. Dr. Reinhold Haux
Universität Heidelberg
Institut für Medizinische Biometrie und
Medizinische Informatik
Im Neuenheimer Feld 400, D-6900 Heidelberg 1

PD Dr. rer. nat. Karl-Heinz Jöckel
Bremer Institut für Präventionsforschung
und Sozialmedizin (BIPS)
St.-Jürgen-Straße 1, D-2800 Bremen 1

CIP-Titelaufnahme der Deutschen Bibliothek

Fortschritte der Statistik-Software 2 / SOFTSTAT '89, 5.
Konferenz über d. Wiss. Anwendung von Statistik-Software,
Heidelberg, 1989. Hrsg. von F. Faulbaum ... – Stuttgart ; New
York : Fischer, 1990
   ISBN 3-437-50335-9
NE: Faulbaum, Frank [Hrsg.]; SOFTSTAT <05, 1989, Heidelberg>

© Gustav Fischer Verlag · Stuttgart · New York ·1990
Wollgrasweg 49, D-7000 Stuttgart 70 (Hohenheim)
Das Werk einschließlich aller seiner Teile ist urheberrechtlich geschützt. Jeder Verwertung außerhalb der engen Grenzen des Urheberrechtsgesetzes ist ohne Zustimmung des Verlags unzulässig und strafbar. Das gilt insbesondere für Vervielfältigungen, Übersetzungen, Mikroverfilmungen und die Einspeicherung und Verarbeitung in elektronischen Systemen.
Druck: Gulde-Druck GmbH, 7400 Tübingen
Einband: Heinrich Koch KG, 7400 Tübingen
Printed in Germany

Vorwort

Die 5. Konferenz über die wissenschaftliche Anwendung von Statistik-Software (SoftStat '89) fand vom 2. - 6. April 1989 wiederum in den Veranstaltungsräumen des Unterrichtsbereichs Medizin und des Hörsaalgebäudes Physik der Universität Heidelberg statt. Sie wurde organisiert durch das Zentrum für Umfragen, Methoden und Analysen (ZUMA) in Zusammenarbeit mit der Arbeitsgruppe "Statistische Auswertungssysteme" der Deutschen Gesellschaft für Medizinische Dokumentation, Informatik und Statistik (GMDS) sowie der Arbeitsgruppe "Computational Statistics" der Deutschen Region der Internationalen Biometrischen Gesellschaft. Die Tagung wurde von ca. 650 Teilnehmern aus dem In- und Ausland besucht, was eine weitere Steigerung der Teilnehmerzahl gegenüber der 4. Konferenz bedeutet. Neben über 100 Vorträgen gab es 32 Softwaredemonstrationen. Die Konferenz wurde von einer Ausstellung begleitet, an der sich 20 namhafte Software-Firmen beteiligten.

Die SoftStat-Konferenzen befassen sich mit dem Einsatz und der Untersuchung von Methoden und Werkzeugen der Informatik für die Statistik, insbesondere mit der Anwendung und mit dem Vergleich von statistischen Auswertungssystemen.

Neben den Schwerpunktthemen der letzten Konferenz, wie "Statistik-Programme in Datenmanagement und Datenanalyse", "Individuelle Modellierung mit Statistik-Software", "Exploratorische Datenanalyse", "Simulation", "Kartographie und Geographische Informationssysteme", "Statistik und linguistische Datenverarbeitung" sowie "Statistik und Datenerhebung" traten als neue Themenbereiche "Einsatz von Graphik-Software in der Statistik" (Schwerpunkt Präsentationsgraphik), "Rechnernetze und Datenfernverarbeitung in der statistischen Datenanalyse", "Statistische Auswertungssysteme für die Verarbeitung von Massendaten" sowie "Statistikausbildung und Statistik-Software" hinzu. Der zuletzt genannte Bereich zog besonders viele Referenten an, was wohl vornehmlich auf die anhaltende Zunahme des PC-Einsatzes in der Statistik-Ausbildung zurückzuführen ist.

Die in diesem Band vereinigten Beiträge wurden im Rahmen eines Begutachtungsverfahrens, das pro Beitrag zwei unabhängige Gutachter vorsah, akzeptiert. Einige Beiträge betreffen Produktvorstellungen von Mitarbeitern kommerzieller Hersteller oder von Wissenschaftlern, die das von ihnen entwickelte Produkt auch kommerziell vertreiben. Diese Beiträge sind durch den Buchstaben "H" im Inhaltsverzeichnis besonders gekennzeichnet.

Die Herausgeber, der Tagungsleiter und die Leiter der Arbeitsgruppen der beteiligten Fachgesellschaften möchten sich an dieser Stelle bei allen Mitgliedern des Programmausschusses für ihre Mitarbeit an der wissenschaftlichen und organisatorischen Gestaltung der Konferenz bedanken. Dem Programmausschuß gehörten diesmal neben den Herausgebern die folgenden Mitglieder an: Carol Cassidy (ZUMA), Allmut Hörmann (GSF München), Ulrich Küsters (Scientific Center IBM, Pisa), Walter Lehmacher (GSF München), Peter Ph. Mohler (ZUMA), Heiner Ritter (ZUMA), Elisabeth Schach (Universität Dortmund), Klaus G. Troitzsch (EWH Rheinland-Pfalz) und H.-M. Uehlinger (Hochschule St. Gallen). Auch den Mitgliedern des zur reibungslosen Abwicklung der Konferenz ZUMA-intern gebildeten Koordinationsausschusses, dem neben den ZUMA-Mitgliedern des Programmausschusses auch die Herren Volker Neureither (ZUMA) und Frowin Gensch (ZUMA) angehörten, gilt unser Dank.

Zur Sicherung des Qualitätsniveaus der Konferenz trugen ferner eine Reihe von Wissenschaftlern bei, die bei der Zusammenstellung von Arbeitsgruppen und bei der Einwerbung von Beiträgen trotz ihrer kostbaren Zeit mit großem Engagement mitgearbeitet haben. Hier sind an erster Stelle die Herren Volker Kreibich und Siegfried Schach (beide Universität Dortmund) sowie Günther Sawitzki (Universität Heidelberg) zu nennen, denen wir ebenfalls zu besonderem Dank verpflichtet sind.

Die Durchführung einer großen Konferenz ist nicht denkbar ohne den engagierten Einsatz vieler weiterer Mitarbeiter, die an dieser Stelle leider nicht einzeln erwähnt werden können und denen wir sehr herzlich für ihre Bereitschaft zur Mitwirkung an der Konferenzorganisation zu danken haben. Besonders erwähnt werden muß jedoch die besondere Einsatzbereitschaft unserer Konferenzsekretärin, Frau Lisbeth Koch.

Unser abschließender Dank gilt Herrn Dr. W. Scholz und Herrn Dipl.-Phys. H. Bernot vom Theoretikum der Universität Heidelberg, die zusammen mit ihren Mitarbeitern die Voraussetzungen für einen reibungslosen Ablauf der Konferenz in Heidelberg geschaffen haben.

Im März 1990

Frank Faulbaum
Reinhold Haux
Karl-Heinz Jöckel

Inhaltsverzeichnis

Eröffnungsreferat

I.W. Molenaar
Producing, Purchasing and Evaluating Statistical Scientific Software:
Intellectual and Commercial Challenges — 3

Statistische Auswertungssysteme für Datenverwaltung und Datenanalyse

Ch. Alt, D. Bender, W. Bien und E. Lorenz
Informationssystem - Eine komplexe Struktur von Datenbanken,
Dokumentationen und Schnittstellen — 13

G. Arminger und R.J. Schoenberg
LINCS - A Program für Linear Mean and Covariance Structure Analysis (H) — 21

E. Aufhauser
Discrete Response Models: Some Comments on Statistical Software — 31

H. Becher und M. Blettner
Comparison of Some Software Packages for the Analysis of Cohort Studies — 39

Bentler, P.M.
EQS Version 3: New Statistics and Computations (H) — 47

B. Dose und W. Holtbrügge
Data Management mit CLINTRIAL bei klinischen Prüfungen — 57

K. Fehres und F. Marschall
Verfahren und Probleme bei der Analyse von Meßwiederholungsdesigns
mit SPSS-X, MANOVA und BMDP4V — 66

W.M. Hartmann
Proc CALIS: Analysis of Covariance Structures (H) — 74

M. Herold
New SAS Facilities for Design of Experiments compared to RS/1 and
STATGRAPHICS — 82

M.A. Hill
A Graphical Study of Health, Economic, and Military Data from Ten Dozen
Countries — 90

K.G. Jöreskog
New Developments in LISREL (H) — 100

R. Kosfeld
Möglichkeiten und Probleme einer Zeitreihenanalyse und Prognose
mit Micro TSP   108

P. Kremser
Statistik auf dem Macintosh   121

U. Küsters und A. Schepers
LISCOMP - A Program to Analyze Linear Structural Equations with
Non-metric Indicators   126

S. Mustonen
SURVO 84C - General Environment for Statistical Computing (H)   136

T. Rudas
DISTAN for Discrete Statistical Analysis   144

O. Schechtner und K. Zelle
Statistical-Prospective Information Systems (STAPIS): Integrated
Management of Statistical and Prospective Data, Methods and Models   155

E.J. Zimmermann
Daten- und Dateimanagement in P-STAT (H)   165

Individuelle Modellierung mit Statistik-Software

L. Knüsel
Numerische Berechnung von elementaren statistischen Verteilungen   177

H.-P. Altenburg und G. Rosenkranz
Analysis of Dose Response Data with SAS   183

H.-J. Andreß
Econometric Models for Event Count Data   191

B. Engel
Individuelle Programmierung in SPSS^X: The USERCODE-Facility   199

A. Eymann und M. Kukuk
Computerprogramme für Discrete Choice-Modelle in GAUSS und SAS/IML   204

L. Fahrmeir, H. Frost, W. Hennevogl, H. Kaufmann (†) und T. Kranert
GLAMOUR: Analysis of Cross-sectional and Longitudinal Data
with Generalized Linear Models (H)   212

S. Gabler
SuSa - Ein GAUSS Programm zur Stichprobentheorie   220

M.G. Schimek
Non-Parametric Spline Regression by BATHSPLINE: Foundations
and Application   224

Graphik und Explorative Datenanalyse

G. Sawitzki
Tools and Concepts in Data Analysis   237

G. Held und A. Lehmann
Advances in Graphical Data Analysis from SAS Institute (H)   249

M. Korn und A. Lamers
STATGRAPHICS (H)   259

M. Nagel
Graphische Methoden der Datenanalyse: Exploration, Analyse und Präsentation   270

G. Wills, A. Unwin, J. Haslett und P. Craig
Dynamic Interactive Graphics for Spatially Referenced Data   278

Expertensysteme in der Statistik

P. Naeve
Is there Something New that Can Be Learned or Solved by Building
Statistical Expert Systems?   291

J. Boucelham
Encompassing: "The Right Track in Building Statistical Expert Systems?"   300

K.A. Fröschl
Automated Protocolling of Statistical Data Analyses   308

W. Klösgen
The Integration of Knowledge-Based and Statistical Methods in a
Statistics Interpreter   316

C.M. O'Brien
A Knowledge-Base for Generalized Linear Modelling (H)   324

D. Rasch, V. Guiard und G. Nürnberg
Present and Planned Future of the Expert System CADEMO (H)   332

Kartographie und geographische Informationssysteme

V. Kreibich
Desktop Kartographie?   343

J.H.P. Hoffmeyer-Zlotnik und H. Ritter
Erstellung von Regionalkarten für MAP-MASTER und Analyse
regionalisierter Umfragedaten mit SPSS/PC+   351

P. Ludäscher
Geographisches Informationssystem und Computerkartographie   359

M. Tettweiler
KARIN2 - Redesign eines erfolgreichen Kartographieprogramms auf
der Basis des geographischen Informationssystems ARC/INFO (H)   365

Statistik und Datenerhebung

E. Schach
Aspekte der Datenqualität bei computerunterstützten Interviews   375

B. Engel und S. Becker
CATI in der Medienforschung   386

H.-J. Hippler, F. Meier und N. Schwarz
Praktische Einsatzmöglichkeiten eines interaktiven Befragungs- und
Instruktionssystems bei Experimenten und in Umfragen   397

F. Meier
Rechnergestützte Untersuchungen in der humanpharmakologischen
Forschung (H)   405

Simulation

M. Möhring
Concepts of Simulation Languages   417

A. Flache und V. Schmidt
IPMOS - Ein Softwarewerkzeug zur Mikromodellierung und Simulation
interagierender Populationen   426

O. Hellwig
Current Status and Developments in Microsimulation Software   434

S. Karczewski
PES - A Modular Gaming Simulation Development System with Functional
and Relational Aspects   442

W. Tettweiler
MAPLIS - die matrixorientierte interaktive Simulation für die
Sozialwissenschaften (H)   451

Skalierung und Klassifikation

H. Giegler und J. Rost
Ordinale manifeste Variablen - Nominale latente Variablen -
Latent Class Analyse für ordinale Daten (H)   461

M.C.J. Lina und R. Popping
The Computer Program AGREE For Nominal Scale Agreement (H)   471

Statistik und linguistische Datenverarbeitung

R. Glas
Sprachverarbeitung mit AWK 479

H. Klein
New Possibilities and Developments of Text Analysis with INTEXT/PC 487

U. Kuckartz
Computerunterstützte Suche nach Typologien in qualitativen Interviews 495

R. Mathes und A. Geis
The Classificatory-Hermeneutic Content-Analysis of Guided Interviews
with TEXTPACK 503

E. Mergenthaler und D. Pokorny
Die Wortartenverteilung - Eine linguo-statistische Textanalyse 512

Verarbeitung großer Datenbestände mit statistischen Auswertungssystemen

J. Oldervoll
Analyzing Large Censuses 525

R. Buhler
Data Base Capabilities within a Statistical Package or Why P-RADE? (H) 530

J. Wackerow
Verarbeitung von Dateien mit sehr großen Fallzahlen 534

G.A. Wicke
Die Verkehrsdatenbank des Bundesministers für Verkehr -
Beispiel einer objektorientierten statistischen Datenbank 542

Statistik-Ausbildung und Statistik-Software

A.W. Bowman und D.R. Robinson
Teaching Statistics: Microcomputer Graphics and Computer Illustrated Texts 555

F. Eicker
Beschreibende und exploratorische Statistik mit EDV-Unterstützung 559

L. Afflerbach
Statistik-Praktikum mit dem IBM PC 567

R. Biehler und W. Rach
Software Tools for Statistical Data Analysis in Education and
Teacher Training? 575

F. Böker
On the Statistical Package GSTAT 584

W.-D. Heller und R. Rupprecht
Erfahrungen im Einsatz von Statistiksoftware in der Statistikausbildung   592

J. Kübler
Software-Ausbildung am Fachbereich Statistik der Universität Dortmund   600

T. Marøy
The Concept of Teaching Packages   608

R. Wittenberg
Der Einsatz von Statistik-Software in der einführenden Methodenausbildung   615

M. Zaus
Teaching Computational Statistics in APL   623

Rechnernetze in der Statistik

Lenz
Die Workstation des Statistikers in den 90er Jahren   633

Adressen   641

Eröffnungsreferat

Producing, Purchasing and Evaluating Statistical Scientific Software: Intellectual and Commercial Challenges

I. W. Molenaar

Summary

The rapid growth of data analysis by non-experts has aggravated the problem that the scientific community lacks a suitable system for assessing and controlling the quality of statistical software. This paper argues that our system of rewards and punishments should be modified in order to devote more attention to accomplishment of software reviewing tasks. The analogy with the review and distribution process of scientific books and papers on one hand, and durable goods like cars and household electronics on the other hand, is used to study the mechanisms of quality control and to propose some points of action that could help to achieve a more satisfactory situation.

1. INTRODUCTION

The roots of this paper lie in a quote from Victor (1985, p.114) : "The evaluation of existing software represents a challenge for the computer statistician. Unfortunately, a large part of existing statistical software must be described as deficient. One of the main targets for the future must be to provide information about the quality of available software and thereby, protect the user.(...). General methods to measure the quality of statistical software are still missing."

The quote comes from talks presented by Victor five years ago, but progress in improving the situation has been remarkably slow. This has led me to the following reflections about the processes by which software is produced, purchased and evaluated. It will be argued that there are deficiencies in the system of rewards and punishments, both financial and immaterial ones, used by our society to regulate the distribution process.

Section 2 distinguishes some aspects of software quality (throughout this paper, "software" must be read as "statistical scientific software", although some remarks hold for other software as well), and presents arguments for the importance of assessing and controlling this quality. Then in section 3 the analogy is discussed with the distribution mechanisms of scientific papers and books, but also of durable goods like cars or household electronics. Section 4 tells how the inter-university expertise center ProGAMMA in the Netherlands was founded in an effort to bridge the gap between the adhoc programs of individual researchers and the products suitable for large scale distribution. Because the predictions for the future, given in section 5, are not exactly rosy, the final section 6 was added containing some proposals for action.

2. QUALITY OF SOFTWARE AND ITS IMPORTANCE

It is widely recognized that software quality is not a unidimensional concept. Some important aspects of it are worth mentioning.
SCOPE. What can the software achieve ? Does it incorporate important variants of the methods offered ? Can it handle different data structures ?
PORTABILITY, FLEXIBILITY. Does it run on my machine ? Is it easy to modify ? Does it interface with other software ?
DOCUMENTATION (both introductory and technical, in print and/or electronic).
CORRECTNESS, ACCURACY. Almost all software goes wrong for very pathological data. Some, however, goes wrong for more usual data. Adequate warnings that something goes wrong are very rare.
EASE OF USE. (This itself is probably a multidimensional concept). Ease for the daily user is different from ease at first use, or ease for teaching.
EFFICIENCY. On the one hand the far lower prices of processing and storage have decreased the paramount importance of efficiency. On the other hand users are more demanding w.r.t. complexity of algorithms, data sizes, answer speed, help facilities etc.
SUPPORT. Does the vendor provide adequate help in case of problems ?

This list is not complete, but suffices for our goals. Let us briefly recall why assessment and control of software quality is important.

Figure 1 presents an educated guess about the number of individuals buying and selling statistical software in the years 1960 up to 2000. Anyone who has used, taught or written such software knows how time consuming and irritating the frequently occurring mistakes and misunderstandings are. The consequences of totally wrong conclusions for scientific reporting are even worse. This will be enough to show that improved software quality matters.

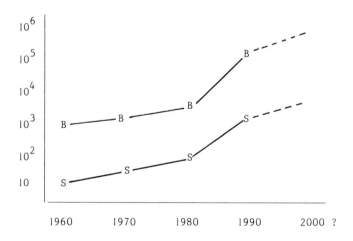

3. SCIENTIFIC OUTPUT - SOFTWARE - DURABLE GOODS

It is instructive to see how society has organized the assessment and control of quality in other areas. Before preparing this section I have consulted seven experts in computational statistics, and I thank them for their helpful answers.

Incentives for writing a scientific paper or book, in an order of importance on which the experts agreed, are divulgence of knowledge, improving one's reputation, covering one's costs, and financial gain (for the author and/or the employer of the author). All agreed that direct financial gain was rare, and therefore not an important motive. One expert also mentioned joy of creating and vanity as motives, vanity denoting feeling flattered, "le plaisir de se voir imprimé" rather than the more rational evaluation of the benefits reaped from an improved reputation.

A computer program is viewed by some experts more as a tool, less as an end product. With a few exceptions, about the same ordering of motives was mentioned for software writing. It is clear that durable goods are produced for money, although joy of creating must have been a major motive when e.g. the first cars were produced individually about a century ago.

Once there is a product, it should reach its intended users. For books and papers one may choose from distributing it oneself (possibly disguised as a firm or foundation of one person), offering it via one's employer (which is how the University Press system was born and later, when some of it was commercialised, the Bulletin series of several institutes and departments), via a learned society (many of which have their own journal) or via a commercial publisher. In this order there are better chances of reaching a wide audience, but more screening, more delay, and less influence of the producer on the final format. For the readers, the non-profit journals of the learned societies like American Statistical Association, International Association for Statistical Computing or Psychometric Society offer the best chances of spending their valuable money and reading time on a well written and innovative product; it is probably no coincidence that such journals often have more prestige and a higher rejection rate than journals run by a commercial publisher. Commercial success of a book or journal is only moderately correlated with scientific innovation; the weird system of some journals to charge the authors for the pleasure of accepting their papers is a clear case of an escape route for rich authors and employers from the strict canon of pure screening on scientific quality.

Roughly the same media exist for the distribution of software, with roughly the same pros and cons. Commercial publishers of books and journals are hesitantly entering the software market, but the alternative here is a contract with a major package distributor.

Passing from scientific books and papers via scientific software to durable goods, we pass from one-or-two-person producing via small group producing to large factories with their own distribution and publicity system. I think that the first and last category of products have reached a stage where the quality control mechanisms generally work well. As argued by Victor and others, this is not the case for software. Although the recency of software as a product provides a partial explanation, it is plausible that there are also some intrinsic properties of software which stand in the way of an effective mechanism for its quality control. This point returns in section 6.

4. ProGAMMA : AN EXAMPLE OF A NEW PHILOSOPHY

Innovative use of computers for data analysis or for other stages of the research process has rapidly gained importance. New models, new estimation methods, new ways of collecting, updating and consulting data, constitute a major portion of the contents of statistical and methodological journals. Such results can only be used by readers if they either build their own software for it or acquire the software used by the author. The former has become too time consuming, given the complexity, and the latter is often disappointing because most authors have worked with adhoc software that is of limited scope, not portable, not well documented, not easy to use, sometimes even inaccurate and inefficient.

The gap between the private software of the author of a method and the quality requirements for professional software has motivated Stokman (1983) to propose a center of expertise for the quality enhancement of such software. The proposal was worked out (Stokman and Van Veen, 1985) by a committee appointed by the Dutch government. At the end of 1987 the foundation ProGAMMA began its work with six staff members, supported by some others on special contracts. It is currently financed by four Dutch universities with an initial subsidy of the government, with the aim of being self-supporting after four years.

The major tasks of ProGAMMA are :
1. Development, implementation, conversion, documentation and distribution of software made at member universities;
2. Research on programming environments and human computer interfaces;
3. Information on and evaluation of external software. ProGAMMA now distributes nine software products, and is working on another ten of them. It has set its standards for documentation, programming, user interface and contracts with interested parties. It offers opportunities for visiting scholars and for practical work by students.

It will be interesting to see whether such an initiative can help to bridge the gap between personal adhoc programs and purely commercial distribution of well established and popular methods, and more generally to increase the awareness of software quality standards. Hopefully it will survive the combined influence of the grim budget position of universities and the general trend of modern western society to demand quick and spectacular results from any investment or initiative.

5. THE FUTURE IS NOT ROSY

For myself, and I am afraid for most of those concerned with the quality of both software and data analysis, the predicted future is not very rosy. Everywhere in our society more and more data are collected, and more and more of the data collection and analysis is done by people without a professional training in statistics, research methodology and computer use. The general greed for quick and spectacular results, combined with the availability of personal computers, cheap software and desktop publishing, has the danger of promoting the quick production of impressive-looking reports based on carelessly collected and carelessly analyzed data.

There is a trend towards massive use of graphics, exploratory methods and simple simulations, without much concern for the very limited scope of generalizability and the dangers of data-mining and over-interpretation that accompany it. In Molenaar (1988a) I have stressed that only well considered plans for collecting and analyzing data can meet the needs for general conclusions of those who read the reports and base their decisions on them. Streitberg (1988), Haux (1989) and Molenaar (1988b) have emphasized that incorporating statistical expertise into software is a very difficult process; software badly doing so is probably more dangerous than oldfashioned software not doing so at all.

6. POINTS OF ACTION

Stokman (1983) has proposed that a computer program be recognized as a specimen of scientific output, like a publication. Although it has been argued that a program is a tool for publications, I share his view : the time involved in writing a good program is such that the indirect reward via future publications is insufficient.

This implies, however, that a screening system for software must be set up. As argued by Victor (1985), this is also important as a means of improving the relations between buyers and sellers of software. I should like to propose a new custom that at the time software is purchased only 80% or 70% of the total price is paid, the remainder not being collectable if the user can demonstrate that the software and the documentation fail to perform in agreement with what was announced. For the software producer, this would be an incentive to be more responsive to complaints of users, an area in which enormous frustrations exist. Even if some producers would simply raise the first payment to the earlier level of the total price, it would be visible that some competitors frequently received the last payment as well, and discussions on quality would become more lively.

If a scientific paper has been written, the customary quality screening process consists of several steps. First the author rereads the paper. Then it is usually given to one or two close colleagues for informal comments. Next it is sent to the editor of a journal, who typically consults two or three expert reviewers (preferably in a doubly anonymous way) before deciding on acceptance, acceptance after changes, rejection with encouragement to revise, or flat rejection. After appearance in print, finally, the paper may still lead to "letters to the editor" in case of incorrectness, incompleteness or unjustified claims of originality.

Now consider the same process for a software product. My experience as researcher, statistical consultant, reviewer, and editor of a major journal, indicates that each of the screening steps described above does not require more than a few hours when a paper is judged. A sound judgement on software, however, taking all quality aspects of section 2 into account, will often require several days. Whereas paper reviewing is only rewarded by words of thanks, being viewed as a normal task of members of the research community, this community will have to offer more rewards for software reviewing. The journal printing the review could pay for it, the reviewer could be allowed to keep the software and documentation (like with books reviewed), perhaps a thorough software review should count for two publications.

The world of computational statistics is very small, and negative reviews will have more visible negative consequences than for papers. This makes anonymity of the reviewer desirable. On the other hand, the editor of the journal in which the review appears may wish to send the review for comment to the software distributor in order to prevent unjustified damage. It will frequently be necessary to have software reviewed both by a substantive expert and by a computer expert. In some cases access to (part of) the source code is desirable, subject to the same ethical constraints that apply to reviewing papers for a scientific journal.

I can only hope that IASC and similar organisations will take actions leading to more serious review practices. Today we see mainly the distributor's announcements in the journals, without independent judgements. Even full sized books like Francis (1981) or Siegel (1985) are mostly like a table of contents, with only limited information on portability or accuracy problems. Sending out free copies for review, like with books, still is very unusual. Today's sofware market is in a sense too easy for the sellers, and certainly too unclear for most of the buyers.

I have asked my seven experts about the desirability of legislation as a means to regulate the software market. They generally expressed that our society only uses this drastic step when the health of people is at stake, like with unsafe cars or exploding TV-sets. Protection by laws against malfunctioning products is less common, although gradually growing. It can only be used on the software market after reaching more agreement on the concept of malfunctioning. The idea of only permitting tested software on the market, in the way in which only tested pharmaceutical products are allowed, is intriguing, but I doubt whether it is feasible or even desirable for the near future.

Where we have legislation, but are unable to enforce it, is in the field of illegal copying. The fatal spiral of more illegal copying provoking higher prices and then still more illegal copying will have to be broken, both for scientific books and for scientific software. Copying being so easy and its detection being so difficult, we probably need a threefold strategy making copying more difficult, detection more easy and most of all inducing a change of mentality in which the immoral aspect is emphasized. The current director of ProGAMMA happens to be an expert in social dilemma research; his preliminary suggestion was to sell only via institutions (campus licenses); reducing the number and anonymity of the participants has been effective in other social dilemma's.

For the more general problem of unprofessional data collection and data analysis, we need a campaign for more education in methodology, statistics, graphicacy, critical report reading. It is particularly important that those who pay for the research and those who base decisions on its results, become convinced that hasty and unprofessional data analysis does more harm than good. The challenge for the professionals is to show to them the returns earned by better software, better data collection and better statistical analysis. This is a formidable challenge, as the deficiencies often remain unnoticed in current practice.

This paper should not create the impression that most software and most data analysis is seriously deficient. Even if this would only hold for a few percent of the cases, however, efforts of the scientific community to build a better system of rewards and punishments are worth the effort. There is a price to that effort, both in time and in money; the community will have to pay that price if it wants to be better protected against malpractice.

References

Francis, I. (1981). Statistical software : a comparative review. New York:Elsevier-Northholland.
Haux, R. (1989). Statistische Expertensysteme. Biometrie und Informatik in Medizin und Biologie, to appear.
Molenaar (1988a). Formal statistics and informal data analysis, or why laziness should be discouraged. Statistica Neerlandica 42 (1988) 83-90.
Molenaar (1988b). Statistical consultants and statistical expert systems. In: D.Edwards & N.E.Raun (eds) COMPSTAT 1988 Proceedings, p.187-192. Würzburg : Physica Verlag.
Siegel, J.B. (1985). Statistical software for microcomputers, a guide to 40 programs. New York : Elsevier-Northholland.
Stokman, F.N. (1983). Twenty years of statistical computing (in Dutch). In : SSS'83, Proceedings of the first statistical software symposium. Utrecht: Center for Data Analysis, Utrecht University.
Stokman, F.N. & van Veen, F. (1985). Software policy for the behavioral and social sciences (in Dutch). The Hague : Distrib.centrum Overheidspubl. DOP.
Streitberg, B. (1988). On the non-existence of statistical expert systems. SSN, 14, 55-62.
Victor, N. (1985) Computational Statistics - Tool or Science ? SSN 10, 105-125.

Statistische Auswertungssysteme
für Datenverwaltung und Datenanalyse

Informationssystem - Eine komplexe Struktur von Datenbanken, Dokumentationen und Schnittstellen

Ch. Alt, D. Bender, W. Bien und E. Lorenz

Summary
Social science handles more and more with complex data. This is only possible by using databases. But it is very often not enough to have a perfect datahandling especially when different analyses had to be done. Which tasks new systems should be able to do and how such a system is realised will explained in the following.

Die Leistungsmöglichkeiten der Datenverarbeitung steigen laufend. In den letzten Jahren hat sich die Entwicklung auf diesem Sektor immer mehr von der Bereitstellung spezieller Hard- und Software auf Konzepte und Möglichkeiten der Integration von Hard- und Software verlagert. Gerade diese Entwicklung ermöglicht inzwischen ein bislang ungeahntes Zusammenspiel von unterschiedlichen Systemen, Datenbanken, statistischen Auswertungspaketen und Graphik- bzw. Präsentationssoftware.

Der Anwender soll jetzt ohne besonderen Aufwand Daten für seine spezifische Analyse bereitgestellt bekommen. Die Unterstützung durch hochentwickelte Software soll den Benutzer ohne Detailkenntnisse in die Lage versetzten auf folgende Fragen selbständig eine Antwort zu finden:

- Welche Daten stehen wo zur Verfügung?
- Wie komme ich an diese Daten heran?
- Wie kann ich diese Daten meinem Analyseinstrument zuführen?
- Wie kann ich meine Ergebnisse präsentieren?

Z.Z. kann noch kein einzelnes Softwarepaket gleichzeitig

optimale Datenhaltung in einer Datenbank sowie hinreichend spezifische benutzerfreundliche Analysealgorithmen in sich vereinigen. Hier ist also Entwicklungsarbeit im Aufbau eines Systems verlangt, wenn man die Leistungen einer Datenbank mit einem Statistikpaket und graphischer Simulations- bzw. Analysesoftware verbinden will. Ein solches System mit verschiedenen Datenbanken, Analysealgorithmen und Übergabespezifikationen wird von uns als Informationssystem bezeichnet.

Der Aufbau eines solchen Informationssystems soll anhand der am Deutschen Jugendinstitut (DJI) installierten Lösung aufgezeigt werden.

Die typischen Aufgaben des DJI liegen auf dem Gebiet der Sozialforschug und Politikberatung für die Bereiche Jugend und Familie. Daraus ergaben sich die Zielvorstellungen für den Aufbau einzelner Datenbanken, die die Verwaltung komplexer strukturbeschreibender Daten ermöglichen. Dabei sollten diese Daten idealerweise so beschaffen sein, daß sie kleinste Einheiten umfassend beschreiben und gleichzeitig durch Umgruppierung, Aggregierung und statistische Bearbeitung auch auf komplexe Fragestellungen Antworten geben, sowie über verschiedene Datenbanken miteinander in Beziehung gesetzt werden können. Am DJI werden deshalb zu ausgewählten Fragestellungen sowohl Umfragedaten als auch Daten der Amtsstatistik auf Kreisebene gesammelt, erhoben und abgelegt (Mikroebene), die später durch geeignete Algorithmen auf nahezu jedes beliebige Analyseniveau aggregiert werden und so auch zu Fragestellungen auf Bundesebene herangezogen werden können (Makroebene). Das Problem bei dieser Konzeption ist nicht allein die Menge der abzulegenden Informationen, sondern der schnelle, flexible Zugriff auf die Daten, eine beliebige inhaltlich sinnvolle Kombinierbarkeit, und die Übergabe an Analysealgorithmen.

Seit 1987 wird am DJI ein solches System entwickelt, das den
Benutzer einerseits im multi-user Betrieb auf einem Hostrechner (Micro VAX Cluster) durch eine mit ORACLE (SQL,Tools)
erzeugte Oberfläche und Struktur unterstützt. Andererseits
aber auch low-end Systeme basierend auf APPLE MACINTOSH oder
IBM AT's enthält, die den einzelnen Benutzern zusätzlich zu
den Daten der zentralen Informationsverwaltung eine individuelle Datenhaltung mit Dokumentationsmöglichkeit anbietet.

Das Informationssystem wird in der Absicht aufgebaut, möglichst ohne besondere Kenntnisse des Betriebssystems oder der
jeweils implementierten Softwarepakete von der Anfrage bis
hin zur Analyse zu gelangen. Mit anderen Worten: Jedem Benutzer sollte es möglich sein, alle am DJI zur Verfügung
stehenden Informationen abzurufen, aufzubereiten und darstellen zu lassen, ohne dabei ein besonderes Expertenwissen für
die vorhandenen Datenverarbeitungsanlagen haben zu müssen.
Dieses Prinzip ist mittlerweile soweit verwirklicht worden,
daß vorhandene Daten angezeigt, statistische Analysen gerechnet, Häufigkeitsauszählungen, Graphiken und Codebücher erstellt werden können.

Das Prinzip hat dort seine Grenzen, wo einzelne Benutzer
spezifische bzw. einmalige besondere Analysen, Recherchen und
Auswertungen vornehmen, die durch eigens dafür geschriebene
oder implementierte Software durchgeführt werden soll. Der
Datentransfer zwischen dieser Spezialsoftware und Datensätzen
mit Spezialsturktur wird durch die Einrichtung entsprechnder
Schnittstellen aus vorgefertigten Modulbausteinen unterstützt.

Eine weitere Voraussetzung für das Funktionieren des Informationssystems betrifft die Ablage von Daten in einer Datenbank. Daten in ORACLE abzulegen heißt in diesem Zusammenhang nicht nur, eine optimale Lösung der Ablage zu haben und die Daten optimal aufbewahren zu können. Hinzu kommt die mindestens gleich gute Möglichkeit, diese Daten aus der Datenbank auch wieder abzufragen. In seiner Konsequenz bedeutet dies, daß jede Zahl, die in die Datenbank aufgenommen werden soll, so ausreichend dokumentiert werden muss, daß sie jederzeit wieder auffindbar ist. Diese Funktion hat in diesem Informationssystem das "Lexikon", in der single-user Version die Dokumentation in der Hypercard. Im Lexikon können die Daten sowohl ausführlich beschrieben als auch später dem Benutzer, z.B. über eine invertierte Schlagwortliste, wieder zur Verfügung gestellt werden. Hypercard, als assoziativer Filemanager, bietet dazu die Möglichkeit von Freitextsuche.

Die folgende Graphik gibt einen Überblick über das gesamte Informationssystem.

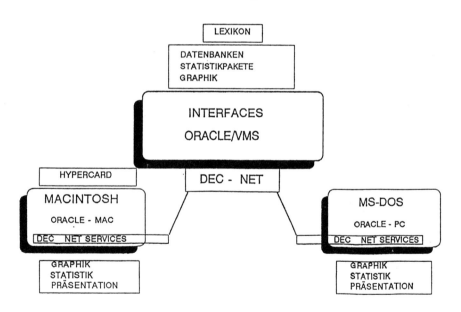

Das Informationssystem am DJI

Die folgende Übersicht zeigt, welche Informationen am Deutschen Jugendinstitut schon vorhanden oder im Aufbau begriffen sind.

DJI - INFORMATIONSSYSTEM	
Infrastruktur	Datenbank

Lexikon   - infobase
             - system
             - database
             - tools
             - links
	Literaturdatenbank
	    -Bücher
	    -Artikel
	    -Dokumente

Tools   -retrieval
            -data input
            -data output
	Statistikdatenbank
	    -Kreisdaten
	    -Länderdaten
	    -Bundesdaten

Links -interfaces	Familiendatenbank
	    -Surveydaten
	    -Jugenddaten

Abfrage und Analyse der Daten werden durch die Möglichkeit einer graphischen Aufbereitung ergänzt.

Mit der graphischen Darstellung soll eine optimalen Präsentationsform komplexer Zusammenhänge erreicht werden, so daß ein leichterer Zugang zu sozialwissenschaftlichen Analysen und damit überhaupt zu komplexen sozialwissenschaftlichen Fragestellungen ermöglicht wird. Eine der künftigen Aufgaben der Sozialwissenschaften wird darin bestehen, aktuelle Daten einer möglichst breiten Öffentlichkeit zur Verfügung zu stellen. Gerade deswegen sollte diese einfache und einsichtige Darstellungsform komplexer Daten mehr Beachtung finden.

Zur Umsetzung des bislang beschriebenen Fragezusammenhanges dienen die folgenden Systemkomponenten.

Das gesamte Schema basiert auf einer zentralen Datenhaltung. Für die Hardwarekofiguration heißt dies , es existiert ein zentraler Rechner (drei Minicomputer der Firma Digital Equipment Compony, die im Cluster laufen), der als Host eingesetzt wird. Die Datenhaltung erfolgt zentral. Da komplexe Auswertungen oder Abfragen i.d.R. über VIEWS (virtuelle Relationen) erfolgen, bringt die zentrale Form der Datenhaltung und der Datenverwaltung den Vorteil mit sich, daß nur ein einziges Mal Modifikationen oder Updates erfolgen müssen, um allen Benutzern entsprechend ihren Fragestellungen aktuelle Daten zur Verfügung stellen zu können.

Die Anbindung intelligenter, dezentraler Knoten sowohl von PC's mit Industriestandart als auch APPLE Computern erfolgt über BACKBONE Ethernet mit nachgeschalteten Ethernet Multiplexern. Zusätzlich werden für den Betrieb der Terminals SERVER eingesetzt, die die Zentralprozessoren im I/O - Bereich entlasten.

Als Netzwerkprotokoll im Ethernet dient DECNET(DEC). Die Low-End Rechner werden mit Serversoftware "SERVICES für MS-DOS" (DEC) und "APPLE-TALK" (APPLE) angebunden, auf deren Grundlage Filetransfer, Printerservice und Mailing möglich sind. Die Organisation der Daten erfolgt über das Relationale Daten Bank Manegement System (RDBMS) ORACLE mit Structured Query Language (SQL).

Die Verarbeitung von Daten im single-user Betrieb mit MACINTOSH - Geräten bietet neben dem Zugriff auf die ORACLE Datenbank Analysenmöglichkeiten und graphische Aufbereitungen, die mit wohldefinierten Schnittstellen des Betriebssystems unter ein und derselben graphischen Oberfläche laufen.

Damit sind über die beschriebene Konfiguration folgende Transformationen möglich:
- mit den Terminals direkt über SQL
- mit den Terminals über eine menugesteuerte Benutzer oberfläche
- über die PC-Welten und das Netz mit der Möglichkeit des Datentransferes und der weiteren Bearbeitung der Daten
- über Interfaces (SPSS,MAP) mit der Möglichkeit der Datenmanipulation, Analyse und Darstellung.
- über Magnetbänder, TK70 (DEC-Kasetten), Disketten

Zusammenfassend lässt sich also sagen, daß man sich bis vor wenigen Jahren vorrangig um Anwendungsprobleme bei der Software kümmern mußte, d.h. man mußte Maschinen und Programme entwickeln, die entsprechenden Leistungsanforderungen gerecht geworden sind.

Jetzt kann man sich Daten halten wie Haustiere. Dabei läßt sich auch die Zahl dieser Kanarienvögel beliebig vergrößern, da das bisherige Problem des zu großen Käfigs in der zu kleinen Wohnung angesichts heutiger Speicherkapazitäten nicht mehr auftaucht. Heute liegen die Probleme eher im schnellen flexiblen Zugriff (wo ist der Vogel, den ich suche) und der beliebigen Kombinierbarkeit der Daten (vertragen sich die verschiedene Vögel miteinander). Ferner gilt es, die vorhandenen Daten mit ihrer vielfältigen Auswertbarkeit einer interessierten, aber fachspezifisch nicht vorgebildeten Öffentlichkeit zugänglich zu machen (wie kann ich die Attraktionen meines Zoos anderen zugänglich machen).

F. Faulbaum, R. Haux und K.-H. Jöckel (Hrsg.) (1990). SoftStat '89
Fortschritte der Statistik-Software 2. Stuttgart: Gustav Fischer, 21 - 30

LINCS - A Program for Linear Mean and Covariance Structure Analysis

G. Arminger and R.J. Schoenberg

Summary

LINCS is a program to estimate the parameters of linear mean and covariance structures written in GAUSS. The program provides novel estimation procedures such as pseudo ML for non-normal data as well as novel test statistics and diagnostic tools. It also handles missing data in a general way without resort to imputation or pairwise correlation methods.

1 Hard and Software Environment

Before we turn to model specification, estimation methods, model diagnostics and a simple example in LINCS, we discuss briefly some hard and software requirements. The present version LINCS 2.0 is implemented in the GAUSS programming language version 2.0.[1] Hence, the use of LINCS is restricted to computers with GAUSS 2.0. However, a compiled version of LINCS 2.0 will be prepared in the near future. At present, GAUSS 2.0 is limited to IBM or IBM compatible personal computers with the MS.DOS operating system, version 2.0 or above. Except for the student version, GAUSS makes use of the mathematical coprocessor.

The standard version of GAUSS can only handle matrices with 8190 or less elements. Since the computation of the estimates of standard errors requires the inversion of an estimate of the information matrix, this restriction of the dimension of a matrix implies that no more than 90 free parameters in a linear covariance structure model can be estimated in the standard version. This restriction on the dimensions of a matrix also limits the dimension of a weight matrix that may be used either in the asymptotically distribution free (ADF) estimation procedure or in the analysis of polychoric and polyserial correlation coefficients similar to the LISREL 7 program (Jöreskog and Sörbom 1988). In the standard version of LINCS such a weight matrix is again restricted to a 90×90 matrix corresponding to the analysis of the covariance matrix of a random vector with no more than 12 components. In the most recent version of GAUSS this restriction on matrix size is relaxed, the number of parameters to be estimated is only restricted by the size of random access memory in the PC. This extended version requires an IBM or IBM compatible personal computer with a 80386 processor and a 80387 mathematical coprocessor as well as a DOS version 3.3 or higher. We point out that a GAUSS version for UNIX operating systems is under preparation so that the availability of LINCS will be greatly enhanced in the near future.

The LINCS program consists of a series of GAUSS procedures. In each run of the LINCS program the matrices of the LINCS model must be specified and the procedures that contain the specific

---

[1] GAUSS is a trademark of Aptech Systems, Inc., 26250 196th Place South East, Kent, Washington 98042, USA. The programming of statistical and numerical procedures in GAUSS is described in Küsters and Arminger (1989). LINCS has been programmed by R. Schoenberg (1989) and may also be obtained from Aptech Systems.

options that are to be used are called. In contrast to programs like EQS (Bentler 1985), LISCOMP (Muthén 1987) and LISREL the GAUSS code of the procedures may be modified or added unto. Hence, parameters such as the precision of the optimization routines may be changed by the user. However, this option should be used only by experienced GAUSS programmers.

2 Model Specification in LINCS

LINCS computes the estimates of the parameters of a linear mean and covariance structure model or equivalently of the first two moments of a $p \times 1$ random vector y defined by the following model:

$$\eta = B\eta + \zeta \ , \tag{1}$$

where η is a $m \times 1$ vector of unobserved variables, ζ is a $m \times 1$ vector of disturbances and B is a matrix of structural regression coefficients. Note that there is no distinction between endogenous and exogenous variables in this structural equation system. However, exogenous variables are easily introduced by equating some η variables with ζ variables which is done by setting the corresponding row in B to 0. The exogenous variables may be coded as metric or as dummy variables while the endogenous variables are metric variables.

We assume that the p observed variables in y are "indicators" of the m latent "variables" η:

$$y = \Lambda \eta + \varepsilon \ , \tag{2}$$

where ε is an error uncorrelated with η, and Λ is the $p \times m$ matrix of "loadings" in a factor analytic measurement model. The observed variables that are "indicators" of endogenous variables are again metric. Consequently, the program cannot be used to estimate the parameters of models which include threshold models of the probit type for censored and ordered categorical variables, unless the program input is a matrix of polychoric and/or polyserial correlation coefficients with the corresponding estimated asymptotic covariance matrix of these coefficients. (In this manner, LINCS may be used like LISREL 7 but it does not include the simultaneous estimation of threshold and covariance structure models as does LISCOMP.)

We further assume that $E(\zeta) = E(\varepsilon) = 0$ and that ζ and ε are uncorrelated. The covariance matrix of ζ is denoted by Ψ, the covariance matrix of ε by Θ. This structure contains the LISREL and therefore all the submodels of the LISREL model as pointed out by several authors including Jöreskog and Sörbom (1988, p. 158). If y contains a component that is constant, e.g. 1 for all observations, then this component may be used to estimate the parameters of models with a regression constant. All the parameters that are to be estimated are collected in a vector ϑ with q components.

We now provide a list of the options of the LINCS program some of which will be discussed in more detail in the later sections of the paper.

- Estimates of the multivariate coefficients of skew and kurtosis of a random vector.
- Estimates of the parameter matrices B, Ψ, Λ and Θ and of their asymptotic variance–covariance matrices. Automatic starting values are provided. As estimation methods

maximum likelihood (ML) estimation, pseudo ML (PML) estimation, unweighted least squares (ULS) estimation, weighted LS with normal theory weights and weighted LS (WLS) with a general weight matrix may be used. The PML option is not included in EQS, LISCOMP and LISREL. Individual data must be provided for this option.

- The vector ϑ may be estimated under general linear or non linear equality and/or inequality restrictions which is not possible in EQS, LISCOMP and LISREL.

- LINCS handles missing data that are missing at random (MAR) in the sense of Little and Rubin (1986) in a completely general way. This option is not included in EQS, LISCOMP and LISREL. Again, individual data must be analyzed.

- Coefficients of the standardized solution.

- Estimates of the total and indirect effects and their asymptotic standard errors.

- Factor score weights using the regression method and Bartlett's method.

- χ^2 statistics such as the Likelihood Ratio test statistic if multivariate normality is assumed or the Mahalanobis distance if the WLS method is used and the weight matrix is a consistent estimate of the inverse of the variance–covariance matrix of the moment matrix that is analyzed. Coefficients of determination are computed for each dependent variable and the set of dependent variables.

- Eigenvalues of the matrix B or its submatrices necessary for the analysis of the stability of an autoregressive system when time dependent data are analyzed.

- To check the model specification a Hausman type test for misspecification may be performed in addition to the computation of the χ^2 statistics. This Hausman type test allows one to check for types of misspecification such as omitted variable bias or wrong functional form bias which cannot be detected the usual goodness of fit statistics or modification indices. The Hausman type test is not available in EQS, LISCOMP and LISREL. Individual data must be provided for this option.

- Residuals and Cook statistics. If the structural equation system includes exogenous variables, standardized residuals for each observed dependent variable may be computed. These statistics are not includes in EQS, LISCOMP and LISREL. This option requires individual data.

- Technical output. During the LINCS run technical information such as the selected numerical algorithms for optimization and for line search are given. The first derivatives for each fixed parameter are printed out to indicate possible candidates for model modification.

3 Estimation Methods and Diagnostic Tools

A statistical analysis with mean and covariance structure models is only valid if the model is correctly specified with regard to the first two moments of y and if the observations $y_i, i = 1, ..., n$ constitute a random sample from one homogeneous population or random samples from a number G of heterogeneous populations indexed by a superscript g,. If certain estimation methods are employed, then additional assumptions must be made. All estimation methods assume that the covariance or second order moment matrix under the model is denoted by Σ and is a function of the parameter matrices B, Γ, Ψ and Θ. The corresponding empirical matrix is denoted by S.

The lower triangular matrices of Σ and S including the diagonal elements may be collected in the vectors σ and s. The estimation methods that can be chosen in LINCS are the following:

1. The ML method minimizes the objective function:

$$Q_{ML}(\vartheta) = 0.5 \cdot [\log \det \Sigma + \text{tr}(S\Sigma^{-1})] \tag{3}$$

In this method, estimates of the asymptotic standard errors are computed on the basis of the Fisher–Information matrix using the second derivatives of the objective function. Only the matrix of second moments of y is needed for the analysis. The assumption of multivariate normality is critical for obtaining correct standard errors and χ^2 statistics.

2. The PML method minimizes the same objective function as the ML method. However, the assumption of multivariate normality is not critical because the standard errors are not computed from the Fisher–Information matrix but rather from the second *and* first derivatives of the objective function. Hence, the error terms may be heavily non–normal. The drawback of this estimation method is that individual data must be provided and analyzed. Note that this method is a good alternative to the asymptotically distribution free (ADF) estimation method of Browne (1984) because it is not necessary to compute and to invert a fourth order moment matrix which makes the ADF method unfeasible for the estimation of the parameters of a large model. The theory of PML estimation has been developed by Gourieroux, Monfort and Trognon (1984) and has been applied to covariance structure models by Arminger and Schoenberg (1989).

3. The WLS method minimizes the objective function:

$$Q_{WLS}(\vartheta) = 0.5 \cdot (s - \sigma)'W^{-1}(s - \sigma) \tag{4}$$

Note that the weight matrix W is a $p(p+1)/2 \times p(p+1)/2$ matrix which becomes very large for models of realistic size. If W is the identity matrix, then the unweighted LS method is used for estimation. If W is a consistent estimate of the variance covariance matrix of s, then the ADF estimation method is used yielding correct standard errors and χ^2 statistics even if the error terms are non–normal. The variance covariance matrix of s may be computed from the second moments of y only when the assumption of multivariate normality is invoked as in the usual GLS estimation. In general this matrix must be computed from the fourth order moments calculated from indidual data. If polychoric and/or polyserial correlation coefficients are to be analyzed the weight matrix is the variance covariance matrix of these correlations. In the GLS method, the weights are provided by LINCS. For the ADF method or for the analysis of polychoric correlation coefficents the weight matrix must be provided by the user like in LISREL 7. Finally we point out that all these methods yield consistent parameter estimates if the model is correctly specified. If results for the parameters differ considerably the model is very likely misspecified.

In all these estimation methods the parameters may be restricted in a completely general way using the concept of fundamental parameters as formulated in McDonald (1980) and Küsters (1987). The parameter vector is assumed to be a continuously differentiable function of a vector γ of fundamental parameters, such that:

$$\vartheta = f(\gamma) \tag{5}$$

Typical examples are equality and order restrictions of the form $\vartheta_1 = \vartheta_2$ and $\vartheta_1 \leq \vartheta_2 \leq \vartheta_3$. These restrictions are easily rewritten for an unrestricted optimization problem using fundamental parameters in the formulation

$$\vartheta_1 = \gamma_1, \quad \vartheta_2 = \gamma_1$$

for the equality restriction and

$$\vartheta_1 = \gamma_1, \vartheta_2 = \gamma_1 + \gamma_2^2, \vartheta_3 = \gamma_1 + \gamma_2^2 + \gamma_3^2,$$

for the order restriction. Much more complicated restrictions arise for instance in the analysis of panel data as shown in Arminger and Müller (1989). While LISREL, EQS and LISCOMP allow only for equality restrictions, LINCS can handle any restriction on parameters that can be written as a continously differentiable function of fundamental parameters.

The implementation of the estimation methods described above uses Newton or Quasi Newton procedures for non linear optimization to minimize the objective function. The procedures used are the Newton–Raphson (NR), the Davidon–Fletcher–Powell (DFP), the Broyden–Fletcher–Goldfarb–Shannon (BFGS) and the Berndt–Hall–Hall–Hausman (BHHH) algorithm. Any of these algorithms may be combined with a line search algorithm choosing a certain steplength. Options are constant steplength of 1, a golden section step search and the method of backstepping. All of these methods are taken from the GAUSS modules for non linear optimization. The numerical procedures may be changed during the LINCS run. Descriptions of these numerical procedures are found in Berndt et al (1974), Kennedy and Gentle (1980) and Thisted (1988).

LINCS provides a multiple group option that allows the estimation of parameters when the data come from heterogeneous populations. In this case, the observed variables y and the parameter matrices B, Γ, Ψ and Θ are indexed by a superscript (g) denoting the g-th population. While the multiple group option in LISREL 7 requires that the empirical covariance matrix computed from each subsample must be positive definite, this requirement need not be met in LINCS. Hence, a group may consist of one member only, a fact that is used to deal with the missing data problem in mean and covariance structure models in a completely general way as proposed by Arminger and Sobel (1989). LINCS computes parameter estimates and consistent standard errors of these estimates when the data that are missing are missing at random (MAR) in the sense of Little and Rubin (1986). It is not necessary to collect the observations into groups of observations with the same pattern of missingness as proposed by Allison (1987) among other authors, the missing data may be missing in any kind of pattern specific for each individual. As a consequence, it is not necessary to use methods such as computing pairwise correlation coefficients and to specify the mean number of observations in the pairwise correlations to deal with missing data. PML estimation in the presence of missing data is based on considering the loglikelihood of the sample as the sum of individual loglikelihoods:

$$Q_{PML} = \sum_i^n Q_i, \quad \text{in which} \tag{6}$$

$$Q_i = 0.5 \cdot \{\log \det(K_i \Sigma K_i + \bar{K}_i) + \operatorname{tr}[(K_i S_i K_i + \bar{K}_i)(K_i \Sigma K_i + \bar{K}_i)^{-1})]\} \tag{7}$$

The matrix S_i is the individual outer product matrix of y_i, that is $y_i y_i'$. The matrix K_i is an individual selection matrix of zeroes with ones on the diagonal if a variable is observed and a zero on the diagonal if a variable is not observed. The matrix $\bar{K}_i = I - K_i$. The objective function and the first and second derivatives now must be computed by individual observations which slows down the numerical procedures considerably.

In addition to the usual goodness of fit statistics such as the likelihood ratio test statistic and measures of determination for each latent and observed dependent variable a Hausman type test statistic is provided to check for omitted variable bias and wrong functional form (Hausman 1978, White 1982). The Hausman type test is based on the observation that the parameters of a correctly specified statistical model may be estimated consistently not only from a random sample but also from a weighted random sample with arbitrarily chosen weights. For the computation of the test statistic, the parameters of the model are estimated from the unweighted sample ($\hat{\vartheta}$) and from the weighted sample ($\tilde{\vartheta}$) (cf. White (1981)). If the model is correctly specified, the two estimates converge in probability to the true vector and the difference between the two estimators converges in probability to 0. Hence, the following Wald statistic is computed:

$$h = (\hat{\vartheta} - \tilde{\vartheta})' V^{-1} (\hat{\vartheta} - \tilde{\vartheta}) \tag{8}$$

The matrix V is the estimated asymptotic variance covariance matrix of the difference of the estimators derived in Arminger and Schoenberg (1989). The test statistic h is under the hypothesis H_0 of no misspecification χ^2 distributed with q degrees of freedom. The same test may be applied to a subvector of ϑ, usually to the structural parameters in B and Λ. The weights for the weighted sample are chosen in such a way that individual observations that are well fitted by the model are lightly weighed while observations that fit badly are heavily weighed. Different types of weights are discussed in Arminger and Schoenberg (1989) and in the LINCS manual. Note that this test relies heavily on asymptotic theory. Therefore, large samples are needed. The use of this test is not advocated as a panacea to detect with misspecification but should rather be used with caution and in combination with other diagnostic tools since extended Monte Carlo simulation studies and long experience with the performance of this test are still missing.

As additional diagnostic tools, residuals and modified Cook statistics are computed for each individual observation. The residuals correspond to the residuals in regression analysis. Hence, only the residuals for observed dependent variables are given. The residuals are standardized. To check whether the results of the estimation are influenced heavily by one specific data point y_i, a modified Cook statistic is calculated by eliminating data point y_i and re-estimating the parameters of the model from the reduced sample. A large difference between the parameter estimates from the full sample and the parameter estimates from the reduced sample indicates that the data point y_i influences heavily the estimation results and should at least be inspected if not even eliminated from the sample. The computation of the modified Cook statistics is very time consuming, since the parameters of the model have to be re-estimated.

4 An Example for PML Estimation

In this section we present a LINCS showing some of the options of LINCS, especially the use of the PML estimation method. We illustrate the differences between the ML and the PML estimate of the asymptotic covariance matrix by generating an input covariance matrix from non–normal errors. The non–normal errors are generated by using the fourth power of standard normal errors and rescaling these non-normal errors in such a way that their covariance matrices are equal to Ψ and Θ. To compute the normal errors the GAUSS procedure for generating uncorrelated normal random numbers has been used. The sample size is $n = 200$. The true covariance structure is given by:

$$\Lambda = \begin{bmatrix} 1.0 & .0 & .0 \\ .9 & .0 & .0 \\ .9 & .0 & .0 \\ .0 & 1.0 & .0 \\ .0 & .8 & .0 \\ .0 & .8 & .0 \\ .0 & .0 & 1.0 \\ .0 & .0 & .7 \\ .0 & .0 & .7 \end{bmatrix} \quad B = \begin{bmatrix} .0 & .4 & .2 \\ .0 & .0 & .5 \\ .0 & .0 & .0 \end{bmatrix}$$

$$\Psi = \begin{bmatrix} 1.5 & .0 & .0 \\ .0 & 1.5 & .0 \\ .0 & .0 & 2.0 \end{bmatrix} \quad \text{diag}\Theta = \{.6\ .6\ .6\ .6\ .6\ .6\ .6\ .6\ .6\}.$$

The elements $\lambda_{11} = \lambda_{42} = \lambda_{73} = 1$ are fixed and will not be estimated. Thus, the first, fourth and seventh observed variables act as the reference indicators for the first, second and third latent variables, respectively. All parameters that are 0 are fixed.

The next lines give the set of LINCS commands that are necessary to perform the mean and covariance structure analysis of the simulated data set described above. Comments for the input lines are given within the @@ and * ... *\ brackets. The directives for printing the output have been left out:

```
library lincs;          @ LOAD GAUSS PROCEDURES FROM LIBRARY    @
call init;              @ INITIALIZE GLOBAL VARIABLES           @
output file=arm1.out reset; @ OUTPUT FILE                       @
vbl=varlbl("V",9);
lbl=varlbl("L",3);      @ LABELS                                @
loadm dat0=arm1;        @ DATA DEFINITION                       @
_data=dat0-meanc(dat0)'; @ REMOVE MEANS                         @
clear dat0;             @ FREE MEMORY                           @

@ ANALYSIS OF DATA FOR KURTOSIS AND SKEW                        @
{kt,pr1,sk,pr2,s,pr3}=mardia(_data,0);

@ PARAMETER SPECIFICATIONS, EACH ROW HAS 3 ELEMENTS             @

let spla= . 0 0   1 0 0   1 0 0   0 . 0   0 1 0   0 1 0   0 0 .   0 0 1   0 0 1;
let spbe= 0 1 1   0 0 1   0 0 0;

{mle,x2,df,pr}=est("XMPL1",0,0,0,1);  @ ESTIMATION              @
```

```
call stand(mle);            @ STANDARDIZED SOLUTION                       @

{fw2,a2}=fsb(mle);          @ FACTOR WEIGHT MATRIX - BARTLETT METHOD      @

vv=vc(mle);                 @ STANDARD ERRORS FROM INFORMATION MATRIX     @
stderr=sqrt(diag(vv));

vvh=wvc(mle,1);             @ ROBUST STANDARD ERRORS                      @
stderr=sqrt(diag(vvh));

{b,se}=totfx(mle,vv);       @ TOTAL EFFECTS                               @

{b,se}=indfx(mle,vv);       @ TOTAL INDIRECT EFFECTS                      @

call fder(mle);             @ FIRST ORDER PARTIAL DERIVATIVES             @

@ HAUSMAN'S TEST                                                          @

{h1,df1,pr1,h2,df2,pr2,dt,wmle}=htst(mle,3,0,0);

call resids(mle,0);         @ ANALYSIS OF RESIDUALS AND OUTLIERS          @
```

The results are given in Tables 1 and 2. The first table gives the summary results. Both the kurtosis and the skew statistics indicate that the data are highly non–normal. Both the LR statistic and the Hausman test statistic for the structural parameters indicate that the model is correctly specified as should be expected from the use of simulated data given the correct model. The Hausman statistic for all parameters shows a poor fit, however this lack of fit results exclusively from the estimates of the variances in Ψ and Θ which are usually of little interest.

Table 1. Summary results from the LINCS run

Kurtosis Statistic: 65.554   Pr =   0.00
Skew Statistic: 21.526   Pr =   0.00

LR statistic: 27.540   df =   24

Hausman statistic for structural parameters only: 0.04, df = 9, Pr = 1.00
Hausman statistic for all parameters: 77.11, df = 21, Pr = 0.00

Table 2 shows the PML estimates and their standard errors. Since the errors are non-normally distributed estimated standard errors computed from the ML method are quite different from the estimated standard deviations computed from the PML method. This example illustrates that the ML estimate of the asymptotic covariance matrix cannot take non-normality into account, whereas the PML method can.

Table 2. Estimated asymptotic standard deviations of parameter estimates from a sample with non-normally distributed errors

Parameter	True value	Estimate	ML Standard error	PML Standard error
λ_{21}	.9	.9234	.0615	.0341
λ_{31}	.9	.8968	.0618	.0408
λ_{52}	.8	.8367	.0655	.0525
λ_{62}	.8	.8401	.0656	.0357
λ_{73}	.7	.6815	.0580	.0395
λ_{83}	.7	.6492	.0560	.0403
β_{12}	.4	.4716	.0922	.0767
β_{13}	.2	.1311	.0799	.0445
β_{23}	.5	.4279	.0720	.0457
ψ_{11}	1.5	1.3883	.1968	1.1503
ψ_{22}	1.5	1.3410	.2014	0.5248
ψ_{33}	1.5	2.1271	.2933	1.0560
Θ_{11}	.6	.5956	.0988	.3074
Θ_{22}	.6	.5542	.0873	.2495
Θ_{33}	.6	.6490	.0914	.2969
Θ_{44}	.6	.6728	.1099	.2348
Θ_{55}	.6	.5976	.0861	.2002
Θ_{66}	.6	.5906	.0859	.2943
Θ_{77}	.6	.6000	.1373	.2546
Θ_{88}	.6	.6344	.0867	.4170
Θ_{99}	.6	.6196	.0822	.4511

References

Allison, P. (1987). Estimation of linear models with incomplete data. *Sociological Methodology 1987*, C.C. Clogg (ed.). Washington. 71–103.

Aptech Systems, Inc, (1988). *GAUSS^{TM}, The GAUSS System Version 2.0*. Kent, Washington.

Arminger, G. and Müller, F. (1989). *Lineare Modelle zur Analyse von Paneldaten*. Erscheint als ZUMA Methodenband, ZUMA Mannheim.

Arminger, G. and Schoenberg, R. (1989). Pseudo maximum likelihood estimation and a test for misspecification in mean and covariance structure models. *Psychometrika*, in press.

Arminger, G. and Sobel, M. E. (1989). Pseudo maximum likelihood estimation of mean and covariance structures with missing data. Forthcoming in *Journal of the American Statistical Association*.

Berndt, E. R., Hall, B. H., Hall R. E. and Hausman, J. A. (1974). Estimation and inference in non linear structural models. *Annals of Economic and Social Measurement*, 3, 653–666.

Bentler, P. M. (1985). *Theory and implementation of EQS, a structural equations program.* Los Angeles: BMDP Statistical Software.

Browne, M. W. (1984). Asymptotic distribution-free methods for the analysis of covariance structures. *British Journal of Mathematical & Statistical Psychology*, 37, 62-83.

Gourieroux, C., Monfort, A., and Trognon, A. (1984). Pseudo maximum likelihood methods: Theory. *Econometrica*, 52, 681-700.

Hausman, J. A. (1978). Specification tests in econometrics. *Econometrica*, 46, 1251-1272.

Jöreskog, K.G. and Sörbom, D. (1988). *LISREL 7 — A Guide to the Program and Applications.* SPSS Inc., Chicago.

Kennedy, W. J. and Gentle, J. E. (1980). *Statistical computing.* New York.

Küsters, U. L. (1987). *Hierarchische Mittelwert- und Kovarianzstrukturmodelle mit nichtmetrischen endogenen Variablen.* Heidelberg.

Küsters, U. L. and Arminger, G. (1989), *Programmieren in GAUSS.* Stuttgart.

Little, R.J.A. and Rubin D. B. (1987). *Statistical analysis with missing data.* New York.

McDonald, R.P. (1980). A simple comprehensive model for the analysis of covariance structures: Some remarks on applications. *British Journal of Mathematical and Statistical Psychology 33*, 161–183.

Muthén, B. (1987). *LISCOMP - Analysis of Linear Equations Using a Comprehensive Measurement Model.* Scientific Software, Inc., Mooresville.

Schoenberg, R. J. (1989). *LINCS: Linear covariance structure analysis. User's guide.* Aptech Systems, Kent, Wahington..

Thisted R. A. (1988). *Elements of statistical computing.* New York – London.

White, H. (1981). Consequences and detection of misspecified nonlinear regression models. *Journal of the American Statistical Association*, 76, 419-433.

White, H. (1982). Maximum likelihood estimation of misspecified models. *Econometrica*, 50, 1–25.

Discrete Response Models: Some Comments on Statistical Software

E. Aufhauser

Summary

In dealing with discrete response models (DRM), substantial differences in the requirements on statistical software arise due to the concrete specification of a DRM, the estimation procedures one may use for a given data structure and the testing procedures one wants to carry out. As each software has to base on some kind of 'standard' assumptions concerning these aspects, all available programs and procedures have at least some limitations in methodological flexibility. The paper gives an overview of possible software choice for typical research requirements.

1. The basic structure of discrete response models

DRM are designed for the analysis of situations in which each individual observation faces a set A of J mutually exclusive and exhaustive discrete response alternatives and has to respond for exactly one of these alternatives. The standard linear regression model for the analysis of continuous responses can be extended to handle such multinomial response situations by introducing a vector of intermediate unobserved (latent) variables y^* and a generalized indicator function which maps the latent variable vector into a vector indexing observed responses. Drawing upon alternative latent variable structures and indicator functions, a rich variety of specific discrete response models may be formulated (e.g. for ordered choice, multivariate responses, dynamic responses; Amemiya, 1981; Heckman, 1981; Small, 1987; McFadden, 1984). In this paper, the standard static multinomial model with unordered response alternatives will be used as a reference.

Let y be a J-vector with $y_j=1$ if response j is observed and $y_j = 0$ otherwise; and T_J the whole set of such vectors. Define the vector of unobserved latent variables by

$$y^* = x\beta + \varepsilon \tag{1}$$

with domain R^J for vector y^* and a multivariate cumulative distribution function $F(\varepsilon|x)$.

The generalized indicator function which maps the latent variable vector into the vector $\underline{y}$ is defined by a partition of R^J into subsets $S_1,\ldots,S_J$ (where S_j is defined to be the set of $\underline{y}^*$ which have $y_j^* \geq y_k^*$; $k \in A$; $k \neq j$; and with some rules for breaking ties), and $Z: R^J \rightarrow T_J$ with $\underline{y}=z(\underline{y}^*)$ satisfying $y_j=1$ if and only if $\underline{y}^* \in S_j$. In this case the (conditional) response probabilities are given by

$$P_j = \text{Prob}(y_j=1|\underline{x},\underline{\beta}) = \text{Prob}(\underline{y}^*=\underline{x}\underline{\beta}+\underline{\varepsilon} \in S_j) = F(\{\varepsilon | y_j^* \geq y_k^*; k \in A; k=j\}|\underline{x}) \qquad (2)$$

The concrete functional form of the link between the response probabilities and the linear predictor in a DRM arises from the assumed (multinomial) cumulative distribution function $F(\varepsilon|\underline{x})$. The most widely used model form is the <u>multinomial logit</u> (MNL)

$$P_j = \frac{\exp(\underline{x}_j\underline{\beta})}{\sum_{k \in A} \exp(\underline{x}_k\underline{\beta})} \qquad (3)$$

which is derived from the general latent variable model by specifying the distribution of the disturbances $\underline{\varepsilon}=(\varepsilon_1,\ldots,\varepsilon_J)$ to be iid type I extreme value.

Perhaps the most general of alternative discrete response models is the <u>multinomial probit</u> (MNP) model, which is derived under the assumption that the vector of random components $\underline{\varepsilon}$ has a multivariate normal distribution with mean 0 and an arbitrary variance-covariance matrix Σ_ε. Although MNP is theoretically quite attractive, it is conceptionally complex, the parametrization of the variance-covariance structure is not straightforward in most empirical applications and it is extremely intractable in computational terms. Due to the fact that the one-dimensional integral for the normal distribution can be evaluated easily and quite precisely, the probit model always was quite popular for binary choice problems and a lot of statistical and econometric software packages includes some binary probit procedures nowadays.

One of the most popular DRM models in applied work is the <u>nested multinomial logit</u> (NMNL) model. As a generalization of multinomial logit, NMNL preserves some of the computational advantages of MNL but accounts for correlation of the disturbances in subsets of the response alternatives (McFadden, 1978). As for most derivatives of the logit model (e.g. most ordered logit models too) consistent (although not efficient) estimation of model parameters is possible with two(and more)-step procedures and standard MNL software. Full-information-maximum-likelihood estimation is more complex although it does not cause principal problems.

2. Methodological aspects of DRM which are important for an evaluation of software

Specificational aspects of DRM

According to the flexibility in existing DRM software one has to differenciate at least on four aspects of the response set: Although a distinction between binary and multinomial response is not fundamental methodologically, the historical development of typical binary versus typical multinomial model forms is still reflected in DRM software. Most multivariate response problems may be reformulated as univariate multinomial response problems. The simplest way of dealing with the resulting correlation structure of error terms is the formulation of nested multinomial logit (NMNL) models which can be estimated consistently with standard logit procedures. Models for ordered discrete responses have to be distinguished theoretically from models for unordered responses. Many different models have been proposed for ordered response alternatives (Agestri, 1984). Most of the logit based model forms can be estimated consistently with standard MNL software (Amemiya, 1981; Small, 1987). One of the most attractive theoretical properties of DRM is that most methodological results apply in the same way whether the response set is identical for all individual observations or not. This allows the explicit consideration of constraints on the individual response set when specifying a DRM.

One feature of the discrete alternatives in the response set which should be considered for in the variance-covariance structure of the disturbances is the unobserved similarity of response alternatives leading to the different functional forms (different links between response probability and linear predictor) of DRM (see section 1.).

The specification of the systematic part (the link between the explanatory variables and parameters) in the latent variable model (1) is crucial in empirical work and is one of the crucial points in distinguishing on the practical flexibility of different DRM software, too. Most of the models in empirical applications are based on a linear-in-parameter specification of the systematic part of the latent variables. As in linear regression models this assumption is not restrictive generally because it allows every kind of nonlinear specifications of variables. Only some DRM software supports Box-Cox resp. Box-Tukey transformation tests easily.

Basically there are three different types of explanatory variables one may use in the specification of DRM models: Individual-specific (socioeconomic) variables are connected with the observation unit only and do not vary with the response alternatives. Alternative-specific variables measure some attributes of the response alternatives and usually do vary in level with the response alternatives as well as the individual observation unit. Pure alternative-specific variables which do not vary across individual observations are named alternative-specific constants. Alternative-specific variables might be connected either with single parameters for each response (alternative-specific parameters) or with one single paramater for all responses (generic parameters). Individual-specific variables can be connected with (up to J-1) alternative-specific parameters only. Similarily, up to J-1 alternativespecific constants can be included in a DRM specification.

Data structure

In social sciences when using survey data the standard data structure when analyzing discrete response will be individual data on all variables. If there are many observations for each combination of responses and values of explanatory variables ('many observations per cell' - grouped data) one can use WLS estimators on so-called 'logit (or probit) transforms' (Amemiya, 1981). A lot of logit or probit procedures in standard statistical packages draws on such logit/probit transforms (and thus grouped data sets).

With simple random and exogenously stratified sampling the maximization of the conditional distribution function $P(j|x,\theta)$ is equivalent to the maximization of the entire likelihood function (including the marginal distribution of X). This result does not extend to more complex sampling schemes in general. Nevertheless, there are some important exceptions: E.g. simple random sample estimation can be used with response based sampling and either sampling fractions equal to the population shares or MNL with J-1 alternative-specific constants (see Manski and Lerman 1977; Coslett 1981). Manski and Lerman's (1977) 'weighted exogenous sample maximum likelihood (WESML) estimator' is essentially equivalent to simple random sample maximum likelihood (except that each observation is weighted by the ratio of the population and sampling fraction for each alternative) and can be used for all DRM models and choice-based sampling.

Output and tests

With output on parameter estimates, the variance-covariance matrix of the parameters and the likelihood at estimated parameter values, basic tests (asymptotic t-tests and likelihood ratio tests) can be performed easily.

Goodness-of-fit measures similar to R^2 resp. $\bar{R}^2$ in standard regression analysis are the likelihood ratio indices rho-squared and rho-squared bar

$$\rho^2 = 1 - L(\beta)/L(\Omega) \qquad \bar{\rho}^2 = 1 - [L(\beta)-K]/L(\Omega) \qquad (4)$$

L(β) likelihood at the estimated parameter vector β
L(Ω) likelihood at the reference model (either the zero-model at $\beta=0$ or the market-share model with all coefficients except J-1 alternative-specific constants set equal to zero)
K number of estimated parameters

Tests on the IIA assumption can be used as a kind of specification test for the MNL model. The most powerful of these tests (the Hausman/ McFadden Test) is based on a comparison of logit models estimated with subsets of alternatives from the universal choice set (Hausman and McFadden, 1984).

Predicted response probabilities are useful for a lot of purposes: outlier analysis, the comparison of the goodness of fit of alternative specifications, the analysis of elasticities and aggregate policy forecasting. As these tasks are quite important in the process of model development, the handling of predicted choice probabilities should be an important aspect in the evalution of DRM software.

Prediction success tables (Ben-Akiva and Lerman, 1985) summarize the aggregate deviations of observed and predicted responses and the ability of a model to replicate observed shares of response alternatives. In interpreting the output of DRM software it is important to distinguish 'success' evaluated at the individual responses with maximum probability and 'success' evaluated at individual response probabilities for all responses.

In contrast to standard linear regression DRM are highly non-linear. Thus, elasticities depend on the value of the response probabilities in general. A disaggregate elasticity represents the responsiveness of an individual response probability to a change in the value of some attribute (an independent variable). Aggregate elasticities summarize the responsiveness of some group of individuals. One has to distinguish between aggregate elasticities computed as the weighted average of the individual level elasticities of the group using the choice probabilities as a weight and aggregate elasticities evaluated at the mean group values of the independent variables.

3. An evaluation of existing DRM software

Within the last ten years discrete response models (DRM) became quite popular in social sciences. The originally used binary probit and logit models were refined, extended and adapted to handle specific research requirements. With some time lag the methodological development was paralleled by an increasing availability of statistical software. Logit and probit procedures are nowadays included in a lot of statistical and econometric software packages. Besides that, special programs were designed explicitly for the estimation and testing of DRM.

The following evalution of programs which has been designed explicitly for the analysis of discrete responses will concentrate exclusively on important aspects of methodological flexibility in different software packages. Aspects of data entry, data handling or manipulation options, user-friendliness, output-presentation etc. are not adressed. It is intended to present some rough decision lines on DRM software for the 'experienced' user of statistical software packages who could deal with some inconvenience in program handling as long as the necessary methodological flexibility is guaranteed. All special DRM software does not possess satisfactory data manipulation features or satisfactory procedures for descriptive data analysis. Nevertheless, special purpose programs are much more flexible on methodological aspects than DRM procedures in multi-purpose software. Thus, the combined use of a general statistical software package for descriptive analysis and/or data manipulation and special DRM software in empirical work seems inevitable at the moment.

The following evaluation survey will be quite selective regarding the included software packages: Neither 'non-public' programs written for special purposes nor general-purpose programs like e.g. Gauss (which in principle allows all necessary computations) are included.

CHOMP/CONFID (Daganzo and Schoenfeld, 1978; Sparman, 1979) is the only (mainframe) package for multinomial probit analysis considered. BLOGIT (Hensher, 1984) is a general multinomial logit software for mainframes, MDA (Lerman, 1985) a general multinomial logit software for PCs. HLOGIT (Börsch-Suppan, 1986) is explicitely designed for three level nested multinomial logit analysis on PCs. LIMDEP (Greene, 1984) is a program for analyzing limited dependent variables in general. The PC version of the program will be considered only. As an example for a multi-purpose statistical program with a 'probit/logit' procedure $SPSS^X$ (SPSS Inc., 1985), as an example for multi-purpose econometric software with a 'logit' procedure IAS (Sonnberger et al, 1986) will be included in the evaluation.

Table 1 gives an overview of what can be done basically within the different software packages. The structuring of the points parallels the methodological aspects of DRM outlined in section 2. Just a few standard assumptions are common to all DRM software: unordered overall response set, linear-in-parameter specification and simple random or exogenously stratified sampling.

Perhaps the most important point for empirical research is the distinction concerning the <u>data structure</u>. E.g. with $SPSS^X$ it is possible to estimate binary logit or probit models if one has 'many observations per combination of explanatory variable values'. LIMDEP on the other hand allows both, estimation with either individual or grouped data. A second important point in empirical research will be the flexibility to estimate arbitrary <u>variable-parameter relations</u>. Programs like MDA and LIMDEP (subroutine DISC) estimate generic variable-parameter relations only, thus needing J alternative-specific variable values for each individual. Although it is possible to include socio-economic (individual-specific) variables, handling of this type of variables is quite troublesome. Programs like $SPSS^X$ and LIMDEP (subroutine LOGIT) draws on individual-specific variables which do not vary with alternatives and allows the estimation of exactly J-1 alternativ-specific parameters for each variable. If one has to deal with individual-specific response sets possible software choice might be BLOGIT, MDA, HLOGIT and the mainframe version of LIMDEP. Despite some inconvenience in data handling and manipulating, LIMDEP might be a good choice if one wants to perform a lot of unconventional testing due to its matrix-operation facilities.

Discrete Response Models · 37

Table 1. What's possible with different software for discrete response models?

		CHOMP/CONFID	BLOGIT	MDA	HLOGIT	LIMDEP	SPSS^X	IAS
general	mainframe	X	X			(X)	X	X
	PC			X	X	X		X
model form	binary logit	X	X	X	X	X	X	X
	binary probit	X				X	X	
	multinomial logit	X	X	X	X	X		X
	multinomial probit	X						
	explicitly ordered logit					X		
	nested logit (FIML) (3 stages)				X			
data structure	individual	X	X	X	X	X		X
	grouped					X	X	
sampling design	WESML				X	X		
response set	individual specific poss.		X	X	X	(X)		
variable-parameter relation	any rel. explicitly to specify	X	X		X^1			X
	generic relations only			X		X		
	J-1 alter.-specific relations only				X	X	X	
output^2	parameter estimates	p	p	p	f	v	p	p
	var.-cov. matrix	p	p	p	f	m	p	p
	likelihood of spec. model	p	p	p	f	m		p
	rho/rho-bar squared		p^3	p^4	f^4	c		p^3
	predicted probabilities			v	f	c		
	prediction success table		p^5		f^6			p^7
	(aggregate) elasticites		p^8		f^9			
special options	Box-Cox/Tukey Test		X					
	linear restrictions on parameter		X					
	fixed parameter restrictions		X		X			
	Hausman-McFadden IIA-Test					X		
	Langrange mult. test, Wald test				X			
	forcasting	X						
	plot of likelihoodfunction				X			

[1] restricted number of arbitrary mappings for individualspecific variables; generic parameters for alternativ-specific variables assumed

[2]
p printed output only
f possible to store on file
v possible to store as a variable
m possible to store as a matrix
c easy to compute within program

[3] likelihood of market-share model used
[4] likelihood of zero-model used

[5] aggregate shares of alternatives based on individual response probabilities
[6] aggregate shares of alternatives based on maximal individual response probabilities
[7] full prediction success table based on individual response probabilities

[8] based on mean values for all variables
[9] based on weighted average across all individuals or on mean values for all variables

References

Agestri A. (1984). Analysis of Ordinal Categorical Variables. Wiley, New York.

Amemiya T. (1981). Qualitative response models: A survey. Journal of Economic Literature, 19,1483-1536.

Ben-Akiva M., Lerman R. (1985). Discrete Choice Analysis: Theory and Application to Travel Demand. MIT Press, Cambridge, Mass. and London.

Börsch-Suppan A. (1986). Hierarchical choice models: Three level nested multinomial logit. Program documentation for version 5.2. of HLOGIT.

Cosslett S.R. (1981). Maximum likelihood estimator for choice-based samples. Econometrica, 49,1289-1316.

Daganzo C. (1980). Multinomial Probit. Academic Press, New York.

Daganzo C.F., Schoenfeld L. (1978). Chomp Users's Manual. Institute of Transportation Studies: Berkely.

Greene W.H. (1984). LIMDEP: Program documentation. New York.

Hausman J.A., McFadden D. (1984). Specification tests for the multinomial logit model. Econometrica, 52, 1219-1240.

Heckman J.J. (1981). Statistical models for discrete panel data. In: Manski C., Mc Fadden D., Structural Analysis of Discrete Data with Econometric Applications. MIT Press, Cambridge, Mass.

Hensher D.A. (1984). BLOGIT - an abridged users' guide - with example program inputs and outputs and interpretative guidelines. Internal Report. Australian Road Research Board: Vermonth South, Victoria.

Lerman S. (1985). Micro Data Analyzer: User's Manual. Compumetrix corporation: Willowdale, Ontario.

Manski C., Lerman S. (1977). The estimation of choice probabilities from choice-based samples. Econometrica, 45, 1977-1988.

McFadden D. (1978). Modelling the choice of residential location. In: Karlsqvist A., Lundqvist L., Snickars F., Weibull J.W., Spatial Interaction Theory and Planning Models. North Holland, Amsterdam, New York and Oxford.

Mc Fadden D. (1984). Econometric analysis of qualitative response models. In: Griliches Z., Intriligator M.D., Handbook of Econometrics, vol.II. Elsvier Science Pub.

Small K.A. (1987). A discrete choice model for ordered alternatives. Econometrica, 55, 2, 409-424.

Sonnberger H. et al (1986). IAS-System Level 3.6. User Reference Manual.Institute for Advanced Studies: Vienna.

Sparman J.M. (1979). Confid User's Manual. Institute of Transportation Studies: Berkely.

SPSS Inc. (1985). SPSS^X User's Guide. McGraw Hill, New York.

Comparison of Some Software Packages for the Analysis of Cohort Studies

H. Becher and M. Blettner

Summary

The development of statistical methods to analyze cohort studies is a relatively new area of research. Therefore, these methods have only partly found their way into big statistical software packages. In this paper we summarize the most important methods to analyze cohort studies, assess their availability in the large packages and present some generally available software products which help to fill some gaps. We compare these products and give some recommendations for practical use.

1. Introduction

Cohort studies are a major study type in cancer epidemiology. Statistical methods to analyze these data have been developed mostly within the last 15 years. Theoretical principles and practical aspects of these studies have been extensively described in [7]. The statistical software is usually not available in standard packages like SAS or BMDP, however, several smaller programs provide some of the necessary computations. This paper briefly describes the most important statistical methods, gives a survey of available software and recommendations for the efficient use of this software in the process of analyzing and modelling data from cohort studies either on PC or on mainframe computers. We concentrate on programs which are generally available and ready to use for the statistician or epidemiologist and which do not require major programming.

2. Definitions, data structures and statistical methods

In a cohort study the mortality or morbidity experience of this population is investigated with respect to the exposure or risk factor of interest. In cancer epidemiology occupational cohorts play an important role to investigate long term effects of certain risk factors. The data collection in a cohort study consists of demographic information of each member of the cohort and of exposure data. Major questions of interest are:
– Is the mortality experience of the study population similar to the general population?
– Are there differences in the mortality rates between subgroups of the cohorts, e.g. have

exposed persons a higher risk of developing the disease of interest than non-exposed persons?
- Is there a dose response relationship between the level or duration of exposure to a potential risk factor and the mortality rates?

Table 1. Data structure (individual data) [DATA 1]

N	Date of birth	Sex	Exposure information period	cat.	other covar.	End of follow-up Date	Cause
1	4 10 1933	1	01 50 05 53	02	x,y,z	01 01 87	000
			06 53 01 73	05			
			02 73 12 86	03			
2	4 12 1923	2	05 45 09 45	12	x,y,z	19 01 80	154
			06 44 12 50	01			
			01 70 05 73	02			

Cause: ICD-Code   if dead
000   if lost to follow-up / end of study
Note: Exposure information is usually given in employment periods, e.g. individual 1 worked from January 1950 to May 1953 in exposure category 02, from June 1953 to January 1973 in exposure category 05, and so on.

The minimum information needed for each member of the cohort is: Date of birth, sex, date of entry into the cohort, date and cause of leaving the cohort and information on the level and duration of exposure. Often further information is collected on other relevant covariates, such as residential or smoking history, to investigate confounding effects. An example of the structure of this data file is given in table 1. This data set will be referred to as DATA 1 in this paper. For certain types of analysis as outlined below, a second data set has to be created from the original data set (DATA 2), containing 'grouped data' (see table 2): The number of person years and the number of events are calculated for selected categories, mainly defined by age, sex, calendar time and exposure level. In some cases DATA 2 may be the only available data set.

Table 2. Data structure (grouped data) [DATA 2]

Category	Observed Deaths	Expected Deaths	Person-Years
01	13	8.301	20654.7
02	18	12.218	22216.7
03	13	10.797	19542.8
04	28	16.105	19521.1
05	22	11.932	8545.0
etc.			

Note: Categories are defined e.g. by age, sex and exposure

If comparison with reference population is carried out, a third data set is required, which includes mortality rates by age, sex and calendar year for the referent population (DATA 3), see [7] p. 358 ff., as an example. The statistical and computational methods can be classified into three groups:
1. Calculations of person years and standardized mortality ratios (SMR),
2. Statistical methods using grouped data (Poisson Regression),
3. Statistical methods using individual data (Cox Regression).

In this paper we briefly describe these methods. A detailed presentation is given in [7].

The Person year calculation includes the exact definition of the cells by age, calendar time and exposure variable, the calculation of the number of person years in each cell and counting the number of events (deaths) in each cell. The statistical analysis includes the calculation of the SMRs (ratio of the observed and the expected numbers), their standard errors, confidence intervals hypothesis testing.

The Poisson regression is based on grouped data (DATA 2). The mortality rate is modelled as a function of covariates. The number of observed deaths in each cell is considered as a Poisson variable. The Poisson regression allows several covariates to be used simultaneously and can be done with or without the use of external rates. If no external rates are available, the mortality rates of different subgroups of the study population are compared (internal comparison). Further details of this analysis including the advantages and problems of using external rates are discussed in [7]. Poisson regression requires grouped data (DATA 2) as input file and the mortality rates of the reference population (DATA 3) resp. the expected number of deaths.

Cox Regression models are used for continuous data, utilizing age, calendar time and exposure measurements in their original form rather than partitioning the data into discrete categories. These models are mainly applications and refinements of the techniques proposed by Cox [8]. In order to apply these models to data from cohort studies the model of Cox is generalized by considering several background mortality functions, one for each stratum. Several extensions can be considered.

a) use of external hazard functions
b) incorporation of time dependent covariates such as cumulative exposure or the cumulated amount of cigarettes smoked.
c) general form of the risk function (additive or mixture models).

Although the Cox regression modeling provides an elegant way to analyze data from cohort studies, it has to be considered that the quality of the data in a cohort study may be very restricted and that therefore the analysis of grouped data is often appropriate and sufficient.

3. Software

The following programs or systems which are available for PC and for mainframe computers have been investigated: GLIM and MANYEARS. SAS [5] and BMDP [3] have not been included in this list although they are widespread and may be used for data editing in connection with the other programs, however, they do not include adequate subroutines for the analysis of data from cohort studies. Both programs include facilities to carry out modelling with the Cox regression approach, but only in the case where no external baseline hazard function is required. In SAS only fixed covariates can be used, while BMDP has some facilities to use time dependent covariates. Furthermore two PC programs have been included, which were specially developed for the analysis of epidemiologic studies: EGRET and PYTAB/AMFIT. Table 3 summarizes the data input steps and the statistical methods.

Table 3. Input data, statistical methods and available software

Input	Possible analysis	Software
Individual data	Person–years calculation	MANYEARS, PYTAB
	Cox Reg. (fixed covariates)	SAS, BMDP, EGRET, GLIM
	Cox Reg. (time dep. covariates)	BMDP, EGRET
Individual data + external rates	Expected number of deaths, SMR	MANYEARS, PYTAB
Grouped data	Poisson Reg. (internal comparison)	AMFIT, GLIM, EGRET
Grouped data + expected no. of deaths	Poisson Reg. (external comparison)	AMFIT, GLIM, EGRET

The following tables summarize the major features of the programs. Technical details will not be given and we will not comment on properties which depend on hardware and computer configuration such as computational speed and storage.

Table 4. MANYEARS

AUTHORS	J. Peto, revised by M.P. Coleman [1]
LANGUAGE	FORTRAN 77, compatible to FORTRAN IV
MACHINE	Mainframe and PC (MS–DOS)
INPUT	Individual records (DATA 1), standard death rates (DATA 3) (optional, if expected numbers of deaths are required), steering file (format description of input files and specification of analysis requirements), FORTRAN subroutine to modify and edit data (optional)
OUTPUT	Labelled tabulations and output file, suitable for GLIM (DATA 2). Person years and observed numbers of deaths for defined categories. With external death rates: expected numbers of deaths from specified causes, ratio of observed and expected numbers, its standard error and test of significance.
SIZE	Storage needed to be declared in main FORTRAN program.

COMMENTS: The use of the new version of the program is uncomplicated, especially for those users who do have some knowledge of FORTRAN. Experience in FORTRAN is necessary if a subroutine for data manipulation is required. Input has to be given in a well-defined format, however, data can be changed with user-defined subroutines. The setup of the steering file is somewhat tedious. The causes of death have to be given in ICD-O code, which may require some restructuring of the data. The tabulations are printed in a clear way and are easy to understand. The possibility of creating an output file for consecutive analysis is valuable.

Table 5. GLIM (Generalized Linear Interactive Modelling)

AUTHORS	Baker, JA & Nelder, JA [2]
ANALYSIS	Poisson regression, Cox Regression
MACHINE	Mainframe and PC (MS-DOS)
INPUT	Poisson regression: input file with grouped data (DATA 2). With external rates: number of expected deaths
	Cox regression: individual records (DATA 1), GLIM Macro required
OUTPUT	Deviance, parameter estimates and standard errors, parameter correlation matrix, fitted values, generalized residuals. Facilities to plot, list or tabulate.
SIZE	Depends on installation. Maximum of 100 user-defined identifiers, 130 model terms and 16 stack levels. Restriction on the dimension on the mainframe changeable by the 'software manager' to allow for large input files.

COMMENTS: GLIM is specially designed to the fitting of generalized linear models (GLM), the Poisson regression being a special case. Although the Cox models are not a direct application of generalized linear models, special MACROS have been written to analyze Cox models within the framework of GLIM [9]. The use of GLIM requires some understanding of the statistical methods. The instructions are powerful, but not always simple. Statisticians who are already familiar with the fitting of generalized linear models, will have no major problems to use GLIM for the analysis of cohort studies, however the special instructions have to be learned. GLIM is mainly useful when used in an exploratory manner, i.e. as a tool for experimenting with the fitting of various models, using different sets of covariables. This generally nice feature of GLIM is somehow limited for the analysis of cohort studies as the INPUT file has to be created before the user can start the modelling step. Complex rearrangements of categories require the input file to be recomputed. Data handling is somewhat more complicated than, for instance, in SAS. Because the language is very compressed, it is difficult to 'read' through programs.

Table 6. PYTAB/AMFIT (Person–Years Tabulation/Additive and Multiplicative Model Fitting)

AUTHORS	Preston, DL & Pierce, DA [4]
ANALYSIS	Person–years calculation, Poisson regression
MACHINE	PC (MS–DOS), mathematical coprocessor required
	a) PYTAB
INPUT	Individual records (DATA 1).
OUTPUT	Multiway, multivariate tables with one or more cross–classified summary variables according to user–defined categories, including fixed categories (e.g. sex), up to three dynamic time variables (e.g. calendar time, age) and time dependent category variables e.g. cumulative dose. Summary variables for each cell: including counts, sums and means for selected variables. For tables with at least one time scale: person years for each cell. Subtables, by collapsing categories. Optional: Output file as INPUT files to GLIM or AMFIT.
	b) AMFIT
INPUT	Grouped data (DATA 2), external mortality rates (DATA 3) (optional).
OUTPUT	Maximum likelihood parameter estimates, standard errors and standardized residuals, likelihood based hypothesis testing in Poisson regression models for standard linear and loglinear models and more general models.
SIZE	To be specified by user (default maximum number of strata is 200)

COMMENTS: Similar to GLIM, AMFIT is a command driven, interactive modelling program and requires a good understanding of the statistical techniques. The possibility of analyzing non–standard models is one of the most interesting features of AMFIT. However, the definition of those models requires some training and experience. More complex modelling or extensive data set may be time consuming. With the new generation of PCs this argument becomes less relevant. Together with PYTAB the program provides a powerful tool in the analysis of cohort studies. One of the strengths of AMFIT (compared to GLIM) is that it is not restricted to relative risk models. It is possible to work with hazard function models in which the additive excess risk is modelled directly and to incorporate data on population rates into the analyses. The program has been developed and used to analyze data from the atomic bomb survivors in Hiroshima and Nagasaki [11].

Table 7. EGRET (Epidemiological GRaphics, Estimation and Testing Package)

AUTHORS	Statistics and Epidemiologic Research Corporation, Seattle, USA. [6], partly based on the program PECAN by Lubin [10], and extended by B.E. Storer et al. [12].
ANALYSIS	Poisson regression, Cox regression
MACHINE	PC (MS–DOS) (menu driven), mathematical coprocessor recommended
INPUT	Input file has to be prepared from a standard ASCII file by a data definition module (first part of the EGRET–package). The file generated by this module must be transferred to the analysis module in which statistical modelling is performed. The data structure used is either individual data (DATA 1) or grouped data (DATA 2) depending on the type of analysis.
OUTPUT	Maximum likelihood estimaters of the parameters, their standard errors, p–values, relative risk and the deviance, score test, residual analysis and diagnostic techniques, including graphics. Cox Regression with fixed or time dependent covariables, stratification for calendar time periods possible.
SIZE	250 variables, practical limit of about 20,000 observations.

COMMENTS: EGRET has been developed in close corporation with epidemiologists and claims to meet the requirements of researchers in this area. It is the most comprehensive package included in our test, and the only one which includes Poisson regression as well as Cox modelling with its special features (mainly time dependent covariables). The menu driven approach is easy to understand. The main disadvantage of the package, however, is the lack of any editing facilities in the main program. Other software is therefore needed when using this product. For instance, it is possible to create an appropriate analysis data file with SAS, and to enter EGRET with this data file.

4. Choice of statistical software and recommendations

As it was shown, none of the presented software packages allow all computations and analyses which are normally required for cohort analysis. Therefore one has to find suitable combinations which are indicated below.

A good combination of two programs is the use of GLIM and MANYEARS, both programs can be either used on PC or on the mainframe. MANYEARS performs person year calculations including SMR analysis, provided the external rates are available in a given format and ICD–coding is used. With MANYEARS the input file for GLIM can be prepared. Because both programs work on PCs as well as on the mainframe, no (error causing) data transfer between two different systems is necessary. In general, the data files from cohort studies are large (often several thousands records e.g. of employees of a company), therefore the mainframe may have advantages compared to a PC. If the data set is smaller or fast PCs are available, the combination of PYTAB and AMFIT is appropriate, and provides better facilities for more complex modelling. Unlike GLIM, AMFIT can deal with non multiplicative models, however, in some circumstances these extensions may not be useful or necessary. Statisticians may be more familiar with GLIM, because it is used for other statistical modelling. The use of PYTAB to calculate Person years and GLIM for the statistical model can be seen as an alternative for those who are working on PCs and familiar with GLIM. EGRET is still under development, a final evaluation is therefore not possible. The major drawback of this package is the missing edit facility. Apart from this, EGRET is a powerful tool. It is very fast, relatively easy to learn and would therefore become the best choice as soon as editing facilities are available.

Acknowledgement

The work of the first author was supported by the Umweltbundesamt, Berlin, under contract no. 106 06 067.

References

A: Software

[1] Baker JA, Nelder JA (1978): The GLIM system, Release 3. Oxford, Numerical Algorithms Group.
[2] Coleman M, Douglas A, Hermon C, Peto J (1986): Cohort study analysis with a FORTRAN computer program. Int. J. Epid. 15, 134–137.
[3] Dixon, WJ (1985): BMDP Biomedical Computer Programs, University of California Press
[4] Preston, DL, Pierce, DA (1987): PYTAB and AMFIT User's Guide. Radiation Effects Research Foundation, Hiroshima, Japan
[5] SAS Institute Inc. (1985): SAS user's guide, Version 5 Edition. Cary, NC
[6] Statistics and Epidemiology Research Corporation (1989): EGRET (pre–release user's manual). Seattle, USA

B: additional references

[7] Breslow, NE, Day NE (1987): Statistical methods in cancer research Vol II: The design and analysis of cohort studies. IARC scientific publications No. 82, Lyon, France
[8] Cox DR (1972): Regression models and life tables. J. R. Stat. Soc. B 34, 187–220
[9] Clayton, D, Cuzick, J (1985): The EM algorithm for Cox's regression model using GLIM. Appl. Stat. 34, 148–156.
[10] Lubin JH (1981): A computer program for the analysis of matched case–control studies. Comp. Biomed. Res. 14:138–143.
[11] Preston DL, Kato H, Kopecky KJ et al. (1987): Studies of the mortality of A–Bomb survivors. 8. Cancer mortality, 1950–1982 Rad. Res. 111: 151–178.
[12] Storer BE, Wacholder S, Breslow NE (1983): Maximum likelihood fitting of general risk models to stratified data. Appl. Stat. 32:172–181.

F. Faulbaum, R. Haux und K.-H. Jöckel (Hrsg.) (1990). SoftStat '89
Fortschritte der Statistik-Software 2. Stuttgart: Gustav Fischer, 47 - 56

EQS Version 3: New Statistics and Computations

P.M. Bentler

Summary

The BMDP-distributed computer program EQS (and EQS/PC and EQS/EM) is one of the most popular programs for linear structural equation modeling, a major methodology for specifying, estimating, and testing hypothesized interrelationships among a set of substantively meaningful variables (see e.g., Bentler, 1986; Bollen, 1989). EQS Version 3 (Bentler, 1989) extends the well-known user-friendly features of the program, as well as the technical analytical capabilities of the methodology.

1. Introduction

The new release of EQS continues its pioneering ease-of-use features while providing the user with a variety of new statistical methods. Although there are many new features to the program, the most important of these for the nontechnical user are again in the interface, especially the on-line help facility, in the ability to run mainframe-size jobs on a PC with EQS/EM, and in the statistics, especially the ability to handle multiple population models, and models with structured means, in a very straightforward way. For example, new multisample and structured means path diagrams are given that make it possible for the first time to visually represent all the parameters of such a model. In the diagrams and the statistics, structured means models are presented directly as models for means and covariances, and the confusing "moment matrices" used in LISREL, which are irrelevant to the theory involved, do not appear. The interpretation of intercepts and means is clarified by principles associated with the effect decomposition that is provided. These new features are used to provide a simple and general approach to modeling with missing data that avoids the various adjustments and "tricks" required by Allison (1987) and Muthén, Kaplan, and Hollis (1987).
The technical user will appreciate new features such as statistics for least-squares estimation, robust standard errors that remain correct under distributional misspecification, the Satorra-Bentler scaled χ^2 statistic, the Lagrange Multiplier (LM) and Wald tests for distribution-free estimation, the ability to vary estimation methods

across groups in multisample covariance structure analysis, the LM test to evaluate cross-group equality constraints, effect decomposition and standard errors for indirect effects, the new noncentrality-based comparative fit index (Bentler, 1988) and Akaike's information criterion, a facility for conducting simulations including the bootstrap and jackknife, improved precision of estimation, the ability to write statistics to external files for further analysis, greater print control, and related improvements. A few of these improvements are discussed in the sections that follow.

2. Robust Statistics

EQS was the first program to make available publically the arbitrary distribution theory generalized least squares (AGLS) methods of covariance structure analysis described by Browne (1982), Chamberlain (1982), Bentler (1983a), and Bentler and Dijkstra (1985). Since AGLS statistics may be difficult or impossible to compute in large models, and in smaller samples there may be a question as to whether the AGLS estimator, standard errors, or test statistics behave as expected, EQS Version 3 extends this methodology by providing statistics for normal theory estimation that are robust to violation of the multivariate normality assumption. The method implemented as METHOD = ML, ROBUST; yields the usual maximum likelihood (ML) estimators of model parameters as well as the ML goodness-of-fit χ^2 statistic and information-matrix based standard error estimates. In addition, however, it provides the robust standard errors described, for example, by Bentler and Dijkstra (1985) that are asymptotically correct even under distributional misspecification. In models without constraints, these standard errors have been the recent focus of an article by Arminger and Schoenberg (1989), and hence further details are not given here.

Satorra and Bentler (1988a,b) developed modifications of the standard goodness-of-fit test T to yield distributional behavior that should more closely approximate χ^2. One of these, the scaled test statistic, is available in EQS. The concept behind the scaled statistic is very old, going back to Bartlett (1937). The idea is to scale the given test statistic with a simple multiplier to yield a new statistic whose mean is closer to that of the reference χ^2 distribution. In particular, Satorra and Bentler (1986) note that the general distribution of T is in fact not χ^2, but rather

$$T \xrightarrow{\mathcal{L}} \Sigma_1^{df} \alpha_i \mathcal{T}_i, \tag{2.1}$$

where α_i is one of the df = (number of data points − number of parameters + number of restrictions) nonnull eigenvalues of the matrix UV_{ss}, $\mathcal{T}_i$ is one of the df independent 1−df χ^2 variates, V_{ss} is the distribution-free asymptotic covariance matrix of the sample variances and covariances, and $U = W - W\dot{\sigma} M\dot{\sigma}' W$ is the residual weight matrix under the model, the constraints, and the weight matrix W used in the estimation method. Additional matrices defining U are $\dot{\sigma}$, the derivatives of the model with respect to the parameters, and M, the residualized matrix $\Delta - \Delta\dot{c}'(\dot{c}\Delta\dot{c}')^{-1}\dot{c}\Delta$, based on the "information matrix" $\Delta = (\dot{\sigma}' W \dot{\sigma})^{-1}$ and the derivatives $\dot{c}$ associated with the constraints $c(\theta) = 0$. The mean of the asymptotic distribution of T is given by trace(UV_{ss}). Now, defining the estimate

$$k = \text{trace}(\hat{U}\hat{V}_{ss})/\text{df}, \qquad (2.2)$$

where $\hat{U}$ is a consistent estimator of U based on the estimate $\hat{\theta}$, and $\hat{V}_{ss}$ is the usual distribution free estimator of V_{ss}, the scaled test statistic is given by

$$\bar{T} = T/k. \qquad (2.3)$$

The Satorra-Bentler statistic (2.3) is referred to a χ^2 distribution with df degrees of freedom.

When all the eigenvalues α_i are equal to one, T is in fact χ^2 distributed and the correction (2.2) has no effect asymptotically; thus, the scaled statistic (2.3) will behave appropriately. When the variables are elliptically distributed, the α_i are all equal to a constant, and (2.2) can be used to provide an estimate of the elliptical kurtosis parameter κ. Specifically, (2.3) will behave appropriately when the variables are elliptical. When the α_i have a high dispersion, the scaled statistic $\bar{T}$ will be only approximately χ^2 distributed. Satorra and Bentler provide a more accurate adjustment to the statistic T to cover this circumstance, but this adjustment is not currently available in EQS.

3. Chi-square Tests for Least Squares (LS) Estimates

The usual goodness-of-fit tests T for model adequacy are not appropriate when a misspecified weight matrix W is used in minimizing a function Q. In least-squares estimation with elliptical (ELS) or normal theory (LS) with sample data based on a sample size of n + 1, $T = n\hat{Q}_E$ (in ELS) or $T = n\hat{Q}_N$ (in LS) at the minimum with $\hat{\theta}$ do not have χ^2 distributions even when the model is correct. Browne (1982, 1984) developed a test based on residuals that was further studied and extended by Satorra and Bentler (1988a,b). This test in its general form is very similar to the linearized test statistic in Bentler (1983b), holding for any distribution of the variables. A variant of the test is used in EQS to reduce the computational burden and the need for very large sample sizes. In this variant, the distribution of the measured variables is assumed to be known, specifically, as normal under LS estimation, and elliptical under ELS estimation.

Let $\hat{\theta}$ be the LS estimator, obtained by minimizing Q_N under the model; $\hat{F}_{ML}$ be the ML function evaluated at $\hat{\theta}$; and $\hat{g}_{ML} = \partial F/\partial \theta$ be the gradient and $\hat{H}_{ML}^-$ be the covariance matrix $\Delta - \Delta \dot{c}'(\dot{c}\Delta\dot{c}')^{-1}\dot{c}\Delta$, all evaluated at $\hat{\theta}$. Then

$$T_{LS} = n(\hat{F}_{ML} - \hat{g}'_{ML}\hat{H}_{ML}^-\hat{g}_{ML}) \tag{3.1}$$

is the statistic computed for the LS solution. Similarly, if $\hat{\theta}$ is the ELS estimator obtained by minimizing the elliptical function Q_E (see Bentler, 1989), $\hat{Q}_{ERLS}$ is the elliptical reweighted least squares function evaluated at $\hat{\theta}$ with $\hat{\kappa}$ and weight matrix $W_2 = \hat{\Sigma}^{-1}$ based on the model, $\hat{g}_{ERLS} = \partial Q_E/\partial \theta$ is the gradient and $\hat{H}_{ERLS}^-$ is the asymptotic covariance matrix, all evaluated at $\hat{\theta}$ with the chosen estimate $\hat{\kappa}$; then

$$T_{ELS} = n(\hat{Q}_{ERLS} - \hat{g}'_{ERLS}\hat{H}_{ERLS}^-\hat{g}_{ERLS}) \tag{3.2}$$

is the statistic computed for the ELS solution. These goodness-of-fit test statistics are evaluated using the usual χ^2 distribution.

4. Lagrange Multiplier (LM) Test

The LM test has been part of EQS for many years now. It gives the uniparameter "modification index" and several multiparameter extensions. The original statistical theory was brought into covariance structure analysis by Lee and Bentler (1980) and was recently discussed by Sörbom (1989). Satorra (1989) and Bentler (1989) provide generalized versions of the usual statistic that hold when the distributional assumption underlying the variables cannot be assumed to be correct. The theory is as follows. When minimizing a function Q subject to the constraints $c(\theta) = 0$, a Lagrangian Multiplier λ_i corresponding to each of the r constraints $c_i(\theta) = 0$ is created. The vector λ of these constraints is defined by the equation

$$g + \dot{c}'\lambda = 0, \tag{4.1}$$

where g is $\partial Q/\partial \theta$. Given an estimator $\hat{\theta}$ that minimizes Q and meets the constraint, the sample vector $\hat{\lambda}$ must meet (4.1), evaluated at $\hat{\theta}$. With s being the vector of sample covariance data, an explicit expression for $\hat{\lambda}$ is

$$\hat{\lambda} = (\dot{c}\Delta\dot{c}')^{-1}\dot{c}\Delta\dot{\sigma}'W(s - \sigma(\hat{\theta})), \qquad (4.2)$$

all evaluated at $\hat{\theta}$. The asymptotic distribution of $\hat{\lambda}$ was given by Bentler and Dijsktra (1985). Using the usual definition of a χ^2 variate in terms of quadratic forms, it follows that

$$\text{LM} = n\hat{\lambda}'(D'\dot{\sigma}'WV_{ss}W\dot{\sigma}D)^{-1}\hat{\lambda} \xrightarrow{\mathcal{L}} \chi^2_{(r)}, \qquad (4.3)$$

where $D = \Delta\dot{c}'(\dot{c}\Delta\dot{c}')^{-1}$. In practice, the matrix in parentheses is evaluated at $\hat{\theta}$. This test statistic, which follows directly from Bentler and Dijkstra (1985), is the Lagrange Multiplier or LM test that evaluates the statistical necessity of the r constraints. Satorra (1989) calls it the generalized score (or LM) test. It is not the classical test statistic described by Lee and Bentler (1980) because it can be applied under misspecification of the distribution of the variables, i.e., even when W is not the optimal weight matrix for the distribution involved. For example, it can be applied under LS estimation with $W = I$ when the distribution of the variables is normal and V_{ss} is the optimal normal theory weight matrix. When W is a consistent estimator of V_{ss}^{-1}, in particular, when the correct distribution of variables is specified, the covariance matrix of $\hat{\lambda}$ simplifies, and (4.3) simplifies to

$$\text{LM} = n\hat{\lambda}'(\dot{c}\Delta\dot{c}')\hat{\lambda}, \qquad (4.4)$$

where, in practice, $(\dot{c}\Delta\dot{c}')$ is evaluated at $\hat{\theta}$. This is the form of the LM test that is currently available in EQS. This statistic, developed by Lee and Bentler (1980) for covariance structure analysis under normality assumptions, is available in EQS for all distributional assumptions, including arbitrary distributions and linearized estimation, as well as for evaluating cross-group equality constraints in multisample models. Appropriate substitution of the relevant estimator $\hat{\theta}$ and the associated Lagrange Multiplier $\hat{\lambda}$ into the equations above produces the correct statistic; see, e.g., Bentler and Dijkstra (1985, Eq. 2.1.8) for the linearized LM test.

5. Wald (W) Test

Let $\hat{\theta}$ be an estimator for a model, and assume that the constraints $c(\theta) = 0$ have *not* been imposed during the estimation. In practice, this means that $c(\hat{\theta}) \neq 0$, and it may be desirable to test the hypothesis that $c(\theta) = 0$. In the simplest case, where the constraint functions simply select given parameters, this hypothesis evaluates whether the selected parameters are zero in the population. From Bentler and Dijkstra (1985, p. 24 last line), correcting a misprint, and the asymptotic equivalence of linearized and fully iterated estimators,

$$\sqrt{n}c(\hat{\theta}) = \dot{c}_+\sqrt{n}(\hat{\theta} - \theta_+) + o_p(1), \tag{5.1}$$

so that, under the null hypothesis, the large sample distribution of (5.1) is given by

$$\sqrt{n}c(\hat{\theta}) \xrightarrow{\mathcal{L}} N(0, [\dot{c}M\dot{\sigma}'WV_{ss}W\dot{\sigma}M\dot{c}']_+). \tag{5.2}$$

It follows that a quadratic form based on (5.2) can be used to test the constraints. Specifically, letting $c(\hat{\theta}) = \hat{c}$, the Wald statistic is given by

$$W = n\hat{c}'(\dot{c}M\dot{\sigma}'WV_{ss}W\dot{\sigma}M\dot{c}')^{-1}\hat{c} \xrightarrow{\mathcal{L}} \chi^2_{(r)}, \tag{5.3}$$

where the matrix in parentheses is evaluated at $\hat{\theta}$. In principle, the W test does not depend on the distribution of variables when V_{ss} is estimated in a distribution-free way. The test is called the generalized Wald test by Satorra (1989), who provides the noncentrality parameter when the null hypothesis is minimally false. In EQS, (5.3) is computed with least squares estimation when a normal or elliptical distribution is assumed, that is, with LS or ELS estimation. It is not computed for other estimators. Rather, the standard Wald test is computed as follows. When the weight matrix W is chosen optimally, $W = V_{ss}^{-1}$ in the typical case asymptotically, and

$$W = n\hat{c}'(\dot{c}\Delta\dot{c}')^{-1}\hat{c} \xrightarrow{\mathcal{L}} \chi^2_{(r)}, \tag{5.4}$$

where, in practice, the matrix in parentheses is evaluated at the unrestricted estimate $\hat{\theta}$. This test is also used when $\hat{\theta}$ is based on linearized estimation, see Bentler and Dijkstra (Eq. 2.2.3). See also Lee (1985), and Satorra (1989). The W test printed out in EQS for all distributional methods except LS and ELS is given by (5.4).

6. Multisample Covariance Structure Analysis

A general approach to multisample covariance structure analysis was given by Bentler, Lee, and Weng (1987), covering the case where there are m sample covariance matrices S_g (with nonredundant elements in the vector s_g) and m corresponding model matrices Σ_g (with vector of nonredundant elements σ_g), one for each of g groups. They solved the statistical problem of estimating all the parameters $\theta = (\theta_1', \theta_2', ..., \theta_m')'$ of the separate models $\sigma_g = \sigma_g(\theta)$ subject to within-sample and between-sample constraints $c(\theta) = 0$, obtaining standard error estimates, and testing goodness of fit of the models to the data. This approach, which generalizes the distribution-free work of Browne (1982, 1984) and Chamberlain (1982) to multiple groups, and permits use of specific distributions, e.g., normal or elliptical, in each of the samples, is implemented in the new release of EQS. More recently, Muthén (1989) has written on this topic.

7. Mean and Covariance Structure Analysis

EQS provides a new and direct way to estimate structured means models by dealing with the covariance/mean sample and model matrices

$$\begin{bmatrix} S & \bar{z} \\ \bar{z}' & 1 \end{bmatrix} \text{ and } \begin{bmatrix} \Sigma & \mu \\ \mu' & 1 \end{bmatrix}, \qquad (7.1)$$

in which S and $\bar{z}$ are sample covariance matrices and mean vectors, and $\Sigma = \Sigma(\theta)$ and $\mu = \mu(\theta)$, i.e., in which both covariances and means are functions of the basic parameter vector θ, in EQS, the parameters of the Bentler-Weeks (1980) model. The data to be modeled are s_2, the vector of lower triangular elements of S, and $s_1 = \bar{z}$. The subscripts indicate the order of moments involved, s_2 referring to 2nd moments about the mean, and s_1 referring to 1st-order moments. Let $s = (s_1'\ s_2')'$, and $\sigma = (\sigma_1'\ \sigma_2')'$ be the corresponding model vectors. Then, EQS approaches the estimation and testing problem by considering $\sigma = \sigma(\theta)$ as usual, and using a general statistical theory for estimating parameters, testing goodness of fit, and so on. The socalled raw moment matrices used by LISREL do not appear in this technical development, and are not used in program input or output. The current version of EQS limits covariance/mean structure models to situations in which the assumption of multivariate normality is appropriate. Only ML estimators and statistics are provided. In this theory, the log likelihood for given model, aside from a constant, is $L = -2^{-1}N[\ln|\Sigma| + \text{tr}S\Sigma^{-1} + (s_1 - \sigma_1)'\Sigma^{-1}(s_1 - \sigma_1)]$ while the corresponding likelihood for a saturated model is $L_s = -2^{-1}N[\ln|S| + p]$. Consequently, maximizing L under choice of estimator $\hat{\theta}$ permits forming the likelihood ratio statistic $\text{LR} = 2(\hat{L}_s - \hat{L})$, given by

$$\text{LR} = N[\ln|\hat{\Sigma}| + \text{tr}S\hat{\Sigma}^{-1} + (s_1 - \hat{\sigma}_1)'\hat{\Sigma}^{-1}(s_1 - \hat{\sigma}_1) - \ln|S| - p]. \qquad (7.2)$$

This function is optimized in EQS. See Bentler (1989) and Muthén (1989) for a more general approach.

8. Simulation

A data generation procedure has been built into EQS to permit simulation studies, which can be used to create artificial data to evaluate the empirical performance of various statistics under controlled conditions. A good overview of simulation methodology is given by Lewis and Orav (1989). A simulation in EQS requires (1) specification of the population, (2) a method of sampling, (3) an estimation run in every sample, (4) specification of the total number of samples, and (5) whether the output raw data files will be saved or what file names will be used. In addition, results from the EQS estimation in each sample may be saved in a file for further analysis.

In EQS, the population is specified in the usual job file; the model in the input file, or the input matrix, defines the population. However, variables in the population may be normal, elliptical, or non-normal continuous variables, or even categorical transformations of normal variables, providing that category thresholds are given. EQS performs two types of sampling: simple random sampling from the population (the default), or resampling with the bootstrap or jackknife (input raw data are taken as the population). Characteristics of each sample, and its EQS estimation, are controlled by the usual statements in a /SPECIFICATIONS section (e.g., estimation method, number of cases). In general, the sample statistics obtained from each sample will vary probabilistically from the population parameters, and a simulation study seeks to describe the sampling results. Most details of the simulation are specified in the new /SIMULATION paragraph, using keywords to create the particular study desired, e.g., the number of replications, the type of transformations desired, or the type of output information to be saved. For example, the following transformations are permissible:

	Uniform distribution	Normal Distribution
1	Uniform or Normal transformation	Normal transformation
2	Skew and/or kurtosis	Skew and/or kurtosis
3	Nonlinear transformation (LOG, EXP, and Power function)	Nonlinear transformation (EXP and Power function)
4	Contaminated normal	Contaminated normal

9. Conclusion

Version 3 of EQS has many new features that make it relevant in a variety of data gathering and statistical investigations. Some of the major new features relevant to the methodologist were summarized above. Of course, other technical changes designed to make the program more efficient and reliable were also made. Such technical details may not be of special interest to the data analyst, who will be more interested in the new user-friendly features such as the interactive on-line help facility that makes the program easier to use than ever before. Such a feature cannot be illustrated in this static summary.

References

Allison, P. D. (1987). Estimation of linear models with incomplete data. In C. Clogg (Ed.), Sociological Methodology 1987 (pp. 71-103). San Francisco: Jossey Bass.

Arminger, G., & Schoenberg, R. J. (1989). Pseudo maximum likelihood estimation and a test for misspecification in mean and covariance structure models. Psychometrika, 54, 409-425.

Bartlett, M. S. (1937). Properties of sufficiency and statistical tests. Proceedings of the Royal Society A, 160, 268-282.

Bentler, P. M. (1983a). Some contributions to efficient statistics for structural models: Specification and estimation of moment structures. Psychometrika, 48, 493-517.

Bentler, P. M. (1983b). Simultaneous equations as moment structure models: With an introduction to latent variable models. Journal of Econometrics, 22, 13-42.

Bentler, P. M. (1986). Structural modeling and Psychometrika: An historical perspective on growth and achievements. Psychometrika, 51, 35-51.

Bentler, P. M. (1988). Comparative fit indexes in structural models. Psychological Bulletin, in press. To appear, March, 1990.

Bentler, P. M. (1989). EQS structural equations program manual. Los Angeles: BMDP Statistical Software.

Bentler, P. M., & Dijkstra, T. (1985). Efficient estimation via linearization in structural models. In P. R. Krishnaiah (Ed.), Multivariate analysis VI (pp. 9-42). Amsterdam: North-Holland.

Bentler, P. M., Lee, S.-Y., & Weng, L.-J. (1987). Multiple population covariance structure analysis under arbitrary distribution theory. Communications in Statistics - Theory, 16, 1951-1964.

Bentler, P. M., & Weeks, D. G. (1980). Linear structural equations with latent variables. Psychometrika, 45, 289-308.

Bollen, K. A. (1989). Structural equations with latent variables. New York: Wiley.

Browne, M. W. (1982). Covariance structures. In D. M. Hawkins (Ed.), Topics in applied multivariate analysis (pp. 72-141). London: Cambridge University Press.

Browne, M. W. (1984). Asymptotically distribution-free methods for the analysis of covariance structures. British Journal of Mathematical and Statistical Psychology, 37, 62-83.

Chamberlain, G. (1982). Multivariate regression models for panel data. Journal of Econometrics, 18, 5-46.

Lee, S.-Y. (1985). On testing functional constraints in structural equation models. Biometrika, 72, 125-131.

Lee, S.-Y., & Bentler, P. M. (1980). Some asymptotic properties of constrained generalized least squares estimation in covariance structure models. South African Statistical Journal, 14, 121-136.

Lewis, P. A. W., & Orav, E. J. (1989). Simulation methodology for statisticians, operations analysts, and engineers. Pacific Grove, CA: Wadsworth.

Muthén, B. (1989). Multiple-group structural modelling with non-normal continuous variables. British Journal of Mathematical and Statistical Psychology, 42, 55-62.

Muthén, B., Kaplan, D., & Hollis, M. (1987). On structural equation modeling with data that are not missing completely at random. Psychometrika, 52, 431-462.

Satorra, A. (1989). Alternative test criteria in covariance structure analysis: A unified approach. Psychometrika, 54, 131-151.

Satorra, A., & Bentler, P. M. (1986). Some robustness properties of goodness of fit statistics in covariance structure analysis. American Statistical Association: Proceedings of the Business & Economic Statistics Section, 549-554.

Satorra, A., & Bentler, P. M. (1988a). Scaling corrections for statistics in covariance structure analysis. Los Angeles: UCLA Statistics Series #2.

Satorra, A., & Bentler, P. M. (1988b). Scaling corrections for chi-square statistics in covariance structure analysis. Proceedings of the American Statistical Association.

Sörbom, D. (1989). Model modification. Psychometrika, 54, 371-384.

… F. Faulbaum, R. Haux und K.-H. Jöckel (Hrsg.) (1990). SoftStat '89
Fortschritte der Statistik-Software 2. Stuttgart: Gustav Fischer, 57 - 65

Data Management mit CLINTRIAL bei klinischen Prüfungen

B. Dose und W. Holtbrügge

CLINTRIAL is an ORACLE based software product, that has been developed to facilitate clinical trials data management.
It supports data entry, definition of standardized database structures and data descriptions as well as tools for quality checks and quality assurance.

Additionally it provides interfaces to statistical software packages as SAS and RS/1.

Besides a description of the general concept and single CLINTRIAL components first experiences of the practical use are discussed.

1. Data Management bei klinischen Prüfungen

Die Entwicklung neuer therapeutischer Präparate und deren zeitgerechte Markteinführung hängt in hohem Maße von der zeitgerechten Erfassung und Verarbeitung komplexer klinischer Informationen ab. Die Anforderungen an die Validität und Qualität der Zulassungsunterlagen für therapeutische Präparate sind in den letzten Jahren stark gestiegen.
Durch die große Anzahl klinischer Prüfungen zu einer Projektsubstanz fallen viele, u.U. gleichartige Daten an, so daß eine Standardisierung der Datenhaltung angestrebt werden sollte.
Nur so werden studienübergreifende Wirksamkeits- und Sicherheitsanalysen ermöglicht, bei denen z.B. seltene Risiken aufgrund größerer Fallzahlen entdeckt werden können oder der Einfluß prognostischer Faktoren ermittelt werden kann.

Die Standardisierungsanforderungen resultieren aber auch aus organisatorischen Gründen: durch gleiche Datenhaltung bei ähnlichem Aufbau einzelner Studien, bei gleichartigen Daten oder Codierungen können viele Arbeitsschritte rationalisiert werden.

Um dieses Ziel zu erreichen, können folgende Bereiche vereinheitlicht werden:

Erhebungsbögen: Manche Bögen können in verschiedenen Studien verwendet werden, z.B. ein Bogen über die Begleitmedikationen oder EKG-Daten.
Variablen: Variablen mit gleicher Bedeutung sollten gleiche Namen, gleiche Codierungen, gleiche Datentypen, etc. zugeordnet werden.
Datenstrukturen, Eingabemasken: Sofern gleichartige Erhebungsbögen studienübergreifend verwendet werden, können Datenstrukturen und Eingabemasken vereinheitlicht werden.
Auswertungsschritte: Sind Datenstrukturen standardisiert, können Teile der Auswertung (beispielsweise zusammenfassende Tabellen) standardisiert werden.

2. Anforderungen an ein Data-Managementsystem

Es lassen sich folgende Anforderungen an ein Data-Managementsystem für klinische Prüfungen stellen:

- Das System sollte einen standardisierten Aufbau der Datenstrukturen und einheitliche Erfassungsmasken unterstützen.
- Um die Studiendurchlaufzeit möglichst gering zu halten und Inkonsistenzen möglichst früh zu erkennen, muß eine studienbegleitende Datenerfassung möglich sein. Zusätzlich sollte das System die Möglichkeit zur Doppelerfassung bieten und dabei Unterschiede zwischen Erst- und Zweiterfassung erkennen.

- Zur Datenvalidierung sollten Mechanismen zur Verfügung stehen, die die Gültigkeit der Daten so früh wie möglich und so ausführlich wie möglich überprüfen. Dadurch lassen sich Fehler in den Daten frühzeitig erkennen und beheben, wodurch die Datenqualität gesteigert wird.
- Änderungen an den Daten müssen vom System protokolliert werden, um diese leicht zurückverfolgen zu können.
- Die Datenhaltung ist so flexibel zu gestalten, daß z.B. nachträgliche Strukturänderungen, Berechnung abgeleiteter Größen, etc. ermöglicht werden.
- Es wird ein adäquates Datenschutzkonzept erwartet, das eine Zuordnung von Zugriffsberechtigungen (recherchieren, erfassen, ändern, löschen) zu Zugriffsberechtigten (Personen) ermöglicht. Das System sollte weiterhin ausreichenden Schutz gegen unbeabsichtigte Zerstörung von Daten bieten.
- Es müssen Schnittstellen zu gängigen statistischen Auswertungssystemen bereitgestellt werden.

3. Aufbau von CLINTRIAL

CLINTRIAL ist ein menu-gesteuertes Datenbankverwaltungssystem, das speziell für klinische Studien von der Firma BBN entwickelt wurde. Auftraggeber waren verschiedene Firmen aus der pharmazeutischen Industrie.
Das System läuft auf den DEC-Rechnern der VAX-Familie unter dem Betriebssystem VMS. Es basiert auf RS/1, einem integrierten Datenanalysesystem, und auf ORACLE, einem relationalen Datenbanksystem.
ORACLE ermöglicht ein flexibles Datenbankdesign, einen hohen Grad an Datenbanksicherheit und stellt SQL als Abfragesprache zur Verfügung.

CLINTRIAL besteht aus folgende Komponenten:

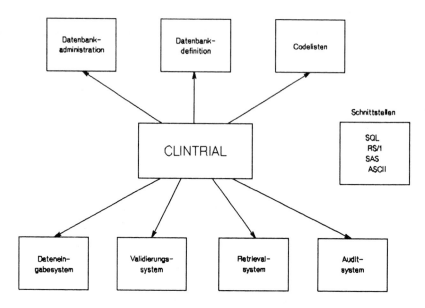

Im folgenden werden zwei CLINTRIAL-Begriffe erläutert, die zum weiteren Verständnis benötigt werden:

PROTOCOL: Ein Clintrial-Protocol ist eine Einheit, in der üblicherweise alle Daten zu einer klinischen Prüfung gespeichert werden.

PANEL: Innerhalb eines Protocols werden in einem Panel die Daten zusammengefaßt, die logisch und/oder zeitlich zusammengehören, z.B. alle Anamnesedaten oder alle Labordaten. Ein Panel entspricht also einer Relation im herkömmlichen Sinne.
Für jedes Panel werden drei ORACLE-Tabellen angelegt: UPDATE-Table, DATA-Table und AUDIT-Table.

In der UPDATE-Table werden die Daten erfaßt. Nach Abschluß der Validierungen werden sie in die DATA-Table überführt. In der AUDIT-Table werden Änderungen protokolliert, die an den Daten in der DATA-Table vorgenommen wurden.

4. Funktionen von CLINTRIAL

4.1 Datenbankadministration

In dieser Komponente werden Benutzer und Benutzergruppen verwaltet, Zugriffsrechte vergeben, Protocols angelegt und der Speicherplatz verwaltet.
Besonders hervorzuheben sind die Sicherheitsaspekte. Für jede der drei Panel-Tabellen Update, Data und Audit können die Rechte SELECT, UPDATE, INSERT und DELETE getrennt vergeben werden. Weiterhin hat man die Möglichkeit, den Zugriff auf einzelne Menüpunkte zu beschränken.

4.2 Datenbankdefinition

Dieses Teilsystem von CLINTRIAL beinhaltet im wesentlichen die Beschreibung der Relationen.

Wie bereits erwähnt, ist CLINTRIAL speziell auf klinische Prüfungen zugeschnitten. Aus diesem Grund muß der Primärschlüssel eine eindeutige Patientenidentifikation und der Sekundärschlüssel die Terminnummer sein. Ausgehend von diesen beiden Variablen unterscheidet CLINTRIAL zwischen fünf verschiedenen Paneltypen :

Typ 1: Pro Patient gibt es genau einen Satz (z.B. Anamnese)
Typ 2: Pro Patient gibt es beliebig viele Sätze (z.B. Vorerkrankungen)
Typ 3: Pro Patient und Termin gibt es genau einen Satz (z.B. Blutdruckwerte)
Typ 4: Pro Patient und Termin gibt es beliebig viele Sätze (z.B. Begleitmedikamente)
Typ 0: Die Daten sind unabhängig von Patient und Termin (z.B. Labornormbereichsgrenzen)

Die resultierenden Bedingungen für den bei der Paneldefinition spezifizierten Typ werden von CLINTRIAL beim Überführen der Daten von der Update-Table in die Data-Table überprüft.

Bei der Datenbankdefinition unterstützt CLINTRIAL eine Standardisierung auf Variablenebene. Man kann festlegen, daß ein Benutzer keine neuen Variablen definieren darf, sondern lediglich aus anderen Protocols kopieren darf. Hierzu ist es sinnvoll, Standardprotocols einzurichten, die nur Variablendefinitionen beinhalten und in denen keine Daten gespeichert werden.

4.3 Codelisten

Eine Codeliste in CLINTRIAL - vergleichbar mit einem SAS-Format - besteht aus den vier Variablen CODE, VALUE, LABEL und LONGLABEL.

Beispiel für eine Codeliste:

Code	Value	Label	Longlabel
1	m	männlich	male
2	w	weiblich	female

Innerhalb eines Protocols muß die Zuordnung zwischen Variable und Codeliste eindeutig sein.
Codelisten in CLINTRIAL werden zentral gehalten, so daß alle Protocols auf alle Codelisten zugreifen können. Um den Aufwand bei der Verwaltung der Codelisten zu minimieren, ist es sinnvoll, die Codelisten studienübergreifend zu standardisieren.
Schließlich ist es möglich, aus den Codelisten direkt SAS-Formate zu generieren.

4.4 Dateneingabesystem

CLINTRIAL unterstützt sowohl eine interaktive Eingabe über Bildschirmmasken als auch das Laden von externen Dateien im Batchmode.
Bei der interaktiven Eingabe können Datentyp-, Codelisten- und Bereichsüberprüfungen durchgeführt werden. Ferner hat man die Möglichkeit, Inhalte einer Maske in eine Folgemaske zu übertragen.
Um eine hohe Qualität der eingegeben Daten zu erreichen, können diese doppelt erfaßt werden. Bei der Zweiterfassung werden vorhandene Inkonsistenzen zur Ersterfassung sofort angezeigt.
Im Batchmode hat man die Möglichkeit, externe ASCII-Files gemäß einer Ladespezifikation in die Datenbank zu laden.

4.5 Validierungssystem

Diese CLINTRIAL-Komponente beinhaltet zwei Funktionen. Zum einen kann man aus Variablen abgeleitete Größen berechnen und zum anderen kann man die Gültigkeit der Daten anhand vorher definierter Regeln überprüfen. Aufgrund dieser Überprüfungen entsteht eine Mängelliste ("Errorlog"), die alle Sätze beinhaltet, die eine Regel verletzt haben.

4.6 Retrievalsystem

Dieses System dient zur Selektion von Daten aus der Datenbank. So können ASCII-Dateien, SAS-Datasets oder RS/1-Tabellen generiert werden. Die Schnittstelle zu SAS bietet sowohl die Möglichkeit SAS-Datasets als auch ASCII-Files plus die dazu passenden SAS-Input-Statements / Formatzuweisungen / Labelanweisungen zu erzeugen.

4.7 Auditsystem

Sobald die Daten aus der Update-Table in die Data-Table überführt worden sind, werden alle weiteren Änderungen protokolliert. Es werden alte und neue Werte, das Datum der Modifikation sowie Identifikation der Eingabeperson gespeichert.

5. Bewertung

Die Anforderungen, die an ein Data-Managementsystem für klinische Prüfungen zu stellen sind, werden grundsätzlich von CLINTRIAL erfüllt.
Positiv erwähnenswert ist das Validierungssystem, durch das die Qualität der Daten sichergestellt werden kann. Interaktive Hilfsfunktionen werden ausreichend zur Verfügung gestellt. Besonders komfortabel ist die Schnittstelle zu SAS. Ein Pluspunkt ist das vorhandene Auditsystem, das hilfreich bei der Zurückverfolgung von Änderungen an den Daten ist.

Andererseits gibt es auch negative Aspekte. So sind die automatisch bei der Validierung erzeugten Mängellisten (Errorlogs) für CLINTRIAL-Laien schwer zu interpretieren. Der Anwender muss sich in mehreren Systemen gleichzeitig auskennen. Er benötigt sowohl SQL-Kenntnisse als auch Kenntnisse über das RS/1-System und dessen Programmiersprache RPL. Die Reportfunktionen sind inflexibel und für die meisten Anwendungen nicht ausreichend (Überschriften der Spalten in den Listen nicht frei wählbar, Tagesdatum und Seitennumerierung nicht möglich, etc.). Wünschenswert wäre eine bessere Dokumentation der Batchdateneingabe. Ein letzter Kritikpunkt liegt in der Beschränkung des Systems auf VAX-Hardware.

Zusammenfassend kann man sagen, daß die Ziele, die mit der Einführung eines Data-Managementsystems angestrebt werden sollten, mit CLINTRIAL zu realisieren sind. Dazu gehören u.a. Pluspunkte wie z.B. die verbesserte Datenqualität durch kontinuierliche Doppelerfassung und Validierung, die übergreifende Nutzung der Daten durch Standardisierung und die Protokollierung der Änderungen an den Daten. Daher sind die positiven Aspekte alles in allem höher zu bewerten als die Schwachstellen des Systems.

References:

BBN Software Products Corp. (1987). CLINTRIAL Users Guide, Cambridge, MA, USA.

BBN Software Products Corp. (1986). RS/1 Users Guide - VAX-VMS/UNIX, Cambridge, MA, USA.

Verfahren und Probleme bei der Analyse von Meßwiederholungsdesigns mit SPSS-X, MANOVA und BMDP4V

K. Fehres und F. Marschall

Repeated measurement designs for analysis of variance have been analysed using the MANOVA procedure in SPSS-X and SPSS/PC, and the P4V procedure in BMDP. Subcommands in MANOVA for generating a user-friendly output are presented. Possible solutions for executing a-posteriori-tests for within-subject measurement, which are not implemented in the aforementioned procedures, are also offered.

1 Problemstellung

Die experimentelle Untersuchung von Lernprozessen beinhaltet i.d.R. die Frage nach der Veränderung spezifischer Leistungs- oder Lernparameter. Dazu werden diese Parameter zumindest zu zwei (Praetest, Posttest), in vielen Untersuchungen jedoch zu drei oder mehr Meßzeitpunkten erhoben. Die statistische Analyse solcher Meßwiederholungsdesigns stellt dabei ein grundsätzliches Problem dar. Dies läßt sich daraus entnehmen, daß in einer Vielzahl von Lernexperimenten die dort verwendeten Verfahren kaum diskutiert werden und darüberhinaus in der angewandten Statistik solche Verfahren theoretisch und pragmatisch nicht besprochen werden. Eine Ursache hierfür liegt darin "(...), daß man die Unterschiede zwischen Zustands- und Prozeßbeschreibung oft ignoriert und sich der Vorstellung hingibt, mit den mehr oder weniger bewährten Methoden der Zustandsbeschreibung auch Veränderungen darstellen zu können" (PETERMANN 1978,11). Ein weiterer Grund ist in der für den Nutzer kaum überschaubaren Plastizität der in verschiedenen Statistikpaketen implementierten Prozeduren zur statistischen Analyse von Meßwiederholungsdesigns zu suchen. Die daraus resultierende Benutzerunfreundlichkeit kann auch von den einschlägigen Handbüchern nicht aufgefangen werden. Dies gilt im besonderen Maße für spezielle Probleme bei der statistischen Analyse von Meßwiederholungsdesigns mit SPSS und BMDP.

In diesem Beitrag sollen am Beispiel der SPSS - Prozedur MANOVA und der BMDP - Prozedur P4V auf einer pragmatischen Ebene nutzerrelevante Lösungsansätze aufgezeigt werden.

Das allgemeine Modell beispielsweise einer zweifaktoriellen Varianzanalyse mit Meßwiederholung beinhaltet den treatment-beeinflußten Faktor A, p-fach gestuft, sowie den Meßwiederholungsfaktor B, q-fach gestuft. Bei einem vollständigen Versuchsplan werden p unabhängige Gruppen zu q Zeitpunkten untersucht. Die statistischen Verfahren zur Analyse von Meßwiederholungsdesigns gehen davon aus, daß die zu den q Zeitpunkten erhobenen Meßwerte jeder Versuchsperson nicht unabhängig voneinander sind. Dieser Voraussetzungsverletzung einer Varianzanalyse **ohne** Meßwiederholung wird bei der Varianzanalyse **mit** Meßwiederholung durch eine entsprechende Quadratsummenzerlegung Rechnung getragen (BORTZ 1985, 404).

2 Zur Gestaltung des MANOVA - Ausdrucks bei univariatem Ansatz

Da die MANOVA-Prozedur Meßwiederholungsanalysen und multivariate Varianzanalysen "formal äquivalent" (BORTZ 1985, 613) behandelt, ist es zunächst notwendig, aus der Vielzahl der in MANOVA möglichen Anweisungen diejenigen auszuwählen, die zum einen eine univariate Meßwiederholungsanalyse in Form eines gemittelten F-Tests **durchführen** und zum anderen die defaults für den multivariaten Ansatz **unterdrücken**. Ein Fehlen dieser zusätzlichen Spezifikationen führt bei der Prozedur MANOVA, zumindest in der Version SPSS-9, zu einer kaum les- und interpretierbaren Flut von z.T. redundanten und für die Fragestellung sogar nutzlosen und den Nutzer verwirrenden Informationen.

Die folgende Darstellung der Anweisungen geht von der Version SPSS-X 2.2 aus.

```
MANOVA  q abhängige Variablen [BY Faktoren (min, max)]    (a)
        /WSFACTORS = Meßzeitpunkte (n)                    (b)
        /PRINT = SIGNIF (AVONLY GG HF)                    (c)
                 HOMOGENEITY (BARTLETT COCHRAN)
```

Abb.1 Struktur der Basis-Anweisungen am Beispiel einer zweifaktoriellen Varianzanalyse mit Meßwiederholung auf einem Faktor

(a) Voraussetzung für die Durchführung der MANOVA - Prozedur stellt eine entsprechende Datenorganisation dar, d.h. pro Meßzeitpunkt muß eine abhängige Variable definiert sein. Entsprechend gehen bei q Meßzeitpunkten q abhängige Variablen in die erste Anweisung ein.

(b) Auf der <u>WSFACTORS</u> - Karte wird eine optionale Bezeichnung für den Meßwiederholungsfaktor mit der in Klammern gesetzten Anzahl der Meßzeitpunkte angegeben.

(c) Mit der <u>PRINT</u>-Karte wird der Inhalt des outputs festgelegt:
- Die Anweisung PRINT = SIGNIF (AVONLY GG HH) berechnet gemittelte F-Tests, sowohl für den Treatment- wie auch den Meßwiederholungsfaktor; GG und HF sorgen für die Berechnung des Signifikanzniveaus auf der Grundlage korrigierter Freiheitsgrade (cf unten).
- Die Anweisung PRINT = HOMOGENEITY (BARTLETT COCHRAN) fordert als univariate Tests Bartlett-Box's F sowie Cochran's C zur Überprüfung der Varianzhomogenität der Gruppen zu jedem Meßzeitpunkt an. Auf den entsprechenden multivariaten Box's M - Test kann verzichtet werden, da bei Verwendung der oben aufgeführten Anweisung PRINT = SIGNIF (AVONLY) der Mauchly's Test of Sphericity zur Überprüfung der Homogenität der Varianz - Kovarianz - Matrix in SPSS-X default ist.

Dies stellt zugleich eine wesentliche Erweiterung zu den für Varianzanalysen ohne Meßwiederholung notwendigen Voraussetzungsprüfungen dar. Bei der Varianzanalyse mit Meßwiederholung wird eine zusätzliche Prüfung der Homogenität der Varianz-Kovarianz-Matrix notwendig. Es wird gefordert, daß neben den Varianzen unter den einzelnen Faktorstufen zusätzlich die Korrelationen zwischen den Faktorstufen homogen sein sollen (BORTZ 1985, 428), was in SPSS-X MANOVA mit dem Sphärizitätstest überprüft wird. Da diese Voraussetzung in Meßwiederholungsdesigns, insbesondere bei Lernexperimenten, in der Regel verletzt ist, erfordert die Varianzanalyse mit Meßwiederholung fast immer hierauf abgestellte Korrekturverfahren, die die Reduktion der Freiheitsgrade durch den Faktor beinhalten. Durch die Anweisung PRINT = SIGNIF(AVONLY) werden drei mögliche Korrekturgrößen für die Freiheitsgrade (Greenhouse-Geisser-ϵ, Huyn-Feldt-ϵ, Lower Bound-ϵ) ausgegeben. Während die durch das Lower Bound-ϵ korrigierten Freiheitsgrade und die daraus errechneten Signifikanzen auf der Annahme einer maximalen Homogenität der Kovarianzen beruhen (entsprechend einem konservativen F - Test), bezieht sich die Berechnung des Greenhouse-Geisser-ϵ und des Huyn-Feldt-ϵ auf die weniger scharfe Annahme, daß die Differenzen zwischen den jeweils zu zwei Meßzeitpunkten (Faktorstufen des Meßwiederholungfaktors) erhobenen Varianzen homogen sind. Hierbei führt die Anwendung des GG-ϵ tendenziell zu den konser-vativeren Ergebnissen. Ab SPSS-X (aber nicht bis zur PC-Vers. 3.0) kann mit PRINT = SIGNIF (AVONLY GG HF) und der ent-sprechenden Modifizierung der Freiheitsgrade unmittelbar das korrigierte Signifikanzniveau berechnet und ausgedruckt werden.

Eine mögliche Alternative zu der Anforderung PRINT = SIGNIF (AVONLY) bildet die Anweisung PRINT = SIGNIF (AVERF). Man erhält damit als erste Varianztafel einen gemittelten Signifikanztest und zugleich die Ergebnisse einer multivariaten Behandlung des Designs. Letzteres kann durch die zusätzliche Anweisung NOPRINT = SIGNIF (MULTIV) unterdrückt werden. Bei dieser Variante ist die Anforderung des Sphärizitätstests weder optional noch default. Vor- und Nachteile der gemittelten Signifikanztests und der multivariaten Herangehensweise sollen hier nicht weiter diskutiert werden (cf. dazu NORUSIS 1985, 266).

Im Anschluß an die Prüfung der Homogenitätsvoraussetzungen finden sich bei der oben beschriebenen Auswahl an Anweisungen zwei Varianzanalyse-Tafeln, wobei in der ersten Tafel treatmentbedingte Haupteffekte, bei mehr als einem Treatmentfaktor auch die entsprechenden Interaktionseffekte, aufgeführt sind (Prüfung auf Unterschied). Die zweite Varianzanalyse-Tafel, die der Berechnung der Korrekturfaktoren für die Freiheitsgrade folgt, beinhaltet alle, die Meßwiederholung betreffenden Effekte, i.e. den Haupteffekt 'Meßzeitpunkte' sowie alle Interaktionseffekte mit den Meßzeitpunkten (Prüfung auf Veränderung). Die jeweiligen varianzanalytischen Prüfgrößen werden (verwirrenderweise) in beiden Tafeln mit der Bezeichnung 'within cells' aufgeführt. Die Berechnung des Constant-Faktors ist default; geprüft wird dabei der Unterschied des Gesamtmittelwertes von Null. Dieser Effekt kann dann von Interesse sein, wenn z. B. die Differenz zwischen empirisch ermittelten Werten und einem auf '0' gesetzten Sollwert statistisch abgesichert werden soll.

Ein ausführlicher Überblick über die Möglichkeiten und Probleme bei einer weiteren Analyse der treatmentbedingten Haupt- und Interaktionseffekte (a posteriori Vergleiche, Analyse der einfachen Haupteffekte etc.), insbesondere auch zur Adjustierung des Signifikanzniveaus bei Mehrfachanalysen, findet sich bei DIEHL (1983). Die daraus resultierenden statistischen Berechnungen können mit den in SPSS-X und BMDP implementierten Prozeduren durchgeführt werden.

Ein grundsätzliches, in beiden Statistikpaketen nicht thematisiertes Problem taucht jedoch bei der statistischen Analyse von a posteriori Vergleichen über Meßzeitpunkte auf.

3   'A Posteriori Vergleiche' über Meßzeitpunkte in SPSS-X MANOVA und BMDP4V

Bei einer Reihe experimenteller Fragestellungen, denen Meßwiederholungsdesigns zugrundeliegen, sind a posteriori Vergleiche über einzelne bzw. Kombinationen von Meßzeitpunkten von Interesse. Dies gilt im besonderen Maße auch für Lernexperimente, in denen etwa Behaltens- oder Vergessensprozesse thematisiert sind.

Während zur Prüfung von a priori Unterschieden bei Orthogonalität der Einzelvergleiche z. B. auch t-Tests für abhängige Stichproben durchgeführt werden können, basiert die Prüfung von a posteriori Unterschieden auf nicht-orthogonalen Vergleichen - analog etwa zum Scheffé-Test bei Varianzanalysen ohne Meßwiederholung. Entgegen den Angaben des deutschen Handbuchs "Die CONTRAST-Angabe gibt die Methode an, nach der die Kontraste (geplante Vergleiche) für einen bestimmten Faktor zu bilden sind. Dies gilt für gewöhnliche wie für WS-Faktoren (Meßwiederholungsfaktoren; d. Verf.)" (SCHUBÖ/UEHLINGER 1986, 303) findet sich im englischsprachigen Manual die Aussage "(...) it is recommended that only orthogonal contrasts be specified on the CONTRAST subcommand for within-subjects factors" (NORUSIS 1985, 286).

In der Tat führt die Anforderung der CONTRAST-Anweisung, die a posteriori Vergleiche über zeitunabhängige Treatmentstufen erlaubt, im Falle des Meßwiederholungsfaktors zu Ergebnissen, die nur für einige wenige Vergleichsstufen nachvollziehbare Aussagen zuläßt. Eine Interpretation des **Gesamt**ausdrucks ist - unabhängig von der Wahl der CONTRAST-Parameter - jedoch nicht möglich und kann nur mit Hilfe von Plausibilitätsüberlegungen unter Berücksichtigung der Datenlage bzw. unter Einbeziehung der orthonormalisierten Transformationsmatrix erfolgen. Die nachvollziehbaren Detailergebnisse sind jeweils identisch mit den Resultaten, die man bei der Verwendung von t-Tests für abhängige Stichproben bzw. beim Anfordern von mehreren, formal voneinander unabhängigen Varianzanalysen mit Meßwiederholung auf 2 Stufen des Meßwiederholungsfaktors erhält. Insgesamt ist diese Vorgehensweise schlichtweg abzulehnen.

Ein Lösungsansatz für das formulierte Problem wird in der SPSS-nahen Zeitschrift PERFORMANCE PLUS (1988) beschrieben. Die dort vorgeschlagene Variante bildet über einen Zwischenschritt eine neue Transformationsmatrix für nicht-orthogonale Kontraste (cf. Abb. 2). Zur besseren Übersichtlichkeit geht das folgende Beispiel von einer einfaktoriellen Varianzanalyse mit Meßwiederholung aus.

```
MANOVA    drug1 to drug4
   /WSFACTORS = drug(4)
MANOVA    drug1 to drug4
   /TRANSFORM = SIMPLE
   /RENAME = cons drug1vs4 drug2vs4 drug3vs4
   /NOPRINT = SIGNIF (UNIV MULTIV)
   /PRINT = TRANSFORM PAR(EST)
```

Abb. 2 MANOVA-Anweisungen zur Analyse (angeblich) nicht-orthogonaler Kontraste über einen Meßwiederholungsfaktor nach PERFORMANCE PLUS (1988)

Es soll bei diesem Beispiel jeweils der Unterschied zwischen den Meßzeitpunkten 1 vs. 4, 2 vs. 4 sowie 3 vs. 4 auf Signifikanz geprüft werden; d.h. der 4. Meßzeitpunkt geht insgesamt dreimal in die statistische Berechnung ein. Die so erhaltenen Ergebnisse sind auf den ersten Blick in der Tat plausibel und interpretationsfähig, sie berücksichtigen jedoch in keiner Weise das durch das mehrfache Eingehen von Faktorstufen erhöhte α-Fehlerrisiko: auch hier wird trotz anderslautender Aussage (cf. PERFORMANCE 1988) von der Orthogonalität der Einzelvergleiche ausgegangen und t-Tests für abhängige Stichproben gerechnet.

Zusammenfassend kann für die Prozedur MANOVA in SPSS-X festgestellt werden, daß nicht-orthogonale Einzelvergleiche über den Meßwiederholungsfaktor **nicht** durchzuführen sind.

Diese Aussage gilt in gleichem Maße für die Prozedur P4V in dem Statistikpaket BMDP.

```
DESIGN FACTOR = drug.
       TYPE = WITHIN; CONTRAST.
       CODE = READ.
       VALUES = 1, 0, 0, -1.
       NAME = drug1vs4./
DESIGN VALUES = 0, 1, 0, -1.
       NAME = drug2vs4./
DESIGN VALUES = 0, 0, 1, -1.
       NAME = drug3vs4./
```

Abb. 3 Anforderung von Kontrasteffekten in BMDP4V (entsprechend der Abb. 2 zugrundeliegenden Fragestellung)

Durch die Parameterwahl im Designparagraphen (cf Abb. 3) könnte leicht der Eindruck entstehen, hier sei die Berechnung nicht-orthogonaler Vergleiche über die Stufen des Meßwiederholungsfaktors möglich. Aber auch hier werden - trotz Angabe von F-Werten im Ausdruck - t-Tests für abhängige Stichproben gerechnet.

Welche Konsequenzen ergeben sich nun für die Prüfung von a posteriori Unterschieden über die Stufen des Meßwiederholungsfaktors? BORTZ (1985) nennt zwei Möglichkeiten zur Verringerung des α-Fehlerrisikos:

(a) die Berücksichtigung der Anzahl der mehrfach eingehenden Faktorstufen durch die Adjustierung des Signifikanzniveaus (ebd., 321f)

(b) beim Vorliegen einer einfaktoriellen Varianzanalyse mit Meßwiederholung die Berechnung eines Scheffé-Tests, wobei die Fehlervarianz durch die Residualvarianz ersetzt wird (ebd., 406). Beide Prüfgrößen sowie ihre Freiheitsgrade finden sich in den Ausdrucken, die Rechnung ist 'per Hand' durchzuführen.

LITERATUR

Bortz, J. (1985). Lehrbuch der Statistik. Springer, Berlin/ Heidelberg/New York/Tokyo.

Diehl, J. M. (1983). Varianzanalyse. Fachbuchhandlung für Psychologie, Frankfurt.

Norusis, M. J. (1985). SPSS-X Advanced Statistics Guide. SPSS Inc., o.O..

Performance Plus (1988). Non-orthogonal Contrasts in MANOVA Repeated Measures Design. Fall, 4-7.

Petermann, F. (1978). Veränderungsmessung. Kohlhammer, Stuttgart/Berlin/Köln/Mainz.

Schubö, W./Uehlinger, H.-M. (1986). SPSS-X. Handbuch der Programmversion 2.2. Gustaf Fischer-Verlag, Stuttgart/New York.

Proc CALIS: Analysis of Covariance Structures

W. M. Hartmann

Abstract

CALIS, a new SAS STAT procedure, fits structural equation models and computes approximate standard errors and hypothesis tests for interval level data. The model is the generalized COSAN model. Equality and inequality constraints on the parameters are allowed. The results of the analysis are saved in output data sets that can be used as input to the procedure in order to modify the analysis by changing initial values, adding or removing constraints, adding or removing parameters, etc. CALIS obtains unweighted least-squares, generalized least-squares, normal-theory maximum-likelihood, weighted least-squares, or diagonally weighted least-squares estimates of the parameters.

Key words: covariance structure analysis, structural equations, simultaneous equations, confirmatory factor analysis, path analysis, COSAN, LISREL, EQS.

1 The Generalized COSAN Model

CALIS can analyze matrix models of the form (Generalized COSAN Model):

$$C = F_1 P_1 F_1^T + \cdots + F_m P_m F_m^T,$$

C : given symmetric correlation or covariance matrix,
F_k, $k = 1, \ldots, m$: product of $n(k)$ matrices $F_{k1}, \ldots, F_{k_{n(k)}}$,
P_k : symmetric coefficient matrices

$$F_k = F_{k_1} \cdots F_{k_{n(k)}}, \quad \text{and} \quad P_k = P_k^T, \quad k = 1, \ldots, m,$$

$$F_{k_j} = \begin{cases} G_{k_j}, \\ G_{k_j}^{-1}, \\ (I - G_{k_j})^{-1}, \end{cases} \quad j = 1, \ldots, n(k), \quad \text{and} \quad P_k = \begin{cases} Q_k, \\ Q_k^{-1}. \end{cases}$$

The matrices G_{k_j} and Q_k contain both constant elements in certain user-specified positions and parameters, which can be summarized in a parameter vector $X = (x_1, \ldots, x_t)$. For a given (corrected or uncorrected) covariance or correlation matrix C, CALIS computes the unweighted least-squares (ULS), generalized least-squares (GLS), normal-theory maximum-likelihood (ML), weighted least-squares (WLS), or diagonally weighted least-squares (DWLS) estimates of the vector X. The weight matrix W for for GLS, WLS, or DWLS estimation can be read from an input data set or set by default (WLS estimation then is identical to Browne's (1982, 1984) asymptotic distribution free estimation).

Some special cases of the Generalized COSAN Model are:

- Original COSAN model of McDonald (1978, 1980),
- RAM model of McArdle (1980),
- EQS model of Bentler & Weeks (1980),
- Keesling - Wiley - Jöreskog LISREL model,
- Hierarchy of Factor Analysis Models.

The very general form of this model allows CALIS to analyze a broad family of problems. In CALIS there are four ways to specify a model:

1. You can specify a generalized COSAN model directly using COSAN and MATRIX statements.
2. If you have a set of structural equations to describe the model, you can use an equation-type LINEQS statement (together with a STD and COV statement) similar to that originally developed by Peter Bentler (1985).
3. You can specify simple path models using an easily-formulated list-type RAM statement (McArdle, 1980).
4. You can do a constrained first-order factor analysis or component analysis using the FACTOR statement.

For example, to specify the first-order autoregressive longitudinal factor model of Mc DONALD (1980) with m = 3 variables, k = 3 occasions, and r = 2 factors,

$$C = BD_1 D_2 T D_2^{-1} D_1^{-1} P D_1^{-T} D_2^{-T} T^T D_2^T D_1^T B^T + U^2,$$

you can use the following COSAN model statement:

```
COSAN B(6,GEN) * D1(6,DIA) * D2(6,DIA) * T(6,LOW) *
      D3(6,DIA,INV) * D4(6,DIA,INV) * P(6,DIA) + U(9,SYM);
```

Simple equality constraints, $x_i = c_i$ and $x_i = x_j$, can be defined in each model by specifying constants or using the same name for parameters constrained to be equal. Boundary constraints, $l_i \leq x_i \leq u_i$, can be specified with the BOUNDS statement. For example, to specify the stability and alienation example of the EQS 2.0 manual you can use the following LINEQS model statement:

```
PROC CALIS COV DATA=WHEATON EDF=931;
TITLE3 'EQS 2. Manual, page 31';
  LINEQS
        V1 =      F1 + E1,
        V2 = .833 F1 + E2,
        V3 =      F2 + E3,
        V4 = .833 F2 + E4,
        V5 =      F3 + E5,
        V6 = LAMB F3 + E6,
        F1 = GAM1 F3 + D1,
```

```
        F2 = BETA F1 + GAM2 F3 + D2;
STD
        E1-E6 = THE1 THE2 THE1-THE4,
        D1-D2 = PSI1 PSI2,
        F3    = PHI;
COV
        E1 E3 = THE5,
        E4 E2 = THE5;
BOUNDS
        THE1-THE4 >= 0.,
        PSI1 PSI2 PHI >= 0;
RUN;
```

More complex linear equality and inequality constraints can be defined by means of programming statements similar to those used in the SAS DATA step. In this case, some of the parameters x_i are not elements of the matrices G_{k_j} and Q_k, but instead are defined in a PARMS statement. Elements of the model matrices then can be computed by programming statements as functions of parameters listed in the PARMS statement. This approach is similar to the classical COSAN program of R. McDonald, implemented by C. Fraser. One advantage of PROC CALIS is that the user does not need to supply code for the derivatives of the specified functions. The analytic derivatives of the user-written functions are computed automatically by PROC CALIS. The specified functions must be continuous and have continuous first-order partial derivatives.

2 Estimation Methods

Five estimation methods are available in CALIS:
- unweighted least-squares (ULS),
- generalized least-squares (GLS),
- normal-theory maximum-likelihood (ML),
- weighted least-squares (WLS),
- diagonally weighted least-squares (DWLS).

In each case the parameter vector X is estimated iteratively by a nonlinear optimization algorithm that minimizes a badness-of-fit criterion F. When S denotes the given sample correlation or covariance matrix for a sample with size N and C denotes the predicted moment matrix, then the fit criterion for unweighted and generalized least-squares estimation is

$$F = .5 Tr[(W(S - C))^2],$$

for maximum-likelihood estimation it is

$$F = Tr(SC^{-1}) - N + log(det(C)) - log(det(S)),$$

for weighted least-squares estimation it is

$$F = Vec(s_{ij} - c_{ij})^T W^{-1} Vec(s_{ij} - c_{ij}),$$

and for diagonally weighted least-squares estimation it is

$$F = Vec(s_{ij} - c_{ij})^T diag(W)^{-1} Vec(s_{ij} - c_{ij}).$$

For ULS, the weight matrix W is the identity matrix I and for GLS, the default weight matrix is the inverse sample moment matrix S^{-1}. For WLS the default weight matrix is one of the asymptotic covariance matrices proposed by Browne (1984) or the asymptotic correlation matrix by DeLeeuw (1983). For DWLS the default weight matrix is the diagonal matrix of the weight matrix used for WLS.

Except for unweighted least-squares, standard errors can be computed as the diagonal elements of the matrix $2H^{-1}/N$, where H is an approximate Hessian matrix of F evaluated at the final estimates. If a given correlation or covariance matrix is singular, CALIS offers two ways to compute a generalized inverse of the information matrix H and therefore two ways to compute standard errors, t values, and modification indices. If the number of parameters to fit is smaller than a specified limit, an expensive Moore-Penrose inverse of H is used; otherwise an inexpensive generalized inverse is computed.

PROC CALIS prints a variety of indices to evaluate the fit of the model. For the ML estimates of the stability and alienation example this output is:

```
         Fit criterion . . . . . . . . . . . . . . . .        0.0145
         Goodness of Fit Index (GFI) . . . . . . . . . .      0.9953
         GFI Adjusted for Degrees of Freedom (AGFI)  . . .    0.9890
         Root Mean Square Residual (RMR) . . . . . . . . .   0.2294
         Chi-square = 13.4860      df = 9      Prob>chi**2 = 0.1418
         Z-Test of Wilson & Hilfrety (1932) . . . . . . .    1.0756
         Akaikes's Information Criterion . . . . . . . . .  -4.5140
         Schwarz's Bayesian Criterion  . . . . . . . . .   -48.0500
         McDonald's Centrality . . . . . . . . . . . . .     0.9976
         Bentler & Bonett's Non-normed Index . . . . . . .   0.9965
         Bentler & Bonett's Normed Index . . . . . . . . .   0.9937
         James, Mulaik, & Brett (1982) Parsimonious Index.   0.5962
         Bollen (1986) Normed Index Rho1 . . . . . . . . .   0.9895
         Bollen (1987) Non-normed Index Delta2 . . . . . .   0.9979
```

PROC CALIS computes a default set of modification indices:

- Univariate Lagrange multiplier test indices for most elements in the model matrices that are constrained to equal constants. Besides the value of the Lagrange multiplier, the corresponding probability ($df = 1$), and the estimated parameter value (should the constant be changed to a parameter) are printed.

- Univariate Wald test indices for those matrix elements which correspond to parameter estimates in the model.

- Univariate Lagrange multiplier test indices which result from the release of equality constraints. Multiple equality constraints containing $n > 2$ parameters are tested successively in n steps each assuming the release of one of the equality-constrained parameters.

- Univariate Lagrange multiplier test indices for releasing active boundary constraints specified by the BOUNDS statement.

- Stepwise multivariate Wald test indices for constraining estimated parameters to zero are computed and printed. Besides the multivariate χ^2 value and its probability, their univariate increments are also printed.

3 Numerical Techniques

There are different default methods available in PROC CALIS for initial estimates of parameters in a linear structural equation model specified by a RAM or LINEQS model statement depending on the form of the specified model:

- two-stage least-squares estimation,
- instrumental variable method,
- approximative factor analysis,
- ordinary least-squares estimation,
- estimation method of McDonald (1988).

For the more general COSAN model there is no default estimation method for the initial values. The RANDOM= or START= option can be used to set otherwise unassigned initial values.

There are four optimization techniques available in CALIS:

- Levenberg-Marquardt (Morè, 1978) algorithm,
- Ridge-stabilized Newton-Raphson algoritm,
- Quasi-Newton methods with several updating algorithms,
- Conjugate gradient methods with several updating algorithms.

Each of them can be modified in several ways by various options in the PROC statement. The Levenberg-Marquardt and Newton-Raphson techniques are usually the most reliable and generally converge after a few iterations to a precise solution. However, for large problems a quasi-Newton or dual quasi-Newton technique, especially with the BFGS update, can be far more efficient. Four different quasi-Newton updates are available:

- BFGS (Broyden, Fletcher, Goldfarb, & Shanno) update,
- DFP (Davidon, Fletcher, & Powell) update,
- Dual BFGS update,
- Dual DFP update.

If memory problems occur, you can use one of the conjugate gradient techniques. Four different conjugate gradient updates are avalilable:

- automatic restart update of Powell (1977) and Beale (1972),
- Fletcher-Reeves update,
- Polak-Ribiere update,
- conjugate descent update of Fletcher (1980).

You can use the GTOL= option to specify an absolute gradient termination criterion. The FTOL= option specifies a relative function convergence criterion. Using the MAXIT= and MAXFU= options, you can specify the maximum number of iterations and function calls in the optimization process. These limits are especially useful in combination with the INRAM= and OUTRAM= options; you can run a few iterations at a time, inspect the results, and then decide whether or not to continue iterating. There are three different line search algorithms available in CALIS for quasi-Newton and conjugate gradient minimization. You are also able to restrict the length of the first minimization steps to avoid overflows.

PROC CALIS offers four different algorithms to compute the information matrix. The fastest algorithm needs the most memory. The other algorithms use utility data sets.

If the information matrix is singular, CALIS does an analysis of the linear dependencies. For example, for an unidentified second order confirmatory factor analysis in McDonald (1985, p.105) CALIS prints:

```
NOTE: Hessian matrix is not full rank. Not all parameters are identified.
      Some parameter estimates are linearly related to other parameter
      estimates as shown in the following equations:

U21 =     1.9083 X1  +  1.9275 X2  +  1.8057 X3  -  1.4081 X10 -  3.4460

U22 =     1.9440 X4  +  1.8542 X5  +  1.6341 X6  -  1.2244 X11 -  3.2255

U23 =     2.8068 X7  +  2.5900 X8  +  2.5288 X9  -  1.6292 X12 -  3.3778

NOTE: Moore-Penrose inverse of information matrix computed.
```

4 Data Processing

As input, you can use raw data, a covariance matrix, a correlation matrix, or a scalar product matrix. Either a (corrected or uncorrected) correlation matrix, or a (corrected or uncorrected) covariance matrix can be analyzed. Assuming all information is given, each type of input data can be transformed to each type of moment matrix for analysis. The BY, FREQ, WEIGHT, PARTIAL, and VARIABLE statement can be used with PROC CALIS the same way as with PROC FACTOR.

If a raw data set is available at input, CALIS prints the mean, standard deviation, skewness, and kurtosis for each variable. It also computes some multivariate kurtosis indices and the observation numbers with largest contributions to Mardia's multivariate kurtosis.

The procedure creates an output data set that completely decribes the model (except for programming statements) and also contains the parameter estimates and standard errors. This data set can be used as input for another execution of CALIS. Small model changes can be made by editing this data set; therefore, you can exploit the old parameter estimates as good starting values in a subsequent analysis. Another output data set contains the analyzed covariance or correlation matrices and the predicted and residual moment matrices of the analysis. You can use this data set as an input data set in a subsequent analysis too.

You can also create a data set containing the weight matrix used in GLS, WLS, or DWLS estimation. This data set too can be used as input data set for another run of CALIS.

Automatic variable selection (using only those variables from the input data set which are used in the model specification) is done in connection with the RAM and LINEQS input statements or when these models are recognized in an input model file. Also in these cases, the covariances of the independent manifest variables are recognized as given constants.

References

[1] Akaike, H. (1987), "Factor Analysis and AIC", *Psychometrika*, **52**, 317-332.

[2] Bentler, P.M. (1985): *Theory and Implementation of EQS A Structural Equations Program*, Manual for Program Version 2.0, Los Angeles: BMDP Statistical Software, Inc.

[3] Bentler, P.M. (1986): "Lagrange Multiplier and Wald Tests for EQS and EQS/PC", Los Angeles: BMDP Statistical Software, Inc.

[4] Bentler, P.M. and Bonett, D.G. (1980), "Significance Tests and Goodness of Fit in the Analysis of Covariance Structures", *Psychological Bulletin*, **88**, 588-606.

[5] Bentler, P.M. and Weeks, D.G. (1980), "Linear Structural Equations with Latent Variables", *Psychometrika*, **45**, 289-308.

[6] Browne, M.W. (1974), "Generalized Least Squares Estimators in the Analysis of Covariance Structures", *South African Statistical Journal*, **8**, 1 - 24.

[7] Browne, M.W. (1982), "Covariance Structures", in *Topics in Multivariate Analyses*, ed. D.M. Hawkins, Cambridge University Press.

[8] Browne, M. W. (1984), "Asymptotically Distribution-free Methods for the Analysis of Covariance Structures", *Br. J. math. statist. Psychol.*, **37**, 62-83.

[9] Buse, A. (1982), "The Likelihood Ratio, Wald, and Lagrange Multiplier Tests: An Expository Note", *The American Statistician*, **36**, 153-157.

[10] Fletcher, R. (1980), *Practical Methods of Optimization*, Vol. 1, Chichester: John Wiley & Sons.

[11] DeLeeuw, J. (1983), Models and Methods for the Analysis of Correlation Coefficients, *Journal of Econometrics*, **22**, 113-137.

[12] Jöreskog, K.G. (1978), "Structural Analysis of Covariance and Correlation Matrices", *Psychometrika*, **43**, 443-477.

[13] Jöreskog, K.G. and Sörbom, D. (1985), *LISREL VI; Analysis of Linear Structural Relationships by Maximum Likelihood, Instrumental Variables, and Least Squares*, Uppsala: University of Uppsala.

[14] Lee, S.Y. and Jennrich, R.I. (1979), "A Study of Algorithms for Covariance Structure Analysis with Specific Comparisons Using Factor Analysis",*Psychometrika*, **44**, 99-113.

[15] McArdle, J.J. (1980), "Causal Modeling Applied to Psychonomic Systems Simulation", *Behavior Research Methods & Instrumentation*,**12**, 193-209.

[16] McArdle, J.J. and McDonald, R.P. (1984), "Some Algebraic Properties of the Reticular Action Model", *Br. J. math. statist. Psychol.*, **37**, 234-251.

[17] McDonald, R.P. (1978), "A Simple Comprehensive Model for the Analysis of Covariance Structures", *Br. J. math. statist. Psychol.*, **31**, 59-72.

[18] McDonald, R.P. (1980), "A Simple Comprehensive Model for the Analysis of Covariance Structures: Some Remarks on Applications", *Br. J. math. statist. Psychol.*, **33**, 161-183.

[19] McDonald, R.P. (1985), *Factor Analysis and Related Methods*, Hillsdale NJ and London: Lawrence Erlbaum Associates.

[20] McDonald, R.P. (1988), "A Procedure for Obtaining Initial Values of Parameters in the RAM Model", Personal Communication.

[21] McDonald, R.P. and Marsh, H.W. (1988), "Choosing a Multivariate Model: Noncentrality and Goodness of Fit", Distributed Paper.

New SAS Facilities for Design of Experiments compared to RS/1 and STATGRAPHICS

M. Herold

Summary

Problems of optimization can be solved by using factorial experimental designs especially in the chemical-pharmaceutical industry but also in other areas of the industrial production.

The new SAS-QC-Experimental Design procedures are useful tools for constructing experimental designs. The FACTEX procedure is a general construction procedure for orthogonally confounded fractional factorial designs. The OPTEX procedure searches for an optimal design from a set of candidate points. Macros and a menu system have been developed for facilitating the construction of design in standard applications.

A brief overview about the conception and the possibilities - including the integrated statistical models - of the SAS-System will be given.

The possibilities of the procedures are compared with other statistical software packages.

1. Aufgabe der statistischen Versuchsplanung

Die Art des Versuchsplans hat einen großen Einfluß auf die Qualität und den Informationsgehalt der Ergebnisse des Versuches. Fehler, die in der Versuchsplanung gemacht wurden, können auch nicht im nachhinein durch aufwendige Auswertungsverfahren kompensiert werden.

Die Ergebnisse der Experimente dienen dem Statistiker u.a. zum Schätzen von deskriptiven Parametern, zum Überprüfen von Hypothesen und der statistischen Modellbildung.

Die Aufgabe der statistischen Versuchsplanung besteht in der Konstruktion optimaler Versuchspläne. In diesen Optimalitätsbegriff gehen u.a. ein:

- möglichst geringe Anzahl von Versuchen,
- Berechnung der Koeffizienten bzw. Parameter des postulierten mathematischen Modells müssen möglich sein,
- geringer Fehler bei Parameterschätzungen,
- hohe Trennschärfe bei statistischen Tests und
- alle Variablen sollen gleichberechtigt sein (Drehbarkeit der Pläne).

2. Computergestützte Versuchsplanung

Ebenso wie der Computer in der Datenanalyse eingesetzt wird, ist er auch ein wichtiges Hilfsmittel bei der Planung von Experimenten. Der Anwender kann sich voll auf die Planung eines Versuches konzentrieren, während der Computer ihm die Berechnungen der entsprechenden Designs abnimmt. Er erspart sich lästige Zahlenrechnung, und die Gefahr von Rechenfehlern ist weit geringer. Darüberhinaus kann der Computer auch Aufgaben wie Decodierung der Faktorwerte und Randomisierung der Versuche abnehmen. Derartige Aufgaben sind, von Hand durchgeführt, häufige Fehlerquellen bei der Entwicklung von Versuchsdesigns. Ein Computer ist unbedingt erforderlich, falls Standardpläne nicht verwendet werden können und optimale Versuchspläne zu berechnen sind.

3. Versuchsplanung mit SAS

SAS stellt zur Konstruktion und Optimierung von Versuchsplänen folgende Hilfsmittel zur Verfügung:

Die Prozeduren

- PLAN,
- FACTEX,
- OPTEX.

Eine Makro-Bibliothek zur Konstruktion, Manipulation und Analyse von Versuchsplänen, die

- ADX-Makros. (Automated Design of Experiments)

Die genannten Prozeduren und Macros sind unter Anwendung des SAS/AF-Moduls in eine Menüumgebung eingebettet worden, den

- ADX-Menüs.

Bis auf PROC PLAN (SAS/STAT) sind die Komponenten im SAS/QC-Modul der PC-Version 6.03 integriert. SAS/QC ist im Moment nur als Testinstallation (Beta-Release) verfügbar. Im PC-Bereich ist die Freigabe der Produktversion im April ´89 geplant. Auf dem Großrechner werden die Prozeduren für Experimental Designs im QC-Modul der Version 6.06 (Freigabe 2. Hälfte ´89) erstmalig verfügbar sein.

Im folgenden werden die einzelnen Komponenten kurz vorgestellt.

3.1 PLAN-Prozedur

Diese Prozedur konstruiert und randomisiert Pläne für Versuche mit Kreuzklassifikation oder hierarchischer Klassifikation.

3.2 FACTEX-Prozedur

Mit dieser Prozedur können Faktor- oder Teilfaktorpläne konstruiert werden. Das vom SAS-System ausgewählte Design ist orthogonal.

Der Anwender kann verschiedene Bedingungen vorgeben, die bei der Wahl des Designs berücksichtigt werden sollen, z.B.:

- Anzahl der Versuche ("Runs"),
- Anzahl der Blöcke,
- schätzbare Effekte.

Die Versuchsdesigns sind nicht in einer internen Tabelle abgespeichert, sondern werden durch einen Algorithmus erzeugt. Dadurch ist z.B. die maximale Anzahl von Faktoren, die das System verarbeiten kann, nur von der verwendeten Hardware (Speicherplatz) abhängig.

Ein großer Vorteil ist die Möglichkeit mit dieser Prozedur auch interaktiv zu arbeiten. Man läßt sich vom System ein Design vorschlagen, untersucht es, ändert Bedingungen, läßt sich ein neues Design erzeugen.

3.3 OPTEX-Prozedur

Überwiegend können Experimente nach Standardversuchsplänen, wie sie die Prozedur FACTEX oder das ADX-System generieren, durchgeführt werden. In Sonderfällen können diese Pläne ungeeignet sein:

- Der Variablenraum ist ungewöhnlich eingeschränkt oder erweitert, die vom Plan vorgeschriebene Variableneinstellung ist nicht realisierbar. Bei Mixtur-Plänen mit unterer und oberer Begrenzung ist für eine größere Anzahl von Komponenten die Anzahl der möglichen Planpunkte so umfangreich, daß eine Selektion für den Plan kompliziert ist.
- Bereits realisierte Versuche sind in einen Plan zu integrieren. Einige Ergebnisse von Versuchen liegen vor, eine begrenzte Anzahl von Versuchen ist so zu ergänzen, daß insgesamt eine maximale Effizienz erreicht wird.
- Es sind Koeffizienten für ein ausgefallenes Modell (z.B. nicht linear) zu schätzen.
- Es bestehen Extremforderungen an eine bestimmte Qualität.

Für diese Probleme, die nicht in Anlehnung an Standardpläne gelöst werden können, sind in der Prozedur OPTEX spezielle Algorithmen implementiert worden. Die Algorithmen

(SEQUENTIAL, EXCHANGE, DETMAX, MODIFIED FEDEROV und FEDEROV) tragen ähnliche Grundzüge. Man geht von einem (zufällig gewählten) Startplan mit N Versuchspunkten aus und fügt den (N+1)-ten Punkt dazu, mit dem das Optimalitätskriterium maximal verbessert wird. Nun streicht man den Punkt, der das Optimalitätskriterium minimal verschlechtert. Es können auch mehrere Punkte zugleich hinzugefügt bzw. gestrichen werden. Es kann eine Menge von Punkten, die vom Austausch ausgeschlossen ist, fest vorgegeben werden. Eine andere Möglichkeit ist die Vorgabe von Punkten ("candidate points"), aus der zu ergänzende Punkte auszusuchen sind.

Als Optimalitätskriterien können in der Prozedur OPTEX
- D-Optimalität und
- A-Optimalität

gewählt werden.

Ist das Ziel der Untersuchungen die größtmögliche Präzision der Koeffizienten, muß man die D-Optimalität der Designmatrix beachten. Im A-optimalen Plan ist die mittlere Varianz der Koeffizientenschätzung minimal.

OPTEX ist, ebenso wie FACTEX, eine Prozedur mit der auch interaktiv gearbeitet werden kann.

3.4 ADX-Makros

SAS bietet dem Anwender die Möglichkeit Makros zu schreiben. Dies sind aus SAS-Anweisungen bestehende Unterprogramme, die in SAS-Programme eingebunden werden können. Man wird für häufig wiederkehrende Programmabläufe oder für spezielle Fragestellungen, die in SAS nicht in Form einer Prozedur oder Funktion implementiert ist, Makros schreiben.

Für die Konstruktion, Manipulation und Analyse von Versuchsplänen stellt das SAS-System innerhalb des QC-Moduls eine Bibliothek von SAS-Makros zur Verfügung.

Diese Makros können vom Anwender, da sie im Quellcode vorhanden sind, nachträglich noch abgeändert oder erweitert werden.

Die Konstruktion folgender Standardversuchspläne ist mit dem ADX-Makro-System möglich:
- Teilfaktorpläne mit und ohne Blockbildung mit bis zu 11 Faktoren und 128 "Runs",
- Plackett-Burman Designs mit bis zu 47 Faktoren,
- Box-Wilson Response Surface Designs mit und ohne Blockbildung mit bis zu 8 Faktoren,
- Mixturpläne.

Ferner stellt die Bibliothek Makros für folgende Funktionen zur Verfügung:
- Randomisierung der Versuchspläne,
- Möglichkeit der Transformation von Variablen,
- Ausdruck des Versuchsplans in Formularform zum Erfassen der Versuchsergebnisse vor Ort,
- Analyse von Teilfaktorplänen (z.B. Ausdruck der Aliasing-Struktur).

3.5 ADX-Menüs

Alle bisher vorgestellten Prozeduren und Makros sind in einem Menüsystem zusammengefaßt. Die Benutzeroberfläche ähnelt in ihrem Aufbau dem SAS/ASSIST. Der Anwender spezifiziert sein Problem über Menüs, die entsprechenden SAS-Anweisungen werden im Hintergrund automatisch erzeugt. Somit ist der Anwender von Programmieraufgaben entbunden, er braucht sich um Syntaxfragen der einzelnen Prozeduren nicht mehr zu kümmern. Ferner steht dem Anwender eine kontext-sensitive Online-Hilfe zur Verfügung.

4. Kurzer Überblick über andere Softwarepakete

In diesem Abschnitt wird kurz dargestellt, welche Verfahren andere ausgewählte statistische Softwarepakete zur Konstruktion und Optimierung von Versuchsplänen zur Verfügung stellen.

4.1 STATGRAPHICS Version 2.6

In dem Programmpaket ist ein Modul EXPERIMENTAL DESIGN integriert. Es stellt folgende Funktionen zur Verfügung:
- Konstruktion von Faktor- oder Teilfaktorplänen. Schätzen von Haupt- und Wechselwirkungseffekten. Randomisierung der Pläne. Die Anzahl der Faktoren ist auf 11, die Anzahl der "Runs" auf 128 begrenzt.
- Konstruktion von Central Composite Designs 2. Ordnung (BOX-WILSON-Designs). Die Anzahl der Variablen ist auf 8 begrenzt.
- Generierung einer Response-Surface-Matrix.
- Bestimmung von Alias-Strukturen einer Design-Matrix.

4.2 RS/1

Innerhalb des RS/1-Systems sind Verfahren zur Konstruktion, Optimierung und Analyse von Versuchsplänen im Modul DISCOVER integriert.

4.3 Vergleich

Die folgende Übersicht gibt einen Eindruck über die Möglichkeiten der drei Statistikpakete im Bereich der statistischen Versuchsplanung.

Tab. 1: RS/DISCOVER, SAS-Experimental Design und STATGRAPHICS im Vergleich

	RS/DISCOVER Version 2	SAS-Exp. Design Version 6	STATGRAPHICS Version 2.6
Designs			
Faktorpläne	●	●	●
Teilfaktorpläne	○ (2^k)	● (q^k)	○ (2^k)
Plackett-Burman	●	●	
Box-Behnken	●	●	
Box-Wilson	●	●	●
Mixtur-Pläne	●	●	
Optimalitätskriterien			
D-Optimalität	●	●	
A-Optimalität		●	
Optimalitätsalgorithmen			
DETMAX	●	●	
SEQUENTIAL		●	
EXCHANGE		●	
FEDEROV		●	
MODIFIED FEDEROV		●	

	RS/DISCOVER Version 2	SAS-Exp. Design Version 6	STATGRAPHICS Version 2.6
Sonstige Routinen			
Randomisierung	●	●	●
Blockbildung	●	●	●
Decodieren des Designs	●	●	
Ausgabe der Alias-Struktur	●	●	●
Formularausdruck	●	●	●
Transformation der Responsevariablen		●	
Analyse von Designs	●	●	
Speichern von Designs	●	●	●
Modifikation von gespeicherten Designs		●	

5. Zusammenfassung

Für den Anwender, der häufig Probleme der Versuchsplanung zu lösen hat, stellen die im SAS/QC-Modul integrierten Prozeduren und Makros zur Konstruktion, Analyse, Optimierung und Verwaltung von Versuchsplänen eine wichtige Erweiterung des SAS-Systems dar.

Für den nicht so erfahrenen SAS-Benutzer sind alle wesentlichen Funktionen zusätzlich in eine menügesteuerten Oberfläche eingebunden. Ausreichende Hilfestellung ist durch eine kontextsensitive Online-Hilfe gewährleistet.

Im Bereich der großen Statistikpakete stellt nur das Paket RS/1 mit dem Modul DISCOVER dem Anwender ähnlich vielfältige Möglichkeiten zur Verfügung.

Literaturverzeichnis

BBN Software Products Corporation (1988). RS/Discover User's Guide.

Box, Hunter & Hunter (1978). Statistics for Experimenters. John Wiley & Sons, New York.

Cochran, W.G., Cox, G.M. (1957). Experimental Designs. Second Edition. John Wiley and Sons, New York.

Davies, O.L. (1954). Design and Analysis of Industrial Experiments. Oliver and Boyd, London.

Held, G. (1988). Future statistical directions of the SAS-System. Proceedings of the Sixth SAS European User's Group International Conference, 111-119.

McLean, R.A., Sanders, R.D. (1987). Experiences with teaching experimental design using the SAS System for Personal Computers. Proceedings of the Twelth Annual User's Group International Conference, Cary, NC: SAS Institute, Inc. ,437-444.

Myers, R.H. (1971). Response Surface Methodology. Allyn and Bacon, Inc., Boston.

SAS Institute Inc. (1988). SAS/QC Experimental Design Procedures. Preliminary Documentation.

Scheffler, E. (1974). Einführung in die Praxis der statistischen Versuchsplanung. 2., stark überarbeitete Auflage. VEB Deutscher Verlag für Grundstoffindustrie, Leipzig.

STSC Inc. (1987). STATGRAPHICS V 2.6 User's Guide.

Wendelberger, J.R. (1986). Using SAS Software in the Design and Analysis of Two-level Fractional Factorial Experiments. Proceedings of the Eleventh Annual SAS User's Group International Conference, Cary, NC: SAS Institute, Inc., 772-777.

A Graphical Study of Health, Economic, and Military Data from Ten Dozen Countries

M.A. Hill

Graphics aid all stages of data analysis. They ease data screening, facilitate communication within the research team, and enhance the reporting of final results. A full range of statistical capabilities should be available with the graphics. As your eye sees a pattern in a display, you may want to support it with statistics. Conversely, when you assess model results, you may want to request a graphical display.

Assume the following scenario: we, the statisticians, plan to join a research team of demographers and political scientists. We only know that they are concerned about differences among United Nations countries associated with

- *type of government:* military regime, despotic, one-party, or multi-party (democracy).
- the *religious preference* of those in power: Protestant, Catholic, Islamic, Marxist, or Eastern.

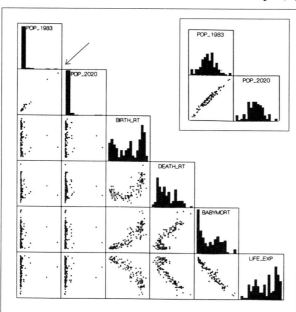

Figure 1

The researchers have sent us data from U.N. Reports for ten dozen or so countries. (Data are provided by the World Game and the graphics and statistical software by SYSTAT.)

We *explore* these data in preparation for our first meeting. We consider transformations, outliers, and homogeneity of the samples. We also assess the amount of missing data and the pattern of incompleteness. We fit

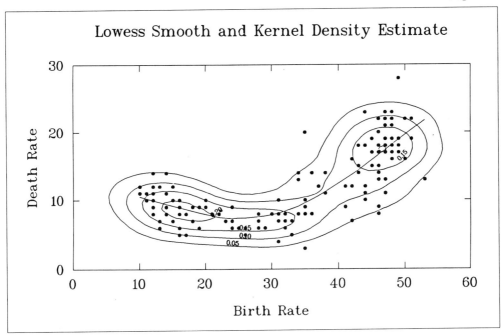

Figure 2

models, *not for final results*, but to show the researchers our "tools" and how we "look" at data and compare results from competing models.

A First Look at Transformations and Outliers. We use Scatter Plot Matrices (SPLOMs) to study univariate and bivariate distributions. In Figure 1, there are 15 bivariate plots with histograms along the diagonal. The row name is the dependent variable, the column name, the independent. The arrow points to POP_2020 (projected population in 2020) versus POP_1983. Points clump at the lower left with 2 stragglers (India and China) floating up to the right. The same population variables after log transformations are replotted in the top insert -- the histograms are now symmetric and linearity has improved.

Transformations may not help all variables. Look at the strange configuration in the DEATH versus BIRTH rate plot. Figure 2 adds density contours and the LOWESS smoother. The smoother indicates a curve with a possible quadratic component, and the contours, a bimodal bivariate distribution. If we repeat this plot (not shown), adding country names and a line for equal BIRTH and DEATH rates, we can identify "developed" nations in the left concentration of density, and "underdeveloped" nations at the right. Countries losing population (points above the line of equal rates) include West Germany, Hungary, Denmark, and Austria. At the other extreme, the

Figure 3

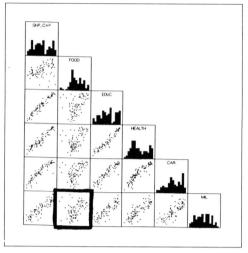

Figure 4

Islamic countries of Libya, Syria, Jordan, Saudi Arabia, and Kuwait have birth rates roughly four times greater than their death rates.

In Figure 3, the histograms for more variables are right-skewed and the points in the plots clump in the lower left corner. After log transformation (Figure 4) the histograms are more symmetric and linearity has improved in all plots except those for FOOD per capita. The plot of MILITARY expenditures per capita versus FOOD has stragglers in the upper left. The highest point is Saudi Arabia -- it spends the most per capita on MILITARY. Tracking this case across plots in the bottom row, we learn that Saudi Arabia is among the big spenders for HEALTH and EDUCATION but has an average number of CARS per 1000 inhabitants. The leftmost straggler is Singapore, which, while low on FOOD, has relatively high values for the other variables.

Incomplete Data. Line printer results were enough to identify missing data problems. EMPLOYMENT is missing for 38% of the countries, ENERGY EXPORTED for 22%, the number of AIDS cases for 20%, the number of CARS for 19%, etc. To check if data are missing randomly, we recoded each value, using "0" if missing and "1" if present, and printed the file sorted by RELIGION. A quick look showed that GNP is missing more frequently for Marxist countries: Poland, Bulgaria, East Germany, Albania, and Czechoslovakia. To check for a bias in missing EMPLOYMENT values, we split the sample into two groups (present and missing) and computed separate variance t-tests for the other variables. Reading the sign of t (t>|3.5|), we learn that countries that omit employment tend to have (compared to those who do report) higher BIRTH, DEATH, and INFANT

MORTALITY rates; a lower LIFE EXPECTANCY and a smaller proportion of OLD PEOPLE; more RURAL area and LAND AREA per capita; lower GNP per capita and ENERGY consumption; and spend considerably less per person on EDUCATION and HEALTH. Underdeveloped countries are underrepresented in the report of employment!

Government Type. The Box Plots for 10 variables in Figure 5 are stratified by type of government. The "box" marks the interquartile range of each distribution; the vertical line inside the box, the median. Contrasting Military regimes versus Democracies (multiparty) produces results parallel to those reported above (missing vs. present for EMPLOYMENT). Quality of life appears to be better in democracies. Look at the scales on the BABYMORT (infant mortality) plot: the bottom scale is in square root units and the top in original units (number of deaths per 1000 births). The median rate for democracies is fewer than 25 deaths per 1000 births; for military regimes, more than 100 deaths per 1000 births. In the last row, the plots have log scales along the bottom and original units along the top.

Religious Preference. Box plots are one way to study subpopulations; plots of cell means are another. In Figure 6, we plot means for dollars per capita expended on HEALTH, EDUCATION, and MILITARY for countries grouped by RELIGION. We wonder whether spending patterns vary by religious preference. *Relative* to the other groups, the Islamic nations, on average, spend more per capita on

Figure 5

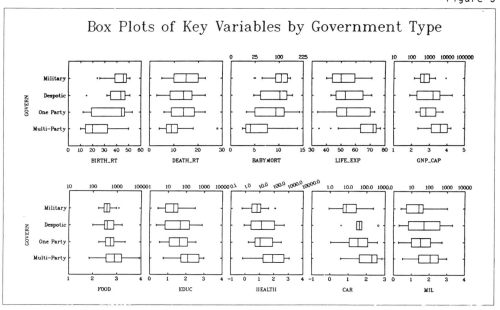

Figure 6

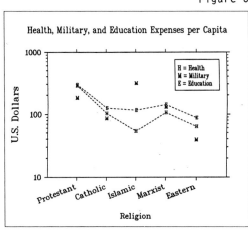

Figure 7

MILITARY than on HEALTH and EDUCATION. We chose not to clutter the plot with standard error bars, but rather to use results from a repeated measures ANOVA to *describe* statistically the observation that the Islamic spending pattediffers from that of other groups. We formed two within-country contrasts across the repeated measures HEALTH, MILITARY, and EDUCATION (coefficients are 1, 0, -1 and 1, -2, 1). The interaction of each contrast with the grouping factor RELIGION was highly significant (p-value<.00005). After removing the Islamic group and repeating the analysis, the interactions are no longer significant (p-values=.12 and .19, respectively). Dollars per capita may not be how the researchers want to measure MILITARY spending. See Figure 7 for a pie chart of total military expenditures using the same groupings.

Figure 8

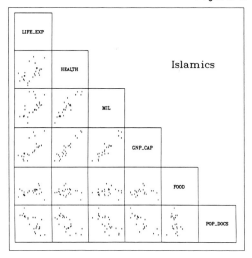

Figure 9

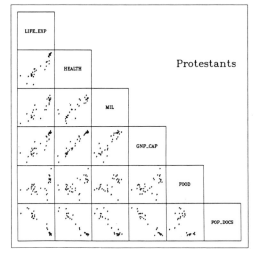

More on Subpopulations. We found differences due to government type and religious preference. But are the groups as defined homogeneous? In the talk, we displayed colored SPLOMs with points for Islamic countries plotted in blue, Protestant in red, etc. From these, slopes and/or intercepts clearly differed among the groups; therefore caution should be exercised about proceeding further with methods based on linear models. Straight lines measure linearity and may mask other anomalies. In Figure 8, note the cluster of four Islamic countries (Saudi Arabia, Oman, Libya, and Kuwait) that is separated from the other points in the plot of GNP versus MILITARY spending. These four countries have high GNP and large MILITARY expenditures. Tracking them through the other plots convinces us that they are unusual and should be mentioned to the researchers.

Look at the plot of POP_DOC (people per doctor) versus FOOD in Figure 9. Note that plot scales are the same in Figures 8 and 9. Tracking the separate cluster of points (on the lower right) back across the POP_DOCS row and up the LIFE_EXP column to the HEALTH by LIFE_EXP plot, we see that the cluster still stands apart. It is easy to identify the countries in this cluster using the

Figure 10

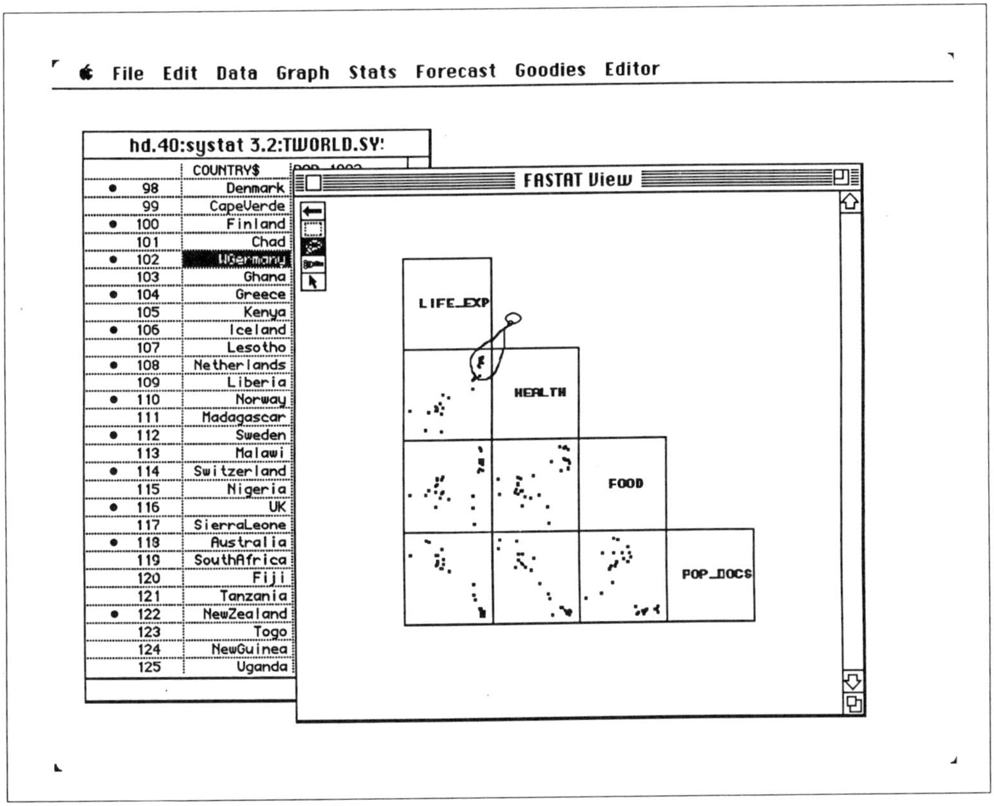

scatterplot brushing tools in the new FASTAT Macintosh product (see Figure 10). We "lasso" the cluster and see these countries light up in other SPLOM plots. The cases are marked by bullets (•) in the editor where we can read their names and check other data values. The "marked" countries may be saved for within-stratum analyses. You can also "click" on a country name, say, West Germany, and see it highlighted in each plot.

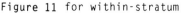

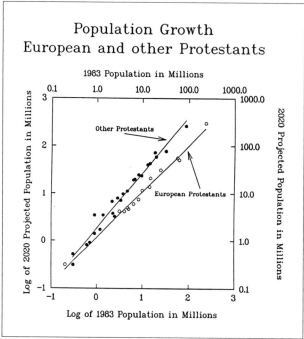

The countries in the cluster are Western European Protestant nations plus the USA, Australia, and New Zealand. In the talk, we explored the Protestant group further using 3D rotations and "freezing" the display when separate clusters appeared. For several variables, "European" Protestants differ from "Other" Protestants. In Figure 11, we plot the projected 2020 population versus 1983 population values, using symbols to distinguish groups, and fit a line to each group. The slope for the Europeans is .97; for the Others, 1.18. An ANCOVA test of parallelism shows that the slopes differ significantly (p=.001). The slope for logged data becomes a power when backtransformed. The difference between groups is striking: the 1983 population for West Germany is 61.7 million; the projection for 2020, 51.3 million. By contrast, Kenya's 1983 population is 18.6 and its 2020 projection is 72.4 million!

Models: Comparisons and Diagnostics. So far we've only explored religious differences bivariately. Discriminant analysis is a useful method for exploring first, which <u>variables</u> among many best separate the groups, and second, which <u>groups</u> are most similar and which differ most. Canonical variable plots (with ellipses of concentration) from two discriminant models are displayed in Figure 12. GNP is included in the first model, but this omits many of the Eastern European Marxist countries. For the second model,

Figure 12

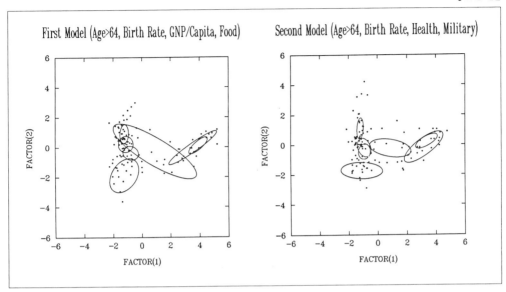

we ignored GNP and allowed HEALTH and MILITARY to enter. Clearly, the assumption of equality of covariance matrices is not met in either model. In the talk we showed a version of this display with group identification. In both models, Islamic nations cluster in the upper left; Eastern nations, in the lower left; and European Protestant and Catholics on the right (their

Figure 13

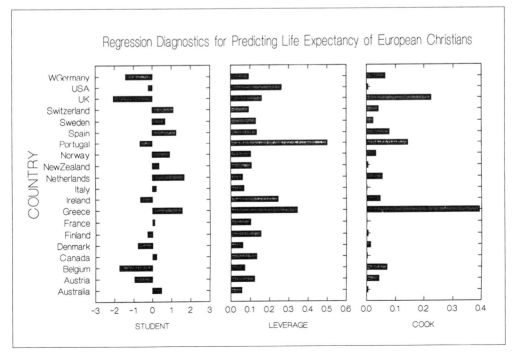

ellipses overlap). The ellipse for Marxist countries extends across the center of each display. A k-means cluster analysis indicated that the Eastern European countries at the right of the Marxist ellipse are much more similar to their Western European neighbors than any other countries.

To give the researchers a sample of diagnostics, we fit several multiple linear regression models. In Figure 13, for a model predicting LIFE EXPECTANCY for European Christians, we display three regression diagnostics side-by-side for each country: a residual, a measure of leverage (outliers in the space of independent variables), and an influence measure (i.e., "influence" on the estimates of the coefficients). We see that LIFE EXPECTANCY is lower for the UK than predicted by the model, while that for the Netherlands is higher. Portugal is an outlier in the space of the independent variables (HEALTH and MILITARY), and Greece's deletion would have the greatest impact on the coefficients. Data analysts often have their own preferences about which diagnostics to use and how to lay them out. For example, they may like Figure 13, but would also like to see *in one graph* both where points fall in the x-space and the size of their residuals. In Figure 14 we use large solid symbols to identify extreme negative residuals (UK) and large open symbols for positive residuals (Greece). The perspective surface in Figure 15 emphasizes curvature -- a plane may not be the best fit.

Figure 14

Figure 15

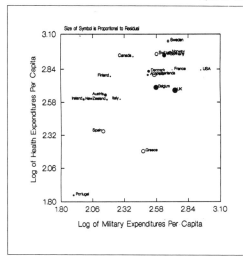
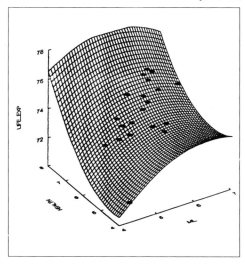

Summary. Throughout all stages of data analysis a broad range of graphical tools is needed. It should be easy to identify unusual points or clusters and isolate them for within-stratum analyses. Sophisticated statistics can't be separated from graphics, because the statistician wants to jump quickly from displays to, say, multivariate statistics and then assess results graphically.

The statistician also needs flexible controls over display size, symbols, plot scales, fonts, placement of titles and legends, and the ability to arrange several displays per page.

Acknowledgements:

Software was provided by SYSTAT (1800 Sherman Ave., Evanston, Illinois, 60201: Telephone (312)864-5670, FAX 312 492-1567) including FASTAT for the Macintosh and SYGRAPH high resolution graphics for IBM PCs and compatibles. Special thanks to Leland Wilkinson for the graphical displays and Anne Marie Wilkinson for help with the manuscript and layout.

Data. Through special arrangement with the U.N., THE WORLD GAME INSTITUTE (University City Science Center, 3508 Market St., Philadelphia, Pennsylvania, 19104: Telephone (215)387-0220) distributes hundreds of variables via floppy disk.

New Developments in LISREL

K. G. Jöreskog

1 Introduction

Two programs will be described: PRELIS and LISREL 7. PRELIS is a program for multivariate data screening and data summarization and a preprocessor for LISREL. LISREL 7 is an extension of LISREL 6. Among the new features of LISREL 7 is its ability to produce correct asymptotic chi-square goodness-of-fit measures and standard errors of parameter estimates under non-normality and when some or all of the variables are ordinal. This paper reviews some of the new features in these programs and discusses in particular the problems associated with the analysis of ordinal variables.

The programs can communicate with each other through files written by one program and read by another. For example, a correlation matrix produced by PRELIS can be read by LISREL.

Each program has its own functionality, and the reason why it is two programs rather than one, is that it is often a good idea to stop and look at the results from one program before proceeding to run another. The programs provide the tools for checking the assumptions on which the analyses are based. Thus, PRELIS checks assumptions about the data on the observed variables and LISREL checks the reasonableness of the hypothesized relationships in the model.

2 Introduction to PRELIS

Users of LISREL should know their data well and be aware of the characteristics and problems in the raw data. In particular, it is important to know the scale type of each variable, the distribution of each variable, the distribution of the variables jointly, and the distribution of missing values over variables and cases. When some or all of the variables are ordinal or censored it is important to choose the right type of correlations to analyze. Failure to do so can lead to considerable bias in estimated LISREL parameters and other quantities. PRELIS has been developed to help LISREL users become aware of these problems. PRELIS reads raw data from a file and computes the appropriate moment matrix (moment matrix, covariance matrix or correlation matrix) to use in LISREL, depending on the type of data.

PRELIS has the following features.

- PRELIS reads raw data of any numeric form, case after case. As the data is not stored in memory, the number of cases (the sample size) is unlimited. PRELIS can also read grouped data and weighted data where each case carries a weight.

- The scale type of each variable may be declared as ordinal, censored, or continuous. Groups of variables (including all variables) of the same scale type may be declared collectively. Ordinal variables may have up to 15 categories.

- A numeric value may be defined for each variable to represent a missing value. Such a numeric value can also be defined collectively for a group of variables or globally for all variables. Moment matrices may be computed either under listwise deletion or pairwise deletion.

- Continuous variables may be transformed using any one of a large family of transformations. Ordinal variables may be recoded or transformed to normal scores, or they may first be recoded and then transformed to normal scores. Maximum and/or minimum values of censored variables may also be transformed to normal scores.

- In addition to moment and covariance matrices based on raw scores or normal scores, the program can compute a number of different types of correlation coefficients: product moment (Pearson), canonical, polychoric (including tetrachoric), polyserial (including biserial), and product moment correlations based on normal or optimal scores. The Spearman rank correlation and Kendall's tau-c coefficient can also be obtained for every pair of ordinal variables. The program can also estimate correlations between censored variables and ordinal variables and between censored variables and continuous variables.

- PRELIS can estimate of the asymptotic (large sample) covariance matrix of the estimated sample variances and covariances under arbitrary non-normal distributions (see Browne, 1982, 1984). This can be used to compute a weight matrix for the WLS (Weighted Least Squares) method in LISREL 7, see Section 7. PRELIS can also compute estimates of the asymptotic variances and covariances of estimated product moment correlations, polychoric correlations and polyserial correlations; these can also be used with WLS in LISREL 7. Optionally, PRELIS may be used to compute a diagonal matrix consisting of estimates of the asymptotic variances of estimated variances, covariances, or correlations. These diagonal matrices can be used with DWLS (Diagonally Weighted Least Squares) in LISREL 7.

3 Treatment of Ordinal and Censored Variables

PRELIS can deal with three types of variables: continuous, ordinal and censored. These types of variables and how PRELIS treats them will now be described.

Observations on continuous variables are assumed to come from an interval or a ratio scale and have metric properties. Means, variances, and higher moments of these variables are computed in the usual way.

Observations on an ordinal variable are assumed to represent responses to a set of ordered categories, such as a five-category Likert scale. Here it is only assumed that a person who responds in one category has more of a characteristic than a person who responds in a lower category. For each ordinal variable x, it is assumed that there is an underlying continuous variable x^* which is normally distributed with mean μ_x and variance σ_x^2. The assumption of normality is not testable given only x; but for each pair of variables where x is involved, PRELIS provides a test of the assumption of bivariate normality of the underlying variables.

Assuming that there are k categories on x, we write $x = i$ to mean that x belongs to category i. The actual score values in the data may be arbitrary and are irrelevant as long as the ordinal information is retained. That is, low scores correspond to low-order categories of x which are associated with smaller values of x^* and high scores correspond to high-order categories which are associated with larger values of x^*.

The connection between x and x^* is

$$x = i \iff \alpha_{i-1} < x^* \leq \alpha_i, \; i = 1, 2, ..., k ,$$

where

$$\alpha_0 = -\infty, \alpha_1 < \alpha_2 < ... < \alpha_{k-1}, \alpha_k = +\infty ,$$

are parameters called threshold values. If there are k categories, there are $k-1$ threshold parameters.

Since only ordinal information is available about x^*, the mean μ_x and variance σ_x^2 are usually not identified and are therefore set to zero and one, respectively. However, when the same ordinal variable is measured one or more times, as in longitudinal or panel studies and in multigroup studies, it is possible to estimate the means and variances of these variables (relative to a fixed origin and scale) by specifying the thresholds to be the same for the same variable over time and/or groups.

A censored variable x represents a latent variable x^* which is observed on an interval scale above a threshold value A. Below A, the value $x = A$ is observed:

$$x = A \text{ if } x^* \leq A$$

$$x = x^* \text{ if } x^* > A.$$

The value A is known and is equal to the smallest observed value of x. The latent variable x^* is assumed to be normally distributed with unknown mean μ and standard deviation σ, which are estimated by the maximum likelihood method.

The censored variable just defined will be said to be censored below. PRELIS can also deal with variables that are censored above:

$$x = x^* \text{ if } x^* < B$$

$$x = B \text{ if } x^* \geq B.$$

Variables that are censored both above and below can also be dealt with.

Censored variables have a high concentration of cases at the lower or upper end of the distribution. The classical example of this is in Tobit analysis where, for example, x = the price of an automobile purchased in the last year, with $x = 0$ if no car was purchased. Here x^* may represent a propensity to consume capital goods. Other examples may be x = number of crimes committed or x = number of days unemployed. Test scores which have a "floor" or a "ceiling" such that a large proportion of cases have no items or all items correct are also censored variables. Attitude questions where a large fraction of the population is expected to have the lowest or highest score or category may also be considered censored variables.

For an ordinal variable, let n_i be the number of cases in the i:th category. The threshold values are estimated from the (marginal) distribution of each variable as

$$\hat{\alpha}_i = \Phi^{-1}(\sum_{j=1}^{i} n_j/N) , \; i = 1,\ldots,k-1 ,$$

where Φ^{-1} is the inverse standard normal distribution function and N is the total number of real observations on the ordinal variable. The normal score z_i corresponding to $x = i$ is the mean of x^* in the interval $\alpha_{i-1} < x^* \leq \alpha_i$, which is (see Johnson and Kotz, 1970, pp. 81-82)

$$z_i = \frac{\phi(\alpha_{i-1}) - \phi(\alpha_i)}{\Phi(\alpha_i) - \Phi(\alpha_{i-1})} ,$$

where ϕ and Φ are the standard normal density and distribution function, respectively. This normal score can be estimated as

$$\hat{z}_i = (N/n_i)[\phi(\hat{\alpha}_{i-1}) - \phi(\hat{\alpha}_i)] .$$

It is readily verified that the weighted mean of the normal scores is zero.

For a variable which is censored below A, PRELIS uses the normal score associated with the interval $x^* \leq A$, which is

$$z_A = \hat{\mu} - \frac{\phi[(A - \hat{\mu})/\hat{\sigma}]}{\Phi[(A - \hat{\mu})/\hat{\sigma}]} \hat{\sigma} ,$$

where $\hat{\mu}$ and $\hat{\sigma}$ are the maximum likelihood estimates of μ and σ. For a variable which is censored above B, the normal score associated with the interval $x^* \geq B$ is

$$z_B = \hat{\mu} + \frac{\phi[(B - \hat{\mu})/\hat{\sigma}]}{\Phi[(B - \hat{\mu})/\hat{\sigma}]} \hat{\sigma} .$$

4 Polychoric and Polyserial Correlations

In order to use ordinal variables in a structural equation model, one must define an a suitable measure of association for every pair of variables. When some variables are ordinal and some are continuous, there are three distinct pairs of variables that can occur (in this context we treat censored variables as continuous after the censored tail has been replaced by its normal score):

O-O Both variables are ordinal.

O-C One variable is ordinal and the other is continuous.

C-C Both variables are continuous.

Each of these cases will be considered in turn.

When two variables x and y are both ordinal with r and s categories, respectively, their marginal distribution in the sample is represented by a contingency table

$$\begin{pmatrix} n_{11} & n_{12} & \cdots & n_{1s} \\ n_{21} & n_{22} & \cdots & n_{2s} \\ \vdots & \vdots & \ddots & \vdots \\ n_{r1} & n_{r2} & \cdots & n_{rs} \end{pmatrix}.$$

The polychoric correlation is the correlation ρ in the bivariate normal distribution of the underlying variables x^* and y^*. This correlation can be estimated by maximizing the log-likelihood of the multinomial distribution, see Olsson (1979),

$$\sum_{i=1}^{r}\sum_{j=1}^{s} n_{ij} \log \pi_{ij},$$

where

$$\pi_{ij} = \int_{\alpha^*_{i-1}}^{\alpha^*_i} \int_{\beta^*_{j-1}}^{\beta^*_j} \phi_2(u,v) du dv,$$

where ϕ_2 is the standard bivariate normal density with correlation ρ. Here,

$$\alpha^*_i = \frac{\alpha_i - \mu_x}{\sigma_x} \quad \beta^*_j = \frac{\beta_j - \mu_y}{\sigma_y},$$

where $\alpha_1, \alpha_2, ..., \alpha_{r-1}$ are the thresholds for x and $\beta_1, \beta_2, ..., \beta_{s-1}$ are the thresholds for y ($\alpha_0 = \beta_0 = -\infty; \alpha_r = \beta_s = +\infty$).

When x is ordinal and y is continuous, the polyserial correlation is the correlation between x^* and y, which are assumed to have a bivariate normal distribution. This correlation can be estimated from bivariate summary statistics consisting of the frequency n_i, the mean $\bar{y}_i$, and the variance s_i^2 of y for each category i of x, see Jöreskog (1986).

When both x and y are continuous, their means, variances, covariance, and correlation can be estimated in the usual way.

5 Types of Moment Matrices

When one or more of the variables to be analyzed are ordinal, it is important to choose the right type of moment matrix to analyze. PRELIS gives six choices:

KMR A matrix of product moment (Pearson) correlations based on raw scores, i. e., with scores 1, 2, 3, ... on ordinal variables treated as if they come from interval-scaled variables. This is the **KM** option in PRELIS when all variables are treated as continuous.

KMN A matrix of product moment (Pearson) correlations with scores on ordinal variables replaced by normal scores determined from the marginal distributions. This is the **KM** option in PRELIS when ordinal variables are declared ordinal.

OM A matrix of product moment (Pearson) correlations with scores on ordinal variables replaced by optimal scores determined for each pair. This is the **OM** option in PRELIS when ordinal variables are declared ordinal.

PM A matrix of polychoric and polyserial correlations. This is the **PM** option in PRELIS when ordinal variables are declared ordinal.

RM A matrix of Spearman rank correlations. This is the **RM** option in PRELIS when ordinal variables are declared ordinal.

TM A matrix of Kendall's tau-c correlations. This is the **TM** option in PRELIS when ordinal variables are declared ordinal.

Monte Carlo studies reported by Jöreskog and Sörbom (1986) suggests that the **PM** matrix is the best one to use when ordinal variables are present, because polychoric and polyserial correlations are the least biased of the six correlations. A recent study to be reported, suggest that these correlations are also robust against departures from bivariate normality of the underlying variables.

6 Introduction to LISREL 7

LISREL 7 has the following new features as compared with LISREL 6.

- A thorough check of the syntax in LISREL input lines in the same way it is done in PRELIS.

- An *admissibility check* of the model with options to stop before iterations begin or after a specified number of iterations if a non-admissible solution is produced.

- Two new estimation methods, WLS and DWLS, have been added to those already available in LISREL 6, and a unified approach to estimation is now taken. WLS requires an asymptotic covariance matrix produced by PRELIS. This method produces asymptotically correct standard errors and χ^2 values under non-normality and when one or more of the observed variables are ordinal. WLS is particularly important when analyzing polychoric and/or polyserial correlations. Note that the computational requirements for WLS become demanding as the number of variables increases. A reasonable compromise between normal theory ML or GLS and non-normal WLS may be DWLS which requires only the asymptotic variances of estimated correlations (or variances and covariances). These asymptotic variances are also obtained by PRELIS.

- Standard errors, t-values, standardized residuals, and χ^2 goodness-of-fit values can now be obtained for method ULS. These are correct under standard normal theory.

- The *Ridge Option* is a new feature in LISREL 7. This option handles covariance and correlation matrices which are not positive definite. If the covariance or correlation matrix to be analyzed is not positive definite, a constant times the diagonal is added to the diagonal before iterations begin. This *Ridge Constant* is automatically determined by the program or can be be specified by the user.

    The Ridge Option is particularly useful in econometric models containing identities and in regression models with high multicollinearity among the regressors; see Chapter 4.

    The Ridge Option may also be chosen even if the covariance or correlation matrix to be analyzed is positive definite (see Section 2.15). This adds a whole new class of estimation methods. The Ridge Option may be used in combination with all the iterative methods ULS, GLS, ML, WLS, and DWLS. Methods IV and TSLS are not affected by the Ridge Option.

- The modification indices will now work with all iterative estimation methods and have been extended and supplied with tables of the estimated change in each parameter potentially to be relaxed. This indicates how sensitive the model is to changes in each parameter and gives information about the power of the χ^2 measure.

- Stemleaf plots of residuals and standardized residuals are obtained in the standard output. These are useful in the assessment of fit.

- Both *indirect* and total effects are given and *standard errors* of these will be obtained by requesting both SE and EF on the OU line.

- In LISREL 7 there are two kinds of standardized solutions: SS (Standardized Solution), in which the latent variables are scaled to have variances equal to one and the *observed variables are still in the original metric* and SC (for Standardized Completely), in which both observed and latent variables are standardized.

- The LISREL model has been extended to include four new parameter matrices (see Chapter 10). Models with mean parameters (intercept terms and mean values of latent variables) can now be specified directly. This makes it much easier to analyze models with mean structures.

7 Weight Matrices and Fit Functions

Estimates of model parameters can be obtained by seven different estimation methods in LISREL 7:

- Instrumental Variables (IV)
- Two-Stage Least Squares (TSLS)
- Unweighted Least Squares (ULS)
- Generalized Least Squares (GLS)
- Maximum Likelihood (ML)
- Generally Weighted Least Squares (WLS)
- Diagonally Weighted Least Squares (DWLS)

Under general assumptions, all seven methods give consistent estimates of parameters. If the model is correct, the parameters will be close to the true parameter values in large samples. The seven types of estimates differ in several respects. The TSLS and IV methods are procedures which are non-iterative and very fast. The ULS, GLS, ML, WLS, and DWLS estimates are obtained by means of an iterative procedure which minimizes a particular fit function by successively improving the parameter estimates. Initial values for the iterative procedures are provided by IV or TSLS.

All fit functions are special cases of a general family of fit functions for analysis of covariance structures which may be written (see, e.g., Browne, 1984)

$$F(\theta) = (s-\sigma)'W^{-1}(s-\sigma) \qquad (1)$$
$$= \sum_{g=1}^{k}\sum_{h=1}^{g}\sum_{i=1}^{k}\sum_{j=1}^{i} w^{gh,ij}(s_{gh}-\sigma_{gh})(s_{ij}-\sigma_{ij}),$$

where

$$\mathbf{s}' = (s_{11}, s_{21}, s_{22}, s_{31}, ..., s_{kk}),$$

is a vector of the elements in the lower half, including the diagonal, of the covariance matrix $\mathbf{S}$ of order $k \times k$ used to fit the model to the data,

$$\boldsymbol{\sigma}' = (\sigma_{11}, \sigma_{21}, \sigma_{22}, \sigma_{31}, ..., \sigma_{kk}),$$

is the vector of corresponding elements of $\boldsymbol{\Sigma}(\boldsymbol{\theta})$ reproduced from the model parameters $\boldsymbol{\theta}$, and $w^{gh,ij}$ is a typical element of a positive definite matrix $\mathbf{W}^{-1}$ of order $u \times u$, where $u = \frac{1}{2}k(k+1)$. In most cases, the elements of $\mathbf{W}^{-1}$ are obtained by inverting a matrix $\mathbf{W}$ whose typical element is denoted $w_{gh,ij}$. The usual way of choosing $\mathbf{W}$ in weighted least squares is to let $w_{gh,ij}$ be a consistent estimate of the asymptotic covariance between s_{gh} and s_{ij}. If this is the case, we say that $\mathbf{W}^{-1}$ is a *correct weight matrix*. To estimate the model parameters $\boldsymbol{\theta}$, the fit function is minimized with respect to $\boldsymbol{\theta}$.

To obtain consistent estimates, any positive definite matrix $\mathbf{W}$ may be used. Under very general assumptions, if the model holds in the population and if the sample variances and covariances in $\mathbf{S}$ converge in probability to the corresponding elements in the population covariance matrix $\boldsymbol{\Sigma}$ as the sample size increases, any fit function with a positive definite $\mathbf{W}$ will give a consistent estimator of $\boldsymbol{\theta}$. In practice, numerical results obtained by one fit function are often close enough to the results that would be obtained by another fit function to give the same substantive interpretations of the results.

Further assumptions must be made, however, if one needs an asymptotically correct chi-square measure of goodness-of-fit and asymptotically correct standard errors of parameter estimates.

"Classical" theory for covariance structures (see e.g., Browne, 1974, or Jöreskog, 1981), assumes that the asymptotic variances and covariances of the elements of $\mathbf{S}$ are of the form

$$ACov(s_{gh}, s_{ij}) = (1/N)(\sigma_{gi}\sigma_{hj} + \sigma_{gj}\sigma_{hi}), \tag{2}$$

where N is the total sample size. This holds, in particular, if the observed variables have a multivariate normal distribution, or if $\mathbf{S}$ has a Wishart distribution. The GLS and ML methods and their chi-square values and standard errors are based on (2). The GLS method corresponds to using a matrix $\mathbf{W}^{-1}$ in (1) whose general element is

$$w^{gh,ij} = N(2 - \delta_{gh})(2 - \delta_{ij})(s^{gi}s^{hj} + s^{gj}s^{hi}), \tag{3}$$

where δ_{gh} and δ_{ij} are Kronecker deltas and the s with superscripts are elements of $\mathbf{S}^{-1}$. The fit function for ML is not of the form (1) but may be shown to be equivalent to using a $\mathbf{W}^{-1}$ of the form (3), with s replaced by an estimate of σ which is updated in each iteration.

In recent fundamental work by Browne (1982, 1984), this classical theory for covariance structures has been generalized to any multivariate distribution for continuous variables satisfying very mild assumptions. This approach uses a $\mathbf{W}$ matrix with typical element

$$w_{gh,ij} = m_{ghij} - s_{gh}s_{ij}, \tag{4}$$

where

$$m_{ghij} = (1/N)\sum_{a=1}^{N}(z_{ag} - \bar{z}_g)(z_{ah} - \bar{z}_h)(z_{ai} - \bar{z}_i)(z_{aj} - \bar{z}_j) \tag{5}$$

are the fourth-order central moments. Using such a $\mathbf{W}$ in (1) gives what Browne calls "asymptotically distribution free best GLS estimators" for which correct asymptotic chi-squares and standard errors may be obtained. As shown by Browne, this $\mathbf{W}$ matrix may also be used to compute correct asymptotic chi-squares and standard errors for estimates which have been obtained by the classical ML and GLS methods. When $\mathbf{W}$ is defined by (4), we call the fit function WLS (Weighted Least Squares), to distinguish it from GLS where $\mathbf{W}$ is defined by (3). WLS and GLS are different forms of weighted least squares: WLS is asymptotically distribution free, while GLS is based on normal theory.

Browne's (1984) development is a theory for sample covariance matrices for continuous variables. In practice, correlation matrices are often analyzed; i.e., covariance matrices scaled by stochastic standard deviations. The elements of such a correlation matrix do not have asymptotic variances and covariances of the form (2), even if S has a Wishart distribution. In PRELIS, we have extended Browne's (1984) work so that an estimate of the asymptotic covariance matrix of estimated correlations can also be obtained under the same general assumptions of non-normality. This approach can also be used when some or all of the variables are ordinal or censored, if the raw scores are replaced by normal scores. PRELIS can also compute estimates of the asymptotic variances and covariances of estimated polychoric and polyserial correlations.

8 References

Browne, M.W. (1974) Generalized least squares estimators in the analysis of covariance structures. *South African Statistical Journal*, 8, 1-24.

Browne, M.W. (1982) Covariance structures. Pp 72-141 in D. M. Hawkins (Ed.): *Topics in applied multivariate analysis*. Cambridge: Cambridge University Press.

Browne, M.W. (1984) Asymptotically distribution-free methods for the analysis of covariance structures. *British Journal of Mathematical and Statistical Psychology*, 37, 62-83.

Cudeck, R. (1989) The analysis of correlation matrices using covariance structure models. *Psychological Bulletin*, 96, in press.

Cudeck, R., and Browne, M. W. (1983) Cross-validation of covariance structures. *Multivariate Behavioral Research*, 18, 147-157.

Johnson, N.L., and Kotz, S. (1970) *Distributions in statistics: Continuous univariate distributions-1*. New York: Wiley.

Jöreskog, K.G. (1981) Analysis of covariance structures. *Scandinavian Journal of Statistics*, 8, 65-92.

Jöreskog, K.G. (1986) Estimation of the polyserial correlation from summary statistics. Research Report 86-2. University of Uppsala, Department of Statistics.

Jöreskog, K.G., and Sörbom, D. (1986) PRELIS *A program for multivariate data screening and data summarization. A preprocessor for* LISREL. Mooresville, Indiana: Scientific Software, Inc.

Jöreskog, K.G., and Sörbom, D. (1988) LISREL 7 *A guide to the program and applications*. Chicago: SPSS Publications.

Olsson, U. (1979) Maximum likelihood estimation of the polychoric correlation coefficient. *Psychometrika*, 44, 443-460.

Möglichkeiten und Probleme einer Zeitreihenanalyse und Prognose mit MicroTSP

R. Kosfeld

Summary

MicroTSP is a program package for time series analysis and regression. It contains a user-friendly surface on which it is easy to use. In this paper we discuss the features of MicroTSP procedures for component models, exponential smoothing, Box-Jenkins methods, and vectorautoregression. Some problems in model fitting and forecasting are outlined and suggestions for improving the program package are given.

1. Allgemeines

Das Programmpaket MicroTSP (TSP Time Series Processor) von Quantitative Micro Software, Irvine, California, enthält Verfahren der Zeitreihen- und Regressionsanalyse bis hin zur Möglichkeit einer Schätzung und Simulation interdependenter Gleichungssysteme. Es ist sowohl auf den Systemen IBM PC, XT, AT als auch auf dem PS/2-System und kompatiblen Rechnern lauffähig. Die neueste Version 6.0, die 1988 freigegeben wurde, setzt eine Mindestspeicherkapazität von 384 KB RAM und zwei Diskettenlaufwerke oder eine Festplatte voraus. Für die hochauflösende Grafik sind alle gängigen Grafik-Adapter zulässig: CGA, EGA, Hercules oder VGA und kompatible Karten. Arithmetische Koprozessoren (8087, 80287 oder 80387) sind zwar nicht erforderlich, jedoch für umfangreichere Auswertungen wünschenswert. MicroTSP kann dialogorientiert konfiguriert werden (CONFIG-Kommando).

Die in MicroTSP verfügbaren Verfahren der Zeitreihenanalyse im engeren Sinne lassen sich in vier Gruppen einteilen:
- Elementare Verfahren (Komponentenmodelle),
- Verfahren der exponentiellen Glättung,
- Box-Jenkins-Verfahren (ARIMA)-Modelle,
- Vektorautoregression.

Als spezielle Verfahren der Regressionsanalyse, die hier nicht behandelt werden sollen, sind Distributed-Lag-Modelle, die Cochran-Orcutt-Methode, nichtlineare Regressionsmodelle, Logit- und Probit-Modelle für binäre Reponsevariablen und diverse Schätzverfahren für simultane Gleichungssysteme verfügbar.

2. Datenmanagement und Dateiverwaltung

Das vorherrschende Datenobjekt in MicroTSP ist die Zeitreihe, jedoch können auch undatierte Reihen verwendet werden, was zu Beginn jeder Sitzung spezifiziert werden muß (CREATE-Anweisung). Als Frequenz kommen für Zeitreihen Jahres-, Quartals- oder Monatsdaten in Betracht. Außerdem muß die Start- und Endperiode bzw. im Falle undatierter Reihen die maximale Anzahl der Beobachtungen angegeben werden. Ebenso wie alle anderen Kommandos kann das CREATE-Kommando vollständig direkt oder aber schrittweise in einem Dialog spezifiziert werden, der sich auch über Funktionstasten initiieren läßt. Mittels des SMPL-Kommandos kann der Analysezeitraum (Stütz- oder Prognosezeitraum) einer Reihe variiert werden. Mit der CONVERT-Anweisung lassen sich Zeitreihen in eine andere Frequenz konvertieren.

Die GENR-Anweisung bietet die Möglichkeit von Datentransformationen, wozu auf diverse interne Funktionen zurückgegriffen werden kann. Außer den üblichen mathematischen Funktionen enthält MicrTSP die Logit-Funktion sowie die Dichte- und Verteilungsfunktion der Standardnormalverteilung. Ein Zufallszahlengenerator für gleich- und normalverteilte Zufallszahlen ist ebenso verfügbar.

Zur Eingabe der Daten einer (Zeit-)Reihe steht ein Daten-Editor zur Verfügung (DATA-Kommando). Die Daten befinden sich zunächst im RAM und können mit STORE extern in Datenbankdateien (data bank files) gespeichert werden. Es handelt sich um ASCII-Dateien, die neben den Beobachtungen vorab noch Informationen über die (Zeit-) Reihe enthalten. Mit FETCH können die Datenbankdateien in den Arbeitsspeicher geladen werden. Darüber hinaus kann MicroTSP andere Dateitypen wie DIF (data interchange files), LOTUS PRN (text files) und Lotus WKS (work sheet files) lesen

(READ-Kommando) und auch Daten in diesen Formaten speichern (WRITE-Kommando).

Vollständige Sitzungen lassen sich mit SAVE speichern und können mit LOAD wieder in den Arbeitsspeicher gebracht werden. Analoge Kommandos gibt es auch für Gleichungen (STOREQ, FETEQ), die ebenso wie Batch-Programme mit MicroTSP-Kommandos mit einem Editor (EDIT-Kommando) bearbeitet werden können. Allgemein steht dieser Editor für Textdateien zur Verfügung. Alle mit ihm erstellten Dateien lassen sich auch mit Textverarbeitungssystemen weiter bearbeiten.

3. Grafik

MicroTSP verfügt über benutzerfreundliche Grafikroutinen, innerhalb derer sich eine Grafik über ein Menü auf einem Matrix- oder Laserdrucker ausdrucken läßt (Kommando PRINT). Alternativ kann eine Grafik in einer Datei gespeichert werden (Kommando SAVE). Mit LGRAPH läßt sie sich später wieder auf dem Bildschirm projizieren und mit PGRAPH ausdrucken. Hochauflösende Grafiken lassen sich zusätzlich mit einem "pen plotter" zeichnen, wenn sie zuvor in einem "HALO File" gespeichert worden sind. Der Benutzer kann Einfluß auf die Gestaltung der Grafiken nehmen, wozu auch eine interaktive Beschriftung gehört. In hochauflösender Grafik können ausschließlich Zeitreihenplots (Kommando PLOT) und Streuungsdiagramme (Kommando SCAT) erstellt werden.

In rudimentärer Grafik (ASCII-Zeichensatz) lassen sich die Autokorrelations- und partielle Autokorrelationsfunktion einer Zeitreihe (IDENT-Kommando) sowie die Kreuzkorrelationen zweier Zeitreihen (CROSS-Kommando) plotten. Darüber hinaus sind diverse rudimentäre Grafiken wie z.B. ein Residuenplot innerhalb spezieller Prozeduren abrufbar.

4. Verfahren der Zeitreihenanalyse
4.1 Elementare Zeitreihenanalyse (Komponentenmodelle)

Unter elementarer Zeitreihenanalyse wird die Zerlegung einer Zeitreihe in eine glatte Komponente, eine Saisonkomponente und eine Residualkomponente verstanden. Die glatte Komponente läßt sich bei ökonomischen Reihen oft noch in eine Trend- und Konjunkturkomponente aufspalten. Neben dem additiven und multiplikativen Komponentenmodell bildet man häufig auch gemischte Modelle bilden. MicroTSP setzt Komponentenmodelle mit einer starren Saisonfigur voraus. Sophistiziertere Komponentenmodelle (s. z.B. Pauly und Schlicht, 1984) lassen sich in MicroTSP nicht oder nur unter extensiver Programmierung schätzen.

Zur Bestimmung der glatten Komponente bzw. des Trends gibt es in MicroTSP keine speziellen Anweisungen. Gleitende Durchschnitte müssen daher über das GENR-Kommandos erzeugt werden. So erhält man z.B. einen zentrierten 4-gliedrigen gleitenden Durchschnitt YG einer Zeitreihe mit dem Variablennamen Y durch die Anweisung

GENR YG = (Y(-2)/2 + Y(-1) + Y + Y(1) + Y(2)/2)/4.

Y(-T) spezifiziert darin einen "lag" und Y(T) einen "lead" von T Perioden. Allerdings muß der Benutzer zuvor den Zeitraum mit Hilfe des SMPL-Kommandos verkürzen.

Für polynomiale Trends steht die LS-Anweisung zur Verfügung, die allgemein zur Schätzung von linearen Regressionsmodellen verwendet wird. Hierzu sind jedoch vorab die "Regressoren" etwas aufwendig nach Definition eines Startwertes mit der GENR-Anweisung unter Variation des Stützzeitraumes zu bestimmen. Ein parabolisches Trendmodell für die Zeitreihe Y läßt sich dann beispielsweise durch die Anweisung

LS Y C T T2

schätzen. C bezeichnet darin das konstante Glied und die "Regressoren" T und T2 enthalten die natürlichen Zahlen von 1 bis n bzw. deren Quadrate. Nichtlineare Trendmodelle in den Parametern können mittels des NLS-Kommandos geschätzt werden, wozu die Gleichungsform zu spezifizieren ist.

Saisonbereinigte Zeitreihen lassen sich dagegen mit dem speziellen Kommando SEAS erzeugen. Die Eingabe des Parameters A indiziert eine Saisonbereinigung für das additive Modell und der Parameter M steht für das multiplikative Modell. Im ersten Fall wird die Differenz zwischen der Ursprungsreihe und und den gleitenden Durchschnitten zur Bestimmung der Saisonkomponente verwendet, im letzteren Fall der Quotient beider Reihen. Die Saisonkomponenten werden dann in der üblichen Form als Durchschnitte der entsprechenden Perioden bestimmt. Hierzu werden nur diejenigen Jahre berücksichtigt, für die die Daten komplett vorliegen. Leider besteht keine Zugriffsmöglichkeit auf die in den Zwischenschritten von SEAS bestimmten gleitenden Durchschnitte und Saisonkomponenten.

4.2 Verfahren der exponentiellen Glättung

MicroTSP enthält folgende Verfahren der exponentiellen Glättung (Parameter in Klammern):
- Einfache exponentielle Glättung (S),
- doppelte exponentielle Glättung (D),
- Holt-Winters-Verfahren ohne Saison (N).
- Holt-Winters-Verfahren mit additiver Saison (A),
- Holt-Winters-Verfahren mit multiplikativer Saison (M)

Bei allen Verfahren werden die Glättungsparameter zunächst mittels der SMOOTH-Anweisung für den Stützzeitraum geschätzt. Die Schätzung erfolgt dabei im Rahmen einer Gittersuche (grid search) durch Minimierung des MSE (mean square errors). Alternativ kann der Benutzer auch einen oder mehrere Parameter vorgeben. Daneben muß ein Variablenname für die geglättete Zeitreihe benannt werden, die dann automatisch vom Programm erzeugt wird. Je nach Verfahren werden neben dem bzw. den Glättungskoeffizienten sowie der Summe der quadrierten Residuen (sum of squared residuals) und dem RMSE (root mean square error) die aktuellen Werte der Niveau-, Trend- und Saisonkomponenten bzw. -faktoren ausgewiesen. Prognosewerte werden automatisch der geglätteten Zeitreihe zugewiesen, so wie der Prognosezeitraum spezifiziert wird. Hierbei kann jedoch aufgrund eines Programmierfehlers ein Problem auftauchen, worauf bei der Modellanpassung und Prognose (Abschn. 5) eingegangen wird.

MicroTSP deckt die wichtigsten Verfahren der exponentiellen Glättung ab. Als Ergänzung kämen für trendbehaftete Zeitreihen ohne Saison das Verfahren von Holt und für saisonale Zeitreihen das Verfahren von Harrison in Betracht. Im Holt-Winters-Verfahren wird die Saisonkomponente nicht weiter aktualisiert. Gilchrist (1976, S. 138-139) hat hierzu ein iteratives Verfahren vorgeschlagen, das unter bestimmten Bedingungen Verbesserungen erwarten läßt. Eine Option für dieses Verfahren wäre ebenfalls wünschenswert.

4.3 Box-Jenkins-Verfahren

MicroTSP bietet die Möglichkeit, multiplikative, saisonale ARIMA-Modelle, ARIMA(p,d,q)x(P,D,Q)$_s$-Modelle, zu schätzen und auf ihrer Basis Prognosen zu erstellen. Zur Identifikation eines SARIMA-Modells ist vom Programm der Box-Jenkins-Ansatz vorgesehen. Zu dem Plot der Autokorrelations- und partiellen Autokorrelationsfunktion einer Zeitreihe liefert das IDENT-Kommando den Standardfehler der Autokorrelationen sowie die Box-Pierce Q-Statistik, die einen Test auf Gültigkeit des Modells erlaubt.

Die Modellschätzung erfolgt mittels des allgemeinen LS-Kommandos, nachdem die Zeitreihe gefiltert worden ist, d.h. nachdem Differenzen der Ordnung d und saisonale Differenzen der Ordnung D gebildet worden sind. Autoregressive Terme werden mit AR, "moving-average"-Terme mit MA bezeichnet, wobei in Klammern der jeweilige Lag anzugeben ist. Entsprechend müssen saisonale autoregressive und "moving-average" Terme durch SAR bzw. SMA spezifiziert werden. Die saisonalen Lags L^s beziehen sich auf die Periodizität der Zeitreihe: bei Quartalsdaten ist L^s aus der Menge {4,8,...}, bei Monatsdaten aus der Menge {12,24,...} zu wählen. Sofern in der LS-Anweisung die Konstante C berücksichtigt wird, bezieht sich die Schätzung auf ein ARIMA-Modell der Zeitreihe $(y_t^{d,D}-c)$, wobei $(y_t^{d,D})$ die gefilterte Zeitreihe (y_t) ist. Sei (u_t) die Zeitreihe der Residuen, die einem "white-noise"-Prozeß gehorchen. Dann wird z.B. durch die Anweisung

LS YD C AR(1) AR(2) MA(1) MA(2)

das ARIMA(2,d,2)-Modell

(4.1) $(1 - \Phi_1 B - \Phi_2 B^2)(y_t^d - c) = (1 + \Theta_1 B + \Theta_2 B^2) u_t$ =>

$y_t^d = c + \Phi_1 (y_{t-1}^d - c) + \Phi_2 (y_{t-2}^d - c) + u_t + \Theta_1 u_{t-1} + \Theta_2 u_{t-2}$

geschätzt. B ist darin der Backshift-Operator, $y_{t-L} = B^L \cdot y_t$, und YD korrespondiert mit der Zeitreihe (y_t^d) der Differenzen der Ordnung d aus (y_t). Entsprechend wird mit der Anweisung

LS YDD C AR(1) AR(2) MA(2) SAR(4) SMA(4)

eine Schätzung des ARIMA(2,d,2)x(1,D,1)$_s$-Modells

(4.2) $(1 - \Phi_1 B - \Phi_2 B^2)(1 - \Phi_1^s B^4)(y_t^{d,D} - c) = (1 + \Theta_2 B^2)(1 + \Theta_1^s B^4) u_t$

$\Rightarrow y_t^{d,D} = c + \Phi_1 (y_{t-1}^{d,D} - c) + \Phi_2 (y_{t-2}^{d,D} - c) + \Phi_1^s (y_{t-4}^{d,D} - c) - \Phi_1^s \Phi_1 (y_{t-5}^{d,D} - c) - \Phi_2^s \Phi_1 (y_{t-6}^{d,D} - c) + u_t + \Theta_2 u_{t-2} + \Theta_1^s u_{t-4} + \Theta_2 \Theta_1^s u_{t-6}$

initiiert. YDD ist darin der Name der Zeitreihe ($y_t^{d,D}$) und die Koeffizienten der saisonalen Terme sind durch das Superskript s gekennzeichnet. Obwohl diesem Modell ein "moving-average"-Prozeß der Ordnung q=2 zugrunde liegt, wird der Parameter Θ_1 nicht geschätzt, da auch die Terme von Prozessen niedrigerer Ordnung explizit mit angegeben werden müssen. Man beachte auch, daß die Terme der MA- und SMA-Polynome vom zweiten Glied ab nicht das übliche negative Vorzeichen haben.

Im Output werden die Schätzer für die Koeffizienten der in der LS-Anweisung explizit spezifizierten Terme mit ihrer Standardabweichung, der t-Statistik und der tatsächlichen Irrtumswahrscheinlichkeit für einen zweiseitigen Signifikanztest ausgewiesen. Weiter sind folgende Informationen verfügbar: Stützzeitraum, Anzahl der Beobachtungen, Anzahl der Iterationen, Bestimmtheitsmaß (unkorrigiert und korrigiert), Standardfehler der Regression, Durbin-Walson-Statistik, logarithmierte Likelihood, Mittelwert und Standardabweichung der Zeitreihe, Summe der quadrierten Residuen, F-Statistik. Mit der Angabe der logarithmierten Likelihood lassen sich auch Akaides Informationskriterien AIC und BIC berechnen, mit denen ein Modell hinsichtlich seiner prognostischen Eignung beurteilt werden kann.

Darüber hinaus kann sich der Benutzer die Kovarianzmatrix anzeigen lassen, jedoch in einer recht unübersichtlichen Form. Eine Darstellung in Form einer unteren oder oberen Dreiecksmatrix wäre adäquater. Zusätzlich kann ein Residuenplot abgerufen werden, der zu jeder Beobachtung die numerischen Werte der Residuen, Zeitreihe und angepaßten Zeitreihe enthält. Die Zeitreihe der Residuen (RESID), die z.B. mit der Anweisung IDENT auf evtl. noch vorhandene Strukturen überprüft werden kann, wird automatisch erzeugt.

Die Modalität der Schätzung von ARIMA-Modellen in MicroTSP ist ausgesprochen vorteilhaft. Die Möglichkeit, die Koeffizienten der zu schätzenden Terme individuell auswählen zu können, entspricht dem *Prinzip der Sparsamkeit*. Sie bietet eine effiziente Modellierung und verringert auch die Gefahr eines "overfittings". Schwierigkeiten wird der Benutzer dagegen bei der Identifikation von ARIMA-Modellen haben, da der Box-Jenkins-Ansatz nur bei reinen AR- und MA-Modellen eine adäquate Strategie ist. Über Ansätze zur Identifikation gemischter Modelle wie z.B. die "corner method" (Beguin, Gourieroux und Montford, 1980) oder Vektorkorrelationen (Streitberg, 1982) verfügt MicroTSP nicht. Dadurch gleicht die Identifikation von ARIMA-Modellen oft einer "pattern recognition without patterns" (Streitberg und Naeve, 1986, S. 131). In dieser Hinsicht unterscheidet sich MicroTSP derzeit aber noch kaum von gängigen ökonometrischen Programmpaketen (wie z.B. RATS) oder Prognosesoftwarepaketen (wie z.B. FORECAST PLUS, PRO CAST). Allerdings werden in letzterer Kategorie zunehmend Möglichkeiten einer automatischen Modellidentifikation bereitgestellt (z.B. in AutoBox Plus, FORECAST PRO), deren Qualität aber noch nicht generell als befriedigend bezeichnet werden kann.

4.4 Vektorautoregression

Bei multiplen Zeitreihen, die miteinander korrelieren, würde man bei der Verwendung von univariaten Zeitreihenverfahren auf Informationen verzichten, die möglicherweise eine Prognose bedeutsam verbessern könnten. Dies wird insbesondere dann der Fall sein, wenn Lagstrukturen zwischen den Variablen relevant sind, d.h. wenn bestimmte Variablen mit zeitlicher Verzögerung auf andere Variablen reagieren. Häufig lassen sich aber die kausalen Variablen nicht einfach identifizieren. Es sei hier nur auf die Problematik der Beziehung zwischen der Geldmenge und dem Sozialprodukt verwiesen (s. z.B. Sims, 1972). Man weiß oft allein nur, daß die Verzögerungsstruktur einer Gruppe von Variablen ihre aktuellen und zukünftigen Realisationen determiniert. Für eine Modellierung und Prognose derart strukturierter multipler Zeitreihen bietet sich die Vektorautoregression an. Es handelt sich dabei um ein Gleichungssystem mit endogen verzögerten Variablen als Regressoren. Jede endogene Variable ist sowohl von ihren eigenen Lag-Werten als auch von den Lag-Werten aller anderen endogenen Variablen für die zu spezifizierenden Verzögerungen abhängig. Optional können exogene Variablen in das System eingeführt werden.

Sei **y** ein qx1-Vektor der endogenen Variablen, **y-** ein px1-Vektor der verzögerten endogenen Variablen, **x** ein mx1-Vektor der exogenen Variablen, **u** ein qx1-Residualvektor und **B** eine qx(p+m+1)-Koeffizientenmatrix. Dann ist eine Vektorautoregression durch das System

$$(5.1) \quad \mathbf{y} = \mathbf{B} \begin{bmatrix} 1 \\ \mathbf{y-} \\ \mathbf{x} \end{bmatrix} + \mathbf{u}.$$

gegeben. Angenommen, für eine bivariate Zeitreihe (y_{1t}, y_{2t}) seien neben einer exogenen Variablen nur der erste und vierte Lag für die Verzögerungsstruktur relevant. Das System (5.1) spezifiziert sich dann zu

$$(5.2) \quad \begin{bmatrix} y_{1t} \\ y_{2t} \end{bmatrix} = \begin{bmatrix} \beta_{10} & \beta_{11} & \beta_{12} & \beta_{13} & \beta_{14} & \beta_{15} \\ \beta_{20} & \beta_{21} & \beta_{22} & \beta_{23} & \beta_{24} & \beta_{25} \end{bmatrix} \begin{bmatrix} 1 \\ y_{1,t-1} \\ y_{1,t-4} \\ y_{2,t-1} \\ y_{2,t-4} \\ x_t \end{bmatrix}$$

und eine Schätzung der Koeffizientenmatrix **B** läßt sich einfach mittels der VAREST-Anweisung durchführen:

    VAREST 1 1 4 4 Y1 Y2 @ X.

Die Zahlenpaare nach dem VAREST-Kommando legen jeweils die Lags oder Lag-Bereiche fest, wodurch eine flexible Lag-Struktur ermöglicht wird. Die darauffolgenden endogenen Variablen (hier: Y1 und Y2) werden durch das Zeichen @ von den exogenen Variablen (hier: X) separiert. Das geschätzte Gleichungssystem, das sich im RAM befindet, muß vor einer Prognose mit dem VARMOD-Kommando in einer Modelldatei (model file) gespeichert werden, z.B. durch

    VARMOD MODELL1,

um anschließend mit dem SOLVE-Kommando

    SOLVE MODELL1

simuliert werden zu können. Natürlich muß der Stützbereich hierzu wiederum erweitert werden, wenn auf der Basis des Modells eine Prognose erstellt werden soll. Schließlich lassen sich mit der VARSTAT-Anweisung Statistiken erzeugen, die zur Interpretation der geschätzten Koeffizientenmatrix relevant sind (Impulsantwortfunktion und Choleski-Dekomposition der Kovarianzmatrix der Residuen).

5. Anpassung und Prognose

Bei univariablen Zeitreihen erfolgt nach einer LS- und NLS-Modellschätzung eine Modellanpassung und Prognose mittels der Anweisungen FIT und FORECST. Im Gegensatz dazu wird die angepaßte Zeitreihe nach Anwendung eines Verfahrens der exponentiellen Glättung automatisch erzeugt und auch die Prognose steht unmittelbar nach Einstellung des Vorhersagezeitraums. Die Simulation einer Vektorautoregression ist im vorhergehenden Abschnitt aufgezeigt worden.

In der Zeitreihenanalyse sind die Anweisungen FIT und FORCST insbesondere für die Anpassung und Prognose eines SARIMA-Modells von Interesse. Während FIT für statische Simulationen eines Modells konzipiert worden ist, soll FORCST dynamische Modellsimulationen ermöglichen (Hall und Lilien, 1988, Abschn. 16.1). Leider ist das Systemverhalten unter diesen Anweisungen für den Benutzer in vielen Fällen nicht überschaubar. Zu beachten ist, daß unter FORCST je nach SMPL-Einstellung völlig unterschiedliche Prognosen resultieren können. Häufig wird der Benutzer mit diesen beiden Anweisungen nicht das gewünschte Ergebnis erzielen.

Tab. 5.1: Verhalten des Systems bei der Modellanpassung und Prognose

	SMPL-Einstellung	
	Stütz- und Prognosezeitraum	Prognosezeitraum
FIT	Erwartete Modellanpassung und Ein-Perioden-Prognose; Mehr-Perioden-Prognosen verzerrt für Perioden, die von verzögerten Variablenwerten innerhalb des Prognosezeitraums abhängig sind	
FORCST	Zeitpfad des Modells bei gegebenen Anfangswerten ohne Berücksichtigung der weiteren Beobachtungswerte	Prognosevariable für Stützzeitraum identisch mit originärer Zeitreihe; erwartete Mehr-Perioden-Prognose

In der Prognosepraxis möchte man in der Regel aufgrund eines Modells eine Zeitreihe erzeugen, die für den Stützzeitraum die Modellanpassung und für den Vorhersagezeitraum die unter dem Modell zu erwartenden Prognosewerte enthält. Wie aus Tab. 5.1 hervorgeht, leistet dies generell weder FIT noch FORCST. Mit FIT erhält man eine korrekte Modellanpassung und eine aufgrund des Modells zu erwartende Ein-Perioden-Prognose. Die Prognose y_{n+k}, $k>1$, ist jedoch verzerrt, wenn sie Prognosewerte aus dem Vorhersagezeitraum voraussetzt: während in den AR-Termen die benötigten Prognosewerte ohne eine Systemmeldung gleich Null gesetzt werden, ist dies in den MA-Termen nur für die Zeitreihenwerte der originären Variablen der Fall. Mithin sind die verzögerten Residuen dann gleich den negativen verzögerten Prognosewerten der entsprechenden Perioden. Mit FORCST erhält man dagegen über dem Stütz- und Prognosezeitraum den Zeitpfad des Modells, der für Prognosen im allgemeinen unbrauchbar ist, da aktuelle Entwicklungen nicht berücksichtigt werden. Sofern als SMPL-Bereich nur der Prognosezeitraum eingestellt ist, liefert FORCST eine aufgrund des Modells zu erwartende Prognose. Da der Prognosevariablen jedoch für den Stützzeitraum die originären Zeitreihenwerte zugewiesen werden, ist damit noch keine Modellanpassung gegeben.

Das hier aufgezeigte Verhalten des Systems kann allerdings durch ein weiteres Problem überlagert werden. Ein über dem Stützzeitraum korrekt angepaßtes Modell mit MA-Termen kann im Falle einer Prognose mit FIT Schwingungen enthalten, die im allgemeinen zu einem starken Anstieg des RMSE führen. Diese Schwingungen können sowohl in einer Subperiode des Stützzeitraumes als auch im Prognosezeitraum auftreten, wobei die übrigen Zeitreihenwerte des Stützzeitraumes unverändert bleiben. Eine Ein-Perioden-Prognose wird aber weiterhin korrekt sein, wenn die Schwingungen ausschließlich im Stützzeitraum auftreten. Diese Unsicherheit im Systemverhalten ist eigentlich nur durch einen Programmierfehler erklärbar, der unter bestimmten Bedingungen zum Tragen kommt. Seltener tritt dieses Verhalten bei den Verfahren der exponentiellen Glättung auf.

6. Konklusionen

MicroTSP enthält die wichtigsten Verfahren der Zeitreihenanalyse zur Prognose univariabler und multipler Zeitreihen. Die Benutzeroberfläche ist übersichtlich gestaltet und gibt Informationen über Zeitreihen, Stützbereich und Kommandos wieder. Abgesehen von Programmierfehlern, die sich in einigen Fällen bei der Modellanpassung und Prognose bemerkbar machen können, gibt es jedoch zusätzlich Unzulänglichkeiten, die gegenwärtig noch eine generelle Empfehlung des Programmpakets zur Zeitreihenanalyse und Prognose problematisch erscheinen lassen:

1. Die Modellanpassung und Prognose ist recht verwirrend und für den Benutzer kaum nachvollziehbar. Ohne genaue Kenntnis des Systemverhaltens können leicht verzerrte Prognosen generiert werden.
2. Die ausschließliche Beschränkung auf den Box-Jenkins-Ansatz ist keine adäquate Strategie zur Identifikation von ARIMA-Modellen. Sie überfordert den Benutzer erheblich bei der Modellwahl.
3. Auch ohne auf Methoden der "Künstlichen Intelligenz" zurückgreifen zu müssen, könnte das Programm Variationen des SMPL-Bereichs häufig selbst übernehmen und den Benutzer damit von lästiger "Rechenarbeit" entlasten.
4. Insbesondere für die Ausbildung und elementare Analyse wäre ein einfacheres "handling" des Komponentenmodells wünschenswert.
5. Spektralanalytische Verfahren zur Zeitreihenanalyse fehlen vollständig.

Der letzte Punkt ist allerdings nur sekundär für Prognosen relevant. Mit spektralanalytischen Verfahren lassen sich aber wertvolle Informationen über die Struktur einer Zeitreihe gewinnen, so daß sie in einem Programmpaket zur Zeitreihenanalyse durchaus nach wie vor von Bedeutung sind. Ausgesprochen positiv ist dagegen die Möglichkeit zu bewerten, speziell die Koeffizienten ausgewählter AR- bzw. SAR- und MA- bzw. SMA-Terme in Box-Jenkins-Modellen schätzen zu können. Dadurch wird eine adäquate Modellierung unter dem Prinzip der Sparsamkeit unterstützt. Wenn die aufgezeigten Probleme beseitigt werden, wird MicroTSP als ein attraktives Programmpaket zur Zeitreihenanalyse und Prognose an Bedeutung gewinnen.

Literatur

Beguin, J.M., Gourieroux, A.M. und Montford, A. (1980), Identification of a Mixed Autoregressive-Moving Average Process: The Corner Method, in: Anderson, O.A. (ed.), Time Series, 423-436, North Holland, Amsterdam.

Gilchrist, W. (1976), Statistical Forecasting, John Wiley & Sons, Chichester.

Hall, R.E. und Lilien, D.M. (1988), MicroTSP Users's Manual, Version 6.0, Quantitative Micro Software, Irvine, California.

Pauly, R. und Schlicht, E. (1984), Zerlegung ökonomischer Zeitreihen: Ein deterministischer und stochastischer Ansatz, Allgemeines Statistisches Archiv, 68, 161-175.

Sims, CH. (1972), Money, Income and Causality, American Economic Review, 62, 540-552.

Streitberg, B. (1980), Vector Correlations of Time Series, Diskussionsbeitrag 4/82, Institut für Quantitative Ökonomik und Statistik, Freie Universität Berlin.

Streitberg, B. und Naeve, P. (1986), A modestly intelligent system for identification, estimation, and forecasting of univariate time series: A⁴: ARIMA, artificial intelligence, and APL2, in: Haux, R. (ed.), Expert Systems in Statistics, Gustav Fischer Verlag, Stuttgart.

F. Faulbaum, R. Haux und K.-H. Jöckel (Hrsg.) (1990). SoftStat '89
Fortschritte der Statistik-Software 2. Stuttgart: Gustav Fischer, 121 - 125

Statistik auf dem Macintosh

P. Kremser

Summary: Inspite of its good graphical and computational possibilities the Macintosh PC does not seem to be very popular among statisticians in germany. This article will describe its role in computational statistics and will give short review of the statistical programs on the Macintosh. There is some information about the programs Excel, Cricket Graph, MacSpin, Statview, Data Desk and Systat. Special attention is paid to Excel and Data Desk.

In Deutschland hat der Macintosh als Werkzeug der Datenanalyse bisher eine untergeordnete Rolle gespielt. Auf der Softstat 87 z.B. gab es einen Vortrag (von G. Sawitzki), bei dem das Macintoshprogramm MacSpin im Mittelpunkt stand; auf der compstat 88 sind mir drei Vorträge bekannt, bei denen der Macintosh eine wesentliche Rolle spielte (von: Murphy/ Bartlett; Nummi/ Nurhonen/ Puntanen; Belsley/Venetoulias/Welsh), und wenige andere, bei denen dieser PC erwähnt wurde. Bei dieser geringen Popularität schien auch ein einfaches Aufzeigen der Möglichkeiten, die ein Macintosh für Statistiker bietet, sinnvoll.

Die Softstat 89 bietet allerdings ein anderes Bild: bei der Sitzung "Exploratorische Datenanalyse" werden in 4 von 6 Vorträgen Macintoshprogramme vorgestellt (Sawitzki; Velleman; Unwin/ Haslett/Craig/Wills; Held); ein Vortrag beschreibt den Einsatz von Statview und Statlab in der Ausbildung (Eggenberger); SPSS kündigt eine Macintoshversion von $SPSS^x$ und SAS das Programm JMP an; einige andere Vorträge verweisen auf den Gebrauch dieser Rechner. Zusätzlich sei hier auf das Programm DIAMOND FAST von Unwin/Wills verwiesen, daß von den Autoren in Ihrem Softstat - Vortrag nicht beschrieben wurde. Es bietet sehr schöne grafische Möglichkeiten zum Vergleich von Zeitverläufen. Unterstrichen wird die wachsende Bedeutung des Macintosh auch von der Tatsache, daß (ebenfalls Anfang April 89) auf dem 21th Symposium on the Interface of Computer Science and Statistics in Orlando, Florida eine Session "Innovative Statistical Software Based on the Macintosh" stattfindet. Der vorliegende Überblick soll die oben angesprochenen Vorträge ergänzen und etwas stärker die Statistikprogramme berücksichtigen, die bei Macintoshbenutzern weit verbreitet sind.

Zum Anfang seien die Programme genannt, die nicht speziell Statistikprogramme sind oder innerhalb der Statistik eine Spezialaufgabe haben: Excel, Cricket Graph und MacSpin.

Excel ist ein Tabellenkalkulationsprogramm mit Datenbankfunktionen und integrierter Grafik, das seit über drei Jahren auf dem Macintosh und seit etwa einem Jahr auch für MS - DOS Rechnern verfügbar ist. Seit Kurzem werden für den Macintosh andere ‚von Ihrem Anspruch noch leistungsstärkere Programme angeboten. Excel bietet zunächst eine komfortable Rechenhilfe z.B. bei der Erstellung von Übungsaufgaben. Grafiken können so mit der Tabelle verknüpft werden, daß sie bei neuen Eingabewerten sofort aktualisiert werden. Somit eignet sich das Programm auch gut zu kleineren Simulationen beziehungsweise zum Demonstrieren der Wirkung von Parameter- oder Datenänderungen auf einfachere, statistische Modelle. Der folgende Screendump zeigt ein Rechenblatt zur geschichteten Stichprobe.

Eine Änderung der Eingabe der Schichtumfänge N $_h$, der Streuungen sig $_h$ oder der Kosten c $_h$ wirkt sich sofort auf die Zwischenergebnisse und auf die grafische Darstellung der kostenoptimalen Stichprobenumfänge aus. Eine der wichtigsten Rollen von Excel bleibt zu nennen: einige Programme verzichten auf eigene, ausgefeiltere Möglichkeiten zur Dateneingabe und Manipulation zugunsten eines Einsatzes von Programmen wie Excel.

Cricket Graph ist ein weit verbreitetes Programm zur Erstellung von Geschäftsgrafiken und statistischen Schaubildern. Recht interessant ist die Geschichte dieses Programms: Aus einem mäßigen Statistikprogramm mit überdurchschnittlich guten Grafikmöglichkeiten (Statworks) ist ein gutes Geschäftsgrafikprogramm mit überdurchschnittlich guten Statistik- und Datenmanipulationsmöglichkeiten geworden. Diese Firma Cricket hat sich noch weiter in Richtung Präsentation entwickelt (Erstellung von Piktogrammen, von Dias usw.).

MacSpin hat innerhalb der (explorativen) Datenanalyse eine spezielle Aufgabe: die Darstellung der Verteilung von drei bzw. vier Variablen mittels (dreidimensionalen) Streuungsdiagrammen. Die Drehung der Punktwolken vermittelt einen räumlichen Eindruck, durch Markieren kann man einzelne Punkte identifizieren und verfolgen. Außerdem kann man nach den Werten einer vierten Variablen die Punkte verdecken bzw. maskieren. Die neueren Versionen können mehrere Fenster verwalten und zusätzlich Oberflächen d.h. Funktionen von $R^2 \to R$ darstellen. MacSpin hatte als erstes low-cost PRIM (projecting, rotating, isolating, masking) Programm eine Vorreiterrolle; inzwischen werden diese Funktionen auch von anderen Programmen z.B. von Data Desk angeboten.

Nun zu den Statistikprogrammen: Das bei Macintoshbenutzern weit verbreitete Programm **Statview** ist einfach zu bedienen, bietet umfassende, gute Grafik und die wichtigsten Statistikprozeduren (Kreuztabellen, Nichtparametrische Verfahren, Regressions-, Varianz- und Faktorenanalyse). Bei Veränderung der Eingabe werden Statistiken und Grafiken sofort aktualisiert. Allerdings bietet Statview keine interaktive statistische Grafik wie MacSpin oder Data Desk und ist von den Prozeduren her auch nicht so umfassend wie Systat. Nach den letzten Updates zu urteilen geht die Entwicklung dieses Programms in Richtung Präsentationsgrafik.

Wenn man PC - Programme von SPSS, SAS oder BMDP im Auge hat, gibt es zur Zeit nur ein Macintoshprogramm, das ein vergleichbares Methodenspektrum bietet: **Systat**. Es bietet standardmäßig sehr viele Grafikmöglichkeiten, Nichtparametrische Verfahren, Kreuztabellen (auch mehrdimensionale Tabellen und loglineare Modelle), Verallgemeinerte Lineare Modelle (einschließlich Regressions-, Varianz-, Diskriminanz-, Kanonischer Korrelationsanalyse), Faktoren- und Hauptkomponentenanalyse, Multidimensionale Skalierung, Cluster- und Zeitreihenanalyse. Zusätzlich sorgt eine mit Basic vergleichbare Programmiersprache für Flexibilität und es sind noch spezialisiertere Programme von Systat erhältlich. Allerdings gibt es keine dynamische Grafik und im Vergleich zu DataDesk keine wesentlich neuen Ideen. Auch in dieser Hinsicht ähnelt es den bekannten Großrechner bzw. MS-DOS Programmen. Da Systat nicht für den Macintosh, sondern möglichst unabhängig von Betriebssystemen entwickelt wurde, ist die Bedienung trotz ordentlichem "Hilfe"- System nicht "Macintosh-like". Vermutlich aus diesem Grund wird von Systat seit Kurzem das Programm Fastat angeboten, daß zwar besser zur Macintosh-Oberfläche paßt, aber nicht mehr den vollen Leistungsumfang bringt.

Data Desk ist ein Programm, das wie kein anderes die Möglichkeiten der interaktiven statistischen Grafik aufzeigt. Alle Objekte (Listen, Kreuztabellen, Grafiken) sind hier verbunden.

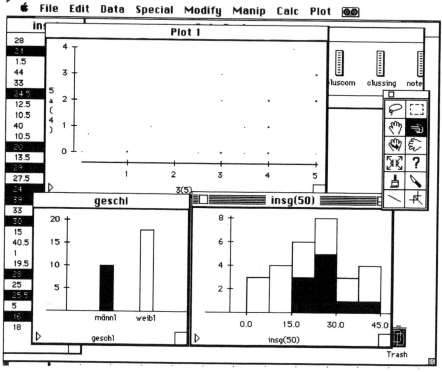

Bei dem vorliegenden Screendump wurde im Balkendiagramm des Merkmals "Geschlecht" der Balken für "männlich" mit der Maus angeklickt. Sofort wurde im Histogramm, im Streuungsdiagramm und in der Liste der Punktezahlen der entsprechende Bereich, die Punkte bzw. die Zahlen markiert. Gegenüber MacSpin kann man nicht nur in dreidimensionalen Streuungsdiagrammen Untersuchungseinheiten markieren, sondern in allen Grafiken, in Wertelisten oder in (Kreuz-)Tabellen. An Statistikprozeduren bietet es im Vergleich zu Statview zusätzlich Clusteranalyse aber kaum Nichtparametrische Verfahren. Macros oder eine Befehlssprache gibt es nicht, allerdings existieren viele Transformationsmöglichkeiten, deren Ergebnisse als spezielle Objekte d.h. Formeln gespeichert werden. Diese Transformationen bzw. Formeln können auch grafisch erzeugt werden. Bei Änderung der Eingabe werden die Ergebnisse sofort aktualisiert. Für die nächste Zukunft ist auch Farbe angekündigt.

Da die Art der Statistikprogramme stark vom Betriebssystem des Macintosh beeinflußt ist, folgen einige Worte zum Betriebssystem. Der Macintosh war Vorreiter für grafische Benutzeroberflächen mit Fenstern, Menüs, Maus usw.. Er hat eine schnelle, gute Grafik. Da er nur im Grafikmodus arbeitet, entfällt das Umschalten von Text- auf Grafikmodus und das Mischen von Text und Grafik wird unproblematisch. Mit dem "clipboard" bzw. der "Zwischenablage" bietet das Betriebssystem eine einfache Möglichkeit, Texte, Grafiken oder Tabellen von einem Programm in ein anderes zu übertragen. Als "Desk Accessories" sind jederzeit kleinere Programme ohne Beendigung des eigentlichen Programms verfügbar. Der "Multifinder" ermöglicht schnelles Wechseln zwischen Programmen und Multitasking. DerMacintosh bietet also eine gute Arbeitsumgebung, die sich durch einfache Bedienung und außergewöhnliche Grafik auszeichnet. Da zwischen Progammen leicht gewechselt und schnell Daten ausgetauscht werden können, können Spezialprogramme wie z.B. MacSpin oder Diamond Fast sinnvoll eingesetzt und in die Umgebung integriert werden.

Zusammenfassend läßt sich sagen, daß die Macintosh-Statistikprogramme sich durch einfache Bedienung und sehr gute Grafik auszeichnen. Wenn man in Bezug auf interaktive statistische Grafik und Benutzeroberfläche den neuesten Stand haben will, ist das Programm Data Desk ein Grund, sich einen Macintosh zu kaufen. An umfassenden, traditionellen Statistikpaketen gibt es zur Zeit keine Auswahl: bis SPSS die angekündigte (für Sommer 1989) Macintoshversion auf den Markt bringt, bleibt dem Benutzer nur Systat. Die hier besprochenen Programme bieten keine Sprache zur Matrixrechnung (wie z.B. GAUSS auf MS - DOS Rechnern). Mit Matlab und Mathematica werden derartige Programme auch für den Macintosh angeboten; ich besitze allerdings keine weitere Infomation zu diesen Programmen.

Literatur:

Edwrds D., Raun N.E. (Ed.) (1988). COMPSTAT Proceedings in Computational Statistics 1988. Physica Verlag, Heidelberg
Faulbaum F.,Uehlinger H.-M. (Ed.) (1987). Fortschritte der Statistik-Software 1. Gustav Fischer Verlag,Stuttgart
Lehman R.S. (1987). Statistics on the Macintosh. In BYTE July 1987
Mac Guide Magazine Inc. (1988). Mac Guide Magazine vol 1, no 4
Microsoft Corporation (1985). Microsoft Excel. Microsoft GmbH
Velleman P.F,Velleman A.Y. (1988). Data Desk Handbook.Odesta Corporation
Wilkinson L. (1987). SYSTAT: The System for Statistics. SYSTAT Inc. ,Evanston,IL,
Woodword A.W., Elliot A.C., Gray H.L., Matlock D.C. (1988). Directory of Statistical Microcomputer Software. New York, Marcel Dekker, Inc.

LISCOMP - A Program to Analyze Linear Structural Equations with Non-metric Indicators

U. Küsters and A. Schepers

1 Introduction and Summary

LISCOMP is a program to estimate linear structural equation models with metric, censored and ordered categorical indicators. The program LISCOMP was designed by Bengt Muthén (1987) to analyze LISREL type models combining threshold relations, factor analytical measurement models and linear simultaneous equations. Other than the LISREL program LISCOMP incorporates explicitly models with non-metric indicators. The program is especially suitable for researchers in disciplines like sociology, economics, psychology and biometrics who formulate causal relations between constructs which may only be measured indirectly by indicators. LISCOMP is implemented in FORTRAN 77. Hence, several versions for different machines ranging from IBM-PC's to mainframes are available. The purpose of this paper is twofold: Firstly, we summarize the statistical components of the LISCOMP model as described in Muthén (1984). Secondly, we evaluate the program by criterions such as the ease of use and error checking. Thirdly, we include the demonstration of a small empirical example. The evaluation is based on the IBM-PC-version 1.1 dated on September, 1987.

2 The statistical formulation of the LISCOMP model

The general model (cf. Muthén 1984) estimated with LISCOMP is a combination of

- *factor analysis* to reduce metric variables to one or several metric latent traits,
- *simultaneous equation systems* to formulate linear causal relations between metric latent traits and exogenous variables and
- *threshold measurement relations* to connect measurable *ordered categorical, truncated* and *censored* variables to the metric latent traits.

A graphical representation of a simple LISCOMP model as a path diagram is shown in figure 1, where unobservable error components are omitted.

The basis of statistical inference for LISCOMP models is a random sample $\{y_n, x_n\}_{n=1,...,N}$ where N is the sample size. y_n is a p-dimensional vector of endogenous variables with components which may be either metric, censored or ordered categorical. The analysis of y_n is performed conditionally on a q-dimensional vector x_n with components which are either metric or dummy-coded. Each component $y_{ni}, i = 1, \ldots, p$ of y_n is connected with an unobservable random variable y_{ni}^* by a threshold relation described below. The latent endogenous vector y_n^* is conditioned on x_n by the distributional assumption

Figure 1: Muthén's LISCOMP-Model

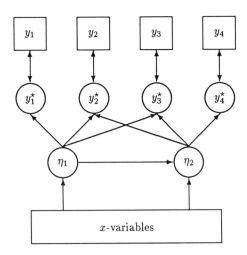

$$y_n^\star | x_n \sim \mathcal{N}_p(\mu(\vartheta) + \Pi(\vartheta) \cdot x_n, \Sigma(\vartheta)) \ .$$

Here $\mu(\vartheta) + \Pi(\vartheta) \cdot x$ is the mean structure and $\Sigma(\vartheta)$ is the covariance structure. Hence, only the mean structure, but not the covariance structure depends on exogeneous variables x. $\mathcal{N}_p$ denotes a p-variate normal distribution. Both moments are generated by a mixture of a factor analytic measurement model with a simultaneous equation model described below. Both models are parametrized by a structural parameter vector ϑ. To simplify the description we will omit the treatment of the multiple group option.

2.1 The threshold relations

Depending on the measurement level each component y_{ni} is connected with $y_{ni}^\star$ by one of the following measurement relations. For convenience of notation the case index $n = 1, \ldots, N$ is omitted.

- y_i metric (identity relation).

  $$y_i = y_i^\star$$

- y_i is ordered categorical with unknown thresholds $\tau_{i,1} < \tau_{i,2} < \ldots < \tau_{i,K_i}$ and categories $y_i = 0, \ldots, K_i$ (ordinal Probit relation, McKelvey and Zavoina 1975).

  $$y_i = k \iff y_i^\star \in [\tau_{i,k}, \tau_{i,k+1}) \quad \text{with} \quad [\tau_{i,0}, \tau_{i,1}) = (-\infty, \tau_{i,1}) \quad \text{and} \quad \tau_{i,K_i} = +\infty.$$

Classified metric variables may be treated in analogy to the ordinal probit relation with the difference that the class limits are used as known thresholds (Stewart 1983).

- y_i is one-sided censored with an a priori known threshold value $\tau_{i,1}$ (Tobit relation, Tobin 1958).

$$y_i = \left\{ \begin{array}{ll} y_i^* & \text{if } y_i^* > \tau_{i,1} \\ \tau_{i,1} & \text{if } y_i^* \leq \tau_{i,1} \end{array} \right\}$$

- y_i is double-sided censored with a priori known threshold values $\tau_{i,1} < \tau_{i,2}$ (Two-Limit-Probit relation, Rosett and Nelson 1975).

$$y_i = \left\{ \begin{array}{ll} \tau_{i,1} & \text{if } y_i^* \leq \tau_{i,1} \\ y_i^* & \text{if } \tau_{i,1} < y_i^* < \tau_{i,2} \\ \tau_{i,2} & \text{if } \tau_{i,2} \leq y_i^* \end{array} \right\}$$

For the case of dichotomous y_i the probit relation may be interpreted as a special case of the random utility maximization principle with two unordered categories $K_i + 1 = 2$ (Nelson 1976, Daganzo 1979).

2.2 The mean and covariance structure

The second component of the LISCOMP model is the parametrization of the expectation $E(y_n^*|x_n, \vartheta)$ and the covariance-matrix $V(y_n^*|x_n, \vartheta)$ in the structural parameter vector ϑ. Analogously to the LISREL model the LISCOMP model is based on a combination of a factor analytic model with a structural equation system:

- *The measurement model*: The latent variable vector y^* is combined with the latent variable vector $\eta \sim m \times 1$ by a classical factor analytic model (Muthén & Christofferson 1981):

$$y^* = \nu + \Lambda\eta + \epsilon$$

$\nu \sim p \times 1$ denotes the general mean of y^* while $\epsilon \sim p \times 1$ denotes the vector of the specific factors with expectation 0 and covariance Θ. The regression structure $\Lambda\eta$ is used to describe the variability of the dependent endogenous variable by a lower number of common factors η_ℓ, which are collected in the vector $\eta = (\eta_1, \ldots, \eta_m)^T$. As in regression analysis it is assumed that the general and specific vectors are independent.

- *Structural equation system*: As in econometrics the stochastic behavior of the vector of common factors η given the exogenous variables x_n is described by the following simultaneous equation system:

$$\eta = \alpha + B\eta + \Gamma x + \zeta$$

The coefficients of the matrix $B \sim m \times m$ describe simultaneous dependencies between the components of η. The diagonal elements of B are set to 0. The components of the common factor vector η depend on exogenous variables x_n through the coefficients in $\Gamma \sim m \times q$. ζ is a case specific error term with expectation 0 and covariance Ψ which is independent of x. Furthermore it is assumed that the matrix $I - B$ is regular.

The combination of the measurement model with the simultaneous equation systems yields the moment structure of $y^\star$ given x:

$$E(y^\star|x,\vartheta) = \nu + \Lambda(I-B)^{-1}\alpha + \Lambda(I-B)^{-1}\Gamma x \equiv \mu(\vartheta) + \Pi(\vartheta)x$$

and

$$V(y^\star|x,\vartheta) = \Lambda(I-B)^{-1}\Psi((I-B)^T)^{-1}\Lambda^T + \Theta \equiv \Sigma(\vartheta).$$

2.3 Identifiability and Estimation

For the identifiability of the structural parameters contained in $\{\tau,\nu,\alpha,\Lambda,B,\Gamma,\Psi,\Theta\}$ certain restrictions like normalization and the exclusion of variables must be imposed. Unfortunately rigorous mathematical identification conditions like the rank and the order conditions are not applicable to the LISCOMP model (see also Dupačová and Wold 1982). Hence researchers are restricted to apply rank checks which reveal at most the state of local identifiability (McDonald and Krane 1977). Due to the general parametrization structure LISCOMP includes many common latent variable models like dichotomous factor analysis (Muthén 1978), variance component models (Wiley, Schmidt & Bramble 1973) and the metric LISREL model (Jöreskog & Sörbom 1988a). Hence especially *all* submodels included in LISREL may also be specified in LISCOMP. In opposite to this generalization further extensions of the LISREL model like hierarchical mean and covariance structure models (Küsters 1987) with more than two levels of latent variables (for example McDonald's (1978, 1980) COSAN model) cannot be estimated by LISCOMP. The direct application of the maximum likelihood method is only feasible for cases with two non-metric indicators. This is due to the fact that each non-metric endogenous indicator introduces an additional integral into the loglikelihood function. Hence each likelihood element contains a p-dimensional normal integral for a LISCOMP model with p ordinal indicators. Accurate and efficent numerical methods for the evaluation of multiple normal integrals are not available. To circumvent this problem LISCOMP utilizes a sequential estimation strategy which may be summarized by the following steps:

1. In the first stage all thresholds τ_i, means μ_i, slopes Π_i and variances Σ_{ii} of the reduced form for each indicator y_i ($i = 1,\ldots,p$) are estimated by regression methods like least squares, Tobit ML and Probit ML depending on the measurement level of the endogenous variable y_i.

2. In the second stage the bivariate likelihood functions of all pairs $(y_i, y_j); i \neq j; i,j = 1,\ldots,p$ are maximized conditional on the results of the first stage with respect to the correlation coefficents $\rho_{ij} = \Sigma_{ij}/\sqrt{\Sigma_{ii}\Sigma_{jj}}$.

3. In the third stage the free structural parameters $\{\tau,\nu,\alpha,\Lambda,B,\Gamma,\Psi,\Theta\}$ summarized in the structural parameter vector ϑ are estimated indirectly by the application of an iterative nonlinear generalized least squares principle to the estimated reduced form coefficients $\hat{\tau},\hat{\mu},\hat{\Pi}$ and $\hat{\Sigma}$ which are obtained as the result of the first two stages.

For general models with more than two endogeneous variables two options for the estimation of the third stage are available in LISCOMP. The first option denoted as weighted least squares allows the incorporation of the asymptotic covariance matrix of the reduced form coefficients to obtain (1) asymptotic efficiency within the class of indirect least squares estimates and (2) the evaluation of standard errors of the structural parameter estimate $\hat{\vartheta}$. This option requires a large amount of memory. A simpler option is the application of the unweighted least squares procedure which has the disadvantage of inefficiency and the impossibility of computing correct standard errors. For models with two endogenous variables the full information maximum likelihood option may be used.

3 Evaluation of the Program System LISCOMP

The most important feature of the LISCOMP system is the fact that it is the only commercially available software system to estimate LISREL type models with ordinal, censored and metric indicators which are conditioned on exogenous variables. The only competitor for the estimation of LISREL type models with non-metric indicators is the system LISREL 7 (Jöreskog & Sörbom1988a) system in conjunction with its preproccessor PRELIS (Jöreskog & Sörbom1988b). Nevertheless the use of the combination of LISREL and PRELIS suffers on the lack of conditioning on exogenous variables. Additionally, it is impossible to compute the correct standard errors. Hence all problems with LISCOMP mentioned in the following evaluation of the PC-version 1.1 should be considered under this background.

LISCOMP's command language is very similar to the directive structure of the LISREL 7 system. Model, data and estimation directives are described by parameters which must be saved in a file. Hence its use is restricted to batch jobs only. Due to the complicated structure of the general LISCOMP model a large number of parameters must be specified which is not always easy to perform. These problems are sometimes caused by the insufficient documentation which suffers from two deficiencies: Firstly, only simple examples are covered in the example section. Secondly and more seriously, the manual does not give sufficient guidance to a suitable parametrization which again is due to the problem that rigorous identification rules for the exclusion and normalization of variables are not available. Additionally, some parameters are always set either to 0 or 1 by default but these defaults are not precisely described.

The numerical procedures are insufficiently described in the manual, but several references to Muthén's papers are given which clarify the general strategy of estimation without details. Hence, it is quite difficult to evaluate the precision and accuracy of the estimates obtained. Nevertheless, the program prints out a warning if no convergence is achieved. Lack of identifiability is usually indicated by a warning that a certain matrix which is not specified further does not possess full rank. Presumably, the algorithm is based on a rank check performed on an approximation of the asymptotic covariance matrix of the structural parameters. Control parameters for the number of iterations and the stopping criteria cannot be specified within a LISCOMP program.

A sophisticated starting value procedure comparable to the instrumental variable estimation method of LISREL 7 is not available in LISCOMP. Hence LISCOMP uses some naive starting values for the parameters which are either set to 0 or 1 depending on the – partially undocumented – default. Nevertheless, these defaults do not usually guarantee convergence of the iteration process. Hence, user provided starting values should be set for the individual structural parameters. LISCOMP users are well advised to try several different starting values to observe the convergence properties of the algorithm because there is no guarantee that the algorithm converges to the true minima within the third stage. Nevertheless within our limited experience we observed no case of multiple local minima but quite often the case that the algorithm did not converge if the starting values were of opposite sign.

The most serious problem which occurs by the application of the PC-version is due to the memory restrictions of MS-DOS. LISCOMP requires a lot of memory especially if the weight matrix option is employed. Hence only models with a small number of cases and a small number of parameters can be sucessfully estimated by the PC-version. Simple examples like a two-factor model with 800 cases, 6 endogenous indicators, 2 factors and 6 exogenous variables can only estimated with the unweighted least squares estimation option excluding the computation of standard errors. The size problem is caused by two factors: First, in general not only the parameters of the covariance but also of the mean structure including thresholds must be estimated. Second, the weight matrix consists of the estimated variance-covariance matrix of the means as well as the covariances so that the number of elements in the weight matrix becomes a quartic function of the number of variables used. To estimate large models one of the available mainframe versions of LISCOMP must be used.

Before proceeding to a simple example it should be emphasized that the combined use of LISREL and PRELIS is by no means restricted to such small models. Nevertheless all users should be aware of the fact that the use of the LISREL/PRELIS combination is an unsuitable substitute for the estimation of LISCOMP models if non-metric indicators occur. Beyond the ommission of the conditioning on exogenous x variables the LISREL/PRELIS conjunction is uncapable to take restrictions within the thresholds into account.

4 Example

As an example we demonstrate the use of LISCOMP to the analysis of a simple multiple indicator – multiple cause model applied to a subset of variables surveyed by the *Allgemeine Bevölkerungsumfrage der Sozialwissenschaften 1984* jointly organized by the *Zentrum für Umfragen, Methoden und Analysen (ZUMA), Mannheim* and the *Zentralarchiv für Empirische Sozialforschung, Köln*. The objective of the following model is the analysis of the attitudes of Germans to *guest workers* measured by several ordinal indicators in dependence on exogenous variables. After eliminating missing cases, a random sample of 496 cases was drawn from the whole sample (consisting of 3004 cases) to circumvent the memory problems mentioned above. To measure the latent attitude toward foreign workers (ATTAGF) indirectly by a factor analytical model the following four items were measured by a Likert-scale ranging from *(0) I strongly object against* to *(6) I strongly coincide*.

- Variable ADAPTION: *Foreign workers should adjust their lifestyle to the lifestyles of Germans.*

- Variable REMIG: *Foreign workers should remigrate if job vacancies become scarce.*

- Variable NOPOL: *Foreign workers should not be allowed to become politically active.*

- Variable COMPAT: *Foreign workers should confine their marriages to compatriotes.*

The explanatory variables are summarized in the following list:

- The variable CONTACT is $\{0,1\}$ coded and describes the private contacts of the German interviewee to foreign workers (0 = contact absent).

- The variable DEGREE is ordered categorical and describes the educational degree of the interviewee. The categories range from *(0) kein Abschluß* (without examination) to *(4) Abitur* (final examination qualifying for university entrance).

- The variable POLINT is a Likert scale to measure political interest. The categories range from *(0) no interest* to *(5) strong interest*.

- The variable GRUENE measures the attitudes toward the *ecology* party *Die Grünen* by a Likert-scale with 11 categories ranging from (0) to (10). Low scores describe strong negative attitudes against the *Grüne*.

To circumvent the problem of building design matrices for the exogeneous variables we handled the variables DEGREE, POLINT and GRUENE like metrically scaled items. To analyze the attitudes of Germans to foreign workers we parametrized the following LISCOMP model, where all redundant parameters are omitted.

Indicators y and exogenous variables x:

$$ y = \begin{pmatrix} \text{ADAPTION} \\ \text{REMIG} \\ \text{NOPOL} \\ \text{COMPAT} \end{pmatrix}, \quad x = \begin{pmatrix} \text{CONTACT} \\ \text{DEGREE} \\ \text{POLINT} \\ \text{GRUENE} \end{pmatrix}. $$

Threshold relations:

$$ y_i = k \iff y_i^* \in [\tau_{i,k}, \tau_{i,k+1}), \quad i = 1, \ldots, 4, \; k = 0, \ldots, 6 \;. $$

Factor analytical model:

$$ \begin{pmatrix} y_1^* \\ y_2^* \\ y_3^* \\ y_4^* \end{pmatrix} = y^* = \Lambda \eta + \epsilon = \begin{pmatrix} 1 \\ \Lambda_{21} \\ \Lambda_{31} \\ \Lambda_{41} \end{pmatrix} \cdot (\text{ATTAGF}) + \begin{pmatrix} \epsilon_1 \\ \epsilon_2 \\ \epsilon_3 \\ \epsilon_4 \end{pmatrix}, $$

with

$$ V(\epsilon) = \Theta = \begin{pmatrix} \Theta_{11} & 0 & 0 & 0 \\ 0 & \Theta_{22} & 0 & 0 \\ 0 & 0 & \Theta_{33} & 0 \\ 0 & 0 & 0 & \Theta_{44} \end{pmatrix}. $$

The regression model as a special case of the simultaneous equation system:

$$ \eta = \Gamma x + \zeta = \begin{pmatrix} \Gamma_{11} & \Gamma_{12} & \Gamma_{13} & \Gamma_{14} \end{pmatrix} \cdot \begin{pmatrix} \text{CONTACT} \\ \text{DEGREE} \\ \text{POLINT} \\ \text{GRUENE} \end{pmatrix} + (\zeta_{11}) \quad \text{with} \quad V(\zeta) = \Psi. $$

The reduced form of the whole model is given by:

$$y^* = \Lambda(\Gamma x + \zeta) + \epsilon \ .$$

Please note that the covariance among ordered categorical indicators is not estimable. This yields the implicit restriction that the diagonal element of $V(y^*|x,\vartheta)$ must be normalized to 1. Hence, the variance parameters Θ_{ii} are not estimable and are given as residuals.

The following program was used to estimate the described LISCOMP model by the LISCOMP system:

```
TI DATA SET: SOFT2.ASC
TI -------------------
DA IY=4 IX=4 NO=496 VT=OT
TE 6 6 6 6
LA    'ADAPTION'  'REMIG'    'NOPOL'     'COMPAT'
      'CONTACT'   'DEGREE'   'POLINT'    'GRUENE'
MO MO=SE P1 P2 P3 NE=1 TA=FR LY=FI GA=FR PS=FR
LL 'ATTAGF'
FR LY(2,1) LY(3,1) LY(4,1)
VA 1.0 LY(1,1) LY(2,1) LY(3,1) LY(4,1)
VA 0.1 PS(1,1)
OU WF TO AL
RA FO UN='SOFT2.ASC'
(4F6.1,18X,2F6.1,6X,F6.1,F6.1,12X,F6.1)
```

The TI directive is used to attach a comment which is printed several times within the output file. The directive DA IY=4 IX=4 NO=496 VT=OT describes the number of indicators (IY=4), the number of exogenous variables (IX=4) and the number of individual cases (NO=496). The statement (VT=OT) specifies a non-metric model with indicators which are neither metrically nor dichotomously scaled. The directive RA FO UN='SOFT2.ASC' specifies that all data are read in their raw form from the file SOFT2.ASC which contains the data in a FORTRAN format specified in the subsequent format-directive (4F6.1,18X,2F6.1,6X,F6.1,F6.1,12X,F6.1). The variable labels are described by the LA directive, while the label of the latent variable η is set by the LL 'ATTAGF' statement. The model-directive MO MO=SE P1 P2 P3 NE=1 TA=FR LY=FI GA=FR PS=FR is used to specify the general model structure in terms of parameters and latent variables. MO=SE P1 P2 P3 specifies that a general structural equation model (MO=SE) with thresholds and means (P1=part 1), slopes (P2=part 2) and covariances (P3=part 3) will be estimated. The statement NE=1 specifies a model with *one* latent variable η, which means that the parameter vector η contains only one component. The parameters τ, Γ and Ψ are set to be free by the statement (TA=FR GA=FR PS=FR) while the parameter Λ is fixed (LY=FI). These settings may be subsequently overwritten by special statements like FR LY(2,1) LY(3,1) LY(4,1) where the elements $\Lambda_{21}, \Lambda_{31}$ and Λ_{41} are freed. The VA directive is used to specify either fixed settings for fixed parameter or starting values for free structural parameters. Hence the directive VA 1.0 LY(1,1) LY(2,1) LY(3,1) LY(4,1) forces the parameter LY(1,1) to be fixed to 1 while the remaining parameters are set to 1 only as starting values. Estimation options etc. are specified within the output-statement OU WF TO AL. The flag WF forces LISCOMP to estimate with the nonlinear iterative *weigthed* least squares algorithm. The flag TO forces an output format with output-width of 80 columns. The flag AL yields the output of *all* results.

Noteworthy is the fact that there are many other directives and flags to specify different models, other input data types like frequencies, correlation and covariance matrices, the specification of simulation runs etc. The output precision can also be set either to 3 or 6 decimal places.

The running of the above program takes approximately 20 minutes on an Olivetti M24 (equipped with 8086/8087 processors and 8 MHz) yielding the following estimates and standard errors. We report only the slightly reorganized results for the structural parameters to save space.

```
              LAMBDA                              PSI
              ATTAGF                              ATTAGF
              --------                            --------
ADAPTION      1.000              ATTAGF           .162
REMIG         1.588
NOPOL         1.663
COMPAT        1.674

              GAMMA
              CONTACT      DEGREE       POLINT        GRUENE
              --------     --------     --------      --------
ATTAGF        -.187        -.154        -.068         -.052

                    STANDARD ERRORS FOR GROUP      1

              LAMBDA                              PSI
              ATTAGF                              ATTAGF
              --------                            --------
ADAPTION      .000               ATTAGF           .031
REMIG         .164
NOPOL         .164
COMPAT        .170

              GAMMA
              CONTACT      DEGREE       POLINT        GRUENE
              --------     --------     --------      --------
ATTAGF        .058         .026         .025          .008
```

The interpretation of these results – which are all significant at the 5% level – is clearcut. Frequent contacts with foreign workers, a high educational degree, strong political interest and a strong favour of the *Grüne* lowers the opposition to foreign workers, which is measured indirectly by a group of four indicators. The factor loadings in Λ indicate that the items REMIG, NOPOL and COMPAT are better indicators for ATTAGF than ADAPTION.

5 Concluding Remarks

The handling of LISCOMP is not easy in comparison to the LISREL system due to the model structure which is much more sophisticated than metric latent variable models. Sociologists, economists, psychologists and biometricians are often involved in the analysis of LISREL type models, in which the dependent variables are non-metric. Because LISCOMP is the only system which enables researcher to do such analysis no computing alternatives remain. Programming of such systems is hard work. Hence, we hope that Bengt Muthén will enlarge the capabilities of LISCOMP by introducing sophisticated start-value routines, more control of the numerical estimation routines and more support to detect underidentified models. Also the documentation should be largely rewritten to enable researcher which are not familiar with the underlying statistics to use the system in a proper way.

References:

Dupačová, J. and Wold, H. (1982). On some identification problems in ML modeling of systems with indirect observation. In: Jöreskog, K.G. and Wold, H. (Ed.). *Systems under Indirect Observation — Causality ⋆ Structure ⋆ Prediction — Part II.* Amsterdam, 293–315.

Jöreskog, K.G. and Sörbom, D. (1988a). *LISREL 7 — A Guide to the Program and Applications.* SPSS Inc., Chicago.

Jöreskog, K.G. and Sörbom, D. (1988b). *PRELIS — A Program for Multivariate Data Screening and Data Summarization.* Scientific Software, Inc. Mooresville, Indiana.

Küsters, U. (1987). *Hierarchische Mittelwert- und Kovarianzstrukturmodelle mit nichtmetrischen endogenen Variablen.* Heidelberg.

McDonald, R.P. (1978). A simple comprehensive model for the analysis of covariance structures. *British Journal of Mathematical and Statistical Psychology 31*, 59–72.

McDonald, R.P. (1980). A simple comprehensive model for the analysis of covariance structures: Some remarks on applications. *British Journal of Mathematical and Statistical Psychology 33*, 161–183.

McKelvey, R.D. and Zavoina, W. (1975). A statistical model for the analysis of ordinal level dependent variables. *Journal of Mathematical Sociology 4*, 103–120.

Muthén, B. (1978). Contributions to factor analysis of dichotomous variables. *Psychometrika 43*, 551–560.

Muthén, B. (1984). A general structural equation model with dichotomous, ordered categorical, and continuous latent variable indicators. *Psychometrika 49*, 115–132.

Muthén, B. (1987). *LISCOMP — Analysis of Linear Equations Using a Comprehensive Measurement Model.* Scientific Software, Inc., Mooresville.

Muthén, B. and Christoffersson, A. (1981). Simultaneous factor analysis of dichotomous variables in several groups. *Psychometrika 46*, 407–419.

Olsson, U. (1979b). Maximum likelihood estimation of the polychoric correlation coefficient. *Psychometrika 44*, 443–460.

Olsson, U., Drasgow, F. and Dorans, N.J. (1982). The polyserial correlation coefficient. *Psychometrika 47*, 337–347.

Rosett, R.N. and Nelson, F.D. (1975). Estimation of the two-limit probit regression model. *Econometrica 43*, 141–146.

Stewart, M.B. (1983). On the least squares estimation when the dependent variable is grouped. *Review of Economic Studies L*, 737–753.

Tobin, J. (1958). Estimation of relationships for limited dependent variables. *Econometrica 26*, 24–36.

Wiley, D.E., Schmidt, W.H. and Bramble, W.J. (1973). Studies of a class of covariance structure models. *Journal of the American Statistical Association 68*, 317–323.

SURVO 84C
General Environment for Statistical Computing

S. Mustonen

Abstract: SURVO 84C is an integrated system for statistical analysis, computing, data base management, graphics, desktop publishing, teaching, etc. Through its unique *editorial interface*, SURVO 84C forms a general environment for many kinds of applications.

Using of SURVO 84C is like working with a powerful text editor with extended capabilities in the above-mentioned areas. In statistical applications, the SURVO 84C Editor is used to control all the stages of the work from data input, screening and editing to data analysis, graphics and report writing. As the last link, the system includes a complete PostScript support. For example, all the SURVO 84C documents are made on the system itself.

1. Introduction

SURVO 84C is a system written for IBM compatible PC's using the C language. Its current version (2.21) includes over 300 system files (programs and other system files) taking over 8 megabytes on the hard disk. As a whole, SURVO 84C forms an integrated system where the programs are loaded to the CPU according to the user's actions automatically. The user has no need to know about the technical details. He/she sees the system as a unified working environment.

All the actions in SURVO 84C are based on text editing. The user types text and commands into an *edit field* which is an area in the memory and always partially visible on the screen. The text editor links the various parts of the system by calling program modules according to the user's activations. All the operations and commands are written in the edit field as well and the user activates them by the ESC key. Likewise, the results are written into the edit field to places indicated by the user. Larger results are automatically saved in matrix and text files. Any result or text file can be loaded to the edit field and used as an input for new operations.

SURVO 84C supports various representations of statistical data sets and bases. Small data sets can be written in the edit field as lists or tables. Larger data sets are saved in data files. Maximum number of variables in one data file can be several thousands and there are no limits for the number of observations except the general restrictions of the operating system for the file size.

A large set of operations is provided for general data management, data input, editing, screening, etc. The variables can be transformed by (conditional) rules defined by the user.

In statistical operations, the variables can be selected in different ways. Also the scale types of the variables can be indicated in data files and the statistical operations will observe whether the scales of selected variables are valid in current analysis. Similarly, observations can be processed conditionally. All the computations are performed in double precision and the intermediate results are saved in matrix files for subsequent studies. A general matrix interpreter and various techniques (*touch mode* and *editorial computing*) related to spreadsheet computing are readily available for subtler analysis of the results.

In many ways, SURVO 84C exceeds the limits of typical statistical packages. One of the main goals is to give the user an opportunity to do most of the things belonging to a statistician's working process with the same tool.

In fact, two different larger models for working with the system can be seen. In the first one, the user creates a series of work schemes (setups in the edit field) to accomplish a typical chain of statistical analyses including graphics, simulation, etc. In the second model, the main target is to produce a multipage printed report with text, tables, and graphical illustrations on the basis of the current data more or less automatically. In more demanding expert applications, usually created as *sucros*, both working models are present.

A sucro is a canned SURVO 84C session with conditional operations and prompts for the user. It is originally constructed by using SURVO 84C under the *tutorial mode* which enables saving of all the user interventions in a selected file. The file can be edited later. This technique permits making of large expert applications based on the existing operations. It also gives good possibilities for using SURVO 84C in teaching of statistics. For example, a set sucros has been developed for the Finnish Science Centre to tell about the principles of statistics.

Since SURVO 84C is a large system, all of its features cannot be covered in a short paper. In the sequel, we shall present a few typical work schemes related to statistical computing and graphics. More detailed documents of the system are mentioned in the list of references.

2. Examples

Influence curves for the correlation coefficient

The following work scheme is intended for plotting a scatter diagram with appropriate contour curves describing the robustness of the correlation coefficient. Actually these influence curves will appear as contours of a raster image of the influence function.

The final graph is produced by a series of 4 different SURVO 84C operations (CORR, PLOT scatter diagram, PLOT contours, and PRINT) given in the next display which is an excerpt from the edit field.

```
12   1 SURVO 84C EDITOR Sun Apr 23 15:28:44 1989         D:\ZUMA\ 100 100 0
 1 *SAVE INF
 2 *
 3 *CORR DECA,4 / VARS=Height,Weight
 4 *Means, std.devs and correlations of DECA  N=48
 5 *Variable  Mean       Std.dev.
 6 *Height    186.9583   5.090493
 7 *Weight     85.56250  6.847600
 8 *Correlations:
 9 *           Height  Weight
10 * Height    1.0000  0.8522
11 * Weight    0.8522  1.0000
12 *..............................................................
13 *r=0.85 mx=186.96 my=85.56 sx=5.09 sy=6.85 n=48
14 *HEADER=Influence_curves_for_correlation_coefficient
15 *PLOT z(x,y)=abs(r*(1-z)+u*v)/w
16 *    u=sqrt(n/(n*n-1))*(x-mx)/sx
17 *    v=sqrt(n/(n*n-1))*(y-my)/sy
18 *    w=sqrt((1+u*u)*(1+v*v))
19 *TYPE=CONTOUR   ZSCALING=20,0       (1/0.05=20)
20 *               SCREEN=NEG
21 *XSCALE=150(10)220 YSCALE=40(10)130 SIZE=1640,1640
22 *x=150,220,0.1    y=40,130,0.1
23 *DEVICE=PS,INF.PS
24 *..............................................................
25 *PLOT DECA,Height,Weight
26 *XSCALE=150(10)220 YSCALE=40(10)130 SIZE=1640,1640
27 *HEADER=
28 *DEVICE=PS,DECA.PS
29 *..............................................................
30 *PRINT 31,35
31 - [Swiss(15)]
32 *SURVO 84C Graphics
33 & 26
34 - picture INF.PS,*,*
35 - picture DECA.PS,*,*
36 *
```

The lines above given with a black background are commands activated. They are highlighted here just for illustration. The SAVE command on the first edit line is used for saving the edit field with its current contents to a file INF. The CORR DECA,4 command computes the means, standard deviations, and correlations of the active variables of a data set DECA and prints the results from the line 4 onwards. Thus, in this case, lines 4-11 are output from the CORR operation. The set of active variables has been limited to Height and Weight by the extra specification VARS= Height,Weight (typed by the user on line 3 as a comment). In fact, extra specifications can appear on any neighbouring lines and the SURVO 84C operations when activated are using them. If a specification is missing, appropriate default values are used instead.

The user has copied the basic statistics obtained by CORR in an abbreviated form to line 13. The PLOT scheme needed for making a contour plot of the influence surface is located on lines 13-23. The actual PLOT command on line 15 plots a function z(x,y) of two variables x,y as a contour plot (specified by TYPE=CONTOUR on line 19). The expression defining z(x,y) depends on the current value of the correlation coefficient r and on three auxiliary functions u,v, and w which in turn depend on parameters n,mx,nx,sx, and sy. These functions are defined as specifications on lines 16-18.

Our function z(x,y) gives the change in the value of correlation coefficient r when a new observation x,y is obtained.

When making the raster image, the values of the function z are mapped continuously to various shades of gray in such a way that 0 corresponds to 'black' and 1 corresponds to 'white'.

If the function value exceeds 1, the shading is selected 'modulo 1'. In this case, the original function values are multiplied by 20 (by ZSCALING=20,0) which gives a complete cycle of shadings when the function value changes by $1/20 = 0.05$. Thus, the final graph will depict contours of r with increments of 0.05 . The SCREEN= NEG specification (on line 20) simply reverses the shadings.

Some plotting parameters, regulating ranges of variables and size of the graph are given on lines 21-22.

DEVICE=PS,INF.PS (on line 23) implies the graph to be produced as a PostScript picture and saved in file INF.PS .

The simpler PLOT scheme on lines 25-29 makes a scatter plot of variables Height and Weight in the data set DECA using the same plotting specifications and saves the picture as a PostScript file DECA.PS .

Finally, the PRINT operation processes the lines 31-35 and produces the following output:

SURVO 84C Graphics

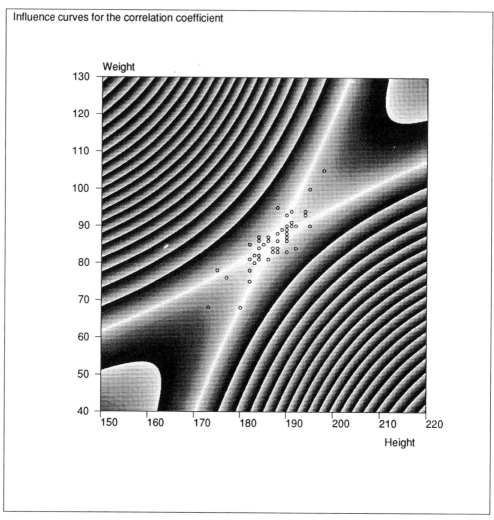

Influence curves for the correlation coefficient

From the graph we can see that, for example, a new observation x=190, y=40 would decrease the original r from 0.85 by 6 × 0.05 to 0.55 .

It should be noted that the setup above, although written for a particular case, gives a general basis for plotting of corresponding contour plots for any other data set as well. By loading the INF edit field, the user can modify the schemes and reactivate them. By supplying explanations within the schemes, the setup could easily be made accessible for users neither very familiar with the system nor with technical details.

Cluster analysis

Our second example demonstrates the behaviour of a certain clustering technique in a simulated heterogeneous data set of two bivariate normal samples. The setup is following:

```
13   1 SURVO 84C EDITOR Sun Apr 23 19:50:45 1989          D:\ZUMA\ 100 100 0
  1 *SAVE CLUSTER
  2 *   Two samples from bivariate normal distribution
  3 *   with different means
  4 *   but same covariance matrix are generated:
  5 *..................................................................
  6 *FILE CREATE N2,32,10,64,7,100
  7 *FIELDS:
  8 *1 N 4 X
  9 *2 N 4 Y
 10 *END
 11 *
 12 *VAR X,Y TO N2
 13 *X=if(ORDER<51)then(X1)else(X2)
 14 *Y=if(ORDER<51)then(Y1)else(Y2)
 15 *X1=Z1      Y1=r*Z1+s*Z2       r=0.8 s=sqrt(1-r*r)
 16 *X2=Z1+2    Y2=r*Z1+s*Z2-2
 17 *Z1=probit(rnd(2))  Z2=probit(rnd(2))
 18 *..................................................................
 19 *VAR G1:1,G2:1,G3:1 TO N2
 20 *   G1=0 G2=0 G3=0
 21 *..................................................................
 22 *   The CLUSTER operation with 10 trials, 2 groups,
 23 *   and random number generator 2
 24 *   gives two different solutions:
 25 *
 26 *MASK=AAGGG    TRIALS=10  GROUPS=2 SEED=2
 27 *CLUSTER N2,28
 28 *Stepwise cluster analysis by Wilk's Lambda criterion
 29 *Data N2   N=100
 30 *Variables: X, Y
 31 *Best clusterings found in 10 trials are saved as follows:
 32 * Lambda       freq   Grouping var
 33 * 0.04496       6     G1
 34 * 0.14945       4     G2
 35 *
 36 *..................................................................
 37 *The result can be checked by plotting the graph:
 38 *GPLOT N2,X,Y
 39 *HEADER=Samples_from_bivariate_normal_distributions
 40 *POINT=G1  (G2 gives the inferior clustering)
 41 *
```

In this experiment, a file N2 of 100 observations is created by FILE CREATE (on lines 6-10) and two samples from a bivariate normal distribution with different means are generated by a VAR operation (on lines 12-17).

Three more variables (G1,G2,G3) are created by another VAR on lines 19-20 to store three different groupings. These variables are initiated by 0's.

The cluster analysis is performed by the CLUSTER operation on lines 26-27 and giving the results on lines 28-34. The variables are selected and their tasks in the analysis are declared by the MASK=AAGGG specification (on line 26). It is an abbreviated form of the VARS specification and determines the roles of variables in the order they appear in the data set. Here 'A' means a variable to be analyzed and 'G' a variable to be used for storing of a clustering.

The analysis is based on the Wilk's lambda criterion and an efficient stepwise procedure developed by Korhonen (1979) is applied. In this procedure, first a random partition of observations into 2 groups (GROUPS=2 on line 26) is selected. Thereafter the procedure tries to move observations from a group to another and if the criterion value is improved, the observation is really moved. This practice will be continued until no single move improves the criterion value.

Since the result depends on the initial random partition, it is good to repeat the procedure several times. In this case 10 different random starts have been taken (TRIALS=10) and two different solutions (G1,G2) are obtained as seen on lines 33-34.

The first solution G1 having the better criterion value is, of course, the true one. The natures of the solutions are clearly revealed by the plots generated by the PLOT scheme on lines 38-40:

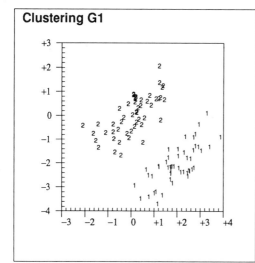
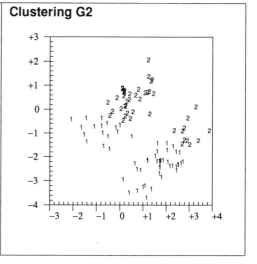

References

P.Korhonen (1979). *A stepwise procedure for multivariate clustering*, Research Reports No.7,
   Computing Centre, University of Helsinki (77 pp.)
S.Mustonen (1987). *SURVO 84C User's Guide*,
   Dept. of Statistics, University of Helsinki (335 pp.)
S.Mustonen (1988). *PostScript Printing in SURVO 84C*, SURVO 84C Contributions 1,
   Dept. of Statistics, University of Helsinki (34 pp.)
S.Mustonen (1988). *Sucros in SURVO 84C*, SURVO 84C Contributions 2,
   Dept. of Statistics, University of Helsinki (28 pp.)
S.Mustonen (1989). *Programming SURVO 84 in C*, SURVO 84C Contributions 3,
   Dept. of Statistics, University of Helsinki (85 pp.)

SURVO 84C functions (in version 2.21):

Text and data management:
   Text typing and editing in the edit field
   General management of text and tables
   Report management and printing
   Desktop publishing on PostScript printers
   Import of text and data as ASCII files
   Export of text, data, results and graphs
      as ASCII and PostScript files, etc.
   Table arithmetics
   Data file management
      Several formats from tiny lists to data bases
      Various tools for data input and editing
   Transformation of variables
      user-defined transformations
      standardized and normalized variables
   Generating data by simulation
   Data sorting and aggregation

Statistical analysis:
   In all forms of analysis
      conditional processing, scale type checking
      results in the edit field, text and matrix files
   Basic statistics
   Means, std.devs and correlations
   Parametric and nonparametric tests
      Fisher's randomization principle in use
   Frequency distributions, histograms and fitting
      univariate distributions (also user-defined)
   Multiway tables of frequencies, means etc.
   Editing of multiway tables
   Log-linear models for frequency data
   Generalized linear models
   Linear and nonlinear regression analysis
   Regression diagnostics
   General nonlinear estimation
   Principal components, canonical correlations,
      discriminant and cluster analysis
   Maximum likelihood and other related solutions
      for factor analysis
   Rotation in factor analysis
      orthogonal and oblique solutions
      interactive graphical and analytical methods
   Semiparametric data smoothing
   Auto- and cross-correlations
   Time series forecasting
   Linear programming
   Special methods as sucros

Graphics:
   Bar and pie charts (several types)
   Histograms
   Correlation diagrams
   Time series, line graphs
   Matrix diagrams
   Scale transformations, probability plots
   Analytical curves, families of curves,
      integral functions
   Contour plots
   Multivariate plotting (Chernoff's faces,
      Andrews' curves, Draftsman's displays, etc.)
   Graphs can be saved in (PostScript) files
      and included in reports in arbitrary size and
      orientation.
   Various forms of graphics can be combined.

Computing:
   Editorial arithmetics
   Arithmetics in touch mode
   Functions related to probability and statistics
   Spreadsheet computing
   Operations with polynomials
   Symbolic derivatives of functions
   General matrix interpreter
      Basic arithmetics with matrices
      Normalizations
      Element by element transformations
      Matrix decompositions (Cholesky, Gram-
         Schmidt, spectral, singular value)
      Linear equations
      Least squares problems
      Partitioned matrices
      Super matrices
      Automatic control for matrix names, column
         and row labels
      Matrix programs

Teaching and user support:
   Extensive on-line help facility
   Tutorial mode
   Ready-made tutorials

F. Faulbaum, R. Haux und K.-H. Jöckel (Hrsg.) (1990). SoftStat '89
Fortschritte der Statistik-Software 2. Stuttgart: Gustav Fischer, 144 - 154

DISTAN for Discrete Statistical Analysis

T. Rudas

SUMMARY

The present paper describes the DISTAN (short for DIscrete STatistical ANalysis) package which has been developed at TARKI (Social Science Informatics Center). The main goal when designing DISTAN was to implement the most important procedures (and develop new ones) for the analysis of categorical (nominal) data. While other packages aimed at both continuous and categorical data are not very parsimonious when storing categorical data, the special file system of DISTAN makes quick reading of large data files possible. The package is completely menu driven and previously filled in menus are available for easy repetition or modification of earlier analyses. Beyond import, export and extensive table transforming and printing modules for the following analyses are available at present: Maximum likelihood estimation of mixed linear and multiplicative models; Fitting compound models by weighted least squares; Boolean factor analysis; Multiple correspondence analysis; Decomposition of mixtures; Cluster analysis for binary data by multivariate embedding; Exploratory methods (in preparation) for both the regression and reduction of dimensionality problems. This research was supported by grant OKKFT TS 3.4.

1. DISTAN: AN OVERVIEW

This introductory section summarizes the main features and philosophy of DISTAN. Later sections will consider these in more detail. The present paper is a short guide to the package, statistical or computational problems will not be considered here: the main aim is to describe what can be done with DISTAN disregarding how it is done. A detailed handbook of DISTAN will be published in the near future. A research report (Rudas 1989b) describing DISTAN can be obtained from the author.

DISTAN differs from most available packages in that it can store, handle and analyse only categorical data. Therefore it does not offer most of the well known multivariate statistical techniques, for these are not suitable to analyse cross classifications. Rather, methods were collected (a few developed) which are suitable for discrete variables. The reason for developing such a package was that, in our experience, generally used multivariate statistical packages do not give as much emphasis to categorical data as these deserve in social, behavioural and a few other sciences.

This insufficiency is twofold. Firstly data are stored in the packages of common use record by record (even in some system files). This is plausible when one thinks of continuous observations: these can be; and generally are, different for each sample unit. However, with categorical data there can be much fewer types of observations and therefore collecting those with the same pattern may result in saving memory when storing and time when processing such data. The second type of insufficiency is more important: the packages that were available to us offered only a few methods for the analysis of categorical data. Moreover changing from one package to the other, for a different type of analysis, required too much effort.

The idea of DISTAN was born in 1985. Having found appropriate financial funding actual work started in early 1986. The Social Science Informatics Center has been housing the project and the moral support received is grafefully acknowledged. Many people have contributed to the Distan project in various ways, all of them on a part time basis.

The main concepts the user has to be fimiliar with when using DISTAN are: the menu program, agenda files, the main program, DISTAN files, utilities, statistical modules, help. These will be described in some detail later on.

The DISTAN package is written in Pascal for IBM PC XT/AT and compatible computers and can be obtained free of charge. A version for IBM mainframe is under development.

2. GENERAL FEATURES

2.1 The menu program and the agenda files

A novel feature of DISTAN is the way in which the utilities of DISTAN and the statistical modules are parametrized. There is an overlay structure and the user can define analyses which activate many modules one after the other. This needs the application of many modules in DISTAN.

Whatever the user wants to do is a defined in a so called agenda file. (There can be many of them in a DISTAN environment under different names.) The agenda file refers to the modules to be activated and contains all the necessary parameters for these modules. The user fills in these agenda files by using the menu program. The menu program asks the questions relevant to the chosen modules. For each DISTAN module the parameters (in a broad sense) that are to be defined are contained in a file (the menu file) and the menu program reads this file to know what to ask. The menu program can not only write agenda files but it can also read them. Whenever an agenda file was read by the menu program, it appears as a series of already filled in menu pages and the user can easily modify the previous analyses and rerun them.

In the sense that many analyses can be defined one after the other DISTAN supports batch processing but the menu itself is completely interactive in the sense that previous choices effect later questions and one can move forward and backward in the menu.

2.2 DISTAN files

Data are stored in special system files called DISTAN files. The format of the data is such that each record contains a definition of a cell of a multiway contingency table (i.e. a list of categories of the defining variables) and a frequency showing the number of observations in that cell. Such a file is called DIB and a 'logical' DISTAN file contains another 'physical' file called DIA. A DIA file contains the names of variables and labels for categories forming the table called the DIB file. DIA and DIB are used as extensions for the different file names under which the user stores his/her data files. The separation of the information into two files is plausible for some operations work only with DIA files. There are also operations that do not affect the DIA file but the DIB file only.

For the sake of saving memory space DIB files can only contain integers (e.g. observed frequencies). The user may want to store non integer numbers in his/her files (see above) and in this case DISTAN produces DIC files. The distinction between DIB and DIC files is technical and the user will not run into this directly when using DISTAN.

2.3 The main program

The agenda files (which contain definitions of different analyses) and the DISTAN files (which contain data and their description) are handled by the main program in an interactive way. These can be listed, DIA files can be looked at, the variable names and category labels can be modified etc.

From the main program the user can also activate the menu program (to fill in a new agenda or to modify an existing one) and analyses defined in an agenda file can be started.

When starting to run DISTAN the user gets into the main program and all DISTAN activities can be mastered from here.

DISTAN matrices that are necessary to parametrize some of the modules can also be handled (including modifications) interactively from the main program.

2.4 Help

DISTAN has an online help facility. At any stage of processing the help button (F1) can be pushed to get into the help environment. Depending on what module was working when help was called one gets into the appropriate part of the help. Within that part (referring to a specific module in DISTAN) one can move just like when editing a file.

There are certain key words in the help file and by typing one of them the user can get into an other part of the help.

3. UTILITIES

3.1 Import and Export

DIA and DIB files can be produced within DISTAN using the import module. Import can read raw data files in either fixed (as specified by the user) or free format and can also read contingency tables.

Export can produce raw data files from DISTAN files (containing either integer or real numbers) which can be the outputs of different analyses performed by DISTAN and can be used as input files for other programs.

3.2 Transform

There are five types of transformations available in DISTAN.

MargTab can form a marginal table of a given contingency table. This can be considered as variable selection. CondTab can form a conditional table of a given contingency table. Here the categories of the conditioning variables are fixed and cross classification of the those individuals in these categories by the rest of the variables is considered. This can be considered as a subsample selection.

CollCat can collapse over specified categories of some of the variables.

KeepCat and LeaveCat will both decrease the number of categories by omitting some of them. The only difference is that with KeepCat the user has to specify which categories to keep, and with LeaveCat, which categories to leave out, whichever is more convenient to list.

3.3 Printing contingency tables

The printing module of DISTAN is called ContPrint. There are two options to print multidimensional contingency tables. One is the conventional way when a k dimensional contingency table is represented as a set of two dimensional tables, all being a conditional table of the original one such that conditioning is upon k-2 variables. The user can 'page' back and forth among these two dimensional tables on the display and when these are bigger then what can be shown on the display the user can also move on each of these pages in any of the four directions. This way of printing a contingency table is called TablePrint in DISTAN.

The other way to represent a multidimensional contingency table is a tree structure. Here each cell is defined by a path through the different categories of the variables and at the end of each path there stands the appropriate frequency. The user can move in any directions on the display over this graph. This way of printing a contingency table is called TreePrint in DISTAN.

4. STATISTICAL MODULES

4.1 Mixed linear and multiplicative models

This module of DISTAN, called MixLinMult is able to fit, by the method of maximum likelihood, various models. The simplest ones among them are the log-linear models (see e.g. Bishop, Fienberg, Holland, 1975). The log-linear models that can be fitted by MixLinMult are more general than the usual ones in the sense that they are defined by a set of partitions. When the partitions are generated by marginals one gets traditional log-linear models, however, other definitions of the partitions may also be necessary. A partition can be defined either by giving the variables the marginals which define a partition or by specifying for each cell the subset into which it belongs. This latter can easily be done with an other utility program of DISTAN called DISTAN Editor or DISEdit. When this program runs the user can fill in the cells in an interactive fashion.

For these log-linear models MixLinMult reports parameter estimates, degrees of freedom of the model, the value of the likelihood ratio statistics and the appropriate probability level. New DISTAN files can be generated which contain the estimated frequencies (these can be printed etc. later on) and the components of the likelihood ratio statistics.

Starting values of the fitting procedure can also be specified by the DISEdit module and beyond handling structural zeros this makes fitting of described conditional interaction models (Rudas, 1987, Leimer, Rudas, 1988) possible.

The other type of models that can be fitted by MixLinMult is a linear model in the sense that linear restrictions on the cell probabilities can be prescribed. Well known examples of models of this kind are symmetry, marginal homogeneity etc. The coefficients can again be defined by the DISEdit module.

Finally, MixLinMult can handle models that are defined by both types of assumptions and computes maximum likelihood estimates and test of fit. The method of obtaining ML estimates in the mixed case is described in a different but comparable set-up in Rudas, 1989.

4.2 Fitting compound models by the method of weighted least squares

This module, called CompWLS, is based on Grizzle, Starmer, Koch, 1969 and Forthofer, Koch, 1973. This is a powerful tool for designing delicately parametrized models for a contingency table.

One can generally suppose that certain functions of the cell probabilities are linear combinations of certain parameters. This model is of the regression type and therefore the parameters can be estimated by the method of weighted least squares.

Matrices are necessary to formulate a hypothesis like this and these can easily be defined, stored and modified by the main program of DISTAN.

Here is a short list of some of the various models that can be formulated in CompWLS: equality of certain cell probabilities or of certain marginals or of certain odds ratios; log-linear and logit models; association models of Goodman, 1981: comparison of groups etc. CompWLS can handle several populations at the same time.

The program reports the estimated asymptotic covariance matrix of the observations, estimated parameter values with their estimated asymptotic covariance matrix and chi square statistics to assess the fit of the model.

4.3 Boolean factor analysis

This module, called BooleFac in DISTAN, can handle binary (i.e. 0-1 valued) data and in its aim is similar to the 8M program of the BMDP package (see Dixon, 1981), although the algorithm implemented was developed independently (Rejt , 1988). The task is to reduce the dimensionality of the data by substituting the original variables with fewer constructed variables using Boolean multiplication. The program reports loading and score matrices. The discrepancies between the data and the estimates are used as a measure of the fit of the model.

Such an analysis may be appropriate when the observed variables can be supposed to be caused by fewer unobserved variables through the following mechanism: whenever someone is positive on an unobserved variable (the score is 1) it will cause positivity on a subset of the observable variables and for each observable variable there is a subset of the unobservable variables that can cause positivity on it. These models can be useful in detecting latent traits, attitudes etc.

4.4 Multiple correspondence analysis

This module, called MultCorr in DISTAN, aims at simultaneous analyses of variables and of the sampling units (Benzecry et al, 1973, Greenacre, 1984). This is done by giving scores to both the variable categories and to the objects in k dimensional spaces, where k is an input parameter. The scores are based on certain factors for both the categories and the objects and for each factor there is a set of scores.

This type of analysis may be useful when metric distances are supposed both within objects and within variable categories and the structures of these spaces are to be understood with reference to each other.

The program reports the scores for both the variable categories and for the objects and gives visual representation in the space of the first two factors (these being the most important ones in a certain sense) of both the variable categories and of the objects. The scores can be written into a (non DISTAN) file for further studies.

4.5 Decomposition of mixtures

This module is called LatCat in DISTAN for the main idea of this analysis has been known in social science as the latent class model (cf. Lazarsfeld, Henry, 1968). The model of interest supposes that the associations among the observed variables are caused by some unobserved variable in the sense that when conditioned upon this unobserved variable the observed ones become independent. This model is parallel to that of factor analysis for continuous data.

Many authors have published algorithms to compute maximum likelihood estimates under this model (see e.g. Goodman, 1974). The output of the module includes an option to create a DISTAN file containing one more variable as compared to the input file, the one showing the estimated membership in the latent categories. The whole file shows the joint distribution of the observed and the uobserved variables.

4.6 Clustering of binary data

This procedure is called BinClus in DISTAN and performs simultaneous clustering of variables and of objects. Variable clusters may be overlapping. All possible response patterns in the sample have a weight, namely their frequencies. The algorithm implemented (Bolla, 1988) tries to find an embedding of all these response patterns into possibly low dimensional Euclidean spaces such a way that similar patterns tends to be embedded into the same space.

The application of this method seems to be reasonable when 1 on a binary variable means possessing a specific property not shared by many other respondents and therefore those giving positive answer are to be analysed (and those with negative answer are of no interest).

The output includes cluster memberships, homogeneity measures for the clusters, dimensionalities of the Euclidean spaces, coordinates of the variables in these spaces and some visual representation in the space of the first two dimensions.

4.7 Statistical modules in preparation

Two exploratory methods will be available soon. One for a version of the discriminant analysis procedure using a Bayesian forecasting rule, partly based on Rudas, 1984. The other is reduction of dimensionality via subset selection, based on Rudas, 1986. Further suggestions are welcome.

5. DISTRIBUTION OF DISTAN

At the present time the version 9 of release 0 of DISTAN is being distributed, free of charge. If you send us an appropriately packed AT compatible (high density) diskette, we will copy DISTAN for you and mail it to your address.

You can also become a registered user of DISTAN. Upon paying a small fee we you will get information on the development of the package regularly and we will react to any problems with DISTAN reported by you.

6. REFERENCES

Benzecry, J. P at al. (1973). L'Analyse des Données, Tome 2 L'Analyse de Correspondances, Dunod, Paris, 1973.

Bishop, Y. M. M., Fienberg, S. E., Holland, P. W. (1975) Discrete Multivariate Analysis: Theory and Practice. MIT Press, Cambridge. Bolla, M. (1988) Spectrum and embedding of hypergraphs. MTA SZTAKI Working paper, MS33, Budapest

Dixon, W. J. (1981) BMDP Statistical Software UCLA Press.

Forthofer, R. N., Koch, G. G. (1973) An analysis for compounded functions of categorical data. Biometrics, 29 143-157.

Goodman, L. A. (1981) Association models and canonical correlation in the analysis of cross-classifications having ordered categories.JASA 76 320-334.

Goodman, L. A. (1974) Exploratory latent structure analysisusing both identifiable and unidentifiable models. Biometrika, 61, 215-231.

Greenacre, M. T. (1984) Correspondence analysis. Academic Press, New York.

Grizzle, J. E., Starmer, C. F., Koch, G. G. (1969) Analysis of categorical data by linear models. Biometrics, 25, 489-504.

Lazarsfeld, P. F., Henry, N. W (1968) Latent structure analysis. Houghton Mifflin, Boston.

Leimer, H.-G., Rudas, T. (1988) Contingency tables with prescribed conditional odds ratios or prescribed log-linear parameters. berg Universitat, Mainz, 88-1.

Rejt , L. (1988) Boolean factor analysis, Manuscript (Hungarian). Rudas, T. (1984) Stepwise discriminant analysis for categorical variables. in: Havranek, Sidak, Novak (eds.) COMPSTAT 84, 389-394, Physica Verlag, Wien.

Rudas, T. (1986) Reduction of dimensionality in categorical data problems via subset selection. Manuscript.

Rudas, T. (1987) Prescribed conditional interaction models for binary contingency tables. in: Prohorov, Sazonov (eds.) Proceedings of the First World Congress of the Bernoulli Society, Vol2, 339-342, VNU Science Press, Utrecht.

Rudas, T. (1989a) Marginal and Partial association models, Social Science Informatics Center, preprint 1989/1.

Rudas, T. (1989b) DISTAN for discrete statistical analysis: an overview, Social Science Informatics Center, preprint 1989/2.

Statistical-Prospective Information Systems (STAPIS): Integrated Management of Statistical and Prospective Data, Methods and Models

O. Schechtner and K. Zelle

Summary

The concepts of a <u>Statistical-Prospective Information System</u> (<u>STAPIS</u>) are presented as an integrated approach to interrelated tasks within a special application area. Based on uniform data definitions STAPIS allows a better exploitation of the public information supply, makes data available by flexible representations, and is able to provide consistent and comparable 'total views' even if detailed data are partly lacking or contradictory. The data base, the method and model base and the system base are pointed out as the main components of STAPIS. Two flexible software tools, the <u>Aggregate Data Management System ADMS</u> for supporting the storage, retrieval, manipulation, processing and exchange of aggregate data, and the <u>General Log-linear Estimation Model AMUP</u> for filling up incomplete tables, for replenishing, transforming and adjusting data, are presented as the instrumental kernel of STAPIS. Finally, the development and operation of STAPIS is illustrated by examples out of three application areas: STAPIS on <u>energy</u>, STAPIS on <u>population and household demography</u>, and STAPIS on <u>labour and education</u>.

1. Introduction

The treatment of many political and economical questions and the support of decision-making processes in different areas require consistent data and specialized quantitative methods and models in order to prepare and process these data. Planning tasks refer to many interrelated subjects, e.g. population, education, employment, housing, building, regional planning, traffic, energy, economy, public budgets etc. Statistical offices, departments and information centers, planning departments of the administration, research institutions and planning offices are faced with a wide range of tasks: answering direct inquiries for data, performing regular or ad-hoc evaluations, preparing regular reports or recent data surveys for planning regions, providing detailed data for research, or performing fundamental planning studies.

Mastering these tasks requires subject competence and creativity, but also well organized data of good quality from statistics and other sources and a set of operative instruments. The experience shows that various problems may cause preventions: Inconsistent data and too restricted software lead to high costs and to unsatisfactory results, and are therefore often a too high barrier for the analytical and prospective work.

In order to overcome these problems this contribution presents the concepts of a <u>Statistical-Prospective Information System</u> (STAPIS) as an integrated approach supporting the various interrelated tasks of evaluation, analysis, monitoring, rating and forecasting by providing a flexible data management and suitable procedures, methods and calculation models.

ADIP-GRAZ has developed the general concepts, the methods and tools of STAPIS during many years of experience in various application areas, e.g. population (see Kaufmann/Zelle, 1981) and household demography (Zelle/Schechtner, 1989), employment and education (Zelle/Schechtner, 1986), energy (Schechtner/Turetschek/Zelle, 1988), economy (Richter/Zelle, 1981), traffic (Sammer/Zelle/Schechtner, 1982; Sammer/Zelle, 1984) and urban planning (Schechtner/Zelle, 1989). The concepts and tools are used within the own activities (ADIP-GRAZ offers e.g. the services of STAPIS-Energy for Austria since 1987) but may also be transferred to users together with the appropriate design and the necessary know-how to operate STAPIS in special application areas.

2. Management and Solution of Planning Problems: STAPIS

Everybody concerned with the information acquisition for planning purposes has become acquainted with some of the usual problems: the deficient survey of the availability of data, gaps in the available data stocks, incomparable and 'scattered' data, inconsistencies, the need of time consuming accumulation and combination of data, difficulties in providing special data by different departments, organizational problems with the acquisition and transfer of data from regional or national statistical offices, time consuming software production or adaptation etc. These are the reasons why fundamental analyses and planning projects are difficult in many cases, why they are performed often only in a very restricted way or remain undone at all. At least two improvements are required for this situation:
- operative and flexible quantitative <u>methods and models</u> and
- consistent, complete and well organized <u>data and planning information</u>.

Well designed procedures, processing methods and computing models are needed to master the described planning tasks, especially for evaluations and analyses (e.g. calculation of indicators, balances), simulations, monitoring and rating (e.g. efficiency control), forecasts and perspective analysis (e.g. detailed population forecasting, budget previews etc.).

Methods and models have to be founded on a data basis of good quality. The most important type of data for planning purposes are <u>aggregate</u> <u>data</u> ('macro-data'), in opposition to individual data ('micro-data') as they are contained e.g. in different registers of the administration (see Cubitt/Westlake, 1987). However, the derivation of the contents of administrative data bases, registers etc. (e.g. by counting, summation, cross tabulating, averaging) is an important source of planning data. These data may be described by the <u>items</u> <u>of</u> <u>data</u> (population, households, firms etc.) and by the <u>origin</u> or <u>source</u> <u>of</u> <u>data</u> (derivations out of current registers of the administration, acquisition of secondary statistics, evaluation of inquiries and polls, results from studies, models or forecasts etc.) All these aggregate data are efficiently represented in the form of one-, two- or <u>more-dimensional</u> <u>tables</u>, e.g. as cross tabulations, stock- and flow-matrices, balance schemata etc. This table representation is of great importance both for the data basis and for the procedures and models. Besides the uniformly organized tables the data basis must contain also the qualitative descriptions of the data with respect to the subject and the structure (<u>meta-data</u>). Two structural aspects are of particular interest: the aspect of the spatial relations and the connected classifications (regions, districts, street segments etc.) and the aspect of time. Not only data of the past and present (<u>statistical</u> <u>data</u>) are essential but also data concerning future developments and data resulting from planning processes (<u>prospective</u> <u>data</u>).

The concepts of the STAPIS were developed as an integrated approach to meet the described requirements. Its two main components, the <u>data</u> <u>base</u> and the <u>method</u> <u>and</u> <u>model</u> <u>base</u>, are founded on uniform terms and definitions. Both are supported by the <u>system</u> <u>base</u> consisting of a suitable configuration of <u>computer</u> <u>hardware</u> starting at the PC level (depending on the actual application area, the volume of data, the scope of interest, the users, and the way of utilization) and of <u>software</u> <u>tools</u> for data management and processing, particularly of the <u>Aggregate</u> <u>Data</u> <u>Management</u> <u>System</u> <u>ADMS</u> (Schechtner/Zelle, 1986, 1987a, 1987b) and the <u>General</u> <u>Log-linear</u> <u>Estimation</u> <u>Model</u> <u>AMUP</u> (Schechtner/Zelle, 1987a).

2.1. The Data Base

The data base of STAPIS consists of the collection data and the underlying data dictionary. The basic data elements in STAPIS are sets of aggregate data represented by general multi-dimensional tables, in which data objects (items of data) are classified by attributes. In STAPIS all the spatial, temporal and subject attributes are treated in an uniform manner. The data dictionary contains the meta-data, i.e. the set of definitions, descriptions and structural information, for

- statistical quantities (the data objects), e.g. population stocks (number of human beings), population flows (births, deaths, migrants), housing stocks (number of dwelling units), changes in housing stocks (gains of dwellings by new constructions, losses by destruction), energy consumption;
- structuring criteria (the sets of attributes of the data objects), e.g. age sex, position in the household, type of household, region, urban district, year of observation, energy sources, energy consumer groups;
- the actual aggregate data tables, e.g. the population stock classified by age, sex, marital status, urban district, and type of household (5-dimensional); the housing stock classified by status of occupancy, size, tenure (3-dimensional); traffic flows classified by source and destination district (2-dimensional); the differentiated table of energy consumption by energy sources, consumer groups, functional types on consumption, useful energy/losses and regions (5-dimensional);
- the relations between these elements and between different data bodies.

Generally, two kinds of aggregate data are distinguished in the STAPIS data base by their origin: Statistical data, resulting from observations in the 'real world', from different public sources like registers, surveys, polls, statistical publications and information systems, and 'synthetical' and 'quasi-statistical' data, resulting from transformation, derivation, integration of separate statistical bodies, estimation, and application of mathematical models. There are many cases where data of the second kind are desirable:

- In order to achieve comparability or integration of statistical data from different sources it may be necessary to transform or adjust the data. Similarly, In order to achieve completeness of statistics it may be necessary to replenish data by estimation.
- Often a disaggregation of data is needed where statistics can supply only data on a higher level of aggregation.

- There may be need for first actual drafts before the final official statistics are published, and therefore recent approximative estimations based on known marginal values may be produced using the tools of STAPIS.
- Last not least forecasts or projections ('prospective data') under certain preconditions and suppositions on trends are required.

It is obvious that for the treatment of questions in practice this type of 'quasi-statistics' is of great importance and therefore forms an essential part of STAPIS. However, both kinds of aggregate data are stored and treated within STAPIS in a formally uniform way.

2.2. The Method and Model Base

The main purpose of STAPIS is the treatment of questions and problems in areas of planning and research and to solve quantitative tasks. This requires data from the data base but also various methods and models that are collected in the method and model base of STAPIS. According to the needs of the users the development of new specific methods and models may be necessary. If they are of common relevance they may be included in the repertory. The aim is to develop standard procedures for special tasks that are founded on the type of aggregate data and observe the modular structure of the method and model base. It is important that the regular and standardized usage of these procedures promotes a steady improvement and innovation within the method base and supports the development of new methods and models. The representation of new connections may provoke new questions and may lead to alternative model dispositions.

Typically the method and model base of STAPIS contains a collection of procedures for the solution of different tasks like data representation, analysis, adjustment, estimation, forecasting and perspective analysis. Some of the standard procedures - especially those dealing with data acquisition, data input and exchange - have to respect the organizational environment of the actual implementation of STAPIS. Thus, the term 'standard procedure' should be seen in a wider sense including also organizational aspects.

3. The Instrumental Kernel of STAPIS: The Software Tools ADMS and AMUP

Tools for manipulating and processing aggregate data are of particular importance for STAPIS. They should perform three main tasks:
- to support the storage, retrieval, manipulation and exchange of data,

- to allow the problem-orientated processing of data,
- to provide means for estimating or adjusting data.

For that aim ADIP-GRAZ has developed two original software tools that form the 'instrumental kernel' of STAPIS (Schechtner/Zelle, 1986, 1987a, 1987b): the <u>Aggregate Data Management System ADMS</u> and the <u>General Log-linear Estimation Model</u> <u>AMUP</u>. ADMS deals with the first two tasks: It allows the user to bild up and to maintain problem-orientated data bases and provides a wide range of processing methods to support all essential steps of problem treatment: searching and collecting of aggregate data, transformation, aggregation and disaggregation of data, preparing analytical or projection methods, processing, storing and presenting results, transferring data to other ADMS data bases, preparing data for other software in order to apply certain methods of data analysis, estimation, evaluation or representation. As ADMS is operational on many different types of computers, especially on every standard personal computer, the user of STAPIS is able to receive the requested data from another STAPIS implementation in an ADMS standard data format and to process these results further with the same instrument according to his own special requirements.

ADMS makes the handling of unwieldy multi-dimensional tables easy and is immediate usable by the statistician and planner without programming experience. (Concerning the former example, e.g. a 3-dimensional table of the population classified by children/adults, sex, and urban district may be derived by one single operation from the 5-dimensional table of the population classified by age, sex, marital status, urban district, and type of household.) ADMS allows the definition of tables, the flexible input of tables in various formats, the updating of structural information and of table values, the searching for tables, the derivation of new tables, the generation of registers of the data base, the representation of tables by flexible output procedures, etc. The functions of ADMS for deriving tables include the aggregation of tables according to the relations between their structuring criteria, marginal aggregation of multidimensional tables, arithmetic operations between tables, calculation of tables of rates with respect to totals, disaggregation of tables by rates, generation of average and ratio tables, transformation of tables in the case of different spatial, temporal or subject structure definitions, extraction of partial tables by selection of particular attributes. Especially for data analysis and representation purposes many other software tools may be used in STAPIS, e.g. statistical analysis packages, graphics software etc. ADMS figures as the data communication tool between all these instruments and supports also an efficient data exchange between STAPIS and other data bases.

For the task of estimation and adjustment STAPIS contains a general log-linear estimation model (Zelle, 1980) represented by the computer program AMUP (Schechtner/Zelle, 1987a). This model is used especially for filling up incomplete tables, for replenishing, transforming and adjusting data and, generally, for establishing statistical systems, i.e. systems of consistent and connected tables. AMUP allows to set up and to solve general log-linear estimation problems. Available information may be used by providing an 'a-priori distribution' for the unknown solution, or by specifying restrictions in form of linear constraints. The set of constraints may be enlarged, reduced or modified in a flexible way. For each model the associated non-linear system of equations is solved numerically, in the present version of the program by a generalization of the so called 'iterative proportional fitting algorithm' (Snickars/Weibull, 1977). AMUP was developed in close connection with the aggregate data management system ADMS and operates on ADMS data bases. When linear constraints are represented by multidimensional tables, they may be prepared by ADMS as well as the 'a-priori distribution'. In the same convenient way AMUP returns the solution as a multidimensional table in ADMS data base format and makes it available for all functions of ADMS. The size of such estimation problems is restricted mainly by the capacity of the computer system, some rather large problems (containing about 30000 to 40000 unknown table cells) have been solved with the program.

4. STAPIS in Practice

The development of a STAPIS starts with a set of interrelated questions and tasks within a special subject area, for example population and housing: consequences of a changing population distribution, household structure estimation, spatial distribution of dwelling units, housing conditions of the population and their future development, implications on traffic flows. The analysis of the questions and of the structure of the required results leads to the definition of the data requirements. In the example, stocks and flows of population and dwellings are needed together with several structuring criteria. This is the basis both for the establishing of the data base and for the development of useful methods and models. The subsequent steps include the data collection, data acquisition, data transfer and translation, loading of the data to the data base (using ADMS), data clearing and consistency checking. The finally available data together with the expert knowledge are decisive for the development of the statistical-computational procedures to achieve the required results. Lacking data must be compensated by additional computations — in the contrary case a good data situation influences the model construction positively. When STAPIS has been made operational in this way, it allows different kinds of utilization:

- In the simplest case, the inquired information exists already in the data base. Then it may be prepared in a suitable form and representation (tabular form, graphics, machine readable form, ADMS format, etc.).
- If necessary, special calculations are performed using methods of STAPIS.
- The treatment of new arising problems and questions may prove the necessity to add new data to the data base or to introduce new methods, models and procedures, e.g. for specific estimations or forecasts using user supplied suppositions, estimations of consequences of interventions.
- Several users of STAPIS have the advantage of comfortable data exchange facilities by using the ADMS standard data format (which represents self-describing files containing data as well as meta-data).
- The growing importance and capacity of microcomputers favours the distributed utilization of STAPIS. Especially the data base may be situated at different locations encouraging the standardized data exchange, e.g. between different offices of an institution.

The following examples may give an impression of the kind of problems and tasks to be treated by various STAPIS applications of ADIP-GRAZ:

STAPIS-Population: The representation of the population, of households and families in multiple classified tables (according to several personal and socio-economic criteria) from different sources; updating of deeply structured demographic data; projection of the population in regional structure; estimation of the consequences of a particular population development (e.g. given by an external projection) on family and household structures.

STAPIS-Labour and Education: A differentiated 'total view' on the basis of the given demographic structure for each region, containing stocks of individuals at the beginning and at the end of a year for a definite set of status kinds (child, education, employed, unemployed, inactive, retired, etc.), flows of individuals between status kinds, integration of stock and flow data ('stock-flow-matrix') in order to show how stocks at the beginning and the end of a year are connected by flows; projections of such a total view in special scenarios under the supposition of given population projections for questions like man power requirements (according to level of qualification), structural change between economic sectors.

STAPIS-Energy: The multiregional energy balance for the regions of Austria, energy balances for smaller regional units (always in full consistency with the totals for the larger regional units); useful energy distributions (market shares for energy sources) and their yearly projections for small regional units, thus providing basic information for regional and communal energy supply and consumption plans; projection of energy balances under scenarios like energy source substitution, saving potentials; estimation of energy flows (volume of supply) between energy supply companies and their monetary equivalents.

5. Conclusion

STAPIS is intended to provide a large variety of relevant data and planning information for a wide range of users: For those who produce and maintain the data the tools of STAPIS should be an efficient aid in the regular work, for those who use them STAPIS should be considered as a recent and efficient complement to the existing statistical publications, data collections and services. STAPIS facilitates the quick processing of ad-hoc inquiries as well as the support of large research and planning projects. The uniform definitions and concepts promote the comparability of data on different levels and from different sources. Results of analyses, previews, planning tasks are presented in a form that may be further processed directly by others. Together with a suitable organizational framework STAPIS may be operated very efficiently at low costs starting at the PC level. It does not need a long implementation and preparation phase and may be utilized directly by the practicioner in planning and research.

With respect to the usual limitations for the solution of planning tasks — restricted time, restricted resources and man-power — the utilization of STAPIS has some very positive aspects: easier access to and better exploitation of available statistical data, saving of time and costs, achieving better quality for planning information. The main effect of STAPIS however is that the process of collecting, systematizing and representing statistical and prospective data in connection with the methods and models causes the stepwise improvement of a broad 'knowledge basis' in an application area.

References

Cubitt R., Westlake A. (ed.) (1987). *Report on the Third International Workshop on Statistical and Scientific Database Management, Luxembourg, 1986.* Statistical Software Newsletter, 13, 3-27.

Kaufmann A., Zelle K. (1981). *Bevölkerungsvorausschätzung Wiens nach Teilräumen.* Projektbericht des Instituts für Stadtforschung. Description of the method in: IS-Informationen 1-2, Wien.

Richter J., Zelle K. (1981). *Interregionale Lieferverflechtungen in Österreich.* Empirica, 1'81, 84-110.

Sammer G., Zelle K. (1984). *A method for updating existing data bases of an origin-destination traffic matrix.* In: Proceedings of the PRTC Summer Annual Meeting, University of Sussex, Brighton, England.

Sammer G., Zelle K., Schechtner O. (1982). *Fortschreibung einer Matrix der Verkehrsbeziehungen mittels Querschnittszählungen.* Straßenverkehrstechnik, 26, 15-20.

Schechtner O., Turetschek K., Zelle K. (1988). *Multiregionale Energiebilanzen für Österreich 1983.* Statistische Nachrichten, 43, 57-69.

Schechtner O., Zelle K. (1986). *ADMS: Aggregate Data Management in Statistics and Planning.* European Political Data Newsletter, 61, 34-40.

Schechtner O., Zelle K. (1987a). *Tools for Aggregate Data Management in Statistics and Planning.* Statistical Software Newsletter, 13, 66-72.

Schechtner O., Zelle K. (1987b). *Aggregatdaten-Management in kommunaler Statistik und Planung.* online/ÖVD, 12/87, 64-68.

Schechtner O., Zelle K. (1989). *A Communal Statistical-Prospective Information System (STAPIS).* In: Proceedings of the 13th Urban Data Management Symposium (UDMS'89), Lisbon, 551-562.

Snickars F., Weibull J.W. (1977). *A Minimum Information Principle - Theory and Practice.* Regional Science and Urban Economics, 7, 137-168.

Zelle K. (1980). *Ein mathematisches Modell zur Schätzung tiefgegliederter Daten für Planung und Statistik.* In: Tagungsbeiträge, 6. Internationaler ADV-Kongreß 'Datenverarbeitung im Europäischen Raum', Wien.

Zelle K., Schechtner O. (1986). *Arbeitskräftegesamtrechnung - Erstellung und Fortschreibung mit Hilfe log-linearer Modelle.* Österreichische Zeitschrift für Statistik und Informatik (ZSI), 16, 56-82.

Zelle K., Schechtner O. (1989). *Neue Modelle für Fortschreibung und Prognose von Haushaltsstrukturen. Entwicklung und Erprobung neuer Modelltypen am Beispiel des Bundeslandes Steiermark und seiner Bezirke.* Österreichische Zeitschrift für Statistik und Informatik (ZSI), 19, 107-138.

Daten- und Dateimanagement in P-STAT

E. J. Zimmermann

Summary

For about 20 years BMDP, SAS, SPSS, and P-STAT have been known as reliable software for statistical analyses. Nowadays samples tend to become larger and larger so that the neccessity for adequate data- and filemanagement features within those packages arises. Besides its traditionally most powerful features in the field of handling sequential datasets P-STAT now is the first to come up with a random access data enhancement to essentially speed up selective processing of large files.
This contribution is intended to discuss P-STAT's data- and filemanagement capabilities under the aspect of its database management features. We come to the conclusion that these are not only well tailored for statistical applications but may also be regarded as a model for the other packages where to go.

Einleitung

In diesem Beitrag soll der Versuch unternommen werden, die umfangreichen Möglichkeiten des Daten- und Dateimanagements in P-STAT unter dem Aspekt "Datenbanksystem-Features in P-STAT" kurz zu umreißen. Dabei sollen im wesentlichen folgende drei Fragen erörtert werden:

1. Was ist ein Datenbanksystem ?

2. Welche Eigenschaften eines Datenbanksystems sind in der statistischen Datenverarbeitung von Nutzen ?

3. Inwieweit verfügt P-STAT über diese Eigenschaften ?

Was also ist ein Datenbanksystem ?

Diese Frage ausführlich zu behandeln würde den Rahmen dieses Beitrages sprengen, so daß hierfür auf die einschlägige Literatur verwiesen werden muß (eg.: STEINMETZ & KAISER, 1982; MARTIN 1981). Für die Zwecke dieses Beitrages soll es genügen, die grundlegenden Eigenschaften, die von einem Datenbanksystem gefordert werden müssen, kurz zu referieren.

Ganz allgemein kann eine Datenbank sicherlich charakterisiert werden als "organisierter Datenhaufen". Einen solchen stellt jedoch jede beliebige Datei genauso dar und es erhebt sich die Frage nach den Unterschieden:

Ein Datenbanksystem umfaßt i.d.R. mehrere Dateien, oft auch Tabellen genannt, zwischen denen (hierarchisch oder relational) definierte Beziehungen bestehen, die einen integralen Bestandteil des Systems darstellen. Desweiteren gehört zu einem Datenbanksystem notwendig ein Pflege- und Verwaltungsprogramm (die Datenbanksoftware), das eine Reihe von Operationen unterstützen muß.

Die in diesem Zusammenhang wesentlichen Operationen sind:
- (1) Erstellen von Dateien
- (2) Ändern/Erweitern von Dateien
- (3) Abfragen der Daten / Erstellen von Reportlisten
- (4) Selegieren von Untermengen

An die Software bzw. das System werden dabei folgende Anforderungen gestellt:
- (5) Schneller Zugriff auf einzelne Fälle
- (6) Reorganisationsfreiheit
- (7) Redundanzfreiheit
- (8) Multi-User-Sicherheit

Diese 8 Punkte bilden somit das Gerüst für die Erörterung der Frage nach dem Nutzen der Features von Datenbanksystemen in der statistischen DV und nach deren Realisation in P-STAT.

1. Erstellen von Dateien

Daß diese Möglichkeit auch in der statistischen DV gegeben sein muß, ist trivial - aber: Ist es damit getan, Daten über eine

Tastatur (sei es maskenorientiert oder sonstwie interaktiv) eingeben zu können? - Sicherlich nicht. Zumindest sollte es möglich sein, Daten aus fest oder frei formatierten ASCII- bzw. EBCDIC-Dateien einzulesen und auch wieder in Form solcher Dateien auszugeben, wodurch eine (Mindest-)Kommunikationsmöglichkeit mit anderen Softwareprodukten gewährleistet ist.
Schöner wäre es natürlich, wenn nicht nur die reinen Daten sondern auch deren Definition, das Data-Dictonary, mit zumindest Feld- oder Variablennamen und -typen direkt kommuniziert werden könnten. Dies jedoch erfordert die Einigung der Software-Hersteller auf einen gewissen Standard, wozu es erfahrungsgemäß eines hinreichenden Druckes seitens der Anwender bedarf. Protagonist und Trendsetter in solchen Dingen war und ist der US-amerikanische Markt - allen voran die Regierungsbehörden einschließlich ARMY und NAVY. Letztere nun hat sich unlängst für den sog. DIF-Standard entschieden, so daß zu hoffen steht, daß dieser Standard in Zukunft zunehmend von den Software-Herstellern übernommen werden wird. Besonderer Vorteil dieses Standards ist, daß DIF-Dateien Character-Dateien sind und somit auch zwischen verschiedenen Rechnern übertragen werden können.
Neben dem DIF-Standard und der direkten interaktiven Datenerfassung unterstützt P-STAT die Übernahme fest und frei formatierter ASCII- bzw. EBCDIC-Dateien und es sind Schnittstellen vorhanden zu BMDP, SAS und SPSS sowie rechnerspezifische Schnittstellen z.B. zu MS-Chart und dBASE auf dem PC, zu ALIS u.ä. auf UNIX-Rechnern, zu BUGRAF auf SIEMENS-Mainframes, zu PlotIT aus DEC- und IBM-Rechnern, usf..
Im Hinblick auf Datenbank-Eigenschaften muß es jedoch nicht nur möglich sein, Daten zu erfassen bzw. zu übernehmen, sondern es muß eine Möglichkeit geben, primäre und sekundäre Schlüsselfelder und - im Fall relationaler Datenbanksysteme - Relationen zwischen den Dateien einer Datenbank zu definieren.
Primär- und Sekundärschlüssel dienen letztendlich dem schnellen Zugriff auf einzelne Fälle unter Anwendung von Direct- bzw. Random-Access-Leseoperationen, während die Möglichkeit, Relationen zwischen verschiedenen Dateien zu definieren für die redundanzfreie und damit ökonomische Speicherung der Daten relevant ist.

Schnelles Auffinden einzelner Fälle spielt in der statistischen DV sicherlich eine geringere Rolle als z.B. bei der Verwaltung eines Großlagers, gewinnt jedoch auch hier immer dann erheblich an Bedeutung, wenn einzelne Datenwerte oft geändert (aktualisiert) werden müssen oder wenn häufig Untergruppen analysiert werden, die - verglichen mit der Gesamtdatei - relativ klein sind.

P-STAT verfügt zu diesem Zweck über einen optionalen Zusatz, das P-STAT Random Access Data Enhancement (P-RADE), das die Definition von Primär- und Sekundärschlüsseln erlaubt und im Random-Access-Verfahren auf die Daten zugreift.

Die Definition von Relationen zwischen Dateien dient immer der Zuordnung von Fällen der einen Datei (Tabelle) zu Fällen einer anderen Datei. Bei P-STAT geschieht dies durch sog. "linking variables", deren Werte die Zuordnung definieren (Fälle mit gleichen Werten in diesen Variablen werden als zueinander gehörig aufgefaßt). In der statistischen DV ist es dabei wenig sinnvoll, die Relationen statisch festzuschreiben, sondern es muß möglich sein, diese neuen Fragestellungen anpassen zu können. Hierzu kann in P-STAT aufgrund des Konzeptes der Verbindung über die Werte der "linking variables" das gesamte Leistungsspektrum der P-STAT Programming Language (PPL) eingesetzt werden. (Die PPL kann als in ein 4. GL-System integrierte vollständige 3.GL-Komponente angesehen werden, deren Möglichkeiten sowohl im Bereich der numerischen wie auch der alphanumerischen Datenmanipulation und -modifikation kaum einen Wunsch offen lassen.) Der Preis für die sich hieraus ergebende große Mächtigkeit und Flexibilität ist, daß der Zugriff auf mehrere Dateien eines Systems nicht durch Zugriff auf die jeweils zueinander gehörigen Sätze verschiedener Dateien oder Tabellen bei Bedarf erfolgen kann, sondern daß die Zuordnung zumindest in einer temporären Datei tatsächlich erfolgen muß (daß hier kaum eine andere Möglichkeit besteht, wird besonders deutlich, wenn man sich vor Augen hält, daß die PPL z.B. auch die Umstrukturierung einer Datei durch Zusammenfassen mehrerer Fälle zu einem Fall bzw. durch Aufspalten eines Falles in mehrere unterstützt)

2. Ändern / Erweitern von Dateien

"Ändern" kann bedeuten
- einzelne Werte bestimmter Fälle ändern
- Variablen entsprechend einer Regel umcodieren
- neue Variablen aus alten ableiten (arithmetisch verknüpfen, durch Manipulation von Zeichenketten erzeugen, usf.)
- Umstrukturieren (mehrere Fälle zu einem Fall zusammenfassen, einen Fall in mehrere aufspalten, eine Datei in Unterdateien zerlegen, usf.)

Die eminente Wichtigkeit dieser Möglichkeiten für die statistische DV bedarf wohl kaum einer näheren Erläuterung. P-STAT unterstützt hier den Benutzer sowohl durch die bereits erwähnte PPL, die auf den Fällen jeweils einer Datei operiert, als auch durch spezielle Kommandos, die auf mehreren Dateien operieren. So stehen z.B. zur Änderung einzelner Werte bestimmter Fälle die Kommandos REVISE (interaktiv) und UPDATE (Batch) zur Verfügung und das Kommando MODIFY in Verbindung mit der PPL erlaubt die regelgesteuerte systematische Änderung einer Datei. Die Kommandos COLLATE, JOIN und LOOKUP wiederum erlauben die Erweiterung einer Datei um die Variablen anderer Dateien - also die "seitliche" Zusammenfassung mehrerer Dateien. Die Verkettung mehrerer Dateien (Erweitern im Sinne von Hinzufügen von Fällen) erfolgt explizit und bei nur teilweise identischen Variablen über das Kommando CONCAT oder aber - identische Variablenstruktur vorausgesetzt - temporär (für die Anwendung nur eines Kommandos auf mehrere Dateien) durch einen Ausdruck der Form

... Datei1 (PPL1) + Datei2 (PPL2) + Datei3 (PPL3) + ...

anstelle eines einzelnen Dateinamens (PPL) bei Aufruf des Kommandos.
Es ist die persönliche, auf langjährige Erfahrung im Umgang mit Statistik-Systemem (BMD/BMDP, DATATEXT, OSIRIS, SAS, SPSS) basierende Meinung des Autors, daß P-STAT insbesondere in diesem Bereich führend ist und Maßstäbe setzt.

3. Abfragen der Dateien / Reportlisten erstellen

Dieser Punkt ist in der statistischen DV sicherlich vergleichsweise unwichtig. Dennoch muß gesagt werden, daß P-STAT auch hier mit den Kommandos LIST und TEXT.WRITER Möglichkeiten bietet, die vom einfachen Datenlisting mit und ohne Aggregationszeilen (Zwischensummen) bis hin zu Integration von Datenwerten in Fließtext und randausgeglichener Ausgabe desselben reichen und weit über dem Standard liegen gehen.

4. Selegieren von Untermengen

In der statistischen DV ist es immer wieder und aus den verschiedensten Gründen notwendig, nur bestimmte Gruppen von Fällen zu analysieren bzw. bestimmte Gruppen von der Analyse auszuschließen. Hierzu dienen in P-STAT PPL-Phrasen wie:
  (IF log.Ausdruck, RETAIN),
  (IF log.Ausdruck, EXCLUDE),
wobei der logische Ausdruck nahezu beliebig komplex sein kann und logische Funktionen unterstützt werden, wie z.B.
  (IF ANY(V1 TO V150) NOTAMONG (1 TO 5, 10), EXCLUDE)
Auch eine einfache Auswahl bestimmter Zeilenbereiche (Fälle) ist möglich:
  (ROWS 1 17 TO 124 244 500 .ON.)
(Zeilen 1, 17-124, 244, 500ff.)
Darüberhinaus steht mit "SEPARATE" ein Kommando zur Aufspaltung einer Datei in mehrere Teildateien zur Verfügung und die meisten Kommandos erlauben durch die Angabe von
  ..., BY Varlist, ...
eine getrennte Bearbeitung der durch die Variablen in "Varlist" definierten Untermengen.

5. Schneller Zugriff auf einzelne Fälle

Wie bereits erwähnt ist dies in der statistischen DV nur dann von Bedeutung, wenn oft einzelne Datenwerte geändert werden müssen oder aber wenn oft vergleichsweise kleine Untergruppen analysiert werden müssen. In diesen Fällen spart das Random-

Access-Read-Write-Verfahren erhebliche Laufzeiten. P-STAT verfügt hierzu, wie bereits weiter oben mehrfach erwähnt, über den optionalen Zusatz P-RADE.

6. Reorganisationsfreiheit

Sofern keine neuen Schlüsselfelder definiert werden, sollte eine Änderung der Daten (Fallselektion, neue Fälle, Recodierung, etc.) möglich sein, ohne eine nachfolgende Reorganisation der Datenbank zu erzwingen (eg. um eine Index-Datei neu zu bilden). Vorausgesetzt, man arbeitet mit einer Datenbankstruktur, ist dieses Feature in der statistischen DV sicherlich sehr wichtig, da gerade hier solche Änderungen der Daten oft erforderlich sind.
Entsprechend erfordert P-RADE auch nur dann einen Reorganisationslauf, wenn neue oder geänderte Schlüsselvariablenwerte den Bereich der vorher definierten Minima/Maxima verlassen.

7. Redundanzfreiheit

Vor dem Hintergrund der Speicherplatzoptimierung ist dies in der statistischen Verarbeitung von Massendaten bezüglich deren Langzeitspeicherung von Bedeutung.
Die Dateimanagement-Möglichkeiten von P-STAT erlauben hier eine minimal redundante Speicherung. Da aber minimale Redundanz immer für den Preis einer schlechteren Laufzeit erkauft wird, bleibt es dem Benutzer überlassen, diese Möglichkeiten auszureizen oder nicht.

8. Multi-User-Sicherheit

Im Bereich der statistischen DV kann dies u.E. nur bedeuten, daß die Benutzer in zwei Klassen eingeteilt werden: Solche, die eine Datei ändern dürfen, und solche, die dies nicht dürfen. Eine Differenzierung bis auf Feldebene hinab unter Berücksichtigung der Problematik der simultanen Änderung eines Datums durch mehrere Benutzer würde u.E. nur einen unnötigen Overhead zu Lasten des Speicherplatzes und der Laufzeit hervorrufen. Insofern ist die Möglichkeit eines Lese- bzw. Schreibpaßwort-Schutzes, wie ihn P-RADE bietet, durchaus angemessen.

Zusammenfassung

Als Ergebnis kann somit festgehalten werden, daß die Daten- und Dateimanipulationsmöglichkeiten von P-STAT in Verbindung mit den Datenbank-Eigenschaften von P-RADE optimal auf die Anforderungen der statistischen DV abgestimmt sind und für andere Systeme, deren Daten- und/oder Dateihandling derzeit weniger elaboriert ist oder die Random-Access-I/O noch nicht unterstützen, durchaus als Vorbild für zukünftige Erweiterungen herangezogen werden können. Besonders richtungweisend sind:

- Das Konzept des Multifiling
  (Jedes Kommando kann auf eine beliebige Datei zugreifen, ohne daß diese explizit eröffnet werden muß.)

- Das Autosave-Konzept
  (Die Speicherung geänderter Dateien sowie die Verwaltung von Sicherheitskopien der jeweils vorletzten Version einer Datei ist vollständig automatisiert.)

- Der Leistungsumfang der Daten- und Dateimanipulationsbefehle
  (PPL, Dateimanagement-Kommandos)

- Der optimale Random-Access-Zusatz P-RADE.

Literatur:

BUHLER, S. (1986): P-STAT 8 User's Manual. Duxbury Press. Bos-Boston, New Jersey.

CODD, E.F. (1970): A Relational Model of Data for large shared Data Banks. Communication of the ACM, 13(6).

GRILL, E. (1982): Relationale Datenbanken: Ziele, Methoden, Lösungen. CW-Publikationen, München.

ISIS Software Report (1986): Systemprogramme. Ausgabe 2.3, Nomina, München.

MARTIN, J. (1981): Einführung in die Datenbanktechnik. Hanser, München.

MICHELS, W., STEINMETZ, G., KAISER, W. (1982): Datenbanken zur rechnerunterstützten Auftragsabwicklung in kleinen und mittleren Unternehmen. CW-Publikationen, München.

STEINMETZ, G. & KAISER, W. (1982): Datenbanksysteme: Konzepte und Modelle. Teubner, Stuttgart.

Individuelle Modellierung mit Statistik-Software

Numerische Berechnung von elementaren statistischen Verteilungen

L. Knüsel

Summary

Even today, the reliable computation of elementary statistical distributions is not yet a matter of course. We present the basic idea of an algorithm to compute Poisson probabilities. The algorithm is claimed to be reliable and efficient for very wide parameter ranges. The same idea can also be applied with the binomial and hypergeometric distribution as well as with the related continuous distributions (Gamma, Chi-Square, Beta, F- and t-distribution in central and non-central form).

1. Einführung

Es ist heute noch nicht selbstverständlich, daß statistische Programmpakete die elementaren statistischen Verteilungen numerisch zuverlässig berechnen. Bei genauerer Überprüfung stellt man selbst bei namhaften Programmpaketen häufig untragbare Unzulänglichkeiten fest, welche den Verzicht auf die altbewährte Tabellensammlung noch nicht als angezeigt erscheinen lassen. Es ist jedoch möglich, die wichtigsten statistischen Verteilungen (Normal-, Chi-Quadrat-, t-, F-, Gamma-, Beta-, Binomial- und Poisson-Verteilung sowie die hypergeometrische Verteilung), ihre Quantile und ihre nichtzentralen Varianten numerisch zuverlässig zu berechnen für sehr große Parameterbereiche (vgl. KNÜSEL(1986 und 1989)). Die Verwendung von Tabellensammlungen für die klassischen Verteilungen wird damit weitgehend überflüssig, und eine Transformation unserer statistischen Probleme auf eine Form, welche die Anwendung der üblichen tabellierten Verteilungen gestattet (Normal-, Chi-Quadrat-, t- und F-Verteilung), erübrigt sich.

Die vorliegende Arbeit soll am Beispiel der Poissonverteilung die Grundidee eines Algorithmus darstellen, der es ermöglicht, obere und untere Verteilungswahrscheinlichkeiten effizient und numerisch stabil zu berechnen für sehr große Parameterbereiche. Der Algorithmus läßt sich ohne weiteres übertragen auf die Binomial- und die hypergeometrische Verteilung. Ferner kann der Algorithmus eingesetzt werden bei der Berechnung der Gamma- und Chi-Quadrat-Verteilung, sowie bei der Beta-, F- und t-Verteilung, da zwischen diesen fünf stetigen Verteilungen und der Poisson- bzw. Binomialverteilung ein funktionaler Zusammenhang besteht (vgl. KNÜSEL(1989)). Schließlich kann der Algorithmus auch eingesetzt werden bei der Berechnung der nichtzentralen Varianten der erwähnten fünf stetigen Verteilungen, da diese dargestellt werden können mit Hilfe der zentralen Verteilungen (vgl. KNÜSEL(1989)).

2. Zielsetzung

Es sei X eine Zufallsgröße mit einer Poisson-Verteilung mit dem Parameter $\lambda > 0$. Dann gilt

$$p_k = I\!P\{X = k\} = \frac{e^{-\lambda}\lambda^k}{k!}, \qquad k = 0, 1, \ldots$$

Unser Ziel besteht darin, zu gegebenem λ und k ($\lambda, k \leq 10^6$ etwa) die folgenden drei Wahrscheinlichkeiten zu berechnen:

    a) Untere Verteilungswahrscheinlichkeit: $I\!P\{X < k\}$
    b) Obere Verteilungswahrscheinlichkeit: $I\!P\{X > k\}$
    c) Einzelwahrscheinlichkeit: $I\!P\{X = k\}$.

Dabei soll jede der drei Wahrscheinlichkeiten mit einer vorgegebenen *relativen* Genauigkeit ε berechnet werden (z.B. $\varepsilon = 10^{-6}$, d.h. jeweils 6 korrekte signifikante Ziffern), solange die exakte Wahrscheinlichkeit größer ist als ein Minimalwert $r_{\min}$ (bei ELV ist $r_{\min} = 10^{-100}$). Man beachte, daß von den beiden Wahrscheinlichkeiten a) und b) nur die kleinere direkt zu berechnen ist, da dann die andere zuverlässig durch Komplementbildung bestimmt werden kann ohne die Gefahr von numerischer Auslöschung.

3. Berechnung der oberen Verteilungswahrscheinlichkeiten

Wir wollen nun zeigen, wie man obere Verteilungswahrscheinlichkeiten zuverlässig berechnen kann. Es gilt die folgende Rekursionsbeziehung:

$$p_k = \frac{\lambda}{k}p_{k-1}, \qquad k = 1, 2, \ldots \qquad (1)$$
$$p_0 = e^{-\lambda}.$$

Aufgrund der Rekursionsformel (1) haben wir

$$p_j = c_j \cdot p_{j-1} \quad \text{mit } c_j = \lambda/j \quad \text{für } j = 1, 2, \ldots$$
$$c_j \downarrow 0 \quad \text{für } j \uparrow \infty \quad \text{(Monotonie der } c_j\text{)}. \qquad (2)$$

Damit ergibt sich für die obere Verteilungswahrscheinlichkeit

$$\begin{aligned}I\!P\{X > k\} &= p_{k+1} + p_{k+2} + p_{k+3} + \cdots \\ &= p_k \cdot c_{k+1} + p_k \cdot c_{k+1}c_{k+2} + p_k \cdot c_{k+1}c_{k+2}c_{k+3} + \cdots \\ &= p_k \cdot I_k\end{aligned}$$

wobei

$$p_k = \frac{e^{-\lambda}\lambda^k}{k!}$$

$$I_k = c_{k+1} + c_{k+1}c_{k+2} + c_{k+1}c_{k+2}c_{k+3} + \cdots$$

Die Berechnung von p_k scheint problemlos zu sein, und wir wenden uns daher zunächst der Berechnung von I_k zu. I_k sieht aus wie eine geometrische Reihe in c (nämlich: $c + c^2 + c^3 + \cdots$), und wegen der Monotonie der c_j ist die Reihe I_k stets konvergent. Aus der Monotonie der c_j und der Definition der I_k ergibt sich sofort

    (i) $I_k \downarrow 0$ für $k \uparrow \infty$
    (ii) $I_{k-1} = c_k(1 + I_k)$ für $k = 1, 2, \ldots$

Wir betrachten nun den folgenden Algorithmus zur Berechnung eines Näherungswertes für I_k bei gegebenem λ und k (offene Rückwärtsrekursion):

> Setze $\tilde{I}_{k+n} = 0$ für eine gewisse natürliche Zahl n.
> Berechne für $j = k+n, k+n-1, \ldots, k+1$:
> $$\tilde{I}_{j-1} = c_j(1 + \tilde{I}_j), \text{ wobei } c_j = \lambda/j.$$
> Dann ist $\tilde{I}_k$ ein Näherungswert für I_k. (3)

Dieser seltsame Algorithmus beginnt irgendwo bei $k+n$ mit einem Startwert $\tilde{I}_{k+n} = 0$, der garantiert falsch ist, und er schreitet dann rückwärts in n Schritten zum Zielwert $\tilde{I}_k$. Wir nennen diesen Algorithmus die *offene Rückwärtsrekursion mit n Schritten*, und haben uns Gedanken zu machen über den Approximationsfehler des Algorithmus. Es gilt offensichtlich

$$I_k = c_{k+1}(1 + I_{k+1})$$
$$\tilde{I}_k = c_{k+1}(1 + \tilde{I}_{k+1}).$$

Daraus folgt
$$I_k - \tilde{I}_k = c_{k+1}(I_{k+1} - \tilde{I}_{k+1}).$$

Durch Wiederholung derselben Überlegung finden wir
$$I_k - \tilde{I}_k = c_{k+1}c_{k+2}\cdots c_{k+n}(I_{k+n} - \tilde{I}_{k+n}).$$

Nun ist aber $\tilde{I}_{k+n} = 0$ und daher ergibt sich
$$\frac{I_k - \tilde{I}_k}{I_k} = c_{k+1}c_{k+2}\cdots c_{k+n}\frac{I_{k+n}}{I_k}.$$

Wegen der Monotonie von I_k ist $I_{k+n} < I_k$ und daher erhalten wir
$$0 < \frac{I_k - \tilde{I}_k}{I_k} < prod,$$

wobei
$$prod = c_{k+1}c_{k+2}\cdots c_{k+n}.$$

Damit ergibt sich das folgende Rezept zur Berechnung von I_k bei gegebenem λ, k ($\lambda > 0, k \geq 1$) und bei gegebener Schranke ε für den relativen Fehler (z.B. $\varepsilon = 10^{-6}$):

1. Bestimme n so, daß
$$prod = c_{k+1}c_{k+2}\cdots c_{k+n} < \varepsilon.$$ (4)
2. Bestimme einen Näherungswert $\tilde{I}_k$ durch die offene Rückwärtsrekursion (3) mit n Schritten.

Dann gilt
$$0 < \frac{I_k - \tilde{I}_k}{I_k} < \varepsilon,$$

d.h. $\tilde{I}_k$ ist dann eine Näherung für I_k mit einem relativen Approximationsfehler $< \varepsilon$. Man beachte, daß der Algorithmus besonders effizient ist, wenn $k \geq \lambda$, da dann alle Koeffizienten $c_{k+1}, \ldots, c_{k+n}$ kleiner als 1 sind. Gerade für $k \geq \lambda$ ist der Algorithmus auch erwünscht, da ja hier die obere Wahrscheinlichkeit im allgemeinen kleiner ist als die untere Wahrscheinlichkeit. Die notwendigen Schrittzahlen für $k = \lambda$ und verschiedene Werte von ε sind aus Tabelle 1 ersichtlich.

Tabelle 1: Notwendige Schrittzahlen bei der Vorwärts- und Rückwärtsrekursion bei gegebenem relativem Fehler ε.
(VR) = Vorwärtsrekursion, (RR) = Rückwärtsrekursion

$\lambda(=k)$	$\varepsilon = 10^{-3}$		$\varepsilon = 10^{-6}$		$\varepsilon = 10^{-9}$	
	(VR)	(RR)	(VR)	(RR)	(VR)	(RR)
100	36	39	49	57	58	71
10000	370	374	522	530	638	651
10^6	3716	3719	5253	5261	6432	6445
$\lambda \to \infty$†	$3.717\sqrt{\lambda}$		$5.257\sqrt{\lambda}$		$6.438\sqrt{\lambda}$	

4. Berechnung der unteren Verteilungswahrscheinlichkeiten

Jetzt wollen wir uns der Berechnung der unteren Verteilungswahrscheinlichkeiten $I\!P\{X < k\}$ zuwenden. Aufgrund der Rekursionsformel (1) haben wir

$$p_{j-1} = d_j \cdot p_j \quad \text{mit } d_j = j/\lambda \quad \text{für } j = 1, 2, \ldots$$
$$d_j \downarrow 0 \quad \text{für } j \downarrow 0 \quad (\text{Monotonie der } c_j).$$

Damit ergibt sich

$$\begin{aligned} I\!P\{X < k\} &= p_{k-1} + p_{k-2} + \cdots + p_0 \\ &= p_k \cdot d_k + p_k \cdot d_k d_{k-1} + \cdots + p_k \cdot d_k d_{k-1} \cdots d_1 \\ &= p_k \cdot J_k \end{aligned}$$

wobei

$$p_k = \frac{e^{-\lambda}\lambda^k}{k!}$$
$$J_k = d_k + d_k d_{k-1} + \cdots + d_k d_{k-1} \cdots d_1$$

Die Beziehung $I\!P\{X < k\} = p_k J_k$ ist auch richtig für $k = 0$, wenn wir $J_0 = 0$ setzen. Aus der Monotonie der d_j und aus der Definition der J_k ergibt sich sofort

(i) $J_k \downarrow 0$ für $k \downarrow 0$
(ii) $J_k = d_k(1 + J_{k-1})$ für $k = 1, 2, \ldots$ $(J_0 = 0)$.

Nun betrachten wir den folgenden Algorithmus zur Berechnung eines Näherungswertes für J_k bei gegebenem λ und k (*offene Vorwärtsrekursion*):

> Setze $\tilde{J}_{k-n} = 0$ für eine gewisse natürliche Zahl n.
> Berechne für $j = k - n + 1, k - n + 2, \ldots, k$:
> $\tilde{J}_j = d_j(1 + \tilde{J}_{j-1})$, wobei $d_j = j/\lambda$.
> Dann ist $\tilde{J}_k$ ein Näherungswert für J_k. (5)

Es gilt offensichtlich

$$J_k = d_k(1 + J_{k-1})$$
$$\tilde{J}_k = d_k(1 + \tilde{J}_{k-1})$$

---

† Die notwendige Schrittzahl für $\lambda \to \infty$ ist $y\sqrt{\lambda}$, wobei $\varepsilon = e^{-y^2/2}$, vgl. KNÜSEL(1986).

und daraus erhalten wir auf iterative Weise

$$J_k - \tilde{J}_k = d_k(J_{k-1} - \tilde{J}_{k-1})$$
$$= d_k d_{k-1} \cdots d_{k-n+1}(J_{k-n} - \tilde{J}_{k-n}).$$

Nun ist aber $\tilde{J}_{k-n} = 0$ und daher ergibt sich

$$\frac{J_k - \tilde{J}_k}{J_k} = d_k d_{k-1} \cdots d_{k-n+1} \frac{J_{k-n}}{J_k}.$$

Wegen der Monotonie von J_k ist $J_{k-n} < J_k$ und daher erhalten wir

$$0 < \frac{J_k - \tilde{J}_k}{J_k} < prod,$$

wobei

$$prod = d_k d_{k-1} \cdots d_{k-n+1}.$$

Damit ergibt sich das folgende Rezept zur Berechnung von J_k bei gegebenem λ, k ($\lambda > 0, k \geq 1$) und bei gegebener Schranke ε für den relativen Fehler:

1. Bestimme n so, daß
$$prod = d_k d_{k-1} \cdots d_{k-n+1} < \varepsilon. \qquad (6)$$

2. Bestimme einen Näherungswert $\tilde{J}_k$ durch die offene Vorwärtsrekursion (5) mit n Schritten.

Dann gilt

$$0 < \frac{J_k - \tilde{J}_k}{J_k} < \varepsilon,$$

d.h. $\tilde{J}_k$ ist dann eine Näherung für J_k mit einem relativen Approximationsfehler $< \varepsilon$. Man beachte, daß hier die notwendige Schrittzahl $n \leq k$ ist; ist $n = k$, so berechnet unser Algorithmus die Größe J_k exakt durch vollständige Rekursion beginnend bei 0; die Berechnung ist in diesem Fall äquivalent zum „Naiven Algorithmus". Man beachte ferner, daß der Algorithmus besonders effizient ist, wenn $k \leq \lambda$, da dann alle Koeffizienten $d_k, \ldots, d_{k-n+1}$ kleiner oder gleich 1 sind. Gerade für $k \leq \lambda$ ist der Algorithmus auch erwünscht, da ja hier die untere Wahrscheinlichkeit im allgemeinen kleiner ist als die obere Wahrscheinlichkeit. Die notwendigen Schrittzahlen für $k = \lambda$ und verschiedene Werte von ε sind aus Tabelle 1 ersichtlich.

5. Berechnung der Einzelwahrscheinlichkeiten

Die Berechnung der Einzelwahrscheinlichkeiten

$$p_k = \mathbb{P}\{X = k\} = \frac{e^{-\lambda}\lambda^k}{k!}$$

scheint problemlos zu sein. Um Unterlaufprobleme bei großen Werten von λ und k zu vermeiden, wird man die logarithmische Berechnungsmethode wählen:

$$\ln(p_k) = k \cdot \ln(\lambda) - \ln(k!) - \lambda.$$

Für $k = \lambda = 10^6$ z.B. erhalten wir

$$\begin{aligned} k \cdot \ln(\lambda) &= 13\,816\,510.6 \\ \ln(k!) + \lambda &= 13\,816\,518.4 \\ \ln(p_k) &= -7.8. \end{aligned}$$

Dieses Beispiel zeigt, daß bei der logarithmischen Berechnung erhebliche numerische Auslöschung auftreten kann. Um in unserem Beispiel p_k mit einem *relativen* Fehler $< \varepsilon = 10^{-6}$ zu berechnen, müßten wir $\ln(p_k)$ mit einem *absoluten* Fehler $< \varepsilon = 10^{-6}$ bestimmen (d.h. mindestens 6 Dezimalstellen nach dem Dezimalpunkt), und dies bedeutet, daß die logarithmische Berechnung mit mindestens 14-stelliger Genauigkeit durchzuführen ist. Neben der Erhöhung der Rechengenauigkeit gibt es allerdings auch andere Methoden zur Reduktion der numerischen Auslöschung (vgl. KNÜSEL(1986)).

Literaturverzeichnis

ABRAMOWITZ, M., STEGUN, I.A.(1964): *Handbook of Mathematical Functions*, Dover Publications: New York.

BABLOK, B.(1988): *Numerische Berechnung nichtzentraler statistischer Verteilungen*, Diplomarbeit am Institut für Statistik und Wissenschaftstheorie, Universität München.

GRIFFITH, P. AND HILL, I.D.(1985): *Applied Statistics Algorithms*, The Royal Statistical Society: London.

KNÜSEL, L.(1986): Computation of the Chi-square and Poisson-distribution, in: *SIAM Journal on Scientific and Statistical Computing* **7**, 1022–1036.

KNÜSEL, L.(1989): *Computergestützte Berechnung statistischer Verteilungen*, Oldenbourg: München.

Analysis of Dose Response Data with SAS

H.-P. Altenburg and G. Rosenkranz

Summary

In the paper is demonstrated how one can analyze dose response trials such as simple quantal response or radioligand assay data. In the case of quantal response the logit, probit or Weibull model is fitted by an iteratively reweighted nonlinear least squares regression procedure yielding maximum likelihood estimators. Radioligand assay data are estimated by a Poisson model whose expectation is given by a four-parameter logit, probit or Weibull function. Moreover a general method for comparing dose response curves of several groups is given. All procedures discussed are implemented in the SAS system.

0 Introduction

Many problems of quantitative inference in biological research concern the relation between a response and an appertained stimulus (dose). In the following paper we want to report on the potentialities of analyzing dose response data with the SAS system. We consider problems related to two kinds of effects each requiring its own estimation technique — the quantal or all-or-nothing effects like disappearance of symptoms and the quantitative effects like the counts in a radioimmunoassay experiment. We point out the requirements for an analysis system and give a resolution of the below formulated problems on the basis of the SAS system.

I Quantal Dose Response Assay

I.1 General Aspects

If the response is quantal, the treated organism is classified at a given time after dosage as having responded or not. Plotting the per cent responses p against the dose x, the resulting curve is usually an asymmetric sigmoid, so that the point of inflexion of the curve is lower than the 50% level. However in plotting the per cent responses against log(dose), we usually arrive at a symmetric sigmoid curve with its point of inflexion at the 50% level.

In most bioassay problems the impact of a drug depends on the intensity of the stimulus. Any object has under controlled conditions a certain intensity with no effect at this level. Such a level is called a *threshold* or *tolerance level*. This tolerance value varies in a given population individually. At very low dose levels we will have no or only few individuals that react with the drug

$$x \approx 0 \quad \Rightarrow \quad p(x) \approx 0,$$

and at high dose levels the portion of effects tends to be near unity

$$x \approx \infty \quad \Rightarrow \quad p(x) \approx 1.$$

Thus a statistical assessment of quantal dose response relations requires model assumptions on an underlying frequency or probability distribution of the portion $p(x)$ of individuals with a tolerance value of at most x:

$$p(x) = \Pr(\text{tolerance value} \leq x) = \begin{cases} G\left((\log x - \mu)/\sigma\right) & \text{for } x > 0 \\ 0 & \text{for } x = 0. \end{cases}$$

$G(z)$ is a distribution function and μ, σ are positive real numbers which have a descriptive interpretation relating closely to the effective dose 50% and the slope of the curve.

The interpretation of the dose response curve as a cumulative distribution of tolerances cannot be regarded as wholly satisfactory, since the evidence so far given for tolerances is indirect. There are, however, certain special circumstances (e.g. in the bioassay of anaesthetizing drugs) in which tolerances, or something very like them, can be observed directly. In the following we will discuss three basic models for the tolerance distribution: the probit model, the logit model and the Weibull model.

The *probit model* (probability unit) assumes that $G(z)$ represents the standard normal distribution

$$G(z) = \Phi(z) = \frac{1}{\sqrt{2\pi}} \int_{-\infty}^{z} \exp(-z^2/2) \, dz,$$

whereas in the *logit model* we have a logistic tolerance distribution function

$$G(z) = 1/(1 + \exp(-z)).$$

The standardized probit and logit distribution agree closely for responses which range from 1 − 99% and however many datas you have, you often have not enough to discriminate between the two models. The differences are mostly at the borders of the curves because the logistic distribution function has longer tails than the normal distribution function. The advantage of the logistic function is that both density and cumulative distribution functions are expressed explicitly in terms of elementary functions.

Theoretical considerations lead in carcinogenesis and some special aquatic toxicity applications (cf. Christensen (1984)) to the *Weibull model*

$$G(z) = 1 - \exp(-e^z),$$

where the parameters are not merely fitting parameters but have a chemical-toxicological significance.

I.2 Computer Programs for Dose Response Assays

Many statistical packages like the SAS system are rather powerful concerning their computational capabilities, but they often lack knowledge about the statistical aspects of a correct data analysis. Moreover they do not satisfy the special requirements of biological or medical research.

A simple and often used method for quantal response analysis is to linearize the model by a probit, logit or Weibull transformation and then to use ordinary least squares techniques for the estimation procedure. The main disadvantage of these methods is the severe distortion of the variance. The transformation stretches the curve but also it stretches any errors. Thus an important standard for an analyzing system is to get unbiased estimators. Further requirements are facilities to evaluate *single and many treatment* trials. Many trials are designed to compare new drugs with a standard treatment, and therefore we require a system that allows for easy comparison procedures, the design of *parallel-line assays* and the computation of *relative potencies* with confidence limits.

On the other hand the statistical analysis procedure should be embedded in an information system, which allows *easy data management*, e.g. input, storage, editing, etc., and *user friendly presentation* with context sensitive help.

The SAS system offers the procedure PROBIT for quantal response analysis. The version 5 procedure calculates maximum-likelihood estimates of the following model equation (probit model)

$$p(x) = \begin{cases} c + (1-c)\Phi(5 + a + bx) & \text{for } x > 0 \\ c & \text{for } x = 0. \end{cases}$$

where a, b are the intercept and slope, c is a natural threshold response rate and x is the dose or log(dose). Optionally the threshold parameter c can be set to constant value and not estimated. The SAS data set used by the procedure PROBIT must include at least three variables specifying the dose, the number of subjects tested at that dose and a variable giving the number of subjects responding to the dose.

The procedure PROBIT prints
- for each iteration of the modified Gauss-Newton algorithm the current parameter estimates (a, b, μ, σ, c);
- the final covariance matrix;
- the estimated effective dose values with 95% fiducial limits for $p = 0.01(0.01)0.1 \ldots (0.05) \ldots 0.9(0.01)0.99$;
- two plots: the empirical probits with the estimated probit-line or the normal probability sigmoid curve versus the dose or log dose.

Though there is a wide range of applicability there are some things which should be improved:
- evaluation of the probit model only;
- no SAS output data set with the final parameter estimates and the covariance matrix;
- only line printer graphics;
- no possibility of a parallel-line assay;
- no relative potencies.

The new feature of version 6 takes some of these aspects into account. Not only the probit model but also the logit and Weibull (Gompertz called) model are then available. Instead of an all-or-nothing response variable one can also use an ordinal scaled dependent variable. There are OUTPUT-options for SAS data sets containing the final parameter estimates, the covariance matrix and predicted values of the sample. In a MODEL-statement the dependent and independent variables and special designs can be specified. To get weighted least squares estimates a WEIGHT-statement is available.

Despite this extension of the PROBIT procedure there are some aspects that can be improved: The specification of interactions is not possible in the MODEL statement. Effective doses are not available on an output data set, which implies difficulties in plotting dose response curves, and the printed output of the effective dose values contains fiducial limits instead of confidence limits. Relative potencies are still not available.

Our intention was to implement the above mentioned requirements on the basis of a standard statistical software package — the SAS system — with regard to the statistical methods published in the recent literature. We chose the SAS system because it is widely used in research and it contains a lot of data management and menu building tools besides highly developed statistical procedures.

The methods described in the following sections are realized in the SAS system by macros embedded in a SAS/AF-menu environment. Thus data management and data analysis occurs within a single SAS shell.

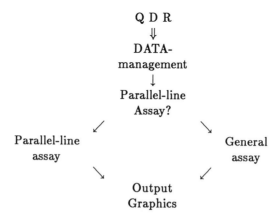

There are only few menu driven decision points which allow to evaluate dose response analysis by rather computer unexperienced users such as experimenters and their assistants. For a detailed discussion of methods and programs we refer to Altenburg and Rosenkranz (1989).

I.3 The Estimation Procedure

We developed the SAS macros for the following common family of quantal dose response models. Let d be the total number of administered doses and n_i the numbers of units treated with dose $x_i, i = 1,\ldots,d$. The number of responders r_i is then binomially distributed with some success probability p_i. It is assumed that the p_i depend on some unknown m-dimensional parameter vector θ according to

$$p_i = p_i^\theta(X) = \Pr(\text{response at dose level } i \mid X, \theta) = G_i(X\theta) \quad i = 1,\ldots,d$$

with the so-called link function G_i and a $d \times m$ design matrix with nonrandom entries. The link function G_i on $\mathcal{R}^d$ is defined in terms of some distribution function as follows:

$$G_i(x) = G(x_i) \quad \text{for every } x = (x_1,\ldots,x_d) \in \mathcal{R}^d.$$

All the distribution functions discussed in the introduction can be inserted for G. The dimension m of the parameter vector θ depends on the problem under consideration (parallel-line or general assay, etc.).

We formulate the theory in a general way because we want to treat different experimental situations like the comparison of several dose response curves or the calculation of relative potencies within the same framework.

The likelihood function of a quantal response experiment is then given by

$$L(X,\theta) = \sum_{i=1}^{d} r_i \log p_i^\theta(X) + (n_i - r_i)\log(1 - p_i^\theta(X)),$$

and following standard likelihood theory an estimate for θ is calculated from the equations

$$\frac{\partial L}{\partial \theta_j} = \sum_{i=1}^{d} \frac{\partial p_i^\theta(X)}{\partial \theta_j} \frac{n_i}{p_i^\theta(X)(1 - p_i^\theta(X))} \left(\frac{r_i}{n_i} - p_i^\theta(X)\right) = 0, \quad j = 1, \ldots, m.$$

According to a result of Jennrich and Moore (1975) maximum likelihood estimation for the exponential family is equivalent to iteratively reweighted nonlinear least squares estimation. Using the SAS procedure NLIN with the options SIGSQ=1 and NOHALVE we obtain the required maximum likelihood estimates from minimizing

$$S(X,\theta) = \sum_{i=1}^{d} w_i \left(\frac{r_i}{n_i} - p_i^\theta(X)\right)^2$$

with the weights

$$w_i = \frac{n_i}{p_i^\theta(X)(1 - p_i^\theta(X))}.$$

In almost all applications the starting values can be set to zero without causing any difficulties for the estimation procedure.

The advantage of the design matrix approach becomes evident if two or more dose response curves have to be fitted and compared. Basically, dose response curves could be estimated seperately. But if the response curves of one assay with several treatments are fitted simultaneously, the parameter estimates become more precise since their estimated variances are smaller than those obtained from separate fits.

Usually several treatments are compared in terms of their relative potencies. If two response curves are parallel ("*parallel-line assay*"), the relative potency is constant otherwise we have to ascertain a relative potency function. Thus in a correct analysis we proceed in two steps:

1. Check whether a parallel-line assumption is consistent with the data.
2a. parallel-line assay: estimate the parameter under this assumption — this reduces the number of parameters and provides estimates which are more precise. Then compute the relative potency.
2b. otherwise: estimate the parameter groupwise and determine the relative potency function.

II Quantitative Dose Response Assay

II.1 General Aspects

In the case of quantitative dose response relations we have similar problems as those discussed in the preceding sections. In many biological experiments like radioimmunoassays (RIA), radioligand assays or radiometric assays (IRMA) the effect of a stimulus (dose) is measured by the bounded or free fraction of radiation counts of the antigens or antibodies. Most of these experiments are perhaps not strictly bioassays, since they do not depend upon responses measured in living organisms or tissues. They are nevertheless so similar in structure that they need consideration from the viewpoint of bioassay.

There are many proposals for the statistical analysis using B_0 and B_∞, the counts in the absence of unlabeled antigens and the non-specific binding counts. Many experimentalists use graphical methods or linear regression fitting in plotting the terms like fraction free or bound against the logarithm of dose. A mathematical model to represent the statistical features of experimental data should preferably concentrate attention on the original observations than on derived functions. We assume that the expectation of the count (RIA-model) is given by a four-parameter sigmoid function:

$$\lambda = E[\text{count} \mid \text{dose} = x] = B_0 + RG(\beta - \gamma \log x),$$

where x denotes the ligand concentration or the administered dose, $R = B_\infty - B_0$ is the range of counts, β, γ are curve parameters (real numbers) with a similar interpretation as in the quantal response case and $G(x)$ is a distribution function (e.g. probit, logit, Weibull, etc.). In an IRMA-model the roles of B_0 and B_∞ have to be interchanged.

The aspects of a computer analyzing system are similar to those mentioned in section I.2 and therefore we direct our attention to the estimation procedure of this four-parameter problem. At present no SAS procedure is available on this topic.

II.2 The Estimation Procedure for the Four – Parameter Model

In a similar manner as in the quantal response case we establish a general model for the analysis of radioimmunoassays. Again the experiment is assumed to be described in terms of a $d \times m$ design matrix X, where d is the number of concentrations and m is the dimension of the parameter vector θ. The two further parameters B_0 and R are supposed to be independent of the design X. Let then $\Theta = (B_0, R, \theta)$ be the parameter vector of interest.

A quite realistic assumption concerning the distribution of counts is that they are realizations of some Poisson process. If there were no measurement errors in the process of recording the counts, maximum likelihood theory could be applied as in the quantal response case. Unfortunately measurement errors occur and the variance is expected to be larger than the variance obtained from a Poisson process. We suppose therefore that the *relative* measurement error is independent of the recorded counts. Thus assuming that the number of counts B_i at concentration x_i conditioned on the errors e_i form a sequence of independent random variables with mean and variance

$$E[B_i \mid X, \Theta, e_i] = \text{Var}[B_i \mid X, \Theta, e_i] = (B_0 + RG(X\theta))e_i$$
$$E[e_i] = 1 \qquad\qquad i = 1, \ldots, d$$
$$\text{Var}[e_i] = \kappa^2 \quad e_i \text{ uncorrelated,}$$

the marginal moments of B_i are given by

$$\lambda_i^\Theta(X) = E[B_i \mid X, \Theta] = B_0 + RG_i(X\theta)$$
$$\Lambda_i^\Theta(X) = \text{Var}[B_i \mid X, \Theta] = \lambda_i^\Theta(X)\left(1 + \kappa^2 \lambda_i^\Theta(X)\right).$$

In contrast to quantal bioassay, we are not able to model the distribution of counts but only its first and second moments. Maximum likelihood estimates are therefore not available. However, quasi-likelihood methods (cf. Wedderburn (1974) and McCullagh (1983)) imply that an estimate $\hat{\Theta}$ of Θ is a root of the equation

$$\sum_{i=1}^{d} \frac{\partial \lambda_i^{\Theta}(X)}{\partial \Theta_j} \frac{B_i - \lambda_i^{\Theta}(X)}{\Lambda_i^{\Theta}(X)} = 0 \qquad j = 1, \ldots, m+2.$$

Quasi-likelihood estimators have similar properties as maximum likelihood estimators (e.g. consistent and asymptotically Gaussian) but in the cases, where maximum likelihood estimators exist, they are less efficient.

To get the quasi-likelihood estimators we can use the SAS procedure NLIN and a corresponding nonlinear least squares technique minimizing the function

$$S(X, \Theta) = \sum_{i=1}^{d} w_i \left(B_i - \lambda_i^{\Theta}(X) \right)^2$$

with the weights

$$w_i = \frac{1}{\Lambda_i^{\Theta}(X)} = \frac{1}{\lambda_i^{\Theta}(X)(1 + \kappa^2 \lambda_i^{\Theta}(X))} \qquad \text{for } i = 1, \ldots, d.$$

There are several parameter estimating methods for dealing with nonlinear regression. In terms of both point estimation, confidence interval coverage (cf. Beal and Sheiner (1988)) and a computational point of view we find that a generalized least squares technique (GLS) is the best tractable one. According to Giltinan, Carroll and Ruppert (1986) the estimators can be obtained in three steps:

Step 1. Ordinary least squares estimator of Θ: Calculate $\hat{\Theta}_0$ such that

$$\sum_{i=1}^{d} \left(B_i - \lambda_i^{\hat{\Theta}_0}(X) \right)^2 = \min.$$

Step 2. Extended least squares estimator of κ^2: Calculate $\hat{\kappa}^2$ such that

$$\sum_{i=1}^{d} \log \Lambda_i^{\hat{\Theta}_0, \hat{\kappa}}(X) + \left(B_i - \lambda_i^{\hat{\Theta}_0}(X) \right)^2 \Big/ \Lambda_i^{\hat{\Theta}_0, \hat{\kappa}}(X)^2 = \min.$$

In our special case of variance Zeger (1988) showed that κ can be obtained by

$$\hat{\kappa}^2 = \sum_{i=1}^{d} \left\{ \left(B_i - \lambda_i^{\hat{\Theta}_0}(X) \right)^2 - \lambda_i^{\hat{\Theta}_0}(X) \right\} \Big/ \sum_{i=1}^{d} \left(\lambda_i^{\hat{\Theta}_0}(X) \right)^2.$$

Step 3. Weighted least squares estimator of Θ given $\hat{\kappa}^2$ and $\hat{\Theta}_0$: Calculate $\hat{\Theta}$ such that

$$\sum_{i=1}^{d} \left(B_i - \lambda_i^{\hat{\Theta}}(X) \right)^2 \Big/ \Lambda_i^{\hat{\Theta}, \hat{\kappa}}(X) = \min.$$

It should be noted that the extended least squares estimator for κ^2 given $\hat{\Theta}_0$ is equivalent to the pseudo-likelihood estimator of Davidian, Carroll and Smith (1988).

They showed in a special case that estimators of this type are more efficient than the modified maximum likelihood estimator proposed by Raab (1981) and Sadler and Smith (1985). Covariance estimators are also available.

Starting values for step 1 of the procedure we get as follows:

$$\widehat{B}_0 = \min(B_1, \ldots, B_d), \quad \widehat{B}_\infty = \max(B_1, \ldots, B_d)$$

and

$$\widehat{R} = \widehat{B}_\infty - \widehat{B}_0.$$

In most applications zero would be again a sufficient starting value for β and γ.

References

H.-P. Altenburg and G. Rosenkranz (1989): Analysis of dose response data. *Schriftenreihe Medizinische Statistik, Biomathematik und Informationsverarbeitung*, Heft 8, Mannheim

S.L. Beal and L.B. Sheiner (1988): Heteroscedastic nonlinear regression. *Technometrics*, 30, 327–338

E.R. Christensen (1984): Dose response functions in aquatic toxicity testing and the Weibull model. *Water Research*, 18, 213–221

E.R. Christensen and Chung-Yuan Cheng (1985): A general noninteractive multiple toxicity model including probit, logit and Weibull transformations. *Biometrics*, 41, 711–725

M. Davidian, R.J. Carroll, and W. Smith (1988): Variance functions and the minimum detectable concentration in assays. *Biometrika*, 75, 549–556

D.J. Finney (1971): *Probit Analysis*. Cambridge University Press, London

D.J. Finney (1976): Radioligand Assay. *Biometrics*, 32, 721–740

D.J. Finney (1979): The computation of results from radioimmunoassays. *Methods of Information in Medicine*, 18, 164–171

D.M. Giltinan, R.J. Carroll, and D. Ruppert (1986): Some new estimation methods for weighted regression when there are possible outliers. *Technometrics*, 28, 219–230

R.I. Jennrich and R.H. Moore (1975): Maximum likelihood estimation by means of nonlinear least squares. *American Statistical Association, 1975 Proceedings of the Statistical Computing Section*, 57–65

P. McCullagh (1983): Quasi-likelihood functions. *Annals of Statistics*, 11, 59–67

G.M. Raab (1981): Estimation of a variance function, with application to radioimmunoassay. *Applied Statistics*, 30, 32–40

D. Rodbard and G.R. Frazier (1975): Statistical analysis of radioligand assay data. *Methods in Enzymology*, 37, 3–22

W.A. Sadler and M.H. Smith (1985): Estimation of the response-error relationship in immunoassay. *Clinical Chemistry*, 31, 1802–1805

SAS Institute Inc. (1988): *SAS/STAT User's Guide*. Version 6 Edition, SAS Institute Inc., Cary, North Carolina

R.W.M. Wedderburn (1974): Quasi-likelihood functions, generalized linear models and the Gauss-Newton method. *Biometrika*, 61, 439–447

S.L. Zeger (1988): A regression model for time series of counts. *Biometrika*, 75, 621–629

Econometric Models for Event Count Data

H.-J. Andreß

1 Summary

The analysis of event-histories and duration data has attained much interest in the social sciences. This fact has been recognized by all major statistical programs (cf. the software reviews in earlier SoftStat proceedings). However, sometimes exact duration data are not available. Instead some kind of aggregate information is observed (e.g. count or change data). This has been the case in a panel study of recurrent unemployment which analyzed a sample of German men leaving unemployment in autumn 1977 (ANDRESS 1989). Five years later at the fourth interview these 250 men were asked to report the number of new unemployment spells since the first interview. This paper discusses methods to estimate models for such count data with standard statistical packages including GLIM, BMDP, and GAUSS. Special attention is paid to the problem of overdispersion and unobserved heterogeneity.

2 Count data models
2.1 Poisson distribution

Let Y_i denote the number of new unemployment spells for the ith of N individuals in the interval from sampling until the 4th panel wave ($Y_i=0,1,2,...$). Assume that events occur with constant rate λ. Then the number of events in an observation period of given length t_i for individual i is Poisson distributed with mean and variance of Y_i equal to $\lambda_i t_i$. A multivariate model is easily specified by equating the mean μ of the distribution log-linearly to a set of p exogenous variables x_{ij} (j=1,...,p including a constant): $\mu_i = \exp(x_i\beta + \ln t_i)$. t_i is included in the model as a known constant (an offset in the terminology of generalized linear models). If the observation period $t_i=t$ is the same for all individuals (i=1,...,N), then this constant can be neglected (it affects only the regression constant). The Poisson model is a standard model in many software packages and therefore presents no practical problems. Table 1 shows the results using GLIM.

Variable		Poisson Estimates	S.E.	Negbin (k=0) Estimates	S.E.
Reference group	Constant	-1,52	0,30	-1,62	0,36
Unempl. spells	1	0,64	0,17	0,67	0,22
	2+	0,73	0,22	0,85	0,31
	Missing	0,52	0,19	0,58	0,24
Vocational train.	No	0,60	0,14	0,68	0,19
Income	Low	0,44	0,16	0,49	0,21
	Missing	0,37	0,35	0,35	0,47
Tenure	3-10 years	0,68	0,29	0,67	0,35
	1- 3 years	0,74	0,30	0,82	0,37
	< 1 year	0,93	0,32	0,99	0,41
	< 3 months	1,02	0,30	1,04	0,36
	Missing	0,36	0,47	0,29	0,60
NB parameter ν				1,58	0,43
Deviance		381,81		244,50	
Degrees of Freedom		238		237	

Reference group: no previous unemployment spell, vocational training, high income, 10+ years tenure

All variables included are significant predictors but the value of the deviance 381.81 compared to the degrees of freedom 238 shows that some heterogeneity remains unexplained. Since most of the explanatory variables were only available for the first interview (1978) while the dependent variable has been measured at the fourth interview (1982), this unobserved heterogeneity may be due to changed conditions during this 4-year period. Data-fit may be improved by using a compound Poisson model including additional nuisance parameters in the equation.

2.2 Negative binomial distribution

A famous special case of such a compound Poisson model is the negative binomial (NB) which is obtained with a gamma-distributed errors ε_i in $\lambda_i = \exp(x_i\beta + \varepsilon_i)$. The gamma distribution $g(\varepsilon_i)$ can be parameterized in numerous ways. I have applied the derivation in CAMERON/ TRIVEDI (1986) who use the "index" parametrization. Therefore

(1) $$g(\varepsilon_i) = (\nu_i \varepsilon_i / \phi_i)^{\nu_i} \exp(-\nu_i \varepsilon_i / \phi_i) / \varepsilon_i \Gamma(\nu_i)$$

and $E(\varepsilon_i) = \phi_i$, $Var(\varepsilon_i) = \phi_i^2 / \nu_i$, $\varepsilon_i > 0$, $\nu_i > 0$, $\phi_i > 0$.

The index parametrization has the advantage that the mean of the distribution is only a function of one parameter, which can be nicely modelled in a regression context. Given this assumption about the unobservables, the marginal distribution of event counts equals the negative binomial

$$(2) \quad Pr(Y_i = y) = \frac{\Gamma(y_i + \nu_i)}{\Gamma(y_i + 1)\Gamma(\nu_i)} \left| \frac{\nu_i}{\nu_i + \phi_i} \right|^{\nu_i} \left| \frac{\phi_i}{\nu_i + \phi_i} \right|^{y}$$

with expected value $E(y) = \phi_i$ and variance $Var(y) = \phi_i + \phi_i^2/\nu_i$. In contrast to the Poisson model, the variance is now larger than the mean and the additional amount of heterogeneity allowed under this assumption equals exactly the gamma variance ϕ_i^2/ν_i. Note again that mean and variance are not independent of each other.

A suitable regression model considers the mean ϕ_i as a function of the exogenous variables. A log-linear specification similar to the Poisson model ensures non-negativity. The second parameter ν_i cannot be estimated independently of ϕ_i. CAMERON and TRIVEDI propose a second reparametrization which allows very flexible variance-mean relationships by letting:

$$(3) \quad \nu_i = [\exp(x_i \beta)]^k / \alpha, \quad \alpha > 0, \; k \text{ arbitrary constant.}$$

In terms of α, k and the exogenous variables the variance of the dependent variable equals

$$(4) \quad Var(y) = \exp(x_i \beta) + \alpha \exp[(2-k) x_i \beta]$$
$$= E(y) + \alpha E(y)^{2-k}.$$

Depending on the choice of k one can model either a variance proportional to the mean (constant coefficient of variation, $k=1$) or a coefficient of variation, which is linear in the mean ($k=0$). The second alternative is usually preferred due to its numerical simplicity with $\nu_i = 1/\alpha$.

3 Estimating the negative binomial distribution
3.1 Maximum Likelihood

The NB distribution is no standard model in any of the widely available program packages. However, many of these packages include nonlinear optimization routines that can be tailored to user-specified models and maximum likelihood estimation. In order to use ML the full likelihood using (2) has to be specified. Depending on the optimization algorithm, first and second derivatives with respect to the parameters must be known as well.

Some programs, however, supply numerical procedures to calculate gradients and/or the hessian matrix. Since y_i is discrete (0, 1, ...), even the Gamma- $\Gamma(z)$ and the Psi-function $\psi(z)=d\ln\Gamma(z)/dz$ can be easily computed by succesive summation over the number of spells. All equations can be obtained from the author on request. Let us now turn to the actual programs: GLIM (PAYNE 1985), GAUSS 1.49 (EDLEFSON/ JONES 1986), and BMDP (1983 version and later) are discussed in this paper. Other alternatives not reviewed here include LIMDEP (GREEN 1983) and the procedure NLIN in SAS.

If the NB parameter ν is known, the NB model can be specified as an "own" model in GLIM, for which the user should be familiar with the GLM philosophy. However, in all realistic cases the parameter ν needs to be estimated. With the first and second derivatives specified, one could program a Newton-Raphson or Fisher's scoring algorithm using GLIM-macros, but this is certainly not very efficient. Besides that, standard errors will be incorrectly estimated. Therefore, GLIM provides no practical solution to direct estimation of the NB model.

The BMDP package supplies two programs that can be used for ML estimation. For the first of them (PAR) it is only necessary to specify the likelihood function while the second (P3R) also needs the first derivatives. These can be specified with the BIMEDT procedure (not available for BMDP-PC), which allows the user to link his/her own code via FORTRAN-statements to the main program. It assumes a compatible FORTRAN-compiler on the host computer. Since this is a problem on some installations the user will probably welcome the fact that with the 1983 version of BMDP it is also possible to specify likelihood and gradients with usual BMDP transformation statements in a separate FUN-paragraph. The corresponding P3R-program consists of the following statements (using the Poisson estimates as start values):

```
/TRANSFORM   DUMMY=1.0.
/REGRESS     DEPENDENT IS DUMMY.
             PARAMETERS ARE 13. LOSS. PRINT=0.
/PARAMETER   INITIAL ARE -1.52, .64, .73, .52, .60, .44, .37, .68,
                         .74, .93,1.02, .36,1.50.
/FUN         MU  =EXP(P1+P2 *V51_2+P3 *V51_3+P4 *V51_6+P5 *AUS_2+
                     P6 *INC_2+P7 *INC_6+P8 *DAU_2+P9 *DAU_3+
```

```
                        P10*DAU_4+P11*DAU_5+P12*DAU_6).
            RES  =AANEU-MU.
            WT   =1+MU/P13.
            A0   =124*LN(P13   )+61*LN(P13+1)+45*LN(P13+2)+
                  25*LN(P13+3)+ 9*LN(P13+4). A0=A0/250.
            A1   =124/P13      +61/(P13+1)   +45/(P13+2)+
                  25/(P13+3)   + 9/(P13+4). A1=A1/250.
            DF1  =         RES/WT.
            DF2  =V51_2*RES/WT.
            DF3  =V51_3*RES/WT.
                  .
                  .
                  .
            DF13=1+LN(P13)+A1-LN(P13+MU)-(P13+AANEU)/(P13+MU).
            F   =AANEU*LN(MU)-(P13+AANEU)*LN(P13+MU)+P13*LN(P13)+A0.
            XLOSS = -F. DUMMY = F + 1.0.
/END
```

PAR uses the same set of statements omitting those for the first derivatives (DF1 ... DF13).

The statistical programming language GAUSS offers a seperate module with a general-purpose program named MAXLIK for the maximization of likelihood functions. Its application is briefly described in the GAUSS newsletter (January 1987). All the user needs to do, is to specify the likelihood function in a procedure named li, supply a set of starting values and read in the data. The program offers two procedures (grad1, hessian) to compute first and second derivatives numerically, which the user can replace by his/her own analytical solutions. This will speed up the computations considerably, especially if analytical gradients are supplied. Although this sounds rather easy to apply, the practical implementation may be not trivial for those users that are not familiar with matrix algebra in general and a matrix-oriented programming language in particular. Special problems arise due to the fact that two different kinds of parameters have have to be handled (the NB parameter ν and p regression parameters β). The following listing shows the GAUSS procedures for calculating the likelihood (li) and the gradients (negb1):

```
proc li(bb);
   local a; a=bb[1,1]; local b; b=bb[2:kd,1];
   retp(y.*x*b - (a+y).*ln(a+exp(x*b)) + a*ln(a) + lnfact(a+y-1)
        - lnfact(a-1) - lnfact(y));
endp;
proc negb1(&li,bb,lb0,dh);
   local a; a=bb[1,1]; local b; b=bb[2:kd,1]; local m; m=exp(x*b);
   retp((-ln(a+m)-(a+y)./(a+m)+ln(a)+1+psi(y,a))~
        (a*x .* (y-m) ./ (a+m)));
```

```
endp;
proc psi(y,a);
   local ax,x,n; let ax=124 61 45 25 9; let x=0 1 2 3 4; n=250;
   retp( (ones(1,5)/n) * (ax./(a+x)) );
endp;
```

The hessian matrix is a rather complicated $(p+1)*(p+1)$ matrix and is much easier computed numerically. The loss in computational speed is negligable. Note that since June 1989 new application modules are available for GAUSS version 2.0. They include a new version of MAXLIK (the older 1.49 modules are not upward compatible) and specialized procedures for count data models.

Table 1 also shows the ML estimates for the NB model using the GAUSS program MAXLIK with analytical gradients specified as in negb1 (BMDP's P3R yields identical parameter and variance estimates up to 2 significant digits, however the NB parameter ν is estimated as 1.47 with standard error 0.23). Note the decrease in deviance compared to the Poisson model. Besides that, standard errors are 20-40% higher. Nevertheless, the structural conclusions from the NB model are identical to those from the Poisson model, since parameter estimates do not differ very much.

3.2 Quasi-Generalised Pseudo Maximum Likelihood

GOURIEROUX/ MONTFORT/ TROGNON (1984, GMT for short) suggest an alternative estimator for compound Poisson models with less distributional assumptions. The statistical derivations are rather involved and therefore the interested reader is referred to the original publication. An application of the GMT estimator to the compound Poisson model consists of the following 2-step-procedure:

1a. Apply the normal distribution (or any other linear exponential family (LEF) distribution) to the data as if it were the true one. Let us call the regression estimates from this first step b_1.
1b. Take the fitted values $\hat{\mu}$ from the first step and the following approximation to the variance of y

$$Var(y) = \mu + \alpha\mu^2$$

to get an estimate of the nuisance parameter α. This is simply done by regressing $V\hat{a}r(y)-\hat{\mu}$ on $\alpha\hat{\mu}^2$.
2. Weigh the observations with the estimate $\hat{\alpha}$ using

$$u_i = (\hat{\mu}_i + \hat{\alpha}\mu_i^2)^{-1}$$

as prior weights for the normal distribution and get a second "improved" fit with regression estimates b_2.

This procedure can be implemented in GLIM with the following macros:

```
$MAC QPMN ! Quasi-Generalized PML:
!          Poisson Compound using NORMAL likelihood
!          Input:  Macro MODL with fit formula
!                  %1 Dependent variable
!          Uses:   %A Nuisance parameter (scalar)
!                  W_ Weight for step 2
!          Output:
!
$YVAR %1 $ERR P $FIT #MODL !            Recycle from Poisson fit
$ERR N $LINK L $SCALE 1 $RECY !         STEP 1: Pseudo ML
$FIT #MODL !                            Define Fit formula in MODL
$CAL %A = %CU( ((%YV-%FV)**2 - %FV) * %FV**2 ) / %CU( %FV**4 ) !
   :  W_ = 1 / (%FV + %A*%FV**2) !
$WEI W_ $FIT . !                        STEP 2: Quasi-Pseudo ML
$$ENDM !
```

4 Conclusion

If one compares the effect of each variable across different models and estimation procedures, no dramatic differences in point estimates occur. For example the effect of training is estimated as follows (see HINDE 1982 for normal compound model):

Model	Deviance	df	Estimate	S.E.
Non-Linear LS	425,73	238	0,53	0,12
Linear model (OLS)	414,48	238	0,74	0,21
Poisson	381,81	238	0,60	0,14
Normal Compound	348,60	237	0,62	0,14
QGPML Normal	304,86	237	0,55	0,16
Neg. Binomial	244,50	237	0,68	0,19
Poisson (Offset t)	216,86	238	0,39	0,13

According to statistical theory all estimators are consistent, provided the true distribution is a LEF member and the mean is correctly specified. Therefore one expects more or less the same estimates since all models equate the mean to $\exp(x_i\beta)$ except the linear model with OLS and the Poisson model with offset t. Accordingly the largest difference is observed for the Poisson with offset t. This model uses a totally different specification for the mean by controlling for time in labor force t_i.

A closer look at the first derivates with respect to the regression coefficients also shows that the analytical structure of all first order conditions is basically the same:

$$\Sigma_i \text{Weight}_i * \text{Residual}_i * x_i = 0$$

with $\text{Residual}_i = y_i - \mu_i$ and weights defined as follows

Poisson:	$\text{Weight}_i = 1$
Neg. Binomial:	$\text{Weight}_i = (1 + \exp(x_i\beta)/\nu)^{-1}$
Linear LS:	$\text{Weight}_i = x_i\beta$
Non-Linear LS:	$\text{Weight}_i = \exp(x_i\beta)$
QGPML Normal:	$\text{Weight}_i = \exp(x_i\beta) / (\mu_i + \alpha\mu_i^2)$.

All weighting schemes are more or less functions of the exogenous variables except the Poisson which assigns equal weights to all observations. This again suggests that estimates should be quite similar. Given these qualifications the choice of model is merely a question of ease of specification and computational speed. In this respect the GMT procedure has clear advantages over the other alternatives.

5   References

Andreß, H.J. (1989): Instabile Karrieren und Erwerbslosigkeit. Ein Vergleich mit der Gruppe der Langzeitarbeitslosen. Theorien, Daten und einige explorative Ergebnisse. MittAB 1: 17-32

Andreß, H.J. (1989): Recurrent unemployment - the West-German experience. An application of count data models to panel data. European Sociological Review 5

Cameron, A.C./ Trivedi, P.K. (1986): Econometric models based on count data: comparisons and applications of some estimators and tests. Journal of Applied Econometrics 1: 29-53

Edlefson, L./ Jones, S. (1986): GAUSS programming language manual. Kent, WA: Aptech Systems Inc.

Gourieroux, C./ Monfort, A./ Trognon, A. (1984): Pseudo maximum likelihood methods: theory. Econometrica 52: 681-700

Gourieroux, C./ Monfort, A./ Trognon, A. (1984): Pseudo maximum likelihood methods: applications to poisson models. Econometrica 52: 701-720

Greene, W.H. (1983): LIMDEP: a program for estimating the parameters of qualitative and limited dependent variables. The American Statistician 37: 170

Hinde, J. (1982): Compound poisson regression models. in: GLIM 1982. Proceedings of the international conference on generalized linear models (Gilchrist, R., ed.). 109-121

Payne, C.D. (1985): The GLIM system. Release 3.77. Oxford: Numerical Algorithm Group

Individuelle Programmierung in SPSS^X: The USERCODE-Facility

B. Engel

Summary

USERPROC and USERGET adds programming flexibility to SPSS^X. The paper shows which problems exist and how to manage the problems. The paper focuses on the general problems of FORTRAN programming within SPSS^X and on the use of the subroutines spread by SPSS. The result is that USERPROC and USERGET is very helpful to solve individual problems - if you are an experienced programmer; the main lack is that you have to use the old fashioned FORTRAN 66 programming standard.

1 Vorbemerkung

Gerade den klassischen Programmpaketen wie SPSS^X wird häufig vorgeworfen, daß sie inflexibel seien für individuelle Programmierung. Der häufig in der Entwicklungsgeschichte der Programmpakete sichtbare Ausweg ist die Makrogenerierung[1], seltener findet sich die Möglichkeit, Programme in einer klassischen Programmiersprache dem Programmpaket hinzuzufügen, was häufig schon deshalb ausgeschlossen ist, weil in aller Regel der Sourcecode der Programmpakete nicht verfügbar ist.

Thema dieses Beitrags ist die individuelle Programmierung innerhalb von SPSS^X mit Hilfe der USERCODE-Facility. In einer kurzen Skizze wird gezeigt, wie welche Daten und Dictionärinformationen in eigenen Programmen weiterverarbeitet werden können und welche Defizite grundsätzlicher Art und im Detail existieren. Auf eine Darstellung von Anwendungsbeispielen - wie sie im Poster der Konferenz gezeigt wurde - ist hier verzichtet worden[2].

Der Schwerpunkt der individuellen Programmierung ist natürlich stark abhängig von den fachlichen bzw. betrieblichen Erfordernissen im Einzelfall, sodaß die Funktion der USERCODEs bzw. USERGETs nicht von generellem Nutzen ist. Die gewählten Beispiele stammen aus den im ZDF programmierten USERPROCs bzw. USERGETs und beinhalten vor allem Datenmanagement-Utilities, die es anderen Entwicklern von Benutzerprozeduren erleichtern sollen zu beurteilen, ob für ihre fachspezifischen Probleme die SPSS^X USERCODE-Facility eine geeignete Lösung ist.

---

[1] Auch in SPSS^X ab Release 3.0 verfügbar; vgl. hierzu SPSS^X User's Guide. 3rd Edition. SPSS, Chicago. Appendix A.
[2] Auf Wunsch können die Beispiele vom Autor angefordert werden.

2 Benutzerprogramme in SPSS^X

Grundsätzlich unterscheidet sich die individuelle Programmierung von USERPROCs und USERGETs von der individuellen Programmierung in anderen statistischen Programmsystemen dadurch, daß die Codierung völlig außerhalb der SPSS^X-Sprache liegt. USERCODE-Programme sind in einer Programmiersprache der 3. Generation zu kodieren, müssen compiliert und gelinkt werden. SPSS^X-Benutzer sollten daher nicht fälschlicherweise annehmen, daß die Programmierung von USERPROCs oder USERGETs auf bereits erworbenen SPSS^X-Kenntnissen aufbauen kann. Eine über Anfängerkenntnisse hinausgehende FORTRAN-Erfahrung ist meines Erachtens dringend erforderlich. Besondere Anforderungen sind sicher notwendig, wenn USERPROCs oder USERGETs so programmiert werden sollen, daß sie von anderen Benutzern gefahrlos und mit Nutzen verwendet werden können.

Ferner sei darauf hingewiesen, daß die individuelle Programmierung derzeit nur unter wenigen Betriebssystemen verfügbar ist, da dem fertigen Lademodul von SPSS^X die benutzerdefinierten Lademodule hinzugefügt werden müssen; dies ist unabhängig vom Releasestand von SPSS^X nicht bei allen Betriebssystemen möglich[3].

3 Beschreibung der notwendigen Arbeitsschritte

Für die Programmierung individueller Prozeduren stehen zahlreiche CALL-Schnittstellen zur Verfügung, die für FORTRAN und COBOL dokumentiert sind[4]. Der Aufbau eines Benutzerprogrammes umfaßt stets folgende Programmierschritte:

- Festlegung des Programmtyps USERGET oder USERPROC; hierbei wird festgelegt, ob das Benutzerprogramm auf einen aktiven SPSS^X-File zugreifen kann oder ob dieser im Programm erzeugt werden soll;
- Festlegung, ob bzw. wie viele neue Variablen im Programmablauf erzeugt werden, die dem aktiven SPSS^X-File hinzugefügt werden sollen;
- Festlegung, ob das Programm über die mitgelieferten Kommando-Prüfroutinen oder mit einer eigenen Prüfroutine verarbeitet wird (Stack-Verarbeitung oder nicht);
- Prüfung der Kommandosyntax;
- Öffnen der Dateien zum Lesen mit der Option, daß der anstehende Lesevorgang der letzte ist;
- Prüfen, ob nur eine Syntaxprüfung erfolgt oder das Programm tatsächlich vollständig ausgeführt wird;
- Lesen der Daten im sogenannten Observation-Vector;
- Auswahl der in der Prozedur zu verarbeitenden Variablen;
- Retrieval der Dictionärinformationen für die zu verarbeitenden Variablen;
- falls vorgesehen: Generierung neuer Variablen und Dictionärinformationen;
- Output.

Danach folgen die Schritte Compilieren und Linken.

---

[3] Derzeit existieren Dokumentationen für IBM/CMS und IBM/MVS sowie Digital VAX/VMS.
[4] Adding User Programs to SPSS^X on IBM MVS and CMS System. SPSS Inc. Reports 1985.

4 USERPROCs und USERGETs im ZDF

Die folgenden Prozeduren geben einen Überblick darüber, für welche Aufgabenstellungen USERPROCs und USERGETs im ZDF entwickelt wurden. Es handelt sich zumeist um Routinen, die sich auch händisch innerhalb der SPSS^X-Sprache erzeugen ließen (z.B. Ermittlung der Fallzahl oder Normierung von Gewichtungsfaktoren). Die händische Erzeugung ist jedoch insbesondere bei Verarbeitung von Dateien, die sich häufig ändern, mühsam und fehleranfällig.

Grundsätzlich ist versucht worden, in den Prozeduren keine Duplizierung von SPSS^X-Befehlen vorzunehmen. So sind beispielsweise für die GINI-Prozedur die Daten mit dem SORT-Befehl zu sortieren oder in der Prozedur FOCW mit einem WRITE-Befehl auf einen File zu schreiben.

Im einzelnen sind derzeit im ZDF folgende Benutzerprogramme in SPSS^X verfügbar:

CASES   ermittelt die Anzahl der Fälle im aktiven SPSS^X-File oder für jede SPLIT FILE-Gruppe;

CONVERT   wandelt eine Variable im A1-Format in ihr numerisches Äquivalent um und etikettiert die numerische Variable mit dem zugehörigen Mnemonic;

DUMP   listet den Dictionary-Inhalt für Fälle (optional für alle Variablen, für Variablen mit gültigen und User missing-Werten oder nur mit gültigen Werten);

FOCR   liest FOCUS-Daten und Hold-File, ergänzt das Dictionary um Informationen der FOCUS Master-Dateibeschreibung und erstellt ein aktives SPSS^X-File mit Dictionary-Informationen (auch als stand alone-Programm in FORTRAN 77 entwickelt);

FOCW   schreibt von einem aktiven SPSS^X-File eine FOCUS Master-Dateibeschreibung;

GINI   errechnet den GINI-Koeffizienten für alle gültigen Fälle oder für jede SPLIT FILE-Gruppe und erstellt ein File für die Werte einer Lorenz-Kurve für die Weiterverarbeitung in einem Grafiksystem;

HDIMP   einfache Hot-Deck-Imputation Prozedur zur Ersetzung fehlender Werte nach dem Verfahren, den letzten gültigen Wert als Ersatzwert zu verwenden;

LABEL   fügt einer numerischen Variablen Value Labels hinzu, die in einer String-Variablen desselben aktiven Files stehen;

NRM   normiert Fallgewichte auf einen Mittelwert von 1 für einen aktiven SPSS^X-File insgesamt oder für jede SPLIT FILE-Gruppe;

TEXT   listet lange String-Variablen, sofern diese nicht Blank sind, und druckt einen zusätzlichen, davon abgetrennten Header nach Benutzervorgabe (zum Beispiel Fallauswahl).

5 Bewertung

5.1 Positive Aspekte

Die grundsätzliche Möglichkeit, USERPROCs schreiben zu können, ist zunächst einmal schon positiv zu bewerten. Ebenso sind einige Details auch nach meinen Erfahrungen auch mit anderen Programmsystemen gut gelöst und sollen hier explizit genannt werden:

- Die Anbindung von USERPROCs und USERGETs ist im Vergleich zu mir sonst bekannten Verfahren[5] schnell (Laufzeit des Linkjobs) und vor allem ohne ein vollständig neues Linken von $SPSS^X$ möglich. Dies scheint mir besonders wichtig, da damit jeder Benutzer - und nicht nur der $SPSS^X$-Systembetreuer - individuelle Programme implementieren kann.

- Die automatische Fehlerbehandlung durch $SPSS^X$ bei Problemen in USERPROCs und USERGETs ist gut. Faktisch alle Benutzerfehler können damit so abgefangen werden, daß $SPSS^X$ nicht "abstürzt".

5.2 Negative Aspekte

5.2.1 Details

Bei der Lösung konkreter Probleme ergeben sich nach meinen Erfahrungen zahlreiche Schwierigkeiten, die hier beispielhaft erwähnt werden:

- Nicht alle Dictionärinformationen sind greifbar; es fehlen die Recordtypen General Information, Documents[6], bzw. auch Detailinformationen hieraus (zum Beispiel File Label).

- Notwendige Informationen während der Verarbeitung sind nicht zugreifbar. Bei der SPLIT FILE-Verarbeitung ist nur ein Wechsel der Gruppe feststellbar, nicht aber, welche Variable für den SPLIT herangezogen wurde, welches die Merkmalsausprägung der aktuell zur Verarbeitung anstehenden Split-Variablen und gegebenenfalls ihr Value Label ist; ebenso sind die Dictionärinformationen der WEIGHT-Variablen nicht zugänglich.

- Die für die Outputgestaltung notwendigen Parameter, die im Customizing festgelegt sind oder mit SET für den jeweiligen Lauf angegeben wurden, sind nicht verfügbar. Die Outputgestaltung ist daher starr oder muß überflüssigerweise in der jeweiligen Prozedur als Befehl eingegeben werden.

5.2.2 Grundsätzliche Kritik

- Ein gravierender und auch nicht zu entschuldigender Mangel ist, daß nach wie vor alle Benutzerprogramme in $SPSS^X$ in dem völlig veralteten FORTRAN Standard 66 geschrieben werden müssen. Gerade für die Verarbeitung von Dictionärinformationen (Textstrings) existieren in ihrer Umständlichkeit kaum

---

5) etwa die Implementation zusätzlicher Routinen in das Grafiksystem TELL-A-GRAF. Vgl. ISSCO Corp. (Hg.) (1989): TELL-A-GRAF User's Manual. Rev. 6.1. o.O.

6) Nähere Informationen zum Aufbau von $SPSS^X$-Systemfiles sind der Dokumentation: SPSS-X Data File Formats. SPSS Inc. Reports 1985 zu entnehmen, die für verschiedene Betriebssysteme vorliegt.

zu überbietende "Krücken". Fertige FORTRAN 77-Programme können somit nicht übernommen werden. Auch eine Adaptierung der von SPSS^X selbst zur Verfügung gestellten Druckertreibersoftware (TBREAD, Programmiersprache FORTRAN 77) ist nicht möglich. Bei USERGETs wird das File-Handling erschwert (fehlender OPEN- bzw. INQUIRE-Befehl in FORTRAN 66).

- USERPROCs können nur auf Daten zugreifen und nicht auf Zwischen- oder Endergebnisse. Meines Erachtens wäre es sinnvoll, neben dem Zugriff auf die Daten auch einen Zugriff auf Prozedurergebnisse zu haben, um eine eigene Druckaufbereitung oder grafische Darstellung[7] der Ergebnisse mit der jeweils verfügbaren Software zu ermöglichen. Diese Starrheit der Weiterverwendung von Output ist bekanntermaßen ein grundsätzlicher Mangel von SPSS^X, der keineswegs nur auf die USERCODE-Facility beschränkt ist. Für bessere Lösungen sei auf die in P-STAT für alle Prozeduren verfügbare Speicherungsmöglichkeit von Ergebnissen als Systemfiles verwiesen[8].

- Die Dokumentation von USERPROCs und USERGETs im INFO-File ist sehr benutzerunfreundlich; eine Update-Utility für INFO-Files oder die Möglichkeit, eigene INFO-Files mit dem SPSS^X INFO-File zu verbinden, könnten hier Abhilfe schaffen.

- Die Dokumentation für die Ersteller von USERPROCs und USERGETs ist unzureichend. Hinweise über die genaue Funktion von Programmen oder Speicherplatzerfordernisse beim Aufruf bestimmter Programme müssen häufig mit erheblichem Zeitaufwand durch Probieren erkundet werden.

Literatur

Horber, Eugene (1986): EDA Exploratory Data Analysis Package for Aggregate Data. Installation Guide an System Administrator Manual Level 1.9. Ms. Geneve.

ISSCO Corp. (Hg.) (1989): TELL-A-GRAF User's Manual. Rev. 6.1. o.O.

P-STAT Inc. (Hg.) (1989): P-STAT Users Manual, Vol I, Vol II, Release 2.11. o.O.

SPSS Inc. (Hg.) (1985): Adding User Programs to SPSS-X on IBM MVS and CMS Systems. SPSS Inc. Reports. o.O.

SPSS Inc. (Hg.) (1988): SPSS^X User's Guide. 3rd edition. SPSS, Chicago.

SPSS Inc. (Hg.) (1985): SPSS^X Data File Formats. SPSS Inc. Reports. o.O.

---

7) vgl. etwa die Realisierung im EDA Package von Horber (1986).
8) P-STAT 8 Users Manual. Vol I, Vol II, Release 2.11 .1989. P-STAT Inc.

Computerprogramme für Discrete Choice-Modelle in GAUSS und SAS/IML

A. Eymann und M. Kukuk

Abstract

The paper describes the estimation procedure of a model of qualitative choice between mutually exclusive categories and its statistical properties. Features of the computer programs in GAUSS and SAS-IML are given, stressing the differences between the two programming languages.

1 Ein mehrstufiges Discrete Choice-Modell

Die in den letzten Jahren zu beobachtende Entwicklung weg von Programmsystemen mit "benutzerfreundlichen", da bequemen black-box-Prozeduren, hin zu flexiblen, jedoch programmieraufwendigen Programmier"sprachen" erlaubt die Schätzung von neuen, differenzierten Modellen nach den Wünschen ihres "Autors".

Am Beispiel der sequentiellen Maximum Likelihood-Schätzung eines mehrstufigen "nested multinomial logit" (NMNL)-Modells[2] sollen die Vorteile der Programmierung in SAS/IML und GAUSS gegenüber der Benutzung vorgefertigter Programmsysteme für Discrete Choice-Modelle wie HLOGIT oder LIMDEP dargestellt werden. Zusätzlich werden die beiden Programmiersprachen in bezug auf die Lösung des vorgegebenen Problems gegeneinander abgewogen.

---

[1] Diese Arbeit entstand im Rahmen des Teilprojekts A2 im SFB 178 "Internationalisierung der Wirtschaft". Wir danken Herrn Prof. Dr. G. Ronning, der die Anregung und viele Hilfestellungen zu dieser Arbeit gegeben hat.

[2] Vgl. z.B. Amemiya (1985), S. 300ff.

Das zu schätzende Modell entstammt der ökonometrischen Nachfrageanalyse für diskrete Alternativen (Discrete Choice-Analyse): Für jede Alternative einer für alle Individuen vorgegebenen (individuenunabhängigen) Alternativenmenge wird die Wahrscheinlichkeit ihrer Wahl (d.h. Nutzenmaximalität) bestimmt. Unterstellt wird eine inter-individuell identische Struktur der (stochastischen) Nutzenfunktion bei Linearität in den Parametern und additiver Separabilität von deterministischem und stochastischem Teil. Die Alternativenmenge läßt sich aufspalten in tiefer verschachtelte Teilmengen von in zunehmendem Maße ähnlichen Alternativen, zwischen denen sich das Individuum sequentiell bis hin zur einzelnen Alternative entscheidet.

Der individuelle Nutzen einer Alternative oder Alternativenteilmenge ergibt sich aus den individuellen (sozioökonomischen) und alternativen(teilmengen)spezifischen Charakteristika. Unbeobachtbare Eigenschaften spiegeln sich im stochastischen Rest wider, für den in Anschluß an McFadden (1981) die Verallgemeinerte Extremwertverteilung[3] unterstellt wird.

Für ein dreistufiges Modell gilt:

$$F(\epsilon_1, \ldots, \epsilon_I) = \exp\Big\{-\sum_l b_l \Big\{\sum_{s \in B_l} a_s \Big[\sum_{j \in B_s} \exp(\rho_s^{-1} \epsilon_j)\Big]^{\frac{\rho_s}{\rho_l}}\Big\}^{\rho_l}\Big\} \qquad (1-1)$$

ϵ_i: Störterm der Alternative i

I: Zahl der Alternativen

a_s, b_l: knotencharakteristischer Parameter

ρ: Unähnlichkeitsparameter

B: Knoten

j: Alternativen der untersten Stufe

s: Knoten der mittleren Stufe

l: Knoten der obersten Stufe

Die im folgenden dargestellte sequentielle Schätzmethode nützt die Tatsache aus,

---

[3] Die Verallgemeinerte Extremwertverteilung (eine Erweiterung der Extremwertverteilung vom Typ B — Bezeichnung nach Johnson und Kotz (1972), S. 251) zeichnet sich durch explizite Integrierbarkeit aus. Zudem erlaubt sie die Modellierung von Korrelationen zwischen den Alternativen bzw. deren Teilmengen.

daß sich die Loglikelihoodfunktion des Gesamtmodells aufspalten läßt in die Summe der Loglikelihoodfunktionen der multinomialen Logit (MNL)-Modelle für jede Teilmenge jeder Stufe des zugrundeliegenden Entscheidungsbaums. Bei der Schätzung kann das einstufige Modell (unter Vernachlässigung von nicht-linearen Parameterrestriktionen) für jeweils unterschiedliche Individuen und unterschiedliche Alternativenteilmengen beliebig häufig verwendet werden; auch komplizierte Baumstrukturen sind (fast) problemlos zu verarbeiten. Für ein dreistufiges Modell gilt:

$$L = \sum_{t=1}^{T} \sum_{j \in B_s} \sum_{s \in B_l} \sum_{l} y_{tjsl} \cdot \ln P_{tjsl} \qquad (1-2)$$

$t: 1, \ldots, T$: Index des Individuums

y_{tjsl}: Indikatorvariable für die Wahl der Alternative j der Knoten s und l

$$y_{tjsl} = \begin{cases} 1 & \text{für } j = i \\ 0 & \text{sonst} \end{cases}$$

i: tatsächlich gewählte Alternative

P_{tjsl}: Auswahlwahrscheinlichkeit der Knoten l und s sowie der Alternative j durch Individuum t

P_{tjsl} läßt sich darstellen als das Produkt der bedingten Auswahlwahrscheinlichkeiten ($P_{tj|sl}$, $P_{ts|l}$ und P_{tl}) für jede Stufe des Entscheidungsbaums:

$$P_{tjsl} = P_{tj|sl} \cdot P_{ts|l} \cdot P_{tl} \qquad (1-3)$$

Als Beispiel sei die Form der Auswahlwahrscheinlichkeit eines Knotens der mittleren Stufe dargestellt:

$$\sum_{s \in B_l} P_{tjs|l} = \frac{b_l \left\{ \sum_{s \in B_l} a_s [\sum_{j \in B_s} \exp(\rho_s^{-1} \overline{U}_{tj})]^{\frac{\rho_s}{\rho_l}} \right\}^{\rho_l}}{\sum_l b_l \left\{ \sum_{s \in B_l} a_s [\sum_{j \in B_s} \exp(\rho_s^{-1} \overline{U}_{tj})]^{\frac{\rho_s}{\rho_l}} \right\}^{\rho_l}} \qquad (1-4)$$

wobei der Wert der (deterministischen) indirekten Nutzenfunktion $\overline{U}_{tj}$ sich wie folgt ermitteln läßt:

$$\overline{U}_{tj} = x^*_{tjsl}\beta + w^*_{tsl}\gamma + r^*_{tl}\lambda + z_t\alpha_{jsl} + y_t\delta_{sl} + v_t\kappa_l \qquad (1-5)$$

x^*_{tjsl}: Charakteristika der Alternativen

w^*_{tsl}: Charakteristika der Teilmenge B_s

r^*_{tl}: Charakteristika der Teilmenge B_l

z_t, y_t, v_t: sozioökonomische Variable

$\alpha_{jsl}, \delta_{sl}, \kappa_l, \beta, \gamma, \lambda$: Parameter

Bemerkenswert ist die Tatsache, daß die verwendete Informationsmenge von Stufe zu Stufe bis zum Ausgangspunkt des Entscheidungsbaums ansteigt, da der Informationsgehalt der Alternativen (bereits geschätzter) nachgelagerter Stufen als alternativencharakteristische Variable ("inclusive value") in die MNL-Schätzung eingeht. (Der im Bereich zwischen null und eins liegende "Unähnlichkeitsparameter" dieser Variable ist ein Maß für die Unähnlichkeit der Alternativen der betrachteten Teilmenge.) Diese Asymmetrie in der Informationsverwendung bewirkt Ineffizienz der (konsistenten) geschätzten Parameter; die Standardfehler sind stark nach unten verzerrt.

Kernstücke der Schätzung sind der individuelle Vektor der Indikatorvariablen, die für die tatsächlich gewählte Alternative den Wert eins (sonst null) annimmt, sowie die Design-Matrix der exogenen Variablen. Diese entsteht durch Stapelung der Teilmatrix der alternativencharakteristischen Variablen auf die normierte Teilmatrix der "Dummyvariablen"[4], die die sozioökonomischen Variablen repräsentieren. Gradient und Hessesche Matrix sind in Matrixschreibweise leicht zu programmieren und ergeben sich wie folgt:

$$\nabla L = \sum_t X_t(Y_t - P_t) \quad (1\text{-}6)$$

$$-\mathrm{E}(H) = \sum_t X_t A_t X'_t; \quad A_t = D(P_t) - P_t P'_t \quad (1\text{-}7)$$

∇L: Gradient

H: Hessesche Matrix

X_t: Matrix der exogenen Variablen des einstufigen Modells

Y_t: Indikatorvariable

P_t: Vektor der individuellen Auswahlwahrscheinlichkeiten

$D(P_t)$: Diagonalmatrix aus P_t

---

[4] Zum Aufbau dieser Matrix siehe auch Abschnitt 2.

Aufwendig hingegen ist die Korrektur der Kovarianzmatrix nach McFadden (1981). Für diese Korrektur sind für jedes MNL-Teil-Modell die Teilmatrizen des Erwartungswerts der gemischten zweiten Ableitungen nach den Parametern der entsprechenden und aller nachgelagerter Stufen zu ermitteln. Mithilfe einer Rekursionsformel ließe sich das Matrizenprodukt aus diesen unteren Dreiecksmatrizen, dem Erwartungswert der Hesseschen Matrizen sowie den transponierten Matrizen der gemischten Ableitungen zeitsparend berechnen.

2 Programmierung der Schätzprozedur

Insgesamt ist die Programmierung eines sequentiell zu schätzenden NMNL-Modells als sehr einfach zu bezeichnen, da derselbe Rechenvorgang der Schätzung eines MNL-Modells beliebig oft und mit beliebiger Zahl von Alternativen und Variablen wiederholt werden kann.

Zur Schätzung des Modells (1-2) konnte trotz der Möglichkeit der sequentiellen Behandlung kein bereits vorhandenes Programm bzw. Modul verwendet werden. Anders als in HLOGIT, das die FIML-Schätzung eines bis zu dreistufigen Modells erlaubt, sind die exogenen Variablen auf allen Stufen des hier behandelten Modells angesiedelt. LIMDEP, mittels dessen nur einstufige MNL-Modelle geschätzt werden können, konnte nicht verwendet werden, da es den "inclusive value", der zur Schätzung der jeweils höheren Stufe benötigt wird, nicht liefert. Die sequentielle Schätzung eines NMNL-Modells ist daher mit diesen Programmsystemen nicht möglich. Innerhalb des GAUSS-Pakets ist die Prozedur $MAXLIK$ zur Maximierung einer Likelihoodfunktion bereitgestellt, doch auch diese konnte nicht verwendet werden, da die Spezifizierung der Likelihoodfunktion (ggf. auch erste und zweite Ableitung) notwendig ist. Gleichung (1-2) zeigt, daß sich für jede Stufe des Modells die Likelihoodfunktion aus der Summierung über alle Personen ergibt:

$$L = \sum_{i=1}^{N} L_i \qquad (2-1)$$

Gleiches gilt für den Gradientenvektor. Dies zeigt die Komplexität der Berechnung der Funktionen gerade bei großen Datenmengen. Daraus ergibt sich die Notwendigkeit der individuellen Programmierung des Lösungsweges. Es wurde in diesem Fall GAUSS gewählt, da die Programmierung in Matrixschreibweise die Schreibarbeit erheblich reduziert. Außerdem ist GAUSS aufgebaut wie andere einfache Programmiersprachen (z.B. Pascal). Exemplarisch seien hier folgende Möglichkeiten genannt:

- Schleifen

- Konditionale Anweisungen

- Unterprogramme (mit lokalen und auch globalen Variablen)

- Elementweise Operationen

Zusätzlich sind für den statistischen Anwender intrinsische Funktionen z.B. zur Invertierung, Determinantenbestimmung, Eigenwertberechnung und Cholesky-Dekomposition von Matrizen von besonderem Interesse.

Der Aufbau des Programms ist ähnlich dem für die Schätzung des multinomialen Logit Modells (MNL). Das Programm wird für jede Stufe separat angewendet. Es besteht aus den vier Unterprogrammen *WMAT, PARAM, INCL* und *COVAR*. In der Prozedur *WMAT* wird die Matrix X_t der Gleichungen (1-6) und (1-7) so aufgebaut, daß die anschließende Parameterschätzung sich nicht von der des MNL Modells unterscheidet. Diese Matrix ergibt sich aus

$$X_t = I \otimes V_{sozio} \quad , \qquad (2-2)$$

wobei $\otimes$ das Kronecker Produkt bezeichnet, was in GAUSS bereitgestellt ist, und V_{sozio} der Vektor der sozioökonomischen Variablen des Individuums t ist. Zeilenweise werden noch die kategorienabhängigen Variablen hinzugefügt[5]. Daraufhin werden die Parameter mit Hilfe der *Scoring Methode* geschätzt. Die Parameter der Iteration $(i+1)$ ergeben sich dabei durch

$$\theta^{(i+1)} = \theta^{(i)} - s \cdot \mathrm{E}(H^{(i)}) \nabla L^{(i)} \qquad (2-3)$$

Der Gradientenvektor ∇L und die *Fisher Informationsmatrix* $-\mathrm{E}(H)$ sind gegeben durch Gleichungen (1-6) und (1-7). GAUSS enthält auch intrinsische Funktionen

---

[5] Vgl. Maddala (1983) S. 75

zur Berechnung von Gradientenvektor und Hessematrix, doch dazu ist die Berechnung der Likelihoodfunktion zu aufwendig. Diese Funktionen berechnen ∇L und H numerisch, so daß Vorsicht bei deren Anwendung geboten ist. Das s in Gleichung (2-3) ist gleich eins, falls $L(\theta^{(i+1)}) > L(\theta^{(i)})$ ist. Wenn dies nicht gegeben ist, wird s solange sukzessiv halbiert, bis sich ein $\theta^{(i+1)}$ ergibt, für das die ebengenannte Bedingung erfüllt ist (*Backtracking-Methode*[6]). Wegen Flachheiten in der global-konkaven Likelihoodfunktion ist der Einbau dieser Backtracking Methode unerläßlich.

Die Prozedur *INCL* berechnet den Inclusive Value. Schließlich ist zur Korrektur der Kovarianzmatrix der Parameter noch die Prozedur *COVAR* nötig. Leider bieten weder GAUSS noch SAS/IML die Möglichkeit der mehr als zweifachen Indizierung, so daß sich bei der Umsetzung der Rekursionsformel für mehrstufige NMNL-Modelle einiger Schreibaufwand ergibt.

GAUSS hat bisher noch die elementare Einschränkung, daß einzelne Matrizen nicht mehr als 8190 Elemente haben dürfen. Bei mehreren Auswahlkategorien und mehreren Einflußvariablen kann diese Grenze leicht erreicht werden. Dies war der Anlaß, mit der Matrixprogrammiersprache IML innerhalb des SAS-Pakets zu arbeiten, welche diese Einschränkung zumindest auf dem Großrechner nicht hat[7]. Außer kleineren syntaktischen Unterschieden ließ sich eine Übereinstimmung zwischen den Programmiersprachen GAUSS und IML feststellen. Eine Konvertierung des GAUSS-Programms in IML war daher lediglich mit Schreibarbeit verbunden.

Literaturverzeichnis

Amemiya, Takeshi (1985): *Advanced Econometrics*. Oxford (Basil Blackwell).

Aptech Systems, Inc. (1988): *GAUSS - The GAUSS System Version 2.0*. Kent, Wash. (Aptech Systems, Inc.).

---

[6]Siehe Dennis und Schnabel (1983)
[7]Besonders bei Anwendung von *VMBATCH*. Dort wird meist mehr Arbeitsspeicher als sonst üblich bereitgestellt.

Börsch-Supan, Axel (1988): *Hierarchical Choice Models: Three Level Nested Multinomial Logit, HLOGIT (Version 5.4)*.

Dennis, J.E.jr. und Schnabel, R. (1983): *Numerical Methods for Unconstrained Optimization and Nonlinear Equations*. Prentice–Hall, Englewood Cliffs, New Jersey.

Greene, William H. (1985): *LIMDEP*, New York.

Johnson, Norman L. und Samuel Kotz (1972): *Distributions in Statistics: Continuous Multivariate Distributions*. New York (Wiley).

Küsters, Ulrich und Arminger, Gerhard (1989): *Programmieren in GAUSS: eine Einführung in das Programmieren statistischer und numerischer Algorithmen*. Stuttgart (Fischer).

Maddala, G. S. (1983): *Limited Dependent and Qualitative Variables in Econometrics*. Cambridge (Cambridge University Press).

Manski, Charles F. und Daniel McFadden (Hrsg.) (1981): *Structural Analysis of Discrete Data with Econometric Applications*. Cambridge, Mass. (MIT Press).

McFadden, Daniel (1981): Econometric Models of Probabilistic Choice. In: Manski, Charles F. und Daniel McFadden (Hrsg.): *Structural Analysis of Discrete Data with Econometric Applications*. Cambridge, Mass. (MIT Press), 198–272.

SAS Institute Inc. (1985): *SAS/IML User's Guide, Version 5 edition*. Cary, NC. (SAS Institute Inc.).

GLAMOUR: Analysis of Cross-sectional and Longitudinal Data with Generalized Linear Models

L. Fahrmeir, H. Frost, W. Hennevogl, H. Kaufmann (†), and T. Kranert

Summary

GLAMOUR is an interactive program for regression analysis of cross-sectional, time series, panel and discrete time survival (event history) data. Response variables may be metric, ordered or unordered multicategorical, or counted. Modelling of data is based on extensions of generalized linear models. Beyond estimation and testing, procedures for variable selection and graphical diagnostics, e.g. for residual and influence analysis, are included.

1. Introduction. Univariate generalized linear models have been introduced by Nelder and Wedderburn (1972) as a unifying family of models for nonstandard regression analysis of cross-sections with normal as well as nonnormal responses. This original class of GLM's has been in extended in various ways by many authors. Multivariate GLM's include multinomial models for unordered or ordered multicategorical data, see. e.g. Amemiya (1986), Tutz (1988). For time series and panel data, dynamic extensions of GLM's of the ARX–(autoregressive with exogenous variables) type are obtained by modelling the current mean of the response conditional on past responses and on current and past covariates. Furthermore, discrete time survival models are closely related to multinomial models for panel data, see Blossfeld, Hamerle and Mayer (1986), Hamerle and Tutz (1989).

The program package GLAMOUR (Generalized Linear Advanced Modelling, University of Regensburg) is designed for analysis in these more general situations. Beyond univariate GLM's, GLAMOUR covers *models* for
- ordered or unordered multicategorical responses, e.g. the multinomial logit model, cumulative (threshold) models, sequential models, two-step response models,
- for time series and panel data,

(†) Heinz L. Kaufmann died in a tragical rock climbing accident on 8/9/1989. His ideas and his work had a most important influence on the development of GLAMOUR. We will never forget him.

- discrete time survival (event history) data, e.g. the grouped Cox model, the model of Aranda–Ordaz, the discrete proportional hazards model.

For these models, the following *statistical procedures* are available:
- estimation and testing, variable selection with several options, graphical diagnostics for residual and influence analysis.

The *user interface* is controlled by menues and masks, allowing convenient handling and description of data, choice of models and statistical procedures, and control of input and output. Currently, GLAMOUR runs under MS-DOS on IBM-compatible microcomputers.

The following sections give a survey on models and statistical procedures contained in GLAMOUR, together with some information concerning its implementation. A detailed exposition may be found in the user's guide to GLAMOUR (Fahrmeir u.a., 1989).

2. Data

All types of data which can be analyzed in GLAMOUR consist in observations on a set of variables which can be metric or (multi-) categorical, with categories ordered or unordered.

For cross-sectional data, time series and panel data, the set of variables consists of a variable of primary interest, the response variable y, and a vector x of covariates.

Due to the distributional assumptions on y, see Section 3, a number of nonstandard regression situations can be handled. Thus responses y may be binary (yes/no) or multicategorical (very good, good,..., bad, very bad) answers in a questionnaire, or counts of purchases, demand of a certain good, occurrence of illness, etc.

(i) Cross-sectional data are observations (y_i, x_i), $i = 1,..., n$, of (y,x) for each unit of a sample of size n, the 'number of cases'. Especially for categorical variables, there may be units with equal values of (y, x). Then the data can be grouped, i.e. only different values of y, x and their frequencies observed in the sample are needed for statistical analysis. Such grouping of data considerably reduces working space and computation time, and GLAMOUR makes efficient use of this possibility. However, for easier notation, this paper is confined to individual data.

(ii) Time series data are observations (y_s, x_s), $s = 1,..., t$, on (y,x), made for a single unit at discrete times s. Whereas classical time series models assume responses to be (approximately) normal, categorical and discrete valued time series, e.g. meteorological data (rain/no rain on days) or purchase data (number of purchases in periods) can be analyzed with GLAMOUR.

(iii) Panel data consist in observations (y_{is}, x_{is}) for each unit i, $i = 1,..., n$, of a population, made at discrete times $s = 1,..., t$. Panel data with categorical responses are obtained e.g. in business tests (as the 'IFO-Konjunkturtest'). On a monthly basis, a large sample of firms answers questions on the tendency ('increase', 'no change', 'decrease') of variables such as production, orders at hand, state of business, etc.

(iv) Discrete time survival or duration times arise in the following situation: For a cross-section of units i, $i = 1,\ldots, n$, it is observed whether a certain event ('death', 'end of unemployment') or one of several absorbing states ('competing risks') has occured within one of t time intervals ('weeks', 'months') $s = 1,\ldots,t$. The data consist in observed discrete survival (or duration) times t_i, covariates x_i, and state variables y_i, $i = 1,\ldots, n$. The state variable y is m-categorical, with values $1,\ldots, m-1$ corresponding to m-1 different absorbing states while $y = m$ stands for a censored observation.

3. Models

3.1 Univariate models for cross-sectional data

This is the situation for which 'classical' univariate GLM's have been introduced. The data (y_i, x_i), $i = 1,\ldots, n$, are assumed to be a sequence of independent observations. The conditional distribution of $y_i | x_i$ is specified in the following way:

(i) Conditional on x_i, the distribution of y_i is a member of a one-dimensional exponential family with mean $\mu_i = E(y_i | x_i)$.

(ii) The mean μ_i is related to the covariate vector x_i

$$\mu_i = h(z_i'\beta), \quad g(\mu_i) = z_i'\beta$$

where

β is a vector of unknown parameters, dim $(\beta) = p$,

z_i is a *design vector*, dim $(z_i) = p$, a function $z_i = z_i(x_i)$ of the covariates

h is a (one-to-one) *response function*,

g the *link function*, the inverse of h.

As an option, a 'nuisance parameter' ϕ can be introduced.

Univariate GLM's are completely specified by choice of the exponential family, the response (link) function and the design vector. The current version of GLAMOUR contains the following options:

1. Exponential families.

– normal, for (non-)linear models with (approximately) normal responses,

– binomial, for binary responses,

– Poisson, for counted data, e.g. frequencies in contingency tables,

– gamma, for nonnegative continuous responses.

2. Response (link) functions.
- linear, for linear normal and nonnormal models,
- logistic, for binary logit models,
- double exponential function, for survival data,
- exponential (logarithmic), for loglinear models,
- inverse function $h(\gamma)$, for gamma distributed responses.

3. The design vector.
It usually contains the '1' to account for a 'grand mean' parameter. Metric covariates can be included directly, while categorical covariates are represented as a vector of dummies. GLAMOUR carries out this coding automatically, with the options of effect or dummy coding. Furthermore, interactions between covariates can be included by a corresponding specification in a 'fit-mask'.

Exponential families, response function and design vectors can be specified independent of each other, the user being responsible for a reasonable combination of the three basic model components.

3.2 Multinomial models for cross-sectional data with categorical responses.
For multicategorical responses, the multinomial distribution is the appropriate member of the exponential family. Responses are coded as vectors $y_i = (y_{i1},...,y_{iq})'$ of (0-1)-dummies for the first $q = m-1$ categories. For multinomial responses, conditional means $\mu_i = (\mu_{i1},...,\mu_{iq})'$, with $\mu_{ij} = E(y_{ij}|x_i), j = 1,...,q$, are conditional response probabilities $\pi_i = (\pi_{i1},...,\pi_{iq})$, with $\pi_{ij} = P(y_{ij} = 1|x_i)$. A multicategorical response model for a sequence of stochastically independent observations is specified by:
$$\mu_i = h(Z_i'\beta),$$
where
    β is a vector of unknown parameters, dim $(\beta) = p$,
    Z_i is a (p x q)-design matrix, a function $Z_i(x_i)$ of the covariates,
    h a q-dimensional response function.

Thus, multinomial models are specified by choice of the response function and the 'design'. The following options are available in GLAMOUR.

1. Response functions.
- linear,
- multivariate logistic,
- cumulative logistic,
- sequential logistic,

– double–cumulative logistic.

The last three response functions are suited for responses with ordered categories.

2. Designs.

The general form of admissible design matrices is

$$Z_i = \begin{bmatrix} z_i' & & & & w_i' \\ & \ddots & & 0 & \vdots \\ & & \ddots & & \vdots \\ & 0 & & \ddots & \vdots \\ & & & & z_i' & w_i' \end{bmatrix}$$

with z_i as a 'category specific' design vector and w_i as a 'global' design vector. Both design vectors are built up as in the univariate case of Section 3.1. However, z_i und w_i must not contain identical covariates. (In particular, the constant '1' must not occur in both.) Either z_i or w_i may be empty.

By appropriate specification of z_i and w_i many useful special designs can be generated, see Fahrmeir et al. (1989) for details. For example, the design $z_i = 1$, w_i a general design vector combined with the cumulative logistic response function results in the cumulative (threshold) logistic model for ordered categories.

3.3 Time Series and Panel Data

Time series (y_s, x_s), $s = 1,..., t$ with normal and nonnormal, e.g. multicategorical, responses can be analyzed in GLAMOUR in dynamic extensions of the models of Sections 3.1, 3.2. In view of the time dependence type of data, it is natural to consider conditional distributions and means of y_s, given present and past covariates and past responses, thereby dropping the independence assumption. In GLAMOUR past covariates and responses can be included in form of a fixed lag structure. Any (conditional) exponential family density is then determined by its conditional mean

$$\mu_s = E(y_s | x_s, ..., x_{s-m}, y_{s-1}, ..., y_{s-k}).$$

This conditional mean is modelled in analogy to the cross–sectional case by

$$\mu_s = h(Z_s' \beta),$$

with the same response functions and the same design as in 3.1, 3.2, however with design vectors z_s, w_s containing past values $y_{s-1}, ..., y_{s-k}$ (and possibly $x_{s-1}, ...$) as additional regressors. For the normal density combined with the linear response function, 'classical' ARX–models are obtained. Multinomial ARX–models for categorical time series are studied in detail in Fahrmeir and Kaufmann (1987), Kaufmann (1987).

Panel data (y_{is}, x_{is}), $i = 1,..., n$, $s = 1,..., t$, can be considered as a cross-section of simultaneous time series. Assuming observations from different units to be independent, models are specified by
$$E(y_{is}| x_{is},..., x_{i,s-m}, y_{i,s-1},..., y_{i,s-k}) = h(Z'_{is}\beta),$$
where the design vectors z_{is}, w_{is} are known functions of covariates $x_{is},...$ and of past responses $y_{i,s-1},...$

3.4 Discrete time survival and event history data

For this kind of data, discrete hazard rates
$$\lambda_{isj} = P(t_i = s, y_i = j| t_i \geq s, x_i), \quad i = 1,..., n, \quad j = 1,..., m-1$$
i.e. the probability that an absorbing state ($j = 1,..., m-1$) is reached in period s given 'survival' up to s and the covariate vector x_i, play a fundamental role in modelling. The process generating the data may be interpreted, for each unit i, as a sequence of multinomial decisions (conditional on 'survival' up to s) between 'survival' and absorption into one of the absorbing states ('competing risks'). This relationship to multinomial models is described in Blossfeld, Hamerle and Mayer (1986) and, in more detail, in Hamerle and Tutz (1989). In analogy to binomial and multinomial models, the vector $\lambda_{is} = (\lambda_{is1},..., \lambda_{is,m-1})$ of hazard rates is modelled by
$$\lambda_{is} = h(Z_{is}'\beta).$$
Due to the particular kind of data, special response functions and designs are implemented in GLAMOUR, including e.g. the grouped Cox model, the discrete proportional hazards model, the model of Aranda-Ordaz, and linear and logistic models for competing risks.

4. Statistical procedures

For each of the models of Section 3, GLAMOUR provides procedures for statistical analysis.

4.1 Estimation

Parameters β can be estimated by the method of (unweighted) least squares or maximum likelihood. Numerically, ML estimation is carried out by Fisher scoring iterations, with initial values obtained from LS estimation as a standard option. In addition to the estimates $\hat{\beta}$, t- and p- values as well as the complete (asymptotic) covariance matrix $[F(\hat{\beta})]^{-1}$ (the inverse of the information matrix $F(\hat{\beta})$) are available.

4.2 Testing

Tests on the significance of a subvector β_r of β, i.e. test of
$$H_0: \beta_r = 0 \text{ against } H_1: \beta_r \neq 0$$

are of special interest since they can be used to test models against submodels. For this testing problem, the likelihood ratio, the Wald and the score statistic are available in GLAMOUR. To compute the LR statistic, ML estimates $\hat{\beta}$ and $\tilde{\beta}_r$ are required, whereas for the Wald resp. score statistic only the estimate $\hat{\beta}$ resp. $\tilde{\beta}_r$ is needed. Thus, to save computing time, it can be of advantage to choose the Wald or the score test. For the more general linear hypothesis

$$H_0: C\beta = \xi \text{ against } H_1: C\beta \neq \xi,$$

with C and ξ to be specified by the user, the Wald test is implemented in GLAMOUR.

4.3 Variable selection

Wald- and score tests of subvectors are the basic tools for the fully automatic backward and forward selection procedures in GLAMOUR. The user can choose between (i) pure backward, pure forward and combined forward/backward selection, and (ii) between

- selection of scalar components of the covariate vector,
- selection of complete variables, i.e. all dummies of multicategorical variables,
- hierarchical selection, i.e. simultaneous selection of main and interaction effects of variables.

Backward and forward steps are carried out by corresponding Wald and score tests for associated parameter subvectors.

4.4 Graphical procedures residual and influence analysis

GLAMOUR contains a number a graphical tools to assess the fit of estimated models, including plots of observed versus fitted values, of fitted and observed values versus index or time, etc. Diagnostic methods of residual and influence analysis by graphical means display model departures, outliers or influential observations. For the normal linear model, Cook and Weisberg (1982) provide an extensive survey of such methods. Several authors extended the ideas to univariate GLM's and multinomial models, see Hennevogl and Kranert (1988) and the references therein. The diagnostic measures in GLAMOUR rest upon a general definition of residuals and hat matrix. The following graphical procedures are available:

- half normal probability plots of absolute (standardized Pearson) residuals,
- χ^2-probability plots of squared residuals,
- residuals versus fitted values,
- residuals versus independent variables,
- residuals versus index,
- Cook distances versus index,
- plot of leverage-values (diagonal elements of the generalized hat matrix) versus

index.

5. Implementation

GLAMOUR is implemented for IBM XT-/AT-personal computers or compatibles with minimum RAM 640 KB and MS-DOS version 2.10 or higher. Further requirements are a screen and printer able to work in graphic or test mode and a hard disk with minimal 2.0 MB free capacity.

The user interface is a specially developed menu- and mask-program. It includes an interactive help-system and interactive checks for errors and plausibility of the user inputs.

There are nearly no size limits on the data that can be analysed with GLAMOUR. The only restriction is the number of estimable parameters, with a maximum of about 350 parameters. Computation time is minimized by grouping of data as an option in all procedures.

References

Amemiya, T. (1985): Advanced econometrics, Harvard Univ. Press, Cambridge, Mass.

Blossfeld, H.P., Hamerle, A., Mayer, K.U. (1986): Ereignisanalyse, Campus Verlag, Frankfurt a.M.

Cook, R., Weisberg, S. (1982): Residuals and influence in regression, Chapman and Hall, London.

Fahrmeir, L., Kaufmann, H. (1987): Regression models for non-stationary categorical time series, J. Time Series Anal. 8, 147-160.

Fahrmeir, L., Frost, H., Hennevogl, W., Kaufmann, H., Kranert, T. (1989): Benutzerhandbuch für GLAMOUR V 2.x.

Hamerle, A., Tutz, G. (1989): Diskrete Modelle zur Analyse von Verweildauern und Lebenszeiten, Campus, Frankfurt a.M.

Hennevogl, W., Kranert, T. (1988): Residual and influence analysis for multicategorical response models. Regensburger Beiträge zur Statistik und Ökonometrie 5.

Kaufmann, H. (1987): Regression models for nonstationary categorical time series: asymptotic estimation theory, Ann. Statist. 15, 79-98.

Nelder, J. Wedderburn, R. (1972): Generalized linear models, Chapman and Hall, London.

Tutz, G. (1988): Modelle für kategoriale Daten mit ordinalem Skalenniveau: Parametrische und nonparametrische Ansätze, Habilitationsschrift, Universität Regensburg.

SuSa - Ein GAUSS Programm zur Stichprobentheorie

S. Gabler

Summary

SuSa is a package of programs and procedures for Survey Sampling. SuSa contains various sampling selection procedures, estimators for the total and variance estimators. It is written in GAUSS 2.0. The basic definitions are similiar to those in W.G.Cochran(1977) "Sampling Techniques" and K.M.Wolter(1985) "Introduction to Variance Estimation".
There is a demo program showing the application and usage of the procedures.

1. Was ist SUSA?

Wer Stichproben aus endlichen Gesamtheiten ziehen möchte, wird auf der Suche nach geeigneten Programmteilen in den gängigen Programmpaketen kaum fündig werden. Dies hat uns veranlaßt, SuSa zu entwickeln. SuSa ist die Abkürzung von **Survey Sampling**. SuSa ist als ergänzendes Modul der Programmiersprache GAUSS Version 2.0 anzusehen und umfaßt die wichtigsten Algorithmen der Stichprobentheorie.
Um eine einheitliche Symbolik zu gewährleisten, sind die

Auswahlverfahren	S_...
Schätzfunktionen	E_...
Varianzen der Schätzfunktionen	Var_...
Schätzungen der Varianzen	V_...

als Procs geschrieben und werden wie Funktionen aufgerufen. Eine Erweiterung der Verfahren ist jederzeit möglich.

Das folgende einfache GAUSS Programm erläutert die Handhabung von SuSa.

Beispiel: Standard Strategie

Gegeben sei eine Erhebungsgesamtheit vom Umfang $N0=5$; $n=3$ Einheiten werden ausgewählt. y0 sei der Vektor der Ausprägungen des interessierenden Merkmals für die

Untersuchungseinheiten (i.a. unbekannt). Zu schätzen ist die Summe dieser Ausprägungen mittels einer Stichprobe vom Umfang n=3. Die Auswahl (simple random sampling) wird durch S_SRS(N0,n) vorgenommen und die ausgewählten Einheiten in s gespeichert. Die Ausprägungen des Untersuchungsmerkmals in der Stichprobe werden in y festgehalten. Der Schätzwert -Stichprobenmittel mal Umfang der Gesamtheit - wird über E_T(y,s) der Variablen e zugeordnet.

Entsprechendes gilt für die Schätzung der Varianz des Schätzers V_T(y,N0) und die Varianz des Schätzers VAR_T(y,N0), die in der Regel wieder unbekannt ist.

```
N0 = 5;
n = 3;
let y0 = 1 3 6 8 9;
s = s_srs(N0,n);
y = y0[s];
e = e_t(y,s);
v = v_t(y,n0);
var = var_t(y0,n);
```

(Mögliches) Resultat:

s = 4 2 5	ausgewählte Einheiten
y = 8 3 9	y-Werte in der Stichprobe
e = 33.333	Schätzung für Merkmalssumme
v = 34.444	Schätzung der Varianz des Schätzers
var = 37.667	Varianz des Schätzers

2. Das DEMO Programm

Ein DEMO Programm, das Beispiele zu verschiedenen Themen(1-7) der Stichprobentheorie enthält, soll die Verwendung und Möglichkeiten von SuSa verdeutlichen. Die Grafiken wurden mittels QUICK GRAPHICS von GAUSS erstellt.

Das Hauptmenü lautet:

TABLE OF CONTENTS

1. **Simple random sampling**
2. **Stratified sampling**
3. **Sampling with unequal probabilities**
4. **RHC-strategy**
5. **Two-phase sampling**
6. **Two-stage sampling**
7. **Systematic sampling**

Der erste Block enthält Beispiele zur uneingeschränkten Zufallsauswahl.

SIMPLE RANDOM SAMPLING

1. SRS (without replacement)
2. SRS (with replacement)
3. Standard strategy
4. Simulation (sample mean)
5. Comparison (standard / ratio strategy)
6. Ratio strategy (confidence intervals)
7. Superpopulation model (ratio estimator)
8. Regression estimator (LS)
9. Regression estimator (slope given)
10. Correlation coefficient (Bootstrapping)

Greifen wir Beispiel 1.6 heraus so erhalten wir:

```
          0.95-CONFIDENCE INTERVALS (RATIO STRATEGY)

    The population consists of   400   units.
    10   units will be selected by SRS.
    The ratio estimator is used to estimate   Σy_i .



           0.95-confidence intervals for   Σy_i  (■)




    80.56 % of the confidence intervals cover the true population total
```

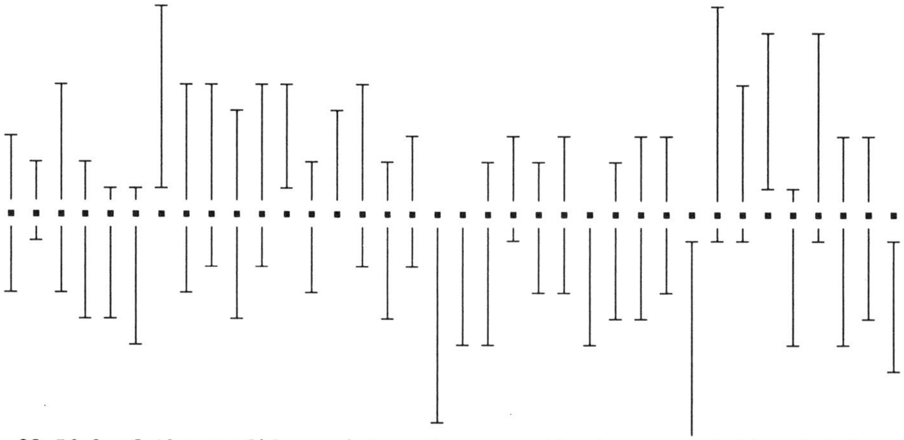

Bild 1: Konfidenzintervalle

Zweistufige Auswahl wird etwa in Beispiel 6.3 in einem Baumdiagramm veranschaulicht.

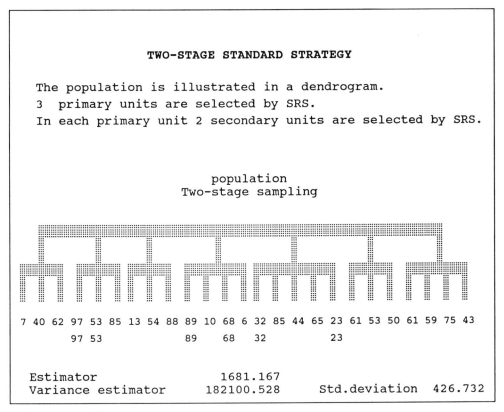

Bild 2: Baumdiagramm

Es lassen sich natürlich beliebig viele weitere Beispiele konstruieren, die zeigen, wie flexibel SuSa eingesetzt werden kann.

Literaturverzeichnis

Cochran W.C.(1977): Sampling Techniques, J.Wiley & Sons, New York.
GAUSS V.2.0 (1988): System and Graphics Manual, Aptech Systems,Inc., Kent.
K.M.Wolter (1985): Introduction to Variance Estimation, Springer, Heidelberg.

Non-Parametric Spline Regression by BATHSPLINE: Foundations and Application

M. G. Schimek

SUMMARY: Spline smoothing approaches for non-parametric regression curve fitting are well known (e.g. WAHBA 1975). However, their application is not widespread. SILVERMAN (1985) has proposed a method based on the special case of natural cubic splines, which is very attractive under both theoretical and practical considerations. Only linear time algorithms are involved. The smoothing parameter can be chosen by an asymptotic generalized cross-validation technique. BATHSPLINE (SILVERMAN & WATTERS 1984) is an interactive spline smoothing package in which the above mentioned methodology is implemented. Additional features are the ability to calculate inference regions and to carry out regression diagnostics. Data input, plot, print and edit facilities are also available. The usual regression model assumption of zero mean uncorrelated errors with a common variance can be relaxed by the assignment of weights to the observations. Unsatisfactory is the restriction to uncorrelated error structures. A spline-like smoothing procedure is considered to overcome this limitation (SCHIMEK 1988b). An empirical example is given in which the automatic choice of the smoothing parameter is essential. Practical experiences with the package are reported.

1 INTRODUCTION

Let us assume an univariate regression problem with one design variable and one response variable. There are three motivations a researcher might have, when carrying out that kind of regression analysis. The first is to explore and model the relationship between the design and the response variable. The second is to make predictions, and the third is to estimate certain properties of the regression curve such as derivatives. The non-parametric spline smoothing methodology we describe in this paper can be best applied when the main emphasis is on the first and third aspect but not on the second. However, spline regression can be a non-parametric tool for the identification of parametric relationships.

In certain situations non-parametric spline regression is not just an interesting alternative to parametric approaches like linear regression. Often it amounts to be the only way to model a functional relationship. This is certainly the case when background information is not obtainable which could lead to the identification of a parametric relationship. The same holds true when our aim is to recover unknown trends and their functionals from noisy observations. Data analytic demands of that sort frequently arise from social science and bio-science applications. There are several well-known spline smoothing approaches to answer these demands, such as those methods proposed by WAHBA (e.g. WAHBA 1975) and co-workers (e.g. CRAVEN & WAHBA 1979). However, their application is not widespread. From our point of view the reason is not so much the level of sophistication of the spline smoothing methodology than the lack of generally available software and the need for high resolution graphics. Such procedures are not included in statistical packages like BMDP or SAS in spite of their practical relevance. We recommend a special package for interactive spline smoothing by SILVERMAN & WATTERS (1984) named BATHSPLINE, which offers the comfort of MINITAB and similar statistical software.

2 NON-PARAMETRIC SPLINE REGRESSION

Let us have a regression problem

$$y_i = g(t_i) + e_i$$

with observations y_i on the response variable, design points t_i satisfying $t_1 \leq t_2 \leq \ldots \leq t_n$, and zero mean uncorrelated errors e_i with a common variance for $i=1,2,\ldots,n$. What we want to estimate is the regression function $g(t_i)$ which is assumed to be smooth. Non-parametric spline smoothing approaches are characterized by the so called modified sum of squares equation

$$SS(g) = \sum_{i=1}^{n} (y_i - g(t_i))^2 + \alpha \int_{t_1}^{t_n} (g^{(m)}(x))^2 \, dx ,$$

which is continuous and consists of an ordinary sum of squares part and a roughness penalty part weighted by a smoothing parameter α ($\alpha > 0$). The smoothing parameter is a central feature of that class of approaches. It controls the exchange between the roughness of the curve as measured by the roughness penalty and the infidelity to the observations as measured by the ordinary sum of squares expression. The curve estimate $\hat{g}_\alpha$, which is obtained by minimizing the above sum of squares equation for a given value of α, is a polynomial smoothing spline of degree 2m. That is, $\hat{g}_\alpha$ is a piecewise polynomial of degree 2m in each of the intervals made up of adjacent knots with the polynomial pieces grafted together so that the first 2m-2 derivatives of the function are continuous. In addition, if we require a polynomial of order m outside the interval $[t_1, t_n]$, the spline is called natural. This leads to the usual estimation problem defined in an infinite-dimensional Bayesian context (KIMELDORF & WAHBA 1970). A much easier estimation problem arises from the restriction to natural splines of order m=2 (cubic) as put forward by SILVERMAN (1985).

3 SILVERMAN'S CUBIC SPLINE APPROACH

SILVERMAN's (1985) cubic spline approach is based on the modified sum of squares equation

$$SS_{cub}(g) = \sum_{i=1}^{n} (y_i - g(t_i))^2 + \alpha \int_{t_1}^{t_n} (g''(x))^2 dx .$$

The regression function is assumed to be continuously twice differentiable and to have a square integrable second derivative. This is a direct consequence of the selected roughness penalty. For a given value of α, the curve estimate $\hat{g}_\alpha$ can be obtained by minimizing the above equation in a finite-dimensional Bayesian framework using linear combinations of specific splines (B-splines). As α goes to infinity, the solution $\hat{g}_\alpha$ tends to the least squares straight line.

There are several consequences, which are most welcome. The computational burden is reduced to linear time algorithms. The finite-dimensional Bayesian context facilitates the deduction and interpretation of inference regions and gives motivation to the prior choice of the smoothing parameter. However, the cubic spline approach can also be motivated from a data-driven point of view. It is the best choice when specific smoothness properties are not desired. This is usually the case in real data analysis. As a result the approach is attractive under both theoretical and practical considerations.

3.1 THE AUTOMATIC CHOICE OF THE SMOOTHING PARAMETER

The determination of the smoothing parameter is difficult unless the appropriate degree of smoothing is known a priori. The required degree of smoothing depends on the properties of the data set. The subjective choice of the value α certainly asks for a lot of experience. SILVERMAN (1984) offers a generalized asymptotic cross-validation method. The method is generalized for computational reasons (the exact trace of the projection matrix is not required) and hence cheaper than comparable cross-validation techniques.

The automatic choice of the smoothing parameter does not only provide for a starting point for further subjective adaptation. It also allows for comparative research tasks (e.g. in quasi-experimentation) and gives a non-subjective reference for outlier detection.

3.2 INFERENCE REGIONS AND REGRESSION DIAGNOSTICS

SILVERMAN's (1985) spline smoothing method can be seen as an empirical Bayes approach (the prior is given by the observations). As a result he was able to introduce posterior probability regions for both the regression curve and functionals of it. Inference regions for the regression curve allow to reduce the class of potential functional forms which can describe the relationship beween the design and the response variable. Inference regions for the derivatives permit the discussion of growth rates of estimated trends.

For regression diagnostics SILVERMAN (1985) proposes generalized studentized residuals (scale independent). Under the additional assumption of independent $N(0,1)$ distributed errors an approximate inference band for the studentized residuals can be calculated. At a 95 per cent confidence level a band of about plus/minus 2 centered around the zero mean is the result.

The automatic choice of the smoothing parameter together with inference bands for the standardized residuals allow to study the causation of outliers in a quasi-experimental setting characterized by a response variable of the following feature. The response variable y_i consists of two components, one, say y_i^c, which presumably depends on the implicit design variable and the other, $y_i^{\bar{c}}$, which definitely does not depend on the implicit design variable. When regression functions for both y_i^c and $y_i^{\bar{c}}$ are estimated under a fixed and automatically chosen smoothing parameter, identified outliers in one regression model should not imply outliers in the other and vice versa. Otherwise the impact of the implicate design variable on the dependent variable y_i^c has to be questioned. A real data example will be given later on.

3.3 ADDITIONAL FEATURES AND LIMITATIONS

The usual error assumptions of non-parametric spline regression are a common variance and uncorrelatedness. SILVERMAN's approach is different in that it allows to consider weighted observations by the adoption of a modified weighted sum of squares equation for a given sequence of weights. The error independence is still required. Dependent error structures (autoregressive or moving average) can be considered in a discrete roughness penalty approach by SCHIMEK (1988b) which assumes equally spaced design points and is formally related to cubic spline smoothing. If the application of this procedure to a data set gives reason to believe that the independence assumption violation is neglectable, SILVERMAN's approach, with all its sought after features, can be applied again.

4 THE BATHSPLINE PACKAGE

BATHSPLINE is an interactive spline smoothing package. It is based on SILVERMAN's cubic spline approach for non-parametric regression curve fitting as described in the previous section. This includes the handling of weighted observations, the cross-validatory choice of the smoothing parameter, inference regions, and regression diagnostics. Additional features are the ability to input, plot, print and edit the data and to control the style of the plots produced. The package expects the data to be read in by pairs (t_i, y_i), one per input line. Its operation is by the input of control words (in ASCII capitals). Each control word must be entered on a separate line as the first word following the prompt '→'. Some of them require one or two numerical codes. As BATHSPLINE is fully interactive, its operation is straight forward (for an example of a terminal session see later). The error messages are self-explanatory. BATHSPLINE has proofed very efficient and of high numerical stability in practice. This can also be said concerning the automatic choice of the smoothing parameter.

BATHSPLINE is implemented in FORTRAN IV. Input and output devices can be addressed by FORTRAN unit numbers. For interactive high resolution graphics one has to supply graphics routines or a graphics package. There is no standard graphics interface. BATHSPLINE can be used on workstations and mainframes. It can be obtained from Prof.B.W.Silverman, University of Bath, School of Mathematical Sciences, GB-BATH BA2 7AY.

5 EMPIRICAL EXAMPLES

The empirical examples are based on a research in social medicine (SCHIMEK 1988a). The task was to evaluate the suicide preventive measure of carbon monoxide reduction in the coal gas supply of a town. The data are monthly overall suicide rates of certain districts and corresponding carbon monoxide (CO) contents (samples of 60 observations). These overall suicide rates can be decomposed each into one part, in which the death was ascribed to carbon monoxide poisoning and into another part comprising all other kinds of death. Hence we can define a quasi-experiment with suicide rates presumably depending on the CO content and complementary suicide rates not depending on the CO content at all. This is exactly the situation to apply cubic spline smoothing in combination with all those features described in subsections 3.1 and 3.2. Each sample of suicide rates (dependent variable) has a common variance and consists of uncorrelated observations. Moreover, their distributions do not substantially depart from normality.

An interactive session analysing the functional relationship between a dependent variable and a design variable represented by a data set in FORTRAN unit 50 could be as follows:

BATHSPLINE	invoke the package
→ UNIT 50	data in FORTRAN unit 50
→ FREAD	read data in fixed format
format?→ (2F5.2)	FORTRAN format (2F5.2)
→ PDATA	plot the data
→ AGXV	estimate and plot the cubic spline following the automatic choice of the smoothing parameter
→ PRESID	calculate and plot studentized residuals
→ PARAMETER 1000	estimate and plot the cubic spline with the smoothing parameter value 1000
→ END	exit the package

To identify the general relationship between the CO contents and the suicide rates attributed to CO poisoning, we apply the mean CO contents (t_i) of all districts together with the corresponding averaged suicide rates (y_i). Our example session produces the following graphical output in **Figure 1**. In plot a we see the data and two regression functions, one for the automatic choice of the smoothing parameter (i.e. $\alpha = 7.25834$) and the other ($\alpha = 1000$) simulating straight line regression. As the plot indicates, the estimated cubic spline for $\alpha = 7.25834$ ($\hat{g}_1$) slightly departs from a linear function ($\hat{g}_2$). Plot b displays the studentized residuals of the 'automatic' spline fit. Three residuals are outside the 95 per cent inference band. These belong to the same observations identified as outliers in standard linear regression. They are caused by other agents than CO under both regression functions ($\hat{g}_1$ or $\hat{g}_2$).

The quasi-experiment is examplified in **Figure 2** for the data of one district. The design variable (t_i) is now time. Plots a and b show the CO suicide rates (y_i^c) and the non-CO suicide rates ($y_i^{\bar{c}}$), respectively, with the 'automatic' spline fits and inference regions based on the same α value. We identify almost linear trends which compensate each other to a certain extent. Plots c and d display the corresponding studentized residuals and their 95 per cent inference bands. The outliers of the fit for y_i^c do not imply outliers of the fit for $y_i^{\bar{c}}$ and vice versa. We conclude that the implicit design variable CO content (the explicit design variable is time) is primarily responsible for the fluctuations in the CO suicide rates. All other fluctuations, especially those of the non-CO suicide rates, can be assumed random.

REFERENCES

CRAVEN,P. and WAHBA,G. (1979). Smoothing noisy data with spline functions: estimating the correct degree of smoothing by the method of generalized cross-validation. Numer.Math., 31, 377-4o3.
KIMELDORF,G.S. and WAHBA,G. (1970). A correspondence between Bayesian estimation and stochastic processes and smoothing by splines. Ann.Math.Statist., 2, 495-502.
SCHIMEK,M.G. (1988a). Ein Evaluationsproblem in der Suizidforschung aus prozeßanalytischer Sicht. In MEIER,F. (ed.). Prozeßforschung in den Sozialwissenschaften. Anwendung zeitreihenanalytischer Methoden. G.Fischer, Stuttgart, 47-75.
SCHIMEK,M.G.(1988b). A roughness penalty regression approach for statistical graphics. In EDWARDS,D.& RAUN,N.E. (eds.). COMPSTAT Proceedings in Computational Statistics 1988. Physica, Heidelberg, 37-43.
SILVERMAN,B.W. (1984). A fast and efficient cross-validation method for smoothing parameter choice in spline regression. J.Amer.Statist.Assoc., 79, 584-589.
SILVERMAN,B.W.(1985). Some aspects of the spline smoothing approach to non-parametric regression curve fitting. JRSS B, 47, 1-52 (with discussion).
SILVERMAN,B.W.& WATTERS,G.W. (1984). BATHSPLINE. An interactive spline smoothing package. University of Bath.
WAHBA,G. (1975). Smoothing noisy data with spline functions. Numer.Math., 24, 383-393.

Figure 1

Plot a: Regression function for $\alpha = 7.25834$ ($\hat{g}_1$) and $\alpha = 1000$ ($\hat{g}_2$)

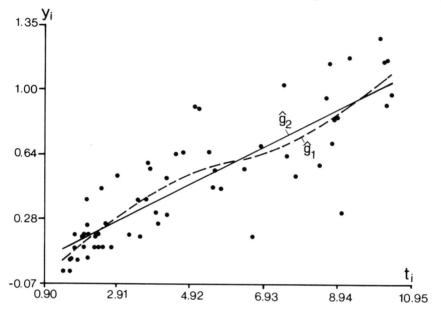

Plot b: Residuals for $\alpha = 7.25834$

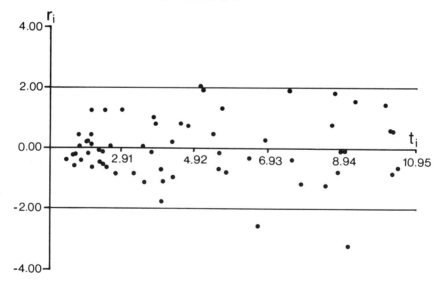

Figure 2

Plot a: Regression function and inference region for CO data ($\alpha=2568.77643$)

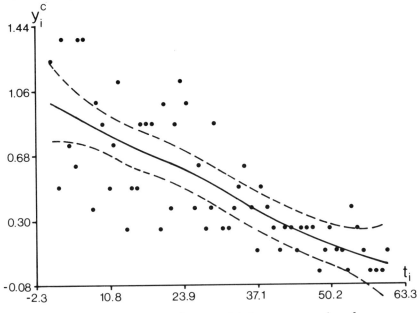

Plot b: Regression function and inference region for non-CO data ($\alpha=2568.7743$)

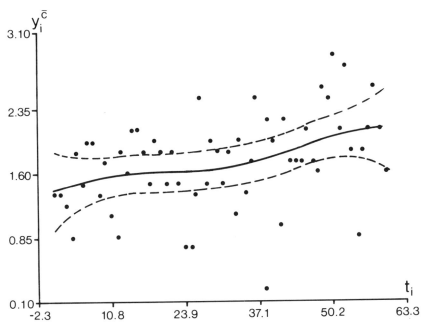

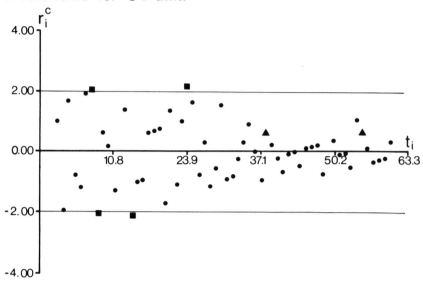

Plot c: Residuals for CO data

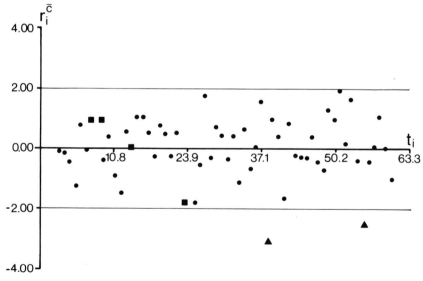

Plot d: Residuals for non-CO data

Graphik und explorative Datenanalyse

F. Faulbaum, R. Haux und K.-H. Jöckel (Hrsg.) (1990). SoftStat '89
Fortschritte der Statistik-Software 2. Stuttgart: Gustav Fischer, 237 - 248

Tools and Concepts in Data Analysis

G. Sawitzki

Summary

Data analysis has two aims: finding informative features in data, and bringing them to human perception. And, in doing this, data analysis has to avoid artifacts coming from random fluctuation, and from perception. Some of the tools, and some of the current concepts in data analysis are reviewed. Diagnostic indices are discussed as special statistics highlighting informative features of data. After an excursion, a look at interactive graphics and some of the statistics involved is given.

1. Introduction

As a spin off of classical statistics, isolated (unidimensional) numbers are often used to express informativity, for example when reporting achievable significance levels. Mere numbers give very restrictive ways to express informativity. The current progress in graphical facilities has made (two dimensional) displays a main utility for data analysis. As a consequence, displays is what data analysis is offering at first sight today.

It is not the point of data analysis to produce a display. The point is to know which displays to look at, and how to look at them. The first part of this talk will start with a classical display, the residual plot, and from here will lead to several diagnostic displays as used in data analysis. The current means to study these displays, namely interactive graphics and linked windows, are the second topic of this talk. In a final part, we will ask for the statistical meaning of these analyses and link back to "classical" aims like testing hypotheses, finding best fits etc.

Let us approach data analysis from well-known grounds and start with a linear regression situation. For illustration, we will use the Scottish Hill Runners' data (Atkinson 1986). This data set allows a substantial analysis by classical tools, while - even for those not trained in data analysis - clearly it is pushing classical approaches to their limits (Figure 1).

Our starting point is the classical linear model
$$Y = X\beta + e \qquad e \sim N(0,\sigma^2) \text{ iid.} \qquad (*)$$
Given a matrix of covariates $X=(X_1,...,X_k)'$, we would estimate the vector of unknown parameters by the least square method, so $\hat{\beta} = (X'X)^{-}X'Y$. This defines a fitting function $\hat{Y}(X) = X\hat{\beta}$ and we can use the residuals $r_i = Y_i - \hat{Y}(X_i)$ to judge the quality of the fit by looking at the coefficient of determination $R^2 = (SSY-SSr) / SSY$, where $SSY = \Sigma (Y_i - \bar{Y})^2$, $SSr = \Sigma (r_i - \bar{r})^2$. To check for the validity of the underlying assumptions (linearity, homoskedasticity, error distri-

bution), the residual scatterplot of r_i against $\hat{Y}(X_i)$ would be consulted. Studying the plot of the residuals (Figure 2) is something any "classical" statistician would do to judge the appropriateness of assumptions of the model.

If the model (*) holds, there is no purpose to do any further analysis. Due to the random fluctuation, we would find structures and systematic features - but they will only be outcomes of random fluctuation. But to find features not covered by the model (*), to look for the unexpected, is a task for data analysis.

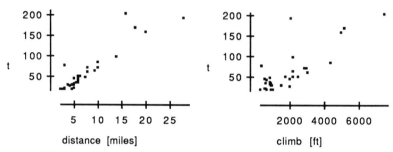

Figure 1: Scottish Hill Runners' data: dcatterplots of the target variable time t [min] against potential regressors distance and climb. Note the clear linear relation in the main regressor's scatterplot (time against distance) with three obvious outliers. What are the effects of these outliers ?

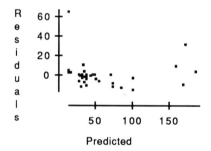

Figure 2: Residual plot for Scottish Hill Runners' data, with obviously non-homogeneous residuals and trend.

2. Diagnostic Indices and Diagnostic Plots

We will start again with the classical residual plot. By defining **diagnostic indices,** the information contained in this plot will be unfolded into several diagnostic plots for data analysis. These plots will exhibit different features inherent in the data.

To study the residual plot, we must define what we are looking for. We have to say what we mean by interesting, or informative events. A first idea would be to look at observations which are **"outliers"**, in the sense of observations which are special with respect to the regression. For this purpose the usual residual plot does not help: since all points affect the regression, any outlier would have influenced the regression, and hence its own residual. In this way, an outlier might produce unduly low residuals and thus hide itself. For outlier detection better residuals $r_{(i)}$ are constructed for data element i by calculating the regression omitting observation i, and then taking scale estimator and residuals from this regression. The "externally studentized residuals" $r_{(i)}/s_{(i)}$ are distributed under the hypothesis as Student's t on (n-p-1) degrees of freedom, and they are not inflated by gross errors in the ith observation. Unfortunately, like the residuals, these are not mutually independent - but there is no help against this. So instead of looking at the raw residual plot, one would look at the externally studentized residual plot when searching for outliers.

We can ask a different question: which observations are of special importance for the regression ? The importance can be potential or factual: again the simple problem splits into two. We can ask which observation are of **potential influence on the regression** - so we would look at the leverage $\partial \hat{Y}(X_i)/\partial Y_i$. For the linear regression situation, since $\hat{Y}(X) = X'\hat{\beta} = X'(X'X)^-X'Y$ this reduces to the leverages $\partial \hat{Y}(X_i)/\partial Y_i = h_i = (X(X'X)^-X')_{ii}$, that is studying the diagonal elements of the "hat matrix" $H := X(X'X)^-X'$, the leverages.

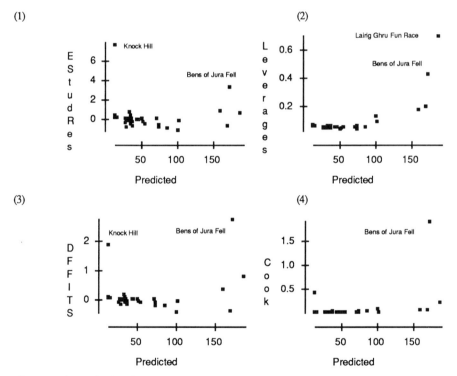

Figure 3: diagnostic plots for studying (1) outliers, observation of potential (2) and factual (3) influence on the fit, and influential observations for parameter estimation (4). The Knock Hill race is the race which is most off with respect to the other data. The highest influence on regression (3) or parameter estimation however comes from the Bens of Jura Fell Race. The most critical race as far as the design (i.e. covaritate values) is concerned is the Lairig Ghru Fun Race.

But we could as well look at the **factual influence on the regression** - of course scaled by the estimated variation. This would lead to considering the DFFITS $\hat{Y}_i - \hat{Y}_{(i)} / s(\hat{Y}_{(i)})$ where $s(\hat{Y}_{(i)})$ is the estimated standard error of $\hat{Y}_{(i)}$

$$\text{DFFITS}_i = \sqrt{\frac{h_i}{1-h_i}} \frac{r_i}{s(i)\sqrt{1-h_i}}$$

Finally, we can interpret the regression problem as an estimation problem. So we ask for the influence of observation i on the **estimation of the parameter** β. A corresponding statistic is Cook's distance D_i which is to be compared with the $F(p+1, n-p-1)$ distribution,

$$D_i = \frac{(\hat{\beta}-\hat{\beta}_{(i)})^t XX^t (\hat{\beta}-\hat{\beta}_{(i)})}{(p+1)\hat{\sigma}^2}$$

We started with one classical display, the residual plot. By making more precise what we mean by "informative" we split up this single display into four different displays - each showing a different aspect of the information. All was contained in the original display. These displays do not add information. But they make information of interest stand out more clearly. For more information on these diagnostic indices see Cook and Weisberg (1982) or Chatterjee and Hadi (1988). The definition of diagnostic indices, adapted to various purposes, is one of the tasks in data analysis. We are not going to study these plots in details as presented by now, because today's dynamical graphics provide better possibilities.

3. Excursion: Validation

So far, the critical issue was outliers. If this were the only problem, robust methods would be appropriate. Data analysis however tries to be prepared for the unexpected. So assumptions about models and distributions as used in robust statistics cannot be the basis of data analysis.

Like any approach in statistics, data analysis has to take care not to be mislead by random fluctuation. Other than the classical statistical approaches, data analysis can rarely draw on predefined model assumptions to check the validity of its findings. In the definition of the externally studentized residuals above we already met a typical approach in data analysis: to use the data at hand to crossvalidate findings. We discarded one observation at a time and calculated the statistic of interest based on the remaining observations.

This approach can be generalized: judge a statistic $T=T(X_1,...,X_n)$ by comparing it to the empirical distribution of corresponding statistics $T'=T(X_{i_1},...,X_{i_m})$, where $i_1,...,i_m$ runs through all subsets of size m<n. This **crossvalidation** idea has been extensively applied and studied in data analysis. If we have a model at hand in which we can estimate the error distribution, we can go a step beyond crossvalidation and **bootstrap** our experiment. Crossvalidation, bootstrap and other resampling plans are a common approaches in data analysis.

4. Excursion: Perception of Graphic Displays

Data analysis tries to find informative features in data, and to bring them to human perception. Appropriate statistics can help finding (or identifying) informative events. Bringing them to human perception is another point. As an illustration, consider the residual plot (figure 4a).

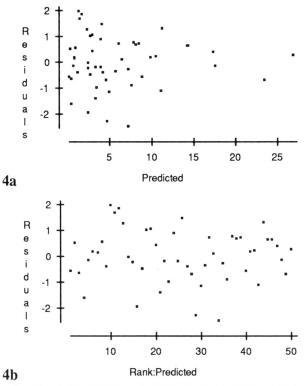

Figure 4: Two views of a residual plot. Note the wedge shaped outline in plot 4a which is not present in plot 4b. Both plots show the same residuals, with the x-axis rank transformed on plot b.

Nearly everybody will immediately see a wedge-shaped structure in this plot. So if you are looking for heterogeneity in variance, you will be alert that variance might not be constant. Now look at figure 4b. There is nothing particularly alerting about this plot. The sad news is: both plots are representing the same residuals. The only difference is that now the residuals are plotted against the rank of the prediction. So the statistical information in both plots is the same. But the concentration of the design points lets the residual plot come out wedge shaped in the first plot. As a matter of fact, these residuals were generated by a simulated simple linear model with homoskedastic normal errors. The skew distribution of the design points makes us perceive plot 4a as different from plot 4b.

The core is: we perceive a shape, or more precisely a "Gestalt". We do not perceive fluctuation (which would be the same in both plots). This is what makes graphical displays a delicate instrument. Data analysis is forced to think carefully of how to communicate informative events to human perception (Tufte, 1983). An example of a particularly successful display construction is John Tukey's Box&Whisker plot. Let us us look at this gem in data analysis displays (figure 5).

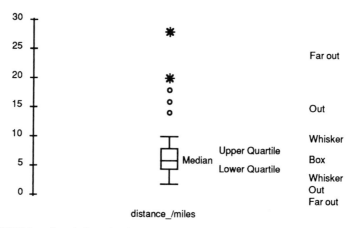

Figure 5: Box&Whisker plot. A *box* showing the quartiles, *whiskers* unto highest data not more than 1.5* interquartile range from upper/lower quartile. *Out* upto 3.0* interquartile range from upper/lower quartile. *Farout* beyond.

The Box&Whisker plots achieve to present general information about the core of the data, with information hiding in this area. On the other hand, they highlight the exceptional. The exceptional data might be just tail effects, or it might be genuine outliers - they are worth a second look anyway. As an application of the Box&Whisker-Plots, figure 6 shows the activity cycle of ants during the day, as observed for a sample of ant colonies. The general characteristic stands out clearly: the "patrollers" are out first, then the nest maintenance ants have their highest activity, and then the foragers. The characteristic time pattern , the "daily round", can be easily perceived from these plots. What is obvious here is very hard to illustrate or find by classical statistical models.

4. Interactive Graphics

After this excursion to dangers and gems of data displays, let us return to the Scottish Hill Runners' data as our leading example. We have split our residual plot into four informative quantities. We now want to make use of their information. What comes to help here is graphical interaction. A common tool in graphical interaction is an identification tool: you move a pointer (linked to a mouse or other input device) across the plot to select a point, press a button and the software replies by showing the identification of the point selected (figure 7).

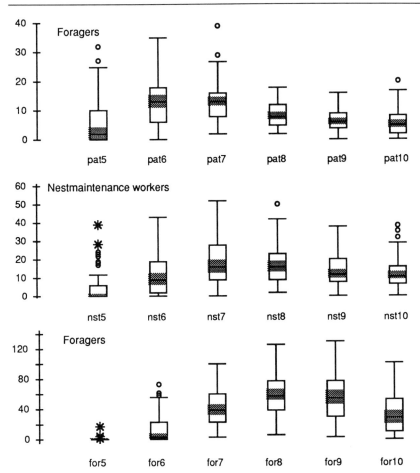

Figure 6: The daily round of ants: activity count of ants, drawn as box&whisker plots, against time of day. Each box&whisker plot represents data from several colonies, by activity group. The different activity patterns of the groups is evident: first activity of patrollers, with maximum at 6:00 (pat6), then main nest maintenance activity with peak at 7:00 (nst7), then foraging with peak at 8:00 (for8). Still to be improved: the shaded bands provide a quick test for pairwise comparison of medians. What would be adequate bands for a profile curve ?

The challenge still is in higher dimensions, and the availability of high computing power made a step in higher dimensions feasible. With a two-dimensional display, one needs a means to reduce dimensionality. There are essentially four ways of reduction:
- put additional dimensions in time and produce a movie representation
- put additional dimensions in space and produce "draftsman's plots"
- put additional dimensions in quality (colour, sound, vibration,...)
- put additional dimensions in interaction.

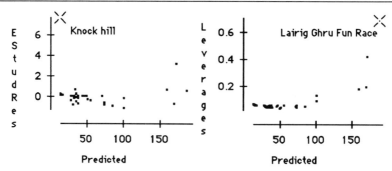

Figure 7: Identification: tag of selected item is shown when selecting with a mouth or an equivalent input device. The main outlier in the in the plot of the externally studentized residuals corresponds to the Knock Hill race; Lairig Ghru Fun Race has exceptional leveerage.

All of them have been tried. The most spectacular one has been the last, as implemented in the PRIM system (PRIM: ADA for Projection, Rotation, Isolation of subgroups, Masking controlled by additional parameters). PRIM was one of the first systems to allow real interaction with data, in particular to allow interactive analysis of (projections of) higher dimensional data sets. The most impressive feature of PRIM was the possibility to rotate a data set in three dimensions. The ISP software package, originally implemented on workstations, provided a link to PRIM-H, thus making it useable for a wider audience. MacSpin was the first program to bring the PRIM facilities down to an affordable budget. By now, the PRIM facilities have become fairly standard in data analysis systems.

Although spectacular at first sight, the PRIM facilities have turned out to be limited in use. PRIM is useful in low dimensional data sets (3-4 dimensions) where you have a large scale structure which can not be reduced to planar models. The diabetes data set of Reaven and Miller (1979) is one of the rare success stories of the PRIM approach. The most fruitful solution so far is the most humble one: just to use a collection of scatterplots (for example to lay out different dimensions in space to produce a draftsman's plot: a matrix of the marginal scatterplots, possibly showing the corresponding histograms in the diagonal) but to **link** the plots. Interactivity is left free to explore the linked windows (figure 8). Once it is realized, this is trivial. But it took someone to have this idea. The earliest reports on interactive graphics for linked windows seems to be Newton (1978, quoted from Becker et al. 1987). A very impressive implementation by John McDonald in the Orion project controlled a "brush" with a mouse. While the brush was moved across one plot, the points under the brush got coloured depending on their distance to the center of the brush. The corresponding representations of the data points in other windows (showing other variables) were coloured in the same colours.

The techniques discussed in this section (Identification, PRIM, linked windows, brushing) are fairly common in graphical data analysis today. For a survey of this area, as seen from Murray Hill, see (Becker et al., 1987).

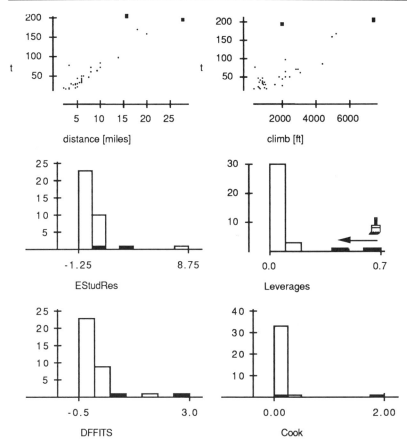

Figure 8: Linked windows with various diagnostic indices. Cases with high leverage are highlighted by a brushing technique in the leverage plot. Corresponding entries in the other plots are highlighted automatically.

5. Statistics of selection and brushing

A new quality in data analysis is gained with the ability to *interact* with the data, especially when there is an immediate graphical response. There is, however, a common overestimation of the importance of the technical tools. The new quality did not arrive with modern high power computer systems. It was already achieved with the first attempts to gain more insight by adding pen strokes and guidelines to pen and paper to help focus on interesting features. It was effectively buried with modern computers providing rapid numerical results, and it is only slowly regained with the new graphical facilities. Two examples for this claim will be given below.

First, let us study the situation of selecting in linked scatterplots. In the simplest situation, we select in one dimension, and look for the response in another dimension. So we can integrate both linked windows in one plot, a ususal scatterplot. Selection acts on one marginal, with response on the other. Again, to simplify in order to make the idea stand out more clearly, we think of a response discretized into bins i=1...k. Any selection yields highlight counts $m_1,...,m_k$ with $\Sigma m_i = m$. Now we can see: checking for a relation corresponds to a classical situation. Under the hypothesis of no relation, i.e. independence, the number of highlighted responses is distributed as multi-hypergeometrical distribution (figure 9).

For example, we can select the upper (or lower) half, and to split the response into two bins at the median (hence we have a hypergeometric distribution with parameters m, m_1, n where m_1=N=m div 2). In a test context, this leads to Quenouille's quadrant test (Quenouille 1952, 1959). The generalization to other selections and discretization of the response and to higher dimensions was already obvious in early times to Quenouille (Quenouille 1959).

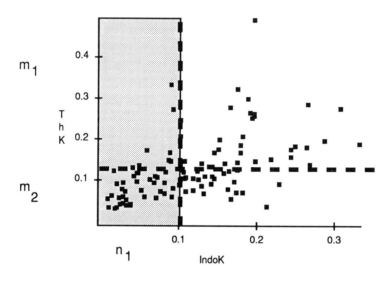

Figure 9: Selecting for an informative event. Here: selecting by medians in IndoK, with reponse split at medians. The informative event is the high occupation count in the lower quadrant. This corresponds to a variant of Quenouille's corner test.

For a second example, let us turn to the dynamic version, i.e. brushing. For simplicity, let us again focus on a one dimensional exploratory variable, with a one dimensional response. We brush in one variable until we see an "informative event" in the other. Again, as a prototype, let us split the response at the median. By brushing, we will get a response on one side of its median. A most obvious informative response is if we jump to the other side of the median (figure 10). In a test context, this again corresponds to a familiar situation: this is Olmstead and Tukey's corner test (Olmstead and Tukey, 1947)

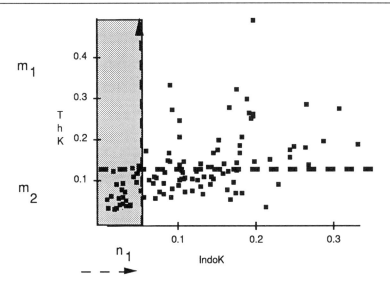

Figure 10: Brushing for an informative event. Here: until a jump over the median occurs in the response. This corresponds to a variant of Tukey's corner test.

6. Data driven modelling

An interesting field is that of data analytical modelling. One wants to go beyond an analysis of the data at hand, aiming for models. There are some approaches. For general regression, for example, there are the popular smoothing approaches, either by using splines or using kernel smoothers, both approaches being closely related (Silverman 1984). The status of the data driven selection of the smoothing parameter, the bandwidth selection, is discussed in (Härdle et al. 1988). CART is a quite distinct approach to tackle regression and classification problems with data analytical methods, essentially tiling the covariate space for homogeneous response. An extensive discussion of this approach can be found in Breiman et al. (1984).

These are data analyitical approaches to modelling. But in general, the relation between data analysis and model building is an open field.

Atkinson, A.C. (1986) Comment: Aspects of Diagnostic Regression Analysis. Statistical Sciences 1, 397 - 402

Becker, R.A., Cleveland, W.S., Wilks, A.R. Dynamic Graphics for Data Analysis (with discussion) Statistical Science 2 (1987) 355-395

Belsely, D., Kuh, E., and Welsch, R.E. (1980) Regression Diagnostics. John Wiley and Sons, NewYork

Breiman, L. and Friedman, J.H. Estimating optimal transformations for multiple regression and correlation (with discussion) J. Amer. Statist. Assoc. 80 (1985) 580-618

Breiman, L., Friedman, J.H., Olshen, R.A. and Stone, C.J (1984) Classification and Regression Trees. Wadsworth, Belmont

Chatterjee, S., and Hadi, A. (1988) Sensitivity Analysis in Linear Regression. John Wiley and Sons, NewYork

Chambers, J. M., Cleveland, W.S., Kleiner, B. and Tukey, P.A. (1983) Graphical Methods for Data Analysis. Wadsworth Statistics/Probability Series. Wadsworth, Belmont.

Cook, R.D. Detection of Influential Observations in Linear Regression. Technometrics 19 (1977) 15-18.

Cook, R. D., and Weisberg, S. (1982) Residuals and Influence in Regression. Chapman and Hall, NewYork.

Gordon, D, M. (1986) The Dynamics of the Daily Round of the Harvester Ant Colony (pogonomyrmex barbatus). Animal Behaviour 34, 1402-1419

Härdle, W., Hall , P., and Marron, J.S. (1988) How far are Automatically Chosen Regression Smoothing Parameters from their Optimum ? (with Discussion). J. Amer. Statist. Assoc. 83, 86-101

Newton, C.M. (1978) Graphics: From alpha to omega in data analysis. In: Graphical Representation of Multivariate Data (P.C.C. Wang, ed.) 59-92. Academic Press, NewYork.

Olmstead, P.S., and Tukey, J.W. (1947) A Corner Test for Association. Ann. Math. Statist 18, 495 - 513

Quenouille, M.H. (1952) Associated Measurements. Butterworth's Scientific Publications.

Reaven, G.M., and Miller, R. (1979) An Attempt to Define the Nature of Chemical Diabetes Using a Multidimensional Analysis. Diabetologia 16, 17-24

Silverman, B.W. Spline Smoothing: the Equivalent Variable Kernel Method. Ann. Statist. 12 (1984) 898-916

Tufte, E. (1983) The Visual Display of Quantitative Information. Graphics Press, Cheshire.

Velleman, P.F. and Hoaglin, D.C. (1981): Applications, Basics and Computing of Exploratory Data Analysis. Duxbury Press, Boston.

The ants activity data (figure 6) are from observations reported in (Gordon 1986). All plots were produced using Paul Velleman's "Data Desk professional" on an Apple Macintosh Plus computer.

F. Faulbaum, R. Haux und K.-H. Jöckel (Hrsg.) (1990). SoftStat '89
Fortschritte der Statistik-Software 2. Stuttgart: Gustav Fischer, 249 - 258

Advances in Graphical Data Analysis from SAS Institute

G. Held and A. Lehmann

1. Summary

In the last few years powerful statistical packages known from the mainframe were introduced to the PC and the UNIX world. Implementation of these packages was done in a more or less traditional way. Based on hardware technologies such as implemented on a Macintosh desktop we see new data analysis packages which open up fascinating possibilities for interactive-style communication with the data.

In this article we will introduce the new product JMP™ from SAS Institute for the Macintosh. JMP (pronounced "jump") is a product grown out of research and development efforts. Using a typical Mac-like interface its emphasis is more on how an analysis can be done rather than what multitude of facilities can be offered.

JMP aims to visualise data primarily through statistical computations. JMP also offers facilities for dynamic graphical analysis such as the scatterplot matrix and the spinning plot. It is the aim of SAS Institute to gradually incorporate the philosophy of JMP into the SAS® System. Some applications will be demonstrated and in this process we will highlight major features of JMP.

2. Background

It is a commonplace that the hardware basis for computing in general, and data analysis in particular, has changed drastically in the last decade. The "hardware revolution" opened up opportunities to distribute the central computing power to smaller departmental computers, and finally to personal computers for the single user. The advantage of having local computing power was counteracted by difficulties of data access (and sometimes restrictions of the PC operating system, PC DOS or MS DOS). Efforts were made to integrate personal computers into networks and/or use more powerful workstations running under UNIX, often in multi-user mode.

The hardware revolution enabled software vendors to offer powerful statistical packages on the PC, a result which could not to be anticipated ten years ago. The way these packages work on the PC as opposed to the mainframe, however, has not been changed dramatically. Most of the PC packages offer some windowing capabilities, but they differ considerably in the way windows can be manipulated (resizing, repositioning, possibility of user-created windows etc.). In addition some packages still appear on the PC mainly as an interface to old-fashioned programming-style applications, primarily batch-oriented, and producing bulky output with little opportunity for annotation or cut-and-paste reporting.

SAS is a registered trademark of SAS Institute Inc., Cary, NC, USA. JMP is a trademark of SAS Institute Inc., Cary, NC, USA.

Meanwhile we see a second "revolutionary" phase, now more focussed on the interface to the computer user. Apple can claim to be the first commercial vendor who offered a user interface which provided a more natural and intuitive way to manipulate data. Using the analogy of a desk and the screen the user is enabled to open and manipulate several documents at a time, documents can be browsed using scroll bars, filed as "icons", printed, and "thrown" into a logical trash can. Being used to traditional ways of computing I was delighted to learn how quickly you can adjust to this "windows-widgets-wonderland" and find it much more logical to the way we think than traditional computing. Obviously this technology is very attractive for a growing user community whose main focus is to solve an application of business, scientific, or technical nature, using a computer as a tool, but not as a profession per se.

This technology was and still is primarily used for applications such as desk top publishing or graphics, but starting in the early seventies (Fowlkes, 1971; Fisherkeller, Friedman, Tukey, 1975) interactive data analysis packages were introduced and were getting very popular recently (see Sawitzki, 1989, in this volume). It seems, however, that these packages were primarily meant for the analyst experienced in descriptive analysis and hypothesis testing, who wanted to "view" the multi-dimensional structure of his data in an exploratory fashion using dynamic graphics as a primary tool (Donoho, Donoho, Gasko, 1986; Young, Kent, and Kuhfeld, 1986). There are two interactive data analysis packages on the market, which cover a broader range of analyses: DATADESK (Velleman, 1989) and JMP from SAS Institute.

3. Introducing JMP Software

JMP is a package from SAS Institute for the Apple Macintosh computer to explore data statistically using visual techniques. JMP combines the following steps into one highly interactive process:

— a spreadsheet for viewing, editing, transforming, and manipulating data

— graphical and statistical methods for data analysis

— options to highlight and display subsets of the data

— tools for moving analysis results between windows or applications for printing

JMP is not the SAS System for the Macintosh. JMP does not attempt to cover all abilities of the SAS System, e.g. it has no programming language, no sophisticated file management, nor does it cover all statistical methods available in the SAS System. It is a software package in its own right: JMP is highly interactive, mouse-driven, and combines a graphical user interface with a common sense approach to statistics.

To use JMP, an Apple Macintosh with 1+ megabyte is required, 2 megabytes are recommended.

Starting a JMP Session. JMP can be activated by double-clicking the JMP icon. When JMP is active you see the following menu bar (Figure 1):

Figure 1.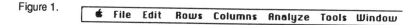

The menu bar serves as the central dispatching point for creating data files and manipulating, analysing, and displaying data. Pointing at any of the entries of the menu bar and clicking, activates a pull-down menu where further specifications can be chosen.

The FILE and EDIT menus offer file handling activities. FILE allows to create, or reshape data tables, import SAS data sets in transport form, close, save or reconstruct data tables, and print statistical and graphical output. Use EDIT to perform standard editing tasks such as cut and copy on selected values in a data table, select rows only, columns only, or choose a combination of both.

When we open a file using the OPEN command in the FILE menu we get a file selection list, from which we select and open a file, e.g. TYPING DATA. The opened file creates a data table in memory that appears in spreadsheet form, with rows and columns as shown in Figure 2. The spreadsheet model of data enables the user to see the data, but to hide the "program" for manipulation of the data. In the spreadsheet there are 17 rows representing typing scores on three brands of word processors.

Figure 2.

		brand (Nom)	speed (Int)
17 Rows	1	REGAL	70
	2	SPEEDYTYPE	87
	3	SPEEDYTYPE	79
	4	REGAL	73
	5	SPEEDYTYPE	77
	6	REGAL	72

Using the Spreadsheet. The JMP spreadsheet allows a variety of data table management functions such as: editing the values in any cell, changing a column width by dragging the column line, hiding columns temporarily or deleting columns permanently, adding new columns (variables) optionally by using a calculator, rearranging the order of rows, selecting a subset of rows for analysis, sorting a data table, and combining data tables. User actions can be performed using the cursor which takes on different forms and performs different activities depending on what kind of table territory it is in.

Level of Measurement and Choosing Variable Roles. When columns of data are selected from a data table, each is assigned a "role" to play in the analysis and a measurement level that specifies how to treat the values. By pointing at the measurement level box the analyst opens up a pop-up menu by which he can define a variable to be interval, ordinal, or nominal. The system chooses reasonable defaults, (e.g. Brand nominal, Speed interval).

Clicking on the variable assignment box allows you to exclude the variable from an analysis, declare it to be a response variable (Y), an independent variable (X), a weight for the response (WEIGHT), a frequency of each row of the data table (FREQ), or a labeling convention for points in plots (LABEL). For now, we declare both columns as Y variables and do not change the default measurement level.

Selecting an Analysis Platform. JMP provides six statistical platforms - each one a stage on which data dramatise their values. Statistical platforms can be chosen through the ANALYZE menu on the menu bar. The following analyses are offered (Figure 3):

- Distribution of Y: describes each column in a data table using histograms and other graphical and textual reports

- Distribution of Y by X: plots with accompanying analysis, for each combination of X and Y variables chosen in the data table

- Fit Y by X's: fit of one Y variable by all the X variables selected, with leverage plots for each effect

- Specify Model: allows model specification for complex effects such as nested factors, interactions, and polynomial terms

- Explore, Spin: Three-dimensional spinning plot of any numeric column in the data table. Three variables can be displayed simultaneously. Principal components can be optionally included in the plot

- Y's by Y's: studies relationship between each pair of response variables (scatterplot matrix) and the relationship between all variables with a multivariate distance outlier plot (Mahalanobis distance).

Figure 3.

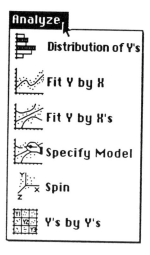

Choosing a measurement level is an important disposition for the analysis: *JMP automatically selects methods appropriate to the measurement level of the data.*

If we select distribution of Y's for our typing data the graphical displays will be shown (Figure 4): histograms of both the brand and speed columns, a mosaic (stacked bar) chart of the nominal variable brand, and a quantile box plot of the interval variable speed.

Figure 4.

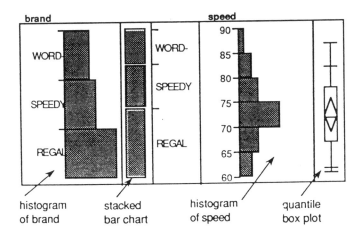

To adjust the histogram bars, select the "hand" from the TOOLS menu. Use the hand to grab the plot you want to change. Moving the hand to the left combines intervals instantly and shows fewer bars. Moving the hand to the right uses a finer division of each interval showing more bars.

Optional text reports can be displayed or hidden by clicking on text report buttons which appear below the graphics. The kinds of statistical reports shown depend once again on the measurement level of the variable. For interval variables such as the speed variable QUANTILES and MOMENTS buttons can be activated. Also, a TEST button displays a t-test that compares the mean of the sample to zero. For nominal and ordinal variables, SUMMARY and PROFILE buttons display the total sample frequency, category frequencies and associated probabilities.

Distribution of Y BY X. We might be interested in any differences in descriptive statistics of the groups formed by the three word processors. To address this question we identify in the spreadsheet the role of brand as X (independent variable) and select Y for speed (dependent variable). To compare the mean typing scores for each brand of word processor, the statistician selects the Distribution of Y BY X platform from the ANALYZE menu.

Distribution of Y by X can be used for four kinds of analyses:

– Categorical analysis when both X and Y have nominal values

– Analysis of variance when X is nominal and Y has interval values

– Logistic regression when X is interval and Y has nominal values

– Regression analysis when both X and Y have interval values.

This reveals another feature of JMP: *JMP is complete with respect to measurement levels. This also applies if multiple factors are specified (Y BY X's platform).*

Once again JMP automatically selects the appropriate analysis from the measurement level of the data. Initially it plots each of the typing test scores for each brand of word processor. More graphical information about the distribution of the speed variable within brands of word processors can be obtained by selecting options form the list displayed by the options triangle.

By selecting all three remaining options we arrive at a plot displayed in Figure 5.

Figure 5.

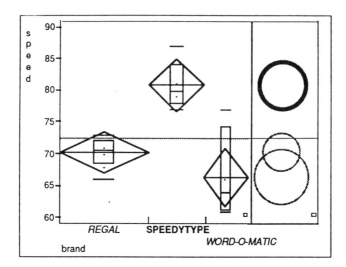

Figure 5 combines four graphical displays: a plot of all data points grouped into the classification variable, a means diamond for each group, a quantiles box plot, and the comparison cycles. For the means diamond a line is drawn at the mean words-per-minute for each brand of word processor. The upper and lower points of the means diamond span a 95% confidence interval computed from the sample values for each machine. The width of each diamond on the horizontal axis is proportional to the group size.

The quantiles box plots give more information about the distribution of speed in the brand groups. The box encompasses the interquartile range of the sample data. Additional horizontal lines are drawn at the 10th, 50th, and 90th percentile. Looking at the quantile box plot and means rectangle together helps you to see whether the data are distributed normally within a group.

The comparison circles displayed to the right of the plot help the statistician visualise whether or not the mean typing scores are significantly different. A circle for each group of points is drawn with the centre of the circle aligned with the mean of the group it represents. The diameter of each circle spans the 95% confidence interval for each group of typing scores. If two circles do not intersect the two group means they represent are significantly different. If the circles do intersect then the confidence intervals overlap and the groups may not be significantly different.

All of the respective information can be obtained by selecting the relevant text reports under the graphic. The main focus of JMP, however, is the graphical message. Generally JMP shows a graph for every statistical test. For example, if given a number of interval level X's and and interval Y variable JMP would display one leverage plot for each X variable which shows the contribution of each observation to the hypothesis test for that term.

Multivariate Analyses. In addition to the General Linear Modeling platforms (Fit Y BY X's, Specify Model) JMP offers two platforms for multivariate analysis: Y's by Y's and the Spinning Plot. For demonstration we use a new spreadsheet, the solubility of chemical substances (rows) in various solutions (columns, Figure 6).

Figure 6.

35 rows / 6 cols	eth	oct	ccl4	hex	Mahal.Distance
1	-.57	-.31	-1.4	-2.1	2.25720667
2	1.80	2.03	0.99	0.46	.991013850
3	-.34	-.17	-2.4	-3.0	2.17630115
4	1.95	1.92	0.57	-.46	1.22617581

Y's BY Y's. This platform is used for basic exploration into how a number of variables relate to each other. The output produced by this platform is divided into two parts. The first part examines the relationship of each pair of response (Y) variables and includes the matrix of product-moment correlation coefficients, and a scatter plot matrix (see Figure 7).

Figure 7.

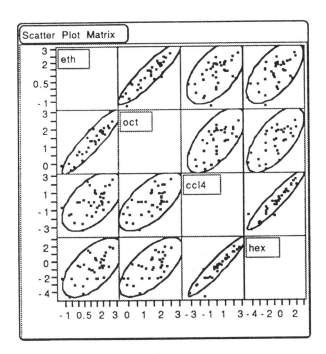

The scatter plot matrix helps to visualise the correlations. A bivariate normal density ellipse is imposed on each scatter plot; if the variables are bivariate normal this ellipse encloses 95% of the points.

To test the relationship of two variables or see density ellipses other than 95%, you can use the Distribution of Y BY X command on the ANALYZE menu.

The second part of the output examines the multivariate relationship between all response variables. This includes the inverse correlation matrix to estimate collinearity, and a multivariate Mahalanobis distance outlier plot (see Figure 8). The outlier distance plot shows the Mahalanobis distance of each point from the multivariate mean (centroid). Multivariate distances are useful for spotting outliers in many dimensions.

Figure 8.

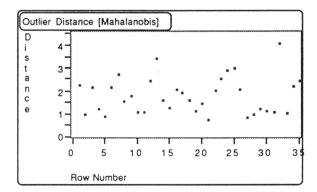

You can highlight points on any scatter plot in the scatter plot matrix, or the outlier distance plot. Using these tools another feature of JMP becomes apparent: *With JMP all objects are active and interdependent.*

This means that if points are highlighted e.g. in a bivariate plot, the same points are also highlighted in all other plots, also in the data table ("linking", see Becker, Cleveland, Wilks, 1987). This way multivariate outliers can be quickly identified for further actions.

SPIN. If more than two dimensions are involved dynamic graphics are an invaluable tool. The SPIN platform of the ANALYZE menu is used to get a three-dimensional view of the data, and an approximation to higher dimensions through principal components. The platform is arranged with a spin control panel at the upper left and the plot frame on the right. When the platform is started, it reads in any variables role-selected as X or Y, scales them, and adds them to the components panel. Alternatively the platform will prompt the user to select variables (Figure 9).

Figure 9.

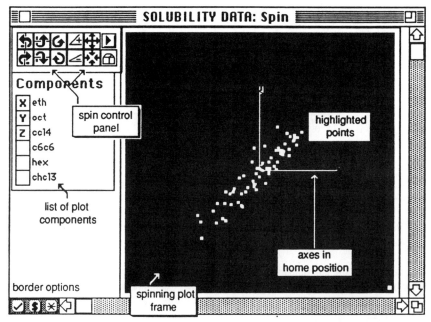

A very convenient way to control the spin is the grabber tool in the TOOLS menu that works like a hand; the rotation tracks the movement of the mouse as you drag it. The directional spin buttons on the control panel are typically used to "fine-tune" the rotation. Further buttons on the control panel add functionalities such as scaling the points, adding colour and markers to points, drawing a box around the plot, etc.

In fact, the SPIN platform is a complete tool for dynamic graphics. It allows us to perform all graphical methods discussed by Becker, Cleveland, and Wilks (1987): identification of points with labels, hiding and deletion of points (outliers), brushing, and showing different subsets of data alternatively ("alternagraphics").

Often it is favourable to view data in more than three dimensions. If more than three variables need to be taken into account, and those variables are somewhat correlated, then principal components can be used to show the most prominent directions of the high-dimensional data.

To get the principal components on the spinning plot, just click on the check icon of the border options and select Principal Components. The principal components will be displayed as new variables in the components control panel, new axes will be included on the plot, and a reveal button appears named PRINCIPAL COMPONENTS. The spinning plot is now a "Biplot" consisting of variables and principal components (Figure 10). Clicking the PRINCIPAL COMPONENTS button we will get a report on the eigenvalues and eigenvectors. In this example using six variables, 97 percent of the variation of the data can be seen in the first three principal components.

Figure 10.

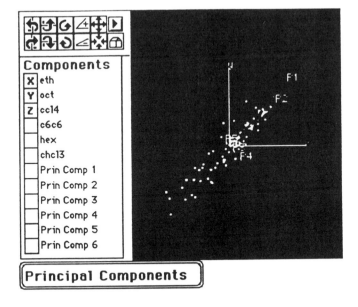

We may summarise the discussion of multivariate analyses with JMP as: *JMP offers comprehensive tools for dynamic graphics in many dimensions: Mahlanobis distance plots, 3D spinning plots, biplots for principle components.*

4. Conclusion

It was our aim to introduce JMP software from SAS Institute using some small examples and to highlight some of the significant features of JMP for interactive data analysis. JMP aims to visualise data in a highly interactive way using a common sense approach to statistics. All analyses are introduced graphically with optional text reports for statistics. JMP automatically selects methods appropriate to the measurement level. It is complete with respect to measurement levels and offers comprehensive tools for dynamic graphics. If multiple analysis platforms are used for the same spreadsheet, then an action on a data point or a subset of points all related windows will also be updated. It was not our intention to describe JMP comprehensively. Further details can be obtained from SAS Institute.

JMP also has a very important function to SAS Institute itself. JMP represents a software technology which is intended to be incorporated gradually into the SAS System. A first move will be taken in Release 6.06 of the SAS System, which will allow the SAS System to run in native windowing environments. This release supports Presentation Manager under OS/2, DECwindows under VMS, and X windows under Unix, initially. In addition, Release 6.06 offers a separate window for graphics which can be moved, resized, and scrolled.

A next step will be the inclusion of statistical graphics capabilities. Statistical graphics in the SAS System are under development for a release after 6.06. Naturally, statistical graphics fit well on a sophisticated hardware environment with high performance as well as suitable screen resolutions. It is therefore considered to implement statistical graphics for UNIX-based workstations and eventually also for OS/2-based personal computers.

REFERENCES

Becker R.A., Cleveland, W.S., Wilks, A.R. (1987): Dynamic Graphics for Data Analysis, Statistical Science, pp. 355-395

Cleveland, W.S., McGill, M.E. (1988): Dynamic Graphics for Statistics, Belmont: Wadsworth and Brooks

Donoho, A.W., Donoho, D.L., Gasko, M. (1986): MACSPIN Graphical Data Analysis Software, Austin, Texas: D2 Software

Fisherkeller, M.A., Friedman, J.H., Tukey, J.W. (1975): PRIM-9: an interactive multidimensional Data Display and Analysis System", Data: its Use, Organization, and Management, pp. 140-145. New York: The Association for Computing Machinery

Fowlkes E.B. (1971): User's Manual for an on-line interactive System for Probability Plotting on the DDP-224 Computer, Technical Memorandum, Murray Hill, NJ: AT&T Bell Laboratories

Sawitzki, G. (1989): Tools and Concepts in Data Analysis, in: Faulbaum, F., Jöckel, K.H., Haux, R: Softstat '89. Fortschritte der Statistiksoftware 2, Stuttgart: Fischer Verlag

Velleman, P.F. (1989): Practical High Interaction Graphics, in: Faulbaum, F., Jöckel, K.H., Haux, R: Softstat '89. Fortschritte der Statistiksoftware 2, Stuttgart: Fischer Verlag

Young, F.W., Kent, D.P., Kuhfeld, W.F. (1986): Visual Exploratory Data Analysis: PROC VISUALS, a User-Written Experimental SAS Procedure, in: SAS Users Group International Proceedings, Cary, NC: SAS Institute Inc., pp. 840 - 845

STATGRAPHICS

M. Korn und A. Lamers

Summary

Topic of this report is demonstrating the power, versatility, graphical qualities and ease of use of STSC Statgraphics, which is beeing used in teaching statistics at the university of Münster in West Germany for some years. All figures printed here are reproductions of the charts generated in an hands-on-demonstration at SoftStat'89 within 20 minutes using the ALLBUS'86 Subset with 1500 Cases.

1. Einführung

Aufgabe des Instituts für Ökonometrie und Wirtschaftsstatistik der Universität Münster, dessen Mitarbeiter die Herren Dr. Korn und Dr. Lamers sind, ist die *Statistik-Ausbildung von Studenten der Wirtschaftswissenschaften*. STATGRAPHICS wird an diesem Institut seit fast drei Jahren intensiv *in Forschung und Lehre* genutzt; es ist heute fester Bestandteil der Lehrpläne des Grund- und Hauptstudiums, wobei die praktische Einführung in den im Rahmen des Computer-Investitions-Programms (CIP) eingerichteten Rechnerpools der Universität Münster erfolgt.

Gründe für die Wahl von STATGRAPHICS sind:

1. das große Spektrum an statistischen Funktionen, das auch die Explorative Datenanalyse sowie Multivariate Verfahren umfaßt;
2. die hohe Qualität der integrierten Graphikfunktionen;
3. die leichte Erlernbarkeit und Bedienbarkeit des Systems und
4. die Möglichkeit zur Bearbeitung relativ großer Dateien.

Mit STATGRAPHICS, Version 3.0 kann der von der ZUMA bereitgestellte ALLBUS'86-Subset mit 11 Variablen und 1500 Objekten umfassend bearbeitet werden. Dies wird möglich durch die Verwendung einer temporären Plattendatei und/oder eines EMS-Speichers nach LIM-Standard 4.0[1].

STATGRAPHICS gestattet, für verschiedene Projekte jeweils ein eigenes *Dateiverzeichnis* zu verwenden; das aktuelle Verzeichnis wird im Tableau **System Profile** festgelegt. Die Liste der vorhandenen Dateien wie auch die Liste der Variablen kann jederzeit ein- oder ausgeblendet werden. Graphiken sind über Optionentableaus mit automatisch gewählten Voreinstellungen und mit Hilfe eines Graphikeditors in weitem Rahmen gestaltbar. Dank eines geräteunabhängigen Graphikformates[2] ist ein Wechsel des Ausgabegerätes – z. B. Bildschirm, Drucker oder Plotter – jederzeit möglich.

Prozeduren können durch Bewegung der Markierung mit Hilfe der Cursortasten und Bestätigung mit [Enter] in einem *zweistufigen Menüsystem* oder direkt durch Eingabe des Prozedurnamens aktiviert werden. Die grundlegende Vorgehensweise und die Geschwindigkeit, mit der aussagefähige Grafiken erstellt werden können, sollen zunächst an der Prozedur **Piechart** erläutert werden.

2. Ein- und mehrdimensionale graphische Darstellungen

Aus der Liste der Variablen kann mit Hilfe der Cursortasten und Bestätigung mit [Enter] der Variablenname **A86.schulab** (Schulabschluß) in das Eingabetableau übertragen werden. STATGRAPHICS kennt – im Gegensatz zu einigen anderen Statistiksystemen – keine automatische Zuordnung von Variablen- oder Werteetiketten. Statt dessen können Kommentare zu den Variablen sowie Textvariablen mit Wertebezeichnungen verwendet werden. Im Feld "Labels" kann der Name einer solchen Textvariablen eingesetzt werden; danach wird die Prozedur gestartet. Das folgende Optionentableau mit Voreinstellungen gestattet zum Beispiel die Wahl eines Offsets für das erste Segment sowie die Veränderung der Position der Legende. Nach Abschluß aller Eingaben braucht man nur Sekunden, um die in *Abbildung 1* gezeigte qualitativ hochwertige Graphik mit einer aussagefähigen Legende zu erstellen.

---

[1] Bei älteren Versionen von STATGRAPHICS ist die Zahl der zu bearbeitenden Objekte auf etwa eintausend begrenzt. Ein weiterer Vorteil der Version 3.0 ist, daß Druck- oder Plotdateien gespeichert und später – ohne STATGRAPHICS – auf einem beliebigen Gerät ausgegeben werden können.

[2] Die Graphiktreiber sind von der Statistical Graphics Corp. lizensiert; der Vorführung auf der SoftStat'89 lag der VGA-Treiber IBMVGA12.SYS zugrunde.

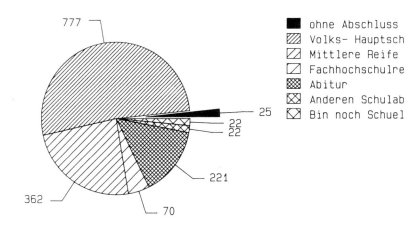

Abb. 1: Aufgliederung der 1500 Objekte nach dem Schulabschluß

Mit der Prozedur **Barchart** können *Balkendiagramme* – z. B. mit den Variablen **A86.fstand** (Familienstand) und **A86.geschlecht** – sehr schnell erstellt werden; das Ergebnis ist in *Abbildung 2* auf der folgenden Seite dargestellt.

Nächstes Beispiel ist ein *dreidimensionales Häufigkeitsdiagramm* mit den Variablen **A86.alter** und **A86.einkomk**. Dabei steht **A86.einkomk** für das klassifizierte Einkommen aus ALLBUS86; die Klasseneinteilung ist in der entsprechenden Textvariablen **L.einkomk** gespeichert. Im Optionentableau der Prozedur **Three-Dimensional Histogram** können die vorgeschlagenen Klasseneinteilungen und/oder Auswertungstypen verändert werden; für **A86.alter** werden die Grenzen 10 und 90 bei 8 Klassen und für **A86.einkomk** wird der Auswertungstyp **Continuous** bei 11 Klassen gewählt.

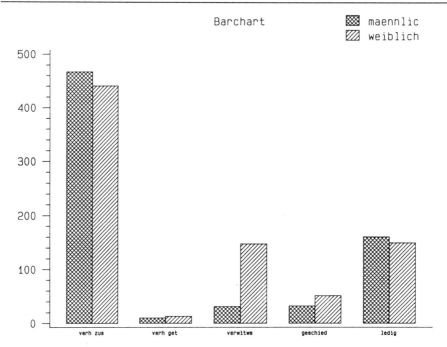

Abb. 2: Aufgliederung der Objekte nach Familienstand und Geschlecht

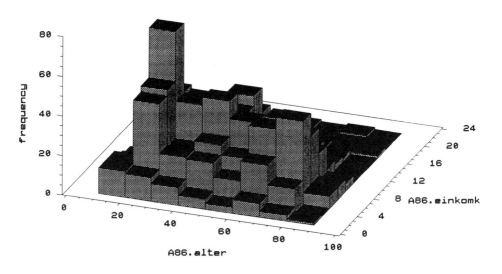

Abb. 3: Gemeinsame Häufigkeiten der Variablen Einkommensklasse und Alter

Die Zeit, die zur Erstellung der in *Abbildung 3* wiedergegebenen Graphik notwendig ist, hängt von der Anzahl der Klassen beider Variablen, der Anzahl der Beobachtungen und von der Geschwindigkeit der Hardware ab. Farben, Schraffuren sowie auch der Blickwinkel können vielfältig variiert werden; auch eine Darstellung kumulierter oder relativer Häufigkeiten ist möglich. Wer die Varianten einer Prozedur nicht kennt, kann ein Fenster mit einem kontextabhängigen englischen Hilfstext aufrufen.

Auch *Streuungsdiagramme* lassen sich durch zahlreiche Gestaltungsmöglichkeiten zu aussagefähigen Graphiken ausbauen. Zunächst werden im Eingabetableau der Prozedur **X-Y Line and Scatterplots** nur die zu berücksichtigenden Variablen **A86.alter** und **A86.einkom** eingetragen. Die neue Variable **A86.einkom** ist aus **A86.einkomk** dadurch entstanden, daß die Einkommenskategorie durch die entsprechende Klassenmitte (Einkommen in DM) ersetzt (recodiert) wird. Das resultierende – hier nicht dargestellte – Streuungsdiagramm ist wenig aussagefähig. Deshalb wird eine farbliche Unterscheidung nach **geschlecht** vorgenommen: Die Vorgabe **geschlecht * 3** im Feld "Point Colors" bewirkt – bei Verwendung einer EGA- oder VGA-Grafikkarte – deutlich unterscheidbare Farben.

Um die Aussagefähigkeit der Grafik weiter zu erhöhen, kann eine *Selektion* nach den Werten beliebiger Variabler, beispielsweise nach dem Schulabschluß, angefordert werden. Wenn die Codierung der Variablen **A86.schulab** nicht geläufig ist, kann mit wenigen Tastendrücken die zugehörige Textvariable auf den Bildschirm eingeblendet werden. Der Bearbeiter sieht, daß Abitur mit 5 kodiert ist; Personen mit Abitur erhält man durch das Selektionskriterium **A86.schulab EQ (equal) 5**. Bei mehrfarbiger Wiedergabe der in Abbildung 4 nur schwarzweiß dargestellten Graphik erkennt man, daß männliche Personen ein tendenziell höheres Einkommen als weibliche aufweisen.

Damit sind die Gestaltungsmöglichkeiten bei weitem nicht erschöpft. Beispielsweise könnte eine logarithmische oder halblogarithmische Darstellung gewählt werden. Auch eine Codierung der Beobachtungen mit einer beliebigen Variablen, beispielsweise mit dem Familienstand, ist leicht möglich: ledige Personen sind dann mit der Ziffer 5, verheiratete zusammenlebende mit der Ziffer 1 markiert. Man erkennt jetzt, daß die höchsten Einkommen von verheirateten Männern (fstand 1) erzielt werden. Wenn die Möglichkeiten des Prozedurtableaus ausgeschöpft sind, kann – evtl. mehrfach – ein zusätzliches

Fenster aktiviert werden. Die erste Option **Plot Options** führt zu einem Tableau, das zum Beispiel die Modifikation der Gesamtüberschrift und der Achsenbezeichnungen sowie Achseneinteilungen gestattet[3]. Nach der Wahl der Option **Replot** erhält man ein publikationsfähiges Diagramm, dessen weitere Ausgestaltung mit dem integrierten *Graphikeditor* erfolgen kann. Beispielsweise können an beliebiger Stelle freie Texte, z. B. der Name des Verfassers und/oder Quellenangaben sowie das Systemdatum bzw. die Systemzeit eingefügt werden; das Ergebnis ist in *Abbildung 4* dargestellt.

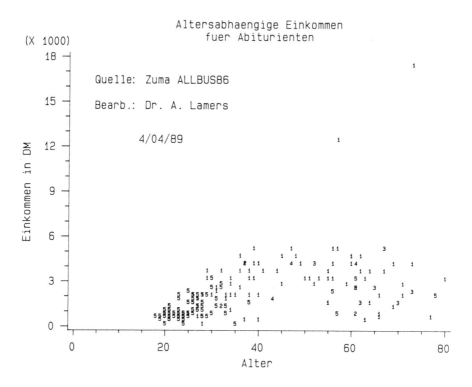

Abb. 4: Altersabhängige Einkommen für Abiturienten, nach Familienstand kodiert

Position, Größe, Orientierung und Farbe sämtlicher Texte in der Graphik können auch nachträglich in weiten Grenzen variiert werden. Alle erzeugten

---

[3] In STATGRAPHICS Version 3.0 werden in diesem Tableau auch deutsche Umlaute und Sonderzeichen akzeptiert. Diese Zeichen werden allerdings von einigen der mitgelieferten Druckertreiber nicht verarbeitet; mit dem VGA-Bildschirmtreiber werden sie jedoch korrekt wiedergegeben.

Graphiken können unter einer vom Anwender wählbaren Nummer gespeichert oder direkt über einen Drucker und/oder Plotter ausgegeben werden.

3. Regressionsanalytische Auswertungen

In STATGRAPHICS sind auch höhere statistische Verfahren implementiert. Als Beispiel für die vielfältigen Möglichkeiten sollen jetzt die im letzten Streuungsdiagramm gezeigten Zusammenhänge schrittweise regressionsanalytisch aufgearbeitet werden.

Erster Schritt ist eine *Einfachregression* zwischen der Variablen **A86.alter** und der Variablen **A86.einkom**. Das Eingabetableau der Prozedur **Simple Regression** bietet die Wahl zwischen den Modelltypen *linear, reciprocal, multiplicative* und *exponential*. Auch die Voreinstellungen (95%) für die Sicherheitsgrade der Prognoseintervalle für die individuelle und die Durchschnittsprognose können verändert werden. Als erstes Ergebnis erhält man das Tableau mit den geschätzten Parametern und die bekannte Varianztabelle. Die Verarbeitungsgeschwindigkeit hängt von der Zahl der zu bearbeitenden Fälle und von der verwendeten Hardware ab, wobei ein eventuell vorhandener mathematischer Coprozessor automatisch berücksichtigt wird. Nach der Berechnung der Parameter folgt die in *Abbildung 5* auf der folgenden Seite wiedergegebene Darstellung der geschätzten Regressionsfunktion und der Prognoseintervalle in der Punktwolke.

Eine sinnvolle Erweiterung der Einfachregression ist die Möglichkeit, Ausreißer interaktiv am Bildschirm aus der Regressionsgleichung zu entfernen. Das Eingabetableau der Prozedur **Interactive Outlier Rejection** unterscheidet sich nur geringfügig von dem vorherigen. Die Bildschirmausgabe dieser Prozedur enthält im unteren Bildteil die wichtigsten geschätzten Parameter der Regressionsfunktion, im oberen Bildteil wird die Regressionsgleichung in der Punktwolke dargestellt. In der Mitte des Bildschirms ist ein Kreuz – der sogenannte Graphikcursor – sichtbar, das durch die Cursortasten gesteuert werden kann. Wird dieses Kreuz in die Nähe eines Objektes gebracht und die Taste [N] betätigt, so erscheint neben dem gewählten Objekt seine laufende Nummer. Alternativ kann – wenn den Punkten sogenannte Objektetiketten (point labels) zugeordnet worden sind – durch Druck der Taste [Q] diese Objektbezeichnung sichtbar gemacht werden.

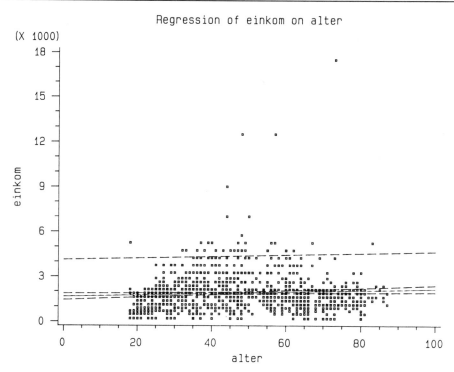

Abb. 5: Streuungsdiagramm, geschätzte Regressionsfunktion und 95%-Prognoseintervalle der Einfachregression zwischen Einkommen und Alter

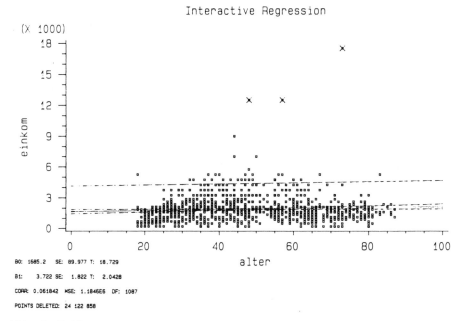

Abb. 6: Tableau zur "Interactive Outlier Rejection" für Einkommen und Alter

Fährt man der Reihe nach die Ausreißerobjekte mit dem Graphikcursor an und betätigt die Taste [E], so werden die entsprechenden Objekte markiert und aus der Regressionsgleichung entfernt. Auf Tastendruck werden die Parameter der Regressionsgleichung neu berechnet und die neue Regressionsfunktion in die Punktwolke eingezeichnet; das Ergebnis ist in *Abbildung 6* auf der vorherigen Seite dargestellt. Jedes aus der Regressionsgleichung entfernte Objekt kann durch Markierung mit der Taste [I] später wieder in die Berechnung einbezogen werden.

Am Beispiel der *Mehrfachregression* mit den Variablen **A86.einkom** als abhängiger und **A86.alter** und **A86.geschlecht** als unabhängigen Variablen können weitere wichtige Möglichkeiten von STATGRAPHICS aufgezeigt werden. Insbesondere kann an diesem Beispiel gezeigt werden, wie sich nominalskalierte Merkmale in Form von Dummyvariablen verarbeiten lassen und wie bei der grafischen Aufbereitung die Technik der Überlagerung von Bildern – Overlay Plotting – genutzt werden kann. Um eine nominalskalierte Variable – hier **A86.geschlecht** – in Dummyvariable zu verschlüsseln, wird sie im Eingabetableau der Prozedur **Multiple Regression** mit dem Schlüsselbegriff **IND** versehen. Der Operator **IND** bewirkt die *automatische Umwandlung* einer nominalskalierten Variablen mit k Ausprägungen (hier k=2) in k-1 Dummyvariable. Zunächst erscheint das übliche Ergebnistableau der Mehrfachregression; weitere Ergebnisse, zum Beispiel Plots der Residuen oder ein graphischer Test auf Normalverteilung der Residuen, können in einem Optionenfenster gewählt werden.

Eine *Darstellung der Regressionsebene* im dreidimensionalen Raum ist nur mit der Prozedur **Response Surface Plotting** möglich. Zunächst werden die Wertebereiche der Achsenabschnitte festgelegt – hier 0 bis 1 für die Variable **A86.geschlecht** und 1 bis 100 für die Variable **A86.alter**. Die zuvor in der Regressionsanalyse bestimmte Schätzfunktion wird vom Anwender als sogenannte *user function* eingegeben; danach erscheint die graphische Darstellung der Regressionsebene. Dieses Bild muß zum Zwecke der Graphiküberlagerung gespeichert werden. In einem zweiten Schritt wird ein dreidimensionales Streuungsdiagramm mit **A86.geschlecht** und **A86.alter** als X- und Y-Variable sowie **einkom** als Z-Variable ohne Referenzlinien erzeugt und ebenfalls gespeichert. Das – hier nicht wiedergegebene – Streuungsdiagramm zeigt die getrennten Punktwolken für die Männer und die Frauen.

Die Prozedur **Splitscreen/Overlay Plotting** ist in der Lage, mehrere Graphiken gleichzeitig neben- bzw. untereinander darzustellen, dabei werden maximal 9 Ausgabepositionen (3 Reihen und 3 Spalten) gleichzeitig berücksichtigt. Innerhalb jeder Position können wiederum bis zu 4 Graphiken überlagert werden. Die *Abbildung 7* zeigt die Überlagerung der zwei im vorgestellten Regressionsbeispiel gespeicherten Graphiken, nämlich der Punktwolke von Männern und Frauen und der berechneten Regressionsebene.

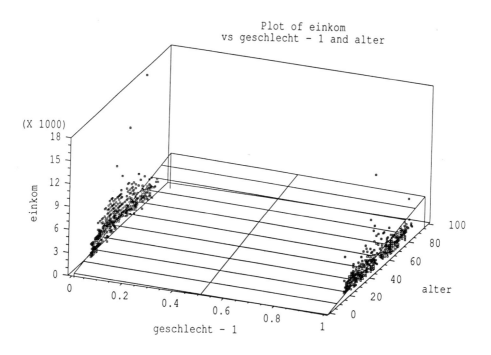

Abb. 7: Punktwolke und Regressionsebene der Mehrfachregression zwischen Einkommen, Alter und Geschlecht

4. Schlußbemerkungen

Als Fazit ist festzustellen, daß sich STATGRAPHICS hervorragend für *kreative Auswertungen* mit unbekannten Daten, also für ein erstes "Durchkneten" der Daten eignet. Viele Prozeduren zur explorativen Datenanalyse und deskriptiven Statistik zusammen mit *hochwertigen Graphiken* erleichtern wesentlich das Verständnis der Daten und die Generierung von Hypothesen. Zur Überprüfung der Hypothesen mit statistischen Tests steht ein breites Spektrum bis hin zu Multivariaten Verfahren zur Verfügung, so daß ein Wechsel zu einem anderen Statistiksystem im allgemeinen nicht notwendig wird.

Die *leicht zu erlernende Menüoberfläche* und die *integrierte Hilfefunktion* erleichtern die Anwendung für unerfahrene oder sporadische Benutzer. Zahlreiche Import- oder Exportfunktionen gestatten den *Datenaustausch* mit Standard-Software wie Lotus 1-2-3 oder Dbase. Auch zu Kartographie- und Präsentationsprogrammen (z. B. Atlas Graphics, Lotus Freelance) existieren Schnittstellen.

Was könnte an STATGRAPHICS verbessert werden? Die Zahl der zu verarbeitenden Objekte könnte durch eine andere Speicherverwaltung oder vielleicht durch eine Umstellung auf OS/2 weiter vergrößert werden, da 1500 Objekte auch in der Version 3.0 hart an der Kapazitätsgrenze liegen. Auch fehlt bislang man die Möglichkeit, Makros zu definieren, um beispielsweise wiederkehrende Routine-Auswertungen automatisch ablaufen zu lassen. Ansonsten ist STATGRAPHICS ein sehr *mächtiges System*, mit dem auch die Studenten der wirtschaftswissenschaftlichen Fakultät der Universität Münster sehr gerne und sehr erfolgreich arbeiten.

Literaturhinweise

Beneke Th., Schippert W. (1989). STSC STATGRAPHICS: Statistik und Graphik für alle Fälle. MS-DOS Welt, 2/89, 127-136.

Bleymüller J. (1988). Programmbeurteilung STATGRAPHICS. WiSt, 3/88, 143-144.

Bleymüller J., Gehlert G., Gülicher H. (1988). Statistik für Wirtschaftswissenschaftler. Vahlen, München.

Hörmann A. (1983). Graphiksoftware als Mittel statistischer Analysen. In: Wilke H. u. a. (Hrsg.). Statistik-Software in der Sozialforschung, Quorum, Berlin, 375-399.

Jungmann N. (1989). SPSS/PC+: Statistik-Gigant im neuen Kleid. PC Magazin, 10/89, 62-70.

Sajuk T., Moreau P. (1989). Graphik statt Zahlen, Statgraphics Statistik-Software. CHIP, 3/89, 132-135.

Schach S. (1988). Mikro-Versionen verbreiteter Statistik-Programmpakete: Ein Vergleich. In: Faulbaum F., Uehlinger H.-M. (Hrsg.). Fortschritte der Statistik-Software 1. G. Fischer, Stuttgart, New York, 137-152.

STSC, Inc. (1988). STATGRAPHICS User's Guide, Rockville (Maryland).

Graphische Methoden der Datenanalyse: Exploration, Analyse und Präsentation

M. Nagel

Summary

Statistical graphics is shown as an essential part of data analysis. Several graphical methods, new and old, for data exploration, for analysis of data, and for communication and presentation are briefly discussed, which improve the way that graphics can be used to aid in exploration, summarization, modelling and communication of data. Especially, high-interaction graphics is an extremely powerful tool to facilitate the discovery of multivariate outliers and multivariate cluster hunting.

1. Die Bedeutung grafischer Methoden in der Statistik

Empirische Forschungsarbeit läßt sich grob in zwei Phasen einteilen: eine explorative Phase, in der der Wissenschaftler Erkenntnisse oder Hypothesen über den Gegenstand seines Interesses aus vorliegenden Daten und über deren Zusammenhänge aufstellt. In einer daran anschließenden konfirmatorischen Phase müssen dann solche hypothetischen Modelle überprüft werden. Fehlen Vorkenntnisse über die Daten, ist über deren Herkunft und Beziehung zu einer möglichen Grundgesamtheit wenig bekannt, ist es sehr schwierig, ein geeignetes Modell aufzustellen oder geeignete Hypothesen zu formulieren: Aus unbekannten Datenstrukturen lassen sich keine weitreichenden Schlüsse ziehen.

Die explorative Datenanalyse ist damit besonders geeignet, unbekannte Datenstrukturen zu enthüllen und dient der Hypothesengewinnung. Eine zentrale Rolle spielt dabei eine aktive grafische Analyse von und Experimentieren mit Daten. Aber auch zu allen anderen Zeitpunkten von statistischen Untersuchungen sind Grafiken sinnvoll. Sei es, daß sie zur Unterstützung von verschiedenen Analysenverfahren oder zur Veranschaulichung von Ergebnissen in anspruchsvoller, kommunikativer Form am Ende einer Untersuchung genutzt werden.

Durch die heute verfügbare Computertechnik am Arbeitsplatz haben sich die Anwendungsschwerpunkte von Grafiken deutlich verschoben: Neben Präsentationsgrafiken als "Endprodukt" stehen heute Echtzeitgrafiken als "Wegwerfgrafiken" auf dem Bildschirm im Vordergrund.

2. Übersicht über grafische Methoden in der Datenanalyse

In nachstehender Tabelle (nach Henschke, 1990) werden wichtige grafische Methoden zusammengestellt. Als Ordnungsprinzip dient die Anzahl der darzustellenden Merkmale. Die Buchstaben E, A, D und P verweisen auf den hauptsächlichen Verwendungszweck der Grafiken (<u>E</u>xploration, <u>A</u>nalyse, <u>D</u>iagnostik, <u>P</u>räsentation).

2.1. GRAFIKEN ZUR UNTERSUCHUNG EINZELNER MERKMALE

<u>Präsentationsgrafik zur Darstellung von Häufigkeitsverhältnissen</u>

Kreisdiagramme   P ⎫
Säulendiagramme   P ⎪
Punkt-Karten   P ⎬ Schmidt, 1954; Tufte, 1983
Linien-Diagramme   P ⎪
Kartogramme   P ⎭

<u>Datenverdichtung</u>   <u>Überprüfung von Verteilungsannahmen für Merkmale</u>

Histogramme   E, P Scott, 1979   Histogrammvergleiche   A ⎫ Hensch-
Häufigkeitspolygone E ⎫ Chambers,   Histogramm und Dichte-   ⎬ ke,
empirische Verteilungs- ⎬ 1983   funktion   A ⎭ 1990
funktion   E ⎭   Wurzeldiagramme   D   Velle-
Wurzeldiagramme   E   Velleman,   man,
                          1981   1981

<u>Vergleich der Verteilung eines Merkmals über mehrere Grundgesamtheiten</u>

Stamm-und-Blatt-Darstellungen zweier Datenmengen   E   Chambers,
                                                         1983, Tufte,
                                                         1983
Mehrfache (eingekerbte) Box-Plots   E, A   Velleman, 1981, Hoaglin,
                                             1983, McGill, 1978
Empirische P-P-Bilder   E   Wilk, 1968
Empirische Q-Q-Bilder   E   Gnanadesikan, 1977
Darstellung von Differenzen und Verhältnissen   E   Chambers, 1981
Mittelwertsvergleiche   A   Andrews, 1980

<u>Diagnostische Darstellungen</u>

Symmetrietests   D, E   Chambers, 1981
Streuung-gegen-Lageparameter   E, D   Chambers, 1981, Hoaglin, 1983

2.2. GRAFIKEN ZUR UNTERSUCHUNG ZWEIER MERKMALE

<u>Streubilder und Variationen</u>

Streubilder und informative Hilfslinien   E   Cleveland, 1984,
                                                Thissen, 1988

Verdichtung von Streubildern   E   Bachi, 1978
Zeitreihendarstellungen   E, A, P DuToit, 1986
Überprüfung der Linearität   A, D, E Hoaglin, 1983

Untersuchung diskreter Merkmale

grafische Darstellungen von Kontingenztafeln   E, A   Snee, 1974
Siebdiagramme   E   Riedwyl, 1983
Zuordnungsanalyse   E   Lebart, 1984

2.3. DIE GLEICHZEITIGE DARSTELLUNG VON MEHR ALS ZWEI MERKMALEN

Symbolisch-schematische Darstellungen von Beobachtungen

Streudiagramme und Streudiagramm-Matrizen   E   Gnanadesikan, 1977
                                                Cleveland, 1988
Glyphen, Metroglyphen, Polygone   E   Anderson, 1966
Andrews-Plots   E   Andrews, 1972
Gesichtsdarstellungen   E   Chernoff, 1973, Flury, 1981

Dimensionsreduktion

empirische Hauptkomponenten   E   Gnanadesikan, 1977
abstandsorientierte Verfahren   E   Gower, 1986
baryzentrische Koordinaten   P, E   Henschke, 1990

Wakimoto-Konstellationsgrafik   E   Wakimoto, 1978, 1980

Analyse der Merkmalsstruktur   E   Gnanadesikan, 1977, Gower, 1966,
                                    1986, Lingoes, 1979

Biplot   E   Gabriel, 1971   Dendrogramm   E   Anderberg, 1972

Bertin-System   E   Bertin, 1983

2.4. HOCH-INTERAKTIVE UND DYNAMISCHE DATENANALYSE

Projektion, Rotation, Identifikation,   E   Cleveland, 1988
Markierung, Brushing
Grafische Inferenz   A, E   Asimov, 1983, Weihs, 1987
Kleine und große Reise   E   Stützle, 1984

3. Hoch-interaktive Grafik

Die direkte Manipulation grafischer Elemente auf dem Bildschirm
und die (virtuell) kontinuierliche Änderung dieser Elemente sind
die wichtigsten Eigenschaften dynamischer oder hoch-interaktiver
Grafik, die zukünftig entscheidend die Datenanalyse beeinflussen
werden: Man sieht mehr, wenn man eine Grafik interaktiv beeinflussen kann, als wenn man sie lediglich betrachtet (Huber, 1983).
Als Vorbild für die heutigen Softwareentwicklungen zur hoch-interaktiven Grafik diente das in Stanford entwickelte System PRIM-9
(Fisherkeller, 1988), wobei PRIM für einige wichtige damit realisierbare Grundoperationen - Projektionen, Rotationen, Isolation
bzw. Identifikation und Markierung bzw. Maskierung von Daten
steht. Durch Rotation wird ein räumlicher Eindruck der Datenstruktur vermittelt. Dabei lassen sich Rotationsgeschwindigkeit,
Drehrichtung, Variablenauswahl interaktiv wählen; die Punktwolke

kann expandieren, geschrumpft und verschoben werden.
Ein wichtiges Hilfsmittel für die Ermittlung von Ausreißern und
die Clusterung ist die Identifikation von Beobachtungen.
Bei einer anderen interaktiven Methode, dem Brushing von Streudiagramm-Matrizen wird ein in Größe und Form frei bestimmbares
Rechteck über den Bildschirm bewegt. Punkte, die in das Rechteck
fallen, werden zeitgleich optisch in allen Feldern der Streudiagramm-Matrix hervorgehoben. Durch diese visuelle Verknüpfung zwischen den einzelnen Variablen werden nicht selten Zusammenhänge
sichtbar, die anderweitig nicht zu entdecken sind. Beispiel: Rotation und Brushing können bei der Bewertung der Umweltgefährlichkeit von Stoffen genutzt werden (Koch, 1989). Als Stoffkenngrößen
werden z. B. Wasserlöslichkeit, Henry-Koeffizient, Verteilungs-
koeffizient Octanol/Wasser, Biokonzentrationsfaktor, Sorptions-
koeffizient, LD 50 und Reaktionsgeschwindigkeit radikalischer
Hydroxylreaktionen herangezogen, wobei eine Bewertung von Umweltgefährlichkeit nur vergleichenden Charakter haben kann. Für ausgewählte Referenzsubstanzen
werden deren einzelne Merkmale mit Hilfe linguisti-
scher Wahrheitsfunktionen
auf das Intervall (0,1) abgebildet. Der zu bewertende
Stoff wird nun in "Rangfol-
ge" dieser Referenzstoffe
eingeordnet: für die Aus-
wahl von 3 Merkmalen kann
der Sachverhalt durch einen
Einheitswürfel veranschaulicht werden (Abb. 1)

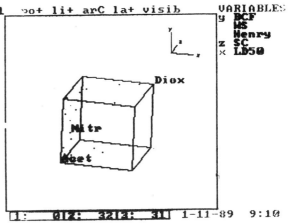

Bei der Bewertung von Substanzen kann sich der Toxikologe die
Lage des interessierenden Stoffes relativ zu den Referenzsubstanzen und unter Berücksichtigung einzelner Merkmale veranschaulichen. Im Bild sind z. B. die Referenzsubstanzen Dioxin, Acetonitril und Nitrofen hervorgehoben.
Für eine Stoffbewertung wäre es wünschenswert, wenn alle transformierten Merkmalswerte möglichst homogen sind. Da das meist
nicht der Fall ist, muß man sich auch alle Merkmalskombinationen
in der Streudiagramm-Matrix (Abb. 2) ansehen. Dabei wurden z. B.

Dioxin (+) und Acetonitril (x) identifiziert. Die Transformation und Visualisierung der Stoffe erfolgte mit Hilfe von PC-ISP bzw. dem dynamischen Grafik-System PC-ISP/DGS (PC-ISP/DGS, 1988) und stellt für den Umweltökologen und Toxikologen eine wichtige Unterstützung bei der Entscheidungshilfe dar.

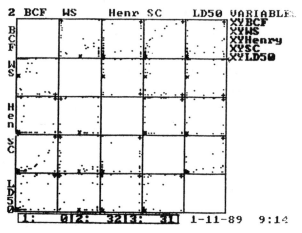

Die PRIM-Operationen sind die bekanntesten Methoden hoch-interaktiver Grafik. Verallgemeinerung von Rotationen (Cleveland, 1988, Asimov, 1983), die Suche nach "interessanten" Projektionen (Projection Pursuit Huber, 1985, 1987), die Nutzung von Bootstrap-Ideen (grafische Inferenz (Buja, 1988) und der Hardware-Möglichkeiten von Workstations mit Lisp-Architektur sowie moderne Benutzeroberflächen (wie z. B. beim Macintosh II) sind interessante Entwicklungsrichtungen der hoch-interaktiven Datenanalyse, deren Einsatzmöglichkeiten noch nicht abzusehen sind. So wären von einer "hoch-interaktiven Kartographie" neue Erkenntnisse aus raumbezogenen Daten zu erwarten.

4. Die visuelle Perzeption von Grafiken

Mit zunehmender Nutzung von Grafiken gewinnt deren Perzeption an Bedeutung: Numerische Werte werden in grafische Ausdrücke transformiert, die wiederum vom Betrachter dekodiert werden. Damit können subjektive Wahrnehmungsfehler auftreten (Tufte, 1983, Cleveland, 1985). Aus gutem Grund gehören deshalb die Untersuchung der Wahrnehmungsmechanismen Grafik Auge – Gehirn zu den interessantesten Forschungsgebieten zur Grafik (Cleveland, 1986). Für die Gestaltung von Grafiken sind die acht visuellen Variablen (Bertin, 1982) in ihrer unterschiedlichen Wertigkeit zu beachten: als Ordnungsvariablen die zwei Koordinaten in der Ebene, Größe, Helligkeitswerte, als trennende Variablen Muster, Farbe, Richtung und Form.

Durch die Kombinationsmöglichkeiten und die Transkription von

Informationskomponenten durch visuelle Variablen ergibt sich eine unendliche Vielfalt von Darstellungsmöglichkeiten, aber die gleichzeitige Wahrnehmung ist auf 3 visuelle Variablen begrenzt. Das spricht für die Nutzung und Weiterentwicklung dynamischer grafischer Methoden.

Literatur

Anderberg, M.R. (1972). Cluster Analysis for Applications. Academic Press, New York

Anderson, E. (1966). A Semigraphical Method for the Analysis of Complex Problems. Technometrics 2, 387 - 91

Andrews, D.F. (1972). Plots of High-dimensional Data. Biometrics 28, 125 - 36

Andrews, H.P., Snee, R.D., Sarner, M.H. (1980). Graphical Display of Means. The American Statistician 34, 195 - 99

Asimov, D. (1983). The Grand Tour. Techn. Report of the Project Orion. Dept. of Statistics, Stanford Univ., Stanford (Cal.)

Bachi, R. (1978). Proposal for the Development of Selected Graphical Methods. In: Graphic Presentation of Statistical Information. Technical Paper 43, U.S. Dept. of Commerce, Bureau of the Census, Washington

Bertin, J. (1982). Graphische Darstellungen. de Gruyter, Berlin (W)

Buja, A., Asinov, D., Hurley, C., McDonald, J.A. Elements of a viewing pipeline for data analysis. In: Cleveland, W.S., McGill, M.E. (Eds.): Dynamic Graphics for Statistics. Wadsworth, Belmont (Cal.), 1988

Chambers, J.M., Cleveland, W.S., Kleiner, B., Tukey, P.A.(1983) Graphical Methods for Data Analysis. Wadsworth, Monterey

Chernoff, H. (1973). The use of faces represent points in k-dimensional space graphically. JASA 68, 361

Cleveland, W.S., McGill, R. (1984). The Many Face of a Scatterplot. JASA 79, 807 - 821

Cleveland, W.S. (1985). The Elements of Graphing Data. Wadsworth, Monterey

Cleveland, W.S., McGill, M.E., McGill, R. (1986). The Shape Parameter of a Two-variable Graph. In: American Stat. Assoc. 1986 Proceedings of the Section on Statistical Graphics. Washington

Cleveland, W.S., McGill, M.E. (Eds.) (1988). Dynamic Graphics for Statistics. Wadsworth, Belmont (Cal.)

Du Toit, S.H.C., Steyn, A.G.W., Stumpf, R.H. (1986). Graphical Exploratory Data Analysis, Springer Verlag, New York

Fisherkeller, M.A., Friedman, J.H., Tukey, J.W. (1988). PRIM-9: An Interactive Multidimensional Data Display and Analysis System. In: The Collected Works of J.W. Tukey; Wadsworth, Belmont (Cal.)

Flury, B., Riedwyl, H. (1981). Graphical representation of multivariate data by means of asymmetrical faces. JASA $\underline{76}$, 757

Gabriel, K.R. (1971). The biplot – graphic display of matrices with application to principal component analysis. Biometrika $\underline{58}$, 453 – 67

Gower, J.C. (1966). Some Distance Properties of latent Root and Vector Methods Used in Multivariate Analysis. Biometrika $\underline{53}$, 325 – 38

Gower, J.C., Digby, P.G.N. (1986). Expressing Complex Relationships in Two Dimensions. In: Barnett, V. (Ed.): Interpreting Multivariate Data. J. Wiley, Chinchester, 83 – 118

Henschke, K., Nagel, M. (1990). Die Exploration, Darstellung und Analyse von Daten: Grafische Methoden. VEB Verlag Volk und Gesundheit (in Vorb.)

Hoaglin, D.C., Mosteller, F., Tukey, J.W. (Eds.) (1983). Understanding Robust and Exploratory Data Analysis. Wiley, New York

Huber, P.J. (1983). Statistical graphics: History and overview. Proc. Fourth Ann. Conf. and Exposition of the National Computer Graphics Assoc. Fairfax (VA), 667 – 676

Huber, P.J. (1985). Projection pursuit; The Annals of Statistics $\underline{13}$, 435 – 475

Huber, P.J. (1987) An illustrated guide to projection pursuit. Draft 1.0 Harvard University

Koch, R., Blüml, T., Nagel, M. (1989). Zur Bewertung der Umweltgefährlichkeit von Chemikalien. Schr.reihe Gesundh. Umw. Bad Elster, im Druck

Lebart, L., Morineau, A., Warwick, K.M. (1984). Multivariate Statistical Description Analysis. John Wiley, New York

Lingoes, J.C., Roksam, E.E., Borg, I. (1979). Geometrical Representations of Relational Data – Reading in Multidimensional Scaling. Mathesis Press, Ann Arbor (Mich.)

McGill, P., Tukey, J.W., Larsen, W.A. (1978). Variations of Boxplots. The American Statistician 32, 12 - 18

PC-ISP/DGS: (1988) Benutzerhandbuch und Befehlsbeschreibung. Artemis-Systems und Datavision

Riedwyl, H., Schuepbach, M. (1983). Siebdiagramme. Techn. Bericht Nr. 12, Inst. für Math. Statistik und Versicherungslehre der Universität Bern, Bern

Schmidt, C.F. (1954). Handbook of Graphical Representation, Second Ed. Ronald-Press, New York

Scott, D.W. (1979). On Optimal and Data Based Histograms. Biometrika 66, 605 - 610

Snee, R.D. (1974). Graphical Display of Two-way-Contingency Tables. The Am. Statistician, 28, 9 - 12

Stützle, W. (1984). GraphischeExploration multivariater Daten am Computer. Allg. Stat. Archiv, 68, 63 - 80

Thissen, D., Baker, L., Wainer, H. (1981). Influence-Enhanced Scatterplots. Psychological Bulletin 90, 179 - 184

Tufte, E. (1983). The visual Display of Quantitative Informations. Graphics Press, Cheshire, (Connecticut)

Velleman, P.F., Hoaglin, D.C. (1981). Applications, Basics and Computing Exploratory Data Analysis. Duxburg Press, Boston

Wakimoto, K. (1980). Sun-Chart Method for Looking Multivariate Data. Annals of the Institute of Statistical Mathematics 32, 303 - 310

Weihs, C. (1987). Dynamic Graphical Methods in Multivariate Exploratory Data Analysis: An Overview. Workshop "Informatik in der Biometrie", Innsbruck (Austria), 13. - 14. 11. 1987

Wilk, M.B., Gnanadesikan, R. (1968). Probability Plotting Methods for the Analysis of Data. Biometrika 55, 1 - 17

F. Faulbaum, R. Haux und K.-H. Jöckel (Hrsg.) (1990). SoftStat '89
Fortschritte der Statistik-Software 2. Stuttgart: Gustav Fischer, 278 - 287

Dynamic Interactive Graphics for Spatially Referenced Data

G. Wills, A. Unwin, J. Haslett, and P. Craig

Summary
Dynamic Interactive Graphics is one of the fastest growing areas of modern statistical research. A substantial body of work has been done on issues such as brushing, information display, 3–D rotations and linked plots. This paper describes the impact of these methods on the field of spatially distributed data, which poses problems for traditional statistical analysis. New methods being developed by the authors for such data are examined, both from practical and theoretical viewpoints, and an overview of computer graphics projects being developed by the authors is given.

1. Spatially Distributed Data

It is necessary for us first to state what we understand by spatially distributed data. We define it as a set of points which have an (x,y) position and n associated variables at each point. It is a common form of data especially in commercial and earth science fields. It is also not an easy form of data to deal with, and the field could be said to be given less attention than its importance suggests.

To look at the types of data commonly studied, we classify them according to the dimension of their geometry :

If the data has no geometrical relation, we term it *0-geometrical data*. If it is linearly related, as in time series, we term it *1-geometrical*, and for data distributed over a plane, we term it *2-geometrical*.

1.1 0-Geometrical Data

0-Geometrical data is data with no spatial or time relationship. The analysis of such data usually involves some form of multivariate analysis, about which there is much literature and for which there are many tools available to the statistician. Here, model building is a much-practised art and choices and tools are many.

As an example of this kind of data, we look at a study conducted at Trinity College Dublin recently, where 820 measurements were made of mineral deposits in water, of which Chrome, Nickel and Zinc were examined. To look at the data, one would usually first examine some summary statistics such as means, standard deviations, correlations, etc., which provide useful information, but for more information, static plots such as those of figures 1 and 2 give more insight.

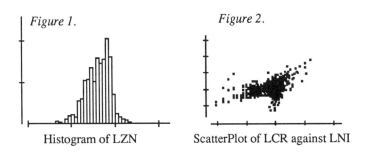

Figure 1. Histogram of LZN

Figure 2. ScatterPlot of LCR against LNI

The two common dynamic methods used for this type of data are scatterplot brushing and rotating plots. These have been presented many times, most notably in papers such as *Dynamic Graphics for Data Analysis* (Becker, Cleveland and Wilks) and *The Use of Brushing and rotation for Data Analysis* (Becker, Cleveland and Weil).

1.2 1-Geometrical Data

Although this is predominantly the realm of time series, spatially 1-dimensionally related data, for example in bore-hole analysis, is also included. There are many modelling techniques available to the statistician for time series, of which ARIMA is perhaps the most popular.

The data collected summarised in figures 3 and 4 give an example of one-dimensional data. These are measurements of means of two metals taken along a stream. Apparent is a visual correlation, and further analysis can be undertaken using standard methods.

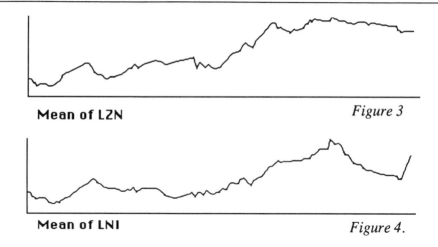

Mean of LZN   *Figure 3*

Mean of LNI   *Figure 4.*

In our analysis, things are generally more complex in this situation. Questions of stationarity arise, and summary statistics tend to be less descriptive than in the previous case; Rather than numbers, we look more at static plots such as :

- Autocorrelation plots
- Partial autocorrelation plots
- Cross-correlation plots
- Residual plots
- Various diagnostic plots.

Also, we not only need our univariate views, but extensions of our univariate tools as well. Instead of just correlations we need plots of auto- and cross-correlations.

In general it is less easy to make decisions - more expertise is required for working with the data, and therefore it is necessary to give the analyst plenty of control over and information about the data. The need for dynamic tools to examine and investigate time series data is becoming more and more clear and is treated, for example, in Unwin and Wills' papers *Eyeballing time series* and *Exploratory time Series graphics*.

1.3 2-Geometrical Data

For spatially distributed data we have two problems; the **point process** itself and the relationship between the **variables** sampled at each point. Here the problem is more complex again. Where we had to consider stationarity in time series, we must consider questions of homogeneity and isotropy. Model building is correspondingly more difficult and requires a lot of expertise and specialised knowledge of the domain of the problem.

In dealing with spatial data, summaries provide little insight and static plots, of which the contour plot is the most common, are also too limited. What is needed is a method of examining the data that embodies the following concepts :

Flexibility.
The type of questions which can be asked about spatial data vary immensely :
> Is there an homogeneous sub-area in the data ?
> Is there an overall trend ?
> Are two areas different in some way ?

Even the types of data vary considerably; we can have information in the form of regions, lines or direction. These give rise to interesting questions such as :
> Does a certain set of points lie closer to some line features than chance dictates ?
> Is a relationship between A and B affected by the underlying region ?

Because of this complexity, any graphic system for studying spatial data must be easily modifiable and applicable to a wide variety of data, as otherwise users will be frustrated by its limitations.

Robustness
The package must recognise unusual features in the data, but must not distort overall patterns due to them. This is necessary given the general non-homogeneity of spatial data.

Ability to incorporate the user's expertise

Computers are a tremendous aid to statistical investigation, but they have great difficulty in pattern recognition as is shown by the failure of Artificial Intelligence research to provide useful tools even for fairly non-complex tasks. For this reason a good program must be able to draw on the user's ability to recognise spatial and other patterns in the data.

For example, relating a pattern of data to a satellite image is tremendously difficult for a computer owing to the vast amount of information such an image conveys, but people have the ability rapidly to perceive which features are interesting, and which are not.

Speed

Because of the high degree of user interaction, rapid calculation and display are necessary. However, a package which can only run on super-computers is of limited use to most of us.

2. SPIDER

With the considerations of §1.3 in mind, the SPIDER package was created. It has been implemented on the Apple Macintosh to take advantage of the WIMP interface. It uses distinct windows for each different view or plot of the data, and a mouse-controlled cursor to enable the user to interact with the data in an efficient manner.

A sample screen is given in figure 5. This data is in fact the metals data shown in the example in §1.1, where the spatial position of each reading has been taken into account. These measurements were taken from streams in a region of central Spain.

At the top left is a window containing a map of the XY positions of the samples. Below is a bar for changing the way the map is displayed and below that is a list of variables observed at each map point, of which those in dark are active variables. At the bottom right is a window containing a scatterplot matrix of LCR and LNI with histograms along diagonals, which was created by selecting the desired variables and using a menu option.

One point to note is that the program displays in colour, and a satellite picture is available behind the map, but it is impossible to represent this faithfully on a black and white page.

2.2 Cross-Highlighting

The best way to explain Spider is by showing how it can be used on the data set given, which consists of several points with Zinc (LZN), Nickel (LNI) and Chromium (LCR) values observed. Logs have been taken of these values.

When we open a data set, we get only the main window. By clicking on LZN and selecting 'Create Histogram' we produce a histogram view. Using the mouse, we select the high values of ZN from the histogram by drawing a box through the bars we want highlighted. This automatically highlights the corresponding points on the map. Note the clusters thus shown.

We can similarly use the scatterplot from figure 5.
Zoom in on one panel (the LCR-LNI scatterplot). We will now investigate this 'V'-shaped scatterplot by selecting one arm as before by drawing a rectangle around it. Instantly we see that this relation occurs only in bottom-left of the map. This is shown in figure 6. In fact there is a different rock type in this area, and so we have visually established the result that the relationship between Chromium and Nickel is substantially affected by the underlying rock type.

2.3 The Brush Trace

Although there are more features which could be shown, possibly the most innovative is the brush trace, which works like this:

By selecting a variable to work with and a statistic to calculate on this variable we select the options for the brush. When the mouse is clicked and dragged along a path, then at repeated intervals the program calculates the statistic on those points within a circle centred at the mouse. These are then recorded as a time series plot. The effect of this is to create a 1-Geometrical view of how the statistic on the variable changes as you move the mouse along a linear feature in the plane.

This is how the figures in §1.2 were created, and as a general method can spot features which are otherwise very tricky to spot. In some streams on the map, Zinc and Chromium are related to a high degree, but overall Zinc and Chromium have a correlation coefficient of only 0.005. It is very difficult to spot this stream correlation using other methods. This subject is given more thorough treatment in a paper by P.Craig : *Moving Graphics - an extension of 'Brushing' for spatial data*

2.3 Future research

Spider has been written in Object-Oriented Pascal, and has been structured so that adding new views of the data and commands which follow the same dynamic ideas as demonstrated above should pose few problems to a competent programmer. The main area of research will be into deciding which tools to implement, and evolving more new tools to take advantage of modern, high powered desktop computers.

New features which are being worked on include more complex views of the data, extension to 3-D data, multivariate tracing statistics such as moving correlations and the ability to work with data sets with different point support, and with linear and regional data.

Spider is currently being used by an environmental research company on geological data. It has been applied to medical problems and it is hoped that further applications should clarify design and structure issues.

3. Conclusion

In this paper the progression from 0-geometrical to 1 and 2-geometrical data has been presented in terms both of analytical and graphical tools. By examining the needs of the analyst and the possibilities that fast interactive graphics offer, our motivation for the Spider package has been given, as well as a brief introduction to the implementation of these techniques in the Spider package.

4. References

Becker, Cleveland and Wilks (1987). Dynamic Graphics for Data Analysis. Statistical Science 2 355-395

Becker, Cleveland and Weil (1987). The use of brushing and rotation for data analysis. Dynamic Graphics for Statistics.

Craig, Haslett, Unwin and Wills (1989). Moving Statistics - an extension of 'Brushing' for spatial data. Interfaces Orlando.

Unwin and Wills (1988). Eyeballing Time Series. Proceedings of 1988 ASA Statistical Graphics section.

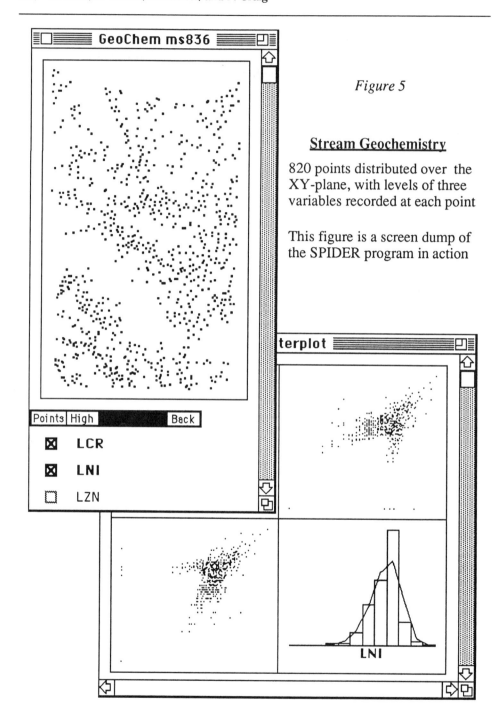

Figure 5

Stream Geochemistry

820 points distributed over the XY-plane, with levels of three variables recorded at each point

This figure is a screen dump of the SPIDER program in action

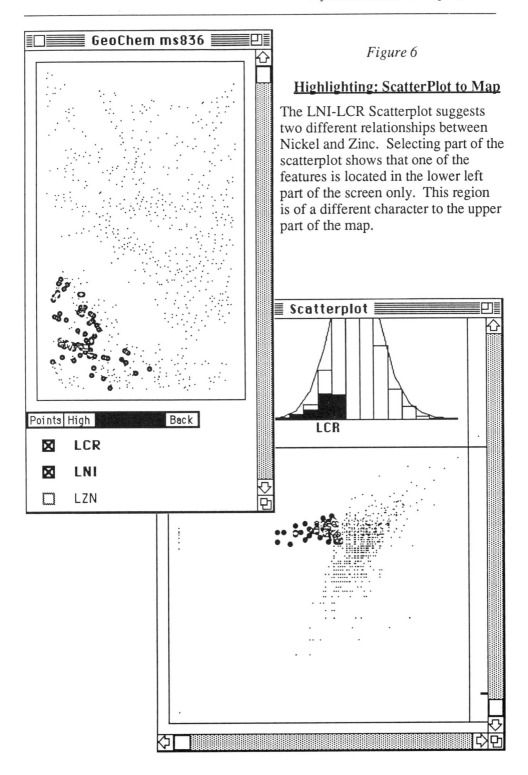

Figure 6

Highlighting: ScatterPlot to Map

The LNI-LCR Scatterplot suggests two different relationships between Nickel and Zinc. Selecting part of the scatterplot shows that one of the features is located in the lower left part of the screen only. This region is of a different character to the upper part of the map.

Expertensysteme in der Statistik

Is there Something New that Can Be Learned or Solved by Building Statistical Expert Systems?

P. Naeve

Summary: Several statistical subjects truely benefit in one way or the othere from all those efforts put into the field of statistical expert systems. Firstly there is a new and very fruitful discussion of the old question "What is statistics?" Secondly we do not only understand better what could be meant by intelligent statistical software but can take the first steps to implement this better understanding. Thirdly we became aware how strongly we depend in our daily work as statisticians on graphical methods of all kinds. These points are worked out and are illustrated by examples.

A wise man's advice. Let me start with a very general answer and - what seems to me more impotant - a warning. I will do this by quoting John Nelder:

> "... We have much to learn about this new kind of software which should not be thought of as a panacea. Procedures unhelpful to the scientists and technologists can be codified as rules just as easily as helpful ones, and we can confidently predict that the misuse of packages will be followed by the misconstruction of expert systems ..."
> (Nelder, 1986)

Learning by doing is a well-known advice. So I am glad my talk is based on experiences I made during a larger research project in the field of statistical expert systems. I will discuss three questions the answers of which might benefit in one way or the other from our efforts on building statistical expert systems. These questions are

What is statistics?
What is intelligent statistical software?
What are we doing with graphics?

There is but one way to tell the truth many people do not want to hear. Say it again and again. So before going into any details let me present my main message again. All those fruitful impulses I will talk about that statistics might get by our working on statistical expert systems might be outnumbered by all evils if we cannot convince the statistical layman that inspite of our working on statistical expert systems there will never be something like a true statistical expert system on the market.

It might be helpful to introduce briefly that research project I mentioned at the beginning.

The (my) background. In the year 1987 the University of Bielefeld and the Nixdorf Computer Company established a joined research project on statistical expert systems. The goal was - at least from Nixdorf's point of view - 'building a statistical expert system with the help of existing, commercially available software'. This will say take a statistical package (the choice was P-STAT because those P-STAT people promised to be cooperative) and a shell (the choice was TWAICE because it is a Nixdorf product). TWAICE belongs to the class of shells constructed according to the EMYCIN paradigm - although the Nixdorf people did not like this classification very much. From the university's point of view we liked to express the goal of the research project somewhat more in line with a scientific attitude. 'Is it possible to build an expert system relying on existing software components?'

It was agreed upon that we should not take special AI-hardware. So the work was done on the university's main frame (a Hitachi computer) and on a HP 9000/320 computer. The operating systems were UTS and UNIX respectively.

Can one give a definition for statistical expert system? Having used the term statistical expert system several times it seems to be mandatory to present a definition. In a somewhat technical way what we were doing was to take an expert system shell and a statistical package as building blocks and to add statistical expertise. So the problem of having a definition for a statistical expert system is changed to 'What is statistical expertise?' Here are the types of expertise we wanted to incorporate into our system.

1. Statistical expertise stands for the ability to find models for the description and analysis of problems. To be sucessful a common background made out of statistics and subject matters must be established among the statistician and client.

2. Statistical expertise stands for methodological knowledge. The statistician knows about the prerequisites, the algorithms, data input and output etc. of statistical procedures. He not only knows how to apply a special procedure but also when to apply this procedure. This includes the knowledge how the interpretation of results should be changed when some prerequisites are not fulfilled.

3. Statistical expertise stands for the ability to describe data. This means the statistician has a concept of an abstract data model from which he deduces the specific model suited for the problem at hand. (The situation resembles somewhat the relation between scheme and subscheme in a data base.)

4. Statistical expertise always incorporates teaching expertise. Hopefully not only a problem is solved during a consultation but the client knows more about statistics then before.

5. Statistical expertise nowadays also stands for statistical software expertise. A software package is not only a collection of useful statistical procedures but usually incorporates some model building strategies. Unfortunately this point is not always made very explicit. And here is the place too to remind us that far to often you have to quite a lot of computer science knowledge to get some statistical package work on your problem.

This is quite an impressive list. But we are convinced that you cannot delete anything from this list without giving up building an expert system in statistics.
Take this list as necessary attributes of a statistical expert system.
If one would insist on having a proper definition I would like to join the one given by John Nelder (Nelder, 1984) in his paper on statistical computing. But I think what has been said so far suffices to make my position clear enough with respect to the question: What is a statistical expert system? So let me deal with the first question.
What is statistics? This question has a long tradition. For instance again and again it was theme of the presidential address in the Royal Statistical Society. For a long time the main problem seemed to be a clear distinction between statistics and mathematical statistics. Nowadays the question sounds like: What are statistical strategies? This shift in focus is due to John Tukey's stressing the importance of explorative statistical analysis.
Speaking about or analysing statistical strategies cannot be done without a suitable language. AI offers many language components which can help to describe knowledge and inference processes involved in statistical strategies.
Two recent papers by Thomas Westerhoff and the author present this point in more details than can be given here (Westerhoff, 1988a,b) But be careful!
Abstraction is not reduction and vice versa. We all know we need language to express our thoughts. And the novel 1984 is a fine example what happens to the people's minds if one only allows for such poor language as 'new speech'. And what about programming languages of all kind? They are still so close to 'new speech' that one faces a danger which I will call reductionism. Let me give you an example.
Recently I found this quote whilst reviewing a paper:

"Wir wollen eine Maschine ... genau dann als Expertensystem bezeichnen, wenn sie Funktionen, die für einen Experten spezifisch sind, übernehmen kann. ... Unter (spezifischen) Funktionen ... verstehen wir diejenigen Fähigkeiten, die, außer von Expertensystemen, nur von Experten übernommen werden können. ..."

This seemed to be a worked out version of the definition for 'intelligent' given by the Merriam Webster (Webster, 1983).

intelligent: able to perform functions of a computer.

In our work we had to face such problems too – especially when you consider that our partner had strong commercial interests. There was always the temptation to abandon what could not be modeled within the possibilities of the shell.

The so called emptiness of the shell was one of the greatest source for this danger of reductionism. A shell is not empty. It has an inference engine which has strong – but not always revealed – views on how your inference processes take place. Those two papers by Thomas Westerhoff und myself deal in some length with this kind of problems.

Having read through many papers reporting on 'building expert systems' I got the impression that more than one author was trapped in this reduction sink.

Reductionism is not just a possibility it is sad fact.

What is intelligent statistical software? There is a long plea for intelligent statistical software. But it is not always clear what is meant by intelligent.

One interpretation seems to be

i) The software should be able to prevent the user from doing something silly e.g. calculate the mean for 0,1 coded sex.

Here AI tools for knowledge representation like frames and rules certainly offer new possibilities. Another interpretation could be

ii) The software should not hinder the statistician doing his analysis the way he wants – it should behave like a slave to his master obeying commands and adapting to new ideas.

Here I doubt if expert system technology really brings something new – at the contrary sometimes it seems as if one goes backward. One of the essential features of expert systems is the ability to explain.

Why this question?
How did we reach this point?
etc.

But when linking the shell TWAICE to P-STAT we soon noticed that this amounts to the shell has to have control over whole dialogue with the user – how should it otherwise understand what was going on. So we had to fall back into the stone age of batch processing with P-STAT.

Although one could pile a lot of critical remarks about software packages their standards are much higher than promoter of expert system technology want us to believe. To mention just on point: interactivity!

Other drawbacks when using shells like lacking interfaces, doing calculations in PROLOG, will be passed just by mentioning. But even within their own domain shells do not have the kind of intelligent software components one should expect. Here are two examples.

How smart are shells with respect to context? This is a very short example showing what has to be done to get something like a 'natural' conversation.

The problem is just this. For a statistician the term variable is something familiar. Variables come along with the problem but not always in the appropriate form at the beginning. Sometimes they have to be transformed. The statistician will speak of using a transformed variable – later on when he is working on the problem for the second time it is just a variable to him. But let us concentrate on the first time. Here is the dialog:

(4) >pH
   Wie lautet der Name der 2. Variable des 1. Modells ?
   ("-", falls keine weitere normale Variable betrachtet werden soll)
(5) >Ca
   Wie lautet der Name der 3. Variable des 1. Modells ?
   ("-", falls keine weitere normale Variable betrachtet werden soll)
(6) >-
   Wie lautet der Name der 1. transformierten Variable im 1. Modell ?
(7) >pHtrans

SETUP sind in diesem Modell bisher folgende Variablen bekannt, die
bei Erzeugung neuer Variablen durch Transformation verwendet werden
duerfen :
Ca
pH

and here is what has to be done to get something like a context dependent conversation.

```
RULE   1221
IF     Variable . ist_transformierte = nein
THEN   Variable . Name = PROC ( prc_frage_normal )
END

RULE   1222
IF     Variable . ist_transformierte = ja
THEN   Variable . Name = PROC ( prc_frage_trans )
END

proc(prc_frage_normal,'Variable',INST,'Name',[],[(_,0)]):-
      dyn_fact(_,'Variable',INST,'Nummer',[(NR,1000)]),
      dyn_son('Variable',INST,'Modell',M_INST),
      dyn_fact(_,'Modell',M_INST,'RELORD',X),
      tw_write(dialog_out,['Wie lautet der Name der ',NR,'. Variable',
      'des ',M_INST,'. Modells ?',nl(1)]),!,
      make_number(NR,Numb),
      Numb > 1,
      tw_write(dialog_out,['("-", falls keine weitere normale Variable',
      'betrachtet werden soll)',nl(1)]),!,fail.

proc(prc_frage_trans,'Variable',INST,'Name',[],[(_,0)]):-
      dyn_fact(_,'Variable',INST,'Nummer',[(NR,1000)]),
      dyn_son('Variable',INST,'Modell',M_INST),
      dyn_fact(_,'Modell',M_INST,'RELORD',X),
      tw_write(dialog_out,['Wie lautet der Name der ',NR,
      '. transformierten Variable im ',M_INST,'. Modell ?',nl(1)]),!,
      make_number(NR,Numb),
      Numb > 1,
      tw_write(dialog_out,['("-", falls keine weitere transformierte',
      'Variable betrachtet werden soll)',nl(1)]),!,fail.
```

Much work just to get the simple phrase 'transformed' at the right place.
Are we really always consistent? This is an example of how the state of the art is lacking behind of what is needed. It is of a more technical nature to make the point of deficiency more explicit.

```
            Bei der von Ihnen gewaehlten Analyse und dem angestrebten
            Ziel schlagen wir als Verfahren "Boxplot" vor.

(18) Sind Sie mit dem vorgeschlagenen Verfahren einverstanden ?
>nein

Bitte waehlen Sie nur aus den folgenden Verfahren aus :
Boxplot
Letter-Values
Stem-and-Leaf

(19) Welches Verfahren waehlen Sie aus ?
>'Letter-Values'
```

The figure exhibits a short part from a dialog SETUP (the name of our 'system') had with the user. It seems quite natural that the user and the system discuss what method should be applied. Obviously we have the possible chains of conversation

       system suggests a method   — user accepts

and

       system suggests a method   — user disagrees
       system offers a list of methods   — user makes his choice.

Due to lack of space I cannot present the code explicitely as I did above. To give you a feeling we had to implement eleven rules (each has approximately the size of those two shown above) and several special objects and attributes to get this little piece of 'natural' dialog. The reason for this is the fact that TWAICE (like all other shells at that time) was very anxious to be consistent, will say: have a consistent knowledge base all the time. Therefore you were not allowed to change an attribute value once it was set. This was one way to stick to TWAICE's design principle: The knowledge base has to be consistent at any moment.

I think especially when doing exploratory statistical analysis we are usually working on top of a large stock of compiled knowledge which is not consistent at all. Hopefully at the end of our work we can come up with a 'consistent piece of work' – just by discarding all parts that would destroy consistency. And expert systems in statistics should allow and support such kind of thinking and working.

What are we doing with graphics? If we had not been aware of the fact that graphics are indispensable tools for statisticians the project would have taught us. I think it is no offend to Roald Buhler when stating that P-STAT is not to famous for its graphical capabilities. But compared to the possibilities allowed for by the shell P-STAT looks like a giant. I will deal with this point in a moment.

First let me briefly summarize how we as statistician work with graphics.

i) We use graphics to present results. A picture is worth thousand words. The many systems for presentation graphics on the market stress this import application of graphics. (In passing I want to say that in my opinion the quality of these products is often more than questionable.) This usage of graphics causes no great problems with respect to statistical expert systems but presentation graphics are of no great value if one considers expert system applications.

ii) We argue with the help of graphics. 'I see linearity in this scatter plot, therefore ...'. 'This point seems to be an outlier ...'. When acting in this way we are looking for something in the displayed data and want to share our observation with our partner, client or supervisor. What are we looking for? The answer is either the expected (the confirmative view on the displayed data) or the unexpected (the explorative view on the displayed data). Especially the later point is now in the focus of the statistical community due to Tukey's EDA (explorative data analysis). Here is a small example how we play around with graphics. The figures are from a forthcoming Ph.D. theses on 'Literate EDA' by P. Wolf (Wolf, 1989).

The well-known data represent measurements of brain-weight (in g) and body-weight (in kg) of different brands of animals (figure 1). Unfortunately I can only show very few of those pictures one would use to tackle the following questions:

1. Are there outliers? This is a two dimensional problem. The scatterplot of the original data suggests the answer yes. But look at the scatterplot of the log-transformed data. Is man an outlier?

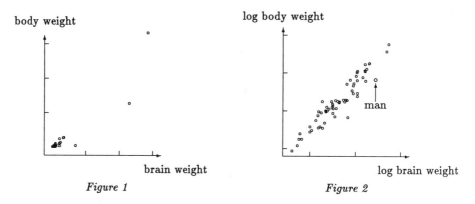

Figure 1   Figure 2

2. Let us turn to a one dimensional problem. Are the log-brain-weight data symmetric? Here is a series of boxplots that might be helpful to get an answer.

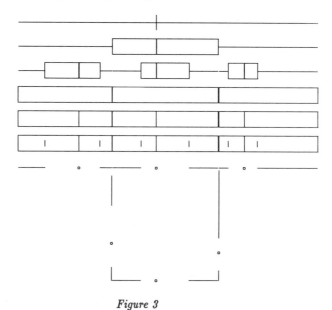

Figure 3

3. Another one dimensional problem is posed by asking what about empty spaces. Here are two plots that might be of use.

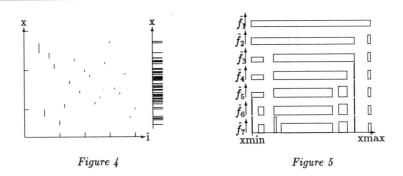

Figure 4   *Figure 5*

4. Are there isolated values? This picture incorporates many ideas of EDA.

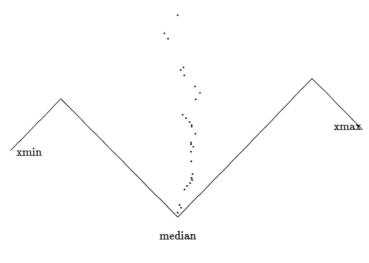

Figure 6

How could such a playing around be done when one of the partners is an expert system?
Here is how we managed the problem to let SETUP see what P-STAT offered as graphical display to the user. We had to provide a numerical analogon for every tupel of problem and graphic so that SETUP could compare the clients answer to question such as 'Does this picture exhibits symmetry' etc. The following lines exhibits the structure behind SETUP's ability to look at a picture. "lastresult" contains the picture the user looks at. "internresult" is needed so that SETUP can pretend to look at the same picture.

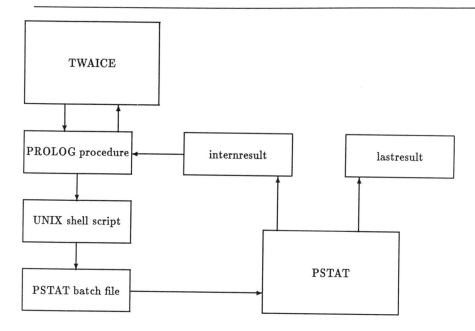

Figure 7: Structure of SETUP's look feature

This is a typical content of the P-STAT batch file (see figure 7).

```
echo "BATCH\$
MAXERROR 1\$
FIND $1, LIBRARY $2\$
PR lastresult\$
PRINT.PARAMETERS lastresult, OUTPUT.WIDTH 80, NO ECHO\$
EDA $1;
BOX.PLOT $3;
\$
PR internresult\$
PRINT.PARAMETERS internresult, OUTPUT.WIDTH 80, NO ECHO\$
EDA $1;
LET $3;
\$
PR\$
END\$" > pstatin
```

This is not a very promising way to do it on a large scale. But it is a good proof for Tukey's claim that we need more cognostics. (P-STAT knows a lot of facts, numerical values etc. about the boxplot shown but there is no possibilty for the user to lay hand on those.)

Where should we go next? I do not want to discuss all kind of repair work to exiting software packages – front-ends might be seen just as such. Neither do I want to deal with small pieces of programs which concentrate on very limited goals. These can be very useful to understand what can be done with expert system technology. But sometimes one cannot help thinking the old saying publish or perish has got a modern version program or perish.

What I want to stress instead is the need for something genuine for statistical work. As I put it elsewhere (Naeve, 1986a). "To make explicit that we are looking for more let us coin a new

name for it. I think statistical environment would be the right name ... – it must contain tools to enlarge the language for personal or common usage."
Our discussion makes us add to the features to be included in a statistical environment

— rules
— frames
— inference strategies i.e. forwared chaining, backward chaining.

Is a statistical environment a dream or could it be reality? I think S (Becker, 1988) is a good prototype of a statistical environment (for all who know my bias towards APL let me say this is a candidate too). So what I intend to do is to enlarge S by adding some AI tools. To be more precise we want to incorporate some frame like structure and mini inference engines.
I had in mind to give some first results. But before you can do this you have to inplement S – the new S.
We did not succeed in finishing this task as fast as we planned.
I do not want to discuss at length why we failed. But you may guess some of the reasons when you hear me stressing: We – the programmers – have not succeeded in writing and documenting correct software. When implementing S we found examples of almost every sin one is warned for in books and lectures on programming and software engineering. So be aware: a statistical expert system is from one point of view just a program. Be humble!
The answer is yes and no I hope to have shown that many things can be learned when working in the field of statistical expert systems. If you do it the right (humble) way you can learn a lot about statistical strategies, statistical software and statistical graphics. And you get a bunch of new and interesting problems. You are on the right way if you are aware of the ever existing danger of reductionism. If you fail to stay on the right way you will increase the large crowd of fooling – most of them do not intend to do but nevertheless do – tailors of the emperor claiming to offer new clothes where there is just nothing. For the message is as stated at the beginning of my talk: ... there will be never anything like a true statistical expert system on the market.

References

Becker R.A., Chambers J.M., Wilks A.R.(1988). The new S language. Pacific Grove

Naeve P.(1986a). Programming languages and opportunities they offer to the statistical community, in: Proceedings of the 1st World Congress of the Bernoulli Society. Y.Y. Prohorov, V.V. Sazonov (eds.), Tashkent

Naeve P. e.a.(1986b). How SETUP was set up. Diskussionspapier 183/1986, Fakultät für Wirtschaftswissenschaften, Universität Bielefeld

Nelder J.A.(1986). Statistics, Science and Technology. JRSS Series A 149, p 109f.

Nelder J.A.(1984). Present position and potential development: Some personal views. Statistical Computing, JRSS Series A 147, p 151f.

Webster's Ninth New Collegiate Dictionary (1983). Merriam Werbster, Springfield

Westerhoff Th., Naeve P.(1988a). On Inference processes. Proceedings in Computational Statistics. COMPSTAT , D. Edwards, N.E. Raun (eds.), Heidelberg, p 193f.

Westerhoff Th., Naeve P.(1988b). Vom menschlichen Inferenzprozeß zum maschinellen Inferenzprozeß am Beispiel statistischer Inferenz und TWAICE-Generationen. Proceedings 2. Anwenderforum Expertensysteme, A.B. Cremers, W. Geisselhardt (eds.), Duisburg , p 307f.

Wolf P.(1989). Grundprobleme der EDA. Literate EDA als Antwort auf Kommunikationsprobleme einer explorativen Datenanalyse. Ph.D. Thesis, Fakultät für Wirtschaftswissenschaften, Universität Bielefeld, to appear

Encompassing: "The Right Track in Building Statistical Expert Systems?"

J. Boucelham

Abstract

The aim of this paper is to emphasize the importance of *encompassing* existing packages and make them less unintelligent Nelder (1977) by allowing various expansions through a collaboration of statisticians and AI engineers. The emphasis is on time series models.

KEYWORDS: Encompassing, Expert systems, Kalman filter, Time series models

1 Introduction

An expert system is an intelligent program with specific high quality knowledge about some area of research.
The interest in AI technology is increasing and applications of AI to different areas of research are reported regularly. Artificial intelligence and experts systems are nowadays natural ingredients for any software product in the market whereas a few years ago they still generated thick clouds of scepticism. This change of attitude is not to dazzle for it has been for generations the way-out of variety of discoveries and the tendancy, as a rule, is the appearance of the specter of misusage. This can in a way explain the ghost of misusage starting from "mis-appellation" (when can a software package merit the *expert system* appellation) to the more complex aspect of functionality, highly qualified guidance, flexibility and implementation which are non-expert users (end-users) deepest expectations.
This paper is based on experience gained while constructing IDENTIFY, a knowledge base for KALMAN (Boucelham, 1989).
KALMAN is a single module of the statistical package SURVO 84C, (Mustonen 1984). It is a routine that computes exact maximum likelihood estimates of seasonal/nonseasonal autoregressive moving average coefficients by means of the Kalman filter, (Kalman, 1969). The identification stage of the prospective SARMA model is carried out independently of this operation using, however, other modules of SURVO 84C. For time series experts, this latter stage is rather

informal (no use of efficient statistical method, rather calls for excessive use of graphical search through the plot of the autocorrelation and partial autocorrelation functions, spectrum, etc,).

For a non-expert user, the identification stage can turn out to be a very difficult phase of model building for the actual routines lack guidance and/or consultancy characteristics which could lead such a class of users towards the *least inappropriate* model. IDENTIFY is designed as a remedy to this deficiency. It is a single module of SURVO 84C but itself consists of various submodules called SUCROS which contain facts and rules about the identification of SARMA models and constitute the knowlegde base (rule based representation) of the IDENTIFY module. The re-structered KALMAN module being now the infernce engine. By *encompassing* in this way the existing KALMAN program, we end up with a less unintelligent and more complete statistical module.

The main goal of this paper is to emphasize the importance of *encompassing* existing packages the way described versus building huge expert systems.

2   Encompassing existing packages

Statisticians are *experts* in planning experiments, analysing data and interpreting final outcomes. On the other hand, most of the steps undertaken during an analysis are based on more or less strong assumptions.

This means that a major part of statisticians' expertise is needed to assert these assumptions in order to safeguard the reliability of the results and allow decision makers to make *better* decisions.

Broadly speaking, the analysis of statistical data varies from simplistic to manageable, complex and miscellaneous. The degree of complexity is dependent on the requirements of the purchaser of the final product (industry, marketing, business,...). This variety can be a tremendous obstacle to the organisation, generation and adaptation of the knowledge base. Besides, even human expertise can fail to generate satisfactory outcomes when the data are generated with a complex data generating mechanism.

Gale (1986) reports that "REX encodes enough knowlegde to do a *simple regression* safely". The specter of merely the knowledge base organisation, maintainance and programming appear huge when regression analysis with varying levels of complexity is merely contemplated.

A realistic wayout is through *encompassing* i.e. expansion of specific parts of existing software packages by means of new programs that generate the knowledge base and accentuate the existing inference engine sights.

This technique has been tried on the statistical package SURVO 84 C Mustonen (1984) which is an integrated interactive system for statistical analysis and producing graphs and reports. It is in itself a collection of programs and, therefore, easy to implement through additional programs.

Using SURVO 84C ready made tools, a little imagination and personal expertise one can make actual modules more expert through regular updating of the knowledge base (SUCROS) as a result of the interface expert-end user.

For time series experts, and once the planning stage of an experiment is completed and the data collected, the following iterative cycle, based mostly on the Box-Jenkins (1970) model building philosophy, is the next phase in analysing and modelling time series processes.

1. **IDENTIFICATION** of the model: Specification of simple regression models versus distributed lag models (regression analysis). Specification of the orders (p,q,P,Q) and the degrees of simple (d) and seasonal (D) differencing (seasonality period s) of the general seasonal multiplicative autoregressive moving average process $SARMA(p,d,q)(P,D,Q)_s$ (time series analysis). Important feature to be borne in mind : *Parsimony principle*.

2. **ESTIMATION** of the specified model.

3. **DIAGNOSTIC CHECKS** are applied to detect any lack of fit in the estimated model: Use of a wide arsenal of statistical tests.

4. **FORECASTING** if the model is accepted.

5. **INTERPRETATION** of final results.

As an example we shall explain how to *encompass* a specialized SURVO 84C module KALMAN (Boucelham, 1989) which computes exact maximum likelihood estimates of $SARMA(p,d,q)(P,D,Q)_s$ (seasonal/nonseasonal autoregressive moving average) coefficients by means of the Kalman filter, (Kalman, 1969) producing thourough diagnostic checks and upon request future values of the series .

A flowchart of the various steps a user should follow in order to be able to estimate a model by the KALMAN operation is given table I.

It is seen from the flowchart that four important tasks at the stage I of the iterative cycle described above are left to the user. Using various other SURVO 84C modules any time series expert can overgo this obstacle (note that the identification and estimation stages necessarily overlap i.e. idenfication-estimation cycle can be repeated as many times as necessary to derive the least unsatisfactory model). For a non-expert user, the identification stage can turn out to be a very difficult phase of model building.

Encompassing this actual operation, KALMAN, by means of a specialized module that would serve as a guide (or merely a consultant) when presented by a user with an identification problem is the achieved improvement of this *unintelligent* routine.

TABLE I KALMAN module, a flowchart.

MODEL IDENTIFICATION. (STEP I)
Transformation and seasonals. User's **first** task
Stationarity condition check. User's **second** task
Identification of **p, d, q, P, D, Q** and s of $SARMA(p,d,q)(P,D,Q)_s$ Model: User's **third** task $\phi_p(B)\Phi_P(B^s)(1-B)^d(1-B^s)^D y_t = \theta_q(B)(q)\Theta_Q(B^s)(q)e_t$ Assumption: $e_t \rightsquigarrow WN(0,\sigma_e^2)$ = Random shocks
Initial values of all identified operators coefficients: User's **fourth** task $\phi_p(B) = 1 - \phi_1 B - \phi_2 B^2 - \cdots - \phi_p B^p$ $\Phi_P(B^s) = 1 - \phi_{1,s}B^s - \phi_{2,s}B^{2s} - \cdots - \phi_{P,s}B^{Ps}$ $\theta_q(B) = 1 - \theta_1 B - \theta_2 B^2 - \cdots - \theta_q B^q$ $\Theta_q(B^s) = 1 - \theta_{1,s}B^s - \theta_{2,s}B^{2s} - \cdots - \theta_{Q,s}B^{Qs}$

KALMAN OPERATION (STEP II)
Uses the Kalman filter to generate exact maximum likelihood estimates of $SARMA(p,d,q)(P,D,Q)_s$ processes coefficients
DIAGNOSTIC CHECKS:
Invertibility non-redundancy (no common factors) Goodness of fit Test of residual randomness
FORECASTING
Includes model stability check.

1. {1, 2, 4, 5 and 6 } Assessment of a predefined set of rules using heuristic strategies and personal judgement.

2. {3 } Use of algorithmic procedures.

Step (3) is, from an interactive point of view, easy to implement, for the user's control can be minimized once the choice of the optimization routine has been made. The remaining steps rely on more or less heuristics principles (dependently on the complexity of the prospective analysis), judgements and analogies and, therefore, are harder to implement.

We apply the encompassing technique and implement an operation called IDENTIFY (not yet a final product) into the existing system. The operation involves the following interactive steps towards genuine guidance in identifying the *least inappropriate* autoregressive moving average model that will fit the series under study:

1. A transformation menu is available allowing for simple transformations: (addition, substraction,..., square root, log, lag, lead, data revision, etc, creation of indicator variables, dummy variables (seasonals), trend, constant, etc). (suggested transformations are motivated and achieved conditional on the user's agreement.)

2. Stationarity of the series is checked. Possible transformations are *suggested* (reasons are given upon request but can be skipped.)

3. Nonseasonal versus seasonal times series: Identification of s (seasonal period). (reasons are given upon request but can be skipped.)

4. Specification the simple and seasonal differencing orders d and D respectively. Plots of autocorrelation and partial autocorrelations are used during the search of adequate values of d and D. (reasons are given upon request but can be skipped.)

5. Suggestion of tentative models i.e. specification of the orders p, q, P, Q. (reasons are given upon request but can be skipped.)

6. Suggestion of initial values. (Simple estimation routine is used.)

7. Switch to robust estimation routine. Discrimination between various suggested models is entertained. (reasons are given upon request but can be skipped)

8. Teaching features are implemented embracing each of the iterative cycle steps: independent submodule.

3 Expert systems versus non-expert systems

In building expert systems, a major distinction on the user's knowledge calibre should be made.
Systems that are designed to serve qualified experts in any scientific branch can be allowed little inquisitive features. PC-GIVE, Hendry (1989) is an example of such a system. It is certainly a powerful tool to any expert econometrician: remarkable diagnostic checks features. Virtually it can work in parallel as a guiding expert and, although the inference engine is very versatile, the way knowledge is organised remains elementary and does not fit in the real structuration of knowlegde based systems.
GLIMPSE, a knowledge front-end for GLIM, (Nelder, 1988), on the other hand offers constructive interaction to the expert-users. To non-experts statisticians, it is, too early to speculate on its genuine assistance, controllability and flexibility.

From an expert point of view, it is much easier to built up expert systems to experts than non-experts users. The latter group is so heterogeneous with varying levels of specific knowledge, unmeasurable perceptive and conceptive abilities that satisfying all its needs in the area is bound to be a difficult task. Systems designed for non-experts should be, apart from informative and strictly explicit, more inquisitive with genuine guidance towards problem solving. REX (Regression EXpert) Gale 1986 is an example of such an expert system. The amount of programming it involves and the statistical topic it tends to cover as well as the scope of users it is aimed at are from an implementation point of view (if genuine expertise is to be gained) very ambitious. In the future we shall certainly learn more about the reliability of such huge expert systems.

4 Conclusion

The importance of human perceptive and conceptual abilities and non-analytical expertise, no doubt, are and remain the ghost in the valley of statistical expert systems builders. While conceptual abilities seem to be a rather solvable programming problem, the perceptive characteristics (expert's personal judgement, rules of thumb, use of analogies), on the other hand, remain the *hole in the loop* in statistical knowledge base acquisition. Ambitious project such as REX (Regression EXpert) Gale (1986) and GLIMPSE Nelder (1988) represent a remarkable breakthrough *the* valley.
Applying existing symbol-manipulation languages (LISP versus PROLOG: to

a certain extent REX versus GLIMPSE) seem to humbly respect this virtual obstacle already mentioned.

On the other hand, the use of problem-oriented languages (FORTRAN, PASCAL, C) with continuous implementation of the constructed system are in the author's opinion, a remedy to the problem. The motivation behind this second approach lies in the uncertainty characterized by the following two questions:

1. How do experts gain their expertise?

2. When is expertise a final product?

Due to its maintenance facility and flexible implementation, the encompassing technique described allow for more attractive features in building intelligent statistical software.

REFERENCES

Boucelham., J (1989). *"Two SURVO 84C Programs: 1). Exact Maximum Likelihood estimation of Autoregressive Moving Average Models by Means of the Kalman Filter. 2). Data Revisions Problem: a Kalman Filter Approach to Generate Optimal Estimates of Final Observations"*, Research Report No 72, Department of Statistics, University of Helsinki.

Box, G. E. P and Jenkins, G. M. (1976). *Time series Analysis: Forecasting and Control.* Revised edition, Holden-Day, San Francisco.

Chambers, J. M., (1981). *"Some Thoughts on Expert Software,"* in Proceedings of the 13th Symposium on the Interface of Computer Science and Statitics, New York Spriner Verlag, pp. 36-40.

Clark, K. L and Mc Cabe, F. G., (1980). *"PROLOG: A Language for Implementing Expert Systems"*, Imperial College, London SW7, November.

Gale, A. W., (1986). *Artificial Intelligence and Statistics.* Addison-Wesley Publishing Company.

Hendry, D. F. (1989). *"PC GIVE. An interactive Econometric Modelling System.* Oxford: University of Oxford.

Kalman, R.E., and Falb, P.L. and Arbib, M.A. (1969). *Topics in Mathematical System Theory,* Academic Press, London.

Mustonen S., (1977). *"SURVO 76: a Statistical Data Processing System",* Research Report No 9, Department of Statistics, University of Helsinki.

Mustonen S., (1987). *SURVO 84C User's Guide. Department of Statistics, University of Helsinki.*

Nelder, J. A. (1977). "*Intelligent Programs, the next Stage in Statistical Computing,*" Recent Developments in Statistics, Proceedings of the European Meeting of Statisticians, pp. 79-108.

Nelder, J. A. (1988). "*How Should the Statistical Expert System and its User See Each Other?*" Proceedings in Compputational Statistics, Compstat 88. Phsica-Verlag, Heidelberg.

Automated Protocolling of Statistical Data Analyses

K. A. Fröschl

Summary

Keeping records of interactive statistical data analyses is a major, but rather neglected, topic in the discussion about "intelligent" statistical software systems. This paper surveys some approaches to (semi-)automatical analysis protocolling and discusses the decisive features of mechanical protocols to be used in knowledge-based systems. A logically oriented protocol model is outlined which tries to create and maintain symbolic representations of an analysis' contextual and temporal dynamics.

1. Motivation

Obviously, statistical consulting is an activity based on communication. To be successful any such communication requires a common understanding shared by each of the participating agents. More precisely, each agent needs to maintain its *own* information base capturing the agent's individual view(s) of the notions and discernments being communicated.

These statements are certainly trivial as long as communication processes between human beings – like the statistical consultant and his client – are considered; we use to keep and update our "mental records" almost unconsciously. However, the scene changes considerably if – for some reason – the human consultant is exchanged for a mechanical device such as an "intelligent" statistical system, e.g. an expert system: in order to be a serious candidate for substituting the human part the system's communicative capabilities somehow *must be made* to resemble the salient features of interpersonal dialogue at least within the boundaries of statistical discourse. Hence, what is required in the first place is a machine representation of the dynamically changing *communication background* of interactive computing sessions as a base for generating sensible, situation-dependent contributions to an analysis on the system's side (see especially [8]).

In contrast to the emphasis commonly laid on the symbolic encoding of statistical knowledge this paper argues that some well-designed means of *automated protocolling* of statistical analyses are of comparable importance for any reasonable intelligent statistical software system intended to offer support or guidance to the user. Apparently, this latter concern has been rather neglected hitherto by the developers of intelligent statistical systems[1] though it would be hardly surprising if a less *ad hoc* strategy of analysis recording (compared to the methods favored up to now) should offer substantial advantages.

---

[1] Potential *users* perceive this deficiency more likely; e.g. cf. [6,14]

Changing the perspective of knowledge-based statistical systems away from machine representations of static, i.e. application-invariant, statistical methodology to the management and maintenance of dynamic, i.e. application-specific, knowledge about particular features of some current analysis implies a coincident shift of focus: instead of the preponderating discussion about competing knowledge representation paradigms (rules vs. frames etc.) now the design of formal models of a dynamic data base functioning as a kind of *mechanical short-term memory* is of primary interest. The essential tasks such a protocol is set up for are

(T1) recording a chronological trace ("what happened": *log* knowledge);
(T2) keeping a structural representation ("what is known": *study* knowledge);
(T3) saving the dynamic interactions between (T1) and (T2) ("why happened what resulting in which new information": *reason maintaining* knowledge)

of a statistical analysis.

Since this protocol is queried for (already recorded) temporal and substantial facts and relationships (and, possibly, some logical consequences thereof) in the course of performing statistical analyses there is an apparent concordance of the protocol's features with several kinds of non-standard logics such as temporal logic, nonmonotonic logic, uncertainty logic, logic of action, and so on. Some proper integration of several such logics certainly would constitute an appreciable calculus of just the sort of *common sense reasoning* (see, e.g., [7]) required for the various purposes the protocol has to meet. However, such calculi unfortunately present us with a plenty of intricate difficulties, and appear to be computationally intractable (at least from a practical point of view), too.[2] A rather pragmatic approach to get out of this dilemma is to devise some purpose-built protocol model capable of supporting the indispensable requirements but abandoning neat logical properties (like deductive completeness) in favor of simplicity and easy tractability. In fact, it is this purposive design of analysis protocols which makes the whole topic belong to the discussion about intelligent *statistical* systems (as opposed to intelligent systems in general).

Before going into the details of a particular protocol model, which is proposed tentatively in section 3 of this paper, some brief remarks about means and ends of analysis protocolling reported in the literature on computational statistics as well as a more concise description of features required of an "intelligent" analysis protocol are dealt with in section 2. Finally, some shortcomings and unresolved problems of the proposed protocol model are considered.

2. Approaches to Analysis Protocolling

Naturally, the desire of keeping protocols of statistical analyses in an automated fashion emerged with the advent of interactive computing: if one considers the powerful statistical software tools available these days, it is a pleasure to produce – by just a few keystrokes – a multitude of analysis outputs hardly to remember in detail even after only half an hour of ongoing work. The freedom to proceed with an analysis beyond the necessity of sticking strictly to a pre-planned course of action, admitting ad lib interesting detours, calls for some disciplined way of recording the actual analysis progress. Consequently,

---

[2] See, e.g. [5,11,15] to get an impression of the state of development in this regard.

attempts have been undertaken to integrate some kind of analysis diary into interactive statistical software systems in order to support the system's users recalling what *they* have already analyzed. For obvious reasons, the computing device suggests itself as a tool for the physical realization of such a diary. Typically, though in general only implicitly, all protocol models assume that any statistical analysis is performed within the scope of the one and only software system actually keeping the diary.

The most elementary strategy of recording a statistical analysis consists of a chronologically ordered trace of commands delivered to the system ("journal"), possibly augmented by a listing of the outputs generated by each command ("transcript"); e.g. cf. [14,1]. This kind of protocol produces a "linear" history of *analytical events* allowing later inspection or even a (modified) re-execution of some section of a journal. A severe disadvantage of these simple chronologies is their inability to capture the *logical structure* of analyses: this requires the representation of which analysis subsections belong to each other in terms of both temporal, and substantial, relationships. Protocol models aiming at a representation of this "spatial" structure of analyses typically are organized as networks. The nodes of such a graph denote (fictitious) objects like sub-analyses, results, and the like;[3] the edges indicate the topological relation between represented objects. Such a purely state-descriptive protocol graph, of course, does not contain any temporal information.

In most suggested models of automated analysis protocolling (e.g. [2,13]) a compromise is preferred which combines temporal and spatial recording of analyses at the cost of losing information in either respect. These "structure saving" protocols maintain a directed graph (occasionally termed *semantic map* [13]) the nodes of which represent whole analysis *states* connected by labelled edges expressing the (mediate) temporal successor relation. The edges' labels carry the information about what effected the state transition between adjacent nodes. In general, each node, or *save state* [2], may become a branching point to which several successor states are attached subsequently. Thus, the protocolled analysis states are partially ordered w.r.t. time, and each path through the semantic map (i.e. chain of states) represents the course of a particular sub-analysis. Visual representations of the network topology (e.g. [2,9]) can help to convey the respective state of elaboration of an analysis efficiently.

What makes semantic protocol networks as described above less suited as *dynamic knowledge bases* of intelligent statistical systems is their insufficient support of self-investigation, i.e. they fail to serve as a system's *own* dynamic memory. Evidently, the strongest demands placed on a protocol destined to achieve this aim are:

(D1) the representation of knowledge entered dynamically into the protocol (tasks T1 and T2) must enable subsequent *mechanical deductions* (at least, however, the retrieval of "facts" w.r.t. time and analytical context);

(D2) the representation must manage to express (or make deducible) various *associative* temporal and substantial relationships between different sub-analyses, analyses and obtained results, prior knowledge and obtained results, introduced assumptions and selected methods, etc. (task T3) in order to keep track of the dynamic evolution of statistical analyses and its underlying rationalization.

Any such protocol, then, both comprises the system's intimate knowledge about a particular analysis in its own terms, and acts as a *deductive* data base to be used directly by

---

[3] E.g., in the GLIMPSE system [16] each alternative linear model corresponds to one such node.

the analyst. Among the major distinguishing features achieved by "integrated" analysis protocols are:

(F1) chronological administration of analytical proceedings already w.r.t. (T3);
(F2) storage of obtained analysis results w.r.t (T2) providing material for subsequent decisions as well as for the assembly of final reports;
(F3) generation of *active* reconstructions of (the analyst's) reasoning having led to particular decisions and analysis strategies;
(F4) information source for "educated," situation–dependent user guidance (as it is proclaimed in expert systems);
(F5) empirical base of data for sifting out *conditional* analysis strategies.

With exception of (F5) all other features mentioned are essential ingredients to any statistical software system intended to participate actively in *statistical problem solving*; moreover, many of these features would also be useful, and, hence, highly appreciated, in systems less involved in problem solving activities focusing instead on convenient support of more experienced analysts.

Feature (F5), eventually, could play a prominent rôle in the formation (either by hand or some means of mechanical induction) of methodological knowledge bases of statistical expert systems.

3. A Logical Framework

The protocol model presented in this section is built upon two fundamental, although quite familiar, assumptions:

(A1) any statistical activity may be decomposed into a finite series of discrete "steps" executed consecutively;
(A2) each "step" transforms the respective analysis state it is applied to into another state deterministically.

Furthermore, let Σ be the set of protocol (or simply: analysis) states and Ω be the set of available elementary *operations*. Then the protocol may be viewed as a (partial) function $\Phi: \Sigma \times \Omega \to \Sigma$. After having carried out n operations, a statistical analysis can be described formally in terms of Φ by (i) some initial state $S_o \in \Sigma$, and (ii) a sequence of operations $\{\omega_i\}_{1 \leq i \leq n}$ such that $S_i = \Phi(S_{i-1}, \omega_i)$, for $1 \leq i \leq n$ (cf. [8]). Since, in general, the admissibility (or, sometimes, preference) of applying some $\omega_{k+1} \in \Omega$ to state $S_k \in \Sigma$ is determined by testing ω_{k+1}'s preconditions against the elements of $\{S_i\}_{0 \leq i \leq k}$ (as, e.g., in [3]), it is reasonable to require some kind of explicit representation of $S_o, S_1, \ldots, S_k$.

With regard to this setup, the protocol has to maintain representations of

(R1) *analysis states* as logical descriptions, i.e. as a finite set of consistent sentences denoting the factual knowledge about the respective analysis, spread among a sequence of states;
(R2) *state transitions*, i.e. the change of factual knowledge about the respective analysis between consecutive states, viz. the update of logical descriptions.

Concerning the logic of statistical analyses, references to absolute time are rather insignificant; any non-metric total ordering of analysis states, or state transitions, resp., will do. In the following, accordingly, the "time" of a state (transition) always refers to the *relative* position of this state (transition) within the protocolled sequence of states (state transitions). By appointment, state transitions are said just to result in *concurrent* analysis states.

Now, the generic structure of analysis protocolling is governed by the following basic principles:

(P1) each activity producing some effect of potential relevance constitutes an operation $\omega \in \Omega$ which, when applied, causes a state transition to be entered into the protocol ("principle of explicity");

(P2) *all* effects of any activity taking place with potential relevance to subsequent analysis phases are entered into the protocol ("principle of state preservation");

(P3) all effects of an activity occur *at once* (i.e. are part of one and the same state transition) without leaving room for any intermittent state change ("principle of synchronism");

(P4) the protocol is updated monotonically, i.e. information entered into the protocol is never withdrawn ("principle of monotony");

(P5) each activity takes place within the scope of some *protocol object*, i.e. the activity's effects are assigned to some object ("principle of reference"; see section 3.2).

Formally, the protocol is organized as a logical data base consisting of a (finite) set of *protocol sentences* $\langle p, s, t \rangle$ where p denotes some proposition which has changed its state to s at time t. The ps are carrying the actual information (e.g. facts obtained by querying the user, computed results, beliefs currently held, introduced assumptions, or hypotheses, etc.) the respective state of which may be $v(=\text{true})$, $f(\text{alse})$, or, else, $u(\text{nknown})$; the latter being true (by default inference) unless a contradicting state change has been protocolled. Thus, the state changes of individual propositions are expressed by formalizing the truth–functional semantics of the set of propositions on the level of object language. Furthermore, by creating protocol entries (i.e. sentences) *only* for the typically rather small set of propositions describing the effects of elementary operations the protocol by and large records nothing but the *state changes* of individual propositions and, hence, is parsimonious as to space complexity.

Complete (w.r.t. the actual protocol frame, i.e. the partial world depicted) descriptions of analysis states, then, are inferred by means of applying (recursively) a deduction rule $\mathcal{T}$ conforming to (P2): let $next(t)$ be the analysis state following immediately the state t, then

$$\mathcal{T}: \quad \frac{\langle p, s, t \rangle, \; T \langle p, s, next(t) \rangle}{\langle p, s, next(t) \rangle}$$

is a kind of temporal *default inference* rule (see [10]) with $T \langle p, s, t' \rangle$ meaning "temporally consistent," i.e. there is no way to derive (from propositions other than p) a state s' for p at time t' such that $s \neq s'$. In plain words, the state of a proposition remains unchanged until another state change is derivable, viz. retrievable due to (P2).

For various cross–referencing purposes it may be useful to augment the primary protocol base with some logical index tables.[4] In particular, an *activity trace* built of pairs $\langle a, t \rangle$ with meaning "the (state changing) activity a took place at (i.e.: ended with) time t" allows easy recollections of the sequence of operations $\{\omega_i\}$ already performed. Since

---

[4] Of course, such tables could be expressed as protocol sentences either but then would be rather clumsy to manage practically.

each activity **a** labels an operation $\omega \in \Omega$ this activity trace provides the vital backbone for explaining the *causes* of state changes (remember that according to (P1) each **a** changes the state of at least one proposition).

3.1 Time Representation

In addition to the total ordering of analysis states it seems worthwhile to have some means of recording the temporal relationship of state transitions. Therefore, a *conceptual time scale* expressing the analytical "proximity" of consecutive analysis states is proposed. In constructing this time scale it is assumed that the state changing activities (*events* for short) are arranged hierarchically as, e.g., expressible by the set of rewrite rules of a formal grammar (cf. [4]). Let e_j be a higher stage event resolved into a sequence of lower stage events (termed *agenda*) $e_{j1}, e_{j2}, \ldots, e_{jn_j}$ by the rule

$$e_j \quad ::= \quad e_{j1} \to e_{j2} \to \cdots \to e_{jn_j} \quad ;$$

then the state transitions achieved by $\{e_{ji}\}_{1 \leq i \leq n_j}$ accumulate to the compound effect of e_j. Viewed distantly, lower level events are just partial contributors to higher level events and, hence, are more likely to be closer related from a procedural point of view than these.

These assumptions provided, each set of events appearing eventually on the same level of the execution hierarchy now can be attached to a corresponding *time level* such that the nesting of time levels mirrors the hierarchical event structure. Formally, if an operation $\omega \in \Omega$ embodies some l–level event e' then the associated time t will be denoted as

$$\boldsymbol{t} = \overset{l}{\underset{d=1}{:}} t^{(d)} = t^{(1)} : t^{(2)} : \cdots : t^{(l)} \; ,$$

$t^{(d)} \in \mathbb{N}$, with $\overset{l-1}{\underset{d=1}{:}} t^{(d)}$ being the time of the event one stage higher e' is contributing to. Within an l–level agenda state transitions are simply enumerated. Due to this convention

$$\boldsymbol{t_1} = \overset{l_1}{\underset{d=1}{:}} t_1^{(d)} \quad < \quad \boldsymbol{t_2} = \overset{l_2}{\underset{d=1}{:}} t_2^{(d)}$$

iff either (i) $\overset{l'}{\underset{d=1}{:}} t_1^{(d)} = \overset{l'}{\underset{d=1}{:}} t_2^{(d)}$ and $t_1^{(l'+1)} < t_2^{(l'+1)}$, for $l_1 \leq l_2$, or (ii) $\overset{l_2}{\underset{d=1}{:}} t_1^{(d)} \leq \boldsymbol{t_2}$, else. Based on this time representation it is fairly easy, e.g., to

(E1) decide the temporal order of any two time points, $\boldsymbol{t_1}$ and $\boldsymbol{t_2}$;
(E2) determine the "conceptual synchronism" of two time points, $\boldsymbol{t_1} \sim \boldsymbol{t_2}$, w.r.t. some time level l' (by checking if $\overset{l'}{\underset{d=1}{:}} t_1^{(d)} = \overset{l'}{\underset{d=1}{:}} t_2^{(d)}$ holds);
(E3) trace analyses at *reduced granularity* by cutting off lower time levels, thus obtaining some sort of "coarse picture" by skipping over sequences of minor state changes.

It should be mentioned that even the temporal interpretation of higher level events (i.e. sequences of elementary operations) as *instants* of time will be in concordance with (P3) although, certainly, such events cover some *duration* with regard to lower time levels.

3.2 The Structure of Propositions: Objects

The "spatial" decomposition of the set of protocol sentences – across analysis states – into semantically defined subsets is accomplished by means of a uniform proposition format as follows.

First, this decomposition comprises two logical stages; to begin with (i) the set of protocol sentences is partitioned into disjoint subsets called *protocol objects*, which, thereupon, (ii) are aggregated to *analytical objects* by creating (overlapping) object hierarchies.

Second, each object is a symbolic entity owning its unique name ι, and consisting of a list of named attributes $\alpha_{\iota 1}, \alpha_{\iota 2}, \ldots, \alpha_{\iota k_\iota}$ to each of which may be assigned some value $\xi_{\iota 1}, \xi_{\iota 2}, \ldots, \xi_{\iota k_\iota}$.

Third, objects are represented as sets of propositions. For this purpose, propositions are interpreted as tuples of a ternary relation p such that each proposition $\boldsymbol{p}$ entered into the protocol appears as $\boldsymbol{p} = p(\iota', \alpha_{\iota' m}, \xi_{\iota' m})$ with meaning "attribute $\alpha_{\iota' m}$ of protocol object ι' holds the value $\xi_{\iota' m}$."

Fourth, object names are non-atomic, set-structured identifiers usually comprising several *components*, i.e.

$$\iota = \{c_{\iota 1}(\kappa_{\iota 1}), c_{\iota 2}(\kappa_{\iota 2}), \ldots, c_{\iota n_\iota}(\kappa_{\iota n_\iota})\}$$

with the c's chosen from a predefined set $\mathcal{C}$ of classes of non-decomposable *basic* objects. Within each class c_i of basic objects individuals are distinguished by unique labels κ_i.

As an example, case 5 of subsample `male` of a sample data set `raw_data` may be identified by

$$\{ ds(\texttt{raw\_data}), ss(\texttt{male}), c(5) \} \ .$$

The generic (i.e. component) structure of object identifiers determines the class of (compound) objects an individual object belongs to; the pattern of basic object labels determines the individual object. All propositions bearing the identifier ι', then, comprise the available information pertaining directly to object ι'. In addition, object ι' is a sub-object of any object ι'' formally iff $\iota'' \subset \iota'$ (in practice, of course, not every subset relation will be meaningful).

Now, the set of protocol sentences with propositions referring to object ι' constitutes the protocol object ι' (at any state of analysis). On top of the set of protocol objects then a (multiple) hierarchy of analytical objects can be arranged by defining a set of meaningful *part-of* relations between compound objects in terms of generic identifier subset relations. Physically each analytical object ι comprehends the entire hierarchy of protocol objects $\iota', \iota'', \ldots$ such that $\iota \subseteq \iota', \iota \subseteq \iota'', \ldots$. This partially ordered, multiple object nesting facilitates a multitude of cross-referential, or associative, relationships between the analytical entities of interest.

Information may be retrieved from the protocol either by "direct" access to individual propositions (due to the flat formal structure of the protocol), or by "projecting" a target object identifier over the whole set of protocol sentences (i.e. testing part-of relations). In this latter case, the retrieval will, in general, result in sets of propositions, resp., objects. Since the analysis protocol records *trajectories* of analytical objects by integrating contextual and temporal structure into protocol sentences, this retrieval can be constrained temporally as well.

4. Concluding Remarks

As a starting point of a straightforward implementation of the protocol model the programming language PROLOG has been chosen. Reasonably, protocol sentences are represented as a quinternary relation; the various retrieval and update functions of the protocol are modelled by taking advantage of PROLOG's meta-language features. Using a logic-based language for implementing another logic calculus certainly simplifies matters, although PROLOG's own semantics sometimes interfere with the designed calculus' inference properties. Also, PROLOG's resolving of retrieval to unification and (indexed, at best) search causes a slight disadvantage. Since the precise wording of formal queries turns out to be rather tedious, quite an extended set of predefined retrieval operations must be provided to exploit the offered flexibility effectively.

Statistical activity may be regarded as an endeavour to increase information, or reduce ignorance, inherently taking place in front of a steadily changing information background. Sometimes, elicited information may become (partially) contradictory and, hence, some rescuing revision is called for. As a consequence, in order to provide sound support for dynamic decisions a protocol has to cope with resolution of inconsistency somehow. Despite the intentions of several proposed reason maintenance systems (e.g. cf. [12]) striving for *absolute* consistency (but, as a rule, avoiding explicit references to time) statistical analysis protocols have to distinguish between merely formal, insignificant inconsistencies and substantially contradicting evidence, or conclusions thereof. How to make this crucial distinction available to mechanical protocol devices is still an open problem.

References

[1] *Becker RA, Chambers JM* "S: An Interactive Environment for Data Analysis and Graphics" Wadsworth, Belmont Ca., 1984
[2] *Cowley PJ, Whiting MA* "Managing Data Analysis through Save–States" Proc. 17th Interface, 1986, pp. 121-127
[3] *Froeschl KA, Grossmann W* "A Model of Meta-Level Data Representation for Advanced Statistical Software Systems" TR-ISI/Stamcom-62, Univ. Vienna, (Dec.) 1988
[4] *Grossmann W, Froeschl KA* "Formale Wissens- und Verfahrensmodellierung in der statistischen Datenverarbeitung" in: Janko W (ed.) "Statistik, Informatik und Ökonomie" Springer, Berlin, 1988, pp. 71-85
[5] *Hobbs JR, Moore RC (eds.)* "Formal Theories of the Commonsense World" Ablex, Norwood NJ, 1985
[6] *Huber PJ* "Environments for Supporting Statistical Strategy" in Gale WA (ed.) "AI & Statistics" Addison Wesley, Reading Ma., 1986, pp. 285-294
[7] *McCarthy J* "What Is Common Sense and How to Formalize It ?" in: GWAI'85, pp. 213-217
[8] *McCarthy J, Hayes PJ* "Some Philosophical Problems from the Standpoint of AI" in: Meltzer B, Michie D (eds.) "Machine Intelligence 4", Edinburgh Univ. Press, 1969, pp. 463-502
[9] *Oldford RW, Peters SC* "Statistically Sophisticated Software and DINDE" Proc. 18th Interface, 1986, pp. 160-167
[10] *Reiter R* "A Logic for Default Reasoning" Artificial Intelligence 13 (1980), pp. 81-132
[11] *Smets P etal (eds.)* "Non-Standard Logics for Automated Reasoning" Academic Press, London, 1988
[12] *Stoyan H (ed.)* "Begründungsverwaltung" Springer Inf. FB 162, Berlin, 1988
[13] *Thisted RA* "Representing Statistical Knowledge for Expert Data Analysis Systems" in: Gale WA (ed.) "AI & Statistics" Addison Wesley, Reading Ma., 1986, pp. 267-284
[14] *Thisted RA* "Computing Environments for Data Analysis" Stat. Science 1 (1986), pp. 259-275
[15] *Turner R.* "Logics for AI" Ellis Horwood, Chichester, 1984
[16] *Wolstenholme DE, Nelder JA* "A Front End for GLIM" in: Haux R (ed.) "Expert Systems in Statistics" G. Fischer, Stuttgart, 1986, pp. 155-177

The Integration of Knowledge-Based and Statistical Methods in a Statistics Interpreter

W. Klösgen

Abstract

The statistics-interpreter EXPLORA is a system for the discovery of interesting facts in statistical databases. The system uses three knowledge-processes to exploit the semantical knowledge about the interesting objects and relations of the domain which has produced the data. First EXPLORA *systematically searches* for statistical results *(facts)* to detect relations within the data which could possibly be overlooked by a human analyst. On the other hand EXPLORA will contribute to overcome the bulk of information which is generally produced when presenting the data. Therefore a second knowledge-process implemented in EXPLORA consists in *discovering messages* about the data by condensing the numerous facts. Approaches of inductive generalization which have been developed for machine learning are utilized to identify common values of attributes of the objects to which the facts relate. Furtheron the system searches for interesting facts by applying *redundancy-rules* and domain-dependent *selection-rules*. In a third process EXPLORA uses methods of discourse-organization to produce a coherent analysis report. The system formulates the messages in terms of the domain, groups and orders them and even provides flexible *navigations* in the *fact-spaces*.

1. The statistics interpreter as an expert system

Most approaches of applying knowledge-based techniques for data analyses concentrate on the context-independent, statistical support. EXPLORA however is developed for the subject- or context-specific interpretation with regard to the contents of the data to be analysed *(content interpretation)*. Besides knowledge about statistical methods such a system needs semantical knowledge about the interesting objects and relations within the domain which has produced the data. Therefore the statistics interpreter can be regarded as a framework-system that can be set up in each special type of application as an expert system for the exploration of a data set using not only statistical but also domain-expertise for its interpretation process.

EXPLORA is a system whose input is a set of data and that produces a content interpretation (Figure 1). The system needs both application specific context knowledge and statistical knowledge for such an interpretation process. The representation of this knowledge in the system requires some effort, therefore we concentrate on a system supporting regular and routine tasks. For those tasks on the other hand a lot of specific experience is available, so that it is much easier to formalize the needed knowledge. When EXPLORA is established for such a task or application, it incorporates the expertise of an experienced data analyst who is familiar with the interpretation of "his" special data set and the interesting statements about the data, and who knows how these statements are verified, what connections exist between these statements and how these are arranged.

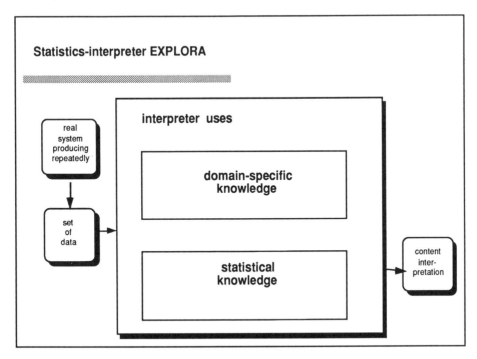

Figure 1: Knowledge sources for content interpretation

There are two approaches for applying knowledge-based techniques for data analysis. The first is given by *consultation systems* that advise their users on the selection and the operation of statistical methods. These systems not only advise the user, but also execute the proposed procedures. Some first examples of this type of statistical expert systems are a prototype consultation system for regression analysis (Gale86), a system for the construction of generalized linear models (Nelder86) and a system for the selection of methods extrapolating time series (Goodrich86). These attempts to model data analysts in statistical expert systems don't aspire to include context. They provide a set of statistically supported conclusions and let the user choose the particular conclusions that are consistent with his knowledge about the context. Because the consultation system holds no semantic knowledge about the application, the subject-specific content interpretation has to be done by its user.

Another approach can be found in the area of *natural language generation systems* (McDonald88). A very long term view of these efforts is the paradigm of a system that can function as an author. Only a few examples in this area like the *stock report generation* system *ANA* (Kukich88) operate in the analysis of data. Such a text generator (Figure 2) for data-exploration incorporates the following knowledge-processes: A *fact-generator* performs arithmetic and statistical computations to produce a stream of facts from the data. Then a *message-generator* infers interesting messages from the facts. The *discourse-organizer* groups messages according to topics and combines and eliminates messages. A *surface-generator* takes the ordered messages and uses lexical, syntactic and grammar knowledge to produce the final report.

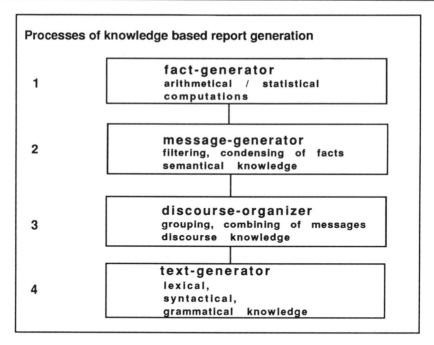

Figure 2: Knowledge processes for text generation

The approaches implemented so far in EXPLORA concentrate on the first two of these processes. The EXPLORA-project is part of a GMD Key Project *Assisting Computer (AC)*. The vision of this key project is the paradigm of the computer as a *personal assisting machine*. The goal of this long-term activity is to create intelligent, active support systems which have the abilities to complete, to render precise and to correct the commands of their users. Furthermore they shall learn and adapt to their users as well as consult and explain. The final result of the AC will be an ensemble of machine assistants adaptable to specific requirements and consisting of universal office assistants, of domain assistants (like EXPLORA) and of communication assistants (Hoschka89).

2. Knowledge-based techniques of EXPLORA

The basis for the interpretation process are the four phases or knowledge processes of Figure 2. They are realized in EXPLORA in the following way.

The generation of facts

Fundamental to this generation is a *pool of statement-types*. For each application-class (compare section 3) all statement-types are collected which can be investigated by the system for verification in the set of data. An example of a statement-type for the application-class *aggregate data analysis* is given by the following template:

Outstanding-behaviour of *result-variable* for *target-group*.

This statement-type has three arguments: *outstanding-behaviour, result-variable, target-group*. An *object-structure* is associated to each argument of a statement-type. Such an object-structure consists of a *set* of objects and of a *partial ordering* on this set. The object-structure *outstanding-behaviour* has as elements several patterns of behaviour like *above the average*. A stronger-relation supplies a partial ordering on this set of behaviour-patterns.

The argument *target-group* refers to a set of basic units of analysis like persons or firms. In this example we are not interested in statements about the individual units of analysis but in statements about some classes of units (aggregates or target-groups). These target-groups are constructed by using the attributes which are available for the units of analysis (e.g. socio-economic characteristics of persons). A partial ordering is defined on the set of all possible attributive generalizations of the units of analysis. A target-group is more general than another, if the attribute-values in its description are more general (referring to the structure defined on the value set of attributes) and/or if its description holds only a subset of the attributes which are used for the other class. Therefore a target-group which is more general than another includes the other more particular target group.

Further a *verification-method* is associated with each type of statement. This method includes statistical criteria used to exclude fortuitous results and to indicate the degree of interest of a concrete *instance* of a statement type (Gebhardt88). It is characteristic for exploratory analyses that the statistical criteria of a verification-method are not rigid tests with strict assertions of significance. An instance of a statement-type is given by an application of the statement-type, where for each of its associated object-structures an element of its object-set is taken as an argument. Some instances of the above statement-type:

Penetration-rate for *Computers* in *Manufacturing and Process* is *below the average*.
Penetration-rate for *General Purpose Computers* in *Manufacturing and Process* in *Northern-Regions* is *much below the average*.

The verification-method checks whether an individual instance of a statement-type is true (in the given data). A verification-method which verifies the above instances e.g. could be based on statistical methods of analysis of contingency-tables. Then a value of the result-variable for a target-group corresponds to a cell in an associated table. This value is compared with its expected value. Depending on the deviation between the value and its expected value in terms of multiples of the standard-deviation the value is classified according to the specified qualitative patterns of behaviour like *much below the average*. A statement-type therefore defines a search-space with dimensions corresponding to the object-structures existing in the statement-type. In the above example we have a three dimensional search-space spanned by the arguments *result-variable, target-group, behaviour*. A *fact* is now defined as a true instance of a statement-type in this search-space.

The generation of messages

Several approaches of redundancy elimination, of inductive generalization and of selection are applied to infer interesting *messages* from the facts.

To *eliminate redundancy* in the space of instances of statements a partial ordering may be defined on this set of instances. This partial ordering is induced by the partial orderings existing in the associated object-structures. The partial ordering on the set of instances of statements is defined as the product of the adapted partial orderings of the associated object-structures. To adapt a given partial ordering of an object-structure one has to define whether this ordering is also essential for the ordering of statements and if so, in what direction (stronger, weaker) it is essential (Latocha89).

As an example of such a redundancy relation let us consider the above statement-type. There are basic partial orderings on the object-structures of behaviour-patterns (a pattern may be stronger than another pattern), of result-variables (let us assume that the result-variables are arranged in a tree-like structure) and of target-groups. Then one instance of this statement is stronger than or equal to another, if the pattern of the first instance is stronger than or equal to the pattern of the second instance, if the result-variable appearing in the first instance is on a higher hierarchical level (or is equal) than the result-variable of the second and if the first target-group is more general than the second. For the tree-structure we can apply one of several possible redundancy rules. In our example this is a heuristic redundancy rule of the form:

If a statement is true for an element in the tree structure, then for all subordinate elements the statement is not interesting.

These are local rules for the individual dimensions (object-structures) in the statement space. They are combined (product-ordering) to deliver a partial ordering in the statement space. A search-algorithm uses this partial ordering to reduce the search for true statements and to present only these non-redundant statements to the user. If this algorithm for instance finds a true statement, it looks for the strongest statements (compared to this true one) which are also true and then can eliminate all still stronger ones (which are false) and all weaker ones (which are redundant).

The two instances of a statement-type presented above are non-redundant. The target-group (Manufacturing and Process) and the result-variable (Penetration-rate of Computers) of the first instance are more general than these of the second instance (Manufacturing and Process in Northern Regions and Penetration-rate of General Purpose Computers) but the behaviour-pattern of the second instance (much below the average) is stronger than the pattern of the first (below the average). Therefore according to the product partial ordering there is no relation between these instances in the sense that one is stronger than the other so that both are selected by the search-algorithm.

The direction which has to be specified for the adaptation of a component partial ordering for the product partial ordering depends on the semantics of the statement-type. Consider the following type:

The *n* units with the *largest* values of a *result-variable* are located in *target-group*.

In this case a statement about a more general target-group is weaker than a statement about a more particular target-group. Therefore the partial ordering on target-groups in this case is used in an inversed direction by the search algorithm compared to the first example of a statement type.

As another technique to reduce the number of presented facts and to combine facts we use *inductive generalization* (or *learning-*) approaches (Michalski86). We mainly apply methods of attributive generalization: The objects of a structure can hold attributes, so that each object takes for each attribute a value out of a structured set of possible values. The goal of the generalization methods is to find classes of objects defined by means of the attribute values with a high density of true statements or with some other measure evaluating the class. These classes are constructed by attributive and relational descriptions.

Let us look at the above example and consider again the argument *target-group*. Now we assume that we have basic statements about single units of analysis like firms. (e.g.: *The best value of result-variable since n fiscal-years for firm A.*) We want to find target-groups with a high density of true statements of this type. Generalization-techniques use the partial ordering on the target-groups and apply evaluation criteria (e.g. LEF-functions, compare Michalski86) to identify interesting target-groups.

We use *selection rules* as another possibility to condense the number of facts and to find interesting messages. These are semantic (context- or application-specific) rules which represent further criteria to select as a filter those facts which shall be presented to the user. In comparison to the verification-method holding primarily statistical criteria these criteria are application-oriented.

The generation of a report

As the result of these two processes we arrive at a set of messages which represent selected or combined or generalized facts. There exist several relations for this set of messages: A message can for instance be an example/counterexample of another message, it can be a message about a subordinate object or about an object that stands in contrast to another object (appearing in another message) etc. These relations can be used in two ways: In an interactive mode the user has the possibility to browse or *navigate* in the spaces of messages. Via these relations he can for instance call (counter-) examples for an *active message*, he can fade in (out) all subordinate messages of selected hierarchies or he can request all the messages about contrasting objects.

On the other hand we apply methods of *text-organisation* (Mann88) to order the set of messages in a coherent report. Ordering- and discourse-rules refer to these relations on messages. The process of *surface-generation* (or text-generation) is represented in EXPLORA only by some elementary techniques, since the topic of *natural language generation* is not of primary interest in our approach. Especially we use *text-templates* to transform the internal representation of the messages into the natural language representation which is presented to the user.

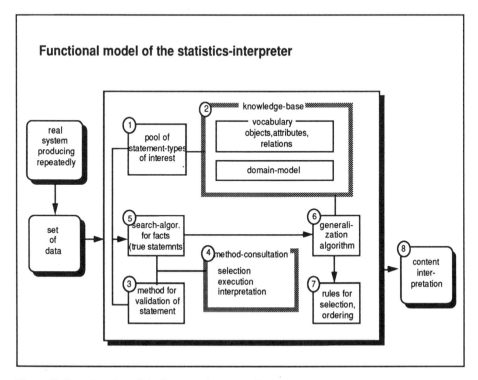

Figure 3: Functional model of content interpretation

3. First applications of EXPLORA

Before a generally available version is distributed, the usefulness of EXPLORA for real applications is evaluated in its beta-test operation. The examples are chosen from the practice of one of the selected pilot-users in the area of survey analysis. They belong to the application-class *aggregate data analysis*. Homogeneous applications of the same structure are gathered in an application-class to facilitate the incorporation of an application into the EXPLORA frame.

The application class *aggregate data analysis*

Data consist of records about units of analysis such as persons, companies or equipment. Variables are collected for a total or a sample of these units. There are result-variables and other variables which characterize the units. Other types and structures of variables are important for selecting relevant statement-types, appropriate statistical tests and parameters. Statements about remarkable patterns of the aggregated result-variables for classes of units are of primary interest. These classes are constructed by the characterizing variables. The files, structured by records (units) and variables, are covered regularly, so that an additional time-dimension is available. Moreover, several files (e.g. for companies and equipment) may be connected (relational data model). In this case several aggregations can be constructed and may appear in a statement-type.

Examples of this application-class are present in marketing research where interviews of establishments concerning their equipment or of persons concerning their buying-behaviour constitute the samples of units. Another example of this type is the analysis of political elections, where the units are given as a total of regional districts; the result-variables are not interview-values, but the actual results for political parties. This example was used as an alpha-test for our first prototype (figure 4).

Results are typically presented in the form of tabulation. Two or three characterizing variables are selected to structure the rows and columns. The aggregated values of a result-variable appear within the tabulation. This is how the notorious bulks of information arise: the users are drowned by tabulations (corresponding to the large number of possible combinations of variables) in which they have to identify remarkable values, e.g. by comparing the values with the margins.

EXPLORA will overcome this situation, so that its user obtains the most interesting messages concerning the data. Interactively he may focus the themes of the exploration and browse through the presented messages. These messages are constructed on the basis of statement-types referring to longitudinal or cross-section analyses.

For the longitudinal analysis some elementary time-series characteristics are applied, such as records and series. The following questions are answered:

Is the present value of a result-variable for any target-group a record, compared to the past values? Is the present value a further link in a series or is any series terminated?

Several partially ordered patterns of records or series are available, so that the redundancy formalism produces statements about a less general target-group only if it shows a stronger pattern.

Cross-sectional analyses can answer the following questions where the redundancy- and generalization-formalisms again reduce the number of generated statements:

For what target-groups are any patterns of behaviours remarkable for any result-variables? What competing objects possess the best (worst) ranks for any result-variable in any target group? In what sections are any cumulative values remarkable for any result-

variable? What functional relations exist between any result-variable and any characterizing variables in any target groups?

The following figure presents an example of the results of our first prototype.

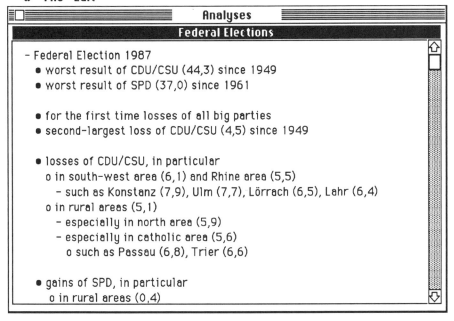

Figure 4: Analysis of the Federal-Election FRG in 1987

References

Gale, W.A. (1986): REX Review. In Gale, W.A. (ed.): Artificial Intelligence and Statistics. 173-227, Reading, Addison Wesley.

Gebhardt, F. (1988): Statistische Fragestellungen bei einem Expertensystem zur explorativen Datenanalyse. Sankt Augustin, GMD, (GMD-Studien 137).

Goodrich, R.L. (1986): FOREX: A time series forecasting expert system. In: Proceedings Sixth International Symposium on Forecasting, Paris.

Hoschka, P. and Klösgen, W. (1989): Assistenzcomputer als Entdeckungshilfe: Die Interpretation von Statistiken durch ein maschinelles System. Sankt Augustin, GMD, (Aus der wissenschaftlichen Arbeit der GMD, Jahresbericht 1988).

Kukich, K. (1988): Fluency in Natural Language Reports. In McDonald, D. and Bolc, L. (ed.): Natural Language Generation Systems. New York, Springer.

Latocha, P. (1989): Exploration von Aussagen-Räumen. Sankt Augustin, GMD, (GMD-Studien, in Vorbereitung).

Mann, W.C. (1988): Text Generation: The Problem of Text Structure. In McDonald, D. and Bolc, L. (ed.): Natural Language Generation Systems. New York, Springer.

McDonald, D. and Bolc, L. (ed., 1988): Natural Language Generation Systems. New York, Springer.

Michalski, R.S. et al. (ed., 1986): Machine Learning II. Morgan Kaufmann, Los Altos.

Nelder, J.A. et al. (1986): A front-end for GLIM. In Haux, R.(ed.): Expert Systems in Statistics. Stuttgart, Fischer.

A Knowledge-Base for Generalized Linear Modelling

C. M. O'Brien

Summary

This paper describes a knowledge-based front-end for the statistics package GLIM 3.77, developed using logic programming methods and tools. Details of the statistical knowledge encoded within the system, the guidance available to a user and a facility for suggesting answers to a user who requires guidance are discussed. The system is suitable for users with different levels of expertise, including those who wish to act independently of the system's advice.

1. Introduction

GLIM is a statistical package (Payne(1985)) developed to facilitate the fitting and assessment of generalized linear models (GLMs). It has its own interpretive language, which allows non-standard analyses to be programmed, plus general facilities for vector arithmetic, plot and histograms.

Although GLIM gives a powerful way of specifying GLMs, together with a general algorithm for fitting them it does not contain any built-in expertise. A statistician must know what he/she wants to do, how to specify it in the GLIM language and how to interpret the resulting output.

2. GLIMPSE - what is it?

GLIMPSE is a knowledge-based front-end for the statistical package

GLIM 3.77. It provides a user with assistance and optional guidance in the application of generalized linear modelling techniques to statistical data sets. It is intended to increase a user's understanding of generalized linear modelling and facilitate use of suitable statistical techniques (c.f. KENS in Hand(1987)).

3. What does GLIMPSE consist of?

GLIMPSE is created from several major components :

- GLIM 3.77, an interactive statistical package providing generalized linear modelling techniques. The package is written in FORTRAN 77 and is available through NAG Ltd.
- sigma-PROLOG, a PROLOG interpreter written in C by LPA Ltd.
- APES, an expert system 'shell' written in PROLOG provided by LBS Ltd.
- a knowledge-based front-end for generalized linear modelling written in PROLOG within the APES environment.

Sigma-PROLOG and APES are two existing logic programming tools that are widely available. Both are discussed by Wolstenholme, O'Brien and Nelder(1988).

4. The objectives of GLIMPSE

GLIMPSE addresses three objectives : to simplify use of the facilities provided by GLIM, to extend these facilities, and to allow the user to access built-in statistical expertise.

For the first two objectives the front-end provides a new command language that allows a user to operate at a much higher level than when using GLIM directly. The commands correspond to useful primitives in an analysis. The front-end provides extensive guidance in the use of this new command language, including menu and question-driven selection for the novice, together with a system of prompted command input for the more experienced user. Explanation is available if a command specified is incorrect in some way. An on-line manual provides additional background information on the command language and on the system in general.

For the third objective the front-end employs the concept of an 'abstract statistician' that watches over the user during an analysis. Where appropriate, the user may request advice on a suitable action to take next in the analysis or help in the interpretation of system output. The advice given is based on previous actions as well as knowledge in the rule-base. The user is free to accept, ignore or request an explanation of the advice proffered. Because the advice may be rejected, the system need not constrain the more experienced user; the advisory facilities are still available if required later.

5. Communicating with GLIMPSE - tasks

The new command language of GLIMPSE comprises a set of tasks permitting various actions to be carried out. The tasks may be divided into two groups :

(i) general tasks - those facilitating general actions such as obtaining help.

(ii) specialised tasks - those enabling a user to perform actions identified as being useful during an analysis.

Each task comprises an initial keyword, which gives a general indication of the action performed when the task is executed, followed by a sequence of additional keywords and variables. The sequence is designed to facilitate prompting and checking. Checking is carried out sequentially in four stages : pattern matching, type checking, context-free checking, and context-sensitive checking. Some of the tasks perform actions which essentially correspond to a single GLIM directive, but the execution of others may involve a complex sequence of GLIM and PROLOG commands.

6. Advice and guidance facilities

The checks and prompts form an essential part of the help and advice facilities offered by the GLIMPSE system. The semantic checks may make use of fairly sophisticated statistical knowledge in order to determine whether the task given is meaningful and, if not, to explain the reason. These checks and prompts may be all the help that the more experienced GLIMPSE user requires. For the less experienced, however, further help may be needed and this will be available in three varieties : help with system organisation, help with statistics and statistical strategy, and help with specifying the correct task.

The intention of help with the system organisation is to advise a user which actions must precede others and what data structures must exist before others can be built upon them.

Wherever it is considered that a user could require statistical or strategic help, appropriate knowledge is incorporated into the system to be used to advise the user as to which task, or sequence of tasks, to execute next. The system bases its advice on the set of rules supplied, together with information obtained as output from previous tasks executed and details supplied by a user through dialogue. Limitations on space do not permit a more detailed discussion but the reader is directed to the text by O'Brien(1989).

7. Outline of GLM modelling

Stages in the statistical analysis of experimental and observational data are conceptualised as distinct activities. Six such activities have been identified
- data input (DI);
- data definition (DD);
- data validation (DV);

- data exploration and transformation (DE);
- model selection and specification (MS);
- model checking and assessment (MC).

As an analyst moves from one activity to another, commands appropriate to that activity become available, and any advice offered is relevant to the activity.

Activity DI is concerned with accessing and storing the numerical values of the response and explanatory variables considered as a data matrix; no distinction is made between the different types of variables at this stage, and each is assigned its own unique reference name. Activity DD is concerned with eliciting as much information as possible about the variables; e.g. whether count, ratio measurement, point scale or continuous; whether extensive or intensive; whether experimental or observational. Activity DV is concerned with the detection of gross errors and inconsistencies in the numerical values of variables, the textual information given in activity DD being assumed correct. The system at this stage does not distinguish between response and explanatory variables. DE establishes basic information about the GLM : the response variate, the set of possible explanatory variables, the link function, the variance function, prior weights and offset; and is concerned with the possible need to transform the explanatory variables. Transformations are determined on the basis of simple graphical techniques but movement to the activity MC allows more formal tests of transformations to be invoked. MS is concerned with the modelling of a chosen response random variable by one or more explanatory variables and searches for suitable sets of terms to include in a linear predictor. Finally, activity MC checks the adequacy of models selected, using various techniques and strategies.

Movement between activities is unrestricted but constrained by a desire for a statistical analysis to be internally consistent.

The strategy of an analysis is summarized by the route taken through the six activities. This reflects the analyst's choice of statistical methods, previous analyses and prior knowledge of the data structure.

8. Help with statistics and statistical strategy

Wherever it is considered that the user could require statistical or strategic help, appropriate knowledge is incorporated into the system to be used to advise the user as to which task, or sequence of tasks, to execute next. The system bases its advice on the set of rules supplied, together with information obtained as output from previous tasks executed and details supplied by the user through dialogue. The statistical advice given is derived from logic rules of the form

> advised-action {_action} if {_conditions}

where an underscore at the beginning of a word, as in '_action', indicates that the word is a PROLOG variable. If, as system developers', it is desired to advise a user to carry out the sequence of individual actions making up a procedure one may describe the procedure by a set of logic rules of this form.

9. Suggested answers - a method of layering advice

When asked a question the user is normally expected to supply the information requested directly. However, where appropriate, the user may, when asked a question, decline to answer directly, and instead ask for a suggested answer from the system (Wolstenholme and O'Brien(1987)). The user may adopt any suggestion as the basis for his or her answer, or may reject it entirely. This feature is particularly useful where the user is expected to have deeper knowledge than the system. For example, in GLIMPSE it is assumed that the user will be better than the system at interpreting graphical output, but GLIMPSE will, if requested, suggest an interpretation based on certain summary statistics.

10. Concluding remarks

The main users who can benefit from the facilities provided by GLIMPSE are analysts working with generalized linear modelling techniques; in particular those already using GLIM or similar packages. GLIMPSE both reduces the time taken for the analysis of data and steers the analyst clear of the most frequent mistakes made by analysts. Considerable improvement of the analysis can result from judicious use of the system(O'Brien(1988)). Educationalists involved in beta-test trials suggest that the system should also be suitable for teaching purposes.

The GLIMPSE system will continue to be developed and enhanced over the coming years. A number of required enhancements to the system have already been identified and work on their development is either planned or underway. A first release of the system is for the Sun 3 workstation operating under UNIX BSD 4.2 (Sun versions 3.2 and 3.5). Two configurations are provided, one makes use of SunTools windowing while the other will run on standard teletype terminals.

Acknowledgement

GLIMPSE was developed by the Numerical Algorithms Group Ltd., and the Departments of Computing and Mathematics, Imperial College, with funding support from the Alvey Directorate (contract ALV/PRJ/IKBS/033).

References

Hand, D.J.(1987). Statistical expert systems research. The Professional Statistician, $\underline{6}$ (issue 10), 10-12.

O'Brien, C.M.(1988). Letters to the editor, 'Discussion of Mallows(1986)'. Technometrics, $\underline{30}$, 135-136.

O'Brien, C.M.(1989). The GLIMPSE System Compendium. To be published.

Payne, C.D.(1985). The GLIM System, Release 3.77, Generalised Linear Interactive Modelling Manual (editor). The Numerical Algorithms Group Limited, Oxford.

Wolstenholme, D.E., O'Brien, C.M.(1987). GLIMPSE - a statistical adventure. Proc. of the 10th Int. Joint Conf. on Art. Intell. (IJCAI 87, Milan, 23-28 August 1987), $\underline{1}$, 596-599.

Wolstenholme, D.E., O'Brien, C.M., Nelder, J.A.(1988). GLIMPSE : a knowledge-based front end for statistical analysis. Knowledge-Based Systems, $\underline{1}$, 173-178.

Present and Planned Future of the Expert System CADEMO

D. Rasch, V. Guiard, and G. Nürnberg

Summary

CADEMO is an expert system for statistical modelling and experimental design. Its present stage is described and demonstrated by the module Bioassay. A list of modules planned in the next future is included.

1. General description of the present state of CADEMO

Experiments are an important tool for gaining knowledge in natural sciences and in technical, medical and agricultural research (fig. 1).

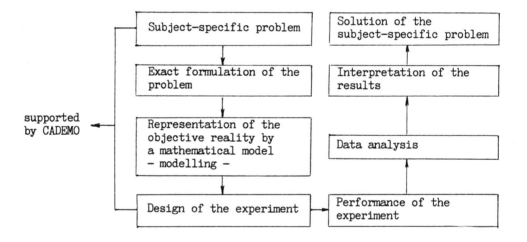

Figure 1. Gaining of knowledge in empirical sciences

Penetrating into the secrets of nature more deeply requires more and more expensive devices, and often just a single observation or measurement is costly. The minimization of experimental costs and the danger of too small a number of experimental units must be weighed against the need for sufficient reliability of the results and, thus, the need to minimize the risk of economic damage resulting from drawing wrong conclusions from the experiments. Most experimental data contain a random component and therefore permit no absolutely reliable inferences, but only probability statements. The smaller the probability of a wrong inference (the risk) the larger the number of experimental units needed. Very often it is possible to calculate the way the risk is related to the number of experimental units. An optimum experimental plan makes it possible to avoid exceeding a given risk with a minimum number of experimental units (see RASCH, 1989).

The results obtained by our research team and those published in the specialist literature have been compiled into a three-volume Library of Procedures for Experimental Design and Evaluation (Verfahrensbibliothek Versuchsplanung und -auswertung. RASCH et al., 1978, 1981) for the rationalization of our advisory work. For four years, about 50 scientists at six universities and three academy institutes representing various fields of application have been working on the problem of making the Library of Procedures and the results of recent research into optimum experimental design and modelling easily, comfortably and quickly accessible by means of an interactive system intended for those engaged in natural, technical, biological and medical research.

The aim is to minimize the knowledge of computer engineering and applied statistics needed to optimize experiments. This is done by making it possible for the user to call for explanations of terms he does not understand during the dialog. Our dialogue or expert system is called CADEMO, an abbrevation of Computer Aided Design of Experiments and Modeling.

CADEMO is intended for those engaged in various fields, starting with the medical researcher, who wants to perform a clinical study through the pharmacists testing a new drug and the plant breeder testing a new variety to the engineer developing a plan for statistical quality control, to mention only a few examples.

Such a wide-ranging expert system will gradually be available in several project stages. The master program of CADEMO will help those inexperienced in experimental design to find the appropriate basic model and the module complex belonging to it. Besides the master program, the first project stage of CADEMO contains the following module complexes (in brackets the number of modules):

- estimating and testing means and probabilities   (2)
- analysis of growth curves   (10)
- bioassay   (1)
- selection procedures   (2)
- statistical quality control and renewal problems   (2)

- field experiments

2. Future modules and module complexes

Besides extending the existing module complexes by adding modules for further tasks, work is in progress on the following module complexes:
- regression with one adjustable explanatory variable
- regression with two or more adjustable explanatory variables
- regression with random explanatory variables
- analysis of variance
- analysis of covariance
- population genetics
- sample survey
- distributions
- clinical and epidemiological studies
- estimating and testing variances
- choice and construction of experimental designs (block designs, row column designs, factorial designs).

It should be noted that CADEMO is not meant to compete with statistics software packages as it serves mainly for modelling and for finding the optimum experimental plan, e.g. the experiment of the smallest size. Figures 2 shows the structure of CADEMO.

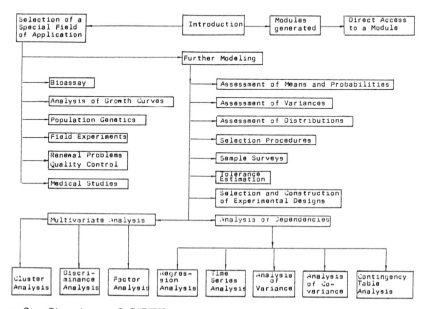

Figure 2. Structure of CADEMO

The first version (1.0) of CADEMO as discussed in RASCH, NÜRNBERG, and BUSCH (1988) was written in FORTRAN 77. Beginning with version 2.0 CADEMO is written in TURBO PASCAL 4.0. The system is available in German, English, Spanish or Hungarian.

3. CADEMO demonstration

We shall demonstrate the use of our expert system by planning an experiment for estimating the potency of a charge of the sexual hormone PMSG (pregnant mare serum gonadotrophin). The potency of PMSG is given in IU (international units), and the IU is defined by the potency of one unit volume of a standard PMSG charge. The experimental question (step 1 in fig. 1) is:

"How many IU's have the same potency as one unit of the charge being investigated?"

This number is called the relative potency, rho.

In an experiment with rats, the question can be answered by comparing the ovary weight of rats treated with graded doses of the standard and the experimental charge respectively. The exact formulation of the problem (step 2 in fig. 1) can after some discussion with the experimenter be formulated as follows:

"The probability that the estimator of rho is between the boundaries 1/1.2 and 1.2 should be about $0.95 = 1-\alpha$".

The value 1.2 is the so-called "limit of error" (l.o.e.).

After starting CADEMO, we see the introductory menu

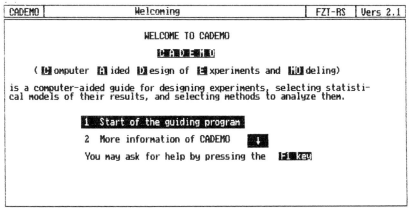

and start the guiding (master) program. This leads us through another menu to the second menu of the guiding program. It can easily be seen

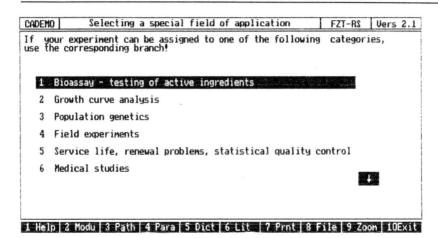

that the first option

"Bioassay – testing of active ingredients"

is needed, and after pressing the "ENTER" key we see the introduction to the module "Bioassay with one quantitative character". We proceed with "PgDn" and get the menu

in which we seek a suitable mathematical model (step 3 in fig. 1). Suppose that the user is not familiar with the different types of dose-response functions. After pressing the F5-key, a window showing a menu with some terms appears, from which the term 'dose-response function' can be chosen. The following explanation then appears:

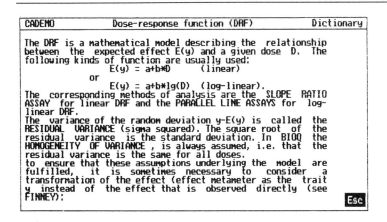

We suppose that the user decides to choose the log-linear model. After "Esc" he (she) is again in the menu presenting different models and selects the first option.

After receiving further explanations, the user must then enter the values of certain parameters by editing in a window. The result is

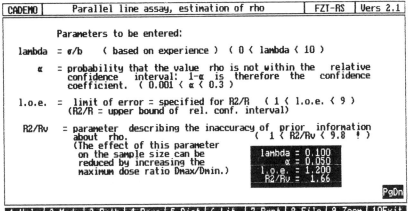

Uncertainties arising during the parameter input can be solved by calling for explanations via the F5-key. The next picture requests data concerning the doses. After these have been entered, we obtain

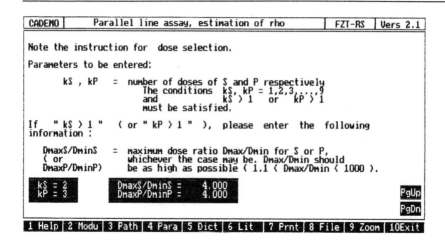

We conclude the data input by "PgDn" and receive the experimental design (step 4 in fig. 1) stating the numbers of rats needed in the different experimental groups.

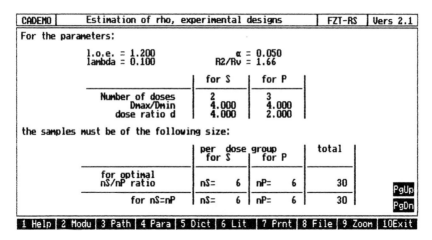

After pressing "PgDn" it is also possible to call for hints relating to the evaluation of the results (step 6 in fig. 1).

If the user is interested in the applied literature, he or she can press the F6-key.

References

Guiard, V. (1984). Versuchsplanung und -auswertung bei der Einstellung und Überprüfung von Präparatechargen mit Hilfe der Parallellinienprüfung (Bioassay). Probleme der angewandten Statistik, Heft 10, AdL der DDR, FZ für Tierproduktion Dummerstorf-Rostock

Rasch, D. (ed.) (1988). Biometrisches Wörterbuch (Erläuterungen und Übersetzungen in acht Sprachen). 3. Aufl., Verlag Harri Deutsch, Frankfurt/M.

Rasch, D., Nürnberg, G., Busch, K. (1988). CADEMO - Ein Expertensystem zur Versuchsplanung. In: Faulbaum, F. und Uehlinger, M. (Hrsg.): Fortschritte der Statistik-Software 1. Gustav Fischer, Stuttgart, 193-201

Rasch, D. (ed.) (1989). Einführung in die Biostatistik. 3. Aufl., Verlag Harri Deutsch, Frankfurt/M.

Rasch, D., Jansch, S. (Federf.) (1989). CADEMO-Handbuch Bd. I und II. FZ für Tierproduktion der AdL, Dummerstorf-Rostock

Kartographie und geographische
Informationssysteme

Desktop Kartographie?

V. Kreibich

Summary

The demand for desktop cartography is analysed and the application of a CAD System (AutoCAD) for thematic mapping demonstrated. By connecting a CAD programm with a databank it can be used as a Geographic Information System.

Das Angebot an Programmsystemen zur kartografischen Darstellung raumbezogener statistischer Informationen wird zusammen mit der Entwicklung neuer Anwendungsfelder immer vielfältiger. Die Bestimmung geeigneter Einsatzbereich gewinnt deshalb für Anbieter und Anwender immer größere Bedeutung. Obwohl die Forschungs- und Entwicklungsschwerpunkte z.T. sehr unterschiedlich sind, lassen sich erstaunliche Anwendungstransfers feststellen. Ein Beispiel ist der Einsatz von CAD-Programmen in der Planungskartografie.

1. Nachfrage

Ein Umbruch der "Qualifikationsbiografien" begünstigt die Nachfrage nach benutzerfreundlichen Anwenderprogrammen. Noch vor wenigen Jahren erfolgte der Einstieg in die EDV-Anwendung durch systematische Einarbeitung und den Erwerb der Fähigkeit zur eigenständigen Programmierung. Der so qualifizierte EDV-Experte bearbeitete Aufträge der Anwender in einer zentralisierten EDV-Organisation.

Heute finden immer mehr Anwender den Zugang zur EDV-Anwendung durch "learning by doing". Sie lernen mehr oder weniger selbständig den Umgang mit Anwenderprogrammen (Textverarbeitung,

Tabellenkalkulation und Statistik). Voraussetzungen sind die zunehmende Computerisierung der Arbeitsplätze, die Dezentralisierung der Hard- und Software; die immer weitergehende Benutzerfreundlichkeit der Programmsysteme.

In der thematischen und Planungskartografie ist dieser Umschwung noch nicht eingetreten. Automatisch gezeichnete Karten werden - zumindest in der öffentlichen Verwaltung - noch weitgehend von Experten im Auftrag erstellt und die Arbeit mit geografischen Informationssystemen am Schreibtisch des Sachbearbeiters ist noch die Ausnahme. Das Angebot an Soft- und Hardware wird die Nachfrage nach "Desktop-Kartografie" aber bald befriedigen können.

2. Angebot

Die Entwicklung des Angebots ist durch widersprüchliche Tendenzen, gekennzeichnet. Großsysteme, die noch für Großrechner entwickelt wurden, werden an die neu entstehende Nachfrage nach PC-Anwendungen angepaßt, für die Statistik z.B. SAS und SPSS, für die Kartografie ARC-Info.

Daneben läßt sich auch die Erschließung neuer Einsatzbereiche für bereits bestehende Progammsysteme feststellen, z.B. die Adaptierung von CAD-Systemen für die Kartografie. Ein solches Multifunktionssystem, das für die speziellen Anforderungen der Planungskartografie verwendet werden kann, ist AutoCAD. Zusätzlich gibt es immer mehr Spezialentwicklungen, z.B. für die Lagerstättenkunde, das Katasterwesen oder die ökologische Forschung und Planung, die z.T. mit neuen Methoden arbeiten (räumliche Datenmodelle, Modellierung unregelmäßiger Oberflächen, Nicht-Standard-Datenbankstrukturen).

3. Desktop-Kartografie?

Kartografie am Arbeitsplatz des Sachbearbeiters war bis vor kurzem noch nicht möglich, weil die Hardware zu aufwendig war (Digitalisierung, Rechengeschwindigkeit, Speicherkapazität, Bildschirmauflösung) und die Software nur für Großrechner bzw. workstations zur Verfügung stand und nur durch Experten angewendet werden konnte. Heute erfolgt mit zunehmender Differenzierung der Aufgaben auch eine immer stärkere Verlagerung an den Arbeitsplatz des Endanwenders (low-end). Typische Aufgabenbereiche für dezentrale Anwendungen sind z.B.:

- Preview thematischer Karten (räumliche Verteilungen)
- Arbeit mit Karten, die nur am Bildschirm benutzt werden (z.B. Leitungsnetze, Grundstückskataster, Routendiagramme)
- Erstellung thematischer Karten für Berichte oder Veröffentlichungen.

Diese Anwendungen sind nur möglich, wenn die Programme folgende Voraussetzungen erfüllen: Menüführung (mit kontextbezogener Hilfsfunktion), interaktive Bearbeitung (auch Editieren) ..., Branchenunterstützung, Unterstützung der Digitalisierung bzw. eines Scanners, Lay-out-Funktionen und Koppelung mit einer Datenbank.

4. Kartografie mit AutoCAD

Das CAD-Programm AutoCad erfüllt alle Anforderungen an ein leistungsfähiges System zur Desktop-Kartografie:

- marktgängige Hardware (Eignung für 268- und 368-Prozessor)
- große Auswahl bei Drucker-, Plotter- und Bildschirmtreibern
- gute Dokumentation, vielfältige Literatur, Lehrbücher, Kursangebote
- weite Verbreitung (Erfahrungsaustausch, add-ons für Branchenlösungen)
- Stabilität (Zuverlässigkeit)

- Benutzerführung (kontextbezogene Hilfefunktion)
- einfaches Digitalisieren
- interne Programmiersprache für Spezialanwendungen.

AutoCAD verfügt über interne und externe Schnittstellen zu Datenbanken, die z.B. die Verwaltung von Stücklisten ermöglichen, für kartografische Zwecke aber bisher noch nicht genutzt worden sind. So wird z.B. in einem Standardwerk zur EDV-Anwendung in der Planung noch festgestellt: "CAD-Programme sind für die Kartografie ungeeignet, da sie nicht in der Lage sind, statistische Informationen mit raumbezogenen Referenzpunkten zu verknüpfen" (Newton, u.a., S. 31).

AutoCAD kann Zusatzinformationen zu den geometrischen Elementen einer Zeichnung, sogenannte Attribute (Punkte, Linien oder Flächen) verwalten: beliebige nicht-geometrische Daten, die einem geometrischen Element zugeordnet sind ("Textinformationen"), z.B.:

- Stücklisten (Katalognummern, Preise, Hersteller)
- Grundstücksdateien (Katasternummern, Grundstücksgröße, Baurecht, Eigentümer)
- Stadtbezirke (Bezeichnung, z.B. Adressenschlüssel, Einwohner, Wohneinheiten, Fläche)

Die Attribute sind an Blöcke gebunden, die als Layer behandelt werden können. Eine thematische Karte könnte z.B. folgende Layer enthalten:

- Polygone für die Grenzen der Gebietseinheiten
- Bezeichnung der Gebietseinheiten
- Schraffurtypen oder Farben
- Legende
- Text (Überschrift)
- Rahmen.

Die Attribute können von AutoCAD mit einer eigenen Datenbank verwaltet werden. Diese Option ist schnell zu erlernen und einfach zu bedienen, ihre Anwendung verlängert aber die Systemzeiten und benötigt viel Speicherplatz. Bei größeren Satzlängen bzw. längeren Attributdateien ist daher die Einrichtung einer externen Datenbank zu empfehlen, was durch eine AutoCAD-Funktion unterstützt wird, die es erlaubt, externe Programme zu starten (z.B. Datenbankprogramme), ohne AutoCAD verlassen zu müssen.

Mit AutoLISP, der internen Programmiersprache von AutoCAD, kann die Geometrie-Datenbank bearbeitet und der Transfer von Attributen zwischen AutoCAD und einem Datenbankprogramm unterstützt werden.

Die Aufgabenstellung, mit der das CAD-Programm AutoCAD als geografisches Informationssystem eingesetzt werden kann, lautet: "Ist es möglich, Informationen aus einer externen Datenbank dazu zu benutzen, um eine existierende AutoCAD-Zeichnung zu verändern, ohne alle Daten von Hand neu eingeben zu müssen? (Jones/Martin, S. 171)

In den USA gibt es inzwischen kommerzielle Zusatzprogramme für AutoCAD, mit denen kartografische Aufgaben bearbeitet werden können (z.B. FMS/AC, Facility Mapping System). Sie werden in öffentlichen und privaten Planungsbüros z.B. für die Flächennutzungsplanung, für die Bearbeitung von Grundstückskatastern, in den Stadtwerken (Leitungsnetzverwaltung) und für Straßenkataster eingesetzt. Diese Systeme arbeiten in der Regel mit einem verbreiteten Datenbanksystem, sind vollkommen menügesteuert, verfügen über aufgabenspezifische Symbolbibliotheken und Suchfunktionen mit Bildschirmanzeige und unterstützen die Digitalisierung.

Die Erfahrungen aus einer Eigenprogrammierung haben gezeigt, daß der Einsatz von AutoCAD für die Planungskartografie und als geografisches Informationssystem tatsächlich ohne großen Aufwand möglich ist. Mit der internen Programmiersprache AutoLISP wurde eine Verbindung zum Datenbankprogramm dBase III+ hergestellt, um thematische Karten zu zeichnen. Dabei wurden folgende Funktionen realisiert:

- Klassifikation von Merkmalsausprägungen,

- Zuweisung von Schraffurtypen zu den Klassen und

- Übertragung der Schraffuren in die Gebietseinheiten der Karte, die nacheinander abgearbeitet werden.

Das Digitalisieren der Grundkarte mit ca. 90 Gebietseinheiten dauerte knapp drei Stunden. Die beiden Abbildungen zeigen ein Strukturdiagramm und ein Beispiel für eine thematische Karte, die mit AutoCAD und automatischer Wertezuweisung aus dBase III+ gezeichnet wurde.

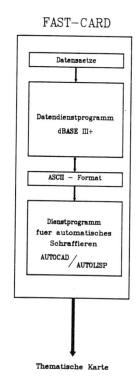

Karte : Anteil der Sozialmietwohnungen am gesamten Wohnungsbestand in den Koelner Stadtteilen 1987 in v.H.

Legende:
- keine Bestaende
- unter 20%
- 20% bis unter 40%
- 40% bis unter 60%
- 60% bis unter 80%
- 80% bis unter 90%
- 90% und mehr

Erlaeuterungen:
Mittelwert: 70,6
Standardabweichung: 28,6
niedrigster Wert: 0%
   im Stadtteil Chorweiler
hoechster Wert: 100%
   im Stadtteil Wahnheide

Quelle: Amt fuer Statistik und Einwohnerwesen, BEBEKO

Literatur

Jones, F. H. und L. Martin: AutoCAD 2.6 organisiert - Techniken professioneller CAD-Datenbankverwaltung, München 1988.

Newton, P.W. u.a. (Hrsg.): Desktop Planning, Melbourne 1988.

Erstellung von Regionalkarten für MAP-MASTER und Analyse regionalisierter Umfragedaten mit SPSS/PC+

J.H.P. Hoffmeyer-Zlotnik und H. Ritter

Summary

In the following article, the digitisation of a complexly structured geographical area is described. The digitisation is accomplished independently of access to specialized hard- and software through the use of the KONMAP program. The resulting material can not only be further processed with the cartographic program MAP-MASTER but also can be enhanced with labels and values from SPSS/PC+ files that are available through the SPSS/PC+ MAPPING interface. How this can be done is illustrated in an example using actual data.

1. Die Ausgangsfragestellung

Durch verschiedene kleine Umfragen (Pretests) liegen Daten vor, die sich regional auf die Ebene von Stadtteilbereichen der Stadt Mannheim beziehen. Von der Analysesoftware auf dem PC liegen in unserem Falle vor allem Erfahrungen mit SPSS/PC+ vor und mit der Schnittstelle SPSS/PC+ MAPPING zum Kartographieprogramm MAP-MASTER ist eine relativ einfache Datenübergabe von SPSS/PC+ in eine Kartendarstellungsform möglich. Die offene Frage war, wie die Digitalisierung der Mannheimer Stadtteilbereiche zu realisieren sei, ohne die optimale Soft- und Hardware hierfür zur Verfügung zu haben. Diese Lösung sowie ein Analysebeispiel soll im folgenden beschrieben werden.

Natürlich ist dies nur eine mögliche Form der Realisierung dieser Fragestellung. So kann z.B. auch SAS/GRAPH zur Lösung benutzt werden. In der Regel ist auch der Einsatz sonstiger Kartographieprogramme möglich. Warum haben wir die "Handvercodung" der digitalisierten Karte gewählt, da es auch hier diverse Möglichkeiten gibt, mit entsprechendem finanziellen Mitteleinsatz, Hardware für die maschinelle Unterstützung der Kartendigitalisierung anzuschaffen bzw. sich fertige, digitalisierte Karten zu kaufen?

Was uns zum beschriebenen Projekt veranlaßte, war die Möglichkeit, auf Grund des vorhandenen Datenmaterials, der Softwarekenntnisse sowie der Möglichkeit, ohne zusätzliche größere Finanzaufwendungen, unter Mitwirkung wissenschaftlicher Hilfskräfte, das Projekt verwirklichen zu können. In diesem Zusammenhang möchten wir Frau Maria Zabula und Herrn Thorsten Borsdorf für ihre Mitarbeit bei der Projektrealisierung danken.

2. Die Kartendigitalisierung mit dem Programm KONMAP

Für das Kartographieprogramm MAP-MASTER[1] werden digitalisierte Kartendaten mitgeliefert, auch für die Bundesrepublik Deutschland. Jedoch ist die tiefste Gliederung die Ebene der Bundesländer. Wie kann also eine selbsterzeugte Karte, in einem Format, das MAP-MASTER einlesen und weiterverarbeiten kann, erstellt werden? Hierfür gibt es vom Amt für Stadtforschung und Statistik der Stadt Nürnberg seit August 1988 das Programm KONMAP[2] in der Version 1.0, mit dem eigenständig erfaßte Karteninformationen in ein für MAP-MASTER geeignetes Format umgesetzt werden können.

In Absprache mit dem Amt für Stadtentwicklung und Statistik der Stadt Mannheim haben wir uns für die Untergliederung des Mannheimer Stadtgebietes in 79 Stadtteilbereiche entschieden. Hierfür überließ uns das Amt eine entsprechende Stadtkarte.

Die eigentliche Kartendigitalisierung erfolgt über die Eingabedateien für das Programm KONMAP. Bei der ersten Datei handelt es sich um eine Koordinatendatei. Darin werden die einzelnen Polygone (inhaltlich: ein Stadtteilbereich) Punkt für Punkt mit x- und y-Koordinatenwerten beschrieben. Der Koordinatenbereich kann in den Grenzen von 0 bis 10.000 liegen. Bei der zweiten Datei handelt es sich um die Polygonbeschreibungsdatei. Hierin werden den einzelnen Polygonen, also den regionalen Kartenuntergliederungen, Namen, eine fortlaufende Nummer, die Startkoordinate des Polygons in der Koordinatendatei (kumuliert) und die Anzahl der Koordinatenpaare angegeben. Über diese Datei werden in der späteren Analyse die Daten aus SPSS/PC+ über die Schnittstelle MAPPING regional zugeordnet. Schließlich werden in der dritten, der Mittelpunktsdatei, den einzelnen Regionsnamen Koordinatenpunkte zugeordnet, die den ungefähren Mittelpunkt eines Polygons beschreiben. Damit werden in MAP-MASTER die Labels für die Regionen zugeordnet. Alle Eingabedateien sind im ASCII-Format abzuspeichern.

Als entscheidend für die spätere Analyse hat sich erwiesen, daß die Namen der Kartenregionen in der Polygonbeschreibungsdatei in einer aufwärts sortierten Reihenfolge vorliegen müssen, da ansonsten die Werte- und Labelübergabe von SPSS/PC+ MAPPING nicht erfolgen kann. Wir entschieden uns als Gebietsnamen für die amtliche dreistellige Ziffer zur Kennzeichnung eines Stadtteilbereiches[3].

Die drei beschriebenen Dateien bauen aufeinander auf, d.h. die Werte aller drei Dateien müssen in derselben logischen Reihenfolge sortiert sein, die jeweiligen

Datenwerte müssen genau stimmen, damit das KONMAP-Programm eine korrekte konvertierte Ergebnisdatei für MAP-MASTER liefert.

Diese konvertierte digitalisierte Kartenformat wird als Boundary-File in MAP-MASTER eingelesen und auf dieser Grundlage können einzelne Karten mit den Grenzen der Mannheimer Stadtteilbereiche gezeichnet werden (siehe Abbildung 1).

Grenzen der Mannheimer Stadtteilbereiche

Relevante Gebiete fuer die Regionalanalyse

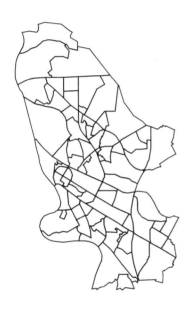
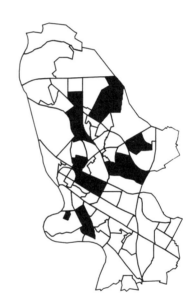

Abbildung 1   Abbildung 2

3. Die Datenübergabe von SPSS/PC+ an MAP-MASTER

Für die Übergabe von Datenwerten und Labels von SPSS/PC+ an MAP-MASTER benötigt man das Zusatzmodul SPSS/PC+ MAPPING. Realisiert wird die Daten-Übergabe mit dem Kommando MAP. Im Kommando müssen als Option die dazustellende Variable (z.B. Bildung) bezogen auf eine Kartengebietseinheit in eine in MAP-MASTER erstellte Grundkarte für das gewünschte Gebiet angegeben werden. Die Variable für die Kartengebietseinheit in unserem Datensatz hatte den Namen GEBIET (die dreistellige amtliche Ziffer der Mannheimer Stadtteilbereiche). Da jedoch MAP-MASTER die 79 Stadtteilbereiche nicht alleine mit dem dreistelligen

Stadtteilschlüssel verwalten kann, fügt MAP-MASTER eine weitere Ziffer für die Gebietskennzeichung hinzu. Dadurch ist der direkte Bezug zwischen der Gebietsvariablen im SPSS/PC+ Datensatz und der internen Gebietsvariablen in der MAP-MASTER Karte nicht mehr gegeben[4]. Daher muß mit einer KEY-Datei gearbeitet werden. Diese KEY-Datei ermöglichst die Zuordnung eines bestimmten Wertes der SPSS/PC+ Gebietsvariablen zu einem bestimmten Wert für ein Gebiet in der MAP-MASTER Karte.

Um nun darzustellen, für welche der 79 Stadtteilbereiche überhaupt Daten vorhanden sind, wurde in SPSS/PC+ das folgende Kommando eingegeben:
   MAP COUNT BY GEBIET (3, KEY='MANNHEIM.KEY') /BASE='ORGINAL'.
"MAP" ist das Kommando für die Schnittstelle von SPSS/PC+ zu MAP-MASTER. "COUNT BY GEBIET" ist eine Option, die bewirkt, daß in der Karte dargestellt wird, für welche Stadtteilbereiche überhaupt die Werte der Gebietsvariablen selbst vorhanden sind. Die "3" nach der Klammer 'auf' kennzeichnet, daß es sich bei der Variablen GEBIET um eine dreistellige Zahl handelt. "KEY='MANNHEIM.KEY'" verweist auf die Datei, in der der Umsetzungsschlüssel für die Werte der Gebietsvariablen in den Daten und der MAP-MASTER internen Gebietsvariablen gespeichert ist und "/BASE='ORGINAL'" benennt die existierende MAP-MASTER Karte ("ORGINAL"), in die die Daten transferiert werden sollen. Das Ergebnis ist in Abbildung 2 dargestellt.
Mit dem Kommando "MAP VALUE(variable) BY GEBIET ..." können dann z.B. auch Variablenwerte übergeben werden.

4. Das Anwendungsbeispiel

Aus der Sicht des Nutzers soll in einem Anwendungsbeispiel demonstriert werden, was eine kartierte Analyse regionalisierter Umfragedaten bei der Veranschaulichung der Ergebnisse bietet.

Das gewählte Anwendungsbeipiel wurde einem von ZUMA 1986 in 11 aus 79 Mannheimer Stadtteilbereichen erhobenen Adressen-Sample von 718 Personen entnommen (vgl. HOFFMEYER-ZLOTNIK 1987: 37-43). Die Auswahl der 11 Stadtteilbereiche war über eine Klassifikation des Gebietsstatus vorgenommen worden. Die in diesem Gebietssample erhobenen Daten einer Studie zu egozentrierten Netzwerken geben sowohl Auskunft über die Befragungsperson selbst als auch zu den von diesen genannten Personen aus deren Netzwerken.

Dieser zur Demonstration gewählte Datensatz ist hinsichtlich seiner Stichprobe nicht untypisch für die Hochschulforschung, da in der Regel Umfragen auf regionaler Ebene entweder nicht flächendeckend oder nur mit wenigen Fällen pro Raumeinheit besetzt sind, denn flächendeckende Erhebungen bei ausreichenden Fallzahlen für die unteren Flächeneinheiten übersteigen oft den verfügbaren Kostenrahmen. Dennoch eignet sich ein Datensatz, wie der des Anwendungsbeispiels, zur regionalisierten Analyse, da die Forschungsfrage die Variable "GEBIET" zu einer zentralen Analyseeinheit erhebt.

Die Ausgangsbedingung für eine Kartierung ist die Reduktion der zu kartierenden Daten auf je einen Wert pro Raumeinheit! Dieses bedeutet, daß zwei Schritte der Datentransformation stattfinden müssen, die man im Gedächtnis behalten sollte:
1. Die Befragungspersonen stellten zwar die Erhebungseinheiten dar, sie sind jedoch nicht mehr die Analyseeinheiten. Die Fälle bei einer Kartierung sind die regionalen Einheiten, im Beispiel die Stadtteilbereiche.
2. Mengen, Anteile, Mittelwerte oder Factorscores, bezogen auf die Stadtteilbereiche, stellen die einer Kartierung zu Grunde liegenden Werte dar.

Häufig dient die Kartierung dazu, Hintergrundmerkmale wie z.B. Geschlecht, Alter, oder andere Merkmale in ihrer regionalen Verteilung darzustellen. Das heißt: Es werden Häufigkeiten oder Anteile einer Gruppenzugehörigkeit kartiert (siehe Abbildung 3).

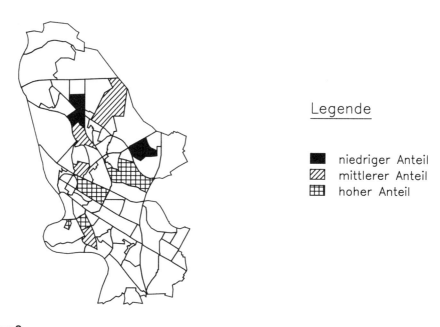

Abbildung 3

Ebenfalls als Hintergrundinformation, und damit oft als Zusatz zu einer befragtenbezogenen Analyse zu sehen, sind komplexere Indikatoren. Hierzu bedarf es allerdings nicht des Vorteils einer Schnittstelle zwischen SPSS und MAP-MASTER.

Eine raumbezogene Analyse stellt z.B. die Faktorialökologie dar (vgl. FRIEDRICHS 1977: 183 ff; HAMM 1977: 94 ff). Die Analyseeinheit ist der Raum - es gilt z.B. städtische Teilgebiete zu klassifizieren, zu typisieren. Der Demonstrationsdatensatz kann entsprechend analysiert werden, da eine Untersuchungsfrage die nach "lokaler Identität" darstellte. Hierzu wurden befragtenbezogene Informationen, demographische sowie relevante Einstellungsdaten, aus der auf dem Großrechner gespeicherten Datei mit der Prozedur "AGGREGATE" und der die Gruppierungsvariable erzeugenden Anweisung "BREAK = VARIABLE 'GEBIET'" in eine stadtteilbezogene Datei transformiert. Diese Transformation wäre bei einem durchgängig auf dem PC bearbeiteten Datensatz für den deskriptiven Part der Analyse noch nicht erforderlich gewesen, sie ist allerdings notwendige Voraussetzung für die Faktorenanalyse.

Bei dieser Transformation wurde nicht mit absoluten Häufigkeiten, sondern mit Mittelwerten gearbeitet. Die Ausgabedatei besteht pro städtischem Teilgebiet und pro Variable aus einem Wert und stellt damit sowohl einen mit SPSS für "Fall = Gebiet" analysierbaren als auch einen in MAP-MASTER einlesbaren Datensatz dar.

Faktor "Subjektive Schichtwahrnehmung"

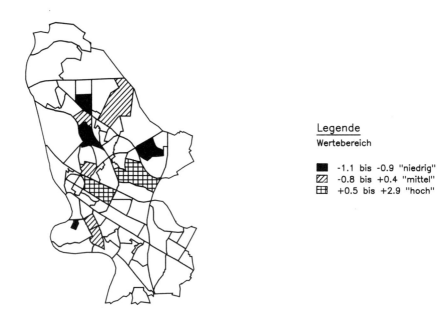

Abbildung 4

Mit den so transformierten Daten kann eine die Gebietseinheiten unterscheidende Analyse durchgeführt werden. Denn bei den nun möglichen Analysen, wobei wir uns nur aus Demonstrationszwecken auf die Faktorenanalyse beschränkt haben, stellen die räumlichen Untereinheiten die Analyseeinheiten dar. Das Beispiel Faktorenanalyse ist in Abbildung 4 demonstriert. Diese zeigt den Faktor "subjektive Schichtwahrnehmung" mit hohen Ladungen auf den Variablen "Schulabschluß der Befragungsperson", "Schichtzuordnung der Nachbarschaft" und "antizipiertes Ansehen des Gebietes in der Bevölkerung". Weitere Analysen mit anderen Prozeduren aus dem breiten Angebot des SPSS-Programpaketes sind möglich - soweit diese entsprechend der Forschungsfrage als sinnvoll anzusehen und bezogen auf die Fallzahl (Anzahl der Gebiete) möglich sind.

5. Schlußbemerkung

Insgesamt gesehen ist hier eine Möglichkeit beschrieben und für die Analyse demonstriert worden, die es dem Stadt- und Regionalforscher erlaubt, mit geringen finanziellen Mitteln und bei erträglichem Aufwand kartierte Analysen regionalisierter Umfragedaten auf eigenverantwortlich erstellten individuellen Karten vorzunehmen. Hierbei hängen die Karten vom Ausgangsmaterial und vom eigenen Arbeitsinput ab; für die Analyse steht das breite Spektrum von SPSS/PC+ zur Verfügung, lediglich eingeschränkt durch die Qualität der eigenen Daten.

Anmerkungen:

1) MAP-MASTER ist ein Ashton-Tate-Produkt. Es ist auch über SPSS Software GmbH zusammen mit der Schnittstelle SPSS/PC+ MAPPING V 3.0 beziehbar und kostet 1.100 DM (ohne MWSt.).

2) Das Programm KONMAP wird im Rahmen des KOSIS-Verbundes (Kommunales Statistisches Informationssystem) vertrieben. Nähere Informationen erhalten Sie bei: Amt für Stadtforschung und Statistik, Herr Stellwag, Unschlittplatz 7a, D-8500 Nürnberg 1, Tel.: 0911/163275. Das Programm KONMAP kostet 150 DM. Informationen über fertig digitalisierte Karten (Gemeindegrenzen, Kreisgrenzen der BRD, dreistellige Postleitzahlbezirke oder auch Karten für spezielle Wünsche) sind auch zu erhalten bei: Universität Gesamthochschule Kassel, FG Empirische Wirtschaftsforschung, Herr Prof. Dr. H.F. Eckey, Nora-Platiel-Str. 4, D-3500 Kassel, Tel.: 0561/80430-38/-45/-46/-47.

3) Mittlerweile gibt es im Programm KONMAP eine Routine MAKECIN, die aus der Koordinatendatei und einer Datei mit den Gebietsnamen die Polygonbeschreibungsdatei und die Mittelpunktsdatei automatisch kreiert. In weiteren Programmverbesserungen soll auch die automatische Sortierung der Polygonbeschreibungsdatei nach Gebietsnamen mit der automatischen Umsortierung der anderen beiden Dateien berücksichtigt werden.

4) Um feststellen zu können, ob die Werte der Gebietsvariablen hinsichtlich der Daten mit denen der internen MAP-MASTER-Karte übereinstimmt, kann in SPSS/PC+ mit dem Kommando "MAP NAME='karte' eine Datei "karte.NAM" erstellt werden, die die Werte der MAP-MASTER internen Gebietsvariablen enthält.

Literatur:

ASHTON TATE CORPORATION (1987). MAP-MASTER User's Manual. Westport.

FRIEDRICHS, J. (1977). Stadtanalyse. Soziale und räumliche Organisation der Gesellschaft. Reinbek.

HAMM, B. (1977). Die Organisation der städtischen Umwelt. Frauenfeld/Stuttgart.

HOFFMEYER-ZLOTNIK, J.H.P. (1987). Egozentrierte Netzwerke im Massenumfragen 1: Zum Design des Methodenforschungsprojektes, in: ZUMANACHRICHTEN 20, S. 37-43.

SPSS INC. (1986). SPSS/PC+ Mapping V 2.0. Chicago.

STADT NÜRNBERG, AMT FÜR STADTFORSCHUNG UND STATISTIK (1988). KONMAP Version 1.0 Programmbeschreibung.

F. Faulbaum, R. Haux und K.-H. Jöckel (Hrsg.) (1990). SoftStat '89
Fortschritte der Statistik-Software 2. Stuttgart: Gustav Fischer, 359 - 364

Geographisches Informationssystem und Computerkartographie

P. Ludäscher

Summary
This paper deals with the experiences made by the conception and realization of a hard- and software-configuration, orientated on the necessaries of scientific research and teaching. For the department of Geography and Geoecology II at the University of Karlsruhe, a hard- and software-conception for these necessities was provided. Therefor the following aims and requirements had to be respected. Concerning software, a relational database management system (RDBMS), a geographical information system (GIS), a statistical program package, a program for designing thematic maps, multi-dimensional graphics as well as profiles and a program for preparation and processing of remote sensing raster data should be part of this system. At last the possibility of data transfer and data conversion between the different program systems has to be secured. Additional all these programs should run under the same operating-system. Furthermore, if possible, all programs had to be installed on one computer system. The following paper tries to give an overview on solving these problems.

Für das Institut für Geographie und Geoökologie II der Universität Karlsruhe war ein Hard- und Softwarekonzept für Forschung und Lehre zu erstellen. Anlaß war u. a. die Beteiligung des Instituts an einem neuen Forschungsverbundprojekt zur Erstellung eines "Prognosemodells für die Gewässerbelastung durch Stofftransport aus einem kleinen ländlichen Einzugsgebiet" (beteiligt sind Institute der Universität Karlsruhe, das Inst. f. Umweltphysik der Universität Heidelberg und die Landwirtschaftl. Untersuchungs- und Forschungsanstalt Karlsruhe). Zentrale Bedeutung hatte dabei die Einrichtung eines Geographischen Informationssystems i. w. S., was nicht nur die Fähigkeiten von Programmpaketen wie z. B. ARC/INFO oder ERDAS beinhaltet, welche man als Geographische Informationssysteme i. e. S. bezeichnen könnte, sondern einige weitere Eigenschaften, die in nachstehender Auflistung zusammengestellt sind.

Anforderungsprofil an ein GIS i. w. S. :
- Leistungsfähiges relationales Datenbank Management System;
- Statistik-Programmpaket mit allen gebräuchlichen statistischen Prozeduren;
- Programm zur Erstellung thematischer Karten und mehrdimensionaler Graphiken, digitaler Geländemodelle und Profile;
- Programm zur Durchführung spezieller Geostatistik (z. B. Krigging);
- Programm zur Aufbereitung und Verarbeitung von Rasterdaten aus dem Bereich Fernerkundung;

- Möglichkeit des Datentransfers und der Datenkonversion zwischen den einzelnen Programmsystemen;
- Geographisches Informationssystem i. e. S.

Die Geräteausstattung des Instituts für Forschungsaufgaben und die vorhandenen Ausbildungsrechner sollten soweit als möglich in das Konzept integriert werden. Für das Projekt soll eine Graphik-Workstation beschafft werden. Für die Hardwareausstattung lassen sich zusammenfassend folgende Kriterien anführen.

Anforderungen an die Hardware:
- ein Betriebssystem für alle Programmpakete;
- Anbindungsmöglichkeit an Großrechner des RZ;
- Einbindung vorhandener Peripheriegeräte für Ein- und Ausgabe;
- Kompatibilität zu den vorhanden Ausbildungsrechnern.

Neben diesen Anforderungen war zu berücksichtigen, daß bestehendes know how bezüglich bereits vorhandener Programmpakete möglichst weiter nutzbar bleiben sollte. Im Bereich der Softwareanpassung und -transferabilität wurden von Institutsmitarbeitern diverse Datenkonversions- und Adaptionsprogramme in Turbo Pascal geschrieben, so daß inzwischen ein relativ reibungsloser Datentransfer zwischen den meistverwendeten Anwenderprogrammen einschließlich der Raster-Vektorkonversion und vice versa möglich ist.
Im Detail wurden aufgrund der oben aufgeführten Prämissen folgende Lösungen gewählt:

- **Leistungsfähiges relationales Datenbank Management System**
  - **PROFESSIONAL ORACLE**

    Für dieses DBMS hält das Rechenzentrum der Universität Karlsruhe eine Campuslizenz für Großrechner und PCs, somit wurde ORACLE zum Standard DBMS der Universität. Eine Schnittstelle zu ARC/INFO wird fertig angeboten.

- Geographisches Informationssystem i. e. S.
  - ARC/INFO PC

    Seit etwa 2 Jahren besitzt das Institut eine Lizenz für eine PC-Version. Inzwischen findet das Paket Anwendung als Kartographiesoftware. Nachteile der früheren PC-Versionen war der relativ hohe Einarbeitungsaufwand. Zudem ist die PC-Version im Vergleich zu Workstation- und Minirechner-Versionen mit diversen Restriktionen behaftet, stellt aber derzeit aufgrund der langen GIS-Erfahrung von ESRI* immer noch "state of the art" im Bereich Vektor-GIS (Hardwareanforderungen: MS-DOS PC mit min. 640 KB RAM und 30 MB Harddisk) dar.

- **MAP-FOR-THE-PC**

Map Analysis Package (Version 2.0; August 1987) ist ein Rastergraphik-System, basierend auf einem von Dana Tomlin entwickelten Programm, welches vom Geographic Information System Laboratory der Ohio State University weiterentwickelt wurde. Die Stärken dieses Programmes liegen in seiner relativ leichten Erlernbarkeit, daher ist es prädestiniert für den Einsatz in der Lehre. Allerdings ist die Dateneingabe, vor allen Dingen bei größeren Datenmengen sehr zeitraubend und etwas umständlich. Die maximale Auflösung liegt etwas unterhalb der auf einem EGA-Bildschirm darstellbaren Pixel (Hardwarevoraussetzungen: MS-DOS PC mit min. 640 KB RAM).

- **Statistik-Programmpaket mit kartographischen Fähigkeiten**
  - **SAS-PC**

Für dieses Programmpaket hält das Rechenzentrum der Universität Karlsruhe eine Campuslizenz für Großrechner und diverse PC-Lizenzen, somit wurde SAS zum Standard-Statistik-Programmpaket der Universität. Durch das bereits bestehende Rechnerkommunikationsnetz der Universität ist ein nahezu ideales Verbundsystem von Großrechner- und PC-Version dieses Programmsystemes möglich geworden.

- **Farbgraphik-, Geostatistik und Kartographieprogrammsystem**
  - **UNIMAP PC**

Die besonderen Fähigkeiten dieses Rastersystems liegen im Bereich leistungsfähiger geostatistischer Verfahren sowie bei diversen räumlichen Interpolationsverfahren, der Variogrammanalyse, des Krigging etc. Die farbgraphischen Darstellungsmöglichkeiten auch in variabler 3D-Darstellung können als herausragend bezeichnet werden. Als Nachteile sind die sattsam bekannten Restriktionen des MS-DOS zu nennen: Erforderlich war ein AT mit min. 640 KB RAM + 512 KB extended Memory und 20 MB Harddisk. Die PC-Version ist außer zur Einarbeitung in die Programmstruktur und zur Arbeit mit kleinen Datenmengen nicht empfehlenswert und wird von UNIRAS inzwischen auch nicht mehr vertrieben. Als Mindestausstattung kann eine Workstation mit Graphikprozessor angesehen werden.

- **Programm zur Aufbereitung und Verarbeitung von Rasterdaten aus der Fernerkundung**
  - **(geplant: ERDAS-PC)**

---

* ESRI: Environmental Systems Research Institute

- **Programm zum Transfer und zur Konversion von Daten zwischen den einzelnen Programmsystemen**
  - **CONVERT**

    Dieses interaktive Programm zur Konversion von Geometrie- und Attributdaten im ASCII-Format zwischen den Programmen UNIRAS, SAS, ARC/INFO und MAP wurde von Institutsmitarbeitern in Turbo Pascal 4.0. geschrieben. Es besteht aus einer Benutzeroberfläche (siehe Abbildung 1) und mehreren Konvertierungsprozeduren, mit denen die einzelnen Datenkonvertierungen durchgeführt werden können. Diese einzelnen Prozeduren bewirken:

    - den einfachen Austausch von Konventionen zur Markierung von Polygonanfang und -ende (SAS -> UNIMAP, SAS -> ARC/INFO);

    - die Rekonstruktion von geschlossenen Polygonzügen aus den Koordinaten einzelner Segmente (Arcs) und der sog. AAT-Datei bei der Konversion von ARC/INFO -> SAS;

    - die Aufrasterung von Polygonzügen aus dem SAS-Format in das MAP-Rasterformat.

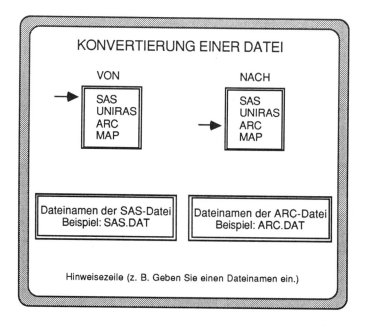

Abbildung 1 : Benutzeroberfläche von "Convert"

Das in Abbildung 2 skizzierte **Softwaresystemkonzept,** welches mit Ausnahme von ERDAS bereits realisiert ist und in der täglichen Praxis gute Dienste leistet, verdankt seine Funktionalität und Leistungsfähigkeit der Möglichkeit des vergleichsweise einfachen Transfers von Daten mit Hilfe des Programmes "CONVERT".

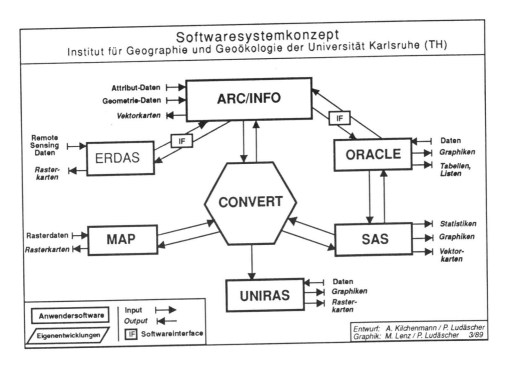

Abbildung 2: Softwaresystemkonzept

Die **EDV-Geräteausstattung** des Instituts befindet sich derzeit auf nachstehend aufgeführtem Stand. Im Ausbildungsbereich wird vorwiegend mit MS-DOS Rechnern gearbeitet. Zum einen, weil der für Ausbildungszwecke zur Verfügung stehende, aus Mitteln des Computer-Investitionsprogramms des Bundes beschaffte "CIP-Pool" ausschließlich aus PCs mit dem Betriebssystem MS-DOS besteht, zum anderen weil derzeit von den gängigsten Programmsystemen in den Bereichen GIS und DBMS sowie Computerkartographie auf der Ebene der Personal-Computer in der Regel nur dieses Betriebssystem unterstützt wird. Die vorhandenen Apple Macintosh und 2GS Rechner werden vor allem zur Erstellung von Publikationen (Desk Top Publishing) und Präsentationsmaterial für Lehrveranstaltungen und Vorträge, sowie für interne Verwaltungszwecke (Haushaltsführung mit Tabellenkalkulationsprogrammen) eingesetzt.

Computer:

Institut:
- 1 PS2/80/314 MB Festplatte
- 2 AT 02
- 1 PC XT
- 2 Macintosh II
- 2 Macintosh SE 2/20
- 1 Macintosh Plus
- (in Beschaffung: Workstation als Projektrechner: IBM RT135, HP9000/835 oder SUN SPARCstation 1)

CIP-Pool:
- 8 AT02 und 2 PS2/80/110 MB Festplatte

Peripherie (Ein- und Ausgabegeräte):

Institut:
- HP-Penplotter (DIN A 3, 6 Farben)
- IBM-Color Inkjet (DIN A 4, 170 dpi)
- HP-PaintJet mit Macintosh-Schnittstelle
- Microtek-Scanner (DIN A 4, 300 dpi)
- Summagraphics-Graphic Tablet (DIN A 3)
- Laser-Writer Plus (DIN A 4, 300 dpi)
- div. Impact Matrixdrucker

CIP-Pool:
- 3 Proprinter (DIN A 4)
- IBM 24-Nadel-Matrixdrucker (DIN A 3)
- HP-Laserjet (DIN A 4, 300 dpi)
- IBM Scanner (DIN A 4)
- Data-Overheadprojektor

Vernetzung (Kommunikationsmöglichkeiten):
- Local Area Network (LAN):
  5 Apple Macintosh, 1 IBM AT 02, Apple Laser Writer Plus, Apple Imagewriter
- Hostrechneranbindung:
  Drei serielle Standleitungen RS232/9600 Baud mit Terminal Emulation auf IBM XT und AT: Kommunikationsnetz "KARLA" des Rechenzentrums der Universität Karlsruhe (ab September 89: Ethernet-Anbindung)
- 1 Koaxial-Standleitung mit Memorex Farbgraphik Terminal zum IBM 3090 Rechner des RZ

Literaturhinweis:

Ludäscher, P. (1989). Ein EDV-Systemkonzept für die Geoinformatik-Ausbildung. Karlsruher Geoinformatik Report, 1/89, 2-5, Karlsruhe.

Ludäscher, P. (1988). Graphische Datenverarbeitung: Raster- oder Vektorverfahren. Karlsruher Geoinformatik Report, 2/88, 6, Karlsruhe.

F. Faulbaum, R. Haux und K.-H. Jöckel (Hrsg.) (1990). SoftStat '89
Fortschritte der Statistik-Software 2. Stuttgart: Gustav Fischer, 365 - 371

KARIN2 - Redesign eines erfolgreichen Kartographieprogramms auf der Basis des geographischen Informationssystems ARC/INFO

M. Tettweiler

Summary

This reading is to introduce KARIN2, a simple-to-use tool for computer aided production of ambitious thematic maps. A short look to its FORTRAN based predecessor KARIN gave evidence of the capabilities of this customer tailored software package designed for and in cooperation with the Munich city council's section for town planning. Its advantages and many different means of representation were pointed out. Next came the introduction of the new concept: the KARIN2 compiler. The functional enhanced problem oriented command language which is invoked either by pull down menus or by editor produced command sequence was demonstrated next. The command language was introduced by means of a small example to be later expanded to its full range. KARIN2 achieves hardware independence by being based on the well known geographic database system ARC/INFO.

Zusammenfassung

Der Vortrag stellte KARIN2 vor, ein Werkzeug zur computergestützten Erzeugung anspruchsvoller thematischer Karten. Kurz wurde der in FORTRAN realisierte Vorläufer KARIN gestreift, eine Auftragsentwicklung für das Münchner Stadtplanungsreferat; Vorteile und beibehaltene Darstellungsmittel daraus wurden aufgezeigt. Danach wurde die neue Konzeption vorgestellt: ein Übersetzer für KARIN2. Ihm folgte die Darstellung der funktionell erweiterten und verbesserten problemorientierten Kommandosprache, welche entweder per Menu oder Editor erzeugte Auftragsbeschreibung ermöglicht. An ein kleines praktisches Beispiel wird sich die Syntax der Kommandosprache in ihrem vollen Umfang anschließen. Maschinenunabhängigkeit erzielt KARIN2 durch Aufsetzen auf dem weitverbreiteten geographischen Informationssystem ARC/INFO.

Historischer Überblick

KARIN wurde in Auftragsarbeit ab 1973 für das Planungsreferat der Stadt München entwickelt. Vom Kleinrechner IBM 1130 ging es bald unter laufender Erweiterung des Funktionsumfangs zu Implementationen auf Großrechnern (PDP 11/70, Siemens 7.750, IBM 360/91, Amdahl 470/V6). Eine seit 1986 nicht mehr gewartete FORTRAN-Version ist nach kundeneigener Portierung auf ein Vaxkluster weiterhin im Einsatz. Das ist nicht zuletzt der Benutzerfreundlichkeit von KARIN und folgenden Eigenschaften zu verdanken:

- Automatische Verknüpfung von Daten und Geographie zur multivariaten Darstellung dieser Daten,
- Flexible Kartengestaltung (Punktekarten, Planquadrat-Karten, schraffierte Graphen, Stromkarten),
- Kuchen-, Balken, Linien- und Viereckdiagramme,
- Benutzerdefinierbare Symbole fester oder variabler Größe,
- Überdeckungsfreiheit der dargestellten Symbole am Stiftplotter,
- Wahl zwischen Standard- oder Spezialegende an beliebigem Ort,
- Textliche Ausgestaltung und Teilkarteneinblendung.

Die Zeichnungen wurden in einer dem GKS-Metafile ähnlichen Datei gespeichert, was Vorausansicht und Nachbearbeitung fertiger Zeichnungen ermöglichte. Zur Ausgabe konnten verschiedene Geräte vom Bildschirm bis zum elektrostatischen Plotter gewählt werden. Grundprogramme zum Erstellen und Fortschreiben der geographischen Kartenbasis und datenbankartige Aufbewahrung von Texten und Symbolen waren ebenfalls bis zu einem gewissen Grad entwickelt.

Die neue Konzeption: ein Übersetzer für KARIN2

Ein nach modernen softwaretechnischen Grundsätzen arbeitender Compilercompiler erzeugt den KARIN2-Übersetzer (in PASCAL) aus einer in einer Datenbank gespeicherten Sprachdefinition, die in einer speziellen CDL (Compiler Description Language) abgefaßt ist und einer LL(1)-Grammatik gehorcht. Softwareentwickler brauchen sich dann bei inhaltlichen und sprachlichen Änderungen nur auf diejenigen Fälle zu konzentrieren, die wirklich Beachtung verdienen und anschließend nachübersetzen. Diese Technik macht auch nationale Sprachanpassungen unproblematisch.

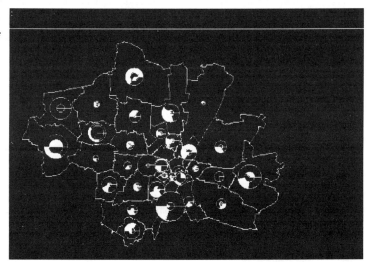

Mit einem Texteditor oder menugeführt mit einem Kommandogenerator erzeugt der Benutzer eine Kommandofolge, die eine inhaltliche Beschreibung

Abb. 1: Vom Kommandofolgenbeispiel erzeugte thematische Karte. (Bildschirmabzug, die Variablen FL86 und FL87 bestimmen die Schalenradien, die Variablen PRI86, MIX86 und GEW86 bestimmen die Prozentanteile (Sektoren) der inneren, die Variablen PRI87, MIX87 und GEW87 die der äußeren Schale)

der gewünschten thematischen Karte darstellt. Diese KARIN2- Kommandofolge wird lexikalisch, syntaktisch und semantisch überprüft, wobei eine Fortsetzung der Bearbeitung nur bei Fehlerfreiheit erfolgt. Die Änderungen der neuen gegenüber der alten KARIN-Sprache sind meist marginal, notwendige Verbesserungen wurden allerdings nicht gescheut.

Funktionell erweiterte und verbesserte Kommandosprache

Die KARIN2-Kommandosprache beinhaltet drei Gruppen von Kommandos: deklarative, vorbereitende und ausführbare Kommandos.

<u>Deklarative Kommandos</u> verändern den Inhalt des Kontextgedächtnisses des Übersetzers. Außerdem dienen sie dem Management und der Aktualisierung der Datenbasen für Layouts, graphische Symbole, Schraffuren und Textbestandteile. Nicht zuletzt definieren sie Verbindungen zwischen symbolischen und realen Namen, z.B. von Dateien oder Gestaltungsmitteln.

Vorbereitende Kommandos machen Layouts und graphische Darstellungsmittel verfügbar. Sie ordnen und rekodieren Daten, die von externen Datenbanken oder Dateien stammen. Das Rekodieren seinerseits geschieht anhand vorbereitend deklarierter und im Kontextgedächtnis gespeicherter Definitionen.

Ausführbare Kommandos ordnen endlich ganz allgemein das Erzeugen eines Graphen an (z.B. das Verbinden von Daten mit graphischen Darstellungsmitteln, wie es beim Herstellen von Gruppen von Kreis- oder Balkendiagrammendiagrammen, größenvariabler Symbole oder Schraffuren notwendig ist), das Erzeugen der Legende oder das Anfügen textlicher Informationen und sonstiger graphischer Details.

```
Zeile   Kommandoinhalt

1       LAYOUT NAME = BEZIRKSGRENZEN DATEI = '86BEZIRK.TOP' ETIKETT = 'Bezirke';
2
3       SCHRAFFURZUORDNUNG SCHRAFFURNAME = L42 SCHRAFFURDATEI = 'L4.SRF'
4           NUMMER = 2 ETIKETT = '0.2 mm Linienschraffur';
5       SCHRAFFURZUORDNUNG SCHRAFFURNAME = L43 SCHRAFFURDATEI = 'L4.SRF'
6           NUMMER = 3 ETIKETT = '0.15 mm Linienschraffur';
7       SCHRAFFURZUORDNUNG SCHRAFFURNAME = L44 SCHRAFFURDATEI = 'L4.SRF'
8           NUMMER = 4 ETIKETT = '0.1 mm Linienschraffur';
9
10      MASSTAB MASSZAHL = 10000.;
11
12      IMPORT DBNAME = 'GEB8687.DBF' KEY = BEZIRK
13          SPALTEN = FL86,PRI86,MIX86,GEW86,FL87,PRI87,MIX87,GEW87;
14      REKODIEREN SPALTEN = PRI86,MIX86,GEW86,PRI87,MIX87,GEW87
15          REGEL = 0 BIS 10 - L42, 10 BIS 100 - L43, 100 BIS 1000 - L44;
16
17      ERGAENZUNGSLAYOUT LAYOUT = BEZIRKSGRENZEN STRICHART = LINIE FARBE = 1;
18
19      KREISDIAGRAMM LAYOUT = BEZIRKSGRENZEN VARIABEL
20          SCHALEN = 2 SEKTOREN = 3
21              RADIUS = FL86,FL87  SCHRAFFUREN = L42,L43,L44
22              ANTEILE = PRI86,MIX86,GEW86,PRI87,MIX87,GEW87;
23
24      ENDE.
```

Beschreibung der Kommandos:

Zeile	Aktion
1	Die Stadtbezirksgrenzen werden verfügbar gemacht.
3-8	Aus einer der Schraffurdateien werden drei Schraffuren ausgewählt.
10	Maßstab der Karte ist 1:10000.
12	Die Daten kommen aus einer Datenbank, die notwendigen Tabellen und deren Sortierung werden vereinbart.
14	Die in den Tabellen enthaltenen Werte werden entsprechend einer Vorschrift rekodiert.
17	Zur Orientierung werden die Stadtbezirksgrenzen gezeichnet.
19	An im Rahmen des Layouts definierten Stellen werden doppelt geschachtelte Kreisdiagramme gewünscht. Radien und Sektorgrößen sind durch die rekodierten Tabellenwerte gegeben.
24	Ende dieser thematischen Karte.

Abb. 2: Kommandofolgenbeispiel: Zweifachkuchendiagramme pro Stadtbezirk.

Als Ergebnis liegt in der ersten Ausbaustufe eine Kommandofolge in ARC-Makrosprache vor. Diese wird der Komponente ARCPLOT des geographischen Datenbanksystems ARC/INFO übergeben. ARCPLOT sorgt dann dafür, daß der eigentliche Graph so erzeugt wird, daß er sich - auch am Stiftplotter - als fehler- und überdeckungsfreie Karte präsentiert. Zur Verbesserung der Bearbeitungsgeschwindigkeit ist geplant, in einer späteren Ausbaustufe ARCPLOT direkt über dessen interne Schnittstellen anzusteuern.

Die Syntax der KARIN2-Sprache, wie in der Datenbank gespeichert

Die Beschreibung der Syntax ist in drei Spalten gegliedert: die erste enthält Nonterminalnamen, die mittlere die zugehörige grammatikalische Einsetzungsvorschrift, die rechte eine kurze inhaltliche Erklärung. (Einige Terminalnamen grundsätzlicher Natur sind nicht näher erläutert: filename, string, varname, id, str, real, float, int und integer.)

Bestandteile der Einsetzungsvorschrift sind frei nach N.Wirth:

EPS bedeutet die leere Kette, d.h. die Kette aus null Zeichen.

Terminalsymbole, z.B. "=", die sich selbst bedeuten, finden sich zwischen Doppelapostrophen und sind ohne diese zu übernehmen.

Andere Terminalsymbole, z.B. "RADIUS" und **Nonterminalnamen** als Bedeutung suggerierende Namen: sind diese nicht selbsterklärend, findet sich die entsprechende Einsetzungsregel normalerweise einige Zeilen weiter unten bei dem entsprechenden Nonterminalnamen in der ersten Spalte.

Der senkrechte Strich "|" trennt **Alternativen** voneinander.

Das Ende einer Einsetzungsvorschrift wird durch das Auftreten eines neuen Nonterminalnamens in der ersten Spalte angezeigt.

Darstellung **optionaler** Bestandteile: [A] bedeutet A | EPS.

Wiederholungen: {A} bedeutet EPS | A | AA | AAA | ...

Runde Klammern dienen der Zusammenfassung.

Formale Definition der Grammatik der KARIN2-Sprache

Nonterminal	Ersetzungsregel (grammatikalische Erklärung)	Inhaltliche Erklärung
karin	{ (layout_verwaltg ";" | symbol_verwalt ";" | schraffurpflege ";")	legende ";" { daten_import ";"	recode_cmd ";"	darstellung ";" }) } ende_cmd	Karin-Grammatik
layout_verwaltg	"LAYOUT" (layout_dekl | layout_undekl)	Beziehungen zu Layouts ermöglichen und trennen
layout_dekl	"NAME" "=" id "DATEI" "=" filename ["ETIKETT" "=" str]	Trägt einen Bezeichner für ein Layout in die Layoutverwaltung ein und ordnet ihm einen Dateinamen und ggf. einen Erläuterungstext zu
layout_undekl	"LOESCHEN" "=" id { "," id }	Bezeichner für Layouts in der Layoutverwaltung tilgen
symbol_verwalt	"SYMBOLVERWALTUNG" (symbol_dekl | symbol_undekl)	Beziehungen zu Symbolen herstellen oder trennen
symbol_dekl	"NAME" "=" id ["SYMBOLDATEI" "=" filename] "NUMMER" "=" int ["ETIKETT" "=" str]	Bezeichner für ein Symbol in die Symbolverwaltung eintragen, Verbindung zu diesem Symbol in einem Font herstellen
symbol_undekl	"LOESCHEN" "=" id { "," id }	Bezeichner für Symbole in der Symbolverwaltung tilgen
schraffurpflege	schraff_wartg	schraff_dekl	schraff_undekl	Schraffuren selbst pflegen oder Beziehungen zu Schraffuren in der Schraffurverwaltung herstellen oder tilgen
schraff_wartg	SCHRAFFURWARTUNG" "DATEI" "=" filename (schraff_def | schraff_repl | schraff_del)	Schraffuren definieren, Schraffurdefinitionen ersetzen oder tilgen
schraff_def	"NUMMER" "=" int schraff_params	Schraffur definieren
schraff_repl	"ERSETZEN" "=" int schraff_params	Schraffurdefinition ersetzen
schraff_del	"LOESCHEN" "=" int	Schraffurdefinition tilgen
schraff_params	"STRICH" "=" schraff_details ["STRICH2" "=" schraff_details] ["ETIKETT" "=" str]	Parameter für eine Schraffur definieren

schraff_details	`"(" "STRICHART" "=" strichart "WINKEL" "=" real "ABSTAND" "=" real ")"`	Details für die Ausführung eines Schraffurstrichs definieren
strichart	`"LINIE"	"ZLINIE"	"DLINIE"	"PUNKTIERT"	"GESTRICHELT"	"(" "SYMBOL" "=" id "RADIUS" "=" real ")"`	Strichart festlegen: einfache, zwei- und dreifache Linie, punktiert, strichliert oder durch Symbole dargestellt
schraff_dekl	`"SCHRAFFURZUORDNUNG" "SCHRAFFURNAME" "=" id "SCHRAFFURDATEI" "=" filename "NUMMER" "=" int [ "ETIKETT" "=" str ]`	Bezeichner für eine Schraffur in die Schraffurverwaltung eintragen, Verbindung zu dieser Schraffur herstellen
schraff_undekl	`"LOESCHEN" "=" id`	Bezeichner für eine Schraffur in die Schraffurverwaltung tilgen
legende	`std_legende	sonder_legende`	Legendenbestandteile einer Zeichnung festlegen
std_legende	`kopf_def	uebers_def	symb_ber_def	schraff_ber_def	komment_def	bearb_def	datum_def	fuss_def	mass_def`	Festlegen von Textbestandteilen in der Standardlegende
kopf_def	`"LEGENDENKOPF" [ schrifthoehe ] mehrfachtext`	Standardkopf anfordern oder Schrifthöhe und Textzeilen für die Standardlegende festlegen
uebers_def	`"UEBERSCHRIFT" [ schrifthoehe ] mehrfachtext`	Überschriftsbereich in der Standardlegende löschen oder Schrifthöhe und Textzeilen für den Überschriftsbereich in der Standardlegende festlegen
symb_ber_def	`"SYMBOLSTDBEREICH" "YVON" "=" real "YBIS" "=" real`	Bereich für Symboletiketten in der Standardlegende festlegen
schraff_ber_def	`"SCHRAFFURSTDBEREICH" "YVON" "=" real "YBIS" "=" real`	Bereich für Schraffuretiketten in der Standardlegende festlegen
komment_def	`"LEGENDENKOMMENTAR" [ schrifthoehe ] mehrfachtext`	Kommentarbereich in der Standardlegende löschen oder Schrifthöhe und Textzeilen für den Kommentarbereich in der Kommentarbereich in der Standardlegende festlegen
bearb_def	`"BEARBEITER" [ schrifthoehe ] einzeltext`	Bearbeitername in der Standardlegende löschen oder Schrifthöhe und Bearbeiternamen in der Standardlegende festlegen
datum_def	`"DATUM" [ schrifthoehe ] einzeltext`	Datumsangabe in der Standardlegende löschen oder Schrifthöhe und Datumsangabe in der Standardlegende festlegen
fuss_def	`"LEGENDENFUSS" [ schrifthoehe ] mehrfachtext`	Standardfußzeilen anfordern oder Schrifthöhe und Textzeilen für die Standardlegende festlegen
mass_def	`"MASSTAB" "MASSZAHL" "=" real [ einzeltext ]`	
sonder_legende	`text_etikett	symbol_etikett	schraff_etikett	masskette`	Festlegen von nicht durch die Standardlegende bestimmbaren Legendenbestandteilen
text_etikett	`"TEXTETIKETT" "X" "=" real "Y" "=" real [ schrifthoehe ] [ schreibwinkel ] einzeltext`	Festlegen eines an beliebig bestimmbarem Ort anzubringenden Schriftzugs
symbol_etikett	`"SYMBOLETIKETT" "X" "=" real "Y" "=" real "SYMBOL" "=" id "RADIUS" "=" real [ [ schrifthoehe ] [ schreibwinkel ] einzeltext]`	Festlegen eines, ggf. zusammen mit einem Schriftzug versehenen, an einem beliebig bestimmbaren Ort anzubringenden Symbols
schraff_etikett	`"SCHRAFFURETIKETT" "SCHRAFFUR" "=" id "X" "=" real "Y" "=" real [ "BREITE" "=" real ] [ "HOEHE" "=" real ] [ [ schrifthoehe ] einzeltext ]`	Festlegen einer, ggf. mit einem Text zu versehenden, an beliebig bestimmbarem Ort anzubringenden Musterschraffur in einem Rechteck
masskette	`"MASSKETTE" "X" "=" real "Y" "=" real [ schrifthoehe ] [ schreibwinkel ] einzeltext`	Festlegen eines an beliebig bestimmbarem Ort anzubringenden Schriftzugs
schrifthoehe	`"SCHRIFTHOEHE" "=" real`	Schrifthöhe im Zusammenhang mit Text- und Etikettendefinitionen festlegen
schreibwinkel	`"SCHREIBWINKEL" "=" real`	Schreibwinkel im Zusammenhang mit Text- und Etikettdefinitionen festlegen
einzeltext	`"TEXT" "=" str`	Einzelnen Text bekanntgeben
mehrfachtext	`"TEXT" "=" str { "," str }`	Text aus mehreren Zeilen festlegen
daten_import	`"IMPORT" [ "TABELLE" "=" id ] ( db_import | seq_import )`	Daten aus Datenbank oder aus zeilenstrukturiertem sequentiellem File, ggf. spaltenselektiv in den Arbeitsspeicher importieren, ggf. Bezeichner dafür definieren
db_import	`"DBNAME" "=" filename "KEY" "=" varname "SPALTEN" "=" (varname { "," varname }	"(" varname ["=" id] { "," varname ["=" id] } ")")`	Daten aus Datenbank, ggf. auch spaltenselektiv importieren, Keyvariable sowie Namen verwendeter Variabler bzw. diesen zugeordnete, frei wählbare Bezeichner deklarieren
seq_import	`"DATEI" "=" filename "KEYPOS" "=" int "KEYLEN" "=" int ["KEYTYP" "=" ("CHAR"	"NONSTD")] "SPALTEN" "=" (spaltendef	"(" spaltendef { "," spaltendef } ")")`	Daten spaltenselektiv aus zeilenstrukturiertem sequentiellem File importieren und zugehörige Bezeichner deklarieren

spaltendef	id int "-" int ["(" ("CHAR" | "INTEGER" | "REAL" ["DEC" int]) ")"]	Bezeichner und zugehörige Spaltenselektion sowie Datenkonvertierung deklarieren
recode_cmd	"REKODIEREN" "SPALTEN" "=" spalten_id { "," spalten_id } "REGEL" "=" recode_def "-" id { "," recode_def "-" id }	Für ausgewählte Spalten Zuordnung von Daten zu Darstellungsmitteln vornehmen, Einzeldaten, für keine Zuordnung erfolgt, bleiben bei der Darstellung unberücksichtigt
spalten_id	id ["." id]	Spaltenbezeichner, bzw. falls mehrere Tabellen identische Bezeichner enthalten, Tabellennamen mit Spaltenbezeichner deklarieren
recode_def	(str { "," str }) | ((int ["BIS" int]) { "," (int ["BIS" int]) }) | ((real ["BIS" real]) { "," (real ["BIS" real]) })	Einzelwerte bzw. Wertebereiche für die Zuordnung zu Darstellungsmitteln deklarieren
darstellung	beschriftung | stabdiagramm | liniendiagramm | balkendiagr | ergaenzlayout | kreuzdiagr | kreisdiagr | piktogramm | rechteckdiagr | symbol | kartogramm | legendenart	Darstellung unter Berücksichtigung der vorangegangenen Festlegungen definieren
beschriftung	freier_textd | beschr_dateid | layout_key_anz	Freie Texte an beliebigen oder an durch Identifikatoren bezeichneten Stellen in der Zeichnung anbringen
freier_text	"FREIER_TEXT" "X" "=" spalten_id "Y" "=" spalten_id ["XDIFF" "=" real] ["YDIFF" "=" real] ["WINKEL" "=" (real | spalten_id)] ["SCHRIFTHOEHE" "=" (real | spalten_id)] ["FARBE" "=" (int | spalten_id)]	Freie Texte, deren Attribute wählbar sind, an beliebigen Stellen in der Zeichnung anbringen
beschr_datei	"BESCHRIFTUNGSDATEI" "LAYOUT" "=" id "KEY" "=" spalten_id ["XDIFF" "=" real] ["YDIFF" "=" real] ["WINKEL" "=" (real | spalten_id)] ["SCHRIFTHOEHE" "=" (real | spalten_id)] ["FARBE" "=" (int | spalten_id)]	Freie Texte, deren Attribute wählbar sind, an beliebigen Stellen in der Zeichnung anbringen
layout_key_anz	"KEY_ANZEIGE" "LAYOUT" "=" id ["XDIFF" "=" real] ["YDIFF" "=" real] ["WINKEL" "=" real] ["SCHRIFTHOEHE" "=" real] ["FARBE" "=" int]	Freie Texte, deren Attribute wählbar sind, an beliebigen Stellen in der Zeichnung anbringen
stabdiagramm	"STABDIAGRAMM" position "STABBREITE" "=" real ["STABABSTAND" "=" real] (einf_stabdiag | grupp_stabdiag | komp_stabdiag)	Daten in Form eines Stabdiagramms darstellen, Breite und Abstand der Stäbe zueinander festlegen
einf_stabdiag	"VARIABLE" "=" var_mit_darst { "," var_mit_darst }	Datenvariable und Darstellungsmittel für ein einfaches Stabdiagramm festlegen
grupp_stabdiag	"GRUPPEN" "=" "(" var_mit_darst { "," var_mit_darst } ")" { "," "(" var_mit_darst { "," var_mit_darst } ")" }	Datenvariable und Darstellungsmittel für ein Gruppenstabdiagramm festlegen
komp_stabdiag	"KOMPONENTEN" "=" "(" var_mit_darst { "," var_mit_darst } ")" { "," "(" var_mit_darst { "," var_mit_darst } ")" }	Datenvariable und Darstellungsmittel für ein Komponentenstabdiagramm festlegen
liniendiagr	"LINIENDIAGRAMM" position (stuetz_lindiag | linien_lindiag)	Daten als Liniendiagramm darstellen
stuetz_lindiag	"STUETZWERTE" "=" "(" spalten_id { "," spalten_id } ")" { "," "(" spalten_id { "," spalten_id } ")" } ["STRICHART" "=" strichart { "," strichart }]	Stützwertvariable für je einen Stützpunkt sowie Stricharten eines Liniendiagramms festlegen
linien_lindiag	"LINIE" "=" "(" spalten_id { "," spalten_id } ["STRICHART" "=" strichart] ")" { "," "(" spalten_id { "," spalten_id } ["STRICHART" "=" strichart] ")" }	Stützwertvariable und Stricharten für alle Linien eines Liniendiagramms festlegen
balkendiagr	"BALKENDIAGRAMM" position (einf_balkdiag | paar_balkdiag | piktogramm)	Daten in Form eines Balkendiagramms darstellen
einf_balkdiag	"VARIABLE" "=" var_mit_darst { "," var_mit_darst }	Datenvariable und Darstellungsmittel für ein einfaches Balkendiagramm festlegen
paar_balkdiag	"PAARE" "=" "(" var_mit_darst "," var_mit_darst ")" { "," "(" var_mit_darst "," var_mit_darst ")" }	Datenvariablenpaare und Darstellungsmittel für ein Paarbalkendiagramm festlegen
kreuzdiagr	"KREUZDIAGRAMM" position "VARIABLE" "=" var_mit_darst "," var_mit_darst "," var_mit_darst ["ART" "=" ("QUADRAT" | "KREIS" | "DREIECK")]	Daten in Form eines Kreuzdiagramms darstellen. Datenvariable, Darstellungsmittel und Gestalt der Quadratfigur festlegen
kreisdiagr	"KREISDIAGRAMM" position ("EINFACH" | "VARIABEL") ["SCHALEN" "=" int] ["SEKTOREN" "=" int] ["POLAR") krdiag_gestalt	Daten in Form eines Kreisdiagramms darstellen
piktogramm	"PIKTOGRAMM" position "VARIABLE" "=" spalten_id "SYMBOL" "=" id ["RADIUS" "=" real] ["ABSTAND" "=" real] (stab_piktogramm | balk_piktogramm)	Datenvariable und Darstellungsmittel für ein Komponentenstabdiagramm festlegen
stab_piktogramm	"ZEILENMAXIMUM" "=" int	Maximale Anzahl Symbole je Stab festlegen. Wird das Maximum überschritten, wird in einem weiteren Stab rechts davon fortgesetzt
balk_piktogramm	"SPALTENMAXIMUM" "=" int	Maximale Anzahl Symbole je Balken festlegen, wird das Maximum überschritten, wird in einem weiteren Balken darüber fortgesetzt
rechteckdiagr	"RECHTECKDIAGRAMM" position "RADIUS" "=" spalten_id ["UEBERHOEHUNG" "=" real] "ANTEILE" "=" var_mit_darst { "," var_mit_darst } ["KONTUR" "=" (int | spalten_id)]	Daten in Form eines Rechteckdiagramms darstellen

symbol	"SYMBOL" position (variab_symbol | festes_symbol)	Daten durch Symbol darstellen
festes_symbol	("KREIS" | "NAME" " = " id) "RADIUS" " = " (real ["(" id ")"] | var_mit_darst) ["KONTUR" " = " (int | spalten_id)]	Daten durch einen Kreis oder ein bestimmtes Symbol, ggf. größenvariabel darstellen
variab_symbol	"VARIABLE" " = " var_mit_darst "RADIUS" " = " (real | spalten_id) ["KONTUR" " = " (int | spalten_id)]	Daten durch ihm jeweils entsprechendes Symbol, ggf. größenvariabel darstellen
kartogramm	"KARTOGRAMM" "LAYOUT" " = " id (schraffieren | punktekarte)	Layout als Kartogramm darstellen
schraffieren	"SCHRAFFURVARIABLE" " = " spalten_id ["FARBE" " = " int { "," int }] ["FARBE2" " = " int { "," int }]	Variable, mit dem je Datum das entsprechende Darstellungsmittel selektiert wird und Farben festlegen
punktekarte	"PUNKTANZAHL" " = " spalten_id ["LAGE" " = " ("ZENTRAL" | "UMGRIFFSBESCHRAENKT")] ["FARBE" " = " int]	Variable, in der die darzustellende Punkteanzahl enthalten ist, und Farbe festlegen
ergaenzlayout	"ERGAENZUNGSLAYOUT" "LAYOUT" " = " id "STRICHART" " = " strichart "FARBE" " = " int	Ergänzungslayout mit der angegebenen Strichart und Farbe darstellen
legendenart	"LEGENDE" "LAGE" " = " ("RECHTS" | "LINKS") ["EXTRA" " = " extras { "," extras }]	
extras	"PASSKREUZE" | "RAHMEN"	
position	"LAYOUT" " = " id | "X" " = " spalten_id "Y" " = " spalten_id	Position für die Darstellung der Datenvariablen definieren (Stabdiagramme: linke untere Ecke, sonst: Mittelpunkt des Darstellungsmittels)
var_mit_darst	spalten_id ["(" id ")"]	Darzustellende Datenvariable und ggf. zu verwendende Schraffur definieren
krdiag_gestalt	"RADIUS" " = " (real | var_mit_darst { "," var_mit_darst }) "SCHRAFFUREN" " = " var_mit_darst { "," var_mit_darst } ["WINKELBEREICH" " = " real "BIS" real] "ANTEILE" " = " var_mit_darst { "," var_mit_darst } ["KONTUR" " = " (int | spalten_id)]	Gestalt eines einfachen (anteilsvariablen) Kreisdiagramms
ende_cmd	"ENDE" "."	Übersetzungslauf beenden

Literaturverzeichnis

ARC/INFO: Users Manual, Version 3.2. Environmental Systems Research Institute.
   Redlands (Ca): 1986.

ARCPLOT: Users Manual, Version 3.2. Environmental Systems Research Institute.
   Redlands (Ca): 1986.

RECHENBERG,P./MÖSSENBÖCK,H.:Ein Compilergenerator für Mikrocomputer.
   München,Wien: 1985.

TETTWEILER,M.:15 Jahre KARIN.
   In: FAULBAUM,F./UEHLINGER,H.-M.:Fortschritte der Statistiksoftware 1.
   Stuttgart,New York:1988.

Statistik und Datenerhebung

F. Faulbaum, R. Haux und K.-H. Jöckel (Hrsg.) (1990). SoftStat '89
Fortschritte der Statistik-Software 2. Stuttgart: Gustav Fischer, 375 - 385

Aspekte der Datenqualität bei computerunterstützten Interviews

E. Schach

Zusammenfassung

Mittlerweile profitieren alle Arbeitsschritte der empirischen Sozialforschung von der Unterstützung durch Rechner. Neben der Programmunterstützung sind dafür vor allem eine weitgehende Parallelisierung von Arbeitsschritten von Bedeutung. Die sich dadurch ergebenden Veränderungen hinsichtlich von Stichprobeneigenschaften und Datenqualität werden anhand des Erhebungsmaterials zweier rechnerunterstützter Studien erläutert.

Summary

Each aspect of current social research may profit from the use of computer technology. Program support and parallel processing are the prime contributors to this development. These technological advances are apt to modify sample characteristics and data quality of empirical studies. The paper describes these aspects in quantitative terms using data from two computer-assisted telephone studies.

1. Rechnereinsatz in der empirischen Sozialforschung

Rechnereinsatz in der empirischen Sozialforschung hat eine lange Tradition. Karweit and Meyers (1983) stellten seinen Einsatz tabellarisch zusammen (Tabelle 1). Dabei dachten sie vorwiegend an ein sequentielles Vorgehen, bei dem im Batchbetrieb arbeitende, zentral aufgestellte Großrechner die verschiedenen Arbeitsschritte jeweils im Nachgang begleiteten. Als Folge der heute möglichen interaktiven Arbeitsweise auf dezentral verfügbaren Rechnern haben sich die Einsatzarten für die empirische Sozialforschung vermehrt. Insbesondere können heute dank interaktiver Rechnerunterstützung einige der in der Tabelle genannten Arbeitsschritte parallel durchgeführt werden (z.B. Datenerhebung und Datenreinigung).

Tabelle 1. Gebiete des Rechnereinsatzes in der empirischen Sozialforschung

- Entwurf von Instrumenten
- Stichprobenplanung
- Feldüberwachung
- Kodierung, Editieren
- Datenerhebung
- Datenbereinigung
- Skalen-, Indexbildung, Gruppierung
- Datensatzorganisation, Dateiverwaltung
- Bildung von Dateiauszügen
- Statistische Analyse
- Dokumentation
- Abfassung von Berichten, Publikationen
- Archivierung
- Datenweitergabe

2. Stichproben- und Datenqualität bei CATI-Interviews

Im folgenden wollen wir uns besonders mit Stichprobenaspekten und solchen der Datenqualität bei computerunterstützten Telefoninterviews beschäftigen. Lyberg (1985) unterscheidet die folgenden Arten von computerunterstützter Datenerhebung (computer assisted data collection - CADAC): computer assisted personal interviews -CAPI-, computer assisted telephone interviews -CATI-, computer assisted self-administered questionnaires - CSAQ-. Alle drei Arten von Erhebungen werden mit zunehmender Verbreitung ihre spezifischen Anwendungsfelder finden. Für telefonische Erhebungen liegen bereits seit 1971 Erfahrungen vor. Zwei Bücher (Groves and Kahn, 1979; Groves, Biemer, Lyberg, et al. 1988) stellen diese einer breiten Öffentlichkeit vor. Außerdem gibt es auf dem Markt mehrere kommerziell verfügbare CATI-Systeme. CATI-Erhebungen sind Online-Erhebungen, die interaktiv mit Rechnerunterstützung vorgenommen werden (Nicholls and Groves, 1986).

Die Fähigkeiten von verfügbaren CATI-Systemen liegen nach Groves und Nicholls (1986) auf folgenden Gebieten:

- Stichprobenziehung
- Verwaltung der Anrufe und Probandenzuordnung zu Interviewern
- Durchführung von Interviews
- Monitoring von Interviews durch den Supervisor, womöglich auch durch Audio-Unterstützung
- Automatische Aufzeichnung der Ereignisse während des Erhebungsablaufs
- Herstellung von Datensätzen.

Beim Vergleich von herkömmlichen Verfahren mit CATI spielen folgende Gesichtspunkte eine Rolle (Nicholls and Groves, 1986):

- Kosten der Installation und Wartung von CATI-Systemen
- Einfluß von CATI auf Planungs- und Durchführungszeiten von Bevölkerungserhebungen
- Einfluß von CATI auf Kosten von Bevölkerungserhebungen
- Einfluß von CATI auf die Datenqualität
- Besondere Vor- und Nachteile von CATI im Vergleich zu alternativen Verfahren
- Kombinationsmöglichkeiten von CATI mit anderen Methoden bei Bevölkerungserhebungen.

Da herkömmliche Erhebungen vor allem damit Schwierigkeiten haben, Eigenschaften von Stichproben und Daten empirisch zu verdeutlichen, um damit die Datenqualität zu dokumentieren, interessiert in unserem Zusammenhang, in welcher Weise ein CATI-System dazu in der Lage ist.

Sofern die wichtigste Voraussetzung für den breiten Einsatz von Telefoninterviews, die Telefonverfügbarkeit, in einer Bevölkerung gegeben ist, kann, unserer Erfahrung nach, die Kontrolle der Stichprobe durch zentral gesteuerte Telefoninterview-Methodik verbessert werden. Das ist, nach unseren Beobachtungen, aus folgenden Gründen der Fall:

- Vermeidung des Oversampling, um angestrebte Kollektivgrößen zu erreichen,
- Ausgabe von Telefonnummern durch das System in Wellen, wobei vor Ausgabe einer weiteren Welle erst die vorherige vollständig abgearbeitet sein muß,
- Sicherstellung, daß tatsächlich gezogene Haushalte befragt werden,
- Sicherstellung, daß im Haushalt, tatsächlich die Zielpersonen befragt werden.

Alle genannten Gesichtspunkte wirken in Richtung auf eine Verminderung von Verzerrungen in den Daten. Weitere Verbesserungsmöglichkeiten sind gegeben durch:

- Verringerung der bei persönlichen Interviews üblichen räumlichen Klumpung von Zielpersonen zwecks Reduktion der Variabilität,
- die Tatsache, daß für die Auswahl Listen nicht erforderlich sind, im Extremfall auch keine Telefonbücher, obwohl man ohne letztere eine gewisse Ineffizienz in Kauf nähme,
- CATI läßt die Realisierung weiterer Stichprobenpläne zu, die durch persönliche Interviews schwieriger zu verwirklichen wären (z.B. bundesweite, disproportionale Auswahlen).

Alle diese Vorteile können sowohl durch zentrale als auch durch dezentrale Organisation realisiert werden. In jedem Fall sollte die Einhaltung der gewünschten Stichprobeneigenschaften im Rahmen einer Studie empirisch überprüft werden. Ein solches Monitoring lassen einige der verfügbaren CATI-Systeme zu.

Unter den Aspekten von CATI, die dazu geeignet sind die Datenqualität zu verbessern, seien folgende genannt:

- Automatisierung des Interviewablaufs
- Automatische Filter- und Sprungkontrollen
- Verfügbarmachung der Interviewanweisungen auf Anfrage oder automatisch
- Erhebung von schwer zu erhebenden Daten durch die Anwendung von Fragenschichten, z.B. bei der Erhebung des Einkommens zunächst die Abfrage von Einkommensbeträgen; wenn dort keine Antwort erfolgt, Erfragen des Einkommens in Klassen; wenn auch dazu die Antwort verweigert wird, Ermittlung der Einkommensquelle
- Mitführung umfangreicher Listen in Hintergrunddateien, um exakte Erhebungen (z.B. von Arzneimitteln) zu ermöglichen
- Ziehung von Unterstichproben mit festen Auswahlraten unter Probanden mit Eigenschaften, die erst im Interview erhoben werden (z.B. jede dritte Person mit Schmerzen)
- Erhebung von probandenspezifischen Sachverhalten mit dafür spezifischen Instrumenten (z.B. arbeitsplatzspezifische oder berufsspezifische Belastungsprofile je nach angegebenem Beruf)

3. Ausgewählte empirische Ergebnisse bei der Stichprobenziehung und hinsichtlich der Datenqualität von CATI-Interviews

Die hier berichteten Ergebnisse stammen aus den methodischen Erfahrungen bei zwei Telefonerhebungen, die kürzlich in der Bundesrepublik Deutschland durchgeführt wurden.

Raucherstudie im Saarland 1986/87

Die Studie suchte das Zigarettenrauchverhalten für eine Stichprobe der erwachsenen (35 - 64 Jahre) Bevölkerung des Saarlandes zu erfragen. Sie wurde im Auftrag des Saarländischen Sozialministeriums von Dornier und FORSA, Dortmund, als Erhebungsinstitution, durchgeführt. Die Studie fand (zwischen Dezember 1986 und März 1987) als CATI-Erhebung bei 16 242 Zielpersonen statt, was einer Responserate von 82,3 % entsprach. Die Zielpersonen wurden aus 22 Regionen des Saarlandes wie folgt ausgewählt: aus den Telefonnummern der einzelnen Regionen wurde eine Auswahl von existierenden Nummern gezogen. Bei den gezogenen Nummern wurden die letzten Ziffern zufällig verändert und die so entstandenen Nummern angewählt. Wenn es sich um einen Privathaushalt handelte, wurde eine Zielperson zufällig aus dem Haushalt gezogen (Schach, S. 1987)

Medikamenteneinnahme durch Kinder in Nordrhein-Westfalen 1988

Die Erhebung hatte zum Ziel, die Medikamenteneinnahme (innerhalb der letzten 4 Wochen) durch Kinder, deren Krankheiten und mögliche Verhaltensauffälligkeiten und damit zusammenhängenden Medikamentenkonsum zu erfassen. Es wurden 4800 Kinder im Alter zwischen 6 und 14 Jahren systematisch aus der Altersgruppe der Wohnbevölkerung gezogen. Die Kinder verteilten sich letztendlich auf 133 Gemeinden des Landes. Die Gemeinden wurden um die Zusendung festgelegter Anzahlen von Adressen von Haushalten mit mindestens einem Kind in der Altersgruppe gebeten. Zu den gelieferten Adressen wurden Telefonnummern herausgesucht und die entsprechenden Haushalte angerufen. Die Erhebung erstreckte sich über mehrere Monate im Frühjahr und Sommer 1988. Sie wurde von FORSA, Dortmund, als CATI-Erhebung durchgeführt, wobei nur erfahrene Interviewer eingesetzt wurden. Die Erhebung richtete sich an ein zufällig ausgewähltes Kind im Haushalt, für das vorwiegend die Mutter antwortete. Für eine Unterstichprobe von 1/4 der Probanden wurde nach Verhaltensstörungen und deren Bewältigung gefragt. Die Responserate betrug 71,3 % (Voß, Klein, Schach, et al., 1989).

3.2. Analysedatensätze

Die rechnerunterstützte Datenerhebung gestattet es uns, den Status aller angewählten Telefonnummern abzuspeichern. So erhalten wir beispielsweise Daten über die Effizienz des gewählten Auswahlverfahrens (nur 5,3 % der Telefonnummern führten nach 9 Anrufversuchen zu keinem Kontakt) oder die Ausfallrate wegen Nichtbefragbarkeit (Schwerhörigkeit, Ausländer mit ungenügenden Deutschkenntnissen - 0,2 % der Probanden -, jeweils Raucherstudie Saarland (Schach, S. 1987)). Abbildung 1 zeigt den Status der angewählten Nummern im einzelnen. Von 31 541 ausgewählten Telephonnummern bilden 43,4 % den endgültigen Datensatz von 16 242 (Abbildung 1). Eine detaillierte Analyse dieser Daten gestattet es uns, die Bedingungen zu beschreiben, unter denen erfolgreiche Interviews zustande kommen (Schach, S. 1987).

In der Studie 'Kinder und Medikamente' wurden vorher bestimmte Anzahlen von Adressen von den Gemeinden erbeten, deren Telefonnummern herausgesucht und dann angerufen wurden. Dieser Angang an die Zielpersonen war wegen der Seltenheit des Untersuchungsgegenstands und des geringen Bevölkerungsanteils der Zielgruppe an der Gesamtbevölkerumg notwendig. Er gestattete uns auch eine Überprüfung der Übereinstimmung von Telefonbüchern und Melderegisterdaten, aus denen die Adressen stammten. Auch hier wurde der Verbleib der Adressen genau verfolgt (Abbildung 2). Ausgehend von 100% gezogener Adressenanzahlen lieferten die Gemeinden 86,5% nach wiederholten Kontakten und z.T. nur gegen Erstattung von Gebühren. Für 69,27% der Adressen wurden Telefonnummern gefunden, 68,04% der Haushalte wurden angerufen. Es ergaben sich 9,42% Ausfälle. Nach diesen Arbeitsschritten verblieben 41,79% oder 2006 Kinder im entsprechenden Alter in der Studie (Voß, Klein, Schach, et al., 1989). Besonders bedenklich war der Schwund von Probanden, weil die Telefonnummern nicht aufgefunden werden konnten. Damit entsteht die Frage der Aktualität der Einwohnermeldedateien.

3.3. Responseraten

Bei Feldstudien ist der Nachweis über den Verbleib der gezogenen Stichprobe oft ein umstrittenes Thema zwischen Auftragnehmer und Auftraggeber, denn die eingeschränkte Repräsentativität des Materials aus Bevölkerungserhebungen mit reduzierten Responseraten schränkt die Verallgemeinerungsfähigkeit von Studienergebnissen ein. Auch nichtrepräsentative Stichproben, die durch Oversampling zustande kommen, gehören in diese Kategorie.

Aus diesem Grund ist es bei Feldstudien von großer Wichtigkeit, den Verbleib der gezogenen Probanden zu beschreiben, damit man sich über die Aussagefähigkeit der Ergebnisse ein Bild machen kann. Wie oben schon bemerkt, war die Responserate in der Raucherstudie (d.h. vollständige Interviews an den um die schon befragten Zielpersonen, den Haushalten ohne Person in der Alters- und Geschlechtsgruppe und Haushalten, bei denen niemand zur Wohnbevölkerung gehörte, reduzierten angewählten Haushalten) 82,3% (Schach, S. 1987). Die Daten geben weiterhin Auskunft darüber, welche Gründe oder besonderen Bedingungen zu Ablehnungen führen und welche besonderen Gegebenheiten sich günstig auf die Befragungssituation auswirken.

In der Studie 'Kinder und Medikamente' beobachteten wir einen Schwund von Haushalten/Zielpersonen auf etwa 42% der anfänglichen Größenordnung. Setzt man diese zu den angewählten Haushalten einschließlich der Verweigerer in Beziehung, so erhält man eine Responserate von 71,3%. Dies macht die Problematik der Berichte über Responseraten deutlich, wenn über die ursprüngliche Kollektivgröße unzureichend Auskunft erteilt wird. Anders gesagt, es kann bei zufriedenstellender Responserate dennoch eine Verzerrung in den Daten vorliegen.

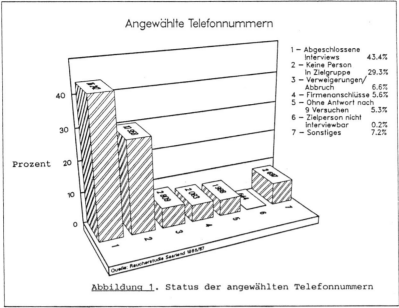

Abbildung 1. Status der angewählten Telefonnummern

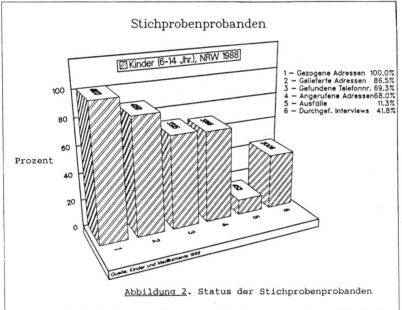

Abbildung 2. Status der Stichprobenprobanden

Bei computerunterstützten Interviews kann man eine Reihe von Stichproben- und Dateneigenschaften automatisch registrieren und sich nach deren Analyse im nachhinein ein Bild von der Qualität der Erhebungsdaten machen. Man kann z.B. aufzeichnen, nach dem wievielten Anrufversuch ein Interview tatsächlich zustandekommt. Das ist insofern wichtig als erfolgreiche Interviews beim ersten Anrufversuch eine andere Gruppe von Probanden repräsentieren als erfolgreiche Interviews erst nach dem 9. Versuch. Sind nun die Anteile der erfolgreichen Erstinterviews in einer Studie zu hoch (durch Oversampling), so sind deren Ergebnisse verzerrt. Es zeigt sich auch, daß sich die Interviews, die nach 3 Versuchen erzielt werden, in ihren Merkmalen deutlich von allen Probanden nach 9 Anrufversuchen unterscheiden. Ausgewählte Schätzer der Raucherstudie nach Anrufversuchen bis zum erfolgreichen Interview sind in Tabelle 2 dargestellt. Diese Darstellung verdeutlicht, wie wichtig es ist, den genauen Status der einzelnen Interviews einer Studie zu dokumentieren. Obwohl dies in herkömmlichen Erhebungen grundsätzlich auch möglich wäre, sind derartige Studieneigenschaften kaum in Methodikteilen veröffentlicht worden. Unter den geschätzten Merkmalen werden große Unterschiede in Abhängigkeit von der Anzahl der Anrufversuche beobachtet. Der Frauenanteil nimmt mit zunehmenden Anrufversuchen ab, die Anteile von Berufstätigen, Rauchern und von Personen mit Abitur nehmen zu. Dies galt trotz restriktiver Ausgabe neuer Telefonnummern und einer hohen Anrufwiederholfrequenz (Schach, S., 1987).

Tabelle 2. Schätzer in Abhängigkeit von der Anzahl der Anrufversuche bis zum erfolgreichen Interview. Raucherstudie Saarland 1986/87.

Schätzer in %	bei Interviews nach Anzahl der Anrufversuche bis zum erfolgreichen Interview			
	1	4	7	10
Anteil Frauen	59,4	48,2	35,9	40,2
Anteil berufstätig	42,4	57,2	71,1	65,5
Anteil Raucher	24,2	28,8	33,9	33,8
Anteil mit Abitur	8,0	10,0	7,8	15,7

Quelle: Schach, 1987

Die Daten der Studie 'Kinder und Medikamente' zeigen gleichlautende Ergebnisse. Während im Laufe des Eingangs der Interviews die Anteile von Kindern, die Medikamente nehmen und von Anteilen von Familien, in denen beide Partner eine Lehre haben, über die 4 Studienabschnitte hin etwa gleich blieben, vermindern sich von den ersten 500 Interviews zu allen Interviews die Anteile von Personen, die chronisch krank sind und erhöhen sich die Anteile von Familien, in denen beide Partner das Abitur haben (Tabelle 3).

Tabelle 3. Schätzer in Abhängigkeit vom Intervieweingang. Kinder und Medikamente, Nordrheinwestfalen 1988.

Schätzer in %	bei Interviews (in der Reihenfolge ihres Eingangs)			
	500	1000	1500	2006
Personen, die Medikamente nehmen	29,6	28,5	28,5	28,6
Chronisch Kranke	16,7	12,2	12,6	11,6
Beide Erwachsene haben Lehre	39,4	37,2	38,6	39,1
Beide Erwachsene haben Hochschulabschluß	4,8	5,5	5,9	6,3

Quelle: Voß, Klein, Schach, et al., 1989

4. Schluß

Computerunterstützte Erhebungsmethoden gestatten es uns, Stichproben- und Datenqualität von Felderhebungen zu verbessern, weil sie das Monitoring von dazu notwendigen Merkmalen rechnerunterstützt vorsehen. Der Befragungsinstitution obliegen dabei die Durchführung von Stichproben-, Erhebungsablaufkontrolle, Dokumentation von Stichprobe und Erhebung und der Datentransfer schon vor Ablauf einer Studie. Will der Auftraggeber gegenüber der Befragungsinstitution die ihm gegebenen Möglichkeiten der Datenqualitätsverbesserung ausnützen, so benötigt er Kenntnisse der Möglichkeiten und der Arbeitsweise der verwandten Software. Im Gegensatz zu herkömmlichen Erhebungen kann der Auftraggeber dann bei computerunterstützten Interviews Anforderungen an Merkmale für Stichproben-, Erhebungsablaufkontrolle und deren Dokumentation formulieren, die der Auftragnehmer erfüllen können sollte. Abbildung 3 zeigt diese Möglichkeiten schematisch auf. Somit bieten computerunterstützte Datenerhebungsmethoden die Möglichkeit, die Stichproben- und Datenqualität von Erhebungen beträchtlich zu verbessern. Es ist zu hoffen, daß Auftraggeber von Erhebungen sich dieser Möglichkeiten bedienen.

Abbildung 3. Verantwortlichkeiten bei computerunterstützten Interviews.

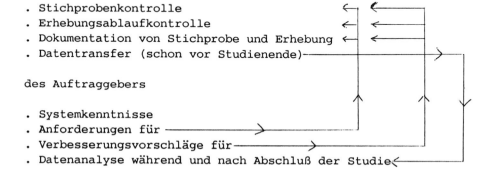

Verantwortlichkeiten

der Erhebungsinstitution

- Stichprobenkontrolle
- Erhebungsablaufkontrolle
- Dokumentation von Stichprobe und Erhebung
- Datentransfer (schon vor Studienende)

des Auftraggebers

- Systemkenntnisse
- Anforderungen für
- Verbesserungsvorschläge für
- Datenanalyse während und nach Abschluß der Studie

<u>Literatur</u>

Groves, R.M., Biemer, P.P., Lyberg, L.E., Massey, J.T., Nicholls, W.T. II, and J.Waksberg (Eds.) 1988. Telephone Survey Methodology. New York: Wiley.

Groves, R.M. and R.L. Kahn. 1979. Surveys by Telephone - a national comparison with personal interviews. New York: Academic Press.

Groves, R.M. and W.L. Nicholls. 1986. The status of computer-assisted telephone interviewing: part II - Data quality issues. Journal of Official Statistics 2: 117-134.

Karweit, N. and E.D. Meyers, Jr. 1983. Computers in Survey Research. in P. Rossi, J.D. Wright and A.B. Anderson (Eds). Handbook of Survey Research. New York: Academic Press: 379-414.

Lyberg, L. 1985. Plans for computer-assisted data collection at Statistics Sweden. Proceedings of the 45th Session. International Statistical Institute, Book III, Topic 18.2, pp: 1-11.

Nicholls, W.L. and R.M. Groves. 1986. The status of computer-assisted telephone interviewing: part I - Introduction and impact on cost and timeliness of survey data. Journal of Official Statistics 2: 93-115.

Schach, S. 1987. Methodische Aspekte der telefonischen Bevölkerungsbefragung - Allgemeine Überlegungen und Ergebnisse einer empirischen Untersuchung. Dortmund: Fachbereich Statistik. Forschungsbericht 87/7

Voß, R., Klein, H-W., Schach, E., Glaeske, G. und FORSA. 1989. Medikamentengebrauch und auffälliges Verhalten von Kindern im Alter von 6 - 14 Jahren in Nordrhein-Westfalen 1988. Düsseldorf: Der Minister für Arbeit, Gesundheit und Soziales des Landes NRW.

… CATI in der Medienforschung

S. Becker und B. Engel

Summary

The paper discusses how to use different standard software as tools for computer assisted telephone interviewing. A catalog of criteria for the evaluation of CATI-systems is developed with respect to practical application, data analysis and costs. Both mainframe and PC-solution show that standard software is suited to develop CATI-systems without spending money for special CATI software.

1 CATI in der Medienforschung beim ZDF und bei der Forschungsgruppe Wahlen (FGW)[1]

Zunächst möchten wir kurz erläutern, wieso hier ein gemeinsamer Beitrag von Zweitem Deutschen Fernsehen (ZDF) und Forschungsgruppe Wahlen (FGW) vorgelegt wird. Die FGW ist im Bereich der Wahlforschung, aber auch bei regelmäßigen Untersuchungen, wie den monatlichen Politbarometerbefragungen exklusiv für das ZDF tätig. Für diese Zwecke stellt das ZDF der FGW Ressourcen für die Datenverarbeitung zur Verfügung. Aus dieser Kooperation ist auch die Zusammenarbeit zwischen ZDF und FGW bei Umfragen aus dem Bereich der Medienforschung entstanden; zudem sind die in der Wahlforschung erreichten Qualitätsstandards für andere Erhebungen der empirischen Sozialwissenschaft von Vorteil.

Die besonderen Anforderungen an computerunterstützte Telefoninterviews im Bereich der Medienforschung ergeben sich vor allem durch die zeitliche Gebundenheit der Feldphase, insbesondere bei Fragen der Programmforschung. Typische Fragestellungen sind hier beispielsweise geplante Fernsehrezeption oder der Stand der Vorinformation über das Programm bzw. einzelne Sendungen oder Serien bei sogenannten Vorbefragungen oder deren Rezeption und qualitative Bewertung in sogenannten Nachbefragungen. Die Realisierung solcher Erhebungen liefert nur dann verläßliche Ergebnisse, wenn die Befragung möglichst nahe beim Ereignis, nämlich der Ausstrahlung der Sendung liegt. Telefonische Interviews bieten hier die bei weitem beste Möglichkeit, die Verhaltensinvarianz der Befragten in der Interviewsituation zu gewährleisten.

Die Zielsetzungen beim Aufbau der CATI-Systeme im ZDF und bei der FGW lassen sich dahingehend unterscheiden, daß im ZDF für quantitativ kleine Stichproben ad hoc insbesondere zur Evaluation des Programm-Vorinformationsstandes und zur Rezeption neuer Serien Befragungen durchgeführt werden. Häufig erfüllen diese Pilotumfragen auch die Aufgabe, für repräsentative Erhebungen Befragungsinstrumente zu testen. Demgegenüber werden bei der FGW im Bereich Medienforschung vor allem repräsentative Bevölkerungsumfragen durchgeführt, die Know how zur Ziehung repräsentativer Stichproben und eine ständige Feldorganisation erfordern. Aus den Zielsetzungen der Systeme folgt auch die unterschiedliche Gewichtung

---

[1] Alle Schaubilder befinden sich am Ende des Textes.

der in Abschnitt 3 näher beschriebenen Bewertungskriterien.

Zunächst stellen wir in Abschnitt 2 Bewertungskriterien für CATI-Systeme in der Medienforschung auf und vergleichen in Abschnitt 3 die CATI-Systeme des ZDF und der FGW. Wir folgen dabei den Phasen einer empirischen Erhebung und berücksichtigen, inwieweit die Anforderungen verschiedener am Forschungsprozeß Beteiligter (Programmierer, Interviewer, Auswerter) erfüllt werden, und ziehen hieraus in Abschnitt 4 ein kurzes Fazit.

Im Vergleich zu den anderen Beiträgen in diesem Band über telefonische Erhebungsverfahren liegt unser Interesse darin zu zeigen, wie mit ganz unterschiedlichen "Werkzeugen" pragmatisch CATI-Systeme aufgebaut wurden, deren Einsatz sich in der Praxis bereits bewährt hat. Freilich ist die Entwicklung solcher Systeme organisch gewachsen und baut auf vorhandenen Strukturen und Ressourcen auf, so daß hier keine idealtypischen Systeme vorgestellt werden. Auf eine ausführliche Darstellung von Literatur ist deshalb an dieser Stelle verzichtet worden.[2])

2 Bewertungskriterien für CATI in der Medienforschung

Bewertungskriterien für die CATI-Systeme des ZDF und der FGW haben wir zu den Bereichen der Systemumgebung, Fragebogenprogrammierung, Kontaktphase, Interview, Feldsteuerung/-kontrolle und Datenanalyse herangezogen. Das relative Gewicht dieser Kriterien und damit ein eindeutiges Gesamturteil läßt sich sicher nicht generell festlegen, da diese sowohl von den Zielsetzungen als auch von vorhandenen personellen Ressourcen abhängen.

Unter dem Stichwort Systemumgebung betrachten wir die Kriterien Kosten für Hard- und Software sowie die Abhängigkeit der Systeme vom Operating. Bei der Programmierung liegt der wesentliche Punkt in der Abwägung zwischen Aufwand und Ertrag: Wie schwierig ist die Programmierung zu erlernen? Welche automatischen Generierungsmöglichkeiten gibt es? Welche Möglichkeiten der individuellen Gestaltung existieren? Welcher Aufwand ist bei Änderungen notwendig? Im Bereich Kontaktphase vergleichen wir die Möglichkeiten der Zielpersonenauswahl und der Protokollierung der Kontaktphase. Für das Interview sind vor allem die Sicherheit im Ablauf und der Bedienungskomfort für den Erfolg der Erhebungen wichtig. Ebenso ist es wünschenswert, während der Feldphase den Fortgang der Erhebung zu beobachten und eventuell Steuerungsmöglichkeiten zu nutzen. Da unseres Erachtens ein CATI-System nicht gleichzeitig auch ein Auswertungssystem sein muß, ziehen wir als Kriterium für den Bereich der Datenanalyse den Aufwand heran, der erforderlich ist, um die Daten und gegebenenfalls ihre Beschreibung in ein statistisches Analysesystem zu überführen (eine tabellarische Übersicht der Kriterien findet sich in Abschnitt 4).

3 Darstellung der CATI-Systeme

3.1 Systemumgebung

ZDF: Da Telefoninterviews nur an etwa 10 bis 12 Tagen des Jahres durchgeführt werden, wird ausschließlich Hard- und Software verwendet, die auch für andere Zwecke eingesetzt wird. Als Hardware stehen zur Zeit bis

---

2) Vgl. hierzu die Literaturübersicht der AG Methodenforschung des Statistischen Bundesamtes (1985) (erstellt von Sylke Becker).

zu 12 Terminals des Typs IBM 3192 G[3] in den Räumen der Medienforschung bzw. einem Benutzerzentrum zur Verfügung, die an einer IBM 3084 Q unter MVS/XA angeschlossen sind. Als Software dient eine sogenannte Sprache der 4. Generation, "FOCUS"[4], die unter anderem auch für das hauseigene Hotelreservierungssystem und das Berichtswesen für die Geschäftsleitung genutzt wird. FOCUS unterstützt die oben genannte Hardware, das heißt, Masken sind im Format 32 Zeilen mal 80 Zeichen farbig und mit Grafikattributen gestaltbar. Eine ebenfalls verfügbare FOCUS-Zusatzoption ermöglicht einen sogenannten Simultanous Usage-Betrieb, das heißt, beliebig viele (maximal 255) Benutzer können gleichzeitig Lese- und vor allem Schreibzugriffe auf eine Datenbank durchführen. Für die Auswertungen der Telefoninterviews steht SPSS-X R3.0 zur Verfügung, das mit einer selbstentwickelten USERGET-Prozedur[5] Zugriff auf FOCUS-Datenbankretrievals und -Dictionaries ermöglicht. Die Kosten für FOCUS betragen etwa 150000 DM (Kaufpreis) zuzüglich Kosten für Updates und Systemunterstützung. Alle FOCUS-Aktivitäten mit Ausnahme der erstmaligen Erstellung von Datenbanken im SU-Betrieb können vom Endbenutzer unter TSO/ISPF vorgenommen werden. Die hohe Betriebssicherheit des ZDF-Rechenzentrums läßt die grundsätzliche Abhängigkeit, insbesondere des SU-Betriebs vom Operating faktisch nicht spürbar werden. Durch die Mehrfachnutzung der Hard- und Software ist eine Zuordnung der Kosten zu den Telefoninterviews nicht möglich.

FGW: Seit Ende 1987 werden computergestützte Interviews im eigenen Telefonstudio durchgeführt. 1988 wurden bei 26 Telefonumfragen ca. 22000 Interviews realisiert. Dabei handelte es sich ausnahmslos um voll standardisierte und strukturierte Interviews. Das Telefonstudio verfügt über 46 Interviewerarbeitsplätze. Jeder Arbeitsplatz ist mit einem ATARI PC 520 bzw. 1040 ST F, einem ATARI SM 124 monochrom Monitor, einem Mikro-Floppy-Diskettenlaufwerk und einer Maus ausgestattet. Alle Geräte arbeiten unabhängig voneinander, so daß natürlich keine negativen Einflüsse des Operating vorkommen können. Das Betriebssystem des ATARI, TOS, beinhaltet die Bedienoberfläche GEM, die aus grafischen Elementen besteht. Dies ermöglicht eine mausgestützte Durchführung aller Operationen während des Interviews. Die Kosten pro Arbeitsplatz belaufen sich auf etwa 1300 DM.

Die Software für die telefonische Erhebung ist eine hauseigene Entwicklung, die mehrere Komponenten umfaßt:
- das Fragebogenprogramm TIPSY (Telefon Interview Programm System), das in der Programmiersprache C geschrieben ist,
- ein Codeplanprogramm, das zum Teil auf Betriebssystemebene, zum Teil in STandardBaseIII arbeitet,
- ein Sammelprogramm, das im Betriebssystem abläuft und
- ein Grundauszählungsprogramm, das in STandardBaseIII vorbereitet und in SPSS auf einem IBM PC abgearbeitet wird.

Bei STandardBaseIII handelt es sich um ein Datenbankprogramm für ATARI ST. Es ist kompatibel zu dBaseIII, dem Datenbankprogramm für IBM PC. Die erste Bearbeitung des Rohdatenfiles erfolgt zur Zeit mit SPSS-X, wird aber in Zukunft auf SPSS PC+ 3.0 umgestellt. Die eigentliche Auswertung, das heißt Berechnungen und Erstellung von Tabellen wird mit dem Tabellierungsprogramm FGWTAB durchgeführt, ebenfalls einer hauseigenen Entwicklung.

---

3) Grafische Farbbildschirme mit einem 80 Zeichen mal 32 Zeilen Display.
4) Information Builders, Inc. (1988): FOCUS Users Manual Release 5.5. New York.
5) Vgl. hierzu den Beitrag von Engel (in diesem Band) zur individuellen Programmierung in SPSS-X.

3.2 Programmierung der Erhebungsinstrumente und Speicherung der Daten

Wichtige Kriterien für die Beurteilung der Leistungsfähigkeit eines CATI-Programmes sind die Unterstützung, die es bei der Programmierung des Fragebogens bietet, die Gestaltungsmöglichkeiten für das Layout, um den Interviewer sicher durch den Fragebogen zu führen, und die Änderungsmöglichkeiten im laufenden Betrieb.

ZDF: Alle Programmierungen werden integriert in FOCUS vorgenommen. Die Hauptbestandteile von FOCUS sind eine relationale Datenbank, Befehle für deren Modifikation und Retrieval sowie Programmiermöglichkeiten zur Systemsteuerung auf der FOCUS-Kommandoebene. Eine Vielzahl weiterer Möglichkeiten (zum Beispiel differenzierte Datenschutzfunktionen) werden für das CATI-System nicht genutzt. Die Dateimodifikationsmöglichkeiten umfassen auch einen Maskengenerator, der wahlweise über eine Full Screen-Eingabe oder mit jedem beliebigen Texteditor geschrieben werden kann (zum Maskenbild und zur Maskeneingabe siehe Schaubild 1a). Die Programmiermöglichkeiten sind äußerst flexibel; die nach Erstellung des Data-Dictionary mögliche Erzeugung von Defaults ist für Telefoninterviews nicht brauchbar. Die Ablaufsteuerung erfolgt durch eine Caselogik (Schaubild 2a), die Filterführung durch eine über das Maß anderer Programmiersprachen deutlich hinausgehende IF THEN ELSE-Logik und einen VALIDATE-Befehl; der Blättermodus wird durch Function-Keys gesteuert. Für die Erstellung der Datenbank ist ein Data Dictionary erforderlich, in dem Variablendefinitionen und -etikettierungen vorgenommen werden können. Die Datenbank für CATI-Anwendungen umfaßt derzeit drei Segmente, und zwar für die Bruttostichprobe der Adressen, die Kontaktprotokolle und die Interviews. Diese Datenbank ist über eine sogenannte dynamische Kreuzreferenz, das heißt für Auswertungen, mit einer Datenbank über regionale Strukturinformationen verbunden. Das Erlernen von FOCUS nimmt durchaus Zeit in Anspruch; Detailarbeiten, wie zum Beispiel die Eingabe von Masken, lassen sich jedoch faktisch ohne eine spezielle Einarbeitung in FOCUS durchführen.

FGW: Mit Hilfe des Fragebogenprogramms TIPSY wird auf der Basis vorgefertigter Programmbausteine ein ablauffähiger CATI-Fragebogen erzeugt. Editiert wird der Fragebogen über das Textverarbeitungssystem BeckerText (vgl. Schaubild 1b). Der Maskenaufbau und die Filterführung werden mit einigen wenigen Steuerzeichen festgelegt (vgl. Schaubild 2b). Variabel gestaltbar ist die Bildschirmaufteilung (horizontale oder vertikale Teilung zur Trennung von Frage- und Antworttext) und die Schriftart (fett oder blaß gedruckt als Hinweis für den Interviewer, welcher Text vorgelesen werden soll und welcher Text nicht, da es sich um einen monochromen Monitor handelt). Eine vertikal geteilte Bildschirmmaske umfaßt zweimal 15 Zeilen à 32 Spalten, eine horizontal geteilte Maske 5 Zeilen à 60 Spalten für den Fragetext und 8 Zeilen à 60 Spalten für Antwortkategorien. Für die Eingabe der Intervieweridentifikation zum Beispiel oder anderer Zahlen ist zusätzlich eine numerische Eingabe vorgesehen, mit der ein Nummernblock erzeugt wird, der die Eingabe aller Ziffern nebeneinander erlaubt und zur Kontrolle zusätzlich über ein Display der eingegebenen Zahl verfügt. Jede Frage ist mit einer Adresse versehen, die während des Interviewablaufs sukzessive angesteuert und abgearbeitet werden. Die Filterführung wird durch eine entsprechende Änderung der Nachfolgeadresse bei der Programmierung festgelegt. Das bedeutet für den Interviewer, daß er keine Filterfehler mehr machen kann, weil ihm automatisch die richtige Folgefrage entsprechend der vorangegangenen Antwort vorgelegt wird. Die Antworten müssen dabei weder vom Programmierer noch vom Interviewer vercodet werden. Der gesamte Fragebogenablauf einschließlich der Filterführung reagiert auf Antwortmarkierungen, denen intern vom Programm ein Wert zugeschrieben wird. Da das gesamte Interview mausgestützt abläuft, werden ausschließlich geschlossene Fragen mit Einfach- oder Mehrfachantworten gestellt und Fragen, die bereits vorvercodet sind. Ein weiterer Fragetyp sind Skalen, zum Beispiel für die Beurteilung verschiedener Fensehserien. Sie werden nacheinander auf einer Bildschirmseite vorgelegt, maximal 8 Skalen pro Seite. Das Programm verfügt über die Fähigkeit, die Abfrage von Batterien, zum Beispiel für ein Eigenschaftsprofil zu randomisieren, damit die Reihenfolge der Abfrage zufällig ist und somit Einfluß auf das Antwortverhalten durch die Stellung eines Items ausgeschlossen ist. Bei der Editierung des Fragebogens können beliebig viele Zeitmessungen eingebaut werden. Zu Beginn eines jeden Interviews wird die Uhrzeit festgehalten. Alle anderen Zeitmessungen erfolgen in Sekunden relativ zu dieser Anfangszeit. Damit kann bei Bedarf der zeitliche Aufwand für jede einzelne Frage oder für einzelne Interviewabschnitte, zum Beispiel für die Kontaktphase, festgehalten werden. Ad hoc-Änderungen des Fragebogens in der Erhebungsphase sind nur von einem auf den anderen Tag möglich, da der geänderte Fragebogenfile neu auf jede Diskette überspielt werden muß. Eine Fragebibliothek ist zur Zeit noch im Aufbau. Die Planung geht dahin, Interviewstandardteile als Gesamtfiles in dieser Bibliothek abzulegen und bei Bedarf durch Verweis auf den Katalogeintrag in den Fragebogen einzubauen.

3.3 Kontaktphase

CATI-Systeme bieten die Möglichkeit, die Kontaktphase systematischer und präziser als bei anderen Interviewverfahren in den Gesamtablauf der Erhebung einzubeziehen. Um dies zu gewährleisten, ist die Protokollierung der Aktivitäten in der Kontaktphase und - je nach Stichprobenverfahren - die Möglichkeit der Zielpersonenauswahl notwendig.

ZDR Es ist versucht worden, alle Phasen einer Erhebung, also auch die Kontaktphase, computerunterstützt ablaufen zu lassen. Der Einstieg in die Kontaktphase beginnt mit der Festlegung des Auswahlverfahrens; hierbei stehen die Kombination aus Quote und Kontaktversuch (Standardeinstellung), eine Terminvereinbarung und eine eindeutige Fallidentifikation zur Verfügung. Entsprechend den Eingaben wird der erste in Frage kommende Fall angezeigt; danach ist zu entscheiden, ob für diesen Fall der Kontakt beginnen soll oder der nächste Fall nach gleichen Auswahlkriterien angezeigt werden soll. Im weiteren Verlauf der Kontaktphase ist die Möglichkeit der Terminvereinbarung bzw. des Abbruchs gegeben. Jeder Kontaktversuch wird mit Datum, Uhrzeit etc. in der Datenbank gespeichert. Das einzige hier bisher bekannte Problem besteht darin, daß in unseren Bruttostichproben häufig mehrere Personen eines Haushalts befragt werden sollen, dies aber im Laufe der Kontaktphase dem Interviewer nicht bekannt ist. Ferner ist es notwendig, die vereinbarten Termine selbst auszuwählen, da kein ständiger Zeitabgleich erfolgt. Ebenso ist der Wählvorgang durch die Interviewer von Hand vorzunehmen.

FGW Die gesamte Stichprobenverwaltung läuft auf Papier ab, weil alle ATARIs zur Zeit noch unabhängig voneinander arbeiten. Grundlage einer Repräsentativbefragung ist eine Zufallsauswahl von Telefonnummern, die in einem gesonderten Schritt generiert werden und auf Kontaktbogen vorliegen; die zu befragende Person im Haushalt wird nach dem Geburtstagsschlüssel ausgewählt.

TIPSY beinhaltet die Möglichkeit, das Kontaktprotokoll über den Bildschirm einzugeben. Vorgesehen ist die Protokollierung des Ergebnisses für jeden Wählversuch. Die Verbindung zur Telefonnummer erfolgt über eine Kontaktbogen-Identifikationsnummer, die vom Interviewer eingegeben wird. Sie ist mit einer Prüfziffer versehen. Eine Prüfziffernroutine meldet dem Interviewer, wenn die Eingabe falsch ist. Die Kontaktbogenprotokollierung unterstützt die manuelle Stichprobensteuerung dahingehend, daß täglich die Anzahl der bereits bearbeiteten Telefonnummern und die damit erzielten Resultate ausgewertet werden können. Die Wahrnehmung von Terminen sowie die Streuung von Kontaktversuchen über die Feldzeit wird zur Zeit noch manuell gesteuert.

3.4 Interview

Im Interview kommt es darauf an, daß die Durchführung für den Interviewer einfach zu handhaben, der Ablauf für ihn völlig durchstrukturiert ist, er also keinen Spielraum bei der Durchführung hat.

ZDF: Der Einstieg in das Interview erfolgt für den Programmierer über eine in FOCUS programmierte Menüoberfläche. Nach der Auswahl wird der gesamte Fragebogen (einschließlich Kontaktphase) vollständig in einen eigenen Speicherbereich geladen; hierdurch gibt es faktisch keine Responsezeiten. Das Interview selbst wird über die Eingabe der Antworten gesteuert, das heißt, nach den Eingaben ist ausschließlich die Datenfreigabe-Taste zu betätigen. Für Notfälle bzw. nachträgliche Korrekturen von Antworten kann der "Blättermodus" verwendet werden. Grundsätzlich sind die Antworten auf vorausgegangene Fragen in jeder Folgefrage verwendbar, zum Beispiel zur vollständigen Vorstrukturierung des Interviews (Sie haben vorhin gesagt, daß Sie ....). Nach dem Ende (ordnungsgemäß oder durch Abbruch) sind die Daten gespeichert; ein erneuter Kontaktversuch (oder eine Änderung der Eingaben) ist durch die Interviewer nicht möglich.

FGW: Das Fragebogenprogramm TIPSY wird zu Beginn einer Sitzung von Diskette auf jeden PC geladen. Es greift auf den Fragebogenfile zu und legt dem Interviewer Frage für Frage vor. Dieser gibt zu Beginn seine Interviewer-ID ein. Das Programm vergleicht sie mit den Angaben in einer Interviewerdatei, die ebenfalls auf jeder Diskette gespeichert ist. Zur Kontrolle wird der Name des Interviewers auf einem Display angezeigt. Die ID bleibt für die gesamte Sitzung erhalten.

Während des Interviews erledigt der Interviewer alle Operationen mit der Maus. Er benötigt also weder EDV- noch Schreibmaschinenkenntnisse. Damit er keine Frage selbständig überspringt, kann er sich nur mittels einer Antworteingabe vorwärts bewegen. Sogenannte Pull Down-Menüs ermöglichen ihm auch, im Fragebogen rückwärts zu blättern, entweder Frage für Frage oder bis zum Anfang des Fragebogens, um Korrekturen durchzuführen. Alle Antworten bleiben bei diesem Vorgang erhalten, durch Korrekturen geänderte Filterführung wird berücksichtigt.

Nach Beendigung eines Interviews (ordnungsgemäße Durchführung oder Abbruch) oder Abschluß eines Protokolls werden die Daten sequentiell aus dem Arbeitsspeicher in einen Ausgabefile auf Diskette herausgeschrieben. Dafür wird vom Fragebogenprogramm TIPSY automatisch ein Datenfile angelegt. Das Interview kann danach nicht mehr geladen werden. Deshalb können Interviews auch nicht unterbrochen und zu einem späteren Zeitpunkt fortgeführt werden.

Da alle PCs unabhängig voneinander arbeiten, auf jedem das Fragebogenprogramm geladen ist und ein separater Datenfile angelegt wird, beeinträchtigt der Defekt eines Gerätes den Arbeitsablauf der anderen nicht.

3.5 Feldkontrolle und Feldsteuerung

Zur Sicherung der Qualität von Erhebungen sind Feldkontrolle und Feldsteuerung wichtige Werkzeuge.

ZDF: Der simultane Lese- und Schreibzugriff erlaubt eine ausgezeichnete Feldkontrolle und Feldsteuerung. Es existieren hierfür einige FOCUS-Standardroutinen, die Einblick in die Ausschöpfung des Adressenvorrates, die durchschnittliche Interviewzeit oder die derzeit laufenden Interviews geben. Verwendet wird die Möglichkeit der Feldbeobachtung zur Steuerung der gleichmäßigen Ausschöpfung der Quoten; bei der kleinen Anzahl der Interviewer ist eine Feldkontrolle nicht notwendig.

FGW: Die Kontrolle über den Stand der Erhebung ist tageweise möglich. Nach Beendigung eines jeden Erhebungstages werden die Daten von 46 Disketten in einen Datenbankfile im Datenbankprogramm STandardBase überspielt. Auf der Basis dieses Rohdatenfiles wird mit einem Grundauszählungsprogramm ein

SPSS-File und ein Listenfile erstellt, der eine Häufigkeitsauszählung für alle erhobenen Variablen enthält. Ebenso sind Kreuztabellen möglich, zum Beispiel um festzustellen, wie viele Interviews Interviewer X pro Feldtag gemacht hat.

Zur Kontrolle der Interviewer dient außerdem die Auswertung der Kontaktprotokolle, die Auskunft über die Anzahl der Kontaktversuche und die daraus resultierenden Einzelergebnisse gibt. Zusätzlich kann anhand der Zeitmessungen festgestellt werden, wie lange ein Interviewer für das einzelne Interview gebraucht hat. Nach einem weiteren Berechnungsschritt kann außerdem die Ausschöpfungsquote pro Interviewer herangezogen werden.

Da die FGW ausschließlich mit einem Repräsentativansatz arbeitet, ist eine Feldsteuerung, beispielsweise zur Aussteuerung bestimmter Quotenmerkmale, nicht notwendig. Eine Steuerung bezieht sich lediglich auf die Verarbeitung der Stichprobe insgesamt, das heißt die Kontaktbogenausgabe, die Streuung von Kontaktversuchen über die Feldzeit oder die Steuerung der Anzahl der Kontaktversuche. Dies geschieht manuell auf der Grundlage der Auswertung aller Kontaktprotokolle.

3.6 Auswertungsschnittstelle

Auswertungen der Interviews sollen schnell und ohne großen Zusatzaufwand möglich sein. Daher werden im folgenden die mögliche Zeitnähe der Auswertungen und der Aufwand der Übertragung in statistische Analysepakete betrachtet.

ZDF: Die Programmiersprache FOCUS besitzt selbst eine umfangreiche und komfortable Reporting-Möglichkeit, die jedoch nur in geringem Umfang statistische Verfahren enthält. Für das ZDF CATI-System existiert eine spezielle SPSS-X USERGET-Schnittstelle, die einen sofortigen Zugriff auf die FOCUS-Datenbank zuläßt und neben den Daten auch alle verfügbaren Data Dictionary-Informationen in den aktiven SPSS-File überträgt. Da die FOCUS-Datenbank relational aufgebaut ist, können nur rechteckige Datenbankauszüge nach SPSS übertragen werden. Ferner ist bei der Anlage der FOCUS-Datenbank zu berücksichtigen, daß SPSS nicht alle Möglichkeiten der Formatgestaltung (zum Beispiel negative Zahlen in Klammern, manche Datumsformate) bzw. Variablennamenvergabe (Variablenlänge bis zu 14 Zeichen) nutzen kann, da die von der Schnittstelle vorgenommenen Ersatzlösungen notwendigerweise suboptimal sein müssen. Insgesamt hat sich die Schnittstelle jedoch sehr gut bewährt und erlaubt ohne Aufwand den Zugriff auf die Erhebungsdaten bereits während der Feldphase.

FGW: Das CATI-System der FGW ist kein Auswertungssystem. Die Auswertungsschnittstelle zu SPSS führt über die Erzeugung eines STandardBase Files. Da STandardBase kompatibel zu dBaseIII ist, kann dieser Rohdatenfile auf einem IBM PC von SPSS ohne Modifikationen gelesen werden. Mit dem Grundauszählungsprogramm in SPSS wird ein SPSS-Exportfile erzeugt, der zur Weiterverarbeitung im SPSS genutzt wird und ein Listenfile, der zur unmittelbaren Feldkontrolle während der Erhebungsphase dient.

Bei einer Standarderhebung kann die Auswertung mit SPSS in Form von Häufigkeitsauszählungen und Kreuztabellen einen Tag nach Beendigung der Erhebung fertiggestellt werden.

4 Fazit

Vergleicht man die CATI-Systeme von ZDF und FGW zusammenfassend, so ergibt sich nach unseren Ausführungen das folgende Bild:

CATI im ZDF und bei der FGW

Phase	Kriterien	ZDF	FGW
Systemumgebung	Kosten	-	+
	Abhängigkeit vom Operating	+	+
Programmierung	Erlernbarkeit	(+)	+
	Voreinstellung	-	0
	individuelle Gestaltung	+	+
	Aufbau von Fragebibliotheken	0	+
	ad hoc-Änderungen	+	-
Kontaktphase	Auswahl der Zielpersonen	+	*
	Protokoll der Aktivitäten	+	+
Interview	Sicherheit im Ablauf	+	+
	Bedienungskomfort	+	+
Feldsteuerung/-kontrolle	Überblick über den Stand der Erhebung	+	0
	Interviewerkontrolle	+	+
Auswertungsschnittstelle	Zeitnähe der Auswertung	+	+
	Aufwand für die Erstellung von Systemfiles	+	+

+ positive Bewertung
- negative Bewertung
0 weder positiv noch negativ
() mit Einschränkungen
* trifft nicht zu

Sicher unterliegen die Bewertungen den speziellen Bedingungen beim ZDF und der FGW und würden unter anderen Anwendungsbedingungen unter Umständen anders ausfallen. Die Kriterien selbst erscheinen uns jedoch für jeden Anwender von CATI-Systemen hilfreich, die Leistungsfähigkeit "seines" oder anderer Systeme zu beurteilen.

Literatur

Statistisches Bundesamt (1985): Literaturübersicht zum Thema CATI, zusammengestellt von Sylke Becker. (Manuskript).

Information Builders, Inc. (1988): FOCUS Users Manual Release 5.5. New York.

Schaubild 1a: Maskenbild und Maskeneingabe im ZDF CATI

```
User: DV43   Panel                                    Fallnummer: 0004711

Fragetyp 1: standardisierte Frage      | 1 Antwortmöglichkeit 1  |   ▮
mit einer Antwortmöglichkeit           | 2 Antwortmöglichkeit 2  |
                                       | 3 Antwortmöglichkeit 3  |

Fragetyp 2: standardisierte Frage      | Antwort 1               |   ▮
mit Mehrfachnennungen                  | Antwort 2               |   ▮
                                       | Antwort 3               |   ▮

Fragetyp 3: offene Texteingabe         |   ▮                     |   ▮
Variablenlänge A24                     |   ▮

Fragetyp 4: Zeitskala

Interviewerhinweis:
Offene Angabe mit einem grossen 'X' auf der Skala markieren
```

wegen fehlender Farbreproduktionsmöglichkeit in diesem Band sind die Farben durch Schrifthinterlegungen kenntlich gemacht: **weiss**, aqua, **rot**, blau

```
<.W.><1>User: <.DW.UID/4> Panel: Muster        <58>Fallnummer:<.DW.CASEID>˜
<.BU.><78><.B.>˜
<.B.><40>  |<67>  |˜
Fragetyp 1: standardisierte Frage              1 Antwortmöglichkeit 1             |<.TR.N1>˜
mit einer Antwortmöglichkeit                   2 Antwortmöglichkeit 2             ˜
                                               3 Antwortmöglichkeit 3
<.BU.><40>  |<67>  |<78><.B.>˜
<.B.><40>  |<67>  |˜
Fragetyp 2: standardisierte Frage              Antwort 1                          |<.TR.M1>˜
mit Mehrfachnennungen                          Antwort 2                          |<.TR.M2>˜
                                               Antwort 3                          |<.TR.M3>˜
<.BU.><40>  |<67>  |<78><.B.>˜
<.B.><40>                                      <67>˜
Fragetyp 3: offene Texteingabe                 <.R.>˜<:C1.TR.A1>˜<.B.>˜
Variablenlänge A24                             <.R.>˜<.TR.A2>˜<.B.>˜
<.BU.><40>  |<78><.B.>˜

Fragetyp 4: Zeitskala˜

<.A.><1>Interviewerhinweis<.B.>˜
<.A.><1>Offene Angabe mit einem großen 'X' auf der Skala markieren<.B.>˜

  <.TR.SKALA>˜
<.R.> 16      17      18      19      20      21      22      23      24˜
<.B.>
<1><.BU.><78><.B.>˜
```

Schaubild 1b: Maskenbild im FGW CATI

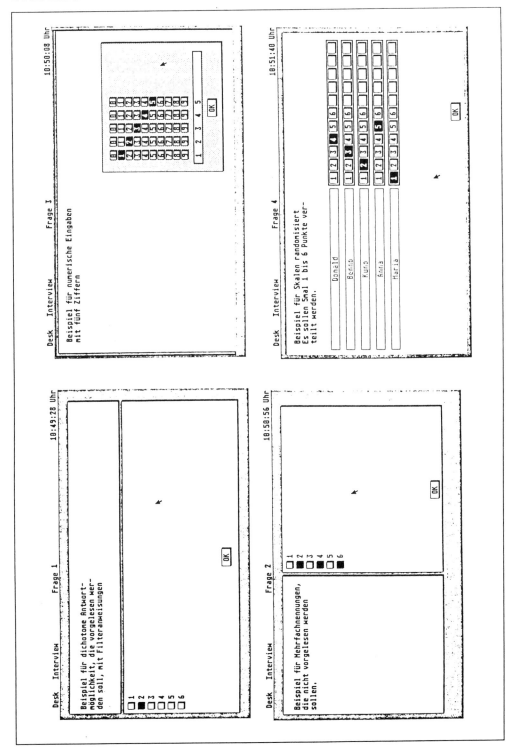

Schaubild 2a: Caselogik im ZDF CATI

```
MODIFY FILE EUROCOP
CHECK 1
GOTO T00
CASE AT START
 -INCLUDE TSTART
ENDCASE
CASE T00
 -INCLUDE T00
GOTO T01
ENDCASE
CASE T01
 -INCLUDE T01
ENDCASE
         :
CASE T99
 -INCLUDE T99
ENDCASE
END
```

Schaubild 2b: Fragebogenaufbau im FGW CATI

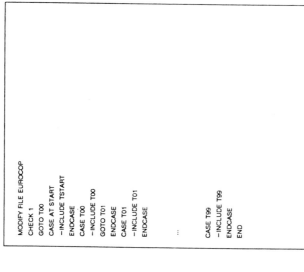

```
#_____START
|  TESTFRAGEBOGEN
#1
Beispiel für dichotome Antwort-
möglichkeit, die vorgelesen wer-
den soll, mit Filteranweisungen
*>2 1
*>3 2
*>3 3
*>3 4
*>3 5
 >3 6
 >3
#2,M
Beispiel für Mehrfachnennungen,
die nicht vorgelesen werden
sollen.
+ 1
+ 2
+ 3
+ 4
+ 5
+ 6
#3,N5
Beispiel für numerische Eingaben
mit fünf Ziffern
#4 S /R
Beispiel für Skalen randomisiert
Es sollen 5mal 1 bis 6 Punkte ver-
teilt werden.
*.1
*.2
*.3
*.4
*.5
*.6
? Anna
? Maria
? Kuno
? Benno
? Donald
```

Praktische Einsatzmöglichkeiten eines interaktiven Befragungs- und Instruktionssystems bei Experimenten und in Umfragen

H.-J. Hippler, F. Meier und N. Schwarz

Summary

Computer assisted telephone and personal interviewing has received considerable attention over the last years. In the present paper, we will provide a short review of these developments and will present the software package "IBIS", that is designed to handle computer assisted telephone, personal, and self-administered interviews. The use of IBIS will be illustrated with a number of experiments on response effects in surveys, and issues of survey administration, data coding, and analysis within IBIS will be discussed. Finally, future developments of computer assisted self-surveying systems are touched.

1. Entwicklungstendenzen im Umfragebereich

In den letzten Jahren läßt sich in der Umfrageforschung eine zunehmende Tendenz feststellen, schriftliche und telefonische Befragungsmethoden als Alternative zum persönlich-mündlichen Interview zumindest in die Designüberlegungen von Untersuchungen miteinzubeziehen.

Diese Entwicklung geht zur Zeit noch weiter: in zunehmenden Maße geschieht eine Hinwendung zu computerunterstützten Telefonumfragen, zu sogenannten CATI- Systemen (Computer Assisted Telephone Interviewing). Obwohl das erste CATI-Interview in den USA bereits vor etwa 15 Jahren durchgeführt wurde (Fink 1983), ist die Verbreitung der Methode in der Bundesrepublik noch relativ gering (zu einem Überblick vgl. Hagstotz 1985). Erst mit dem zunehmenden Einsatz von Telefonumfragen allgemein (und der Erkenntnis ihrer unabweisbaren Vorteile), als auch durch die schnelle technische Entwicklung im Computerbereich (insbesondere im PC-Sektor) zeichnet sich jetzt ein weiterer Trend zu computerunterstützten Telefoninterviews ab (vgl. Groves et al. 1988).

2. "CATI"- und "CAPI"- Systeme

Gleichzeitig hat die Entwicklung in Richtung computerunterstützter Telefoninterviews bewirkt, daß man darüber nachdenkt, diese Systeme auch für Untersuchungen ohne Mitwirkung von Interviewern, also für Selbstbefragungen bzw. Experimente nutzbar zu machen. Nicholls & Groves (1986) definieren in Ergänzung von CATI-Systemen deshalb zwei weitere Möglichkeiten: (1) "Computer Assisted Personal Interviewing" mit Computerterminals, Portablen oder Laptops (CAPI); (2) "Computerized Self-Administered Questionnaires (CSAQ)" bei dem der Befragte selbst die Geräte bedient. Zu letzterem existiert in den Niederlanden ein bisher außerordentlich erfolgreicher Versuch (SARIS 1988) mit Hilfe von Heimcomputern (Philips MSX2) komplexere Selbstbefragungen mit täglichem Datenabruf (per Akkustikkoppler und Telefon) von einem Zentralcomputer aus zu implementieren. In den USA werden mehrere spezifisch für Experimente konzipierte Selbstbefragungssysteme angeboten. So enthält z.B. eines der ausgereiftesten Interviewsysteme, das CI2-System ein spezifisch für Marktforschungszwecke entwickeltes Unterprogramm zur Selbstbefragung. Auch in der Bundesrepublik beginnt sich hierzu ein Markt zu entwickeln

3. Die Vorteile computerunterstützten Interviewens

Die generellen Vorteile computerunterstützten Interviewens, sei es mit Hilfe von CATI oder CAPI- Systemen sind folgende:

- Interviewanweisungen, Fragen und Antwortalternativen werden vom System vorgegeben. Der Interviewer trägt die Antworten entweder offen oder nach vorgegeben Codes ein, bzw. er bewegt den "Cursor" bis zur genannten Antwort und bestätigt sie;

- Antworten aus vorangegangenen Fragen können während des Interviews wieder auf dem Bildschirm abgebildet und zur Motivations- und Kommunikationsverbesserung, zu Nachfragen bzw. zur Kontrolle verwendet werden;

- Bei der Eingabe numerischer oder alphanumerischer Codes kann eine Prüfung der Bandbreite und Gültigkeit der Antworten vorgenommen werden.

- Darüber hinaus kann während des Interviews eine Konsistenzprüfung (stimmen die gegebenen Antworten mit vorher erhobenen Informationen überein?) erfolgen; bei der Feststellung von eventuellen Inkonsistenzen können diese während des Interviews beim Befragten rückgefragt und evt. verbessert werden;

- Fehlerhafte Eingaben werden entweder nicht angenommen (nochmalige Eingabe) oder resultieren in weiteren Unterfragen ("probes") oder Fragen;

- Die Datenaufnahme erfolgt während der laufenden Interviews und die Daten liegen jederzeit in kontrollierter Form vor; Längere Antworttexte auf offene Fragen können direkt eingegeben werden und stehen anschließend sofort "maschinenlesbar" zur Verfügung;

- Komplexe Filtersprünge, Rückfilter ("sie haben vorhin gesagt...") oder das Auslassen einzelner Items geschieht automatisch, d.h. systemgesteuert;

- In einzelnen Fragenkomplexen, in denen Kontexteffekte erwartbar sind, können "Randomisierungen" der Fragenabfolge vorgenommen werden; ebenso sind längere Itembatterien randomisiert abfragbar;

- Es können Antwortzeiten, die beispielsweise Aussagen über Verständlichkeit etc. einzelner Fragen zulassen, miterfaßt werden;

- Die Daten können direkt in ein Analysesystem übergeführt werden. Ergebnisse sind zu jedem Zeitpunkt der Befragung abrufbar.

4. Das IBIS-System

Die technischen Einzelheiten des für unsere Untersuchung benutzten IBIS-Systems sind an anderer Stelle ausführlicher dargestellt (Hippler et al., 1988; Meier, 1989 in diesem Band). Deshalb nur ein grober Systemüberblick:

Das IBIS System verfügt über alle der bereits dargestellten Vorteile computerunterstützter (Telefon-)Befragungssysteme und eignet sich sowohl für computerunterstützte telefonische oder mündliche Befragungen, als auch für Selbstbefragungen. Es ist ein modular aufgebautes Softwaresystem, das mit einer hochfunktionalen Anweisungssprache eine Benutzeroberfläche für die Entwicklung von Befragungs- und Lehrprogrammen bietet (Meier, 1988a, b). Es können Programme für Einplatz- und Gruppenanwendungen erstellt werden. Bei der Entwicklung wurden vor allem

Gesichtspunkte sozialwissenschaftlicher Befragungs- und psychologisch-experimenteller Untersuchungsmethoden berücksichtigt.

Damit der Anwender Befragungen, Untersuchungen und Unterweisungen mit großer Flexibilität und Entwurfsfreiheit entwickeln kann, steht eine deutsche Anweisungssprache zur Verfügung, die die Begrenztheit menügeführter Benutzeroberflächen nicht kennt.

Kernstück des Systems ist der IBIS-Prozessor, der zahlreiche Steuerungsfunktionen koordiniert und ausführt. Allgemein wird der Untersuchungsablauf durch zahlreiche Anweisungen und deren Spezifikationen gesteuert, die in einer Steuerdatei mit einem Editor zusammengestellt werden. Die Anweisungen einer Steuerdatei werden vom IBIS ausgewertet und die entsprechenden Funktionsmodule – Untersuchungsablauf, Bildschirmdarstellung, Antwortauswertung und Ergebnisausgabe – aktiviert.

Der modulare Funktionsaufbau des IBIS gestattet weiterhin die Steuerung verschiedener peripherer Hardwaresysteme, wie die Fernsteuerung von Videorekorder, Bildplatte oder Diaprojektor. Die Steuerung von Arbeitsplatz- rechner oder Handterminals, sogenannten Portables, ermöglicht den Einsatz des IBIS in Untersuchungs- und Unterrichtsgruppen und bietet sowohl individuelle als auch gruppenbezogene Aufgabenstellungen und Befragungen, Antworterhebungen und Rückmeldungen.

Alle Abläufe und Daten werden in Ergebnisdateien festgehalten Entwurf und Aufbau einer Steuerdatei für eine Befragungsuntersuchung sind in einfacher Weise mit jedem beliebigen Text- oder Programmiereditor möglich.

5. Die Experimente

Zur Überprüfung der praktischen Einsatzmöglichkeiten des IBIS-Systems wurden aus dem ZUMA-Forschungsschwerpunkt "Kognition und Umfrageforschung" insgesamt fünf Experimente ausgewählt und in einem Untersuchungsdurchgang erhoben.

Experiment 1 prüfte, ob die zum Nachdenken verfügbare Zeit die Erinnerung an das Datum eines Ereignisses begünstigt (hier: Afghanistan-Intervention der UDSSR; Falklandkrieg Großbritanniens und Tschernobylkatastrophe). Die Nachdenkzeit wurde durch einen 15 Sekunden stehenden Bildschirm vs. eine direkte Antwortmöglichkeit manipuliert. Parallel wurde die Zeit gemessen und den Befragten zum Ende der Befragung (nach Rückkopplung Ihrer am Anfang des Interviews geäußerten Antwort) für jedes vorher genannte Datum die Möglichkeit einer Korrektur gegeben.

In Experiment 2 wurde der Einfluß unterschiedlicher Kontextfragen auf die Interpretation einer "fiktiven" Frage untersucht (Schuman/Presser 1984; Strack et al. 1987; Strack/Martin 1987). Ein sonst bei schriftlichen Interviews mögliches Zurückblättern und dadurch Verändern des Kontexts war nicht möglich, auch hier wurde - wie übrigens bei allen Fragen - die Zeit gemessen.

In Experiment 3 wurden die Befragten gefragt, ob sie zu einem bestimmten Themengegenstand (hier Gesundheitsreform) eine Meinung hätten, äußerten sie keine Meinung zu haben, wurden sie dennoch danach gefragt. Durch die durch jeweils neuen Bildschirmaufbau mögliche Trennung von Filterfrage und Meinungsfrage war dies ebenfalls einfacher möglich, als in einem schriftlichen Interview.

In zwei weiteren Experimenten wurden der Einfluß unterschiedlicher Skalenvorgaben und unterschiedlicher Frageabfolgen auf das Antwortverhalten überprüft.

Insgesamt mußten sechs unterschiedlichen Versionen von Fragebögen bzw. Frageablaufsteuerungen entwickelt werden.

6. Implementation und Durchführung

Nach Erarbeitung einer Grundversion und einem ersten Test wurden die weiteren fünf Versionen erstellt.
Durch die Vielzahl normierter Standardskalen (5- und 7 Punkte-Skalen) die vom System zur Verfügung gestellt werden, waren nur noch die Endpunkte der Skalen zu benennen bzw. war nur noch die gewünschte Verbalskala aufzurufen.

Das bei Experimenten mit schriftlichen Fragebögen auftretende Problem der Notwendigkeit der Wiederholung von Fragetextbestandteilen im Stimulusmaterial von Skalen "für wie typisch deutsch halten Sie...." trat nicht mehr auf.

Die Stimulusvorgabe konnte "reizkonsistent", d.h. ohne störende Bildschirmvorgaben wie beispielsweise "Menüsteuerungen" erfolgen.

Die Filtersteuerung war nicht sichtbar und einfach steuerbar, d.h der/die Befragte erlebte einen unterbrechungsfreien Durchgang.

Schließlich konnte die Datenablage so erfolgen, daß auch bei sehr unterschiedlichem Stimulusmaterial (etwa: offene Antwortmöglichkeit, Skala mit hohen Frequenzvorgaben, Skala mit niederen Frequenzvorgaben) alle Antworten auf einem Datenpunkt gesammelt und dann direkt weiterverarbeitet werden konnten. Somit entfiel das ansonsten bei Experimenten übliche "Vorvercoden" und "Recodieren" der Variablen im Datensatz.

Die eigentliche Untersuchung wurde an den Universitäten Konstanz und Mannheim mit insgesamt 156 Versuchspersonen, allesamt Studenten durchgeführt.

7. Erfahrungen bei der Durchführung, der Datenaufbereitung und Datenanalyse

Die durchschnittliche Zeit für die Bearbeitung der Untersuchung durch die Studenten lag bei etwa 15 Minuten. Ganz im Gegensatz zu ähnlich langen, mit schriftlichen Fragebögen durchgeführten Experimenten wurde diese Zeit von den Versuchspersonen aber als wesentlich geringer eingeschätzt. Ein ähnlicher Effekt zeigt sich bei der von den Befragten zum Schluß der Befragung anzugebenden Zahl der von ihnen zu bearbeitenden Fragen. Mit einer durchschnittlichen Zahl von 29 Fragen wurde die reale Anzahl um 100 % unterschätzt.

Die Versuchspersonen hatten mit den Eingaberoutinen(tasten) durch die intensive Anfangsanweisung und die bei jeder Frage zusätzlich gegebenen Hinweise keine Schwierigkeiten. Selbst Befragte, die noch niemals zuvor an einem PC gesessen hatten, berichteten keine Bedienungsprobleme.

Die Befragung wurde insgesamt von den Studenten als außerordentlich positiv empfunden. Diese positive Beurteilung bezog sich

dabei weniger auf die Inhalte, als auf die "ungewöhnliche" Art der Befragung ("mal was anderes").
Bei der Befragung selbst war eine sehr konzentrierte Atmosphäre festzustellen, die durch die Notwendigkeit entstand, mit einem weitgehend unbekannten Instrument "klarzukommen".

Die Zusammenführung der auf den einzelnen Computern abgespeicherten Befragungsdaten (der Daten der einzelnen Versionen) war problemlos. Jeder neuen Versuchsperson wurde vom System eine Identifikationsnummer und eine Versionskennzeichnung zugeteilt. Die Daten konnten deshalb nach Beendigung der Befragung einfach zusammenkopiert werden.

Ansonsten notwendige Filterprüfungen oder Konsistenzchecks bzw. das Suchen nach fehlerhaften Kodierungen entfielen.

Die Daten lagen als zwei Datensätze vor: ein Textdatensatz (in diesem Experiment lediglich das Studienfach) und ein Datensatz mit den Antworten zu den offenen und geschlossenen Fragen sowie den Zeitmessungen zu jeder einzelnen Frage. Da die Datensätze in "fixed-format" ausgegeben werden, war eine direkte Überführung in statistische Softwarepakete wie beispielsweise SPSS-PC oder STATGRAPH mit einem vorbereitetem Setup ohne Schwierigkeiten möglich. Die Analysen konnten so direkt nach Abschluß der Befragungen durchgeführt werden.

8. Zukünftige Entwicklungen bei interaktiven Selbstbefragungssystemen

Auf der Grundlage dieser ersten Erfahrungen mit dem interaktiven Befragungssystem IBIS, stellt sich generell die Frage nach den Entwicklungsmöglichkeiten derartiger Systeme. Durch die ständige Weiterentwicklung der technischen Möglichkeiten im PC-Bereich (Portables, Laptops etc.) und die gleichzeitige kostengünstige Entwicklung wird es sicherlich in unmittelbarer Zukunft zu einem verstärkten Einsatz von Computern bei persönlich-mündlichen Interviews (unter Einsatz von Interviewern) kommen. Schon heute werden von Versicherungen tragbare PC's zur Kundenberatung oder

Datenaufnahme eingesetzt die durch Akkustikkoppler bei Bedarf mit dem Zentralcomputer verbunden werden können. Aber auch die Methode, daß Befragte selbst mit dem Computer arbeiten, rückt in den Bereich des Möglichen. Da in der empirischen Sozialforschung zunehmende Tendenzen zur Befragung von Spezialpopulationen, zu immer komplexeren Instrumenten und Abfragetechniken sowie zu Befragungen über längere Zeiträume festzustellen sind, wird auch hier ein Bedarf nach -schon jetzt möglicher, aber noch zu kostspieliger- Technikunterstützung entstehen. Die teilweise "rasant" zu nennende Entwicklung bei computerunterstützten Telefoninterviewsystemen bestätigt dies (Groves et al. 1988).

Literatur

Fink, J.C., 1983: CATI's first decade: The Chilton experience. Sociological Methods and Research 12:153-168.

Groves, R.M./Biemer, P.P./Lyberg, L.E./Massey, J.T./Nicholls II, W.L./Waksberg, J. (Hrsg.), 1988: Telephone Survey Methodology. New York: Wiley.

Hagstotz, W., 1985: Bestandsaufnahme der Anwender von CATI-Systemen. ZUMA-Technischer Bericht T85/15.

Hippler, H.J./Meier, F./Schwarz, N., 1987: Erste Erfahrungen mit der Erprobung eines interaktiven Befragungs-und Instruktionssystems (IBIS). ZUMA-Nachrichten 23: 79-91.

Meier, F., 1989: Rechnergestützte Untersuchungen in der humanpharmakologischen Forschung (in diesem Band).

Meier, F., 1988a: Konzeption und Realisation eines rechnergestützten Befragungssystems, S.105-113, in: F. Faulbaum/H.M. Uehlinger (Hrsg.), Fortschritte der Statistik-Software 1. Stuttgart: Fischer Verlag.

Meier, F., 1988b: Computerunterstütztes Lehren und Lehrer-Schüler-Beziehung: Gegensatz oder Ergänzung? Versicherungswirtschaft 43:575-578.

Nicholls II, W.L./Groves, R.M., 1986: The status of computer-assisted telephone interviewing: Part I - Introduction and impact on cost and timeliness of survey data. Journal of Official Statistics 2:93-115.

Saris, W.E. 1988: A full automatic procedure for data collection: Tele interviewing, S.93-104, in: F. Faulbaum/H.M. Uehlinger (Hrsg.), Fortschritte der Statistik-Software 1. Stuttgart: Fischer Verlag.

Schuman, H./Presser, S., 1984: Questions and answers in attitude surveys. Experiments on question form, wording and context. New York: Academic Press.

Strack, F./Martin, L.L., 1987: Thinking, judging, and communicating: A process account of context effects in attitude surveys, S.123-148, in: H.J. Hippler/N. Schwarz/S. Sudman (Hrsg.), Social information processing and survey methodology. New York: Springer Verlag.

Strack, F./Martin, L.L./Schwarz, N., 1987: The context paradox in attitude surveys: Assimilation or contrast? ZUMA-Arbeitsbericht 87/07.

Rechnergestützte Untersuchungen in der humanpharmakologischen Forschung

F. Meier

Summary: The application of the interactive research and instruction system IBIS to the domain of pharmacological clinical research and testing is demonstrated in this article. IBIS provides the researcher with a user oriented command language as a programming tool for study control, self-administered questionnaires, and computer-based instructions with controlling of peripheral systems like video recorder, CD-player etc. As a professional tool, IBIS is not menue-driven and therefore of high functionality and flexibility for many research problems in all domains of human sciences.

1. Einleitung

Die humanpharmakologische Forschung benötigt für die klinische Prüfung der Wirkung von Medikamenten auf wesentliche Funktionen der Wahrnehmung, Aufmerksamkeit, psychomotorischen Steuerung, des Befindens und des Denkens zunehmend psychometrisch-diagnostische Methoden. Um einerseits die Untersuchungen mit hohem Standard zu fahren und andererseits den Untersuchungsablauf zu optimieren, bietet sich der Einsatz rechnergestützter Erhebungs- und Protokolltechniken an.

Das Interaktive Befragungs- und Instruktionssystem IBIS, gestattet nicht nur die Ablaufprogrammierung von Befragungen (vgl. Hippler et al., 1988 und Hippler in diesem Band, Meier, 1989a) und Unterweisungen (vgl. Meier, 1989b), sondern ebenso die voll rechnergestützte Steuerung von Untersuchungsphasen einer humanpharmakologischen Studie bis hin zur simultanen und synchronisierten psychophysiologischen Messung.

IBIS ist ein modular aufgebautes Softwaresystem, das eine hochfunktionale Benutzeroberfläche für die Entwicklung von Befragungs- und Untersuchungsprogrammen darstellt. Dem Anwender bietet eine deutsche Anweisungssprache als Benutzeroberfläche große Flexibilität und Entwurfsfreiheit für die Erstellung von Befragungen, Studien und Instruktionen. Derzeit ist IBIS für IBM-PC/AT und kompatible Rechner mit dem Betriebssystem MS-DOS der Microsoft GmbH sowie für die Rechnersysteme VAX und PDP-11 mit den Betriebssystemen VMS und RSX der Digital Equipment GmbH verfügbar. Für die Klinische Prüfung wird IBIS beispielsweise im humanpharmakologischen Labor der KNOLL AG, Ludwigshafen, auf einer VAX unter VMS mit mehreren Laborplätzen und einem zentralen Überwachungsplatz eingesetzt.

Der Untersuchungsablauf wird mit verschiedenen IBIS-Anweisungen und deren Spezifikationen in einer Steuerdatei beschrieben. Dazu kann jeder verfügbare Editor verwendet werden. Eine den professionellen Anwender einengende Menüführung ist nicht erforderlich. Die Anweisungen einer Steuerdatei werden von IBIS ausgewertet und die entsprechenden Funktionsmodule aktiviert. Neben der Zeitsteuerung des Ablaufs sind Sprungfunktionen wichtige Hilfsmittel der Ablaufgestaltung eines Untersuchungsprogramms.

Die Steuerung der Bildschirmdarstellung ist eine zentrale Systemfunktion und dient der Darbietung von Informationen und Fragen in beliebiger Form auf dem Systemmonitor des Computers. Zahlreiche Bildschirmanweisungen ermöglichen die Verwendung der auf dem jeweiligen Rechner vorhandenen Bildschirmattribute und Farben. Zuvor erhobene Eingaben des Probanden können diesem als Rückmeldung wieder dargeboten werden.

Die Antwortauswertung kann alphanumerische, ganzzahlige, dezimale und offene Antworten akzeptieren. Standardisierte Anworten können mithilfe von Antwortskalen vom Probanden eingegeben werden. Hierfür sind in IBIS bereits vielfältige Skalenformen vorhanden. Die Antworten lassen sich dann variabel kodieren und zusammenfassen, so daß beispielsweise Summenwerte als Subtestwerte berechnet werden können. Die Antwortzeiten werden automatisch gemessen und registriert. Die Befragungs- bzw. Untersuchungsergebnisse werden in verschiedene Dateien ausgegeben (vgl. Abbildung 1).

In einer Protokolldatei wird der gesamte Befragungsablauf abgebildet, so daß nach Ablaufunterbrechungen durch den Benutzer oder Untersuchungsleiter, aber auch nach einem Systemabsturz des Computers, das Untersuchungsprogramm ohne Wiederholungen fortgesetzt werden kann.

In eine Datendatei werden die numerischen Ergebnisse zusammen mit den Bearbeitungszeiten abgelegt, über alle Untersuchungen gesammelt und mit einer aufsteigenden Probandennummer versehen.

In einer Ergebnisdatei können die Antworten bzw. Leistungen eines einzelnen Probanden in übersichtlicher Form zusammengestellt und ausgegeben werden. Dazu wird eine Formulardatei entworfen und im Programmverlauf aufgerufen. In dieser Formulardatei sind der Text des Ergebnisblattes und Anweisungen zur Nutzung verschiedener Druckerattribute enthalten, sowie die Kennzeichnung der Variablenwerte und Bearbeitungszeiten, die ausgegeben werden sollen. Diese Formulardatei wird im Programmablauf mit den individuellen Probandendaten aktualisiert und als Ergebnisdatei ausgegeben.

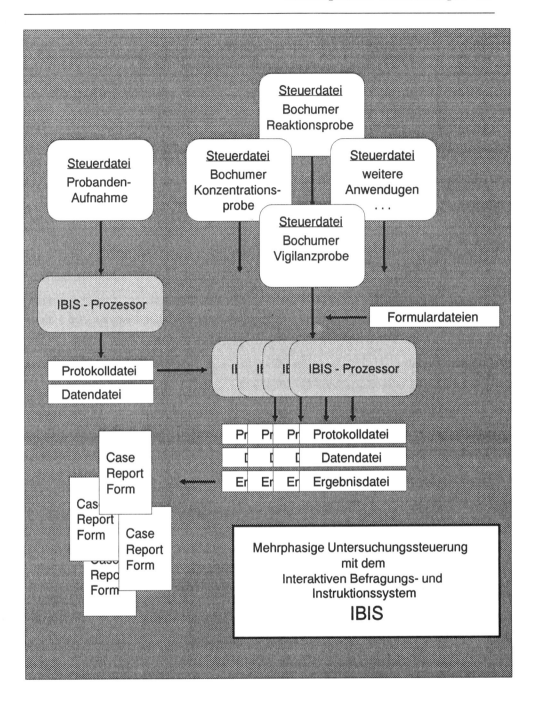

Abbildung 1

Die Steuerung von Diaprojektionen, Videosystemen oder Bildplatte sind hochfunktionale Ergänzungen des IBIS für Beanspruchungsuntersuchungen im Wahrnehmungs- und Aufmerksamkeitsbereich, insbesondere für komplexe Reizvorgaben und Simulationen.

Die funktionellen Anforderungen an ein rechnergestütztes interaktives Untersuchungssteuerungssystem und die damit verbundenen Einsatzmöglichkeiten des IBIS in der humanpharmakologischen Forschung für die Klinische Prüfung von Präparaten sollen nachfolgend erläutert werden.

2. Zeitsteuerung und Kontrolle von Untersuchungsabläufen

Pharmakokinetische und pharmakodynamische Untersuchungen erfordern die zeitgenaue Applikation von Prüfpräparaten und deren Wirkungskontrolle, um die Einhaltung der zur Studiendurchführung entwickelten Prüfpläne zu gewährleisten. Eine rechnergestützte Untersuchungsführung kann hierzu die verschiedenen Labortätigkeiten zeitgenau anfordern und die ermittelten Meßwerte erheben und protokollieren. IBIS bietet verschiedene Funktionen der zeitlichen Ablaufsteuerung und Protokollierung der Normalzeit in Abhängigkeit von bestimmten Eingaben und Antworten.

3. Einweisung von Laborpersonal und Probanden

Einweisungen in die Labortätigkeit und Aufgaben für die Probanden sollten rechnergestützt dargeboten und kontrolliert werden, so daß ein Höchstmaß an Instruktionsverständnis gesichert wird. IBIS stellt zahlreiche Funktionen der Bildschirmsteuerung und -darstellung bereit, um Informationen über den Untersuchungsablauf oder die Aufgabenstellung gezielt und mittels Antwortprüfungen kontrolliert darzubieten. Die mündlichen Einweisungen eines Versuchsleiters können somit auf ein Mindestmaß reduziert und die Untersuchungsbedingungen auf ein Höchstmaß standardisiert werden.

Zusätzlich erlaubt IBIS die ergonomisch sinnvolle Führung und Dokumentation von Probandendaten während eines ganzen Studienablaufs (vgl. Abbildung 1). So können zunächst die wesentlichen biographischen Daten (Alter, Geschlecht, Gewicht usw.) eines Probanden und die Studienmerkmale (Untersuchungsleiter, Probandennummer, Aufgabenauswahl usw.) aufgenommen bzw. vom Laborpersonal eingegeben werden. Diese werden dann in eine Protokolldatei gespeichert und können von jeder weiteren Anwendung des IBIS unter der Probandennummer abgerufen werden.

Alle Eingaben sind also nur einmalig vorzunehmen und stehen jeder weiteren Anwendung zur Vervollständigung des Datensatzes zur Verfügung.

Abbildung 2

4. Psychometrische Untersuchungen

Die Wirkungsprüfung von Testpräparaten auf Wahrnehmung, Aufmerksamkeit, Psychomotorik, Befinden und Denken kann mittels verschiedener psychometrischer Testverfahren in standardisierter Form vorgenommen werden. Eine rechnergestützte Testdurchführung erfordert keinen Versuchsleiter und vermeidet daher Registrierfehler und Versuchsleitereffekte. Zusätzlich können Meßwerte kontinuierlich in schneller Folge erfaßt und gespeichert werden. Mit der Anweisungssprache des IBIS lassen sich beliebige Fragestellungen und Aufgaben für den Probanden formulieren. Darüberhinaus stehen zeitkritische Anwendungen bereits als Programmmodule zur Verfügung (vgl. Abbildung 1):

für Untersuchungen der Aufmerksamkeitsleistung die Bochumer Vigilanzprobe (vgl. Abbildung 2), für Untersuchungen der Konzentrationsleistung bei mentaler Dauerbelastung die Bochumer Konzentrationsprobe und für Untersuchungen der Reaktionsleistung bei unterschiedlich komplexen Stimuli die Bochumer Reaktionsprobe. Entwickelt werden derzeit eine sprachfreie Intelligenzprobe und eine psychomotorische Koordinationsprobe. Untersuchungsverfahren zum aktuellen Befinden können vom Anwender selbst in beliebiger Form gestaltet werden.

5. Aufgabensynchrone Steuerung psychophysiologischer Langzeitmessungen

Die psychometrische Aufgabenstellung als Dauerbeanspruchung kann nur mittels rechnergestützter Untersuchungsführung zeitsynchron mit verschiedenen kontinuierlichen psychophysiologischen Messungen gekoppelt werden, um dynamische Regulationsmuster als Indikator für psychosomatische Beanspruchungen und Präparatewirkung in Langzeitmessungen gewinnen zu können. Spezielle Programmodule des IBIS unterstützen in einer Untersuchungsführung simultan die Aufgabendarbietung für den Probanden, die Kontrolle der richtigen Antwort und gewährleisten, daß je nach Meßrate bzw. anlog-digitaler Abtastgeschwindigkeit der physiologischen Meßkanäle der anfallende Datenstrom mittels Laborrechner registriert, gespeichert, parametrisiert und analysiert wird (vgl. Meier, 1986).

6. Ergebnisdarstellung in Case-Report-Form (CRF)

Individuelle Untersuchungsergebnisse können übersichtlich auf dem Bildschirm dargestellt und als Ergebnisprotokolle in Case-Report-Form (CRF) ausgegeben werden. Abbildung 1 zeigt, daß

```
KNOLL AG
Humanpharmakologie
                                Bochumer Konzentrationsprobe


        Study              : Esopamilin

        Investigator       : H. Bunsen

        Subject            : W. Brenner
        Number             : 123

        Experimental Task  : Bochumer Konzentrationsprobe
                             Concentration test

        Timing
          date             : 13. 4.1989
          starting time    :  9:17
          duration         : 1802 seconds

        Results
          total solutions  : 244
          true solutions   : 238
          false solutions  :   6
          false/total (F%) : 2.4%
```

Abbildung 3

von jeder Anwendung vorbereitete Formulare aus Formulardateien aufrufbar sind, die gegebenenfalls an Vordrucke angepaßt sind. Diese Formulare werden mit den individuellen Ergebnissen und Versuchsbedingungen ergänzt und als CRF fertig ausgedruckt. Wie alle Steuer- und Ergebnisdateien sind auch die Formulare mit einem Editor leicht zu entwickeln und zu modifizieren. Sie können demzufolge auch entsprechend den Anforderungen der amerikanischen Food and Drug Administration (FDA) entworfen werden. Abbildung 3 veranschaulicht die Ergebnisdarstellung auf dem Bildschirm bzw. als Formularausdruck in Case-Report-Form.

7. Datenerhebung und Ablaufprotokollierung der Untersuchung

Die fehlerfreie und zeitgenaue Ablaufprotokollierung der Untersuchung und Meßdatenerhebung ist für die Durchführungskontrolle der entwickelten Prüfpläne einer Studie unerläßlich. Einerseits ist jeder einzelne Versuch in Protokollblättern (Case Report Form) zu dokumentieren, andererseits sollen statistische Aussagen anhand von Datenaggregaten gemacht werden. IBIS erstellt für jeden Probanden eine Protokolldatei, in der alle Ereignisse und Antworten der Untersuchung sequentiell notiert werden. Diese Angaben können in weiteren Untersuchungsprogrammen wieder aufgerufen und verwendet werden. Sie dienen darüberhinaus zum Restart eines willentlich oder unwillentlich abgebrochenen Untersuchungsprogramms.

Zusätzlich werden die Untersuchungsantworten aller Probanden einer Studie für die statistische Analyse mit einem der verfügbaren statistischen Programmsysteme in eine Datendatei festformatiert eingetragen. Arbeitsphasen der Datenaufbereitung und -prüfung entfallen und verkürzen die Datenauswertung.

8. Übersicht der IBIS Systemfunktionen

Mit der Version 2.0 hat die Forschungsgruppe IBIS die funktionale Vielfalt des Interaktiven Befragungs- und Instruktionssystems IBIS um wesentliche Möglichkeiten erweitert. Neben den tatsächlich freien Sprüngen und Verzweigungen innerhalb des gesamten Anwenderprogramms ist die Definition und die Verwendung von Anweisungsblöcken, wie es in modernen Programmiersprachen üblich ist, eine herausragende Neuerung der IBIS Version 2.0. Die mit diesen zusätzlichen Funktionen erzielbare elegante und leichte Anwendungsprogrammierung wird durch die völlig neue Compiler-Struktur des IBIS-Prozessors erreicht. Das gesamte Anwendungsprogramm ist zur Laufzeit resident und erreicht sehr schnelle Ablaufgeschwindigkeiten. Mit dem Übergang von der Interpreter-Struktur der IBIS Version 1.6 zur Compiler-Struktur der IBIS Version 2.0 sind für den Anwender deutlich sichtbare, qualitative Neuerungen vorgenommen worden, die es ihm gestatten, Laboruntersuchungen, Befragungen, Telefoninterviews, Unterweisungen usw. noch effizienter zu gestalten. Die IBIS Systemfunktionen der Version 2.0 sind:

Ablaufsteuerung

❑ **Zeitsteuerung,**

alle Befragungssequenzen und das Antwortverhalten können zeitlich genau kontrolliert und protokolliert werden,

❑ **freier Variablenzugriff,**

die vom Befragten oder Probanden gegebenen numerischen und alphanumerischen Antworten können Variablen in beliebiger Abfolge zugewiesen werden,

❑ **freie Sprungführung und Ablaufverzweigungen,**

im gesamten Umfang eines Befragungs- oder Untersuchungsprogrammes läßt sich mittels Sprung und Verzweigung eine differenzierte Ablaufführung in Abhängigkeit der gegebenen Antworten erstellen,

❑ **Blockdefinitionen,**

häufig benutzte Bildschirminhalte und Bildschirmausschnitte, z.B. Bildschirmfenster können an beliebiger Stelle des Anwendungsprogramms als Programmblock definiert oder von einer Datei eingelesen werden,

❑ **Blockaufruf und -ausführung,**

definierte Anweisungsblöcke lassen sich entsprechend einer objektorientierten Ablaufprogrammierung an beliebiger Position des Anwenderprogramms aufrufen und schachteln,

❑ **Randomisierung,**

mittels Zufallsgenerator kann die Abfolge von Anweisungsblöcken zur Laufzeit bestimmt werden, um z.B. Sequenzeffekte in Fragelisten zu vermeiden,

❑ **Restartfunktion bei gewollter oder ungewollter Programmunterbrechung,**

vom Benutzer können Positionen im Ablaufprogramm frei gewählt werden, von denen aus IBIS nach Programmabbruch oder Programmunterbrechung den Untersuchungsablauf wieder fortsetzt,

❑ **Rundlauffunktion für wiederholte Befragungen,**

für vollautomatische Befragungen ohne Interviewerbeteiligung oder Versuchsleiterkontrolle besteht die Möglichkeit nach einem Programmdurchlauf sofort wieder zu starten,

❑ **Zugriff auf Hilfssteuerdateien (z.B. Fragensammlung),**

Teile des Anwendungsprogramms können in Dateien gesondert abgelegt und an beliebiger Stelle eingelesen werden, so daß Fragen und Bildschirminhalte in verschiedenen Untersuchungen verfügbar sind,

❑ **Videosteuerung,**

mit zusätzlicher Hardware und einem IBIS-Modul für die Steuerung von Videorekordern lassen sich Fragekontexte hervorragend veranschaulichen und fokussieren,

❑ **Diasteuerung,**

für bestimmte Anwendungen in wissenschaftlichen Untersuchungen steuert ein IBIS-Modul die Darbietung von Diaprojektionsbildern für qualitativ hochwertige Reizkonfigurationen,

❑ **Handterminal- bzw. Portablesteuerung für Gruppenuntersuchungen,**

für Gruppenuntersuchungen und den rechnergestützten Gruppenunterricht bietet ein IBIS-Modul die Möglichkeit zur Steuerung mehrerer Arbeitsplatzrechner oder -terminals zur Verwirklichung einer hocheffizienten Gruppenunterweisung,

Bildschirmdarstellung

❑ **graphische und farbige Bildschirmattribute,**

alle verfügbaren Graphikattribute lassen sich mit der IBIS Anweisungssprache einsetzen,

❑ **freie Textpositionierung,**

der Bildschirm kann frei mit Texten und Graphiken gestaltet und schrittweise ergänzt werden,

❑ **Ausgabe von Antwortvariablen und -texten,**

alle erhobenen Antworten können dem Befragten wieder vorgelegt werden,

❑ **Vorgabe standardisierter Skalen,**

eine Sammlung von Antwortskalen sind zur standardisierten Beantwortung in IBIS bereits enthalten, weitere können vom Anwender selbst leicht und schnell entworfen werden,

❑ **Blockdefinition von wiederholt aufrufbaren Bildschirmfenstern,**

häufig benutzte Bildschirminhalte, wie Fenster und Graphiken können in Anweisungsblöcken definiert werden und sind dann als Objekte frei verfügbar,

Antworterhebung

❑ **alphanumerische Eingaben,**

Texte aus offenen Antworten können erhoben, gespeichert und gegebenenfalls dem Befragten wieder vorgelegt werden,

❑ **numerische Eingaben,**

ganzzahlige und dezimale Eingaben können erhoben und Variablen frei zugeordnet werden,

❑ **Antwortübernahme aus vorhergehenden Untersuchungen,**

werden Probanden in mehreren Untersuchungsphasen einbezogen, so können bereits erhobene Antworten zur Erstellung eines konsistenten Datensatzes oder aber zur bedingten Verzweigung in dem aktuellen Ablaufprogramm aus vorhergehenden Untersuchungen übernommen werden,

Antwortauswertung

❑ **Wertebereichsprüfung,**

selbstverständlich werden alle Eingaben auf ihre Gültigkeit hin überprüft und unzulässige Eingaben schon bei der Eingabe nicht akzeptiert,

❑ **Prüfung auf Richtigkeit von Antworttexten,**

alphanumerische Antworten können auf Richtigkeit geprüft werden, z.B. in Lückentests oder Satzergänzungen,

- **Precoding,**
  alphanumerische Antworten können nach vorgegebenen Textelementen untersucht und numerisch codiert werden,
- **Erfassung von Beantwortungszeiten,**
  alle Beantwortungszeiten werden automatisch ermittelt und mit den Antwortdaten abgespeichert,
- **Summenwertbildung,**
  frei auswählbare numerische Antworten und Bearbeitungszeiten können aufsummiert werden,

Ergebnisausgabe

- **Protokoll des Untersuchungsablaufes,**
  alle Phasen des Befragungs- bzw. Untersuchungsablaufes werden in einer Protokolldatei aufgezeichnet und sind rekonstruierbar,
- **Datendatei,**
  alle Antworten einer Untersuchungsstichprobe werden in einer Datendatei gesammelt. Die Probandennummern können automatisch oder manuell vergeben werden. Die Datendatei enthält die festformatierte Ausgabe von Antwortwerten, Bearbeitungszeiten und Antworttexten.
- **Ergebnisdatei,**
  ein Formularprozessor ermöglicht die Ausgabe der indviduellen Untersuchungsergebnisse in eine Ergebnisdatei als frei gestaltbare Protokollformulare, wie Case-Report-Forms, Leistungsbescheinigungen, usw.

9. Literatur

Hippler, H.j., Meier, F. & Schwarz, N. (1988). Erste Erfahrungen mit der Erprobung eines interaktiven Befragungs- und Instruktionssystems (IBIS). ZUMA-Nachrichten 23, 79 - 91.

Meier, F. (1986). Zweistufige Parametrisierung digitaler Messungen in psychophysiologischen Langzeituntersuchungen. Zeitschrift für Arbeitswissenschaft, 40 (N.F.12), 13-18.

Meier, F. (1989a). Computergestützte Befragung in der Marktforschung und Verkaufsförderung mit dem interaktiven Informationssystem IBIS. Marktforschung & Management, 33, 14 - 18.

Meier, F. (1989b). Computerunterstützte Unterweisung in der Arbeitssicherheit. In: Ludborzs, B. (Hrsg.), Psychologie der Arbeitssicherheit. 4. Workshop 1988. Berufsgenossenschaft der chemischen Industrie. Heidelberg, Asanger, 119 - 126.

Simulation

Concepts of Simulation Languages

M. Möhring

summary:

The main topics in this paper are the presentation of criteria to characterize existing simulation systems and the introduction of some new ideas for future developments in this area. Starting from a general — desirable — system structure, the discussion is focussed on the two most important system components, the *model description* language and the *experimental frame*.

Describing simulation as a complex and interactive process for the validation and analysis of models, the development of a structured and interactive simulation environment is suggested in which all the components of a simulation system (e.g. model, model initialization, simulation parameter) can easily be combined. As a well suited realization of this kind of experimental frames, window-oriented user interfaces are introduced.

Simulation systems can be characterized, for instance, by the time base of models, the general software structure, and the conceptual distance between model design and model description. Beside the fact that for special applications, only simulation systems with a restricted modelling flexibility are necessary, there is a need for tools which cover a wide range of modelling techniques and at the same time do not burden the modeller with a lot of programming and implementation details. Some useful help can be given by new language paradigms, like those in functional and object-oriented programming languages. Some of these paradigms are considered in the model description language of MIMOSE, from which a short example is finally presented.

1 The structure of simulation systems

For the purpose of this paper we choose a frequent definition of *simulation*: "experimentation with models" [Korn/Wait 1978] or "the generation of temporal behavior of a model" [Zeigler 1976]. Therefore simulation is a method to analyze models, which does not result in a complete description of the model behavior — in contrast to analytic methods like the solving of differential equations — but merely in a trajectory of model states, calculated step-by-step over time. This temporal behavior depends on a limited set of circumstances under which the model is subjected to experimentation.

To support such a model analysis technique, real simulation systems should contain some basic components:

- a formal *model description* language

- an *experimental frame* for model validation and analysis, which allows

  - the initialization of model parameters
    (e.g. model attributes, model environment parameters),
  - the preparation of simulation runs
    (e.g. definition of time steps, interruption and termination points of a simulation),
  - the execution of simulation runs, and
  - the presentation of simulation results
    (e.g. graphics, statistics)

- general systems components
  (e.g. model, data, and method management, interfaces to external systems, facilities for system tests and maintenance)

Existing simulation systems consist more or less completely of these components, which are, however, not equally comfortable in their use. But most of these systems do not support an explicit separation of one component from the other, to give users a more structured view of the whole system and a better orientation within the different phases of the modelling and simulation process.

A second deficiency refers to the state of the art of experimental frames. In the past the development of simulation systems concentrated on the evolution and the improvement of the model description language. But performing modelling and simulation is a complex and highly interactive process, which requires a lot of simulation runs with different model structures and a high variation of model and simulation parameters. Therefore, the design and realization of the experimental frame is as important for a satisfying system usage as, for instance, a powerful model description language. Instead of the prevailing batch-oriented experimental frames, simulation systems need interactive user interfaces with flexible access to the different system components to combine and alter complete simulation models.

2 Classifications of simulation software

2.1 Time base of models

There exist many partly overlapping classification schemes for simulation systems (e.g. in [Zeigler 1976], [Kreutzer 1986], [Schmidt 1986], [Kheir 1988], [Hilty 1985]). One of the most frequently mentionend criteria is the time base on which model events occur.

- *continuous*
  A model is called a continuous time model when the model clock advances the time continuously through the real numbers (e.g. differential equation systems). Because of the discrete time organisation of computer systems, simulations of continuous models (e.g. in ACSL) must be "simulated" by choosing very small time intervals and the approximation of the model behavior within these intervals by special integration functions (e.g. Runge-Kutta).

- *discrete*
  In a discrete time model the time advances in jumps. A further distinction is made between *equidistant time intervals* as in systems which simulate difference equations (e.g. DYNAMO) and the initiation of time jumps by *events or processes* which occurs during the model behavior (e.g. queueing models in GPSS).

- *continuous/discrete*
  The strict distinction between continuous and discrete time models has its origin in their application within different sciences (e.g. continuous models in physics). It seems to be a better and a more realistic approach to combine both modelling techniques in one model, because reality consists of continiuous *and* discrete processes too (i.e if the continuous variable temperature in a technical process reaches a certain mark, it cause an discrete alarm). In simulation system combined models could be, for instance, realized on the bases of continuous models with additionally provided threshold functions (e.g. SLAM II).

2.2 General structure of software

Another criterion for the distinction of simulation systems is the way in which the software system is realized:

- *packages*
  Simulation facilities are provided by collections of functions like subroutine libraries, which are accessible through a separate main program (e.g. GASP, GPSS-FORTRAN, SICOS) or by extensions of an ordinary programming language (e.g. SIMPAS, TURBOSIM). The main advantage of packages is the flexibility to develop simulation programs and to adapt them to special user requirements, because the user works with the system

on a "source code" level. This includes the extension of system facilities by the user. On the contrary, working with these systems is difficult for unexperienced users, because it requires a good knowledge and experience of simulation programming.

- *languages*

  Modelling and simulation tasks are expressed by statements of an independent language (e.g. SIMSCRIPT, GPSS, DYNAMO, ACSL), which has neither the flexibility nor the complexity of an ordinary programming language. The restricted capabilities of languages allow a definite support of modelling and simulation (e.g. modelling techniques) in a more problem-oriented way. User-defined language extensions overcome these restrictions. Existing simulation languages, however, are not provided with this facility.

The development of simulation systems should combine the advantages of both approaches: The definition of a wide range of modelling and simulation problems in a flexible *and* problem-oriented way, including system extensions by the user.

2.3 Conceptual distance between model design and model description

The third criterion for the distinction of simulation systems refers to the difference between the process of developing a model, that is, to find an " 'appropriate' representation of structures and processes of a miniworld, instantiating some aspects of theory" [Kreutzer 1986, p. 3], and transforming it into the formalism of a concrete simulation system (Kreutzer calls it "model coding" [Kreutzer 1986, p. 4]). This description formalism, which the modeller has to consider, can have a greater or smaller distance to the model design process. A modeller therefore needs — besides some handling experience, which every user of software systems has to learn — special knowledge to perform a formal description for using the simulation facilities. The amount of the required knowledge depends on the simulation system and it has an important influence on the acceptance of such systems.

level 0: ordinary programming languages
(PASCAL, FORTRAN, C)
On this level the user gets neither support in modelling nor in simulation. But if he/she knows one of these languages, the development of flexible simulation programs for special needs is possible.

level 1: simulation support languages
(SIMULA, SIMSCRIPT, GASP)
These systems, which have almost the same power as those on the former level, additionally provide features to support some general simulation program facilities like program structuring components (e.g. classes in SIMULA) or random number generators.

level 2: modelling support languages
    (GPSS, GPSS-FORTRAN, SLAM, DYNAMO, CAPAS)
    Simulation systems on this level provide modelling and simulation facilities for special model classes (e.g. see [Troitzsch 1989]), like derivatives of continuous functions, integral functions to approximate continuous model behavior (see chapter 2.1) or queue, server and agenda structures to describe discrete event models.
    A more restricted usage on this level provide parameter-driven simu-la-tion systems in which the modeller "describes" a model by setting only its parameter values (e.g. the number of servers in CAPAS).
    The concentration of special modelling techniques diminishes the modelling flexibility of these systems, but for the supported techniques it provides a smaller distance to the model design process.

level 3: application support languages
    (RAILSIM, HOSPSIM, XCERT, CINEMA)
    Usually simulation is used for concrete applications (e.g. simulation of computer systems, manufacturing systems, chemical processes) on the bases of a modelling technique. For example, both a computer system and a manufacturing system could be modelled as a discrete event queueing system. Therefore, systems on this level concentrate on special modelling techniques, but they provide additional support to adapt these techniques for the application (e.g. application-oriented terminology, graphical presentation of models, execution of simulation by animation).

From level 0 up to 4 the user gets more and more support to develop his/her simulation program but at the same time the restrictions of the modelling flexibility increases as well. Beside the fact that special applications only need restricted but more problem-oriented simulation tools, another reason for the development of systems on level 2 and 3 is *efficiency*. Simulation covers a wide range of techniques with different requirements for the development of a software system. Systems for special simulation problems can be implemented more efficiently (speed, storage) than general tools (e.g. microsimulation needs the implementation of birth/death processes and the managment of populations with large numbers of members).

On the other hand, there is a need for simulation tools which cover a wide range of modelling techniques and at the same time do not burden the modeller with a lot of details which are not related to the subject of his research (Why should a social scientist have to know FORTRAN to use simulation?). Examples for this kind of applications are the exploration of collective phenomena, the behavior of chaotic systems or self-organizing processes (e.g. in [Weidlich/Haag 1983] [Troitzsch 1989] [Haken 1988]).

3 Trends in developing simulation systems

The preceding chapters pointed out requirements for the development of simulation systems. Referring to the general system structure, some suggestions to realize these requirements will be given.

The design of model description languages, which have a high degree of flexibility in using different modelling techniques and at the same time do not consider programming and implementation details by the user, requires new language concepts. Some useful help can be given by new programming language paradigms, like those in *functional languages* [Ebert 1986] and *object-oriented languages* [Stoyan/Görz], in which the user describes his applications in a more declarative form. This means to describe *what* the program should do rather than *how* it should be done.

Instead of a general description of these language paradigms, which cannot be given here, the realization of a specific language following some of these paradigms is introduced in the next chapter.

The demand for a simulation environment, which supports an explicit distinction of the system components and which at the same time allows a flexible, interactive combination of these components to simulation programs (e.g. model description, model initialization, simulation parameters) can be satisfied by a window- and menu-oriented user interface (e.g. DYNAMIS in [Häuslein/Nowak/Slottke]), to structure user input and system responses in different "logical screens". The following set of windows suggest a concrete realization of such an interface:

- *permanent windows*

    - model description (supported by a syntax editor)
    - model initialization with multiple initialization sets for each model
    - preparation of a simulation run with multiple parameter sets for each model
    - user workspace to define functions, to change model attribute values and parameter values during a simulation run, and to perform local calculations

- *temporary windows*

    - presentation of simulation results during and after simulation runs (statistics, graphics)
    - system messages (e.g. user errors)
    - interfaces to external systems (e.g. graphic system, statistical analysis systems, data base, operating system)
    - graphical representation of models

The integration of models, data (empirical, generated by simulation) and methods (e.g. for simulation and statistical analysis) in a uniform environment provides additional flexibility (as in [Klösgen/Schwarz/Honermeier]).

4 Model description in MIMOSE

MIMOSE (micro and multilevel modelling software) is a project to design and develop a modelling and simulation system[1], which satisfies some of the requirements mentioned in the preceding chapters. The greatest attention is given to the design of a flexible and powerful model description language, covering a wide range of model classes and at the same time supporting the model design process of the user. At this point only an overview of the main characteristics of this language can be given (for a broader description see [Möhring 1989]):

- uniform language concept
  (functional-applicative paradigm)

- small number of language constructs which can be easily combined

- dataflow-driven evaluation of expressions

- description of model objects and their relationship on different abstraction levels (e.g. individuals, groups, organizations)

- dynamic creation and deletion of model objects

- dynamic modification of object relationships

- interruption of simulation runs with modifications of model parameter values

- user defined functions

A model in MIMOSE consists of a set of different object types of which concrete objects will be created. Each object type again consists of a set of attributes which describe the possible state space of created objects. If an expression is assigned to an attribute, it is evaluated within every simulation step, generating new object states. Attributes without assigned expressions are called *constant* and they get a value once at the simulation start. The concrete relations between objects can vary within a simulation, because they are expressed by attribute definitions too.

The following figure shows an application of the model description language of MIMOSE. In the described model ([Weidlich/Haag 1983]) some individuals (*person*) can make a decision (*dec*), which is realized by user defined state transition functions (*my1, my2*). The decision of an individual depends on the decision of the same individual in the simulation step before (dec_1) and on the state ($state\_1$) of the whole population, which is described as a second object type (*pop*). The calculation of this population state, again depends on the decisions of all individuals. Thus, a feed-back mechanism between processes on an individual level and on the macro level *pop* is defined. The relations between the two object types are realized by attribute definitions too (*p, group*). The population attribute *out* denotes a dynamically growing list in which all generated

---
[1] MIMOSE is funded by the Deutsche Forschungsgemeinschaft (DFG) since November 1988

states of the population are stored.

```
pop :=
{
    out     : list of real
            := append(out_1, state);
    state   : real
            := (2 * number(group[$1.dec = pro])) /
               number(group) − 1;
    group   : list of person
};

person :=
{
    dec     : (pro,contra)
            := case dec_1 of
               pro : contra
                  if my1(p.state_1) < unif(0.0, 1.0) else pro;
               contra : pro
                  if my2(p.state_1) < unif(0.0, 1.0) else contra;
               end;
    p       : pop
}
```

$my1$: real → real
:= fct x to $ny * exp(-(pi + kappa * x))$ end;
$my2$: real → real
:= fct x to $ny * exp(pi + kappa * x)$ end;

Actually a first version of the MIMOSE language is implemented (C, UNIX). The design and development of a user interface, whose main characteristics are presented in chapter 3, has started and first results will be expected in 1990.

References

[Ebert 1986] J. Ebert. *Element funktionaler Programmiersprachen.* in: J. Perl (Hrsg.). Neue Konzepte von Programmiersprachen. Universität Mainz, 1986. Informatik-Bericht 1/86

[Haken 1988] H. Haken. *Information and self-organization: a macroscopic approach to computer systems.* Berlin: Springer, 1988.

[Häuslein/Nowak/Slottke] A. Häuslein, C. Nowak, K. Slottke. *Modellbildung mit System Dynamics am Beispiel der Eutrophierung eines Sees.* in: B. Page (Hrsg.). Informatik im Umweltschutz. München: Oldenbourg, 1986. S. 251–283.

[Hilty 1985] L. Hilty. *Benutzergerechte Modellierungssysteme.* Universität Hamburg. Fachbereich Informatik. Diplomarbeit 1985.

[Kheir 1988] N.A. Kheir. *System modelling and computer simulation.* New York: Dekker, 1988.

[Klösgen/Schwarz/Honermeier] W. Klösgen, W. Schwarz, A. Honermeier. *Modellbanksystem (MBS).* Bonn: GMD, 1983. Arbeitspapiere der GMD, Nr. 32.

[Korn/Wait 1978] G.A. Korn, J.V. Wait. *Digital Continous-System Simulation.* Englewood Cliffs: Prentice-Hall, 1978.

[Kreutzer 1986] W. Kreutzer. *System Simulation. Programming Styles and Languages.* Sydney: Addison-Wesley, 1986

[Möhring 1989] M. Möhring. *MIMOSE — Eine funktionale Sprache zur Beschreibung und Simulation individuellen Verhaltens in interagierenden Populationen.* in: H. Kreutz (Hrsg.). 3. Symposium zur Sozialwissenschaftlichen Computersimulation, Nürnberg, 28.6.–30.6.88. Opladen: Leske + Budrich, 1989.

[Schmidt 1986] B. Schmidt. *Classification of simulation software.* in: Journal of mathematical modelling and simulation. 3(1986)2. S. 133–140.

[Stoyan/Görz] H. Stoyan, G. Görz. *Was ist objektorientierte Programmierung?.* in: H. Stoyan, H. Wedekind. Objektorientierte Software- und Hardwarearchitekturen. Stuttgart: Teubner, 1983. S.9–31.

[Troitzsch 1989] K.G. Troitzsch. *Modellbildung und Simulation in den Sozialwissenschaften.* Opladen: Westdeutscher Verlag, 1989.

[Weidlich/Haag 1983] W. Weidlich, G. Haag. *Concepts and Models o a Semi-Quantitative Sociology.* Berlin: Springer, 1983.

[Zeigler 1976] B. Zeigler. *Theory of modelling and simulation.* Malabar: Krieger, 1985, 1976.

F. Faulbaum, R. Haux und K.-H. Jöckel (Hrsg.) (1990). SoftStat '89
Fortschritte der Statistik-Software 2. Stuttgart: Gustav Fischer, 426 - 433

IPMOS - Ein Softwarewerkzeug zur Mikromodellierung und Simulation interagierender Populationen

A. Flache und V. Schmidt

Summary

This paper describes the approach of a " Quantitative Sociology " (Weidlich and Haag, 1983) shortly. Using a simple migration model of Weidlich and Haag as an example, we introduce our software tool IPMOS for the modeling and simulation of this class of micromodels and give an impression of its usage and abilities.

1 Ursprung und Merkmale des Ansatzes

Michael Möhring stellt in seinem Vortrag unterschiedliche Methoden der formalen Modellierung sozialer Systeme vor. Wir werden im folgenden näher auf den Ansatz eingehen, den Wolfgang Weidlich und Günther Haag 1983 unter dem Titel „ Concepts and Models of a Quantitative Sociology, The Dynamics of Interacting Populations " (Weidlich, Haag, 1983) präsentierten. Es handelt sich dabei um stochastische 2 - Ebenen Modelle mit diskretem Zustandsraum, deren Zustandsänderung sich in diskreten Zeitschritten vollzieht.

„ The Dynamics of Interacting Populations " ist eine Anwendung des, von Haken zunächst für die Naturwissenschaften (Haken, 1977) entwickelten, Konzeptes der Synergetik auf die Sozialwissenschaften. „ Synergetics, an interdisciplinary field of research, is concerned with the cooperation of individual parts of a system that produces macroscopic spatial, temporal or functional structures. It deals with deterministic as well as stochastic processes " (Haken in : Weidlich, Haag, 1983).

2 Das Konzept der 'Quantitativen Sociology'

2.1 Elemente der Modellbeschreibung und deren Formalisierung

Weidlich und Haag betrachten *Individuen* als kleinste Einheit sozialer Systeme. Für alle Individuen bestehen dieselben, endlich vielen, verschiedenen Verhaltensmöglichkeiten, die den „ *attitude space* " bilden. Bei einem einfachen Migrationsmodell könnte dieser individuelle Einstellungsraum z.B. eine Dimension ' Gebiet ' mit den Ausprägungen ' Süd ' und ' Nord ' haben. In der formalen IPMOS Notation wird dies ausgedrückt durch :
gebiet[süd , nord] .

Es gibt aber auch individuelle Eigenschaften, die nicht in dieser Weise als Einstellung modellierbar sind, etwa die Bereitschaft den Wohnort zu wechseln, oder die Neigung, sich den Mehrheitsverhältnissen anzupassen. Als *Population* wird daher die Menge aller Individuen betrachtet, die in diesen Eigenschaften übereinstimmen. D.h., die Individuen innerhalb einer Population unterscheiden sich nur durch ihre Position im Einstellungsraum. Zu einer formalen Modellbeschreibung gehört somit die Aufzählung der Populationsnamen (s. Bild 1).
Um den Zustand eines Systems vollständig zu beschreiben, ist es erforderlich für jede Population die Verteilung der Individuen im Einstellungsraum anzugeben. Bei dem einfachen Migrationsmodell mit 2 Populationen ist diese „ *socio-configuration* " ein 4 - Tupel $(x_{11}, x_{12}, x_{21}, x_{22})$ wobei x_{ij} die Anzahl der Individuen der Population i mit Einstellung j (Süd = 1, Nord = 2) angibt.
Die Soziokonfiguration beschreibt den Systemzustand, aber nicht, wie er sich ändert. Die Dynamik des Systems beruht darauf, daß in jedem Zeitschritt ein Individuum zufällig ausgewählt und untersucht wird, ob und wie dieses Individuum seine Einstellung ändert. Die individuellen Einstellungsänderungen bestimmen also die Veränderung des Systemzustandes. Wandert z.B. ein Individuum der Population 1 von Süd nach Nord, so verändert sich die Soziokonfiguration von $(x_{11}, x_{12}, x_{21}, x_{22})$ zu $(x_{11}-1, x_{12}+1, x_{21}, x_{22})$.

Wann findet ein solcher Einstellungswechsel statt ? Die Wahrscheinlichkeit μ_{ij} für einen Übergang von Einstellung i zu Einstellung j ist eine Funktion des aktuellen Systemzustandes und der Eigenschaften des Individuums, d.h. der Population, zu der es gehört.
Es ist also zur Beschreibung eines Modells erforderlich, für jede Population und jeden möglichen Übergang eine *Übergangswahrscheinlichkeitsfunktion* anzugeben. Die Wahrscheinlichkeit μ_{ii} auf einem Einstellungspunkt zu verharren, kann dabei aus der Gegenwahrscheinlichkeit zu einem Einstellungswechsel bestimmt werden : $\mu_{ii} = 1 - \sum_{i \neq j} \mu_{ij}$ (i fest, j über alle Einstellungspunkte variierend). In unserem Beispiel sind also 4 Funktionen anzugeben, für jede der beiden Populationen die Funktionen für μ_{12} und μ_{21}.
Wie kann eine solche Funktion aussehen ? Zur Erleichterung der mathematischen Formulierung soll zunächst der Zustand p_i einer Population i durch den Index :

$$p_i = \frac{x_{i2} - x_{i1}}{x_{i1} + x_{i2}}$$

ausgedrückt werden. $p_i = -1$ bedeutet dann, daß alle Individuen der Population i im Gebiet Süd wohnen, $p_i = +1$ das Gegenteil und $p_i = 0$ Gleichverteilung.
Die individuellen Eigenschaften gehen in die Funktionen über sogenannte *Trendparameter* ein, in diesem Falle ν, φ, κ und δ. Für eine detaillierte Interpretation der Parameter s. (Weidlich, Haag, 19^3, S.95).
Die nicht - lineare Funktion $\mu_{12} = \nu \exp(\varphi + \kappa p_1 + \delta p_2)$ beschreibt nun mathematisch, daß (solange κ und δ positiv sind) die Individuen dazu neigen das zu tun, was die Mehrheit tut. Entsprechend ist $\mu_{21} = \nu \exp(-(\varphi + \kappa p_1 + \delta p_2))$.
Dabei bestimmen die Parameter κ und δ die Stärke dieser Anpassungsneigungen, die man auch als interne (κ) und externe (δ) Sympathie, bzw. bei negativen Werten Antipathie, bezeichnen kann.
Bild 1 zeigt eine vollständige Modelldefinition für das behandelte Beispiel in der IPMOS Eingabesprache. Der Text zwischen zwei „ # " ist Kommentar, der vom Programm nicht verarbeitet wird.

```
# Einfaches Migrationsmodell mit 2 Populationen und    #
# 2 Gebieten,       vgl. Weidlich/Haag 1983            #


# Populationsnamen #  population1;population2.

# Einstellungsraum #  gebiet[sued,nord].

# Standardnummerierung des Einstellungsraumes : #
# sued = 1 #
# nord = 2 #

# Trendparameter : #

# Flexibilitaet #                       ny;
# Praeferenz ( phi ) #                  p;
# interne Sympathie (kappa) #           k;
# externe Sympathie (delta) #           d;
# Index fuer Zustand der Population 1 # pop1;
# Index fuer Zustand der Population 2 # pop2;

# pop1 und pop2 muessen durch die Initialisierung dieser    #
# ' Parameter ' so definiert werden, dass gilt :            #
# Fuer beide Indizes heisst -1 : Alle Individuen sind in ' sued ' #
#                            0 : Gleiche Zahl in beiden Gebieten #
#                            1 : Alle Individuen sind in ' nord ' #
```

```
# Uebergangswahrscheinlichkeiten  :  #


# Population 1 : #

# 1 -> 2 #   ny * exp( + ( p + k * pop1 + d * pop2));
# 2 -> 1 #   ny * exp( - ( p + k * pop1 + d * pop2));


# Population 2    #

# 1 -> 2 #   ny * exp( + ( p + k * pop2 + d * pop1));
# 2 -> 1 #   ny * exp( - ( p + k * pop2 + d * pop1));
```

Modelldefinition als IPMOS Eingabe
Bild 1

Mit dieser Eingabe ist nur die Modellstruktur festgelegt, für die vollständige Beschreibung des dynamischen Verhaltens ist noch eine Modellinitialisierung erforderlich, die eine Anfangssoziokonfiguration und für jede Population Werte der definierten Parameter umfaßt.
In IPMOS können die Parameter auch als Funktionen der Zeit, der Soziokonfiguration und anderer Parameter initialisiert werden.

2.2 Bedeutung und Reichweite des Ansatzes

Offensichtlich kann mit diesem Formalismus nur ein Teil der relevanten Aspekte sozialer Systeme befriedigend modelliert werden :

- Der individuelle Einstellungsraum muß relativ klein sein, da die Anzahl der zu definierenden Übergangswahrscheinlichkeitsfunktionen quadratisch mit der Größe des Einstellungsraumes wächst.

- Die Individualität der ' Individuen ' ist begrenzt, denn es kann , abgesehen von stochastischen Einflüssen, nur soviel unterschiedliche Verhaltensweisen geben, wie es Elemente der Soziokonfiguration gibt (Produkt aus Populationszahl und Größe des Einstellungsraumes).

Dennoch erlaubt es dieser Ansatz „ a principle insight into the role and effect of certain trends " (Weidlich, Haag, 1983, S.15) für die Dynamik eines Systems zu bekommen, was im folgenden noch an Beispielen deutlich werden soll.
Ein anderes Problem besteht darin, daß bei mathematisch schwierigen Funktionen die analytische Ermittlung der Modelldynamik oft nicht mehr möglich ist. In dieser Situation kann ein Simulationswerkzeug weiterhelfen.

3 IPMOS

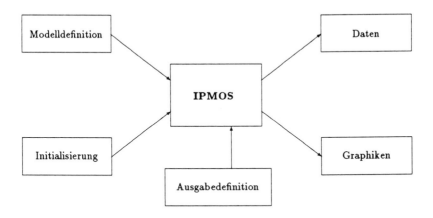

Bild 2

Bild 2 zeigt, was IPMOS im wesentlichen tut. Das Definieren, Initialisieren und Simulieren eines Modells kann im Dialog mit dem Programm erfolgen. Graphische Ausgaben werden während des Simulationslaufes erzeugt, können aber auch später wieder aus den abgespeicherten Simulationsergebnissen rekonstruiert werden.
Mit ' Ausgabedefinition ' ist gemeint, daß die Darstellung von Graphiken und die Art der ausgegebenen Daten vom Benutzer variiert werden kann. Genauere Informationen über den Umgang mit IPMOS können dem Benutzerhandbuch entnommen werden (Flache, Schmidt, 1988).

4 Simulationsergebnisse am Beispiel des Migrationsmodells

In diesem Abschnitt soll gezeigt werden, was für Informationen über das dynamische Verhalten eines Modells durch die Simulation gewonnen werden können.
In einem ersten Simulationslauf haben die Parameter κ und δ in beiden Populationen relativ niedrige Werte, wobei in Population 2 δ negativ ist. D.h., daß die Individuen der Population 2 die Angehörigen ihrer eigenen Population ' mögen ', also mit möglichst vielen von diesen zusammen wohnen möchten, die der anderen hingegen nicht.
Bild 3 zeigt die Trajektorien von 5 identischen Systemen mit der Anfangssoziokonfiguration (70,30,70,30).
Trotz der Antipathie der Individuen der Population 2 gegen die der Population 1 bewegen sich alle Systeme in die Umgebung des Zustandes (50,50,50,50) und verlassen diese auch nicht mehr. Nach endlicher Zeit hat also die Wahrscheinlichkeitsdichtefunktion des Systemverhaltens ein Maximum in diesem Punkt. Verstärkt man die Sympathien und Antipathien ($\kappa = 1.2$, $\delta = 1.0$), so ergibt sich ein vollkommen anderes Verhalten (Bild 4). Jetzt fliehen die Individuen von Population 2 vor ' den anderen ', jene wiederum folgen ihnen nach, was auf einen stabilen Grenzzyklus führt, auf dem sich das System nach endlicher Zeit bewegt.

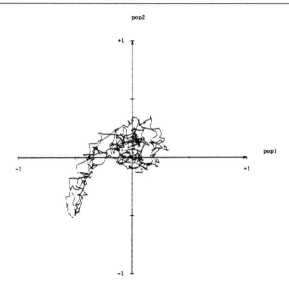

Dynamik des Migrationsmodells bei niedrigen Sympathie- und Antipathiewerten
Bild 3

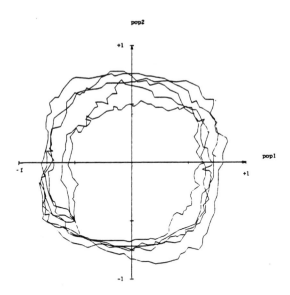

Dynamik des Migrationsmodells bei hohen Sympathie- und Antipathiewerten
Bild 4

Diese Ergebnisse könnten auch ohne Simulation ermittelt werden, Weidlich und Haag zeigen sogar, wie auf analytischem Wege die stationäre Wahrscheinlichkeitsdichtefunktion des Systemverhaltens bestimmt werden kann, was weitaus mehr Informationen über die Dynamik des Systems liefert, als eine Simulation. Für die analytische Methode ist es aber wichtig, daß die Übergangswahrscheinlichkeiten günstige mathematische Eigenschaften haben, wie z.B. Exponential- oder lineare Funktionen. Im nächsten Beispiel ist diese Bedingung nach Kenntnis der Autoren nicht mehr erfüllt. Die Übergangswahrscheinlichkeiten von Population 1 sollen unverändert bleiben, die von Population 2 eine kompliziertere Struktur erhalten :

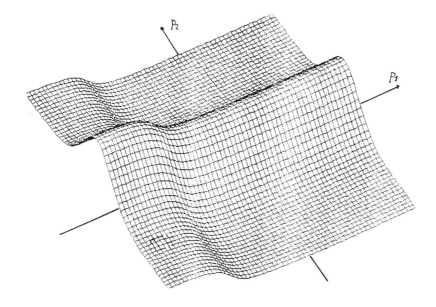

Geänderte Übergangswahrscheinlichkeit μ_{12}
für ein Individuum der Population 2 :

$$\mu_{12} = \nu \left(\frac{1}{\sqrt{2\pi\kappa}} \exp(-\frac{1}{2}\frac{p_2{}^2}{\kappa}) + \nu_{ex} \left(\arctan(-\delta(p_1 + \varphi_{ex})) + \frac{1}{2}\pi \right) \right.$$

Bild 5

Das durch diese Funktion beschriebene Verhalten ist etwa : ' Die anderen stören mich nicht, solange sie nicht zuviele werden, meine eigenen Leute stören mich nicht, wenn sie viel oder wenig sind '. Wir haben diese Funktion natürlich nicht wegen der (fragwürdigen) soziologischen Bedeutung gewählt, sondern um die Komplexität der Ausdrücke zu demonstrieren, die mit IPMOS verwendet werden können.
Die Rolle der Parameter κ und δ entspricht etwa der bei den vorherigen Funktion. Daher wurden für den ersten Simulationslauf wieder niedrige Werte gewählt, und es zeigt sich eine Dynamik, die der des ersten Modells ähnelt (Bild 6). Die Erhöhung der Sympathien und Antipathien führt dazu, daß die Systeme wieder in einen Zyklus geraten, diesen Zyklus aber teilweise verlassen um dem Zustand (50,50,50,50) zuzustreben (Bild 7). Durch Erhöhung der Anzahl der Realisierungen und Verlängerung der Simulationszeit könnte ein genaueres Bild der Dynamik gewonnen werden, all dies ist mit Hilfe von IPMOS ebenfalls möglich.

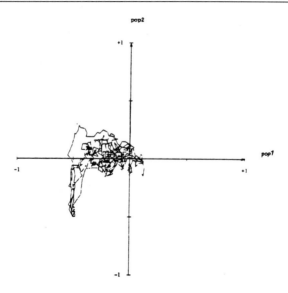

Dynamik des geänderten Modells bei niedrigen Sympathie- und Antipathiewerten
Bild 6

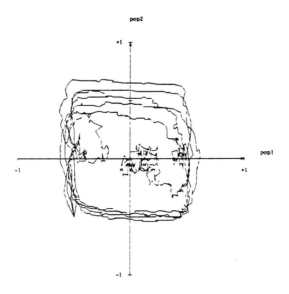

Dynamik des geänderten Modells bei hohen Sympathie- und Antipathiewerten
Bild 7

5 Abschließende Bemerkungen

- Unsere Beschreibung des Modellierungskonzeptes von Weidlich und Haag ist bereits auf die Umsetzung in eine Modellbeschreibungssprache hin orientiert. Daher bestehen gewisse Unterschiede zum Originalansatz, z.B. sind Differentialgleichungen für veränderliche Trendparameter im Modellbeschreibungsformalismus von IPMOS nicht vorgesehen.

- Nicht alle Möglichkeiten, die dieser Ansatz bzw. IPMOS bieten, konnten in diesem Rahmen vorgestellt werden. Z.B. können auch Geburts- und Todesprozesse modelliert werden, oder Wechsel von einer Population zur anderen.

- Diese Modelle sind nicht dafür gedacht, Vorhersagen über das Verhalten realer sozialer Systeme zu machen. Dafür ist die Komplexität, die auf sinnvolle Weise noch beschrieben werden kann, viel zu gering. Wie wir hoffen gezeigt zu haben, kann aber ein qualitatives Verständnis der Rolle individueller Eigenschaften in der Interaktion von Populationen gewonnen oder vertieft werden.

- Obwohl weitaus mächtigere Simulationswerkzeuge existieren bzw. entwickelt werden, wie z.B. MIMOSE (vgl. Vortrag v. Möhring), ist IPMOS speziell für diese Klasse formaler Mikromodelle ein flexibles und leicht anwendbares Instrument, zumal es auf den allermeisten PC (IBM Standard) lauffähig ist und ein Simulationslauf der oben beschriebenen Art, je nach Hardwarekonfiguration, c. 5 - 15 min dauert.

Weitere Informationen über das Programm, oder das Programm selbst, sind über die Autoren oder Prof. Dr. Klaus G. Troitzsch, EWH Koblenz erhältlich.

6 Literatur

1. Weidlich, Wolfgang, Günther Haag
   „Concepts and Models of a Quantitative Sociology.
   The Dynamics of Interacting Populations"
   Berlin/Heidelberg/New York 1983

2. Haken, Herrman
   „Synergetics, an Introduction "
   Berlin/Heidelberg/New York 1977

3. Flache, Andreas, Vera Schmidt
   „ Benutzerhandbuch IPMOS "
   in : dies. , „ IPMOS ", Studienarbeit EWH Koblenz 1988

Current Status and Developments in Microsimulation Software

O. Hellwig

1. Introduction

Microanalytic simulation models were suggested by Orcutt as early as 1957. This type of model ages a microdata base which is a sample of micro-units (e.g. persons and households) by using behavioural assumptions (e.g. marriage probabilities and consumption functions). The aged microdata base is then analyzed in order to generate the results of interest. Although microanalytic simulation is a general modelling paradigm almost all applications relate to households or firms for which demographic and socio-economic aspects are modelled.

Microanalytic simulation models impose high requirements on their software (the microsimulator):
- efficiency since the microdata bases typically contain between 10.000 and 150.000 persons with 50 to 200 variables each. In addition the modelling is often complex as well as comprehensive.
- flexibility since with changing applications generally the modelling and often the microdata base change.
- portability because the development of a microsimulator is quite expensive. For this reason microsimulators are mostly used over a long period of time on changing computer equipment.
- user-friendliness because the programs are generally used by the modellers or by analysts who are social scientists rather then programers.
- low cost of development.

For these reasons software has been a major limiting factor for the further dissemination and application of microanalytic models. Partly for the same reason and partly because of modelling problems simplified types of microanalytic models have been developed, see Krupp and Wagner (1982) and Hellwig (to be published). The main types of microanalytic models are:
- dynamic aging models are the original proposal of Orcutt and explicitly simulate the demographic processes which are difficult to program since the structure of the microdata base changes during the simulation. For example, when simulating death a person has to be deleted, at marriage persons interact and form new households etc., cf. Hellwig (1989). Dynamic aging models are typically comprehensive and simulate demographic processes, education, workforce participation, income, taxes, social security, consumption and savings. However, a few models are restricted to demographic processes.

- static aging models simulate the demographic processes implicitly by using weighting factors for the persons and households which adjust the microdata base to some exogenous forecast of the population, cf. Bungers (1981). For this reason, static aging models can be used for short to medium range forecasts only. These models are typically partial models, simulating only the process of primary interest in an explicit way. In most cases this is social security or the income tax law, which are then modelled in very great detail.
- longitudinal models are a special subtype of dynamic aging models. Here each person is completely processed (for all simulation periods) before the next person is simulated. By contrast, the ordinary dynamic aging models simulate the complete microdata base for one period after the other, these models are also called cross sectional models.

2. Survey on microsimulators

Now we will briefly describe some microsimulators. Beforehand a few recommendations for additional reading seem appropriate. An interesting report on software aspects of some major US microsimulators was provided by Pankoke-Babatz (1980a). Krupp and Wagner (1982) include a good survey of microanalytic models, but software aspects are not covered. Many microsimulation models are presented in Havemann and Hollenbeck (1980) and Orcutt et al. (1986). However, in most cases no information is given for the software. In order to get such information one has to consult technical working papers and documentations. More general work on problems of microsimulation software can be found in Klösgen (1986) and Müller (1986). In selecting a few microsimulators to be described here, we concentrate on software which is still in use. However, some lessons can be learned from experience made with some of the earlier implementations.

1. SUSSEX was the first microsimulator and was developed from 1957 to 1961 for the U.S.A., cf. Orcutt et al. (1961). The object of the project was to demonstrate that dynamic microanalytic simulation models are computationally feasible. The program was written in ASSEMBLER on an IBM 704 with 8192 words of core storage and the same "amount" of disk storage. The simulation of only a few demographic processes required about 1 hour of CPU for one simulation period and 7788 persons.
2. RIM was the second static microsimulator (the tax model of the treasury department was the first one, see Harris (1977)) and was developed for the U.S.A. in 1968, cf. McClung (1970). RIM was developed by the President's Commission on Income Maintenance for the analysis of alternative income transfer plans. It was programmed under great time pressure and had been reprogrammed several times in order to simulate the many alternative plans. The hasty development and constant reprogramming led to some programming errors. For this reason the Urban Institute, which took the microsimulator in house, decided to develop a new microsimulator: TRIM.
3. TRIM, a redesign of RIM, was developed from 1971 to 1973 at the Urban Institute, cf. McClung et al. 1971. The major aim of the development was flexibility. However, in order to reach this goal to a

large extent the software became very complicated. This in turn reduced the flexibility as the programs were quite difficult to understand and therefore to modify. For this reason the system was redesigned a second time (TRIM2) from 1978 to 1980, cf. Webb et al. 1987. The primary goal was to make the system easy to understand. TRIM, or TRIM2, has been in almost constant operation, and many projects have been carried out using it. Altogether several million Dollars have been invested in TRIM. The program is tailored to the needs of the Urban Institute. It is written in FORTRAN, ASSEMBLER and COBOL and requires only 1 to 10 minutes CPU for 180.000 persons on a IBM 3090. There are several off-shoots of TRIM, e.g. MATH see Beebout (1977) and KGB, see Betson et al (1980).

4. DYNASIM, the first comprehensive dynamic microsimulation model, was developed for the USA from 1969 to 1976, mainly at the Urban Institute, cf. Orcutt et al 1976. The first implementation, called MASH, see Sadowski (1977) was a sophisticated, comfortable, interactive system but too slow for professional application. It was written in FORTRAN, ASSEMBLER and COBOL and required several hours to be processed on a PDP 10. MASH can be considered to be a microsimulation shell to some degree. Later DYNASIM was implemented as MASS, cf. Orcutt and Glazer (1980) and as MICROSIM, cf. McKay (1978). These are simplified and more efficient systems programmed mainly in PL/1 for IBM 360/370 computers. Especially MICROSIM is a very modular system and seems to be quite flexible and easy to understand. On the other hand almost no user comfort is provided. MASS and especially MICROSIM have been used for a couple of applications. In addition MICROSIM has been taken in house and applied by some ministries. The system have been dormant for a few years. Some years ago, DYNASIM2 was developed by the Urban Institute, see Wertheimer et al (1986). This system is a combined cross-sectional and longitudinal microsimulator and therefore is more efficient than purely cross-sectional models. As with static models, this type of microanalytic simulation model was developed mainly for computational reasons. In other words, the possibilities of modelling are restricted due to technical restriction of required computer time. The hope of Sadowski (1977) that through the rapid development of hardware even costly microsimulators could be processed in reasonable time obviously did not become reality. Computers certainly became much faster, but new versions of operating systems and compilers use up a share of the additional power. Furthermore the microdata bases and models became bigger and bigger so that the required CPU times were not reduced as much as had been anticipated.

5. BAFPLAN is a static micromodel for analysis and policy evaluation of the German Training Assistance Act. It was developed by the non-profit research corporation for mathematics and computing, GMD, for a ministry, cf. Bungers and Quinke (1986). The model is programmed in FORTRAN and imbedded in the model bank system MBS which supports model and data management, model execution and result generation. BAFPLAN is constantly updated by the GMD and continuously used by some analysts of the ministry. However, some analysts prefer having the simulations performed by the staff of the GMD. One simulation run takes only a few minutes on a SIEMENS 7541 when using 10.000 persons. The developers of BAFPLAN argue that short run times and excellent

support for simulations are essential for acceptance by policy makers as the results generally have to be available within a few hours to a few days in order to be used in political discussions. The GMD has also developed a static microsimulator named APF for analysis of family allowances by another ministry, cf. Quinke (1988). APF is imbedded in MBS just as BAFPLAN is.

DPMS, a dynamic microsimulation model was developed for West Germany between 1980 to 1986 at Darmstadt University, cf. Heike, Hellwig and Kaufmann (1987) and Hellwig (1989). The project is aimed at methodological studies of micro modelling and microsimulation software. The microsimulator was developed using the techniques of software engineering, e.g. task-oriented design, centralization and localisation, structured and standardized programming and data hiding. Furthermore, several program levels have been created through hierarchical structuring. It can be viewed as a microsimulation shell to a certain degree. For these reasons the microsimulator is quite flexible and portable. It has been running on various computers such as VAX, UNIVAC and IBM and has been transferred to the Hungarian Central Statistical Office, which used it as a base to develop a dynamic microsimulator for Hungary. This proves the high standard of quality of the DPMS. However, the microsimulator is very complex and therefore difficult to handle, cf. Hellwig (1989). Our experience seems to have been quite similar to that of the Urban Institute with TRIM, see point 3 above. The microsimulator is programmed in pseudo code and implemented in FORTRAN. It requires 45 minutes CPU for 127.000 persons and one simulation year on a UNIVAC 1100/91. The demographic modules of the DPMS have recently been transferred to an IBM XT. The complete DPMS would run approx. 68 hours for 127.000 persons on a IBM XT. Using a 386 type processor perhaps one could run the microsimulator within 24 hours. This would be about the same time as the elapsed time on a mainframe: jobs of about one hour CPU are generally processed over night. However, dynamic microsimulation models are often used for long-term projections of 20 to 50 years. While such a run could be processed on a mainframe over a weekend, a PC would require almost 2 months.

CORSIM is the first dynamic microsimulator designed for a PC and was developed from 1986 to 1987 for the U.S.A., cf. Caldwell (1987). It aims to support the development of economic theory. CORSIM is programmed in C and is userfriendly as it is menu driven. 20 minutes are required to process 20.000 persons for one simulation year on a 386 desktop. However, modelling is yet not very differentiated or comprehensive. A more complete micro model would certainly require much more time. The development of the microsimulator as well as of the micro modell (which is based on DYNASIM2) are continuing.

The HCSO dynamic microsimulator has been being developed from 1984 to the present time by the Hungarian Central Statistical Office, cf. Zafir (1987) and Cicsman and Papp (1987). This project was supported by the Darmstadt microsimulation group, cf. Hellwig (1989). A multipurpose utilization of the microsimulator is planned: policy exploration and forecasting, substitution of surveys (that is, the time between taking a specific survey will be increased. For the years for which no survey is available the last survey, aged by the microsimulator, will be used), correction and merging of survey data. Aims of the software are flexibility (because many different applications are planned) and user-friendliness (as the users are mainly social scientists and statisticians with very little experience in programming). The microsimulator is based on the DPMS software and is programmed in FORTRAN, PL/1 and ASSEMBLY and uses the relational data base RAPID. 1 hour CPU is required on an IBM 4361. RAPID proved to be too slow and will be replaced by direct access files. This coincides with some earlier experiments with file-handling systems for microsimulation, see Hellwig (1989). There the use of sequential files or, at the most, direct-access files with a self-programmed specific system to handle pointer variables were suggested. Applications include an analysis of the proposed income tax for the Ministry of Finance and an analysis of family aid. The development of microanalytic models for the health-care system and for private companies is planned. It is hoped that the existing microsimulator for households can be adapted for these tasks.

9. NEDYMAS, a dynamic microanalytic model for the Netherlands has been being developed from 1985 to the present, cf. Nelissen (1987). The model is aimed at analysis of the redistributive impact of social security on life-time income. However, NEDYMAS is a quite comprehensive model and can be used for analysis of other topics as well. The program ist rather compactly coded in ALGOL 68 and requires 6 minutes CPU for 10.000 persons on a VAX 8.700.

10. SPSD/M is a static microsimulator developed by Statistics Canada from 1984 until recently cf. Statistics Canada (no date). SPSD/M is based on anonymized micro-data and models taxes and transfer income. The microsimulator is programmed in C for PC's with MS-DOS and requires 8 minutes on a COMPAQ 386/25 for 160.000 persons having compressed the data from 70 MB to 5 MB. An outstanding feature of SPSD/M is that it can be bought for $ 5000 (including the microdata base) from Statistics Canada. In addition, Statistics Canada has developed a longitudinal demographic microsimulator, cf. Wolfson (1989a) and has just started the development of a dynamic cross-sectional microsimulator, cf. Wolfson (1989b).

Other major microsimulation projects are the well-known German "Frankfurt Model" of the Sfb3, cf. Galler (1988) and Sfb3 (1989) and the Swedish MOSES, the only micro-analytic model of the firm sector, cf. Eliasson (1985). DEMOD is a new development for Cechoslovakia, cf. Vano (1988). Furthermore the tax ministries of most industrialized countries use static tax models, cf. Lietmeyer (1986). In addition tax simulations are performed at many universities and research institutions . A great variety of dynamic microsimulators (cross-sectional as well as longitudinal models) has been developed for purely demographic analyses, cf. Orcutt et al. (1976), p. 11. Typically these microsimulators are specially tailored programs having as their major aim computing efficiency. Most of these models had only a few academic applications and then seem to have vanished.

3. Summary and outlook

To sum up, microanalytic models cause a great computational burden, they have a common structure and many functions (e.g. for Monte Carlo simulation) are generally used. However, there are several subtypes of models and the modelling greatly differs for the various projects. Microsimulation software was developed in most cases under great time pressure and was specially tailored for the specific modelling project at hand, whereby sophisticated techniques of software engineering were rarely used.

Almost all microsimulators under review are more or less specially tailored programs. Most microsimulators have been developed by the modellers (who are generally social scientists) or by programmers rather then by computer specialists with a higher degree in informatics. Only very few models are implemented using more advanced software or a somewhat more general microsimulation software which was developed for them. The model bank system MBS well supports the static microsimulators BAFPLAN and APF. It is to be doubted whether MBS in its current form can support comprehensive dynamic models efficiently.

None of the existing microsimulators is based on a general simulation language such as SIMULA or on a general simulation package such as GPSS. First, the efficiency of such tools is considered to be insufficient for microanalytic models and, second, most functions required for these models are not supported by general simulation software, cf. Hellwig (1989). Also, a specific microsimulation language, cf. the proposal of Pankoke-Babatz (1980b), has not been developed. Conventional program languages have generally been used to develop specially tailored programs. A few relatively simple static micro models are implemented using a statistical package such as SPSS or SAS. Recent work has started to use object-oriented programming languages for simulation models, cf. Zeigler (1987) and Möhring (1989). For reasons of efficiency microanalytic simulation models will not be able to work in such programming environments which are based on object-oriented languages within the near future. However, I hope that the outstanding capabilities of such languages can be used for the development of microsimulators in the long run.

Advanced tools have rarely been used for the development of microsimulators, as has been described above. As a result, existing microsimulators have rarely been taken over by new microsimulation projects. Each project group had to program their own microsimulator. Some exceptions are reported for the USA where some models have been implemented through personnal transfer. That is, some institutions have hired microsimulation specialists who brought microsimulators with them and used this software to create a new microsimulator. It is to be hoped that recent advances in software quality of microsimulators continue so that new microsimulation projects do not have to keep reinventing the wheel and programming the microsimulators from scratch.

For the near future I expect that most microsimulators will continue to use conventional program languages and mainframe computers. The application of techniques of software engineering hopefully will increase. Future work should concentrate on creating an efficient, portable and flexible microsimulation shell rather than on specific microsimulators. Such a system (MBS, see point 5 above) already exists for static micromodelsd. The task of developing a shell for dynamic micromodels will be more demanding than doing so for static micromodels.

PC's will increasingly be used for static micromodels. These programs are typically written in C or in Pascal, the program languages which are mainly used on PC's. I expect that dynamic microsimulators will not be run on PC's within the near future with the following exceptions: partial models (e.g. for demographic analyses) and methodologic studies (possibly with reduced microdata bases) without extreme time pressure. Perhaps work stations will prove to be a good alternative to mainframes.

References

Beebout, H. (1977): Microsimulation as a Policy Tool: The MATH Model, Policy Analysis Series No. 14, Mathematica Policy Research Inc., Washington, D.C.

Betson, D., Greenberg, D., Kasten, R. (1980): A Microsimulation Model for Analyzing Alternative Welfare Reform Proposals: An Application to the Program for Better Jobs and Income, in Haveman and Hollenbeck (1980).

Bungers, D. (1981): Microanalytic Simulation Models as Tools for Legislative, Simulation 36:4, 111-118.

Bungers, D., Quinke, H. (1986): A Microsimulation Model for the German Federal Training Assistance Act-Principles, Problems and Experiences, in Orcutt et al. (1986).

Caldwell, S. (1987): How Can Microsimulation Help Develop Better Theories?, (presented at the International Workshop for Demographic Microsimulation of the IIASA, Budapest, to appear in the forthcoming proceedings).

Cicsman, J., Papp, E. (1987): The Software Prepared for the Household Statistics Microsimulation in the HCSO, (presented at the International Workshop for Demographic Microsimulation of the IIASA, Budapest, to appear in the forthcoming proceedings).

Eliasson, G. (1985): The Firm and Financial Markets in the Swedish Micro to Macro Model-Theory, Model and Verfication, IUI, Stockholm.

Galler, H.P. (1988): Microsimulation of Household Formation and Dissolution, in Nico Keilman, Anton Kuijsten, Ad Vossen (Eds.), Modelling Household Formation and Dissolution, Clarendon Press, Oxford.

Harris, R. (1977): Microanalytic Simulation Models for Analysis of Public Welfare Policies, The Urban Institute, Washington D.C.

Haveman, R., Hollenbeck, K. (Eds.) (1980): Microeconomic Simulation Models for Public Policy Analysis, New York.

Heike, H.-D., Hellwig, O. and Kaufmann, A. (1987): Experiences with the Darmstadt Microsimulation Model (DPMS), (presented at the International Workshop for Demographic Microsimulation of the IIASA, Budapest, to appear in the forthcoming proceedings).

Hellwig, O. (1989): Programming a Microanalytic Simulation Model, (to be presented at the 4th International Symposium on Computer Simulation in the Social Sciences, Nuremberg, June 27 to 29, 1989).

Hellwig, O. (to be published): Implementing Simultaneity and Markets in Microanalytic Simulation Models.

Klösgen, W. (1986): Software Implementation of Microanalytic Simulation Models - State of the Art and Outlook, in Orcutt et al. (1986).

Krupp, H.-J., Wagner, G. (1982): Grundlagen und Anwendung mikroanalytischer Modelle, in Bendisch, J. and Hoschka, P. (Eds.): Möglichkeiten und Grenzen sozio-ökonomischer Modelle, GMD-Studien No. 68, St. Augustin, F.R.G.

Lietmeyer, V. (1986): Microanalytic Tax Simulation Models in Europe: Development and Experience in the German Federal Ministry of Finance, in Orcutt, Merz and Quinke (1986).

McClung, N. (1970): Estimates of Income Transfer Program Direct Effects, in the President's Commission on Income Maintenance Programs, technical studies, US Government Printing Office, Washington D.C.

McClung, N., Moeller, J., Sigual, E. (1971): Transfers Income Program Evaluation, Urban Institute Paper 950-3, Washington D.C.

McKay, C. (1978): Micro Analytic Simulation System, Technical Documentation of the MICROSIM model, Washington D.C.

Möhring, M. (1989): Konzepte von Simulationssprachen, in this volume.

Müller, G.P. (1986): Data Structure Requirements of Microanalytic Simulation Models, in Orcutt et al. (1986).

Nelissen, J.H.M. (1987): A Microsimulation Model for the Netherlands, Working Paper No. 23, Tilburg University, Department of Sociology.

Orcutt, G.H. (1957): A New Type of Socio-Economic System, The Review of Economics and Statistics, Vol. 58, pp. 773-793.

Orcutt, G.H., Greenberger, M., Korbel, J., Rivlin, A.M. (1961): Microanalysis of Socioeconomic Systems: A Simulation Study, Harper and Row, New York.

Orcutt, G.H., Caldwell, S. and Wertheimer, R. (1976): Policy Exploration Through Microanalytic Simulation, The Urban Institute, Washington D.C.

Orcutt, G.H., Glazer, A. (1980): Microanalytic Modeling and Simulation, in B. Bergmann, G. Eliasson and G. Orcutt (Eds.), Microsimulation-Models, Methods and Applications, IUI Conference Reports 1980, Industrial Institute for Economic and Social Research, Stockholm.

Orcutt, G.H., Merz, J., Quinke, H. (Eds.) (1986): Microanalytic Simulation Models to Support Social and Financial Policy, North-Holland, Amsterdam.

Pankoke-Babatz, U. (1980a): Einsatz mikroanalytischer Simulationsmodelle in den USA; GMD working paper, IPES 80.212, Bonn.

Pankoke-Babatz, U. (1980b): Überlegungen zur Entwicklung eines Softwaresystems zur Mikrosimulation, GMD working paper, IPES 80.213, St. Augustin.

Quinke, H. (1988): Methoden zur Schätzung der Kosten des Familienlastenausgleichs, in B. Felderer (Ed.): Familienlastenausgleich und demographische Entwicklung, Berlin.

Sadowsky, G. (1977): MASH - A Computer System for Microanalytic Simulation for Policy Exploration, The Urban Institute, Washington D.C.

Sfb3 (1989): Handbuch zum Mikrosimulationsmodell, technical documentation, Frankfurt University, F.R.G.

Statistics Canada (no date): SPSD/M - Product Overview, Electronic Data Dissemination Division, Statistics Canada, Ottawa.

Vano, B. (1988): Das mikroökonomische Modell der Bevölkerungs- und Haushaltsentwicklung, unpublished manuscript, VUSEI-AR, Bratislava, Cechoslovakia.

Webb, R.L., Michel, R.C., Bergsman, A.B. (1987): Software Problems in Microsimulation: The Historical Development of the TRIM2 Model, (presented for the Conference on Software Systems and Income Transfer Policy, Washington D.C., to appear in the forthcoming proceedings).

Wertheimer, R.II., Zedlewski, S., Anderson, J., Moore, K. (1986): DYNASIM in Comparison with other Microsimulation Models, in Orcutt et al. (1986).

Wolfson, M.C. (1989a): Divorce, Homemaker Pensions and Lifecycle Analysis, Population Research and Policy Review, Vol. 8, 25-54.

Wolfson, M.C. (1989b): The CEPHID Project: Canada's Elderly - Projecting Health, Income, and Demography, Working paper No. 1, Social and Economic Studies Division, Statistics Canada, Ottawa.

Zafir, M. (1987): Aims and Structure of the Hungarian Microsimulation System on Household Statistics Data, (presented at the International Workshop for Demographic Microsimulation of the IIASA, Budapest, to appear in the forthcoming proceedings).

Zeigler, B.P. (1987): Hierarchical, Modular Discrete-event Modelling in an Object-oriented Environment, Simulation, Vol. 49, No. 5, 219-230.

PES - A Modular Gaming Simulation Development System with Functional and Relational Aspects

S. Karczewski

Summary

There are many games for management, social, political and ecological problems on the market. For implementing the games on the computer a high number of programming languages will still be needed. General programming languages like BASIC (TOPIC from IBM), FORTRAN (INTOP from Thorelli et.al.), COBOL (LUDUS10 from ORBIS Informatik), PL/1 (ORBYD from IBM) and PASCAL (INSIM from Nixdorf) are used. The computer part of new games usually will not be made in a special language for games. Depending on these aspects PES (PES is the German abbreviation of gaming simulation development system) will develop and implement an architecture for the software components of games taking aspects of computer sience (functional programming, relational database system) into consideration. PES will supply a problem oriented language for the designer of a game and the teams which have to play the game. The designer can construct the access grants for the teams conceputual independent from the underlying model. The teams can read data for information and write data for decision making. The system will automatically check the definitions of access grants and the permission of access by the teams.

After specification gaming simulation (gaming, Planspiel) (1.), the presentation of the software components of games (2.) and the functional simulation system MIMOSE, which will be used inside PES (3.), we introduce the relational system PES which exists really as a prototype (4.). The survey (5.) shows the actual development and planned components of PES.

1. Gaming simulation (gaming, Planspiel)

Distinction between the gaming simulation method and other similar social science methods

There are many words used as titles for gaming simulation and other similar social science methods (Baumann 1988, 54ff.; Böhret/Wordelmann 1975, 24ff.; Diekmann/Leppert 1978, 3ff.; Harbordt 1974, 18f.; Herrmann 1987, 21ff.; Kaiser 1973, 70ff.; Rohn 1964, 134ff.; Shubik 1983, 16f.; Taylor/Walford 1974, 22ff.; Vagt 1978, 16ff.). We need central criteria to distinguish between **gaming simulation**, **computer simulation**, **role play** and **games used in game theory**. All enumerated methods build a section of a real situation, in which one part (**rule system**) will be modelled by a fixed algorithm —

usually by machine. In the other part there are human beings, whose possibilities of actions will be described by an **organization system**. The criteria of distinction are:

a. Degree of formalism in the rule system
b. Degree of formalism in the organization system
c. Time structure

a): Gaming simulation, computer simulation and games used in game theory have a formal rule system, which is given as mathematical equations or in another formal language, which can be computed. The rule system of a role play is informal or perhaps given as textual role cards.

b): The organization system of a gaming simulation is partly formalized. The information and decision variables for the teams are formal and refer to the rule system. But there are also conferences and other informal discussions which have no connection to the rule system. This informal part can be influenced by the selection and variability of the formal part of the organization system. Role plays have only an informal organization system. In games used in game theory the facts are reversed. There is only a formal organization system with no discussion between teams and no variabilty in the formal part. A typical computer simulation has no organization system. Possibly the experimentator or designer of the model can change parameters while the simulation is interrupted. But in contrast to a gaming simulation there is only one person who can interfere.

c): Computer simulation and gaming simulation have a time structure which is dynamic and divided into periods. Role plays have their own dynamic character. There is no periodic cycle in which new decisions of the players directly produce results which can be valid for subsequent actions. Games used in game theory are static. Sometimes they seem to have a dynamic structure, but the appearances are deceptive because one game is only played with frequent repetition.

Application aims of gaming simulation

Gaming simulation will be used

- in **teaching and training** (Adamowsky 1964, 9ff.; Ahorner/Lech 1980, 48; Baumann 1988, 64f.; Böhret/Wordelmann 1975, 42ff.; Diekmann/Leppert 1978, 14ff.; Eckardt/Stiegeler 1973, 7ff.; Lienhard/Steiger/Weber 1975, 43; Shubik 1975, 3ff.; Troitzsch 1989, 17),
- in **practice** (prognosis, personal judgement, decision preparation) (Ahorner/Lech 1980, 55; Böhret/Wordelmann 1975, 39ff.; Troitzsch 1989, 17; Lienhard/Steiger/Weber 1975, 44) and
- in **research** (Adamowsky 1964, 9; Ahorner/Lech 1980, 49; Baumann 1988, 63; Bleicher 1962, 94ff.; Böhret/Wordelmann 1975, 32ff.; Lienhard/Steiger/Weber 1975, 43; Shubik 1975, 10f.).

Gaming simulation is a method in which the whole man is challenged. Complex situations can be played without the cost of practice tests. The model shows immediate response to the decisions, so that the players can correct their faults.

One can have different views on gaming simulation. It can be seen as a role play in which the reactions come from a formal model or as an expanded computer simulation in which parts of the model, which cannot yet be written in a formal manner, are replaced by human actors. The latter form will be used in research, the former in teaching and training.

Parties to gaming

There are different persons concerned in gaming, **the designer, the director**, who has not to be the same person, and the **player** or **teams**. The designer frames the model and specifies access grants of the teams. The director has the same rights as the teams and can in addition start the simulation and change access grants of the teams. He should not change anything arbitrarily. The player or teams can be solo, parallel, in competition or in cooperation with other players or teams. They obtain information and make decisions.

2. Software components of gaming simulation

A gaming simulation consists of two systems which alternate, the rule system and the organization system. The communication between the two systems is achieved via a database. Every game designer knows this partition of the systems, nevertheless the produced program code mixes the components, so that it is impossible to change access grants in a simple manner. Only the designer can change the access rules by changing the program code.

Rule system

The rule system is the frame of a gaming simulation. The game world (**formal modeling**) and the **behaviour of the model** will be described in this system.

Organization system

There are two central tasks in the organization system. The **formal team description** says what information the players get from the rule system and which decisions they can take. The team actions (**update, select** data), too, are part of the organization system.

Database

The interface between rule and organization system is **a database** with data for **initializing** the simulation and holding the **results of the simulation** and supplying the **information data** for the teams and receiving the **decisions of the teams**.

Figure 1 shows the connections between the central software components of gaming simulation.

Figure 1: Rule and organization system with database

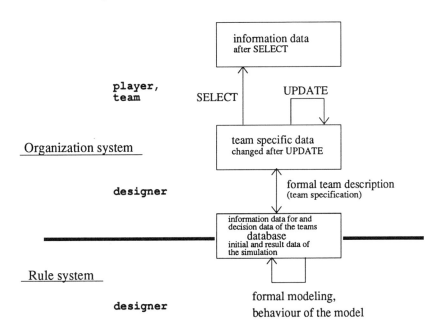

3. Simulation system MIMOSE

In PES, the simulation system MIMOSE (the abbreviation stands for micro and multilevel modeling software engineering) of Troitzsch and Möhring is used (Möhring 1988). MIMOSE allows the formal modeling and the initializing of models and simulations. MIMOSE follows the functional programming language paradigm (Ebert 1986, Glaser/Hankin/Till 1984).

Model specification

A model in MIMOSE is a set of objects (see Figure 2). Objects (in Figure 2 there is only "INSURANCE" an objecttype) can refer mutually and to the environment. An object consists of attributes (In Figure 2 the attributes NAME, IND, DIR, DIS, COM, RATE, M_NUM, M_PORT and INSURANCES exist).

Behaviour of the model

The values of the attributes determine the state of the objects. The behaviour of the model consists of attaching a calculation instruction as a function call to attributes of objects. The attributes get new values for every time step. The references between objects consist in the application of attributes as parameters inside the function call (In Figure 2 the attribute M_NUM of INSURANCE gets its value for every time step by application of function f to the values IND, DIR, DIS, COM, RATE of the same object. The function f will not declared in this text.). MIMOSE makes the use of past attribute values as parameter of functions possible. This simple language allows manifold modeling.

Initially all constant attributes, which have no function call on the right side of their declaration, get explicit actual values. In Figure 2 one can see the initializing after the key word "init". "INSURANCE [2]" says that two objects of type INSURANCE exist.

Figure 2: Model specification and initializing in MIMOSE
(The abbreviations IND, DIR, DIS, COM stand for investment in indirect, direct measures, measures of distribution and communication of health insurance. RATE stands for contribution rate. M_NUM and M_PORT are number and portion of members.)

```
INSURANCE :=
{
   NAME : string;
   IND : int;
   DIR : int;
   DIS: int;
   COM : int;
   RATE : real;
   M_NUM : int := f (IND, DIR, DIS, COM, RATE);
   M_PORT : real := M_NUM / sum (INSURANCES.M_NUM);
   INSURANCES : list of INSURANCE;
}

init INSURANCE [2]
(
   NAME := ['HI1', 'HI2'];
   IND := [50, 75];
   DIR := [80, 50]
   DIS := [65, 35];
   COM := [40, 85];
   RATE := [12.5, 13.0];
)
```

MIMOSE supplies the result data of every simulation step in a file. This file is the interface between the simulation system MIMOSE and the organization system PES (see Figure 1 on page 4).

4. Organisation system PES

Different persons have different rights of data definition and manipulation. The (virtual) data definition language and the data manipulation language take their pattern from the relational database language SQL (Date 1986, 93ff., 173ff.; DIN ISO 1987). The most important advantage in using this language in contrast to procedural languages is the descriptive manipulation. The user has to describe what and not how to do. The internal representation is not important for the teams, the director and the designer.

An object of PES (for example "INSURANCE") is a table; attributes of objects are the rows of the table. All attribute values of a column determine an object value. Attribute values are table entries in the corresponding row of the attribute (see Figure 3).

Figure 3: Relational View on the data

		'HI1'	'HI2'
INSURANCE.	NAME		
INSURANCE.	IND	50	75
INSURANCE.	DIR	80	50
INSURANCE.	DIS	65	35
INSURANCE.	COM	40	85
INSURANCE.	RATE	12.5	13.0
INSURANCE.	M_NUM	11525	10845
INSURANCE.	M_PORT	0.52	0.48

Organisation possibilities of the designer and the director

The game designer can divide the physical data in **views**. Views are not really existing (virtual) tables, but they can be used like real tables. The designer makes partitions of all tables to give access grants in accordance with content aspects.

The director can cancel or change views if the environment for the teams should change. In particular this option is necessary if the simulation system allows the generation of new objecttypes or attributes.

Before the player or teams can operate on the data, the designer (and later on the director) has to give them **access grants**. The definition of access grants (select, update) can be done specifiying the object (for example "INSURANCE") or relative to the defined virtual tables.

There exists an internal consistency test which makes it impossible to allow two teams the UPDATE-grant to one value. In this case the simulation result is dependent on the moment in which the teams decide. This is undesirable in gaming simulation. If the designer gives more than one UPDATE-grant, only the team which obtains it last can update. This is justified because the changing of rights is allowed.

The combination of view definition and access grant defines the gaming frame for the teams. The file with the result data of simulation is divided into team-specific data (see Figure 1 on page 4). Figure 4 shows one team specification for the previous example.

Figure 4a: View definition and SELECT- and UPDATE-grant of the designer

create view k1A **as select** IND, DIR, DIS, COM, RATE **from** INSURANCE **where** NAME = 'HI1'
grant select, update **on** k1A **to** Team1

		'HI1'	'HI2'
INSURANCE.	NAME		
INSURANCE.	IND	50	75
INSURANCE.	DIR	80	50
INSURANCE.	DIS	65	35
INSURANCE.	COM	40	85
INSURANCE.	RATE	12.5	13.0
INSURANCE.	M_NUM	11525	10845
INSURANCE.	M_PORT	0.52	0.48

The attribute values in the black box (☐) can be selected and updated by the team named "Team1".

Figure 4b: View definition and SELECT-grant of the designer

create view k1B as select NAME, M_NUM, M_PORT from INSURANCE where NAME = 'HI1'
grant select on k1B to Team1

INSURANCE.	NAME	'HI1'	'HI2'
INSURANCE.	IND	50	75
INSURANCE.	DIR	80	50
INSURANCE.	DIS	65	35
INSURANCE.	COM	40	85
INSURANCE.	RATE	12.5	13.0
INSURANCE.	M_NUM	11525	10845
INSURANCE.	M_PORT	0.52	0.48

The attribute values in the black boxes (□) can be selected by the team named "Team1".

"Team2" can be defined analogously.

Access grants of the teams

The teams can **select** and **update** the designer-defined scopes (see Figure 1 on page 4). Every manipulation will be filtered by the designers' team specification. The data manipulation language takes its pattern from SQL like the designers' language.

Figure 5 shows a SELECT-instruction of a team, Figure 6 an UPDATE- followed by a SELECT-command.

Figure 5: SELECT-instruction of the team named "Team2"

select NAME, M_PORT from INSURANCE where M_PORT < 0.5 for Team2

INSURANCE.	NAME	**	'HI2'
INSURANCE.	IND	**	***
INSURANCE.	DIR	**	***
INSURANCE.	DIS	**	***
INSURANCE.	COM	**	***
INSURANCE.	RATE	**	***
INSURANCE.	M_NUM	**	***
INSURANCE.	M_PORT	**	0.48

Figure 6: UPDATE- and SELECT-instruction of the team named "Team2"

update INSURANCE set IND = 100, DIR = 40 **for** Team2
select * from INSURANCE **for** Team2

INSURANCE.	NAME	**	'HI2'
INSURANCE.	IND	**	->100
INSURANCE.	DIR	**	-> 40
INSURANCE.	DIS	**	35
INSURANCE.	COM	**	85
INSURANCE.	RATE	**	13.0
INSURANCE.	M_NUM	**	10845
INSURANCE.	M_PORT	**	0.48

"Select *" means that all attributes of the object INSURANCE will be selected. The values with an arrow (->) were changed by the UPDATE-instruction.

The black boxes (▢) in Figure 5 and Figure 6 show the SELECT-scope for "Team2". The output has two asterisks ('**') in a value field, if there is no authorization for selecting and three asterisks ('***'), if the condition of the team's inquiry is not performed or the value of the attribute is not enquired. If there are values canceled during simulation (for example if modeling death processes) the output of the value field is one asterisk ('*').

The SELECT- and UPDATE-instructions allow a multi-grade manipulation. Depending on the knowledge about the game the teams can obtain access to whole objects or to single or multiple attributes.

5. Survey

PES is implemented on a SUN workstation in the computer language "C" and with the software tools LEX and YACC. Constructed on the present prototype a **window oriented** user interface is being developed. Every team gets different windows on the screen with the gaming information and actions being supplied in a straightforward manner.

An expansion of the system is planned allowing the team abilities relating to local variable definition and definition of macros. In future, previous testing of decisions for the teams will be possible.

Literature:

Adamowsky, S.: Das Planspiel; Frankfurt: Agenor-Verlag, 1964

Ahorner, K.; Lech, G.: Sichere Entscheidungs-Methodik; Heidelberg: Sauer-Verlag, 1980

Baumann, H.: Konstruktion und Einsatz makroökonomischer Simulationsmodelle im Rahmen der computerunterstützten Wirtschaftsförderung und wirtschaftswissenschaftlichen Ausbildung; Fischer, 1988

Bleicher, K.: Unternehmungsspiele; Baden-Baden: Verlag für Unternehmensführung, 1962

Böhret, C.; Wordelmann, P.: Das Planspiel als Methode der Fortbildung; Köln, Bonn: Heymanns, 1975

Date, C.J.: An Introduction to Database Systems (Vol. I); Reading: Addison-Wesley, 1986

Diekmann, P.; Leppert, H.: Planspiel und Planspiel-Simulation in der Raumplanung; Basel, Stuttgart: Birkhäuser, 1978

DIN ISO 9075 Informationsverarbeitung, Datenbanksprache SQL, 1987

Eckardt, P.; Stiegeler, A.: Das Planspiel in der politischen Bildung; Frankfurt, Berlin, München: Diesterweg, 1973

Ebert, J.: Elemente funktionaler Programmiersprachen; in: J. Perl (Hrsg.) Neue Konzepte von Programmiersprachen; Universität Mainz; Informatik-Bericht 1/86

Glaser, H.; Hankin, C.; Till, D.: Principles of Functional Programming; Englewood Cliffs: Prentice-Hall, 1984

Harbordt, S.: Computersimulation in den Sozialwissenschaften (Bd. I); Reinbek: Rowohlt, 1974

Herrmann, H.-J.: Simulationsspiele als Methode eines bankbetrieblichen Entscheidungstrainings; Düsseldorf: Verlagsanstalt Handwerk, 1987

Kaiser, F.-J.: Entscheidungstrainig; Bad Heilbrunn: Julius Klinkhardt, 1973

Lienhard, H.; Steiger, F.; Weber, K.: Planspiel Elektrizitätswirtschaft; Bern, Stuttgart: Paul Haupt, 1975

Möhring, M.: MIMOSE — Eine funktionale Sprache zur Modellierung und Simulation individuellen Verhaltens in interagierenden Populationen, Interner Bericht, EWH Koblenz, Sozialwissenschaftliche Informatik, 1988

Rohn, W. E.: Führungsentscheidungen im Unternehmensplanspiel; Essen: W. Girardet, 1964

Shubik, M.: Games for Society, Business an War; New, York, Oxford, Amsterdam: Elsevier, 1975

Shubik, M.: Gaming: A State-Of-The-Art Survey; in: J. Stahl (Ed.) Operational Gaming; Oxford, et. al.: Pergamon Press, 1983; 13–22

Taylor, J. L.; Walford, R.: Simulationsspiele im Unterricht; Ravensburg: O. Maier, 1974

Troitzsch, K. G.: Modellbildung und Simulation in den Sozialwissenschaften, Opladen: Westdeutscher Verlag, 1989

Vagt, R.: Planspiel; Rheinstetten: Schindele-Verlag, 1978

MAPLIS - die matrixorientierte interaktive Simulation für die Sozialwissenschaften

W. Tettweiler

Summary

The use of simulation techniques in the field of social sciences is now as ever not quite common. That might be due to the fact that the concepts of conventional simulation languages and the objects of their data are by far not complementary to concepts and objects dealt with in established statistical languages.

This report aims to eliminate preoccupations against simulation techniques that are common with social scientists. Selected examples will be used to demonstrate the correlations that exist in one respect in the language concepts of the (statistics based) simulation language MAPLIS and the statistical language SPSS and on the otehr side in the data processing concepts of MAPLIS and P-STAT. Familiarity with the use of either of these languages is highly useful for understanding and working with MAPLIS. The applications presented here show furthermore that the use of MAPLIS simulation models is nothing else but another method to create and alter contents of objects by means of model based algorithms as it is done with statistical functions.

Zusammenfassung

Die Anwendung der Simulationstechnik ist in den Sozialwissenschaften nach wie vor noch nicht besonders weit verbreitet. Dies wohl vornehmlich deshalb, weil die Konzepte der gebräuchlichen Simulationssprachen und ihre die Anwenderdaten enthaltenden Objekte nicht hinreichend komplementär sind zu den Konzepten und Objekten der in den Sozialwissenschaften verbreiteten Statistiksprachen.

Dem daraus entstandenen Vorurteil vieler Sozialwissenschaftler gegenüber Simulation soll mit diesem Vortrag abgeholfen werden. Anhand einiger ausgewählter Beispiele wird gezeigt, daß einerseits zwischen der (Statistik-)datenbasierten Simulationssprache MAPLIS und der Statistiksprache SPSS vom Sprachkonzept her, andererseits zwischen MAPLIS und P-STAT vom Datenbehandlungskonzept her einige wesentliche Verwandtschaften bestehen. Die Gewöhnung an die Anwendung dieser Statistiksprachen ist daher für Verständnis und Gebrauch der MAPLIS-Sprache sehr hilfreich. Außerdem zeigen die Beispiele, daß der Einsatz von MAPLIS-Simulationsmodellen nichts anderes als ist eine weitere Methode, mit der - wie mit statistischen Auswertungsfunktionen - lediglich aufgrund modellhafter Algorithmen Inhalte von Objekten verändert oder erzeugt werden.

1 Vorbemerkung

Dieser Vortrag setzt dort fort, wo die Sprache MAPLIS in einem Vortrag des Autors anläßlich der letzten Statistiksoftwarekonferenz (1987) vorgestellt wurde. Ihre hauptsächlichen Eigenschaften seien hier in Erinnerung gebracht:

- die Modellzeit basiert auf äquidistanten Zeitintervallen (periodenorientiert à la DYNAMO)

- entsprechend haben Datenobjekte die Funktion von Bestands- und Flußgrößen

- die Datenobjekte sind vom Typ Tensor (null- bis n-dimensional)

- der Initialisierungsteil für Simulation ist externalisiert

- der Simulationsteil (Modelldefinitionen) ist durch Folgen von Zuweisungsgleichungen dargestellt

- der Ausgabeteil für Simulationsergebnisse ist sehr sparsam, Auswertungen erfolgen extern

- die Benutzerschnittstelle ist dialogfähig sowohl in der Modelldefinitionsphase wie auch während des Simulationslaufs.

Ziel dieses Vortrages ist nicht, das Ergebnis einer exakten semantischen Analyse der in Statistik, Modellbildung und Simulation gebräuchlichen formalen Sprachen vorzustellen. Auch soll keine erschöpfende Übersicht oder vollständige Aufzählung erfolgen, geschweige denn eine Bewertung vorgenommen werden. Vielmehr wird anhand von in den Sprachen SPSS, P-STAT und MAPLIS formulierten Beispielen aus dem Bereich des Datenaustauschs gezeigt, daß einige nicht unwesentliche Ähnlichkeiten bestehen.

2 Sprachkonzepte und deren Funktionen

Allen drei genannten Sprachen ist gemeinsam, daß sie eine mathematisch orientierte Grammatik haben und - um die Akzeptanz zu erhöhen - leicht erlernbar sind. Damit wiederum geht einher, daß sie im Bereich der Programmstrukturierung verhältnismäßig schwach ausgebaut sind, worauf nachfolgend näher eingegangen wird.

2.1 SPSS

Diese Statistiksprache ist - den Datenmodifikationsteile ausgenommen - von ihrem Konzept her eine Assemblersprache. Jede Anweisung einer Anweisungsfolge wird eigenständig ausgeführt. Dies dient der Einsparung von Übersetzungs- und Binderläufen.

Die Datenmodifikationsanweisungen ermöglichen die algebraische Verknüpfung von Daten auf der Basis von Skalaren (COMPUTE, COUNT, IF) einschließlich Transformationsoperationen (RECODE). Es gibt einige primitive zusammengesetzte Anweisungen (DO REPEAT, DO IF, LOOP).

Die übrigen Anweisungen bewerkstelligen den Import und Export des Inhalts des gerade bearbeiteten Datenobjektes (Arbeitsdatei, FILE HANDLE) und - eigentlicher Zweck einer Statistiksprache - sie rufen (vordefinierte) Statistik-Prozeduren auf. Besondere Beachtung unter diesen verdienen für unsere Betrachtungen jene zum Aggregieren (AGGREGATE) und zur Kreuztabulierung (CROSSTABS mit Option 10 sowie PROCEDURE OUTPUT-Angabe), mit denen neue Datenobjekte hergestellt werden. Entweder ersetzen sie die Arbeitsdatei oder ihr Inhalt wird exportiert, beispielsweise, um in der MAPLIS-Sprache formulierten Modellen als Bestandsgrößen (z.B. AGGREGATE mit Anwendung der function SUM erzeugt) oder Flußgrößen (entsprechend mit CROSSTABS mit der Option 3 oder 4 erzeugt) zu dienen.

2.2 P-STAT

Diese Statistiksprache ist im o.g. Sinn gleichfalls eine Assemblersprache.

Auch hier sind Anweisungen für algebraische Verknüpfungen auf Skalarbasis (in der PPL = P-STAT Programming Language) vorhanden sowie für IF- und FOR-Sprachkonstrukte zusammengesetzte Anweisungen. Darüberhinaus ist der Kontrollfluß beeinflußbar (GOTO-Anweisung) und ein sehr weitgehendes Makrokonzept (MACRO- und RUN-Anweisung) realisiert. Da alle Datenobjekte (s.u.) vom Typ (zweidimensionale) Matrix sind, stehen die entsprechenden Matrixoperationen Anweisungen (E.ADD bis E. TRANSPOSE) zur Verfügung.

Die übrigen Anweisungen dienen der Herstellung der für Auswertungen erforderlichen Systemumgebung (z.B. Import und Export von Daten und Makros) sowie zur Durchführung von Datenauswertungen. Unter diesen ist auch hier wieder die Funktion der AGGREGATION-Anweisung mit der Selektion COUNT für unsere Betrachtungen von besonderem Interesse: Mit ihr können Daten dergestalt aggregiert werden, daß sie als Bestandsgrößen für MAPLIS-Simulationsläufe verwendet werden können. Über die Möglichkeiten von SPSS hinausgehend ist bei P-STAT das Konzept, daß Auswertungsergebnisse stets als neue Datenobjekte zur Verfügung gestellt werden und sofort wieder Eingang in die nächste Auswertung finden können. Dies ist sehr nützlich, weil z.B. durch die TABLES-Anweisung erzeugte Objekte, deren Inhalte in Simulationsläufen als Flußgröße verwendet werden sollen, <u>unmittelbar</u> mit den in P-STAT verfügbaren Darstellungsmitteln bearbeitet und überprüft werden können.

2.3 MAPLIS

Die Simulationssprache MAPLIS verfügt über die elementare Anweisung der Wertzuweisung sowie einige primitive zusammengesetzte Anweisungen (implizites-Konstrukt im jeweiligen Hauptmodell, einfaches IF-Konstrukt), ferner über das wichtige Konzept des Haupt- und Untermodells (entsprechend dem Makrokonzept von P-STAT), dargestellt durch Prozedurvereinbarungen (ADD MODEL bzw. REPLACE MODEL) und Aufrufe (CALL MODEL). Dies dient der Formulierung von Simulationsmodellen, die als Objekte in einer sog. Modellbasis abgelegt werden. Anspruchsvolle Programmstrukturen lassen sich damit - wie bei den Statistiksprachen - allerdings auch nicht aufbauen.

Weitere elementare Anweisungen (AGGREGATE, DISAGGREGATE) dienen dem Aggregationsniveauwechsel in <u>beiden</u> Richtungen: beim Aggregieren (d.i. in MAPLIS ein Teil- und Randsummenbilden) von Bestandsgrößen kann man die den jeweiligen Zellen zugehörigen relativen Häufigkeiten speichern. Interpretiert man sie nun auch als Wahrscheinlichkeiten von diskreten Verteilungen, können diesen gemäß Bestände wieder geteilt (disaggregiert) werden, womit sie die Bedeutung von Flußgrößen erhalten. Für den Disaggregationsvorgang sind verschiedene Algorithmen verfügbar: mit der simplen Multiplikation beginnend bis hin zur Ganzzahligen Verteilung mit monte-carlo-Methoden, ggf. auch zielverteilungsorientiert, um die beste Nutzung zur Verfügung stehender Ressourcen zu erreichen.

Die übrigen Anweisungen bewerkstelligen den Import und Export von Objekten der Modell- und der Datenbasis.

Über die Möglichkeiten der Statistiksprachen hinausgehend ist die dem Fortgang der Modellzeit entsprechende periodische Fortschreibung der Datenobjekte und ihre (theoretisch) unbeschränkte Dimensionenzahl. Aus der ersten Eigenschaft ergibt sich, daß die TIME SERIES-Anweisung nicht mehr als ein Zusammenfassen einer Reihe von Datenobjekten zu einem Vektor bewirkt (und das entstandene Objekt besitzt die zusätzliche Dimension Zeit). Aus der zweiten Eigenschaft folgt, daß das geschlossene Durchspielen mehrerer Planungsalternativen in ein und demselben Simulationslauf möglich ist. Allen einschlägigen Datenobjekten gibt man eine Dimension mehr, deren Wertevorrat durch die Anzahl der Planungsalternativen bestimmt ist. Die Suche nach dem Optimum läuft darauf hinaus, daß in einer Ergebnisgröße die Zelle mit dem Minimum/Maximum aufgesucht wird. Deren entsprechende Indexwerte bezeichnen das gefundene Optimum.

Im folgenden Beispiel wird ein sehr einfaches Modell der Entwicklung einer Schülerpopulation deklariert. In diesem haben die Bestandsgrößen die Namen s (Schülerzahl insgesamt), sdiv (Schülerzahl differenziert nach erfolgreich/nicht erfolgreich), serf (Erfolgreiche), swdh (Wiederholer) und svers (Versetzte), die einzige

Flußgröße ist mit perf (Wahrscheinlichkeit, differenziert nach erfolgreich/nicht erfolgreich) bezeichnet. Die Schlüsselworte der MAPLIS-Sprache (deren Ähnlichkeit mit SPSS 7 gewollt ist) sind in Großbuchstaben wiedergegeben:

```
ADD MODEL      sdfsim Schülerdurchflußmodell
COMMENT        1. Schritt: Teilen des Schülerstroms
DISAGGREGATE   RESULT=sdiv SOURCE=s DISTRIBUTION=perf
COMMENT        2. Schritt: Erfolgreiche und Wiederholer separieren
SUBMATRIX      RESULT=serf, SOURCE=sdiv, VALUE=1
SUBMATRIX      RESULT=swdh, SOURCE=sdiv, VALUE=2
COMMENT        3. Schritt: Erfolgreiche versetzen
COMPUTE        svers = SHIFT(serf,'KL',1)
COMMENT        4. Schritt: Klassen neu zusammenstellen
COMPUTE        s = svers + swdh
END MODEL
```

Dieses Modell funktioniert unabhängig von der im jeweils konkreten Fall vorliegenden Dimensionalität seiner Objekte: sind s, serf, swdh und svers Skalare (nulldimensional) sowie sdiv und perf Zwei-Elemente-Vektoren (eindimensional), wird eine einzelne Klasse simuliert. Tritt überall die Dimension "Klassenstufe" (hier mit KL bezeichnet) hinzu, simuliert man eine einzügige Schule. Nimmt man noch Dimensionen für Zügigkeit, Schulart, Standort der Schule, auch Geschlecht und Sozialstatus der Schüler hinzu, kommt man sehr schnell auf eine vieldimensionale Simulation, deren Kern die entsprechend vieldimensionale Verteilungsmatrix perf ist (allerdings fällt das entsprechende Simulationsmodell dann wahrscheinlich nicht mehr ganz so einfach aus).

3 Objekte und Inhalte

Wir beschränken uns bei der folgenden vergleichenden Betrachtung auf Objekte, die quantitative Daten enthalten. Sie entstammen wiederum formalen Sprachen der Anwendungsbereiche Statistik und Simulation. Der Darstellung der verschiedenen Sprachkonstrukte dient die sehr weit verbreitete Programmiersprache PASCAL, deren Schlüsselworte in Großbuchstaben erscheinen.

3.1 Objekte in Statistiksprachen

Die gebräuchlichsten Typen der mit Statistiksprachen behandelten Datenobjekte sind
```
satz_typ = ARRAY (. 1..number_of_variables .) OF REAL;
```
und darauf aufbauend
```
systemfile_typ = FILE OF satz_typ;
```
repräsentierend eine Rechteckmatrix (Fortentwicklungen der Statistiksprachen ermöglichen komplexere Datenstrukturen, auf die hier nicht näher eingegangen werden soll).

In P-STAT haben Objekte darüberhinaus den Typ
```
psfile_typ = ARRAY (. 1..n_of_rows, 1..n_of_colums .) OF REAL;
```
bei dem die zweidimensionale Struktur leichter erkennbar ist.

Die oben bereits beschriebenen Funktionen führen Datenobjekte unter Beibehaltung ihres Typs ineinander über.

3.2 Objekte in Simulationssprachen

Simulationssprachen sind klassische Programmiersprachen, teilweise mit sog. "abstrakten Datentypen" (die auch die Funktionen mit umfassen, die einen Zugriff darauf realisieren, z.B. in SIMULA). Entsprechend vielfältig sind die Typen der Datenobjekte.

In kontinuierlichen Simulationssprachen sind dies:
```
skalar_typ  = REAL;
vektor_typ  = ARRAY (. ... .) OF REAL;
tabellen_typ = ARRAY (. ... .) OF vektor_typ;
```
darüberhinaus haben in DYNAMO Objekte eine spezielle Vektorstruktur, die zeitliche Vor- und Rückgriffe ermöglichen, MAPLIS schließlich kennt den Typ Tensor (der mit Pascal- Sprachelementen nicht exakt darstellbar ist, daher das nachfolgende Provisorium):
```
tensor_typ = ARRAY (. 1..n1, ..., 1..nn .) OF REAL;
```
Werte, die Objekte erhalten - insbesondere, soweit sie Anfangswerte, Parameterwerte, Schranken, Veränderungsraten (Quoten, Wahrscheinlichkeiten), Abbruchkriterien etc. betreffen - sind nur mit höheren statistischen Methoden (Regressions- , Varianz-, Faktoranalyse usw.) zu bestimmen. Dies stellt normalerweise hohe Anforderungen an den Modelldesigner als Statistiker bzw. an den Statistiker als Modelldesigner. Lediglich die von MAPLIS bearbeiteten Objekte enthalten entweder Ergebnisse von MAPLIS-Funktionen oder Ergebnisse einfacherer multivariater Verfahren oder - falls die Dimensionen der Tensoren jenen eines multivariaten Versuchsplans entsprechen - einfache Eingaben, die Schätzungen von Experten sind. (Dies ist eine Weiterentwicklung der Idee, die den im Management häufig eingesetzten Tabellenkalkulationsprogrammen zugrunde liegt.) Die folgende Abbildung zeigt die jeweils verwendeten statistischen Verfahren zur Wertermittlung:

Statistiken	(High level statistics) Regression analysis, analysis of variance, factor analysis ..	(Multivariate statistics) Crosstabs, breakdown, t-test, correlation analysis, ...
Graph. Darstellg. des Verfahrens der Wertermittlung	(Scatterplot of points)	.30 | .35 | .35 1.00 | .0 | .0
Formale Darstellg.	D = f(I) + r D=dependent I=independent	f(i,...,k); TOTALSUM(f) = N p(j); SUM(p(j)) = 1. or p(i,...,k); SUM(SUM...) = 1.
Objekte	(Makrosimulation) Skalare für Differenzen-/Differential-gleichungen	Matrizen, Tensoren
Sprache	MIMIC, CSMP, CSSL, ACSL, DYNAMO	APL, MAPLIS, MATSYS

In diskreten Simulationssprachen sind die Typen der Datenobjekte weitgehend dieselben wie die der kontinuierlichen. Hinzu kommt der Typ Zeiger und auf diesem aufbauend Liste (Warteschlange):

```
ref_liste = ^liste_typ;
liste_typ = RECORD
... (Irgendwelche Informationen) ...;
nachfolger: ref_liste;
END;
```

Zur Bearbeitung von Objekten dieses Typs sind algebraische und simulationsspezifische Funktionen verfügbar. Diese basieren auf den Konzepten "Ereignis" (SIMSCRIPT), "Transaktion" (GPSS) oder "Prozeß" (SIMULA), auf die hier nicht näher eingegangen werden kann.

Die Inhalte der Objekte (u.a. oben mit "irgendwelche Informationen" bezeichnet) sind häufig statistische Größen, die vergleichsweise leichter zu gewinnen sind als jene der kontinuierlichen Simulationssprachen, da "einfache" statistische Auswertungsverfahren eingesetzt werden können. Die folgende Abbildung fügt der vorigen eine weitere Spalte hinzu:

```
+----------+--------------------------------+
|          |                                |
| Stati-   | (Raw data)                     |
| stiken   | Descriptive statistics,        |
|          | one-way frequency distributions|
|          |                                |
+----------+--------------------------------+
|          |                                |
| Graph.   | +-------+-------+-------+      |
| Dar-     | I 4017 I 98723 I   102 I      |   <= Randsummen, auf denen die
| stellg.  | +-------+-------+-------+      |      in den Objekten verwendeten
| des Ver- |                                |      Verteilungen p(i) beruhen
| fahrens  | +-------+-------+-------+      |
| der      | I  164 I  9850 I     1 I      |
| Wert-    | I 2740 I  1665 I    12 I      |
| ermitt-  | I  998 I 10354 I     7 I      |
| lung     |                                |
|          |      ...                       |
|          |                                |
+----------+--------------------------------+
|          |                                |
| Formale  | f(i); SUM(f(i)) = N            |
| Dar-     |                                |
| stellg.  | p(i); SUM(p(i)) = 1.           |
|          |                                |
+----------+--------------------------------+
|          |                                |
| Objekte  | (Mikrosimulation) Skalare zur  |
|          | Darstellung von Verteilungen,  |
|          | Attributen, Events, Queues, ...|
|          |                                |
+----------+--------------------------------+
|          |                                |
| Sprache  | SIMSCRIPT, GPSS, SIMULA        |
|          |                                |
+----------+--------------------------------+
```

3.2 Objekte in MAPLIS

Bei der vorausgegangenen Betrachtung hatte man den Eindruck gewinnen können, daß sich MAPLIS unwesentlich "näher" an den Statistiksprachen befindet als jede andere Simulationssprache. Beim Betrieb vom MAPLIS zur Erstellung oder Ausführung eines Simulationsmodells finden sich jedoch sehr wohl einige Parallelen.

3.2.1 Vergleich mit SPSS

Von SPSS (NIE75) wurde die Struktur der Datenmatrix (Fälle mal Variable) <u>nicht</u> übernommen, jedoch die Angabe der Ausdehnung in der jeweiligen Dimension. In SPSS wird mit N OF CASES <u>eine</u> von zwei Dimensionen festgelegt, in MAPLIS leistet dies N OF VALUES für <u>jede</u> beliebige Dimension. Dokumentations- und Lesehilfen für Druckausgaben wie z.B. FILE NAME, VAR LABELS, VALUE LABELS und DOCUMENT wurden identisch übernommen, ebenso Datenmanagementanweisungen wie ADD VARS, DELETE VARS, REORDER VARS, SAVE FILE und GET FILE, allerdings ergänzt durch ADD MODEL, DELETE MODEL, SAVE DATABASE und GET DATABASE. Dem AGGREGATE wurde das komplementäre DISAGGREGATE zugefügt. Modulare Zerlegung wird unterstützt durch CALL MODEL.

Die Möglichkeit, fehlende Werte (MISSING VALUES) zu berücksichtigen, wurde aus zwei Gründen übernommen: einmal, um bei schwach besetzten Matrizen Speicherplatz zu sparen; andererseits, um Fehler bei der Modellkonstruktion zu entdecken (ein automatisches Umordnen der Gleichungen wie beispielsweise in DYNAMO findet in MAPLIS nicht statt). Wenn bei einem Verrechnen in den Eingabewerten mindestens ein fehlender Wert angetroffen wird, erhält entweder das Ergebnis ebenfalls diesen Wert (Fortpflanzung) oder der Anwender wird durch eine entsprechende Meldung gewarnt.

Statistische Auswertungen von SPSS innerhalb von MAPLIS übernehmen zu lassen, gelang mangels geeigneter Schnittstellenbeschreibungen bislang nicht. Hingegen ist eine Kommunikation zwischen SPSS und MAPLIS und umgekehrt über Zwischendateien sehr wohl möglich:

```
SPSS:     ...
SORT CASES BY V1, ... ,VN (Werte werden Indexwerte für MAPLIS)
AGGREGATE ... / BREAK = V1, ... , VN
          / ANZAHL = N (absolute Häufigkeiten
    ...                                         ausgeben)

MAPLIS: ...
N OF VALUES    X1(...), ... ,XN(...)  (entsprechend den Werte-
    ...                                bereichen von V1 bis VN)
ADD VARIABLES  V(X1,...,XN)
READ DATA      V (INDEXED)
    ...
```

(Anstelle absoluter könnte SPSS auch relative Häufigkeiten liefern.)

```
MAPLIS: ...
WRITE DATA     V (INDEXED)
    ...

SPSS:    ...
DATA LIST ... / N ... V1 ... VN
WEIGHT BY N
    ...
```

3.2.2 Vergleich mit P-STAT

Das Prinzip, die Ausgabe jeder beliebigen Operation zugleich Eingabe in eine andere Operation sein lassen zu können, wurde von P-STAT voll übernommen. P-STAT geht bei der Speicherung dokumentarischer Information sogar noch einen Schritt weiter als MAPLIS: die sog. Description File ist vom selben Datentyp wie alle anderen Objekte. Damit geht eine Beschränkung der Textlängen einher, die in MAPLIS nicht tolerabel wäre.

Eine unmittelbare Schnittstelle zwischen MAPLIS und P-STAT existiert ebenfalls nicht. Auch hier muß die Kommunikation über Zwischendateien abgewickelt werden:

```
P-STAT  ...
SORT V, BY V1 ... VN, OUT S$
AGGREGATE S (GENERATE T = 1), BY V1 ... VN,
    COUNT, OUT P$ (cell counts bereitstellen für MAPLIS
FILE.OUT P, FILE = ... $
    ...

MAPLIS: ...
N OF VALUES     X1(...), ... ,XN(...) (entsprechend den Werte-
    ...                               bereichen von V1 bis VN)
ADD VARIABLES   V(X1,...,XN)
READ DATA       V (INDEXED)
    ...
```

(Anstelle absoluter könnte P-STAT auch relative Häufigkeiten liefern.)

```
MAPLIS: ...
WRITE DATA      V (INDEXED)
    ...

P-STAT  ...
FILE.IN, FILE = ... , NV n_plus_eins, OUT = V ... $
MODIFY V, WEIGHT VAR1 $
    ...
```

Vorsicht: Die Variablen V1 bis VN heißen jetzt VAR2 bis VARn_plus_eins!

4 Ausblick

Die vorgestellten Beispiele sollten lediglich Schlaglichter auf die Simulationsszene aus Sicht des Statistikers werfen. Sie haben sich deshalb auf Verwandtes zwischen beiden Bereichen konzentriert. Wenn der - sich mit der Zeit zwangsläufig ergebende - Wandel der Bedeutungen semantischer Einheiten diese Verwandtschaften verdichtete, wäre zu erwarten, daß Simulation auch in den Sozialwissenschaften eine höhere Akzeptanz erfährt. Der Statistiker wäre dann eher in der Lage, die Bedeutung simulationssprachlicher Elemente aus jenen der ihm geläufigen Statistiksprachelemente zu erkennen. Simulation wäre für ihn nichts anderes als Fortsetzung der Statistik mit anderen formalsprachlichen Mitteln.

Skalierung und Klassifikation

F. Faulbaum, R. Haux und K.-H. Jöckel (Hrsg.) (1990). SoftStat '89
Fortschritte der Statistik-Software 2. Stuttgart: Gustav Fischer, 461 - 470

Ordinale manifeste Variablen - Nominale latente Variablen - Latent Class Analyse für ordinale Daten

H. Giegler und J. Rost

Summary

The model of latent class analysis is described and contrasted with traditional statistical methods like factor and cluster analysis. An extension of the model for the application to ordinal manifest variables is outlined. This extension is done by introducing eight different linear constraints for the threshold probabilities. The output of the computer program LACORD is illustrated by means of a data example from the ALLBUS-86 survey.

1. Einleitung

In den empirischen Sozialwissenschaften lassen sich zwei Strategien der Datenanalyse unterscheiden: Erstens, empirische, d.h. beobachtete oder "manifeste" Merkmale werden mit anderen empirischen Merkmalen in Verbindung gebracht. Zweitens, empirische Merkmale werden mit postulierten latenten Merkmalen in Verbindung gebracht: die empirisch beobachteten Merkmale haben in diesem Fall die Funktion von Indikatoren für die postulierten latenten Merkmale.

Auf den ersten Blick scheint die zweite Strategie nicht recht einleuchtend zu sein: warum - so könnte man in guter behavioristischer Tradition fragen - sollte die (scheinbar) "unmittelbar gegebene empirische Basis" zugunsten eines "nur postulierten latenten Überbaues" verlassen werden? Dafür ließen sich nun eine ganze Reihe von Gründen ins Feld führen. Ein Hauptgrund ist der, daß in den Sozialwissenschaften sehr häufig mit Begriffen gearbeitet wird, die sich zwar in empirisch konstatierbaren Handlungen niederschlagen, in diesen aber nicht in einem 1:1-Verhältnis aufgehen. So z.B., wenn die Psychologie von "mathematischer Begabung" oder von "Depressivität", die Soziologie von "Autoritarismus" oder von "Entfremdung", die Politikwissenschaft von "Konservatismus" oder von "Liberalität" sprechen.

Die "klassischen" multivariaten Analysestrategien, die hier normalerweise zum Einsatz kommen, sind die verschiedenen Spielarten der Faktorenanalyse, der Clusteranalyse und der multidimensionalen Skalierung. Bei allen Unterschiedlichkeiten weisen diese Analysestrategien dennoch eine Gemeinsamkeit auf, die keineswegs als völlig problemlos gelten kann: Sie bauen alle auf bivariaten Ähnlichkeits- oder Distanzmaßen auf. Damit sind jedoch einige Probleme verbunden:

1. Postuliertes Skalenniveau: Es stellt sich die Alternative, entweder die Information über die Größe der Differenzen bei den involvierten Merkmalsausprägungen voll auszuschöpfen, d.h. die in die Analyse eingehenden Merkmale (in der Regel ungeprüft) wie metrische Merkmale zu behandeln (z.B. bei der Berechnung von Produkt-Moment-Korrelationen oder "Euklidischen Distanzen"); oder, die Information über die Größe der Differenzen bei den involvierten Merkmalsausprägungen nicht voll auszuschöpfen und diese nur als Ranginformation zu behandeln (z.B. bei der Berechnung von Kendalls' tau oder "Gamma-Koeffizienten").

2. Beschränkung auf bivariate Assoziationen: In den genannten multivariaten Analysemethoden werden nur bivariate Assoziationen in Rechnung gestellt. Multivariate Assoziationen, wie z.B. Interaktionseffekte im Sinne der Varianzanalyse oder Moderatoreffekte von Drittvariablen bleiben unberücksichtigt, bzw. werden nur in ihrem "Niederschlag" auf die bivariaten Assoziationen erfasst.

3. Polytome nominale Merkmale und Merkmale mit unterschiedlichen Skalenniveaus: Polytome nominale Merkmale sind entweder gar nicht oder nur mit großem technischen Aufwand (Bildung von Dummy-Variablen) analysierbar. Assoziationskoeffizienten für Merkmale mit unterschiedlichem Skalenniveau sind noch problematischer.

Genau in diesen Punkten unterscheidet sich die **latent class Analyse (LCA)** grundlegend: sie benötigt keine bivariaten Assoziations- oder Distanzmaße, sondern geht - wie bei der log-linearen Analyse - unmittelbar von den aufgetretenen Häufigkeiten in den Zellen einer mehrdimensionalen Kreuztabelle aus, wobei jedes empirische Merkmal einer Dimension entspricht. Ähnlich wie bei der Faktorenanalyse wird ein zusätzliches, nicht beobachtetes und daher "latentes" Merkmal postuliert, das für die multivariaten Assoziationen in der Kreuztabelle "verantwortlich" ist. Dieses latente Merkmal ist im Gegensatz zur Faktorenanalyse, Rasch-Modell oder LISREL-Modell nicht metrisch sondern nominal skaliert, definiert also "latente Klassen" anstelle latenter Dimensionen.

LACORD ist ein Computerprogramm, das speziell für die **LA**tent Class Analyse bei **ORD**inalen manifesten Merkmalen entwickelt wurde, und damit insbesondere auch dem ersten der drei oben genannten Problembereiche Rechnung trägt.

2. Grundgedanken von LACORD

Ein typischer Anwendungsfall von LACORD sind Daten, die mit den in den Sozialwissenschaften nach wie vor gängigen Ratingskalen, z.B: "nie, selten, manchmal, oft, sehr oft" oder "überhaupt nicht, wenig, mittelmäßig, stark, sehr stark" erhoben wurden. Anstatt ungeprüft Intervallskalenniveau dieser Daten anzunehmen oder lediglich die Ranginformation in diesen Daten zu nutzen, werden die Wahrscheinlichkeiten, von einer Kategorie der Ratingskala zur nächst höheren zu "springen", zum Gegenstand der Modellbildung und Datenanalyse gemacht. Diese Wahrscheinlichkeiten heißen **"Schwellenwahrscheinlichkeiten"** (Sw) und bieten einen "genialen" Ansatzpunkt, mit ordinalen Daten umzugehen: In die Definition der Sw geht einerseits ein, was die Ordinalskala von der Nominalskala unterscheidet, nämlich die Information, welches die "nächst höhere", also benachbarte Kategorie ist. Andererseits brauchen keine ungeprüften Annahmen über die Abstände dieser Kategorien gemacht zu werden. Vielmehr geben die Sw als **Ergebnis** der Datenanalyse indirekt Auskunft über die Kategorienabstände auf der Ratingskala: Je höher die Sw, desto "größer" oder "breiter" ist die höher gelegene Kategorie im Vergleich zur niedrigeren. Die Sw ist folgendermaßen definiert:

$$Sw = P_x / (P_x + P_{x-1}),$$

wenn P_x die Wahrscheinlichkeit ist, in Kategorie x zu antworten. Die folgende Abbildung zeigt ein Beispiel für eine 6-kategorielle Ratingskala, in dem P_x durch die Breite der Kästchen symbolisiert ist.

P_x	0.1	0.2	0.2	0.3	.15	.05
x	0	1	2	3	4	5
Sw	.66	.5	.6	.33	.25	

Im Unterschied zu den Kategorienwahrscheinlichkeiten P_x, die der Restriktion unterliegen, sich zu 1 zu addieren, können die Sw beliebige Werte im Interval [0,1] annehmen.

LACORD führt diese Sw auf additiv zusammenwirkende Komponenten zurück, die - je nach Modell - vom Item i, der latenten Klasse g und der Antwortkategorie x abhängen. Da eine additive Zerlegung der Sw selbst - wegen ihrer Beschränkung auf das Intervall [0,1] - nicht möglich ist, wird die Zerlegung - wie beim Rasch-Modell - für die logistisch transformierten Parameter durchgeführt:

$$Sw = \exp(f_{gix}) / (1 + \exp(f_{gix})).$$

Die Art der additiven Zerlegung der logistischen Sw-Parameter f_{gix} ergibt die 8 unterschiedlichen Modelle von LACORD. Modell 7, welches für das im nächsten Abschnitt beschriebene Datenbeispiel am besten paßt, hat die folgende Zerlegung:

Modell 7: $\quad f_{gix} = \mu_{ig} + \tau_{xg} + (m+1-2x)\,\delta_{ig}.$

Hierbei sind die μ_{ig} die **Leichtigkeitsparameter** der Items für Personen aus der latenten Klasse g: je höher diese Itemleichtigkeit ist, desto leichter fällt es den Personen **alle** Schwellen auf der Ratingskala zu passieren, desto größer sind also die Antwortwahrscheinlichkeiten am oberen Ende der Skala. Die τ_{xg}-Parameter sind die **Leichtigkeiten der Ratingkategorien in Klasse g**, d.h. je größer ein τ_{xg} ist, desto häufiger sind Antworten in dieser Kategorie **im Vergleich zur vorangehenden Kategorie** (deswegen gibt es auch kein τ_{0g} !). Die **Dispersionsparameter** δ_{ig} der Items in Klasse g sind etwas schwierig nachzuvollziehen: ihr Koeffizient (m+1-2x) bewirkt, daß die **Abstände** der durch die τ_{xg} vorgegebenen Schwellenleichtigkeiten für ein Item um den doppelten Betrag von δ_{ig} vergrößert bzw. verkleinert werden. Damit steuert dieser Parameter die Dispersion des Items in einer Klasse, d.h. je **größer** δ_{ig}, desto **steiler** die Verteilung (desto kleiner die Dispersion).

3. Datenbeispiel

Der im folgenden in Auszügen dargestellte LACORD-Output beruht auf Daten aus dem "ALLBUS 86". Der ALLBUS (Allgemeine BevölkerungsUmfrage der Sozialwissenschaften) ist eine, alle zwei Jahre wiederholte repräsentative Bevölkerungsumfrage der BRD zu verschiedenen, teils wiederkehrenden, teils veränderten Themenbereichen, und dient in erster Linie der Forschung und Lehre in den Sozialwissenschaften. Die Grundgesamtheit ist definiert als alle Personen mit deutscher Staatsangehörigkeit, die in der BRD oder in West-Berlin zum Zeitpunkt der Erhebung gelebt und das 18. Lebensjahr vollendet haben.

Aus dieser Umfrage wurde die Frage 5 ausgewählt, in der nach der subjektiven Wichtigkeit von Lebensbereichen gefragt wurde. Die vorgegebenen Antwortmöglichkeiten erstreckten sich zwischen den Codes 1 (unwichtig) und 7 (sehr wichtig). Die subjektive Wichtigkeit folgender Lebensbereiche wurde erfragt:

1. Eigene Familie und Kinder
2. Beruf und Arbeit
3. Freizeit und Erholung
4. Freunde und Bekannte
5. Verwandtschaft
6. Religion und Kirche
7. Politik und öffentliches Leben
8. Nachbarschaft.

Im folgenden ist der LACORD-Output für die 5-Klassenlösung unter der Annahme von Modell 7 wiedergegeben:

```
LACORD * NUMBER OF CLASSES = 5 * MODEL 7
******************************************

CLASS SIZE        *    EXPECTATION VALUES
  1.CL:  0.237    *    5.73  4.72  4.78  4.80  4.57  3.80  3.78  4.33
  2.CL:  0.122    *    4.59  3.22  3.32  2.84  2.59  2.41  2.21  2.60
  3.CL:  0.155    *    4.54  5.07  5.48  5.09  2.86  1.05  3.67  2.68
  4.CL:  0.241    *    5.23  4.57  4.20  3.85  3.17  2.60  3.05  3.02
  5.CL:  0.245    *    5.64  4.92  5.13  5.32  4.76  3.97  4.09  4.88
```

Die als erstes ausgedruckten Erwartungswerte geben für jedes Item an, an welcher Stelle der Ratingskala in einer latenten Klasse der Erwartungswert der Antwortverteilung liegt. Hierbei ist zu beachten, daß die Antwortvariable stets mit dem Wert 0 beginnt, hier also von 0 bis 6, statt von 1 bis 7 wie im Fragebogen. Diese Werte eignen sich am besten für eine inhaltliche Interpretation der latenten Klassen.

Demnach zeichnen sich die 24,5% der befragten Personen in **Klasse 5** dadurch aus, daß sie allen Lebensbereichen eine sehr hohe Wichtigkeit beimessen, bei den letzten 5 Items sogar die höchste von allen Klassen. Das Gegenstück hierzu ist **Klasse 2**, in der mit der Ausnahme von "Religion und Kirche" allen Bereichen die geringste Wichtigkeit - verglichen mit den anderen Klassen - beigemessen wird. Diese Klasse umfaßt nur 12,2% der Personen.

Wesentlich spannender sind die anderen drei Klassen. So enthält **Klasse 3** jene 15.5% der befragten Personen, die den Lebensbereichen "Beruf und Arbeit" (5.07), "Freizeit und Erholung" (5.48) und "Freunde und Bekannte" (5.09) einen relativ hohen, den Lebensbereichen "Religion und Kirche" (1.05) und "Nachbarschaft" (2.68) hingegen einen relativ geringen Stellenwert beimessen. **Klasse 1** setzt mit dem absolut höchsten Erwartungswert von 5.73 einen deutlichen Akzent auf die "eigene Familie und Kinder" und zeigt ansonsten (alle Erwartungswerte unter 5 !) ein eher indifferentes, mittelhohes Antwortverhalten. Von diesen immerhin 23,7% der Personen unterscheidet sich die ebenfalls sehr große **4. Klasse** (24,1%) grob gesehen nur im

Niveau der Antworten, der deutliche Akzent auf der Familie ist auch hier gegeben.

```
CLASS SIZE    *  CATEGORY PROBABILITIES

1.CL  0.237 *0*  0.007  0.041  0.000  0.000  0.000  0.029  0.008  0.000
            *1*  0.003  0.034  0.002  0.000  0.000  0.060  0.035  0.003
            *2*  0.002  0.034  0.015  0.001  0.006  0.098  0.098  0.028
            *3*  0.006  0.066  0.086  0.039  0.093  0.200  0.258  0.168
            *4*  0.018  0.110  0.213  0.250  0.313  0.224  0.283  0.320
            *5*  0.146  0.314  0.460  0.584  0.493  0.284  0.265  0.397
            *6*  0.817  0.402  0.223  0.126  0.093  0.104  0.054  0.083

2.CL  0.122 *0*  0.095  0.207  0.055  0.082  0.143  0.279  0.246  0.168
            *1*  0.047  0.113  0.096  0.136  0.164  0.160  0.186  0.162
            *2*  0.035  0.080  0.142  0.179  0.169  0.110  0.145  0.152
            *3*  0.056  0.107  0.254  0.274  0.227  0.130  0.169  0.201
            *4*  0.070  0.097  0.196  0.172  0.142  0.095  0.105  0.133
            *5*  0.155  0.136  0.153  0.104  0.095  0.099  0.081  0.103
            *6*  0.542  0.260  0.104  0.052  0.060  0.128  0.067  0.081

3.CL  0.155 *0*  0.067  0.004  0.000  0.000  0.103  0.484  0.036  0.109
            *1*  0.032  0.006  0.000  0.001  0.095  0.194  0.045  0.106
            *2*  0.049  0.023  0.002  0.012  0.185  0.167  0.121  0.208
            *3*  0.090  0.077  0.020  0.069  0.272  0.109  0.246  0.287
            *4*  0.125  0.150  0.094  0.177  0.196  0.036  0.247  0.183
            *5*  0.189  0.246  0.263  0.292  0.099  0.008  0.177  0.077
            *6*  0.449  0.494  0.622  0.447  0.051  0.002  0.129  0.031

4.CL  0.241 *0*  0.004  0.001  0.000  0.000  0.008  0.083  0.010  0.013
            *1*  0.009  0.008  0.002  0.003  0.055  0.159  0.066  0.075
            *2*  0.022  0.040  0.030  0.053  0.200  0.234  0.223  0.227
            *3*  0.053  0.138  0.195  0.289  0.360  0.253  0.369  0.356
            *4*  0.113  0.261  0.400  0.430  0.269  0.168  0.247  0.240
            *5*  0.226  0.291  0.280  0.190  0.089  0.073  0.072  0.075
            *6*  0.573  0.261  0.092  0.034  0.018  0.029  0.013  0.015

5.CL  0.245 *0*  0.017  0.093  0.014  0.008  0.025  0.093  0.069  0.021
            *1*  0.004  0.016  0.008  0.005  0.014  0.037  0.032  0.012
            *2*  0.006  0.020  0.022  0.015  0.037  0.069  0.066  0.032
            *3*  0.023  0.052  0.095  0.072  0.141  0.192  0.199  0.126
            *4*  0.038  0.062  0.127  0.108  0.161  0.169  0.180  0.151
            *5*  0.065  0.075  0.122  0.118  0.127  0.105  0.112  0.127
            *6*  0.847  0.681  0.612  0.674  0.494  0.336  0.342  0.532
```

Wesentlich detaillierter als die Erwartungswerte geben die vollständigen Antwortverteilungen in den latenten Klassen die Ergebnisse der Analyse wieder (category probabilities). Regelmäßigkeiten oder Unregelmäßigkeiten bezüglich der **Form** der Verteilungen, z.B. hinsichtlich der Größe der Kategorien oder der Dispersion der Items lassen sich jedoch leichter an den Schwellenparametern ablesen.

```
THRESHOLD PARAMETERS
********************

LOGISTIC ITEM EASINESS PARAMETERS
ITEM NO.:    1     2     3     4     5     6     7     8
1.CL :     0.79  0.38  1.13  2.54  1.75  0.21  0.33  1.02
2.CL :     0.29  0.04  0.11 -0.08 -0.14 -0.13 -0.22 -0.12
3.CL :     0.32  0.79  1.87  1.19 -0.12 -0.92  0.21 -0.21
4.CL :     0.82  0.93  1.28  1.03  0.14 -0.18  0.04  0.02
5.CL :     0.65  0.33  0.64  0.74  0.50  0.21  0.27  0.54

LOGISTIC CATEGORY EASINESS PARAMETERS
CATEGORY  X= 1      2       3       4       5       6
1.CL.:     1.074   0.625   0.611  -0.211  -0.317  -1.782
2.CL.:    -0.093  -0.046   0.365  -0.254  -0.027   0.055
3.CL.:    -0.063   0.729   0.484  -0.191  -0.505  -0.453
4.CL.:     1.571   1.009   0.403  -0.385  -1.098  -1.500
5.CL.:    -1.359   0.280   0.773  -0.300  -0.559   1.165

ITEM DISPERSION PARAMETERS
ITEM NO.:   1      2      3      4      5      6      7      8
1.CL.:   -0.542 -0.329  0.015  0.457  0.326 -0.114  0.026  0.160
2.CL.:   -0.181 -0.111  0.110  0.134  0.074 -0.067  0.006  0.035
3.CL.:   -0.200 -0.072  0.112  0.062  0.020  0.014  0.015  0.050
4.CL.:   -0.322 -0.093  0.180  0.251  0.047 -0.149  0.058  0.029
5.CL.:   -0.149 -0.140  0.038  0.032  0.060  0.043  0.062  0.054
```

Die **Itemleichtigkeiten** liegen auf einer logistischen Skala und können z.B. direkt mit den Ergebnissen einer Rasch-Analyse derselben Daten verglichen werden. Für eine inhaltliche Interpretation der Klassen eignen sie sich weniger, da sie nur unter Berücksichtigung der beiden anderen Parameterarten präzise Aussagen machen, und dann in der Regel dieselben wie die Erwartungswerte.

Die **Kategorienleichtigkeiten** sagen etwas über die "Größe" der Ratingkategorien aus. In Klasse 1 und 4, also jenen fast 50% der Personen, die der eigenen Familie die höchste Wichtigkeit einräumen, sind die Schwellen nach absteigender Leichtigkeit geordnet. Dies entspricht dem "Idealfall" der Benutzung von Ratingskalen, da man es geradezu als Definitionsmerkmal von Ratingskalen verstehen kann, daß die Schwellen "von Stufe zu Stufe höher", d.h. schwerer werden. Auf jeden Fall garantieren sinkende Schwellenleichtigkeiten stets unimodale Antwortverteilungen, was nur durch große negative

Dispersionsparameter wieder zunichte gemacht werden kann (siehe z.B. das zweite Item in Klasse 1).

In Klasse 2 sind die beiden ersten und beiden letzten Kategorienleichtigkeiten nahe bei Null und relativ nichtssagend. Dagegen ist die Schwelle zur dritten Kategorie sehr leicht (0.365) und die Schwelle zur vierten Kategorie sehr schwer (-0.254). Das bedeutet, daß in dieser Klasse eine Antworttendenz zur Mitte vorliegt, da die Personen "leicht" in die mittlere Kategorie hinein, aber "schwer" wieder hinaus finden. Dementsprechend finden sich in den Kategorienwahrscheinlichkeiten der 2. Klasse überstarke Besetzungen der mittleren Kategorie (z.B. 0.169 beim 7. Item). Aufgrund analoger Argumentation gibt es in Klasse 3 eine Tendenz zur extremen Antwort, genauer: einzelne Lebensbereiche für völlig unwichtig zu halten. Dies deshalb, weil die erste Schwelle - gemessen am Kriterium sinkender Leichtigkeiten - viel zu schwer ist (-0.063). Klasse 5 hat sogar an beiden Enden der Ratingskala eine Tendenz zum extremen Urteil (erste Schwelle schwer, letzte Schwelle leicht). Die Konsequenz einer trimodalen Verteilung zeigt sich besonders ausgeprägt bei Item 6 und 7 in dieser Klasse.

Auf die Interpretation der **Dispersionsparameter** soll hier verzichtet werden, da auch hier - wie bei den Itemleichtigkeiten - jeweils die beiden anderen Parameterarten mit zu berücksichtigen sind und die inhaltliche "Ausbeute" bei diesem Datenbeispiel relativ gering zu sein scheint.

```
GOODNESS OF FIT STATISTICS:
****************************

MODEL* LOG-LIKELI * PARMS *LIKELI.RATIO* DEG.OF FR. * AIC-INDEX
    3 * -38619.578 *    56 *  29309.977 *   5764744  * 77351.156
    4 * -38529.035 *    84 *  29128.891 *   5764716  * 77226.070
    7 * -37912.840 *   104 *  27896.500 *   5764696  * 76033.680
    8 * -37800.937 *   244 *  27672.695 *   5764556  * 76089.875
SAT.M. -23964.590 *
```

Am Ende stehen verschiedene **Goodness of Fit Maße**. Diese liefern Hinweise dafür, welches Modell am besten mit den Daten vereinbar ist. Auf den ersten Blick scheint die "Log-Likelihood" für das Modell 8 am größten zu sein; das ist allerdings auch kein Wunder, weil hier die meisten Parameter für die Schätzung der Zellenhäufigkeiten zur Verfügung stehen. Genau dies berücksichtigt der "AIC-Index", in den die Anzahl der zu schätzenden Parameter eingeht. Nach dem AIC-Kriterium paßt Modell 7 am besten auf die Daten, da für dieses Modell der Wert am kleinsten ist.

Sofern die Bedingungen für Likelihood-Qoutienten-Tests erfüllt sind (nicht zu viele erwartete Häufigkeiten unter 1) kann der "Likelihood-Ratio" als inferenzstatistisches Maß herangezogen werden. Im vorliegenden Datenbeispiel sind diese Bedingungen ganz gewiß nicht erfüllt, denn von den 5 764 801 Zellen der Kreuztabelle sind nur 2858 bestetzt.

Literatur

ROST, J.: Quantitative und qualitative probabilistische Testtheorie. Bern: Huber, 1988.

ROST, J.: Rating scale analysis with latent class models. Psychometrika 1988, 53, 3 327-348.

ROST, J.: Test theory with qualitative and quantitative latent variables. In: LANGEHEINE, R. & ROST, J.: Latent trait and latent class models. New York: Plenum, 1988.

ROST, J.: Measuring Attitudes with a threshold model drawing on a traditional scaling concept. Applied Pschological Measurement 1988, 12, 4, 397-409

ROST, J.: LACORD - Latent class analysis for ordinal variables - A FORTRAN program. Kiel: IPN, 1988.

Das Programm LACORD ist erhältlich bei: Jürgen Rost, IPN, Olshausenstr. 62, 2300 Kiel 1

The Computer Program AGREE for Nominal Scale Agreement

M.C.J. Lina and R. Popping

1. Introduction

In order to introduce the term agreement a simple example is given: In an investigation it is necessary to assign a sample of subjects to the categories in favor or against something. This is done by two coders. When they have finished their task the assignments are compared. The number of times the both assigned a statement to the same category is a starting point for computing the reliability. If this reliability, which is called agreement, is sufficient, the investigator can continue using the assignments by one of the coders. If he were to use the assignments by the other coder, he would get (nearly) the same results.

Agreement is very often considered as a special kind of association. There are differences however. It is important to determine the similarity of the content of behavior (in a broad sense) between coders in general with the degree of identity of this behavior. The behavior of one coder does not have to be predicted from that of the other. In case of association the strength of the linear relationship between the variables is investigated. Here the goal is to predict the values of one variable from those of the other.

Very often the coders have to assign the subjects to a variable having a nominal scale. When a subject is assigned to a category, it will be called an entity.

In the situation where a measure of nominal scale agreement is to be computed, the choice of the agreement index is determined by whether or not the response categories were known a priori to the coders.

When the categories are known, they are equal for all coders, and all entities would be assigned to one of these categories. Another situation is when the response categories have to be developed by the coders during the assigning process. In this situation each coder may finish with a different set and number of categories. This situation arises most in pilot studies, where the investigator wishes to find a set of response categories that will be used in the main investigation.

Popping (1988) has shown that in the first situation the agreement kappa (Cohen, 1960) performs best, while in the second situation the index D2 (Popping, 1983) performs best. Extensions of these indices are available for nearly all research situations that are realistic. Review papers with regard to nominal scale agreement are Landis and Koch (1975), Bartko and Carpenter (1976), and Fleiss (1981).

This paper describes the computer package AGREE which can be used in computing the two indices kappa and D2 in many research situations.

2. Definition of indices

The basic formulas of kappa and D2 for computing the agreement between two coders, whose classifications are represented in an agreement table, are presented here. Suppose that for the computation of kappa, N entities have been assigned to c categories by the two coders. The number of entities assigned by one coder to category i is denoted $f_{i.}$, and the number of entities assigned by the other coder to category j by $f_{.j}$. The number of assignments by the first coder to category i and by the second one to category j is denoted by f_{ij}. The formula for kappa is

$$K = (P_o - P_e) / (N - P_e),$$

where

$$P_o = \sum_{i=1}^{c} f_{ii};$$

$$P_e = \sum_{i=1}^{c} f_{i.} f_{.i} / N.$$

In this formula P_o is the amount of observed agreement. In case of independence, given the marginals, there would already be the amount of agreement P_e. Therefore, a correction is made for this amount of agreement. In order that the index assumes the value 1 in case of perfect agreement, this correction is also made in the denominator.

The D2-index is based on the same principle. Because the sets of response categories, as developed by the coders, can refer to different contents, it is not possible just to consider the entities on the diagonal of the agreement-table. Instead pairs of entities have to be compared. The N(N-1)/2 pairs of entities per coder can be assigned to the classes: 'same' category and 'different' category. Now the pairs can be placed in a 2*2 table in which cell 'same-same' denotes the pairs on which there is agreement among the coders. Here this cell denotes the amount of observed agreement.

Since the coders may have used not only categories referring to a different content, but also a different number of categories, it is assumed that one coder uses again c categories, and the other one r categories. D2 is defined as

$$D2 = (D_o - D_e) / (D_m - D_e),$$

where

$$D_o = \sum_{i=1}^{r} \sum_{j=1}^{c} f_{ij} (f_{ij} - 1) / 2;$$

$$D_e = \sum_{i=1}^{r} \sum_{j=1}^{c} c_{ij},$$

$$c_{ij} = g_{ij} (h_{ij} - 0.5 \, g_{ij} - 0.5),$$

$$h_{ij} = f_{i.} \, f_{.j} / N,$$

$$g_{ij} = \text{entier} (h_{ij});$$

$$D_m = \max (D_r, D_c),$$

$$D_r = \sum_{i=1}^{r} f_{i.} (f_{i.} - 1) / 2,$$

$$D_c = \sum_{j=1}^{c} f_{.j} (f_{.j} - 1) / 2.$$

3. Program features

The AGREE-package is available on IBM personal computers and compatibles. The program needs almost 360 kB, the help-file almost 36 kB.

The program should be used interactively, but batch usage is possible. The keywords are entered from a batch file then. The program is 'user friendly'. It has a keyword structure. In case of problems it is possible to enter the HELP-command. In case of errors a clear message is given.

3.1. Input

The program has the possibility to enter both agreement-tables and data matrices, i.e. matrices with entities for the rows and coders (and items) for the columns. The data can be entered as part of the set up via the programs own spreadsheet, but they can also be copied from any file. When the necessary analyses have been performed on these data, it is possible to enter new data.

3.2. Output

The standard output consists of the value computed for the agreement index requested, and the number of entities that have been used in the computations. Optionally the observed and expected amount of agreement are given as output, and/or the variance and null-variance of the index.

It is possible to copy results of the analyses to an output file. This file can be send to a line printer when the session is finished.

3.3. Analyses

In the program an agreement-table is considered as a data matrix containing the assignments by two coders. The program offers the possibility of doing several analyses after each other. These can be analyses on different parts of the data matrix. Missing values can be considered as such, in which case the corresponding entities will be kept out of the analyses; they can also be considered as zeroes. The program offers some facilities for datamanipulation.

The types of analyses that can be performed are among others the computation of:
- (weighted) agreement between two coders;
- (weighted) agreement between more than two coders, based on the mean observed and null expected agreement;
- (weighted) agreement between several coders and a standard;

- simultaneous agreement between coders;
- majority agreement between coders;
- (weighted) agreement in the situation where per assignment the coder is not known;
- simultaneous agreement for the same situation;
- majority agreement for that situation;
- agreement per category can be computed for the above situations (except majority agreement);
- agreement between clusters of coders;
- the contribution to agreement of an extra coder.

It is also possible to select the best coder, and to compare lateral distributions.

3.4. Capabilities and limitations

The datamatrix can contain the assignments by 250 coders. These can be assignments by a number of coders to one or more items (remember: analyses can be performed on only a part of the data matrix). At most 10.000 entities are allowed. Per analysis the assignments by 40 coders can be entered. The coders may have assigned the entities to 16 different categories, which are indicated by numbers in the range 1 to 999 (in case weights are used, the range is 1 to 16).

3.5. Availability

The AGREE package is distributed by iec ProGAMMA, Kraneweg 8, 9718 JP Groningen, The Netherlands. An extended description is Popping (1989).

4. References

Bartko, J.J. & Carpenter, W.T., 1976
    'Methods and Theory of Reliability.' **Journal of Nervous and Mental Disease**, 163, 307-317.

Cohen, J., 1960
    'A Coefficient of Agreement for Nominal Scales.' **Educational and Psychological Measurement**, 20, 37-46.

Fleiss, J.L., 1981
    Statistical Methods for Rates and Proportions. New York: Wiley.

Landis, J.R. & Koch, G.G., 1975
    'A Review of Statistical Methods in the Analysis of Data Arising from ObserverReliabilityStudies.' StatisticaNeerlandica,29,101-123,151-161.

Popping, R., 1983
'Traces of Agreement. On the Dot-Product as a Coefficient of Agreement.' **Quality & Quantity**, 17, 1-18.

Popping, R., 1988
'On Agreement Indices for Nominal Data'. In: Saris, W.E. & Gallhofer, I.N. (eds.), **Sociometric Research**, Vol. I., London: McMillan, 90-105.

Popping, R., 1989
ComputingAgreementforNominalData.TheComputerProgramAGREE 5.0. Groningen : iec ProGAMMA.

Statistik und linguistische Datenverarbeitung

Sprachverarbeitung mit AWK

R. Glas

Summary
This article introduces to the use of the AWK programming language for linguistic purposes. A short overview of the language is followed by a number of practical AWK programmes treating various aspects of linguistic analysis. It is further demonstrated that applications written in AWK are, due to their brevity, much easier to work with than other application requiring modification or reformatting of the data.

Sprachverarbeitung mit AWK

1. Der Name der Sprache AWK leitet sich von ihren Autoren her: Aho, Kernighan und Weinberger. Eine erste Version lag 1977 vor. Eine erweiterte Version erschien 1985. Sie wird von den genannten Autoren in dem vorzüglichen Handbuch "The AWK Programming Language" beschrieben[1]. AWK ist Bestandteil von UNIX, es liegt aber mittlerweile auch eine MS-DOS-Version vor, die entweder als Bestandteil von MKS-Toolkit oder einzeln erhältlich ist und der neuen, im Handbuch beschriebenen AWK-Version entspricht.[2] Der hauptsächliche Unterschied zwischen der alten und der neuen AWK-Version besteht darin, daß die neue Version dem Anwender die Möglichkeit gibt, selbst Funktionen zu schreiben.

2. Die Stärke von AWK bei der Sprachverarbeitung liegt vor allem in zwei Bereichen: einmal in der Flexibilität und Schnelligkeit beim "pattern matching", zum anderen in der Leichtigkeit der Programmierung. AWK-Programme sind außergewöhnlich kurz[3] und sind, gerade wenn es um die Verarbeitung sprachlicher Daten geht, schnell zu erstellen. Als Haupteinsatzgebiete für AWK empfehlen sich
- "pattern matching"
- elementare sprachstatistische Untersuchungen
- die Erstellung von zusammenfassenden Berichten und tabellarischen Übersichten
- philologische Standardanwendungen wie die Erstellung von Indices und Konkordanzen

- vorbereitende Arbeiten im Bereich der linguistischen Datenverarbeitung
  wie Umkodieren, Fehlersuche in Texten, Testen von Syntaxregeln etc.
AWK-Programme eignen sie sich auch besonders gut für Programme, die nur einmal gebraucht werden.

Die Kürze von AWK-Programmen hat mehrere Gründe: zum einen entfällt die Vereinbarung von Variablentypen: der Typ einer Variablen wird aus ihrem Verwendungskontext erkannt. Auch die Initalisierung von Variablen ist oft entbehrlich; sie werden durch Gebrauch ins Leben gerufen und erhalten Null bzw. Leerstring als Startwert. Ebenso entfallen weitgehend Anweisungen zum Öffnen und Schließen von Dateien. Wird nichts anderes bestimmt, so werden die Eingabedateien, die beim Aufruf von AWK angegeben wurden, sequentiell gelesen und verarbeitet. Weiterhin verfügt AWK über mehrere vordefinierte Variablen und Funktionen, die gerade die Verarbeitung sprachlicher Daten sehr erleichtern.

3. AWK ist ein Interpreter mit einer C-ähnlichen Syntax. Ein AWK-Programm besteht aus maximal drei Teilen: einem Anfangs-, einem Mittel- und einem Schlußteil. Jeder dieser drei Teile ist optional. Der Anfangsteil wird als solcher festgelegt durch das reservierte Wort BEGIN und enthält alle Wertzuweisungen und Anweisungen, die ausgeführt werden, bevor die Eingabedatei gelesen wird; der Mittelteil, der nicht eigens gekennzeichnet wird, enthält alle Anweisungen, die ausgeführt werden, solange die Eingabedatei gelesen wird; der Schlußteil, der durch das reservierte Wort END gekennzeichnet ist, enthält alle Anweisungen, die nach dem Lesen der Eingabedatei zur Ausführung kommen. Hierzu ein Beispiel:

(1) # Ermittelt den längsten Satz und gibt ihn aus
    BEGIN { RS = "/" }
    NF > maxlaenge { maxlaenge = NF }
    END   { print "Der längste Satz hat",maxlaenge,"Wortformen" }

Zu Beginn wird der vordefinierten Variablen RS (Record Separator), die auf Zeilenende voreingestellt ist, ein neuer Wert zugewiesen (hier die Satz-endemarke "/", s. dazu Abschnitt 3.3). Dann, im Mittelteil, werden die Eingabedaten sequentiell gelesen und verarbeitet. Die einzelnen Verarbeitungsschritte werden formuliert als eine Folge von "pattern {action}"-Anweisungen. Liegt das "pattern" (hier: NF > maxlaenge) vor, wird die "action" (hier: {maxlaenge = NF}) ausgeführt, andernfalls wird zur nächsten Anweisung übergegangen oder, falls keine Anweisung mehr folgt, der

nächste Datensatz verarbeitet. Im Schlußteil des Beispiels wird dann der Wert, den die Variable maxlaenge nach dem Lesen der gesamten Eingabedaten hat, ausgegeben.
Die beiden Teile einer "pattern {action}"-Anweisung sind optional: eine Anweisung kann nur aus einer "action" bestehen oder sie kann auch nur aus einem "pattern" bestehen (in diesem Falle wird die "print"-Anweisung ausgeführt).

3.1 Beispiel (1) macht neben RS noch von einer weiteren vordefinierten Variablen Gebrauch, von NF (Number of Fields). Diese Variable wird für jeden gelesenen Datensatz jeweils neu berechnet und zwar nach Maßgabe von RS (Record Separator) und FS (Field Separator, voreingestellt auf das Leer- bzw. das Tabulatorzeichen). Entsprechend zu NF gibt es auch die vordefinierte Variable NR (Number of Records). Das folgende Beispiel benutzt NF zur Berechnung der Summe der Tokens in einem Text:

(2) { tokens += NF }
    END { print "Summe der Tokens:", tokens }

In Entsprechung zu NF gibt es auch eine vordefinierte Variable NR (Number of Records). So gibt beispielsweise das folgende AWK-Programm die Anzahl der Zeilen eines Textes oder, falls RS entsprechend gewählt wurde, auch die Anzahl der Sätze eines Textes aus:

(3) END { print NR }

Das Beispiel mag befremden, da es nur aus dem Schlußteil besteht, aber, wie schon gesagt, die drei Teile eines AWK-Programms sind optional, und das angeführte Beispiel ist, so wie es hier präsentiert wird, lauffähig.
Das folgende Beispiel benutzt NR, um die Anzahl der Wortformen pro Satz und einige weitere Werte zu berechnen, wobei auch einige der vordefinierten numerischen Funktionen zum Einsatz kommen:

```
(4) { RS = "/" }
    NF > 0 { sum += NF ; sumq += NF**2 }
    END { if (NR > 1)
              printf("Anzahl der Sätze:     %8.2f\n", NR)
              m = ((NR*sumq)-sum**2); n = (NR*(NR-1)); v = (m/n)
              printf("Mittlere Satzlänge: %8.2f\n", sum/NR)
              printf("Varianz:              %8.2f\n", v)
              printf("Standardabweichung: %8.2f\n", sqrt(v) ) }
```

Angewandt auf die Satire "Auch ich war in Arkadien" von Joseph von Eichendorff, die ich im folgenden als Beispieltext verwende, erhält man als Ausgabe:

Anzahl der Sätze: 301.00
Mittlere Satzlänge: 20.08
Varianz: 161.71
Standardabweichung: 12.72

3.2 Der bereits erwähnte Feldbegrenzer FS läßt sich frei festlegen, auch mehrere Alternativen sind zulässig. Diese Möglichkeit läßt sich unter anderem dazu nutzen, Satzzeichen zu übergehen, wie folgendes Beispiel zeigt:

```
(5) BEGIN { FS = ",[ ]+|,[ ]+|\.[ ]+|[ ]+" }
    { for (i=1;i<=NF;i++) print $i }
```

Das Programmbeispiel erzeugt eine Wortformenliste, aus der alle Satzzeichen entfernt sind. Dabei wurden die folgenden Metazeichen verwendet:

+   ein oder mehrere Vorkommen (linksgerichtet)
\   Fluchtsymbol (rechtsgerichtet)
| Alternative
[]   hier zur Darstellung des Leerzeichens verwendet, sonst alternative Zeichen einschließend, z.B. [Gg]

In Beispiel (5) wird außerdem eine weitere vordefinierte Variable benutzt, die Variable $i. Sie ermöglicht es, auf bestimmte einzelne Felder zuzugreifen, mit $1 auf das erste Feld (im allgemeinen die erste Wortform einer Zeile), mit $2 auf das zweite Feld, mit $NF auf das letzte Feld. So gibt beispielsweise das folgende Programm die beiden Positionen einer Liste in umgekehrter Reihenfolge aus:

```
(6) { print $2, $1 }
```

Hier ein weiteres Beispiel für die Verwendungsmöglichkeiten der vordefinierten Variablen $i :

(7) BEGIN { RS = "/" }
    {for (i=1;i<(NF-1);i++) print($i, $(i+1)) | "sort | uniq -c" }

Das Programm erzeugt eine Liste, die alle innerhalb der Satzgrenzen unmittelbar aufeinanderfolgenden Wortformenpaare enthält, sortiert diese Liste und gibt die verschiedenen Wortformenpaare und die Anzahl ihrer Vorkommen aus. Auf ähnliche Weise lassen sich auch Wortformentripel auflisten. Zieht man nur die mehrfach belegten Fälle in Betracht, so erhält man für den genannten Beispieltext die folgende Liste:

```
2 Auf einmal blieb              2 ich an den
2 Brei im Kessel                3 ich in der
2 Da hatte ich                  2 ich war in
2 Finsternis, nieder mit        2 ich weiß nicht,
2 Gasthofe Zum goldenen         2 im Saale auf
2 In demselben Augenblick       2 in das dickste
2 Saale auf und                 2 in der Angst
2 Und in der                    2 in der Eile
2 Währenddes war der            2 in der Luft
4 Zeit zu Zeit                  3 in der Tat
2 Zum goldenen Zeitgeist        2 in der Tat,
2 am Ende noch                  3 mir der Professor
2 an, wie er                    2 mit der Zeit
2 auf dem Rücken                2 mitten durch das
2 auf und nieder,               2 nach allen Seiten
2 aus dem Munde                 2 nach und nach
2 daß ich in                    2 nieder mit der
2 dem Rücken des                2 rief mir der
2 der Professor in              2 sich in die
2 der Tat nicht                 2 sie schnell auf
3 der öffentlichen Meinung      2 und immer wieder
2 die Augen wieder              3 von Zeit zu
2 die Finsternis, nieder        3 von allen Seiten
2 die Oberpriester und          2 von der Stirn
3 die öffentliche Meinung       2 war der Professor
2 er mir den                    2 weiche die Finsternis,
2 ganz rotblau im               2 weiß nicht, ob
2 hatte ich denn
```

Wie man sogleich sieht, bedarf eine solche Liste der Nachbearbeitung, da mehrfach belegte Wortformenfolgen aus mehr als drei Elementen in einer solchen Liste mehrfach und an verschiedenen Stellen vorkommen. In obiger Liste ist dies z.B. der Fall bei *von Zeit zu Zeit*. Dennoch sind solche Listen sehr nützlich, beispielsweise um feste Syntagmen zu erkennen wie *nach und nach*, mehrteilige Namen wie *Zum goldenen Zeitgeist* (hier der Name eines Gasthauses), häufig gebrauchte Formulierungsmuster, soweit sie nicht flektiert vorkommen etc. Darüberhinaus geben solche Listen Aufschluß über die Stereotypie eines Textes; das allerdings nur mit Einschränkung, da diejenigen Fälle, die sich nur durch die Flexion unterscheiden, unberücksichtigt bleiben.

Es besteht übrigens nicht nur die Möglichkeit, die Ausgabe an ein anderes UNIX-Kommando zu übergeben, wie es hier (Beispiel 7) geschah, sondern die Übergabe kann auch an ein weiteres AWK-Programm erfolgen.

3.3 Die vordefinierte Variable RS ermöglicht es, auch mit langen Zeichenketten zu arbeiten, unter UNIX in der Regel mit Ketten, die bis zu 3000 Zeichen lang sind. Im Unterschied zu FS sind aber die Wertzuweisungsmöglichkeiten an die Variable RS begrenzter und abhängig von der jeweiligen AWK-Version. Im ungünstigsten Falle ist nur die Zuweisung eines einzelnen Zeichens möglich. Für diesen Fall empfiehlt es sich, von dem zu bearbeitenden Text eine Arbeitsversion zu erstellen, in der das auf das Satzende folgende Leerzeichen durch ein einheitliches Zeichen, etwa "/", wie hier in einigen Beispielen, ersetzt ist. Das ist keineswegs erforderlich, bedeutet aber für einige Anwendungen größeren Komfort. Die Zeichensubstitution kann auf unterschiedliche Weise erfolgen: durch die Zeichenkettenfunktion "gsub" (global substitution) oder "substr" (substring), oder durch eine Anweisung vom Typ "pattern {action}", wie im folgenden Beispiel:

```
(8) { for (i = 1;i <= NF;i++)  {
         $i ~ /\!$|;$|\?$|\.$/ ?  $i = $i "/" : $i = $i " "
         printf $i }  }
    { printf "\n" }
```

Noch nicht erwähnte Metazeichen:
  `^` Beginn der Zeichenkette (rechtsgerichtet)
  $ Ende einer Zeichenkette (linksgerichtet)
  ! Negationsoperator
  ~ "matching operator"

Zu erwähnen ist ferner der konditionale Operator "?", der aus C bekannt ist; ferner die Tatsache, daß AWK keinen eigenen Operator für die Konkatenation besitzt; die Konkatenation wird einfach durch das Nebeneinander dargestellt ($i "/" bzw. $i " ").

3.4 Die Funktion "getline" bewirkt das Lesen einer neuen Zeile. Die Funktion liefert den Wert 1, wenn der Lesevorgang erfolgreich war. Im folgenden Beispiel wird sie zur Steuerung des Programmablaufs benutzt. Das Beispielprogramm sucht alle Belege von *gold...* in einem Text und gibt sie in einem dreizeiligen Kontext mit vorangestellter Seitenangabe aus:

```
(9) $0 ~ /^[0-9]+/   { seite = $0; getline }
    ausgabe == "ja"  { printf "%s\n\n", $0; ausgabe = "nein" }
    /[Gg]old/        { printf("\n%s\n%s\n%s\n", seite, zeile1, $0)
                       ausgabe = "ja"; n++ }
    END              { printf "Anzahl der Belege: %d\n", n }
```

Angewandt auf den genannten Beispieltext erhält man unter anderem:

.....
732
einem dicken Buche über Urrecht und Menschheitswohl, wie ich an
den großen goldnen Buchstaben auf dem Rücken des Buches erkennen
konnte. Ein Oberpriester im Talar eines ägyptischen Weisen

738
Als ich die Augen wieder aufschlug, lag ich ruhig in dem Gasthofe
Zum goldenen Zeitgeist im Bett. Die Sonne schien schon hell
ins Zimmer, der fatale Kellner stand neben mir und lächelte

Anzahl der Belege: 6

3.5 Eine Besonderheit von AWK sind die Reihungen. Im Unterschied zu gewöhnlichen "arrays" werden die Indizes von Zeichenkettenkonstanten gebildet. Das heißt, ein Programm wie das folgende

```
(10)      { anfang[$1] }
    END   { for (i in anfang) print i }
```

würde die Ausgabe aller gleichen Zeilenanfänge veranlassen, wobei die for-Schleife unter Verwendung einer Variablen das Auslesen der Indizes bewirkt. Alle gleichen Zeilenanfänge kommen also in der so erzeugten Liste nur einmal vor.
Zur Verdeutlichung noch ein weiteres Beispiel. Zunächst werden alle Satz- und Sonderzeichen mittels der Funktion "gsub" unterdrückt, dann (2. Zeile) wird die Reihung gebildet und im Endteil ausgegeben:

```
(11) { gsub(/,|;|:|\.|\?|\!|\(|\)|\-|\&|<|>/,"",$0) }
     { for (i = 1;i <= NF;i++)  ++wortform[$i] }
     END { for (w in wortform) printf "%d\t%s\n", wortform[w], w }
```

Das Programm erzeugt eine Liste, die die Types (w) und ihre absolute Häufigkeit (wortform[w]) enthält. Da die Reihung immer nur die Types enthält, ist es offensichtlich, daß sich auf diese Weise auch die TTR berechnen läßt, vorausgesetzt allerdings, man verfügt, wenn es sich um einen langen Text handelt, über einen ausreichend großen Arbeitsspeicher. Natürlich lassen sich Type-Listen in AWK auch auf andere Weise erzeugen, aber der Gebrauch von Reihungen ist der kürzeste Weg. Es gibt allenfalls eine noch kürzere Verfahrensweise, wenn man voraussetzt, daß die Satz- und Sonderzeichen bereits entfernt sind: man weist RS das Leerzeichen als Wert zu:

(12) awk '{ RS = " "; print }' eingabe.dat | sort | uniq

Zum Schluß noch ein Programmbeispiel für die Verwendung einer Stopwortliste:

(13) BEGIN { FS = ",[ ]|;[ ]|\.[ ]|[ ]"
              while (getline <"stopwort.dat" > 0) stopwort[$0] }
     {for (i=1;i<=NF;i++) {if ($i in stopwort) ; else print $i } }

Das Beispiel zeigt, wie die Prüfung auf Enthaltensein bei einer Reihung erfolgt (if ($i in stopwort)), und wie die Funktion "getline" und die leere Anweisung ";" verwendet werden kann. Das Ergebnis ist ein um die Elemente der Stopwortliste verkürzter vertikalisierter Text.

4. Die Kürze von AWK-Programmen macht sie nicht nur geeignet für Arbeiten, die nur einmal anfallen. Vielmehr ist im Einzelfall zu erwägen, ob es nicht ökonomischer ist, ein AWK-Programm zu schreiben oder ein vorhandenes zu ändern, als einen Text, der verarbeitet werden soll, den Anforderungen eines Anwenderprogramms anzupassen.

Anmerkungen
[1]) Alfred V. Aho/Brian W. Kernighan/Peter J. Weinberger: The AWK Programming Language. Reading, Mass.: Addison-Wesley Publishing Company. 1988

[2]) Mortice Kern Systems Inc., 35 King Street North, Waterloo, Ontario, Canada. Der Preis für AWK beträgt einschl. Handbuch ca. 99 US-Dollar

[3]) Das Handbuch gibt auf S.123 anhand eines KWIC-Index-Programms ein eindrucksvolles Beispiel. Zum Laufzeitverhalten von AWK s. S.183

Für Hinweise und Anregungen danke ich dem HRZ der Universität Dortmund.

F. Faulbaum, R. Haux und K.-H. Jöckel (Hrsg.) (1990). SoftStat '89
Fortschritte der Statistik-Software 2. Stuttgart: Gustav Fischer, 487 - 494

New Possibilities and Developments of Text Analysis with INTEXT/PC

H. Klein

1 Summary

INTEXT/PC is a program package for the analysis of texts in both the humanities and the social sciences. It's written in C, runs under MS-DOS and requires 384 KB RAM. A harddisk is recommended but not absolutely necessary, colour monitors are supported. A German and an English version are available, the manual is in German only. A version for the Apple Macintosh is planned.

The package is controlled by IS, the INTEXT supervisor, therefore it's not necessary to know the structure and dependencies of the package. Via a project name the file names are automatically generated – thus the user does not have to enter the file names too often – and documented on the screen and the log files.

The main tasks of INTEXT/PC are the generating of an index, an index of a lemmatized version of the index (only for German words, LEMMA2 program is required), a reverse order index, keyword-in-context (KWIC) lines of variable length (up to 255 characters in a line), readability analysis with 8 different formulas. The content analysis can be done with ignoring upper-/lowercase, control of single and multiple negation and interactive coding of ambigious search entries. These search entries can be a word, any part of it and multiple words. Words may contain joker symbols like '*' and '?'. Interactive coding shows the current text unit, the search entry (highlighted), the category and its label. It's possible to accept the suggested code, to change the code or not to code. Statistical packages (currently SAS and SPSS) are supported by a setup including var and value labels. The statistical analysis can be done directly from the supervisor (needs 512 KB RAM then).

Systemdatei	Exploration	Analyse	Management	Drucken	MS-DOS	Optionen	Ende
	Wörterbuch erstellen		Systemdatei			Beep an	
	Wörterbücher vergleichen		Wörterbuch			Beep aus	
	KeyWords-in-Context (KWIC)		Kategoriensystem			Zeilenzähler an	
	KeyWords-out of Context (KWOC)		KWICs			Zeilenzähler aus	
	Restwörterbuch erstellen		KWOCs			interaktiver Modus	
	Lemmabuch		Wordcomp-Output			Hintergrundmodus	
						Optionen speichern	
						Projektkennung	

2 INTEXT/PC – neue Möglichkeiten und Entwicklungen

INTEXT/PC ist ein aus insgesamt 11 Routinen bestehendes Programmsystem, das Textanalysen vielfältiger Art ermöglicht. Die Erstentwicklung erfolgte auf einem Großrechner in PL/1, die PC-Version ist in C geschrieben.

Das System benötigt mit Supervisor 384 KB Hauptspeicher, ohne nur 256 KB. Eine Festplatte erleichtert die Anwendung, ist aber softwaremäßig keine Voraussetzung. Farbmonitore werden unterstützt.

2.1 Anwendungen in den Geistes- und Sozialwissenschaften

Die Anwendungen liegen schwerpunktmäßig in den Geistes- und Sozialwissenschaften:

- Inhaltsanalyse massenmedialer Texte (z.B. Zeitung, Fernsehen)
- Verschlüsselung offener Fragen in der Umfrageforschung
- Vergleich großer Textmengen, Wortschatzvergleiche
- Stilanalyse (für Literaturwissenschaft und Linguistik)
- Analyse von Intensivintervies (z.B. in der Psychologie)

2.2 Aufbau von INTEXT/PC: der Supervisor IS

INTEXT/PC besteht aus einer Sammlung von Routinen, die Dateien ausgeben, die andere dieser Routinen (oder auch andere Programme) weiter verarbeiten können. Die Integration dieser Routinen übernimmt der Supervisor, so daß eine Kenntnis der Struktur von INTEXT/PC nicht notwendig ist. Mit den Cursortasten wird die entsprechende Funktion (z.B. Häufigkeitswörterbuch, KWICs, KWOCs, Codierung) angewählt und die entsprechende(n) Routine(n) aufgerufen. Dateinamen werden mit einer speziellen Systematik gebildet, dazu wird anfangs eine Projektkennung eingegeben, aus der dann die entsprechenden Dateinamen gebildet werden. Die Eingabe von Dateinamen für die Eingabe- und Ausgabedateien entfällt damit weitestgehend. Selbstverständlich können die Namen für die Ausgabedateien auch frei gewählt werden. Aus den Protokolldateien und der Bildschirmausgabe können die generierten Dateinamen entnommen werden.

Integriert in den Supervisor sind die statistische Analyse mit einem entsprechenden Programmpaket (zur Zeit werden die PC-Versionen von SAS und SPSS unterstützt) und die Lemmatisierung mit dem Programm LEMMA2 von Gerd Willée (Bonn). [1]

Sobald der Text maschinenlesbar vorliegt, ist es mit geringem Zeitaufwand möglich, die zur Identifizierung dienenden INTEXT-Steuerzeichen einzufügen. Sowohl relative als auch absolute Setzung dieser Identifikatonszahlen (maximal 3, jeweils sechsstellig) sind möglich.

3 Exploration des Textes

Um sich mit einem Text vertraut zu machen, gibt es mehrere Möglichkeiten:

Rückläufiges Wörterbuch ist für linguistische Anwendungen eine interessante Möglichkeit. Ein rückläufiges Wörterbuch kann sowohl in der rückläufigen Form als auch in der ursprünglichen Form ausgegeben werden.

Erzeugung eines Lemmabuches Eine weitere Möglichkeit, die Wörter eines Textes kennenzulernen, besteht darin, sich nicht ein Wörterbuch aller im Text vorkommenden Zeichenketten (Häufigkeitswörterbuch) ausgeben zu lassen, sondern ein Wörterbuch mit den Lemmata der Zeichenketten (Lemmabuch). Benutzt wird dazu das Lemmatisierungsprogramm LEMMA2 von Gerd Willée (Bonn). LEMMA2 ist voll in den Supervisor eingebunden. Für größere Textmengen wird allerdings sehr viel Plattenplatz und Rechenzeit gebraucht.

Key-Words-In-Context (KWIC) Keywords-in-Context (KWICs) sind sowohl mit einzelnen Zeichenketten als auch mit Wortstammfolgen (SIC = Search Units in Context) möglich. Wahlweise können diese mit Identifikationsnummern oder ohne ausgegeben werden, die Länge einer KWIC/SIC-Zeile darf zwischen 40 und 255 Zeichen liegen. Gedruckt wird mit IPRINT, wobei die Suchbegriffe hervorgehoben werden (**fett**, *kursiv* oder <u>unterstrichen</u>) können.

Key-Words-Out-of-Context (KWOC) Für die Kontrolle mehrdeutiger Suchbegriffe können diejenigen Texteinheiten, in der mindestens ein Suchbegriff gefunden wurde, so ausgegeben werden, daß hinter

---
[1] Willée, Gerd (1988): LEMMA2-Handbuch. Bonn: Eigendruck.

dem Suchbegriff (der fett, kursiv oder unterstrichen gedruckt werden kann) die Kategoriennummer und das für die Kategorie gültige Etikett steht. Diese Art der Darstellung heißt bei INTEXT KWOC.

Manipulation von Häufigkeitswörterbüchern In Häufigkeitswörterbüchern kann gesucht werden, als Suchbegriffe sind Zeichenketten zugelassen, die an jeder Position innerhalb des Wortes stehen können. Diese Suchbegriffe (GO-Wörter) können interaktiv eingegeben oder aus einer Datei eingelesen werden, die gefundenen Wörter in eine Ausgabedatei geschrieben werden. Weiterhin kann ein Häufigkeitswörterbuch verkleinert werden, in dem Wörter nach Länge und/oder Häufigkeit oder durch Abgleich mit einem Stop-Wörterbuch ausgeschlossen werden. Bei großen Datenmengen können verschiedene Teilwörterbücher gemischt werden.

Die Erzeugung eines Kategoriensystems auf der Basis des Häufigkeitswörterbuches ist möglich. Dabei werden die Optionen für das Ignorieren der Groß-/Kleinschreibung und für die Mehrdeutigkeit von Suchbegriffen entweder für alle Suchbegriffe einmal am Anfang oder für jeden einzelnen Suchbegriff abgefragt. Die für die interaktive Codierung notwendige Datei der Kategorienetiketten wird dabei gleich mit erzeugt.

4 Neue Arbeitstechniken

Besonders bei der Generierung von Häufigkeitswörterbüchern großer Texte ist es effektiver, erst nur Teilwörterbücher zu erstellen und diese dann miteinander zu mischen. INTEXT/PC stellt die dazu notwendigen Routinen bereit, der Supervisor unterstützt diese Arbeitstechnik. Diese Vorgehensweise stellt sich immer dann, wenn beispielsweise auf einer Festplatte nicht mehr genügend Platz ist (bei Textdateien mit mehreren Megabytes).

Da INTEXT/PC als Suchbegriffe Wortteile an beliebiger Stelle innerhalb eines Wortes zuläßt, ist es nützlich zu wissen, welche Wörter eines Textes nicht codiert werden (besonders bei der Verschlüsselung offener Fragen). Das Restwörterbuch enthält alle Zeichenketten, in denen kein Suchbegriff vorkommt. Vorher oder nachher kann man das Häufigkeitswörterbuch auch um die STOP-Wörter verkleinern, das sind oft Wörter, die als Einzelwörter keine Bedeutung haben (z.B. Artikel, Pronomina, Interjektionen, Konjunktionen). Diese Analysetechnik empfiehlt sich für die heute gebräuchliche Form der Einzelwortanalyse.

5 Datenanalyse

Bei der Datenanalyse wird immer dann ein Code zugewiesen, wenn ein Suchbegriff gefunden wurde. Ein Suchbegriff kann ein Teil eines Wortes an beliebiger Stelle innerhalb dieses Wortes sein, ein ganzes Wort, eine Folge von Worten oder eine Wortstammfolge. Eine Wortstammfolge heißt, daß der 1. Teil einer Wortstammfolge innerhalb des Textes vorkommen muß, der jeweils nächstes Teil der Wortstammfolge im direkt darauffolgenden Wort innerhalb des Textes. Ein Beispiel:

Sollen Zeichenketten wie 'guter Politiker' oder 'gute Finanzpolitik' von einem Suchbegriff gefunden werden, so ist das mit der Wortstammfolge 'gut> <politik>' möglich. Im Parameter derselben ist dann die Option U (für Uppercase, Ignorieren der Groß-/Kleinschreibung) zu setzen.

Außerdem können innerhalb von Suchbegriffen auch ein Stern (*) und beliebig viele Fragezeichen (?) verwendet werden. So werden z.B. beim Suchbegriff 'Ver????ung' die Wörter Versuchung, Verletzung, Verbleiung gefunden, nicht aber Verbeamtung. Das wird mit dem Suchbegriff 'Ver*ung' gefunden.

5.1 Codierprobleme

Bei der Codierung von Einzelworten, teils auch bei Wortstammfolgen, treten verschiedene Probleme auf, die die Validität der Codierung in Frage stellen. Zum einen ist die Mehrdeutigkeit von Suchbegriffen für sehr viele Suchbegriffe ein Problem. Hier hilft nur, sich diese Suchbegriffe im Kontext (KWIC = Key-Word-in-Context) ausgeben zu lassen.

5.2 Negation

Ein weiteres Problem tritt mit der Negation auf. Bei einem Suchbegriff 'attraktiv' soll codiert werden, aber wenn davor ein 'nicht' steht, ist es eventuell nicht mehr erwünscht oder soll in eine andere Kategorie eingeordnet werden. Dabei wird mit einer Liste von Indikatoren gearbeitet, die in einer Datei frei zugänglich sind. Deren Vorkommen wird in den Wörtern vor dem Suchbegriff gezählt. Die Negation wird von INTEXT/PC erkannt, und zwar auch dann, wenn eine mehrfache vorliegt. Sollte ein doppelte Negation (Litotes) vorliegen, die gleichbedeutend mit einer verstärkten Bejahung ist, so wird diese auch erkannt, der Code wird zugewiesen, während bei einfacher (oder dreifacher Verneinung) kein Code zugewiesen wird.

5.3 Routine SUWACO – Neue Möglichkeiten der Codierung

Die Routine SUWACO (Search Units in Word And COntext Coding) verarbeitet Suchbegriffe und gibt die Ergebnisse in KWICs, KWOCs und statistischen Dateien aus. Zur Zeit können zwischen 2000 und 3000 Suchbegriffe in einer Analyse verarbeitet werden, je nach Anzahl der Auswertungsdateien und Länge der Suchbegriffe.

5.3.1 Kategorienetiketten

Für bestimmte Optionen bei der Codierung von Suchbegriffen wird eine Datei der Kategorienetiketten benötigt, die die Kategorien inhaltlich beschreiben. Beim Generieren des Setups werden daraus die Var Labels extrahiert, bei der interaktiven Codierung erscheinen nicht nur der Code, sondern auch dessen Etikett auf dem Bildschirm. Die Datei der Kategorienetiketten kann bei der interaktiven Generierung eines Kategoriensystems aus einem Häufigkeitswörterbuch erzeugt werden.

5.3.2 Ausgabe der Ergebnisse

Neben den Analyseergebnissen sind auch vielfältige Arten des Protokolls möglich: dabei können die Texteinheiten, bei denen kein Suchbegriff (REST), bei denen mindestens ein Suchbegriff (CODED) gefunden wurde und/oder bei denen das Negationsproblem auftrat (NEG), in eine separate Datei ausgegeben werden. Bei der Datei der codierten Texteinheiten können die Suchbegriffe im Druck hervorgehoben werden, hinter den Suchbegriffen stehen die Codes und dahinter die dazugehörigen Kategorienetiketten, so daß der Codiervorgang gut kontrolliert werden kann.

5.3.3 Interaktiver Codiermodus

Neu ist auch die interaktive Codierung bei potentiell mehrdeutigen Suchbegriffen, die entsprechend markiert werden müssen. Beim Codieren werden die nicht markierten Suchbegriffe automatisch codiert, während die potentiell mehrdeutigen auf dem Bildschirm angezeigt werden. Zusätzlich erscheinen die Identifikationsnummern und der darstellbare Teil der Texteinheit. Suchbegriff, Code und Kategorienetikett sind hervorgehoben, auch die bereits codierten Suchbegriffe erscheinen mit Code und Kategorienetikett. Codiert werden kann mit dem vorgeschlagenen Code, überhaupt nicht oder mit einem anderen Code.

Diese Möglichkeiten verwischen die Unterschiede zwischen konventioneller und computerunterstützter Inhaltsanalyse, zwischen qualitativ und quantitativ. Sie eröffnen neue Anwendungsbereiche und Arbeitstechniken, deren Möglichkeiten zur Zeit kaum abzuschätzen sind.

6 Ausdruck der Ergebnisse

Für die von INTEXT/PC erzeugten Dateien gibt es ein Druckprogramm, das eine Überschrift, Seitennummerierung, verschiedene Zeilenabstände und das mehrspaltige (bis zu sechs Spalten) Ausdrucke eines Häufigkeitswörterbuches erlaubt. Ränder sind auf den Millimeter genau angebbar, Einzelblattverarbeitung und automatische Einzelblatteinzüge werden unterstützt, der Satzspiegel ist permanent speicherbar.

7 Leistung und Performance

Hier eine LOG-Datei einer Inhaltanalyse. Sie wurde auf einem 80386-AT mit 25 MHz (Landmark 28 MHz) gerechnet. Die Eingabedatei des Codierlaufes ist 571 Kilobytes groß, die Ergebnisdatei 1108 Kilobytes.

```
INTEXT/PC Routine SUWACO 23.08.1989
Eingabedatei      kontakt.itx
DIC-Datei         kontakt.dic
TAB-Datei         D:\KONTAKT\kontakt.TAB
LAB-Datei         D:\KONTAKT\kontakt.LAB
Job für SPSS/PC+ in Datei STAT.JOB


- I 01:       6316 Texteinheiten gelesen
- I 02:      63963 Wörter gelesen
- I 03:        797 Suchbegriffe verarbeitet
- I 11:      12457 codierte Suchbegriffe in TAB-Datei
- I 22:       6316 Ausgabesätze in TAB-Datei
- I 23:       6316 Codiereinheiten
- I 24:       1679 nicht codierte Codiereinheiten
- I 25:       4637 codierte Codiereinheiten
SUWACO Start: 15:43:37
SUWACO Ende:  16:37:19
SUWACO brauchte 3222 Sekunden CPU-Zeit
```

8 Ausblick

Die Weiterentwicklung wird nicht stehenbleiben. Texte werden durch due weitere Verbreitung optischer Speichermedien verfügbar sein, als ein einheitliches Formal könnte sich PostScript entwickeln.

Die Benutzeroberfläche der Software wird sich an die heterogene Benutzerschar anpassen müssen: menuorientierte für gelegentliche und neue Benutzer, Batch-Modus für Standardanwendungen und für die Experten. Hier setzt INTEXT/PC Standards.

Für die computerunterstützte Inhaltsanalyse ist die Analyse mit Einzelwörtern seit 20 Jahren Standard, eine Weiterentwicklung ist wünschenswert. Die Wortstammfolgen von INTEXT/PC sind ein Anfang, geplant sind Suchelementfolgen als Suchbegriffe, in denen dann Listen von Kategorien kombiniert werden können.

Die von UNIX her bekannten 'regular expressions' sind ebenfalls eine mächtige Möglichkeit, Suchbegriffe zu formulieren.

Syntaktische Informationen lassen sich mittels linguistischer Ansätze gewinnen. Hier ist mit der Integration von LEMMA2 eine Möglichkeit gegeben, syntaktische Informationen mit semantischen zu kombinieren und neue Analysetechniken zu entwickeln.

ns. SoftStat '89
Fortschritte der Statistik-Software 2. Stuttgart: Gustav Fischer, 495 - 502

Computerunterstützte Suche nach Typologien in qualitativen Interviews

U. Kuckartz

Summary

The article discusses a model for the effective use of computers for finding natural typologies in qualitative interviews. MAX is a new program system especially designed for the combination of qualitative and quantitative data analysis. MAX follows the data base approach and runs as an executable program on the IBM PC and PS/2 under the DOS operating system. The paper highlights how MAX can be used to link hermeneutics with cluster analysis.

1. Einleitung

In den letzten Jahren sind verschiedene Möglichkeiten des Computereinsatzes bei der Auswertung qualitativer Interviews diskutiert worden (vgl. CONRAD/REINHARZ 1984), doch hat sich auch in den USA noch kein Software-Programm als "Standard" etablieren können. Die von BRENT u.a. 1987 publizierte Studie über die Computernutzung von qualitativ arbeitenden Sozialforschern in den USA zeigte, daß nur zwei Programme genannt wurden, die von zwei Forschern benutzt wurden, alle anderen der 26 genannten Programme wurden nur einmal erwähnt.

MAX ist ein Textanalyseprogramm, das primär auf eine Verbindung von qualitativer und quantitativer Analyse und auf eine kontrollierte Form der Typenbildung abzielt. Das größte Problem bei der Auswertung qualitativer Interviews ist nach wie vor die Materialfülle, der "data overload" (HUBERMANN/MILES 1983:285), d.h. es gibt eine kaum zu überblickende Textmenge, die nur schwer geordnet, zugänglich gemacht und reduziert werden kann. Gleichzeitig stellt man fest, daß in qualitativen Studien immer wieder "quasi-statistisch" argumentiert wird. Begriffe wie "häufig", "meist", "typisch" oder "charakteristisch" tauchen, wie Christel Hopf zeigte (HOPF 1982), regelmäßig in qualitativen Arbeiten auf. Solche quantifizierenden Begriffe sind meist jedoch eher intuitiv fundiert und nicht Resultat eines kontrollierten Verfahrens der quantitativen Analyse.

Das hier vorgestellte computerunterstützte Verfahren der Typenbildung ist aufgrund von Überlegungen zur soziologischen Analyse von Interviewtexten erarbeitet worden (KUCKARTZ 1988a); diese hat es anders als die quantitative Inhaltsanalyse, bei der der **manifeste** Inhalt von Texten im Vordergrund steht, vor allem mit dem **latenten** Inhalt, den Deutungsmustern der Befragten zu tun. Die folgende Beschreibung zeigt, wie mit MAX im Verbund mit einem Statistikprogramm (hier SYSTAT) natürliche Typologien in qualitativen Daten entdeckt werden können.

2. MAX - ein Analysesystem für verbale Daten

MAX ist die PC-Version eines originär für mainframes entwickelten Auswertungsprogramms (vgl. KUCKARTZ 1988b). Während das mainframe-Programm aus einer Sammlung von SIR/DBMS Retrieval-Programmen bestand, ist MAX ein eigenständiges, Menue-gesteuertes Programm (vgl. Abb.1), das auf allen IBM PC und PS/2 Geräten mit 640 kB Hauptspeicher läuft. MAX benötigt eine Festplatte und DOS ab Version 3. Das Programmdesign sieht eine enge Zusammenarbeit mit einem Textverarbeitungsprogramm (z.B. WORD 4) einerseits und einem Statistik-Programmpaket (z.B. SYSTAT, SPSS) andererseits vor; ein beliebiger Editor läßt sich in MAX einbinden, hervorragend geeignet hierzu ist der IBM PE2.

Abbildung 1   Das Hauptmenue von MAX

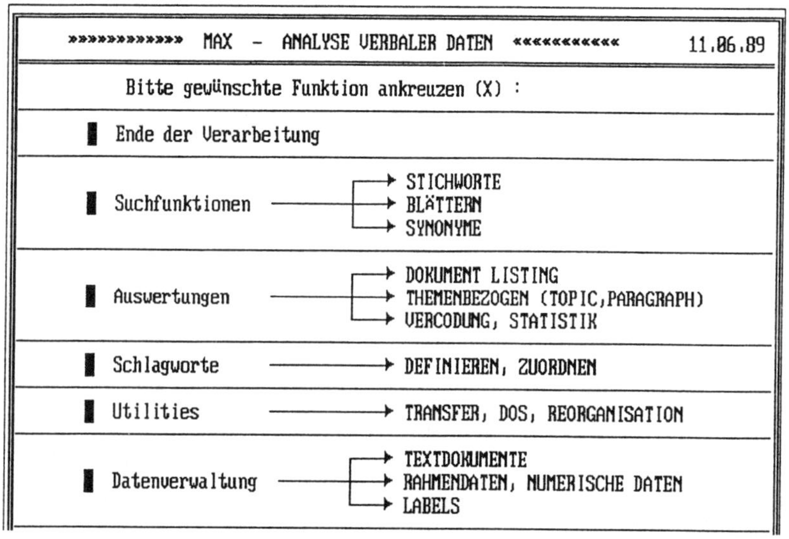

```
»»»»»»»»»»»»    MAX  -  ANALYSE VERBALER DATEN   ««««««««««««       11.06.89

          Bitte gewünschte Funktion ankreuzen (X) :

   ▌ Ende der Verarbeitung

                              ┌─→ STICHWORTE
   ▌ Suchfunktionen ──────────┼─→ BLÄTTERN
                              └─→ SYNONYME

                              ┌─→ DOKUMENT LISTING
   ▌ Auswertungen  ───────────┼─→ THEMENBEZOGEN (TOPIC,PARAGRAPH)
                              └─→ VERCODUNG, STATISTIK

   ▌ Schlagworte   ───────────→ DEFINIEREN, ZUORDNEN

   ▌ Utilities     ───────────→ TRANSFER, DOS, REORGANISATION

                              ┌─→ TEXTDOKUMENTE
   ▌ Datenverwaltung ─────────┼─→ RAHMENDATEN, NUMERISCHE DATEN
                              └─→ LABELS
```

Fünf Gruppen von Funktionen bzw. Auswertungsprozeduren werden unterschieden:

o Suchfunktionen zur on-line-Recherche in den Texten
o verschiedene Arten der Datenanalyse
o Funktionen zur Erstellung und Verwaltung eines Systems von Schlagworten und Schlagwortverweisen
o Funktionen des Datenmanagements für die verschiedenen Datenarten (Text-Dokumente, Rahmendaten, numerische Daten)
o Utility Funktionen wie Datenimport/-export, Datenbankstatistik, Datenbankreorganisation und Durchreichen von DOS-Befehlen

Nach Aufruf einer dieser fünf Funktionsarten erscheint auf dem Bildschirm das entsprechende Untermenue, das weitere Auswahlmöglichkeiten anbietet. Ausgangsbasis für MAX sind **Texte**, z. B. ein transkribiertes Interview, die Antworttexte eines Befragten aus offene Fragen in einem Fragebogen, ein Beobachtungsprotokoll oder irgendeine Art von Geschriebenem. In der Terminologie von MAX heißt ein solcher Text "**Dokument**" - bis zu 1000 Dokumente können gleichzeitig verwaltet und bearbeitet werden. Die Dokumente können eine innere Gliederung in "**Paragraphen**" aufweisen; diese entsprechen etwa den Kapiteln in Büchern, den Themen eines Interviewleitfadens oder den offenen Fragen einer Fragebogenerhebung. Jedes Dokument kann in maximal 99 Paragraphen gegliedert werden, diese dürfen einen maximalen Umfang von 1000 Zeilen mit einer Länge von 60 Zeichen haben.

3. Vier analytische Schritte bei der Suche nach Typologien

Die Leistungsfähigkeit von MAX zeigt sich besonders bei der Suche nach natürlichen Typologien; der analytische Prozeß durchläuft **vier Phasen:**
Im **ersten Schritt** werden einfache Retrievals durchgeführt. Gewissermaßen in Analogie zur Terminologie der quantitativen Sozialforschung kann man die mit Hilfe eines Interview-Leitfadens erhobenen Interviewtexte als "Datenmatrix" betrachten. Die Zeilen der Matrix werden durch die Fälle, d.h. die Befragten gebildet, die Spalten bestehen aus den Leitfadenpunkten und Unterpunkten.
Nun lassen sich zwei prinzipielle Arten von Retrievals unterscheiden: horizontale und vertikale Retrievals. Horizontal bedeutet Fall-orientiertes Text-Listing, während vertikal das Auffinden von Textsegmenten zu bestimmten Themen bzw. Leitfadenpunkten bedeutet. Zunächst wird jedes In-

terview in der Reihenfolge der Themen im Interview-Leitfaden ausgegeben, d.h. die Reihenfolge der Textpassagen wird verändert, so daß ein "standardized data display" im Sinne von HUBERMANN/MILES produziert wird.
Im Anschluß daran werden vertikale Retrievals für alle Leitfadenpunkte durchgeführt, d.h. die Textsegmente aller Interviews zu einem bestimmten Leitfadenpunkt werden ausgegeben bzw. gedruckt.

Der **zweite Schritt** der Analyse besteht in der Erzeugung einer Sekundärstruktur der Interviewtexte. Die Interviews werden erneut durchgelesen und aufgrund dieser Lektüre werden Stichworte definiert; in einem weiteren Arbeitsgang werden Textpassagen auf den Ausdrucken markiert und Stichworte zugeordnet. Am Ende dieses "Indexierungsprozesses" werden die Daten zu den Stichwortreferenzen schließlich in einem Eingabedialog in MAX eingespeist. Durch diese Form der Textbearbeitung wird neben der ursprünglich durch den Interviewleitfaden gegebenen Struktur des Textes eine neue, zweite Struktur erzeugt: ein Netz von Text-erschließenden Stichworten wird gewissermaßen über den Text gelegt.
Im Anschluß an den Indexierungsprozeß lassen sich nun neue themenbezogenen Auswertungen ("vertikale Retrievals") durchführen. In verschiedenen Abschnitten des Interviews findet man Textsegmente, die sich auf ein bestimmtes Stichwort beziehen. All diese markierten Textpassagen zu einem Stichwort werden aus den Interviews extrahiert und auf eine externe Daten geschrieben, die am Bildschirm oder auf dem Drucker ausgegeben werden kann. Dieser Bearbeitungsvorgang ist die computerunterstützte Form der GLASER/STRAUSS beschriebenen "mechanischen" Auswertungstechniken des Markieren, Codieren, Ausschneiden und Aufkleben.

Im **dritten Analyseschritt** gehen wir einen Schritt weiter als qualitative Sozialforscher üblicherweise gehen: die themenbezogenen Auswertungen der Stichworte und der Themen des Interviewleitfadens dienen als Grundlage für einen Klassifikations- und Codierungsprozeß. Zunächst wird ein Attribut wie beispielsweise das Item "Religiöse Orientierung" in einer Studie über türkische Migrantenfamilien definiert und alle Antworten aller Befragten zu diesem Themenkomplex werden ausgedruckt. Dies erleichtert es sehr, Muster in den Antworttexten aufzufinden und Codes zu bestimmen. Eine einfache Form der Codierung besteht in der Definition dichotomer Merkmale: jeder Fall (=Interview) wird hinsichtlich eines Merkmals nach dem Kriterium vorhanden/nicht vorhanden klassifiziert. Nachdem die Codes in die numerische Datenbank von MAX eingegeben worden sind, können deskriptive Statistiken für diese Merkmale berechnet werden und Kreuztabellen angefertigt werden. Hervorzuheben ist die Möglichkeit, diese codierten Daten in der Analyse mit den Interviewtexten zu verknüpfen. Abhängig vom Vorhandensein bestimmter Merkmale oder Merkmalskombinationen werden Subgruppen von Befragten selektiert und aus den Interviews dieser Befragten Textsegmente zu interessierenden Stichworten ausgegeben.

Im **vierten Analyseschritt** werden nun diese durch die Klassifikation und Codierung erzeugten Daten genutzt, um natürliche Typologien, multivariate Merkmalskonstellationen in den Daten aufzuspüren. Ein nützliches und bewährtes Hilfsmittel zum Auffinden von Typologien ist das statistische Verfahren der Clusteranalyse. Obwohl das Verfahren gerade für die typologisch denkende Sozialwissenschaft sehr gut geeignet ist (vgl. KUCKARTZ 1988a:204ff), haben die marktführenden Statistik-Programmpakete die Clusteranalyse lange vernachlässigt; auch heute bietet beispielsweise SPSS noch keine iterative Methode der Clusteranalyse an.

Ein leitender Gesichtspunkt bei der Konzeption von MAX war, eine schnelle und problemlose Zusammenarbeit mit Statistik-Software zu ermöglichen. Dies funktioniert im Prinzip mit allen Programmen, die ASCII-Dateien oder dBase III-Dateien als Eingabe akzeptieren. Hervorragend gestaltet sich die Zusammenarbeit mit dem SYSTAT-Programm. SYSTAT ist ein leicht handhabbares, sehr schnelles Statistikprogramm und - was für die Typenanalyse wichtig ist - SYSTAT offeriert neben den hierarchischen Formen der Clusteranalyse das iterative K-Means Verfahren.

Der Datentransfer von MAX zu SYSTAT ist denkbar leicht (siehe Abbildung 2): die numerischen Daten werden von MAX in eine dBase III-kompatible Datenbank transformiert, die vom SYSTAT Data-Modul einfach importiert werden kann - dazu sind lediglich folgende Befehle nötig:

    save filename
    import "c:\max\numeri.sta" /type=dbase3
    use filename

Danach ist die gesamte Datenbank inclusive der Variablennamen in SYSTAT verfügbar, d.h. es muß keine weitere Daten- oder Formatbeschreibung eingegeben werden, sondern man kann sofort mit einer Clusteranalyse fortfahren. Auch bei größeren Samples vergehen zwischen dem Beginn des Datenexports in MAX und dem Ende des Datenimports in SYSTAT weniger als 60 Sekunden.

Es wird nun mit einer hierarchischen Clusteranalyse begonnen. Hat man zu einem Themenkomplex eine Reihe dichotomer Merkmale definiert, so wird ein Prozentmaß als Distantzkoeffizient benutzt. Der Distanzkoeffizient bedeutet in diesem Fall den Prozentsatz der Nichtübereinstimmung zwischen zwei Merkmalsprofilen, d.h. der Koeffizient ist sehr anschaulich interpretierbar: wenn zwei Befragte in allen Merkmalen übereinstimmen beträgt der Koeffizient 0, wenn sie bei allen Merkmalen differieren beträgt der Distanzkoeffizient 100. Aus dem Baumdiagramm des clusteranalytischen Agglomerationsprozesses läßt sich bereits entnehmen, welche Fälle sich stark ähneln und welche Fälle sich extrem von allen anderen unterscheiden. Das Cluster-Modul von SYSTAT ist sehr leicht zu handhaben und stellt auch für die in der Handhabung von Statistik-Software oftmals wenig erfahrenen qualitativen Sozialforscher kein Problem dar. Als zweite Stufe der Clusteranalyse wird eine iterative Methode eingesetzt. Hierbei werden die Fälle des Samples einer vorab festgesetzten Anzahl von nicht-überlappenden Clustern zugeordnet. Das Verfahren iteriert, bis alle Fälle erfolgreich geclustert sind, d.h. bis sich jeder Fall in dem Cluster befindet, zu dem er die größte Ähnlichkeit aufweist. Diese an sich simpel klingende Anforderung wird von keinem hierarchischen Verfahren erfüllt, hier besteht immer das Problem, daß die in einem frühen Stadium der Analyse vorgenommenen Zuordnungen der Fälle zu Clustern in einem späteren Stadium der Analyse nicht mehr korrigiert werden können.

Die Anzahl der Typen (=Cluster) ist nach dem gewünschten Differenzierungsgrad, der Samplegröße und aufgrund der Interpretation von Analysen mit unterschiedlicher Anzahl von Clustern zu bestimmen. Die Summary-Statistik für die schlußendlich ausgewählte Analyse gibt einen Überblick über den Diskriminierungswert der einzelnen Merkmale und über die Charakteristika jedes Clusters. Für jedes Cluster werden die Fall-Kennummern seiner Mitglieder, ihr jeweiliger Distanzkoeffizient zum Cluster-Centroid und die Verteilung der Merkmale im Cluster wiedergegeben. Nach der Interpretation der Resultate der Analyse können typische Fälle durch Evaluation der Distanzkoeffizienten zwischen Fällen und Clustern identifiziert werden. Die Cluster-Zugehörigkeiten, d.h. die Nummer des Typs, dem jeder Fall zugeordnet wurde, können von SYSTAT gespeichert werden und mit Hilfe des DATA-Moduls mit den Ausgangsdaten zusammengeführt werden. Im letzten Abschnitt der Analyse wird die Cluster-Zugehörigkeit zu MAX zurück transferiert (Abbildung 2).

Abbildung 2   Kommunikation zwischen MAX und anderer Software

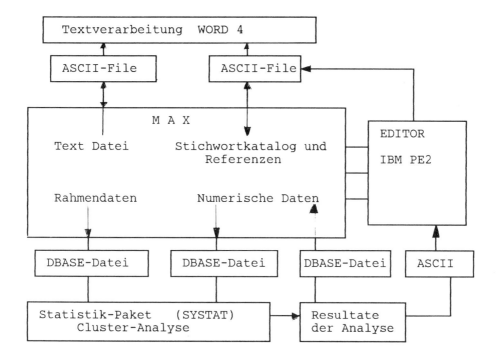

Nun lassen sich die gefundenen natürlichen Typologien weiter analysieren und veranschaulichen: für jedes Cluster oder für typische Fälle werden ausgewählte Interviewsegmente interpretiert. Die Behauptung, daß ein Argumentationsmuster oder ein Deutungsmuster eines Befragten "typisch" ist, kann nun streng empirisch kontrolliert werden, sie ist nicht mehr bloß intuitiv fundiert.

4. Schlußbemerkung

Auch wenn in diesem Beitrag primär der Software-Aspekt bei der Suche nach Typologien focussiert wird, muß nachdrücklich betont werden, daß mit dem Computereinsatz keineswegs irgendeine Form **automatischer** Analyse intendiert ist, vielmehr läßt sich die analytisch Vorgehensweise als "hermeneutisch informierte Sozialforschung" (SMITH 1988) beschreiben. In der Geschichte der Sozialforschung lassen sich in der Tradition von MAX WEBER eine Reihe von empirischen Studien finden, die zeigen, daß qualitative und quantitative Analyse sehr wohl verbunden werden können und keineswegs sich wechselseitig ausschließende Forschungskonzepte sind. Diese Konzeption des Auswertungsprozesses, mit der Interpretation der einzelnen Fälle zu beginnen und über Merkmalsdefinition, Klassifizierung und Quantifizierung zu Typologien und zu Verallgemeinerungen fortzuschreiten, versucht die Vorteile der qualitativen Methodik, die Detailfülle und die verständliche Deutung des Einzelfalls beizubehalten und gleichzeitig die Nachteile dieser Forschungsstrategie, den Mangel an interner Validität, zu beseitigen.

Bislang war keine Software verfügbar, die einen solchen Forschungsansatz wirksam unterstützte - MAX versucht diese Lücke zu schließen. Das Vorhandensein dieses Analyseprogramms soll gleichzeitig dazu beitragen, diesen methodischen Ansatz, der Verstehen und Erklären, hermeneutische und statistische Argumentation verbinden will, auch in die Praxis in empirischer Sozialforschung umsetzen zu können.

Literatur

Brent E., Scott J., Spencer J. (1987). The use of computers by qualitative researchers. Qualitative Sociology, 10, 309-313.

Conrad P., Reinharz S. (eds.) (1984). Computers and qualitative data. Human Sciences Press, New York.

Hopf Ch. (1982). Norm und Interpretation. Einige methodische und theoretische Probleme der Erhebung und Analyse subjektiver Interpretationen in qualitativen Untersuchungen. Zeitschrift für Soziologie, 11, 307-329.

Hubermann A.M., Miles M. (1983). Drawing valid meaning form qualitative data: some techniques of data reduction and display. Quality and Quantity, 17, 281-339.

Kuckartz U., Maurer A. (1989). MAX-Analysesystem für verbale Daten. Handbuch zur Programmversion 2. Hektographiertes Manuskript, Berlin.

Kuckartz U. (1988a). Computer und verbale Daten. Chancen zur Innovation sozialwissenschaftlicher Forschungstechniken. Peter Lang, Frankfurt/Bern/New York.

Kuckartz U. (1988b). Computer aided analysis of qualitative interviews. CAIA: a software solution with SIR/DBMS. Paper presented at the International Social Research Methodology Conference Dubrovnik (June).

Smith R.B. (1987). Linking quality and quantity. Part I. Understanding and explanation. Quality and Quantity, 21, 291-311.

The Classificatory-Hermeneutic Content-Analysis of Guided Interviews with TEXTPACK

R. Mathes and A. Geis

Summary

Classificatory-hermeneutic content analysis integrates hermeneutic, interpretive and classificatory, quantitative analysis in one method. In the first step of the research procedure, the texts (mostly guided interviews) are transcribed and a text-data-file is set up. In the second step of the research procedure, the texts are classified and coded in a multi-dimensional way e.g. considering various different aspects, and a numeric data-file is set up. The text-data-file and the numeric data-file are connected with identifiers. We pursue an interactive strategy for the text-analysis: The quantitative analysis of the classified text characteristics -- which are in the numeric data-file -- is combined with the hermeneutic interpretation of the relevant passages of the text -- which are in the text-data-file. This combination enables us to conduct multi-level text-analysis. The method was developed in order to analyze large amounts of text normally resulting from guided interviews in an adequate manner.

Concept and Procedures

With reflect to methodological issues in the social sciences, there seems to be a contradiction between hermeneutic text interpretation and quantitative content analysis. Quantitative and qualitative methods of text-analysis are introduced as alternatives, each with specific advantages and limitations. In general, "qualitative" social scientists consider their method as the more valid one, whereas "quantitative" social scientists emphasize the greater precision and intersubjectivity of empirical methods. In the dispute over the "right", analytically adequate method, quantitative and qualitative social science has mainly emphasized the differences between the two methods, neglecting their similarities and coincidences (Küchler 1980, Mohler 1981). Since the mid-seventies, qualitative and quantitative methods of text-analysis have been combined in one method at ZUMA (Mohler 1978, 1987). In this article, we would like to introduce a variant of this method-combination which is conducted with the aid of the text-analysis program TEXTPACK (Mohler, Züll 1986). This method is called classificatory-hermeneutic content analysis (Mathes 1988a). It was developed for analyzing the large amounts of texts resulting from guided interviews in an adequate manner.

The classificatory-hermeneutic content analysis of guided interviews consists of two parts. In the first part, the tape-recorded, qualitative interviews (e.g. guided interviews, narrative interviews) are transcribed and a *text-data-file* is set up. The text-data-file contains the entire texts of all interviews including their identifiers which mark the text units. TEXTPACK allows for the administration and computer-aided content analysis of the texts during the entire procedure of the analysis. In the second part of the analysis, a "conventional", quantitative content analysis of the text is conducted and a *numeric data-file* is set up. It contains the relevant formal and contextual characteristics of the text classified in numeric codes.

Text-data-file and numeric data-file are connected through identifiers, which are set at the beginning of each text unit in the text-data-file, and in the corresponding coding unit in the numeric data-file. One coding unit can refer to one or more text units. The identifiers allow for a connection between the text passages and their coded versions at any time during the text-analysis, so the reference to the original text is never lost. With the identifiers, we differentiate between text-references and context-references. The text-reference refers to the directly coded passage of the text. The context-reference denotes the wider context, which is necessary or helpful for the interpretation of this text passage.

For the text-analysis, we pursue an *interactive strategy*; the quantitative analysis of the classified text characteristics -- which are in the numeric data-file -- is combined with a qualitative hermeneutic interpretation of selected, relevant parts of the text -- which are in the text-data-file. The quantitative-qualitative interactive analysis strategy is carried out in several steps. In the first step, a quantitative analysis of coded text characteristics is done. It supplies basic information on the relevant structural characteristics of the texts such as frequency and manner of discussed topics, aspects or evaluations as well as relations between these text elements. This *quantitative structure analysis* gives the researcher an overview of the relevant text characteristics and their quantitative importance. In a second step, a systematic selection of interviews respectively parts of interviews for the *hermeneutic detail-analysis* is conducted with the results of the quantitative structure analysis in mind. Thus, the selection can concentrate on particularly frequent, typical cases, or on relatively rare cases with specific combinations of characteristics. The researcher can, for example, let the text-analysis program select all parts of the interviews, in which a certain topic is mentioned, a certain perspective is included or a certain evaluation is expressed. The text-retrieval possibilities offered by TEXTPACK have the advantage that the text can be systematized according to a large number of criteria, and that different criteria for selection can be combined and changed as often as necessary and desired. The selected text passages offer the basis for a more in-depth interpretation of their manifest and latent contents. The hermeneutic detail-analysis is necessary in those cases in which the analysis of larger, contextual relations should come in focus, or the detailed analysis of characteristics not included in the quantitative analysis is asked for.

In a third step, the results of the hermeneutic detail-analysis are included in the quantitative analysis strategy. For example, the frequency of certain patterns identified in the hermeneutic detail-analysis of one case can be examined in other cases. This interaction between quantitative and qualitative analysis steps allows for the conduction of multi-level analysis and for the reaching of deeper, more detailed levels of analysis. Figure 1 gives an overview of the structure of classificatory-hermeneutic content analysis.

Figure 1

Classificatory-Hermeneutic Content Analysis
Overview of the combination of computer-aided and conventional content analysis

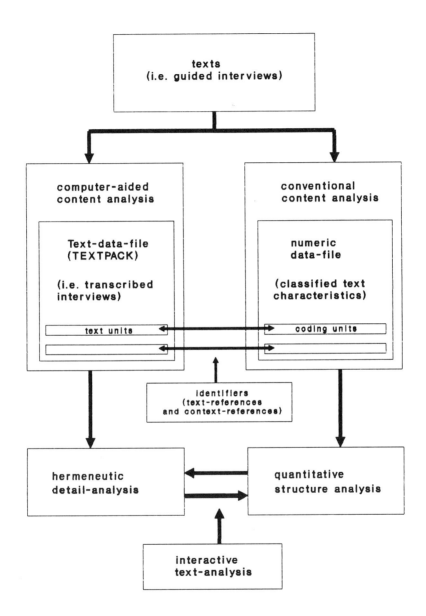

Applied coding techniques

For classificatory-hermeneutic content analysis simply or complexly structured coding techniques can be applied. Simply structured coding systems are only able to distinguish and code one or few text characteristics. Complexly structured, multi-dimensional category-systems are distinguished by their ability to code several characteristics in combination for each part of the text. A simply structured category system can for example consist of a list of topics dealt with in the interview. In this case, the coding for each text part only notes which specific topic was discussed. The quantitative structure analysis with SPSS or another data-analysis program then can calculate how often certain topics are mentioned and which socio-demographic data these respondents have. For the hermeneutic detail-analysis TEXTPACK allows us to sort out all text passages refering to one or more specific topics from the text-data-file, and to view them for analyzing more in detail.

When using complex coding techniques, not only the topic as such can be coded, but also the perspective from which it is discussed, the evaluation of the topic, the named actors and their functions,etc. The quantitative structure analysis then can precisely determine the perspectives under which a topic is discussed, and the evaluation of certain topics and actors, and so on. For the hermeneutic detail-analysis the text parts can be selected according to different characteristics, e.g. such as all text parts in which a topic is presented from a certain perspective and with a certain evaluation.

Since these complex methods are especially interesting in combination with hermeneutic-interpretatory procedures, they are introduced more in detail in the following. So called *relational category-systems* are distinguished by their ability to record an almost unlimited number of interrelating characteristics of messages as well as the relations between these characteristics. As the name already indicates, this type of category-system is marked out by its relational logic: The individual characteristics are coded in their connections and relations amongst each other. Instead of using the conventional coding logic, where the individual text elements are coded in an isolated manner with "or"-connections, numerous "and"-connections are established, which can record the relations between different characteristics respectively text elements. In other words, the conventional coding logic is replaced by a synthetic coding logic. The meaning of the messages is preserved and can be reconstructed in the data-analysis.

An example for such complexly structured category-systems is the *network-technique* which summarizes functionally defined classes of categories to category-nets. The individual category-nets are woven into a network, with the connections between the nets reflecting the relations between the text characteristics. The net-like connections allow a clear reconstruction of the context of argument even for complex statements, making the network-technique especially adequate for these. The number and form of recorded relations can be varied in accordance with the analytical goal of the research project.

As an example for the application of the network-technique, we will briefly introduce the category-network with which we analyzed the conceptions and opinions people expressed in extensive guided interviews on the welfare state (Mathes 1988b). The category-network was developed as part of a research project to record conceptions associated with the term "welfare state" on one hand, and on the other hand to record the multiple and partially interrelating evaluations and reasons given for these conceptions (Kaase et.al. 1988). In this case, the network-technique was combined with a multi-level analysis. On the level of the entire interview, we investigated the central, comprehensive elements and concepts attributed to the welfare state which were summed up in several types of understanding. Here we coded whether the term "welfare state" was associated to state interventions for realizing social security, or with other conceptions.

On the level of the individual statements and chains of arguments, the mentioned objects and their evaluations were coded in a differentiated manner. In the *object net* we coded the objects -- that is: which goals (intended effects), measures and principles -- people ascribed to the welfare state. More detailed information was coded about the responsible institutions, the extent and amount of social measures, which target groups they should cover and which criteria should be used for their distribution. In the *evaluation net*, we recorded evaluations the respondents gave of the welfare state, differentiating between functioning and general acceptance. In the statements on the functioning of the welfare state, we distinguished responsible and irresponsible usage by different groups of users. Detailed information was coded on the consequences attributed to the welfare state, again differentiating between intended effects (goals) and not-intended effects (undesired side-effects). The three types of evaluations could also be coded in combination. Acceptance of the welfare state, for instance, was often substantiated by goal attainment, whereas the reasons given for non-acceptance often were abuse and/or negative side-effects. In addition, aspects given as frames of reference to the individual objects and evaluations were coded.

The coding logic can be explained by a statement that contains several object aspects and connected evaluations. "As we see from the model Sweden, high social benefits in the welfare state are to costly, ruin the state and are mostly abused anyway. I categorically reject the welfare state." In this case, the general object "welfare state" is labeled with the specific object aspect "social benefits" and the specific object condition "high", which is given as the reason for a specific form of use ("abuse"), and this in turn is the reason named for the negative side-effect "ruin of the state" used to substantiate the rejection of the welfare state. Figure 2 provides an overview of the category system.

Performance with TEXTPACK

The classificatory-hermeneutic content analysis is conducted with the text-analysis program TEXTPACK, which was developed at ZUMA, in combination with a data-analysis program (such as SPSS or SAS). The methodologically necessary connection between the text-data-file and the numeric data-file can be reached by two different procedures. The first procedure

Figure 2
Network of Categories for the Analysis of Perceptions and Opinions on the Welfare State

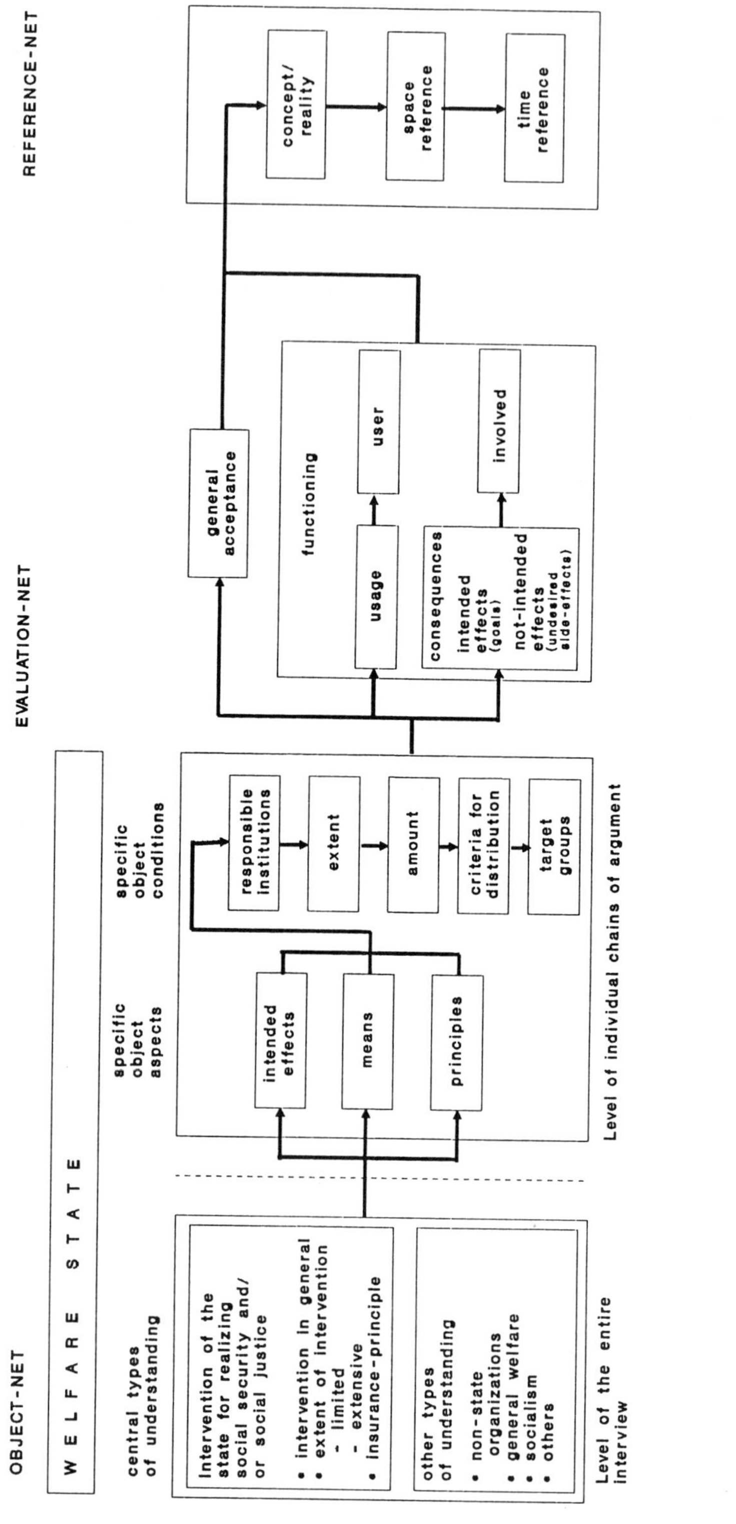

starts out from the coding and then marks the corresponding passages in the text-data-file. The second procedure starts out from defined text units such as sentences or paragraphs, and then marks in the numeric data-file what the coding refers to. In the first case, the connection is established through defined coding units written in the text-data-file, in the second case through defined text units noted in the numeric data-file. We are developing a program for the first form of connection at ZUMA in the moment. The plan is to do the coding directly at the terminal, with the accomplished coding being connected to the corresponding part of the text. This program also allows for complex, multidimensional coding. Furthermore the program will include help-functions (e.g. recall of parts of the category-system, such as category-definitions) to faciliate terminal coding.

The second form of connection can already be realized with the existing TEXTPACK version. Precondition is the setting up of text-data-file with defined text units. Size and classification of the text units must be as differentiated as reference to the text is asked for. Possible text units in interviews are e.g. respondent, question, speaker and sentence. TEXTPACK allows for three identifiers of which the third can be generated automatically. Second, during the coding procedure not only the codes for the contextual characteristics of the text parts must be noted, but also the identifiers for the text units to which the coding refers. Then SPSS or any other data-analysis program can count out the identifiers of all text units which contain previously defined contextual characteristics or combinations of characteristics. The TEXTPACK subprogram SUBSEL then sets up a new text-data-file with help from the identifier list, which contains all texts with the requested characteristics.

Figure 3 shows an example for the structure of such a data-file. It contains information about the text units to which the coding refers as well as the contextual characteristics of the text units. The data-file is from the already mentioned project on the welfare state. In this case, the text units were marked through three identifiers. The number of the respondent was the first, the number of the question the second identifier. The third identifier numbered each sentence successively from 01 to 99. As additional information, an added third number marked the speaker (1=interview, 2=respondent, 3=other person, 9=commentary during the transcription). For each coding, up to three text-units could be registered. Since SUBSEL up to now only allows for one text-identifier as criteria for selection, a second data-file was set up, in which the coding corresponding to each single text-unit was repeated. Figure 3 shows the original data-file.

Analytical Possibilities
The combination of advanced content analytical methods and hermeneutic interpretations offers new research perspectives and more in-depth understanding. Classificatory-hermeneutic content analysis has three important advantages compared to the predominating qualitative analysis of guided interviews. First, it is possible to analyze a rather large number of guided interviews. The number of cases is more or less unlimited. Indeed, there are financial and time expending limits since the transcribing and coding - particularly with very complex category

systems - is very time-consuming and thus rather expensive. Yet 200 to 300 guided interviews are a realistic amount. Representative research designs and samples now come within reach of qualitative social science research, creating the preconditions for a generalization of the results.

Second, the procedure allows for a systematic selection of cases for the hermeneutic detail-analysis. One problem of qualitative social research mostly is to select a few cases for the analysis from a large number of unknown cases -- illustrating: a "qualitative" social scientist will tend to grope about "through the fog". Classificatory-hermeneutic content analysis enables a systematic selection of cases on the basis of the results from the quantitative structure analysis.

Third, the interaction between quantitative and qualitative analysis enables us to include rather large amounts of text in the qualitative analysis - the "information overload" which normally occurs in the analysis of guided interviews can be mastered. The text can be structured according to an infinite number of search-strategies which can be modified at any time. The "nets" of criteria, with which the texts are explored can be defined either as closely or widely knit. Summarizing we can note that the classificatory-hermeneutic content analysis of guided interviews with TEXTPACK combines hermeneutic, case-oriented with classifying, quantitative procedures, thus creating the preconditions for the analysis of a greater number of cases with representative samples, allowing for a generalization of the results. Yet it must be noted that the procedure of classificatory-hermeneutic content analysis is very time consuming and - as far as the costs for coding are concerned - rather expensive. Yet this disadvantage is outweighed by a wider range of possibilities for the analysis.

Figure 3
Example for the Structure of the Numeric Data-File

Text Identifiers			Coding (classified text characteristics)			
respondent Id	number of question	identifier of text-unit	object net	evaluation net		frame of reference
3169	1	032 042	110 21	2	161 201	8
3169	2	092 102	110 37	2	182 220	3
3169	3	082 092 102	110 24	1	173 201	9

The coded, contexual characteristics refer to the sentences 8, 9 and 10, which respondent Nr. 3169 mentioned to question 3.

The respondent, who thinks the welfare state should only intervene on a limited scale to insure social security, criticizes in this passage, that too much unemployment aid only makes people lazy, and that he is against higher unemployment aid.

References

Kaase, M./Maag, G./Roller, E./Westle, B. (1988). Projektbericht: Politisierung und Depolitisierung von Wohlfahrtansprüchen. ZUMA-Nachrichten 21, 78-91

Küchler, M. (1980). Qualitative Sozialforschung. Modetrend oder Neuanfang? Kölner Zeitschrift für Soziologie und Sozialpsychologie 32, 373-386

Mathes, R. (1988a). "Quantitative" Analyse "qualitativ" erhobener Daten? Die hermeneutisch-klassifikatorische Inhaltsanalyse von Leitfadengesprächen. ZUMA-Nachrichten 22, 60-78

Mathes, R. (1988b). Dokumentation zur Inhaltsanalyse "Verständnis und Bewertung von Sozialstaat und Wohlfahrtsstaat". ZUMA-Technischer Bericht Nr. T 88/14, Mannheim

Mohler, P.Ph. (1978). Abitur 1917-1971. Bern, P. Lang

Mohler, P.Ph. (1981). Zur Pragmatik qualitativer und quantitativer Sozialforschung. Kölner Zeitschrift für Soziologie und Sozialpsychologie 33, 716-734

Mohler, P.Ph. (1987). Cycles of Value Change, European Journal of Political Research, 15, 155-165

Mohler, P.Ph./Züll, C. (1986). TEXTPACK V. Mannheim, ZUMA

Smith, R.B. (1988). Linking Quality and Quantity, Quality and Quantity 22, 3ff.

Die Wortartenverteilung -
Eine linguo-statistische Textanalyse

E. Mergenthaler und D. Pokorny

Summary

Properties of the system of parts of speech (e.g. noun, verb, adjective, etc.) are discussed. Based on a sample of 27 sessions from a psychotherapeutic treatment it will be shown, that these linguistic variables are subject to change significantly over time. Furthermore parts of speech seem to be a sensitive measure to differentiate individuals.The statistics used comprised descriptive methods, ANOVA, loglinear models with contingency tables, time series, and multivariate analysis.

1. Vorbemerkung

Diese Arbeit entstand im Rahmen der ULMER TEXTBANK, einer wissenschaftlichen Dienstleistungseinrichtung zum Archivieren, Ausleihen und Auswerten von Texten. Sie wurde mit Unterstützung der Deutschen Forschungsgemeinschaft im Rahmen des Sonderforschungsbereiches 129 an der Abteilung Psychotherapie der Universität Ulm aufgebaut. Das verwaltete Textmaterial stammt vornehmlich aus der psychotherapeutischen Situation. Für Vergleichszwecke sind aber auch Texte aus soziologisch orientierten Erhebungen enthalten. Eine der über die ULMER TEXT-BANK angebotenen Methoden bietet die Möglichkeit, die Verteilung von Wortarten zu einem Text zu ermitteln. Grundlagen und Besonderheiten der statistischen Anaylse derartiger Daten, mit Hilfe des BMDP-Paketes (Dixon, 1988) durchgeführt, werden im folgenden erörtert.

2. Zum Gebrauch der Wortarten.

Der Gebrauch von Wortarten ist ein alltäglicher und zumeist kaum beachteter Vorgang. Wer sich mit jemandem unterhält reflektiert üblicherweise nicht, in welchen Wortarten er seine Information verpacken und seinem Gesprächspartner zukommen lassen will. Genausowenig ist es beim Hören üblich, darauf zu achten, welche Wortarten vom Gegenüber eingesetzt werden. Tatsächlich weisen

Gespräche aber eine hohe Variabilität bezüglich dieses Kriteriums auf. Die bedingenden Variablen können vielfältiger Art sein.

Bild 1 (s. Löffelad, 1989 S.276) zeigt die mittlere Anzahl (bezogen auf Textblöcke zu je 200 Wörtern) der von einer Patientin vor und nach dem Wechsel ihres Therapeuten (nach Stunde 6) verwendeten Adjektive (Auswahl). Zum Vergleich ist die Bandbreite einer vergleichbaren Normalpopulation (graues Band) mit eingetragen. Es zeigt sich, daß der Gebrauch dieser spezifischen Wortart in der Dyade mit der ersten Therapeutin eher unterrepräsentiert ist und dann bei dem die Behandlung fortführenden Psychoanalytiker sprunghaft ansteigt. Unter dem Aspekt der Veränderung eines Patienten im Verlaufe seiner Behandlung wäre im Übrigen zu erwarten, daß er sich bei erfolgreichem Ausgang in Richtung der Bandbreite seiner vergleichbaren Population entwickelt. Im vorliegenden Beispiel konnte dieser Effekt im weiteren Verlauf der Behandlung ebenfalls beobachtet werden.

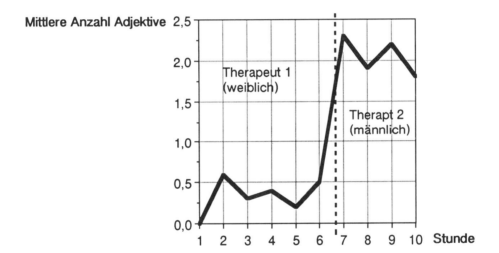

Bild 1: Mittlere Anzahl Adjektive je 200 Wort für eine Patientin mit zwei verschiedenen Therapeuten (nach Löffelad 1989 S.276)

Ein anderes Beispiel (Mergenthaler und Kächele, 1985) zeigt die Abhängigkeit der Wortartwahl vom Thema während einer psychoanalytischen Behandlungsstunde. Das Thema wechselt in der untersuchten Stunde von eher unpersönlichen, die Patientin nicht betreffenden Sachverhalten zu persönlichen, ihren Konflikt betreffenden Überlegungen. In dem Maße wie die Verben abnehmen, nehmen die

Substantive und Adjektive zu. Persönliches, die Patientin Berührendes wird von ihr also eher statisch durch Nomina als dynamisch durch Verben geäußert.

Obwohl es offensichtlich ist, daß die Wortarten vielseitig Aufschluß über den Zustand und die Veränderung eines Sprechers zu geben vermögen, sind bisher wenig wissenschaftliche Untersuchungen zu diesem Thema bekanntgeworden. Eine der wenigen Arbeiten stammt von Lorenz und Cobb (1975) die von diesem Gedanken ausgehend zeigten, daß Neurotiker mehr Verben, jedoch weniger Konjunktionen als eine zum Vergleich herangezogene Normalpopulation benutzten. Im Bereich der Psychologie und der Psycholinguistik wurde den Wortarten als Persönlichkeitsvariablen bisher keine Aufmerksamkeit geschenkt. Bei den Sprachwissenschaftlern dagegen gibt es eine Reihe von Untersuchungen die insbesondere den Gebrauch einzelner Wortarten in Abhängigkeit der Variablen Geschlecht, Landschaft, Beruf und Thema zum Gegenstand haben (Ruoff, 1973, Eisenmann, 1973). Am beeindruckendsten ist hier, daß das Geschlecht am stärksten zum unterschiedlichen Gebrauch etwa der Konjunktionen beiträgt.

3. Das System der Wortarten

Im Rahmen dieser Studie werden die Wortarten in 13 Klassen unterteilt. Tabelle 1 gibt eine Übersicht zu deren Bezeichnung, je ein Beispiel, den geschätzten prozentualen Anteil am gesamten deutschen Wortschatz nach (Erben, 1968), sowie die mittlere Auftretenshäufigkeit in allen von der Ulmer Textbank verwalteten Korpora. Unter der Rubrik "unbekannt" sind abgebrochene Wortformen wie sie durch Stottern, Selbstkorrektur oder Unterbrechung zustande kommen zusammengefasst. Die "Sonstigen" sind zumeist Eigennamen, Abkürzungen und unverständliche Wortformen.

Die empirisch-statistischen Eigenschaften dieser Klassen sind sehr unterschiedlich. Sehr mächtigen Wortklassen wie die der Nomina stehen Wortarten mit nur wenigen Wortformen gegenüber. Die mittleren Auftretenshäufigkeiten variieren sehr stark über die einzelnen Klassen. Außerdem sind nicht alle Wortarten unabhängig voneinander. Während Interjektionen (z.B. äh, mhm) jederzeit in ein Gespräch eingestreut werden können, sind die Artikel stark an das Vorhandensein eines Substantivs gebunden. Ebenfalls bilden die Negationen, Konjunktionen, Adverbien, Pronomina und Verben eine deutlich untereinander korrelierende Gruppe. Andererseits sind diese Gruppen wiederum negativ miteinander korreliert, schließen sich also gegenseitig weitgehend aus.

	Bezeichnung	% Vokabular	Beispiel	% Textbank
1	Nomen	50-60	haben Sie den *Bogen* raus?	10.1
2	Verb	25	hab was *gekriegt*.	18.5
3	Adjektiv	10	ein *schlimmes* Wort	7.5
4	Adverb	5-10	bin *vielleicht* fort	9.6
5	Pronomen	<1	*ich* weiß nicht so recht	15.6
6	Numerale	<1	im *zwölften* Lebensjahr	1.5
7	Negation	<1	kann ich *nicht* sagen	2.3
8	Artikel	<1	das ist *der* Druck	8.4
9	Präposition	<1	es liegt *auf* dem Tisch	4.7
10	Konjunktion	<1	Katz *und* Maus	15.5
11	Interjektion	<1	*ah* ja, da haben Sie	5.3
12	Sonstige		in / gewesen	0.7
13	unbekannt		das war *ge-* äh versprochen	0.3

Tabelle 1: Das Wortartensystem

Nach (Ruoff, 1973) bedarf es mindestens einer Textblocklänge von 200 Wörtern, um sprachnotwendige Erscheinungen beobachten zu können. Die Länge einer Äußerung eines Sprechers ist damit entscheidend für die Auftretenswahrscheinlichkeit einer Wortart. Am Beispiel von 60 Sprachproben, die anläßlich eines psychologischen Tests (Holtzmann-Inkblot) erhalten wurden, kann dies verdeutlicht werden. Der Textumfang der Antworten variierte zwischen 280 und 1615 Wörtern. Mit dieser unterschiedlichen Sprechaktivität war auch ein unterschiedlicher Gebrauch der Wortarten verbunden. Tabelle 2 zeigt die nach dem Korrelationskoeffizienten geordneten Wortarten. Soweit nicht anders vermerkt, sind alle Korrelationen hoch signifikant.

Nomen	-.78		Präposition	.36
unbekannt	-.56		Adjektiv	.37
Artikel	-.42		Negation	.48
			Konjunktion	.55
Sonstige	-.00	(n.s.)	Adverb	.61
Numerale	.08	(n.s.)	Pronomen	.72
Interjektion	.25	(n.s.)	Verb	.78

Tabelle 2: Korrelation zwischen relativer Auftretenshäufigkeit von Wortarten und Textumfang (n=60).

Wie erwartet nehmen die absoluten Auftretenshäufigkeiten der Wortarten mit dem Textumfang zu. Die Ergebnisse aus Tabelle 2 können damit wie folgt interpretiert werden: Nomina und Artikel sind Grundelemente der Sprache, geeignet um kürzeste Antworten zu bilden. Je länger eine Antwort ausfällt, desto mehr kommen die Adjektive, die Partikeln (Adverbien, Konjunktionen und Präpositionen) und die Interjektionen zum Tragen. Diese Wortarten eignen sich, detailiertere Beschreibungen zu erstellen. Für die längsten Äußerungen ist der Gebrauch von Verben und Pronomina typisch, ein Zeichen für das Vorhandensein von ganzen Sätzen mit eingestreuten Relativsätzen. Komplexe Handlungen und Zusammenhänge zwischen Objekten können mit ihnen beschrieben werden. Verschiedene Häufigkeitsvektoren von Wortarten lassen sich damit aber auch unterschiedlichen Sprechstilen zuordnen. Die nachfolgenden Auszüge aus dem kürzesten sowie dem längsten Test-Protokoll für die Beschreibung derselben Bildtafel mögen dies verdeutlichen:

> **Proband A** (Gesamttext 280 Wörter): Rattenkopf, Fuß, Bein. Der Umriß.
>
> **Proband B** (Gesamttext 1615 Wörter): Pflanze, Baum, dünner, zierlicher Baum, Äste, andere Seite auch, aber schlechter zu erkennen, ich schließe nur von der einen Seite, hätte ich es allein gesehen, hätte ich es nicht gesagt. Zwischen den Bäumen ein Weg. Öde Landschaft, ziemlich düster. Ekelhaftes grade aus, durchdacht, neuzeitlich. Guckt auf den Weg runter, die rechte Figur, die linke guckt zur Seite, auch ein Tiermenschmonster, hat auch eine Waffe, aber primitiver, sieht nicht so gefährlich aus.

Das System der Wortarten kann als mehrfach determiniert angesehen werden. Neben den systemisch bedingten Aspekten wie etwa dem korrelativen Zusammenhang zwischen Artikeln und Nomina, kommen persönliche Charakteristika der Sprecher hinzu. Es kann davon ausgegangen werden, daß verschiedene Personen auch verschiedene Vektoren aufweisen.

4 Wortart und Interaktion

Während im vorausgegangenen Abschnitt am Beispiel der Test-Protokolle das Sprechverhalten in einer nicht-dialogischen Situation zugrunde gelegt wurde, sollen nun Einflüße betrachtet werden, die durch die Interaktion zweier Sprecher bedingt sind. Es wird davon ausgegangen, daß in einer Kommunikationssituation Tendenzen der gegenseitigen Anpassung der beteiligten Sprecher zu erwarten sind. Dieser Effekt wird als umso deutlicher angesehen, je verschiedener die Wortart-Vektoren der Gesprächspartner sind und je länger bzw. öfter diese Kommunikationssituationen bestehen.

Die Datenanalyse erfolgt am Beispiel einer Kuztherapie die sich über 29 Sitzungen erstreckte (Materialien, 1988). Dies entspricht einer Behandlungsdauer von neun Monaten. Die Sitzung 20 wurde nicht in die Auswertung mit aufgenommen, da in dieser Stunde die Freundin des Patienten mit anwesend war und sich am Gespräch beteiligt hat. Sitzung 23 wurde aus technischen Gründen nicht aufgezeichnet, so daß schließlich 27 Verbatimprotokolle zur Auswertung kamen. Über den Methodenzweig der ULMER TEXTBANK wurde die Wortartenverteilung zu diesem Korpus für jede einzelne Sitzung, getrennt nach Patient und Therapeut, ermittelt und als Rohdaten-Datei an einer Schnittstelle zum BMDP-Paket, das in dieser Studie für die Datenanalyse fast ausschließlich eingesetzt wurde, bereit gestellt.

4.1 Die Kontingenztafel

Die drei Dimensionen Person, Sitzung und Wortart (P, S und W) bilden eine 2 x 27 x 13 Kontingenztafel mit 702 Zellen. Untersucht wurden die Randhäufigkeiten und Partialtabellen sowie log-lineare Modelle. In den Dimensionen Person vs. Wortart wurden überzeugende Unterschiede zwischen Patient und Therapeut gefunden. Dies war auch bei den Dimensionen Person vs. Sitzung der Fall, die hohen Signifikanzen wurden aber nicht interpretiert, da für diese Tabelle die Forderung nach Unabhängikeit der Daten, und somit die Voraussetzung des multinominalen Erhebungsschemas, nicht erfüllt war.

Das Modell mit allen Interaktionen zweiter Ordnung (PS, PW, SW) wurde hoch signifikant zurückgewiesen, so daß lediglich das saturierte Modell (PSW) angenommen werden kann. Das heißt aber, daß die Unterschiede zwischen Patient und Therapeut komplexer Natur sind, indem Veränderungen über die Zeit für Patient und Therapeut unterschiedlich verlaufen.

4.2 Sprecherunterschiede

Ausgehend von den relativen Häufigkeiten der Wortarten je Sitzung wurden die Wortart-Vektoren von Patient und Therapeut verglichen.

4.2.1 Varianzanalyse

Die Varianzanalyse (t-Test für verbundene und unverbundene Stichproben sowohl univariat als auch über Hotelling's T^2) sowie robuste als auch nicht-parametrische Verfahren zeigten die vom Therapeut bzw. Patient jeweils bevorzugten Wortarten. Dieselben Ergebnisse ließen sich auch über die zweidimensionale Kontingenztafel Person. vs. Wortart finden.

PATIENT		THERAPEUT		NEUTRAL	
Pronomen	-17.6	Nomen	28.7	unbekannt	0.0
Konjunktion	-11.3	Interjektion	11.0	Artikel	-0.7
Adjektiv	-10.2			Numerale	-0.7
Negation	-8.1			Verb	-0.8
				Adverb	-1.3
				Sonstige	1.1
Hotellings T^2-Verfahren: $F_{12,41}=149.8$ $p<0.0001$				Präposition	1.4

Tabelle 3: T-Test für unabhängige Stichproben (t-Statistik mit 52 Freiheitsgraden, kritischer Wert 2.00; Signifikanzniveau 0.05 zweiseitig).

Hinter diesen Unterschieden verbergen sich unterschiedliche Sprechstile. So kennzeichnet etwa der bevorzugte Gebrauch der Interjektionen durch den Therapeuten dessen stützende Rolle, indem er dem Patienten durch sogenannte Hörersignale (z. B. mhm) sein Interesse bekundet. Die für den Therapeut ebenfalls spezifische Kategorie "unbekannt", die ja weitgehend aus abgebrochenen Wortformen besteht, erklärt sich mit dessen Bereitschaft, mitten im Satz und Wort abzubrechen, wenn der Patient unvermittelt das Wort ergreift.

4.2.2 Diskriminanzanalyse

Die schrittweise Diskriminanzanalyse zeigte, daß die Unterschiede zwischen beiden Sprechern so deutlich sind, daß eine (jackknife) Klassifikation für Therapeut und Patient in allen 27 Sitzungen ohne Fehler möglich ist.

4.2.3 Clusteranalyse

Eine nicht hierarchische (K-means) Clusteranalyse der Fälle schließlich teilte alle 54 Wortart-Vektoren in zwei Cluster auf - nämlich genau in diejenigen des Therapeuten bzw. des Patienten.

Aufgrund dieser Ergebnisse sollte es mit hoher Wahrscheinlichkeit möglich sein, diese beiden Personen auch in weiteren therapeutischen Gesprächen lediglich auf der Basis ihrer Wortart-Vektoren zu unterscheiden. Dagegen kann zur Unterscheidungsmöglichkeit hinsichtlich weiterer (dritter) Personen aber auch bezüglich dieser beiden Personen in anderen Gesprächssituationen (z. B. Begegnung auf der Straße oder Telefongespräch) keine Aussage getroffen werden.

4.2.4 Äußerungslänge

Nach diesen doch eher eindrücklichen Ergebnissen bleibt zu fragen, ob diese nicht mit der Äußerungslänge i. S. einer Störvariable erklärt werden können und damit eher ein Artefakt darstellen. Wie oben bereits gezeigt wurde, hängt die Wortartenverteilung ja mit der Sprechaktivität zusammen. Tatsächlich ist der Redeanteil des Therapeuten deutlich geringer als der des Patienten. Die Analyse der zweidimensionalen Tabellen für Person vs. Wortart (für die ersten fünf Sitzungen), getrennt nach den verschiedenen Äußerungslängen, sollte Klarheit schaffen. Als Ergebnis zeigte sich, daß für alle untersuchten Längenklassen Unterschiede bestehen. Die Muster der bevorzugten Wortarten sind jedoch geringfügig verschieden. So stellte sich die vom Therapeuten bevorzugte Wortart der Nomina erst bei Äußerungen mit mehr als drei Wörtern ein. Bei 1,2 und 3-Wort Äußerungen dominierten bei ihm die Interjektionen.

4.3 Zeitreihen

Nachdem die Unterschiedlichkeit beider Sprecher hinsichtlich dem Gebrauch der Wortarten gezeigt ist, stellt sich nun die Frage, ob es bei einem oder bei beiden Gesprächspartnern Veränderungen während der Behandlungsdauer gegeben hat. Zu erwarten wäre, daß der Patient, der sich ja hinsichtlich seiner psychisch bedingten Problematik von der Behandlung in jedem Fall eine Veränderung erhofft, diese auch in seinem Sprechstil zu manifestieren vermag. Eine Zeitreihenanalyse des Gebrauchs der einzelnen Wortarten ergab jedoch kein klares Bild, so daß ein Maß gesucht wurde, das alle 13 Wortarten zu integrieren vermag. Dies läßt sich mit einer Distanzfunktion, die als Chi^2-Statistik aus der Tabelle mit den *relativen* Häufigkeiten für Therapeut und Patient je Sitzung errechnet wurde, ablesen. Wegen der beträchtlichen Unterschiede zwischen Therapeut und Patient, wie sie oben bereits herausgestellt wurden, war es außerdem möglich, für einen der Sprecher jeweils die Werte aus allen Sitzungen zu einem Globalwert zusammenzufassen und dann den anderen Sprecher damit Sitzung für Sitzung mit Hilfe der Chi^2-Funktion zu vergleichen. Diese Funktion entspricht formal der Chi^2-Statistik für eine Stichprobe, angewandt auf den Vektor der relativen Häufigkeiten des jeweils untersuchten Sprechers. Auf diese Weise läßt sich die Veränderung des einen Sprechers in Bezug auf seinen Gesprächspartner beschreiben.

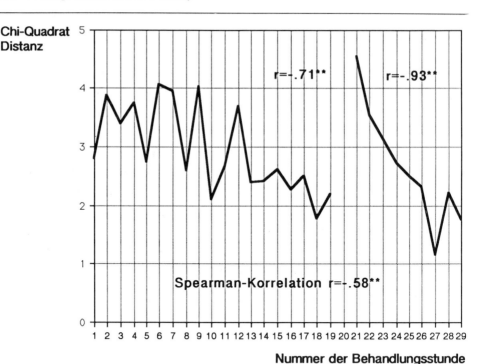

Bild 2: Chi²-Distanzen Therapeut-Patient

Bild 2 gibt zunächst einen Überblick zu dem Vergleich Therapeut-Patient pro Sitzung. Die Introspektion des Verlaufs der Kurve zeigt insgesamt eine deutliche Abnahme mit einem auffälligen Sprung nach der Sitzung 20. Es liegt nahe, unter diesem Eindruck zwei Phasen mit einem Schnitt zwischen Sitzung 19 und 21 zu unterscheiden. In beiden Phasen findet eine signifikante Annäherung statt. Wie aus Bild 3 und den entsprechenden Spearman'schen Korrelationskoeffizienten deutlich wird, ist dies in der ersten Phase jedoch weitgehend auf eine Veränderung des Therapeuten ($r_t = -.77$, $p<0.01$) zurückzuführen, während der Patient um einen Mittelwert pendelt ($r_p = .07$, n.s.). In der zweiten Phase wird innerhalb von 9 Sitzungen dasselbe Ausmaß an Annäherung erreicht, wie zuvor in 19 Sitzungen, diesmal jedoch tragen beide Gesprächspartner zur Verringerung der Unterschiede bei ($r_t = -.93$, $p<0.01$; $r_p = -.67$, n.s.) wenngleich beim Patienten dieser Effekt noch nicht signifikant ist.

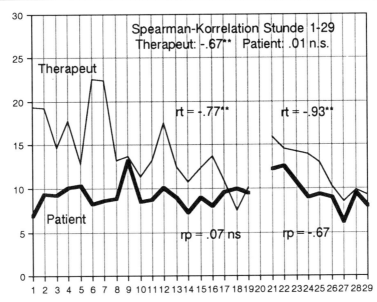

Bild 3: Chi²-Distanzen für Patient und Therapeut

5 Schlußbemerkungen

Der Wortarten-Vektor hat sich am Beispiel einer Querschnitts- als auch einer Längsschnittstudie als charakteristisches Persönlichkeitsmaß erwiesen. Er ist geeignet, Veränderungen über die Zeit, aber auch interaktionelle Einflüße aufzuzeigen.

Literatur

Dixon W. J. (1988). BMDP Statistical Software Manual. University of California Press, Berkeley, Los Angeles, London.

Eisenmann F. (1973). Die Satzkonjunktionen in gesprochener Sprache. Niemeyer, Tübingen.

Erben J. (1968). Deutsche Grammatik. Fischer Taschenbuch Verlag, Frankfurt a. M.

Löffelad M. (1989). Die Adjektive in gesprochener Sprache. Niemeyer, Tübingen.

Lorenz M., Cobb S. (1975). Language and a woman´s place. Harper/Row, New York.

Materialien (1988). Der Student. Verbatimprotokolle einer Kurztherapie. Teil 1 und 2. Ulmer Textbank, Universität Ulm.

Mergenthaler E., Kächele H. (1985). Changes of latent meaning structures in psychoanalysis. Sprache und Datenverarbeitung, 9, 21-28.

Ruoff A. (1973). Grundlagen und Methoden der Untersuchung gesprochener Sprache. Niemeyer, Tübingen.

Verarbeitung großer Datenbestände mit statistischen Auswertungssystemen

Analyzing Large Censuses

J. Oldervoll

In Norway, there are a large amount of historical data available in the computer. Most of it is nominal data on individuals. The 1801 census were computerized in the early 70-ies, at the History Department in Bergen, under my own auspices. The later are worked on for the time being, at an institution called Registreringssentralen for historiske data (not quite accurately translated into Norwegian Historical Data Archives) at the University of Tromsø.

The data is available to the public, and is very widely used. It is impossible to say how many people actually are using it. But we are able to say what kind of people. They can be divided into three categories. The first group, but not the largest, is the professionals, at the universities, colleges and local area historians. Most of them are historians, but there are a very wide group of actual and potential users.

The second group is the educational sector, from university downwards to probably fourth or fifth grade. This group is growing steadily.

The third group consists of what we can call family historians, or perhaps better, people being interested in their ancestors. This is by far the largest user group. It can probably be counted in thousands.

If we look at the *number* of user, the Norwegian computerized censuses is very well used. But still, there are problems. The most important is that the professional historians don't use the data as much as they could or should. This goes both for research and teaching. The most important task in the years to come, must be to establish the computerized censuses in the minds of the university historians. The crucial point will be to deliver the software needed. But software can only be seen in light of the methods used.

The methods are usually rather simple. There are two reasons for this. One is that the data is nominal. There are a rather limited statistical repertoire available for nominal data. The other reason is that most of the users have very limited statistical knowledge. The most widely used methods are cross tables and presentation graphics.

One solution is to use a commercial package like SPSS. But this is creating a lot of problems. One is that packages are expensive, another that SPSS is difficult to use. But most important, in my opinion, is the speed, or rather, the lack of speed. I tried SPSS on the coded version of the 1801 census on an VAC8600, and asked around on the time consumption on a AT, and got results as in table 1.

Table 1: The time consumption in the making of a cross table from the 1801 Census by SPSS.

# of cases	Vax 8600	AT
500	107 seconds	1 minute?
10.000	10 minutes?	20 minutes?
1.000.000	15 hours?	30 hours?

The only number actually measured, is the 107 seconds, all other is based on the estimates of people using SPSS.

The important thing is that if you want to use SPSS on large censuses, you are counting time consumption in hours. This has very serious consequences for your research. If you need to analyze some 100.000 individuals, making a simple cross table would take hours. You could probably not make more than one a day. Some of them would be wrong and have to be remade. A production of 2-3 tables a week would be maximum. The lack of speed would affect the progress of your research negatively. You would use much time waiting for the computer to make your table. But still more important, the lousy speed will affect the way you are using the computer in your research. Very simply, research can be divided into to parts; *hypothesis creation* and *hypothesis testing*. Normally, the first takes most time and would profit mostly from the use of computer. But the problem is that you probably had to make lots of table, just to be acquainted with the material. In the *hypothesis creation* process, you should play around with the data, using it more or less like a playground. But this is impossible with SPSS and a large dataset. The result is that the data will mostly be used in *hypothesis testing*. This can be compared to an anthropologist working on Africa. Who could imagine that he would work out an hypothesis at home and than go to Africa, living there for a year and being interested only in what could confirm or affirm his original hypothesis confirm of invalidate a hypothesis. Of course he wouldn't work like that. It would be a terribly waste of time and money. Using data in the same way is of course the same waste of resources.

A solution to this problem would of course be to make a sample. But this is not satisfying. Even a 1% sample would be very slow if one would analyze the whole country. But more important, it would rise methodological problems. A sample is always more inaccurate then a population. Many of the users haven't statistical knowledge to handle a sample. And what about the small groups, like the bishops? They can't be handle in a sample. A sample is a very bad solution when you have the whole population in the computer.

After having dismissed the commercial systems, I sat down and developed my own. It had to fulfil three requirements; it must run an a regular PC, it had to have a very friendly user interface and it had to run fast. These requirements are fulfilled in a program I have called CensSys (CENSus SYStem).

SPSS is able to crosstable approx. 10 or 20 records a second. CensSys runs through from 8.000 to 20.000 a second on my Olivetti M280 (more or less regular AT). It is approx. 1000 times as fast as SPSS which fulfils the speed requirement.

Some people will probably be interested in how this is done. In my opinion it is more interesting to know how SPSS is able to throw away the amount of computer power they do. I am not able to answer that question. But I can answer the former. The answer is *simple*. Keep it simple.

In a computer "time" can be divided into two components, I/O-time and CPU-time.

In other to save I/O-time, the most important thing is to reduce the number of bytes shuffled between the disk and RAM. If you store the variable *sex* in SPSS, it will be stored in a *real* variable, or *48 bits*. But sex may only have two values, and can be stored in *one bits*.

In a compact version of CensSys, which only keeps coded data, 18 variables with an average of 30 values in each variables, are stored in 35 bits, or 5 bytes. 1.000.000 cases are stored in 5Mb. In SPSS the same data would be stored in approx. 100Mb.

When data is stored in 5% of the disk space, you also use only 5% of the I/O-time. You may also save doubly, because when the data is compact, it may also be possible to store it permanently in RAM. The second time you need the data, you don't use any I/O-time at all.

What have been said up to now, applies to numerical data only. But there are also things to be done to alphanumerical data. In a census, the same alphanumerical information will often be repeated many times. There may be hundreds of individuals with the same occupation, spelled exactly the same. In a population of 10.000 individuals there are probably not more than 3-400 different occupations. If they have a maximum length of 100 letters, they would need 1Mb storage in SPSS. If you store the list of names separately and only a pointer to the list in the record, the storage can be reduced to apr. 25kb, or 1/40th of the storage needed in SPSS. The records will then consist of numbers. The number will point to an entity in a textual list. The textual data will look exactly like coded data, which consist of numbers pointing to an entity in a code book, which is a textual list. In addition to saving storage and I/O-time, you also get your data structured in a way which makes it very easy to write programs. Making cross tables based on the textual data is as fast as if you make it on coded data, since there are no differences between the two.

But there are other ways to save I/O-time. If you are going to make a cross table, you usually only need two variables. If there are 100 variables in your dataset, the other 98 should remain on the disk. SPSS reads them all into RAM, CensSys doesn't. Depending on your data, there are lots of time saved here. But to make full advantage of this, one has to organize the data by variable, not by record like it is usually done. Otherwise you will loose on seek time, what you win on transfer time.

Reducing CPU-time can be done by making the program simple. The fewer lines of program, the faster the program runs. The most important thing is to move all tests outside loops and to avoid data conversions.

CensSys could even be made to run faster. But it hasn't a very high priority. It is running fast enough for the kind of data it is supposed to handle in the near future.

It isn't much to be said about the interface. It is completely menu-driven. Making subsets of the data is easy. The tables can be edited.

At this point, CensSys is a program that does what SPSS does to census type data, but does it easier and and very much faster. But the users want, or should want more.

A census usually contains very much information. The 1801 census, for example, contains 48.000 different ways of expressing the occupations of the 879.020 individuals. To make any kind of analysis, the data has to be coded; the information have to be reduced. The fact that a man is a smith may be expressed in hundreds of ways. These are reduced to one, smith. But than you loose lots of information on the smiths. Making tables is reducing the information even more. In a table you may learn that there are a certain number of male smiths, and a certain number of female, which is less that you learn from the coded version, where you can learn lots of things about the persons, and the household he or she is living in. Statistical measures will reduce the amount of information still more. What you are doing, is to freely giving away information to get a clearer picture. But sometime you wish to recall the information, for example when you find a female smith, and even more if you should find a female general.

With commercial software, this can be done, but it is extremely cumbersome, and will only be done only in extreme cases. In CensSys you only have to push a key, and all information behind a cell in a table will be there. If it is wrong, if the general wasn't female after all, it can be corrected by two or three more pushes. *Fast control and correction of data is a very important feature of CensSys.*

The *coding* is important. In my opinion, there are no such thing as a general, or a neutral, objective coding. When somebody sits down and codes a material, he or she always have some project, some hypothesis or some set of hypothesis in mind. The coding will in principle fit no other hypothesis. What most people do, is that they are changing their hypothesis to fit the coding of the material, or they choose to see the coded variable as some kind of a proxy variable to the real one, which is hiding in the vast amount of information lost in coding. CensSys makes it possible to recode the material at any time, and do it very easily. It is also possible at any time to check what is behind any code in the material. That can be done by looking at the terms which have been added to make up the code, or you can look at the individuals having that code. Terms or individuals can be moved to other codes. *Easy and flexible coding, controlling of coding and recoding of the material is another important feature of CensSys*. This ads very much to the usefulness of the census.

Sometimes you want to use your material as a database. That can be done with CensSys. If you want to find *Ole Larsen*, that can be done very quickly even taking care of the problem that both *Ole* and *Larsen* can be spelled in many different way, one being for example *Oluff Lauritzen*. This could of course be done in a database program like dBase. But the problem is that dbase would need something like 100 times as much storage as CensSys, and very few people have harddisk that could accommodate such a project.

To recapitulate, CensSys is a program that:
- is very fast
- is compressing the data very much, which makes it possible two have large amount of data even on a small hard disk.
- is accommodating both full-text data and coded data at the same time, and makes it very easy to change between the two levels.
- makes it easy to code and recode.
- makes it easy to check whatever you are doing.

But there are also features lacking. For the time being, the program can only be used by a very limited number of sources. You can't just put your data into it. The program has only very limited statistical analyses. The presentation graphics is lacking. Some of it is going to be put into it. But I would think that it would be better to make good interfaces to commercial statistical and graphical packages. But, on the other hand, CensSys is a program that I should like to develop, and in many directions. Like it is now, it can be seen as a very powerful engine, which later on can be put into use in many areas.

Data Base Capabilities within a Statistical Package or Why P-RADE?

R. Buhler

If you need both statistical analysis and data management, it is increasingly possible to:

1) Use an interface between the statistical package and an existing data base management system.

2) Use whatever statistical capabilities are provided as part of a data base management system.

3) Use the data base management capabilities of a statistical package.

The first solution provides the user with the full capabilities of both the DBMS and the statistical package. It is probably the best solution for users who require extensive statistical capabilities and a full fledged DBMS with all the security features for record locking, multiple updates, and extensive relational capabilities.

The advantages come with a price. It is necessary to purchase and learn two packages. The interfaces are, in some cases, not very elegant and can result in some loss of information as data are passed between the packages. This is particularly true of the labelling and character information when the packages have different constraints on admissible character sets and field sizes.

Another issue is the "tightness" of the interface. The best way is for the records to be retrieved from the DBMS and converted into a statistical package system file directly. Unfortunately this is not always the case; some interfaces write the DBMS records to an intermediate file on disk and then, in a separate step, build a system file. The P-STAT/Informix interface to be released in the first quarter of 1990 builds the system file directly. Even so, the information is stored twice: in the DBMS and in P-STAT.

The second solution might be preferred by the user who needs only basic statistics and requires full DBMS capabilities.

We believe that the third solution is best for the user with moderate database needs *REGARDLESS OF THE LEVEL OF HIS STATISTICAL REQUIREMENTS*. The rest of this presentation will focus on our reasons for this statement and will include a description of P-STAT's recent efforts to enhance our already considerable data management capabilities with P-RADE, a direct access form of a P-STAT system file.

Because DBMS packages are designed to handle the very complex designs required by large corporations and in particular to address the problems of security, they are often difficult to learn and require the presence of a database manager to build and manage the data base. This is overkill for the user who 1) has data he needs to process that requires only the security provided by the operating system; 2) would like to have control over his own data sets; and 3) does not need to link multiple files for every operation.

P-STAT has always had good data management capabilities including the ability to handle multiple files and files with a relational structure. However, P-STAT system files are sequential -- processed case by case, starting with the first case in the file. Updates of sequential files are done by reading each case in the file, making changes if needed, and writing the case to a new file.

Sequential processing is fine when files are not large, when the files are static, or when most of the cases are to be changed in some way. Sequential processing is very wasteful of computer resources when the files are very large and only a small percentage of the cases are changed at any one time. It is this last situation for which P-RADE was designed.

WHAT IS P-RADE?

P-RADE is an acronym for P-STAT Random Access Data Enhancement. It is a direct access form of P-STAT system file. Because a P-RADE file is an integral part of P-STAT and provides for multiple key access, it can be read by any P-STAT command in either sequential (i.e., primary key) or secondary key order. All of the statistical capabilities of P-STAT and all the power of the P-STAT programming language are available for use by P-RADE files.

Each case in a P-RADE file must have a unique primary key which can comprise up to 10 numeric and/or character variables. Up to 9 secondary keys can be defined. If the value of a variable used to define one of the keys is changed during an update, the key is also updated at the same time. Secondary keys do not need to have unique values and can even be missing. This means that a secondary key can be used to define a permanent subset. A large file that is often processed by specific subsets might be a good candidate for P-RADE file format even if it is a static file that seldom requires changes.

P-STAT files are compressed very aggressively on a case by case basis to use the minimum amount of disk space. Because a P-RADE file permits a case to be changed in place, a case cannot float in storage as data values are changed. Therefore, every case in the P-RADE file uses the same space as every other case. As a result a P-RADE file requires more disk storage than a P-STAT system file with the same data, particularly when wide character variables are in use.

A P-RADE file has four components: 1) a small P-STAT sequential file which looks like the usual P-STAT system file and contains the full pathnames for the other three components; 2) a direct access DATA file; 3) a direct access INDEX file; 4) and a small direct access CHECKPOINT file. Indexing is done with B* trees which provide for very rapid access of a single case. Even with a very large file a given case can be located with 1 to 5 disk reads.

The checkpoint area is used to protect against disasters during the update process. In sequential processing the original file is still intact and an update can be restarted if a problem such as a power failure occurs. In direct access processing, restarting is not possible as the direct access file changes with each transaction. The checkpoint area provides for clean recovery when a problem occurs.

Checkpointing is simple: an updating transaction might affect only one record, but could affect several if keys are changed or blocks of data are changed due to insertions. The affected blocks are first written to the CHECKPOINT area and a flag is set in the checkpoint area saying these blocks are "live". The blocks are then written into the file itself and the checkpoint flag is reset when the transactions are complete.

Checkpointing, while the default, can be turned off. This will speed up writing into the file. The file should obviously be backed up rigorously if updates are done without checkpointing.

In addition to all the regular P-STAT commands, there are several commands designed for use only with P-RADE files.

1. <u>BUILD.PRADE</u> takes an existing P-STAT file and creates a P-RADE file. The information that is needed to construct the packing of the P-RADE file is provided by a description file containing the ranges for each of the variables in the file. A name for the primary key and the variables that define the primary key are provided at this time.

2. ADDKEY.PRADE adds a secondary key to a P-RADE file. A secondary key may be defined by the values of up to 10 numeric and/or character variables.

3. VERIFY.PRADE checks to make sure that the key structure of a P-RADE file is correct and the data values match the key values.

4. UPDATE.PRADE uses a P-STAT system file of transaction records to add cases, delete cases, or change the values of the variables in a P-RADE file. An extensive report is generated detailing each type of transaction that occurred.

5. REVISE.PRADE is a conversational command to update a P-RADE file using the primary key.

6. MODIFY.PRADE is used to modify a P-RADE file using the P-STAT Programming Language.

7. EXTRACT.PRADE is used to create a P-STAT system file from a P-RADE file using a transaction file to provide information about the cases to be extracted.

8. STATUS.PRADE prints a report about the status of a P-RADE file including the names of the keys, the variables which comprise each key, and the space usage for the data and index areas of the file.

9. MATCH.PRADE is used for case retrieval. An AWK-like pattern matching language is used to select cases whose values on key variables match the pattern.

CURRENT STATUS

An earlier version of P-RADE has been running on IBM mainframes for 7 years. It has been thoroughly tested on files as large as 500,000 cases and 700 variables. The code was re-written in 1988-89 making it able to process character values and also making the code portable to UNIX, VAX, and most other P-STAT supported environments.

F. Faulbaum, R. Haux und K.-H. Jöckel (Hrsg.) (1990). SoftStat '89
Fortschritte der Statistik-Software 2. Stuttgart: Gustav Fischer, 534 - 541

Verarbeitung von Dateien mit sehr großen Fallzahlen

J. Wackerow

Summary

Every year the computers are getting faster, the storage units are growing bulkier and the statistical program packages are more comfortable.

These are quick and efficient tools, if one analyzes some survey data of approx. 2 000 cases. But if you want to process very large files like census data (for instance: the official german micro census has approx. 600 000 cases, 150 variables), you are quickly getting in touch with the limits of a university mainframe. What is to be done, if the CPU time exceeds several thousand seconds, if the jobs are waiting for the night and one is working - as usual - at an urgent matter?

The user can handle this problem by a well prepared data selection, by organizational arrangements, and with the aid of system utilities. The general principles of this procedure are presented system independent. The true analysis should be carried out with the normal statistical packages like SPSSX-X, BMDP, SAS etc.

Moreover a concrete example on a Siemens BS2000 computer describes, how to use the system utility SORT for case and variable selection, and for aggregation of cases in one step. After this essential and fast decrease of the data volume, one can analyze the data for instance with SPSS-X.

By this procedure the total CPU time is considerably diminished, without purchase or development of special software.

1. Probleme bei der Verarbeitung von Massendaten

Die permanente Speicherung von großen Datenmengen ist meist nur auf Band möglich. Nur augenblickliche Arbeitsdateien kann man auf Platte halten. Der Umfang einer Datei ist neben der Datenmenge auch abhängig von der Darstellungsform des einzelnen Datums. Folgende Darstellungsformen wären bei der Abspeicherung von Massendaten denkbar:

- Character (jedes Zeichen = ein Byte) 100 %
- Binär an Wortgrenze (Vier Byte) ca. 267 %
- Binär an Bytegrenze ca. 65%
- Binär ohne Bytegrenze ca. 31%

Die Schätzung des Platzbedarfs bezieht sich auf die bei amtlichen Daten übliche Variablenstruktur. Die Character-Darstellung hat den großen Vorzug, daß man mit jedem Statistik-Programm die Daten lesen kann. Den geringen Platzbedarf der Binärgrenze ohne Orientierung an Bytegrenze müßte man sich mit einer Spezialleseroutine erkaufen (sehr schnelles Programm nur in Assembler möglich).

Auch bei der Organisationsform der Datei ist gegenüber der klassichen Rechteckdatei (ein logischer Satz gleich einem Fall) eine Alternative denkbar: eine Rechteckdatei, bei der jeder logische Satz die Werte einer Variable über alle Fälle beeinhaltet.

```
              F F F                F
              a a a                a
              l l l                l
              l l l                l

              1 2 3 . . . . . . . . m       Prinzip des
                                            selektiven
         V 1  x x x . . . . . . . . x       Variablenzugriffs
--->     V 2  x x x . . . . . . . . x       bei gestürzter
--->     V 3  x x x . . . . . . . . x       Datenmatrix
              . . .                 .
              . . .                 .
              . . .                 .
         V n  x x x . . . . . . . . x
```

Diese Organisationsform hat den Vorteil, daß man nur die Variablen liest, die man tatsächlich benötigt, also man weniger CPU-Zeit für das Einlesen benötigt. Doch auch hier versagen die Standard-Statistik-Programme, eine spezielle Zugriffsroutine wäre nötig.

Die Eingabe in den Arbeitsspeicher stellt einen Engpaß bei der Verarbeitung von großen Datenmengen dar. Die folgenden Tests beleuchten diese Problematik, sie wurden auf einer Siemens-BS2000-Anlage gemacht. Die CPU-Zeiten, die bei den Tests gemessen wurden, sind hier für eine Datei mit 600 000 Personen und einer Satzlänge von 200 Zeichen pro Satz hochgerechnet:

Tabelle 1:

Lesen und Umwandeln	CPU-S.
100 2-stellige Variablen mit FORTRAN-Format 100 I2 in Integervariablen	4 494
Characterfeld mit FORTRAN-Format A200 mit ICONV-Umwandlungsrout. (OSIRIS-Assembler-UP)	1 423
Characterfeld mit FORTRAN-Format A200 mit BINCODE-Umwandlungsrout. (eig. Assembler-UP)	693

Tabelle 2:

Nur Lesen	CPU-S.
Characterfeld mit FORTRAN-Format A200	147
RCHAIO (OSIRIS-Ass.-UP) von FORTRAN aufgerufen	76
Siemens-PAM in Assembler-UP, von FORTRAN aufgerufen (ein Block = 2 048 Bytes)	52
Siemens-PERCON Dienstprogramm mit großer Blockgröße des Datenfiles	23
Siemens-PAM in Assembler-UP, von FORTRAN aufgerufen (16 Blöcke = 32768 Bytes)	11

Das reine Lesen von Daten ist wenig CPU-Zeit-intensiv, besonders wenn systemspezifische Leseroutinen mit großen Puffern verwendet werden. Doch das Umwandeln der Daten in die interne Binärdarstellung ist sehr aufwendig. Daher sollte jede mögliche Datenmengenreduzierung vorher vorgenommen werden.

Die Datenmenge sollte so früh wie möglich auf das für die Analyse Notwendige beschränkt werden. Fall- und Variablenauswahl sowie Aggregierung der Daten sind dafür ein wirksames Instrument. Bei Aggregierung hat man auf der Ebene der ausgewählten Fälle und Variablen keinen Informationsverlust, doch die Datenmenge wird je nach Vielfältigkeit der Merkmalskombinationen meist erheblich vermindert. Ein logischer Satz repräsentiert nicht mehr einen Fall, sondern eine tatsächlich existierende Merkmalskombination mit einem Fallzähler. Dieser Fallzähler muß beim Analyseprogramm als Gewichtungsvariable angegeben werden.

Prinzip der Aggregierung:

Ausgehend von einem Datenfile mit 3 414 Personen.
(Ein Datensatz gleich eine Person)

Kreuztabelle:

		Geschlecht	
		Männer	Frauen
Alter	Altersgruppe 1	456	512
	Altersgruppe 2	783	799
	Altersgruppe 3	429	435

Aggregierte Daten in Vektorform:
(Ein Datensatz gleich einer Kombination von Merkmalsausprägungen)

```
1 1 456
1 2 512
2 1 783
2 2 799
3 1 429
3 2 435
```

Die Aggregierung ist durch eine Supertabelle im Arbeitsspeicher (sehr schnell) leicht realisierbar, doch benötigt man für jede theoretisch angenommene Merkmalskombination einen Speicherplatz, auch wenn die real auftretende Vielfalt viel kleiner ist. Man wird sehr schnell an die Grenze des Arbeitsspeichers gelangen.

Durch Sortieren, Zählen und Streichen von gleichen Fällen ist auch eine Aggregierung der Daten machbar. Dieser Weg hat den Vorteil, daß man hochoptimierte Systemsortierprogramme nutzen kann, und daß die Menge der auftretenden Merkmalskombinationen nur durch die Größe der Arbeitsdatei des Sortierprogramms begrenzt ist.

Meist kann man diese Systemsortierprogramme auch für Fallauswahl, Variablenauswahl und Recodierung nutzen. Diese ganzen Operationen können vor der rechenzeitintensiven Binärumwandlung vorgenommen werden.

2. Schnelle Datenanalyse mit Siemens-SORT und z.B. SPSS-X

SORT liest Daten von Platte wie von Band. SORT nutzt hohe Blockgrößen der Dateien aus und vermindert dadurch die benötigte CPU-Zeit und die Anzahl der Ein-/Ausgabeoperationen. Es können folgende Operationen vorgenommen werden: Fallauswahl, Variablenauswahl, Aggregierung. SORT braucht eine Arbeitsdatei, am besten auf einer Extra-Platte. Die Nachteile von SORT sind die komplizierte Anweisungssprache, man operiert nicht mit Variablen, sondern mit Feldpositionsangaben, eine Recodierung ist nicht möglich (wie z.B. bei VAX-VMS-SORT).

Im folgenden Beispiel wird nach drei Variablen gefiltert, es werden sechs Variablen ausgewählt und die Daten werden aggregiert. In einem weiteren Schritt kann dann die eigentliche Analyse folgen.

Setup eines Beispiellaufes mit SORT:

```
/LOGON
/SYSFILE SYSOUT = JW.ANA.SORT.OUT
/FILE JW.ANA.RAW.DAT, LINK = SORTIN, OPEN = INPUT
/FILE JW.ANA.SORT.DAT, LINK = SORTOUT, SPACE = (1000,1000),    -
/                     BLKSIZE = STD,16)
/FILE JW.WORK, LINK = SORTWK1, SPACE = (1000,1000)
/EXEC $SORT
MODS E03 = (CONV)
ALLOC CORE = MAX
OPTION OPM = CT, MSG = 0, LIST = YES
INCLUDE COND =                                                 -
  (15,1,EQ,'1',    AND,                  "V10 = 1"             -
   9,1,GE,'4',    AND,  9,1,LE,'6', AND, "V5  = 4-6"           -
  32,2,GE,' 2',   AND, 32,2,LE,'11')     "V23 = 2-11"
SORT FIELDS = ((6,1),    "V3"                                  -
               (7,2),    "V4"                                  -
              (12,1),    "V7"                                  -
              (13,1),    "V8"                                  -
              (19,2),    "V14"                                 -
              (32,2),    "V23"                                 -
              ('00000001')), "FALLZAEHLER"                     -
               OPT = SEL
SUM FIELDS = (10,8,ZD)
END
/ERASE JW.WORK
/LOGOFF NOSPOOL
```

Im folgenden werden an zwei Analysen mit SPSS-X die Vorteile der Datenvorbereitung mit SORT dargestellt. Diese Beispiele wurden auf einer Siemens-BS2000-Anlage gerechnet.

Bei der ersten Analyse wurden folgende Aktionen durchgeführt: Selektion, Recodierung, Konstruktion von neuen Variablen, fünf zweidimensionale Kreuztabellen, zwei Regressionen mit jeweils vier unabhängigen Variablen. Die Datei hat 31 Variablen bei 331 608 Fällen und eine Satzlänge von 50 Zeichen. Die Größe des Datenfiles ist 8 112 Pam Pages (16 224 KB).

Tabelle 3:

	CPU Zeit in Sek.	Zahl der IO-Operat.	Anzahl der Sätze f. Analyse
Einlesen von SPSS-X-Systemfile und Analyse mit SPSS-X	1 137	22 028	180 377
Selektion und Aggregierung mit Siemens-SORT	34	853	-
Einlesen von Rohdaten und Analyse mit SPSS-X	+139	+2 764	18 539
Summe	173	3 617	-

Bei der zweiten Analyse wurden folgende Aktionen durchgeführt: Selektion, Recodierung, Häufigkeitsauszählung von fünf Variablen, 25 zweidimensionale Kreuztabellen. Die Datei hat 31 Variablen bei 623 090 Fällen und eine Satzlänge von 342 Zeichen. Die Größe des Datenfiles ist 104 944 Pam Pages (209 888 KB).

Tabelle 4:

	CPU Zeit in Sek.	Zahl der IO-Operat.	Anzahl der Sätze f. Analyse
Einlesen von Rohdaten und Analyse mit SPSS-X	5 838	41 522	606 833
Einlesen von SPSS-X-Systemfile (ohne Keep-Op.), Analyse mit SPSS-X	4 910	382 830	606 833
Einlesen von SPSS-X-Systemfile (mit Keep-Op.), Analyse mit SPSS-X	3 541	111 393	606 833
Selektion und Aggregierung mit Siemens-SORT	169	7 273	-
Einlesen von Rohdaten und Analyse mit SPSS-X	+307	+2 533	35 085
Summe	476	9 806	-

Bei beiden Beispielen sieht man deutlich, daß sich die CPU-Zeiten erheblich (je nach Variablenart) reduzieren lassen. Außerdem nutzt SORT im Gegensatz zu SPSS-X die hohen Blockgrößen aus (weniger Ein-/Ausgabeoperationen), was positive Auswirkungen auf die tatsächliche Verarbeitungszeit und die entstehenden Kosten hat.

3. Schnelle und einfache Datenanalyse mit einem speziellen Programm-Modul für SPSS-X

Bei der Abteilung Mikrodaten von ZUMA wird bis Ende 1989 ein spezielles Programm-Modul für SPSS-X entwickelt, das das Systemsortierprogramm mit SPSS-X verknüpft. Das Modul wird folgende Funktionen umfassen: Schnelles Einlesen von Rohdaten und Verminderung der Datenmenge durch Fallauswahl, Variablenauswahl und Aggregierung mit SORT (als Unterprogramm), sowie Binärumwandlung durch ein schnelles Assemblerprogramm. Die Datenübergabe an SPSS-X findet innerhalb des Arbeitsspeichers statt.

Dieses Modul wird zuerst auf einer Siemens-BS2000-Anlage in Form einer SPSS-X-USERPROC zu Verfügung stehen. Eine Anpassung an IBM-MVS und VAX-VMS ist vorgesehen.

Folgende Syntax ist geplant:

```
/FILE workfile, LINK = WORK, VOLUME = privat disk, ...
/FILE tempfile, LINK = TEMP, VOLUME = privat disk, ...
/FILE filename of module library, LINK = USERLIB
/CALL $SPSSX.SPSSX, LIST = listing file

(FILE HANDLE DICT / NAME = 'filename of dictionary')
(GET FILE DICT)
(USERPROC NAME = GETDICT)
USERGET NAME = REDUCE /
      FILE = 'filename of raw input data' /
      VARIABLES = variable list /
      WEIGHT = case counting variable for the aggregated data or
               weight variable of the raw input data /
      (FORMAT = (format specification) if dictionary is not used /)
      (SELECT = case selection /)
      (FILE1 = 'filename1' /) several input files
         ...
      (FILE99 = 'filename99' /)
      (INDICATOR = possibility of an automatic indicator variable
                   when using several input files /
      (OUTFILE = 'output filename for aggregated data' /)
      (DATA = SPSSX    FILE    BOTH)
```

```
        WEIGHT BY case counting variable of the aggregated data
        SPSS-X-commands
        ...
        FINISH
```

Das Format der Eingabedaten kann entweder direkt über Angabe in der REDUCE-Prozedur spezifiziert werden oder von einem SPSS-X-Systemfile gelesen werden. Dieser Systemfile besteht nur aus Informationen über die Daten, speichert selbst aber keine Daten. Auf diese Weise wird nicht auf Nutzung schon eingebener Format- und Label-Informationen verzichtet.

Es können mehrere Dateien nacheinander gelesen werden. Die Sätze jeder Datei können zusätzlich mit einer eindeutigen Indikatorvariablen versehen werden, was besonders bei Zeitreihen sehr nützlich sein kann.

Literatur:

- SORT (BS2000) Beschreibung.
  Ausgabe 1985 (Siemens Softwareprodukt Sort V7.1A)
  Bestell.-Nr. U1266-J-Z55-3

- SPSS-X User's Guide, SPSS Inc., Chicago 1983

Die Verkehrsdatenbank des Bundesministers für Verkehr - Beispiel einer objektorientierten statistischen Datenbank

G. A. Wicke

Summary: The Traffic Data Base of the Federal Ministry of Transport provides information on rather small regional units of Germany. This information mainly consists of amounts of goods- and passenger-traffic between any two regions as well as structurual data on a single region from 1970 up to 2010. There are also traffic data to and from EC-countries on a rougher regional basis.
An object-oriented database for these data has been developed and is in operation on a mainframe. Retrieval and presentation of data is performed by an Information-System-Shell. It operates on the object-oriented database producing the desired information in tabular form. The retrieval and tabulation facilities are object driven and a query is handled completely within the sphere of the user's subject knowledge.

1. Struktur des Datenbestandes

Die Verkehrsdatenbank (VDB) ist eine Verwaltungsfachdatenbank tiefer räumlicher Gliederung; die kleinste Raumeinheit ist der amtliche Kreis. Der Datenbestand umfaßt Angaben über

- die Verkehrsströme zwischen je zwei Regionen
- die Struktur einer einzelnen Region
- Bezugsdaten generell zu jeder Information.

Verkehrsströme: Sie sind in zweifacher Weise gegliedert, einerseits in Personen- und Güterverkehrsströme, andererseits nach Verkehrsträgern wie Straße, Schiene, Luft oder Wasser.

Dabei gibt es immer eine Quellregion mit Versand und eine Zielregion mit Empfang. Personenverkehrsströme sind zusätzlich in Fahrtzwecke unterteilt, Güterverkehrsströme nach Gütergruppen.

Strukturdaten: Diese bestehen für die amtlichen Kreise aus Angaben über

- Flächen (gegliedert nach Nutzungsarten)
- Bevölkerung (gegliedert nach Altersgruppen und Tätigkeitsbereichen)
- KFZ-Bestände (gegliedert nach Haltergruppen und Fahrzeugarten)
- volkswirtschaftliche Daten (gegliedert nach Wirtschaftsbereichen)
- Personen- und Güterverkehrsmengen (aus oder in die Bezugsregion).

Bezugsdaten: Verkehrsstrom- und Strukturdaten unterliegen grundlegenden Bezügen zu Raum, Zeit, Quelle und Herkunft.

Regionaler Bezug: Es gibt 328 Kreise, 295 Kreisregionen und 79 Planungsregionen in der Bundesrepublik. In Bezug auf diese Raumeinheiten werden alle Daten erhoben, geschätzt oder prognostiziert.

Diese drei Grundelemente der Raumgliederung sind mehr oder weniger Verwaltungseinheiten. Aus ihnen werden andere räumliche Gliederungen abgeleitet, die problembezogen sind, zum Beispiel:

- Regionen mit hoher, mittlerer oder geringer Bevölkerungsdichte
- Regionen mit hoher, mittlerer oder geringer Verkehrsballung
- Grenzregionen.

In der VDB gibt es demnach verwaltungsbezogene und problembezogene Raumeinheiten.

Zeitbezug: Jede Information ist an den Zeitpunkt oder das Intervall ihres Entstehens gebunden. Der Zeitbezug der VDB reicht zurück bis 1970 und geht in die Zukunft bis 2010. Das bedeutet nicht, daß für alle Datengruppen zeitlich lückenlose Bestände vorhanden sind. Die Periodizität der einzelnen Datengruppen ist unterschiedlich.

Quellenbezug: Dieser gibt an, wie die jeweils betrachteten Daten entstanden sind, nämlich ob sie aus einer Erhebung, Schätzung oder aus einer Prognose stammen.

Herkunftsbezug: Es wurden Daten des Statistischen Bundesamtes, des Kraftfahrtbundesamtes und verschiedener Institute wie des DIW (Deutsches Institut für Wirtschaftsforschung), der PLANCO-Consulting oder der PROGNOS AG, Basel, zusammengeführt.

Diese Bezüge zu Raum, Zeit, Quelle und Herkunft bilden neben den Struktur- und Verkehrsstromdaten das Gerüst für die Verkehrsdatenbank.

2. Fachliche Ziele beim Aufbau der Verkehrsdatenbank

Das Bedürfnis nach statistischer Information war wohl seit den Ursprüngen der Statistik verknüpft mit dem Wunsch nach gut erfaßbarer Präsentation der Daten. In der Tat ist auch heute noch die geeignete Präsentation eines vielschichtigen Datenbestandes und seine Verfügbarkeit überhaupt ein Problem.

Für die Verkehrsdatenbank, wie sie hier vorgestellt wird, sind Präsenz und Präsentation ebenfalls wesentliche Gesichtspunkte. Im einzelnen stehen folgende fachliche Vorgaben im Mittelpunkt:
- Präsenz der Daten durch leichte Abrufbarkeit im Rahmen der fachlichen Begriffswelt
- Recherchen auch im Expertenmodus möglich
- Präsentation der Daten in Tabellenform
- automatisches Tabellenlayout mit Nachbearbeitungsmöglichkeit nach Fachvorstellungen
- Recherche-Ergebnisse sind als Tabellen aufzubewahren
- Flexibilität der Datenstruktur.

Die letzte Forderung spiegelt die mit Datenerhebungen häufig verbundene Problematik wider, daß die zu Grunde liegenden Datenstrukturen sich mit der Zeit ändern, weil
- die Gliederung von Datengruppen abgewandelt wird, z.B. aus Datenschutzgesichtspunkten oder wegen Harmonisierungsbemühungen mit anderen Statistiken im europäischen Rahmen
- gewisse Daten nicht mehr erhoben werden, z.B. aus finanziellen Gründen.

Es entsteht der Wunsch nach einfachen Möglichkeiten, solche Änderungen ohne großen Aufwand berücksichtigen zu können.

3. DV-technische Ziele und Methoden

Ziele: Die Fachforderungen führen zu zwei softwaretechnischen Zielsetzungen. Die eine Forderung war, Recherchen rein in der fachlichen Begriffswelt durchführen zu können; dazu muß die Sachlogik dieser Begriffswelt für die Verarbeitung der Daten präsent sein. Die zweite Forderung, Zulassen der Veränderlichkeit der Datenstrukturen, macht eine rigorose Trennung von Daten und ihrer Verarbeitung notwendig. In Programmen dürfen keine datenabhängigen Verarbeitungsschritte verankert sein.

Methoden: Zur Lösung des Problems, wie man neben den Daten selbst auch Wissen über die Daten mitspeichern kann, orientiert man sich an den Vorgehensweisen für Expertensysteme. Als allgemeinstes Mittel zur Darstellung sachlogischer Zusammenhänge kennt man dort "Semantische Netze", "Objekt-Attribut-Wert-Tripel", "Frames und Slots" oder man operiert mit Prädikatenlogik.

An einem Beispiel soll der Begriff des semantischen Netzes erläutert werden, weil ein solches für die Verkehrsdatenbank genutzt wird. Ein semantisches Netz ist, allgemein gesprochen, eine Sammlung von Objekten, die untereinander über Beziehungen verbunden sind. Es gibt Objekte einerseits und Beziehungen andererseits. Abbildung 1 dient der Erläuterung dieser Begriffe.

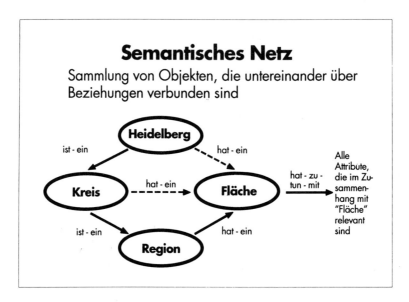

Abbildung 1: Beispiel für semantisches Netz

Heidelberg, Kreis, Region Fläche sind Objekte. Beziehungen zwischen diesen Objekten werden durch "ist-ein", "hat-ein" oder auch "hat-zu-tun-mit" ausgedrückt. Zwischen den Objekten einer Objektmenge wird im allgemeinen mehr als eine Beziehung bestehen.

Diese Sichtweise bietet Vorteile. Alles was für eine Region gilt, gilt auch für einen jeden Kreis und das insbesondere für Heidelberg. Man spricht in diesem Zusammenhang von der Vererbung von Attributen bzgl. einer Begriffshierarchie, die als eine spezielle Beziehung zwischen Objekten interpretiert werden kann. Ein Programm zum Beispiel, das die Fläche einer Region zur Verfügung stellt, wird auch auf dem Datenbestand der Kreise und deren Ausprägungen, wie Heidelberg, operieren können; und es wird erkennbar, daß hier eine beachtliche Ökonomie verborgen liegt, Objektmengen logisch so zu gliedern, daß Gemeinsamkeiten der Objekte nicht nur sichtbar, sondern auch nutzbar werden.

Der Begriff des Objektes kann sehr weit gefaßt werden. Objekte können sein:
- physische Gegenstände (z.B. KFZ, Straßen, Güter)
- gedankliche Elemente (z.B. Regionen, Bruttoinlandsprodukt, Attribut)
- Eigenschaften (z.B. Anzahl Personen, Gesamtfläche, Dezimalzahl).

Zum semantischen Netz gehören Beziehungen zwischen den Objekten. Man benötigt mehrere Beziehungstypen, deshalb spricht man zweckmäßigerweise von "Beziehungsstrukturen der Objekte". Wir beschränken uns hier auf diejenigen, die bei der VDB Anwendung finden. Das sind Beziehungen zur
- Gliederung von Objekten in Klassen: Oberklasse - Unterklasse; Klasse - Instanz (Ausprägung)
- Zuordnung von Eigenschaften zu Objekten: Klasse - Attribut
- Darstellung von Zusammenhängen: Referenzbeziehung.

Auf unser Beispiel bezogen, wäre die Beziehung "Region-Kreis" eine typische Oberklasse-Unterklasse--Beziehung, "Kreis-Heidelberg" wäre eine Klasse-Instanz-Beziehung; Instanzen sind als Ausprägungen so etwas wie einelementige Klassen. "Region hat eine Fläche" ist Beispiel für Klasse-Attribut-Beziehungen. Mit Referenzen beschreibt man losere begriffliche Zusammenhänge.

Mit diesen wenigen Beziehungstypen kann man bereits ein Informationssystem aufbauen, wobei die ersten beiden Beziehungen, also "Oberklasse-Unterklasse" mit "Klasse-Instanz", und die Klasse-Attribut-Beziehung ausreichen, um die sachlogische Datenstruktur darzustellen. Die Referenzbeziehung benötigt man, um dem Benutzer das Zurechtfinden in der Begriffsvielfalt zu erleichtern.

Die Verwendung semantischer Netze kommt auch der zweiten software-technischen Forderung entgegen, nämlich der Entkoppelung von Daten und Verarbeitungsprogrammen. Alles Datenabhängige kann im semantischen Netz niedergelegt werden. Die Programme haben dort, aus dem semantischen Netz, die benötigten Informationen über Datenstrukturen abzurufen. Datenstrukturänderungen werden durch Einträge in das semantische Netz vollzogen, es bedarf dazu keiner Programmierung.

Diese Begriffe, Objekte und Beziehungsstrukturen und Programme, die auf semantischen Netzen operieren, sind Grundlage des objektorientierten Ansatzes.

4. Realisierung der Verkehrsdatenbank

Die VDB wurde mit objektorientierten Methoden realisiert. Dabei wurden die Ideen des objektorientierten Ansatzes mit traditionellem Software Engineering zusammengeführt.

Es war einerseits die Möglichkeit zu schaffen, semantische Netze im Rechner zu speichern. Dazu waren Datenbank-Techniken und objektorientierte Methoden zusammenzuführen zur Konzeption einer objektorientierten Datenbank. Andererseits war ein Programmsystem zu entwickeln, das auf semantischen Netzen operiert und das über Fachbegriffe die Datenselektion bewerkstelligt, ohne von den eigentlichen Daten abhängig zu sein. Eine solche datenunabhängige Programmarchitektur für eine bestimmte Klasse von Anwendungen ist das, was man unter einer Shell versteht.

Die VDB wurde mit Hilfe einer für diesen Zweck entwickelten Shell realisiert. Sie weist überdies die Besonderheit auf, für einen Großrechner konzipiert zu sein. Shells gibt es in Hülle und Fülle für PC und Workstations, nicht aber für Großrechner.

Klasse der mit der Shell realisierbaren Anwendungen: Die Klasse der Informationssysteme, die mit der Shell entwickelt werden können, setzt folgende Eigenschaften des Datenbestandes voraus:
- er ist in Tabellenform darstellbar
- jeder Einzelwert ist als Element einer mehrdimensionalen Matrix auffaßbar
- Werte gleicher Dimension sind in gemeinsamer Matrix darstellbar.

Die Dimension z.B. einer als Tabelle interpretierten zweidimensionalen Matrix ist charakterisierbar durch einen Oberbegriff für Zeilen oder Spalten, dieser Oberbegriff hat im Falle der Spalten die Begriffe der Kopfzeile als Ausprägungen. Das Ganze läßt sich auf mehrdimensionale Matrizen übertragen. Wenn diese Anforderungen an den Datenbestand erfüllt sind - und das wird für statistische Daten oft gegeben sein - dann kann die Shell, die hier beschrieben wird, eingesetzt werden.

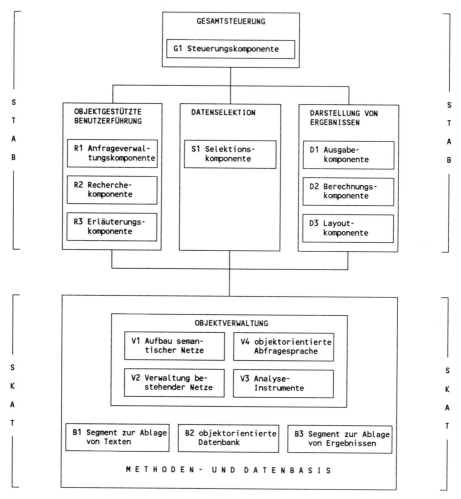

Abbildung 2: Gliederung der Informationssystem-Shell

Komponenten der Informationssystem-Shell: Abbildung 2 vermittelt die Gliederung des Systems, dessen Komponenten im folgenden kommentiert werden. Es besteht aus zwei Hauptteilen:

- SKAT, einer objektorientierten Datenbank mit einem Toolsystem zur Verwaltung und Pflege der Daten- und Wissensbasis und einer Sprache zur objektorientierten Informationsbeschaffung
- STAB, der eigentlichen Shell, mit Komponenten zur Steuerung, zur objektgestützten Benutzerführung, Datenselektion, sowie der Darstellung von Selektionsergebnissen in Tabellenform und ihrer Ablage.

Datenbasis: Sie besteht aus drei Segmenten, zwei traditionellen Datenbank-Segmenten zur Ablage von Texten sowie von Selektionsergebnissen in Form von Tabellen und deren Layout.

Das dritte, weitaus interessantere Segment, ist die objektorientierte Katalog-Datenbank. Sie enthält alle überhaupt in der VDB benötigten Objekte und ihre Beziehungen in Form eines semantischen Netzes. Diese Katalog-Datenbank entspricht der Wissensbasis bei Expertensystemen zur Ablage der sachlogischen Objekte und ihrer verschiedenen Beziehungen. Darüberhinaus werden auch die Datenobjekte

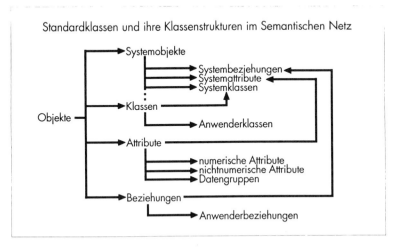

Abbildung 3: Standardklassen im semantischen Netz

in der gleichen Netzstruktur abgelegt und konsequenterweise ebenfalls die benötigten dv-technischen Objekte, schließlich die Beziehungsstruktur aller Objekte überhaupt.

Um einen Eindruck von der Behandlung der dv-technischen Objekte zu geben, zeigt Abbildung 3 die Standardklassen der Shell. Als Standardobjektklassen werden Klassen, Attribute und Beziehungen ge-

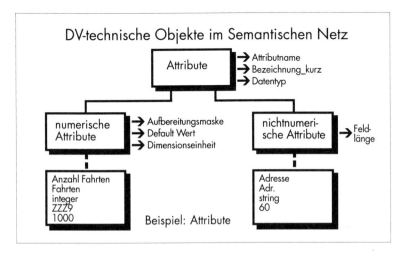

Abbildung 4: Klasse der Attribute als Systemstruktur

führt, um die Anwendung abzubilden. Diese Standardklassen werden auch benutzt, um Systemobjekte, also dv-technische Gegebenheiten, zu beschreiben.

Das soll am Beispiel der Klasse der Attribute näher erläutert werden. Sie gliedert sich in die Unterklassen "numerische Attribute", "nichtnumerische Attribute" und "Datengruppen". Abbildung 4 zeigt, daß die Klasse der Attribute selbst u.a. die Attribute Attributname, Bezeichnung-kurz und Datentyp hat. Bei der Unterklasse der numerischen Attribute kommen hinzu Aufbereitungsmaske, Defaultwerte, Dimension.

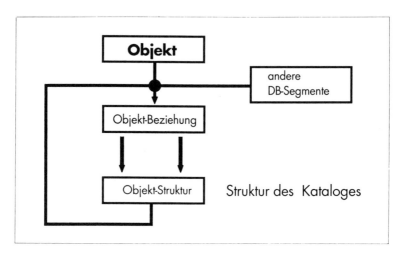

Abbildung 5: Struktur der objektorientierten Katalog-Datenbank

Die Struktur einer Datenbank, die es gestattet, einen solchen objektorientierten Katalog zu speichern, kann relativ einfach gehalten werden; selbstverständlich erwarten wir ein Netzwerk.

Der Satztyp "Objekt", in Abbildung 5 dient der Speicherung der Einzelobjekte. Jedes Objekt kann mehrere Beziehungen eingehen, diese Beziehungen sind in einer Stücklistenstruktur abgelegt, die an den Objekten hängt. Schließlich gibt es noch eine Set-Verbindung zu anderen Datenbank-Segmenten.

Wegen dieser einfachen Datenbankstruktur ist die hier geschilderte Vorgehensweise sehr wenig vom unterlegten Datenbankmanagementsystem abhängig. Für die Verkehrsdatenbank wurde **sds** der systema, Mannheim, wegen seiner Zuverlässigkeit und Flexibilität eingesetzt.

Objektverwaltung: Der Aufbau semantischer Netze erfolgt aus sequentiellen Dateien.

Zur Pflege bestehender Netze sind Editoren, die in der Regel auf sequentiellen oder indexsequentiellen Dateien operieren, überhaupt nicht geeignet. Die Standard-Tools der zugrundeliegenden DBMS sind zu kompliziert in der Anwendung auf Strukturen, die ein semantisches Netz abbilden. Demzufolge waren Instrumente bereitzustellen, die auf das Operieren auf der Struktur des Kataloges (vgl. Abb. 5) und insbesondere der Objektbeziehungen zugeschnitten sind:

- eine deskriptive Retrieval-Sprache SYLLOG
- ein Dialogprogramm zur lokalen Abänderung semantischer Netze
- ein Browser SKATOR zur lokalen und globalen Analyse, mit dem man zum Beispiel alle von einem Objekt im Netz "erreichbaren" Objekte anzeigen kann.

Objektorientierte Benutzerführung: Die Forderung der Datenunabhängigkeit der Programme bedeutet, daß insbesondere die angebotenen Menüinhalte aus dem semantischen Netz zu importieren sind. Dazu wurde eine Beziehung, die "Menue-Menue" genannt wird, implementiert. Der Benutzer bekommt die Netzinhalte sukzessive angeboten, seine Auswahl bewirkt den internen Aufbau einer Schlüsselstruktur der zu suchenden Daten. Diese Schlüsselstruktur steht dann der Selektionskomponente für den effizienten Zugriff auf die Daten selbst zur Verfügung.

Wesentlich ist, daß von der Konzeption her eine Unabhängigkeit des Dialogs von speziellen Datenstrukturen gegeben ist und allein durch Veränderung des Menue-Menue-Netzes Modifikationen der Dialoggestaltung bewirkt werden können.

Datenselektion: Die wesentlichen Informationen, nämlich Datenstruktur und Daten, sind als Objekte und Beziehungen in der Katalog-Datenbank abgelegt. Es wäre nicht sinnvoll, dem Programmierer zuzumuten, auf die logisch komplexen Strukturen der semantischen Netze direkt zuzugreifen. Es waren Operationen bereitzustellen, die diese Zugriffe abwickeln. Diese Operatoren und Funktionen wurden in einer Sprache für objektorientierte Informationsbeschaffung - SYLLOG - zusammengefaßt.

SYLLOG operiert auf Objektmengen und Objektstrukturen. Es ist in der Lage, Beziehungstypen wie "ist-ein", "hat-ein", zu verarbeiten, indem über solche Beziehungen selektiert werden kann. SYLLOG ist SQL-orientiert, es besitzt entsprechende deskriptive Sprachmittel, und das Resultat einer Selektion ist jeweils eine Menge, auf die iterativ wieder SYLLOG-Statements angewandt werden können.

Als Beispiel wird das SELECT-Statement betrachtet:

SELECT (INTO) Mengenbezeichner (Prädikat)

Es muß eine Menge angegeben werden, die das Selektionsresultat aufnimmt. Das Prädikat enthält Selektionsbedingungen, die z.B. durch allgemeine Mengenoperationen definiert werden können; zusätzlich kann man die Netzbeziehungen nutzen mit den Schlüsselwörtern ISA und JND. ISA liefert alle Objekte, die in einer Beziehung **zu** dem Ausgangsobjekt stehen. JND steht für 'joined' und stellt alle Objekte bereit, die **auf** das Ausgangsobjekt als Zielobjekt weisen.

Für ein Beispiel gehe man von der einfachen Struktur aus, daß sich der Oberklasse "KFZ" die Unterklassen "Dieselfahrzeug" und "PKW" unterordnen.

Die Menge, in die selektiert wird, soll m heißen, sie wird präzisiert durch das Prädikat "ISA Dieselfahrzeug AND NOT PKW":

SELECT m ISA Dieselfahrzeug AND NOT PKW

m enthält dann alle dieselgetriebenen KFZ außer Personenkraftwagen.

Der <u>Sprachumfang</u> von SYLLOG beschränkt sich nicht auf Statements dieser Art. Zur Prädikatproduktion gibt es Konkatenationsfunktionen, überhaupt Stringverarbeitungsfunktionen, Boolsche Funktionen, Vergleichsoperatoren und Selektionsprädikate, die es gestatten, über Schlüssel auf die Objekte und Beziehungen zuzugreifen. Es ist neben dem SELECT- auch ein AGGREGATE-Statement vorgesehen, um Aggregationen über Netzstrukturen standardisiert abwickeln zu können.

Die <u>Anwendungsart</u> von SYLLOG-Anweisungsfolgen ist vielseitig. Sie sind vom Bildschirm absetzbar wie Kommandos einer Query-Sprache. Aus Objektstrukturen, Anwenderprogrammen und Dateien können sie im Sinne eines "embedded" SYLLOG verwendet werden, in der vorliegenden Realisierung eingebettet in PASCAL.

Die <u>Funktionsweise</u> von SYLLOG bietet das Erscheinungsbild eines Interpreters. Selektionsfolgen werden zur Laufzeit übersetzt und sofort ausgeführt.

Darstellungskomponente: Zur eigentlichen Präsentation der Daten gibt es drei Teilfunktionen, die dem Anwender für die Darstellung der Ergebnisse zur Verfügung stehen:

Die <u>Ausgabekomponente</u> erstellt aus dem im allgemeinen mehrdimensionalen Anfrageergebnis eine zweidimensionale anzeigbare oder druckbare Tabelle. Diese Tabelle kann dann mit den anderen beiden Komponenten weiterbearbeitet werden.

Die <u>Berechnungskomponente</u> gestattet zeilen- oder spaltenbezogene Zwischensummen, Prozente, Produkte und Quotienten zu berechnen und in die Tabelle aufzunehmen.

Die <u>Layoutkomponente</u> schließlich deckt ab, was an flexibler Tabellengestaltung notwendig ist: Spalten- und Zeilen permutieren oder unterdrücken, Tabelle stürzen, Spaltenbreiten ändern, Texte ändern, Titelzeile ändern, Deckblatt gestalten, Drucker ansteuern.

5. Entwicklungs- und Einsatzumgebung

Das Informationssystem ist auf dem SIEMENS-Rechner 7570 B des Rechenzentrums des Bundesministers für Verkehr und der Bundesanstalt für Straßenwesen (RZ BMV/BASt) unter dem Betriebssystem BS2000 realisiert worden.

Die Programmierung der Software, die der Verkehrsdatenbank zugrundeliegt, erfolgte durch systema, Mannheim, unter Benutzung der PASCAL-Entwicklungsumgebung SPASS des RZ BMV/BASt.

Dabei dient zur objektorientierten Datenhaltung das Datenbankverwaltungssystem **sds** der systema. **sds** ist ablauffähig auf SIEMENS-Rechnern unter dem Betriebssystem BS2000 sowie auf IBM-Rechnern unter MVS. Zur Maskengenerierung wird FHS mit IFG (Interaktiver Format-Generator) der SIEMENS AG verwendet. Die Programmiersprache ist PASCAL-XT der SIEMENS AG.

Die Entwicklungsumgebung SPASS integriert diese Komponenten durch Sprachkonstrukte in Form von PASCAL-Packages zur Bedienung der logischen Datenbankschnittstelle und des Maskengenerators, zur Integration des Data-Dictionaries in den Entwicklungsprozeß und in das Laufzeitsystem der Anwendungssoftware sowie zur Nachrichten- und Memoryverwaltung. SPASS ist als Gemeinschaftsprojekt von systema und BASt entwickelt worden. Durch die Möglichkeiten von SPASS war eine erheblich vereinfachte und komfortable Programmierung der vorliegenden Shell gewährleistet.

Die Abhängigkeit von der speziellen Einsatz- und Entwicklungsumgebung ist nicht besonders hoch. Es liegen dem Gesamtkonzept allgemeine Prinzipien zugrunde, die in anderen Umgebungen analog realisiert werden können.

6. Anwendung und Ausbaufähigkeit der Shell

Liegen die in 4. gennanten Voraussetzungen für eine Anwendung vor, dann sind zum Einrichten eines Informationssystems folgende Schritte erforderlich:

- Entwicklung eines semantischen Netzes nach den Regeln des Objekt-Orientierten-Designs.
- Erstellung von Ladedateien für semantisches Netz und Daten
- Installation der objektorientierten Datenbank und der Shell
- Laden des Netzes und der Daten
- Überarbeiten des semantischen Netzes.

Es handelt sich hier um mehr oder weniger technische Tätigkeiten bis auf die Entwicklung des semantischen Netzes der Anwendung, dessen Design ist zwar kompliziert aber im hohen Maße fachbezogen.

Diese Fachbezogenheit eröffnet die Möglichkeit der intensiven Einbindung des Endanwenders in den Entwicklungsprozeß beim Umsetzen der fachlichen Denkwelt in das logische Modell eines semantischen Netzes.

Im Falle der Verkehrsdatenbank erstreckte sich die Bearbeitung des semantischen Netzes parallel zu allen Phasen der Softwareentwicklung der Shell. Sie wird auch zukünftig andauern.

Die Flexibilität des Systems liegt gerade in der Adaptierbarkeit einer Anwendung allein durch Veränderung der Netzstrukturen. Es ist möglich:

- neue Attribute zu Objekten hinzuzunehmen
- völlig neue Objekte aufzunehmen
- neue Beziehungsstrukturen einzuführen
- speziellen Benutzern eigene Begriffswelten einzurichten.

Neben die <u>Ausbaufähigkeit einer individuellen Anwendung</u> durch Abänderung des semantischen Netzes tritt die <u>Möglichkeit der Weiterentwicklung der Shell</u> in Richtung objektorientierter Methoden.

Man kann daran denken, Beziehungen zwischen Objekten und Operationen einzuführen, um häufig benötigte Informationen abzuleiten. Diese Operationen würden als Objektklassen ebenfalls im semantischen Netz gehalten werden und sind dann in der Lage, sich über geeignete Beziehungen die Objekte zu suchen, auf denen sie operieren können. Ein solches Verfahren läßt sich ausbauen bis hin zum <u>Anschluß eines vollen Inferenzteiles</u>, wie man es bei Expertensystemen kennt.

Ausblick: Die Erweiterungsfähigkeit einer laufenden Anwendung einerseits, die Einsatzfähigkeit der Shell für verschiedene Anwendungen und die volle Berücksichtigung der Denkwelt des Endanwenders sind außerordentlich bemerkenswerte Aspekte dieser Entwicklung.

Die Erfahrungen im Rahmen der Konzeption und Entwicklung der Verkehrsdatenbank weisen eindeutig darauf hin, daß zukünftig die Ideen des objektorientierten Ansatzes auch die traditionelle Programmarchitektur durchdringen werden. Voraussetzung sind geeignete Werkzeuge für Datenhaltung und Datenpflege. Diese können, wie das Projekt Verkehrsdatenbank des Bundesministers für Verkehr zeigt, auch für Großrechner bereitgestellt werden.

<u>Literatur</u>

Semantische Netze:
    Harmon P., King D. (1985,1989). Expertensysteme in der Praxis, Oldenbourg, München u. Wien
    Müller R.A. (1988). Wissensbasierte statistische Planungssysteme. In Faulbaum - H.M. Uehlinger (Hrsg.) Fortschritte der Statistiksoftware 1. Gustav Fischer, Stuttgart.
Objektorientierte Datenbank und Informationssystem-Shell:
    Emmelmann H., Welter J. (1989). Realisierung objektorientierter Datenstrukturen auf der Basis von Datenbankmanagementsystemen unter besonderer Berücksichtigung der Verkehrsdatenbank des BMV. systema, Mannheim.

Statistik-Ausbildung und Statistik-Software

Teaching Statistics: Microcomputer Graphics and Computer Illustrated Texts

A.W. Bowman and D.R. Robinson

Summary

The role of the computer in teaching statistics is not restricted to the performance of calculations or the display of data, but also includes the use of microcomputer graphics in communicating statistical methods and results. Various ways in which this can be achieved are described. The computer can be used to produce attractive and easily modified diagrams; animation can provide striking demonstrations of techniques; statistical rsults can be motivated by the combined use of simulation and graphics; the computer can act as a patient instructor, taking the student through the steps of some key task. These approaches have been used in developing a number of Computer Illustrated Texts on statistics, each work consisting of software and a textbook. The software may additionally be used in lectures, tutorials and practical classes.

1. Introduction

Over the last two decades, the teaching of statistics has benefited enormously from the existence of flexible and easy to use statistical computing packages. Such packages allow students to explore and model data in a way which focusses attention on the purpose of an investigation without the need to expend great effort on detailed calculations. With the arrival of personal computers, some packages have begun to incorporate high resolution graphical facilities and this has further enhanced the role of the computer in exploring data and in teaching data analysis.

The main aim of the vast majority of statistical computing packages is to provide an environment which makes the exploration of data and the performance of standard analyses and calculations a simple matter. The benefits of this to teaching are beyond question. However, one area in which use of computers is somewhat less prominent is in the explanation of statistical techniques, principles and results. For example, it is easy in most packages to perform a two sample t-test or to fit a simple linear regression. It is less common to find software which uses the facilities of the computer to explain what a t-test is or to illustrate the principle of least squares.

Computer assisted learning in its more traditional form has of course been under development for some time. Here the student is usually set a problem by the computer and is invited to give responses to a variety of questions. This has the benefit of giving the student immediate feedback on his understanding of a subject area, although such systems are necessarily somewhat inflexible in the problems which may be tackled.

It has been our aim in the past few years to explore the use of computers in teaching through the development of graphical software whose aim is to explain some of the ideas, principles and techniques of statistics. In each package, software is linked to a book and the two together are known as a "Computer Illustrated Text". The software is menu-driven and is designed for use by a teacher in a lecture demonstration as well as by a student on his own in a self-study, tutorial or lab setting. It is in this second setting that the integration of the text and software comes into effect. The material discussed in this paper is all available for BBC and IBM microcomputers in published form (Robinson & Bowman (1986), Bowman and Robinson (1987), Bowman and Robinson (1990)).

2. The role of microcomputer graphics

The advantages of good graphical facilities in exploring data has already been stressed above. In this section. we will discuss the role of high resolution graphics, such as are commonly available on microcomputers, in explaining statistical ideas.

2.1 The electronic blackboard

This term is used by some to describe the ability of the microcomputer to produce attractive pictures quickly, easily and accurately. In a lecture setting, traditional methods of presentation such as overhead projectors already perform this role but there are considerable advantages in a computer based display. One is the ability to build a picture up step by step rather than presenting all the details of a finished picture. Another is the ability to respond to the particular needs of different groups, or to questions from the floor, by immediately altering the parameter values or datasets which are currently being used.

A simple example of this use of the computer is in displaying Binomial probability distributions (program B&P). It is possible to communicate the meaning and effect of the probability parameter p simply by comparing the shapes of probability distribution produced by varying p while n is held fixed. Further, the adequacy of the Normal approximation to the Binomial distribution can be explored graphically by superimposing the Normal density function and visually assessing the agreement between these two shapes. This is an example of the use of the computer in exploring a theoretical result. Of course, the mathematics underlying this approximation result is illuminating to those students who have the necessary technical background. However, most people find pictures helpful in explaining not only what the result means but also in exploring when the approximation is good enough.

2.2 Animation

One particular graphical technique which can be used to very good effect in a teaching context is animation. Program STEM illustrates the construction of a histogram by taking numbers from a displayed list, "floating" each one across the screen and dropping it into the appropriate "bin" on a scale at the foot of the screen. This "space invaders" style of presentation usually causes some amusement, which itself is no bad thing, but it also communicates the technique with a minimum of verbal explanation. The points are further enhanced by following this up with a demonstration of how to construct a stem-and-leaf plot. Here the numbers are again floated across the screen but the digits then separate to be associated with the stem and the leaf parts of the plot. We believe that such a visual presentation communicates very effectively, and is highly memorable.

2.3 Simulation

This is a very obvious application of computers in teaching which is already much used. Our aim has been to enhance this use by combining both graphics and simulation. One example is program CONF, which aims to assist students in understanding the nature of a confidence interval. The precise meaning of such intervals often causes confusion and in this program the essential features are communicated by repeatedly constructing confidence intervals from simulated sets of data. The collection of intervals so produced are displayed on the screen and illustrate both the random nature of the intervals and the meaning of confidence as the proportion of times these intervals capture the true value.

2.4 Drill and practice

This feature of the use of computers is not, of course, restricted to graphically based material. It is, however, important to stress the advantage of the computer in having infinite patience to repeat a display or solution with the same, or under different, conditions. Program CHISQ allows the user to type in a contingency table of frequency counts. A chi-squared test of no association is then performed step by step, at successive key presses, in great detail. The calculations for each expected value are displayed at the foot of the screen. This allows students to see where answers come from and to repeat the explanations until the principle becomes clearer.

2.5 Illustrating principles

The examples mentioned above illustrate statistical techniques (the construction of a histogram or stem-and-leaf plot), probability models (the Binomial distribution), theoretical results (the Normal approximation to the Binomial distribution) and statistical methods (confidence intervals). However, graphics can also be used to illustrate general principles. Program SCATTER displays simple linear regression data and allows the user to superimpose a straight line on the graph. This line begins in a horizontal position but the user may move it about the screen by pressing the arrow keys. By pressing key R the residuals from the current line are superimposed and the corresponding sum-of-squares displayed at the top of the screen. As the line is moved, we seek to minimise the sum-of-squares function and so to visually communicate the meaning of the least squares principle.

3. Conclusions

The authors are members of the CIText group - a collaborative project bringing together academics in mathematics and statistics who are interested in developing the kind of teaching materials described above. These authors believe that the role of the computer in teaching is not restricted to the performance of calculation or to the display of data, but includes the use of microcomputer graphics in communicating some of the basic ideas of the subject. In particular, the aim is to complement a standard presentation of the subject by using pictures to develop an intuitive "feel" for ideas and techniques which students often lose when material is presented algebraically.

This material is being published in the form of COMPUTER ILLUSTRATED TEXTS. These are text-books in which software is an integral part. As topics are developed, the reader is invited to run the software to provide appropriate graphical illustrations. Exercises are provided to encourage the reader to explore results and build up an understanding through experience. This approach aims to combine the advantages of a book, such as the ability to browse, with the graphical and other advantages of a computer, as discussed above.

Acknowledgements

The authors gratefully acknowledge the support of the Computer Board (through the Computers in Teaching Initiative), IBM and the Leverhulme Trust in supporting the CIText project.

References

Robinson, D.R. and Bowman, A.W. (1986). Introduction to Probability: a computer illustrated text. Adam Hilger: Bristol.

Bowman, A.W. and Robinson, D.R. (1987). Introduction to Statistics: a computer illustrated text. Adam Hilger: Bristol.

Bowman, A.W. and Robinson, D.R. (1987). Introduction to Regression and Analysis of Variance: a computer illustrated text. Adam Hilger: Bristol. To appear.

Beschreibende und exploratorische Statistik mit EDV-Unterstützung

F. Eicker

Summary. Exploratory data analysis (EDA) has become much more powerful and useful through graphical and computational analysis tools and software for PCs and workstations. Since these tools are widespread by now and familiar to most freshmen students they are introduced in an increasing number of elementary data analysis and statistics courses. Also the number of corresponding textbooks increases. Such courses at the Department of Statistics at Dortmund University have met enthusiastic student acceptance, some experiences with them are reported.

Erweitere Vorlesung Deskriptive Statistik

Exploratorische datenanalytische Methoden finden durch die leichtere Verfügbarkeit geeigneter PCs steigendes Interesse bei Statistikern und Anwendern der Statistik. Es wurde deshalb im SS 1988 am Fachbereich Statistik der Universität Dortmund, nachdem CIP-Pools zur Verfügung standen, erstmals versucht, die Vorlesung Deskriptive Statistik (4 Std. Vorlesung, 2 Std. Übung) für Studierende des Hauptfachstudiums Statistik im 2. Semester mit einer Einführung in eine zeitgemäße computergestützte exploratorische Datananalyse (EDA) zu kombinieren.

Wegen der besonderen Denk- und Arbeitsweise der EDA (induktives Arbeiten ausgehend von empirischen Sachverhalten und Daten, Versuch- und Irrtummethoden, zyklisches Durchlaufen verwandter Analyseschritte, empirische Absicherung von Modellierung, Einsatz neuerer Hilfsmittel aus der Informatik, z.B. dynamische Computergrafik, besondere Mensch-Maschine-Kommunikation und Programmierumgebungen, Benützung von Begriffen der Differentialgeometrie, der darstellenden Geome-

trie und der Approximationstheorie) ist es notwendig, die
Studierenden frühzeitig mit diesem Instrumentarium vertraut
zu machen und ihnen während des ganzen Studiums Gelegenheit
zu geben, exploratorische Methoden ergänzend zu anderen
einzusetzen. Da bei manchen EDA-Methoden Wahrscheinlichkeitstheorie nicht benötigt wird, ist es auch möglich, eine erste
Einführung bereits in den ersten Semestern vorzunehmen; Lehrveranstaltungen in höheren Semestern können die Kenntnisse in
EDA mit solchen in Stochastik verbinden. Mathematische Kenntnisse z.B. des zweiten Semesters wie solche aus Analysis I
und Lineare Algebra I sowie der gleichzeitig gehörten Analysis II können herangezogen werden. Es wird zugleich deutlich,
inwieweit sich EDA von der klassischen Beschreibenden Statistik unterscheidet.

Ein Modellversuch am FB Statistik

Außer grafikfähigen PCs wurden grafische Arbeitsstationen mit
dem Betriebssystem UNIX sowie für die EDA besonders geeignete
Hochsprachen, wie z.B. ISP und S-Language eingesetzt; aus di-
daktischen Gründen wurde in der genannten Lehrveranstaltung
des zweiten Semesters das Schwergewicht auf nur eine Sprache,
und zwar auf ISP gelegt. Überraschend war die hohe Akzeptanz
dieser technischen Hilfsmittel durch die Studierenden gerade
auch auf UNIX-Maschinen.

Unser Dortmunder Versuch der Berücksichtigung der EDA möglichst früh im Studium hat Parallelen: Ähnliche Ziele verfolgt z.B. der neuere Leitfaden von Polasek (1988), der sich
insbesondere auch an Studierende der Wirtschafts- und Sozialwissenschaften wendet, auch im Ausland gibt es mehrere
Parallelen. (Einige Literaturhinweise finden sich am Ende des
Beitrages.) Bei Statistik-Hauptfachstudenten kann die Ausbildung auf entsprechend lange Dauer und breite Grundlagen angelegt werden.

Aus dem Obigen folgt, daß die Rolle des Rechners in der EDA sich wesentlich von der Verwendung in Lehrveranstaltungen und Praktika zur Mathematischen Statistik unterscheidet. Die Berücksichtigung der EDA allein in der traditionellen einsemestrigen Standardvorlesung über Beschreibende Statistik kann jedoch nicht als angemessen angesehen werden, da die verfügbare Zeit nicht ausreicht, einen dieser Ausbildungsstufe angemessenen Überblick und Einstieg in die Methodologie zu geben, anspruchsvollere Methoden (Projection Pursuit, Principal Curves, Glättung in höheren Dimensionen, Brushing, Konditionierung, stochastische und strukturelle Fallstudien und Lernbeispiele etc.) müßten ohnehin höheren Semestern vorbehalten bleiben. Der praktische Statistiker von heute benötigt bei Ausbildungsende neben Kenntnissen über mathematische Statistik auch zunehmend solche über anspruchsvollere Anwendung von Methoden der Informatik, wie wissensbasierte Systeme, Expertensysteme, Programmierumgebungen, Mensch-Maschine-Kommunikations- und -Interaktionsmöglichkeiten, insbesondere der Grafik (s. oben). Ferner sollte es im Rahmen eines praktischen statistischen Studienganges möglich sein, als Vertiefungsfach statistische Softwareentwicklung, die wesentlich über numerische Routinen hinausgeht, zu wählen. Es sei an dieser Stelle auf einen gelegentlich zitierten Satz von McDonald und Pederson (1986) hingewiesen, des Inhalts: How we think about data analysis is strongly influenced by the computing environment in which the analysis is done.

Beispiele für EDA-Themen

Zur Behandlung im zweiten Semester und zur praktischen Erprobung auf dem PC eignen sich beispielsweise die folgenden Themen:

1. Variabilität des Aussehens von Histogrammen bei Veränderung der Klassenbreite und des Anfangwertes.

2. Box-Cox-Transformationen mit variablem Exponenten zur Symmetrisierung von Histogrammen und Linearisierung von schwach gekrümmten zwei-dimensionalen Punktwolken bei Regression etc.

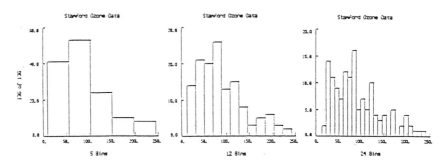

Abb. 1 a-c: Histogrammaussehen bei verschiedener Klassenbreite b zum selben Datensatz; b kontinuierlich veränderbar. (Beispiel 1)

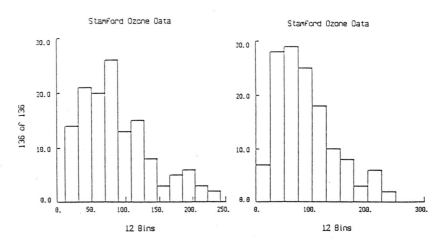

Abb. 2 a,b: Wie Abb. 1. Anfangswert variabel. (Beispiel 1)

3. Vergleich zweier ordinaler Merkmale durch Rücken-an-Rücken Histogramme oder Stamm- und Blattdiagramme.

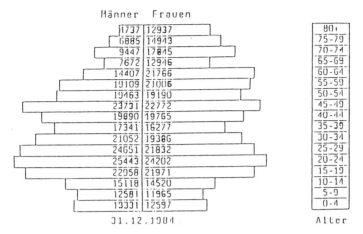

Abb. 3: Ein Rücken-an-Rücken Histogramm. (Beispiel 3)

4. Streudiagramme (Scatterplots) bei voraussetzungsarmer Regressions-, Assoziations- und Clusteranalyse, Konstruktion von Zusammenhangskurven; Residuenanalyse; Glättung.

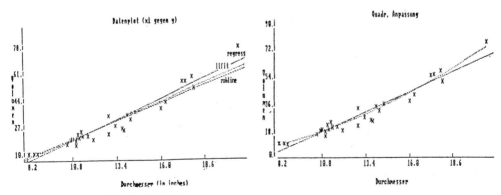

Abb. 4: Glättungen einer Punktewolke. (Beispiel 4)

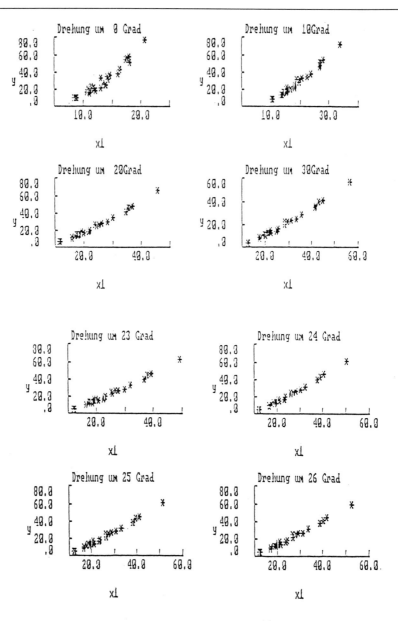

Abb. 5: Begradigung eines 3-dimensionalen Datensatzes durch Drehung um die waagerechte Achse. (Beispiel 4)

5. Veranschaulichung und Parametervariabilität bivariater Histogramme.

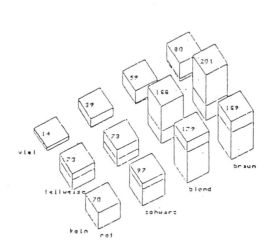

Abb. 6: Bi- bzw. trivariates Histogramm bei ordinalen/ kategoriellen Daten.
(Beispiel 5)

6. Modellfindung und -überprüfung.

7. Box-Plots und vergleichende Box-Plots für eine grobe Analyse multivariater Datensätze.

8. Matrizen von Streudiagrammen als grafisches Hilfsmittel zur Untersuchung multivariater reeller Datensätze sowie ggf. bereits die Technik des Brushing (Konditionierung).

Grafische Computerausdrucke der angegebenen Art werden von Studenten (2. Semester) in der Regel mit ISP in den regulären Übungen erstellt. [1]

Schlußbemerkung

Die Nutzbarmachung des Fortschrittes der Informationstechnologien, die in den meisten Anwendungen der Statistik unverzüglich vor sich geht, erscheint auch in der Hochschulausbildung - und zwar keineswegs nur in der Statistik - als ein Gebot der Stunde. Wegen des z.T. beträchtlichen Aufwandes an Technologie und Informatik bietet sich bei einer solchen, organisatorisch und didaktisch umfangreichen Aufgabe die Team-arbeit an, wie sie seit je auch in entsprechenden mathematischen Lehrveranstaltungen zu finden ist. Wegen der interaktiven Benutzung der Rechner und der experimentierenden Arbeitsweise in der EDA sind jedoch besondere Übungen und Kurse mit gleichzeitiger Rechnerbenutzung in größerem Umfang erforderlich. In einem Team lassen sich die unterschiedlichen Aufgaben auf mehrere Schultern verteilen, z.B. könnte sich der Hochschullehrer (wie im Fall des Autors) mehr auf die allgemein methodischen und prinzipiellen Fragestellungen, auf Interpretationsfragen grafischer Rechneroutputs etc. konzentrieren, die Mitarbeiter und Hilfskräfte die Arbeit an den Rechnern betreuen.

Literaturliste

Afflerbach, L.: Statistikpraktikum mit dem PC. Teubner Studienbuch 1987.
Becker, R.A., J.M. Chambers (1988): The new S Language, Wadsworth & Brooks/Cole.
McDonald, J. und Pederson, J. (1986): Computing environments for data analysis: Part 3: Programming environments. Laboratory for computational statistics, Stanford Technical Report 24.
PC-ISP. Datavision, Postfach 471, CH-7250 Klosters, Schweiz.
Polasek, W.: Explorative Datenanalyse. Einführung in die Deskriptive Statistik. Heidelberger Lehrtexte Wirtschaftswissenschaften. Springer 1988.
S-Plus. Fa. Krause & Becker, Behringstr. 62, 46 Dortmund 50.

1. Herrn A. Benner, der die Übung geleitet hat, wird für die Mithilfe bei der Bereitstellung der Abbildungen gedankt.

Statistik-Praktikum mit dem IBM PC

L. Afflerbach

Summary

A new statistical software package for IBM personal computers is presented. This tutorial software consists of 13 units with 131 exercises. The students have to solve the exercises in a dialogue with the PC. The statistical methods are illustrated by a lot of computer graphics. This tutorial software has been used at different universities with good experiences.

1. Einführung

Heutzutage gibt es wohl kaum einen Bereich, in dem die Statistik nicht in irgendeiner Form von Bedeutung ist. Für die statistische Auswertung von Datensätzen gibt es eine Vielzahl von Software-Paketen. Bei diesen Programmpaketen wird vorausgesetzt, daß die Anwender mit den statistischen Verfahren sinnvoll umgehen können. Deshalb ist es wichtig, daß insbesondere während des Studiums möglichst alle Studenten den richtigen Umgang mit statistischen Verfahren erlernen. Da an den Hochschulen seit einigen Jahren leistungsfähige Personal Computer zur Verfügung stehen, werden neue Lehrformen in der Statistik-Ausbildung möglich.

Es wird hier über die Entwicklung und den Einsatz eines Software-Paketes (s. Afflerbach, 1987b) berichtet. Das Programmpaket, *Statistik-Praktikum mit dem PC*, mit Lernprogrammen zur Statistik-Ausbildung stellt eine völlig neue Art von Statistik-Software dar. Beim Einsatz des Statistik-Praktikums wurde deutlich, daß die 'Verpackung' des Lerninhaltes durch eine Vielzahl von Computer-Graphiken zur Illustration stochastischer Vorgänge und statistischer Verfahren einen recht positiven Einfluß auf das Lerninteresse und die Leistungsbereitschaft der Studenten hat. Aber das Statistik-Praktikum ist nicht einfach eine Zusammenstellung von gewissen Illustrationsprogrammen sondern eine in sich geschlossene, komplette Lehrveranstaltung. Doch bevor die Lernprogramme hier ausführlicher beschrieben werden, soll etwas auf die Entstehung des Statistik-Praktikums eingegangen werden. Dabei wird insbesondere auch aufgezeigt, wie sich in Zusammenarbeit mit den Studenten die jetzige Form des Statistik-Praktikums herausgestellt hat.

2. Die Entstehung des Statistik-Praktikums

An der Technischen Hochschule Darmstadt wird die Statistik-Grundvorlesung für Studenten verschiedener Fachbereiche gemeinsam gehalten. Daher stellt die Stoffauswahl und der zeitliche Umfang von Vorlesung und Übungen gewissermaßen ein Kompromiß dar. Neben der dreistündigen Vorlesung und den einstündigen Rechenübungen sind für die Mathematik-Studenten zusätzlich noch zwei Stunden pro Woche als Tutorium zur Vertiefung des Stoffes vorgesehen. Trotz großer Anstrengungen, dieses Tutorium interessant zu gestalten, blieben die meisten Studenten im Laufe des Semesters dem Tutorium fern. Dies war der Ausgangspunkt für Überlegungen, das Tutorium in Form eines Praktikums abzuhalten. Als erster Versuch wurde im Sommersemester 1985 alternativ zum Tutorium in der damaligen Form ein Praktikum veranstaltet, das sich stark an dem StatLab-Praktikum (Hodges, Krech, Crutchfield, 1975) orientierte. Dieses von drei Professoren der University of California, Berkeley, erstellte Praktikum fand bei den Studenten schon mehr Interesse, auch wenn es gewisse Probleme gab, diese Veranstaltung auf die Vorlesung abzustimmen. Ferner wurde der Arbeitsaufwand mit Taschenrechner, Papier und Bleistift von den Studenten als etwas zu hoch angesehen.

Im Jahr 1986 standen im Hochschulrechenzentrum der Technischen Hochschule Darmstadt 8 IBM PC-AT für die Durchführung von Lehrveranstaltungen zur Verfügung. Dies gab die Anregung, die IBM Personal Computer für Rechnungen und zur Erstellung von Computer-Graphiken (z.B. Histogrammen) zu verwenden. Da der Fachbereich Lehre und Forschung der IBM Deutschland für die Entwicklung des Statistik-Praktikums dankenswerterweise einen Leih-PC zur Verfügung gestellt hatte, war es möglich, eine Vielzahl von Rechen- und Graphik-Programmen zur erstellen, so daß ein völlig neues Praktikum entstand. Es war eine Herausforderung, die Möglichkeiten, die durch die IBM Personal Computer geschaffen wurden, in der Statistik-Ausbildung einzusetzen. Das Statistik-Praktikum mit dem PC wurde dadurch, losgelöst vom StatLab-Praktikum, eine neue Lehrform, die bei den Studenten sehr großes Interesse fand. Lediglich auf die sehr interessanten StatLab-Daten wurde gerne zurückgegriffen, um für die Durchführung der statistischen Untersuchungen reale Daten zur Verfügung zu haben. Da aus zeitlichen Gründen die einzelnen Einheiten erst während des Semesters von Woche zu Woche entstanden, wurden die Lernprogramme stark durch das Interesse und die Leistungsfähigkeit der Studenten geprägt. Die Erprobung des Statistik-Praktikums fand also bereits während seiner Entwicklung statt. Die Studenten nahmen mit so großem Interesse am Praktikum teil, daß von einem Teilnehmerschwund keine Rede mehr sein konnte – ganz im Gegenteil: Auch Studenten anderer Fachrichtungen, in deren Lehrplan eine solche Veranstaltung nicht vorgesehen war, kamen, um an dem Praktikum teilzunehmen. Bei der ersten Version des Statistik-Praktikums mit dem PC im Sommersemester 1986 mußten von den Praktikumsteilnehmern in den einzelnen Einheiten einfache Programme z.B. für die Berechnung von empirischen Lage- und Streuungsmaßzahlen oder zur Durchführung der einzelnen Tests geschrieben werden. Einige Studenten kamen mit dem Programmieren sehr gut zurecht, andere jedoch hatten dabei so große Schwierigkeiten, daß die statistischen Verfahren in der Hintergrund gedrängt wurden. Auch die Möglichkeiten zum Einlesen und Auswerten von eigenen Datensätzen hat sich nicht bewährt. (Auswertungen von anderen Datensätzen mit Programmpaketen wie SPSS werden erst ein Semester nach der Statistik-Grundvorlesung durchgeführt.)

Aufgrund der Erfahrungen bei der ersten Durchführung des Statistik-Praktikums wurden die Programme erheblich umgeschrieben und ergänzt, so daß bei der nun vorliegenden zweiten Version keine Programmierkenntnisse benötigt werden. All die Fragen und Bemerkungen, die bei der ersten Durchführung des Statistik-Praktikums bei den verschiedenen Gruppen immer wieder an die Studenten gerichtet werden mußten, wurden bei der zweiten Version des Praktikums als Aufgaben und Bemerkungen in die Programme integriert. Dabei hat sich die Personalunion von Veranstalter, Programmierer und Betreuer als sehr günstig erwiesen, wenn man einmal von der enormen Arbeitsbelastung absieht. Im nächsten Abschnitt wird eine kurze Beschreibung des Programmpakets mit den Lernprogrammen zum Statistik-Praktikum gegeben.

3. Die Software: *Statistik-Praktikum mit dem PC*

Das Statistik-Praktikum (Afflerbach, 1987b) ist ein Programmpaket mit Lernprogrammen zur Statistik-Ausbildung für Mathematiker, Informatiker, Wirtschaftswissenschaftler, Naturwissenschaftler und Ingenieure. Die Lernprogramme sind aber auch für Studenten aus verschiedenen geisteswissenschaftlichen Fachbereichen geeignet. Mit 13 Einheiten zur Beschreibenden Statistik, Wahrscheinlichkeitstheorie und Schließenden Statistik stellt das Statistik-Praktikum eine komplette Lehrveranstaltung dar, die als Ergänzung zu einer Statistik-Grundvorlesung gedacht ist. Die Einheiten sind so konzipiert, daß sie vorlesungsbegleitend bearbeitet werden können. In jeder Einheit wird jeweils ein recht klar abgegrenzter Themenbereich behandelt:

1. Daten einer Population
2. Darstellung von Meßreihen
3. Empirischer Korrelationskoeffizient
4. Regression
5. Bertrand'sches Paradoxon
6. Verteilungen von Zufallsvariablen
7. Grenzwertsätze
8. χ^2-, t-Verteilungen, graphische Methode
9. Konfidenzintervalle
10. Tests bei Normalverteilungsannahmen
11. χ^2-Anpassungstest
12. Unabhängigkeitstests
13. Verteilungsunabhängige Tests

Durch die strenge thematische Gliederung ist es möglich, ggf. auch nur einzelne Einheiten des Statistik-Praktikums herauszugreifen. Damit läßt sich das Statistik-Praktikum in vielfältiger Weise für die Statistik-Ausbildung in nahezu allen natur- und geisteswissenschaftlichen Fachbereichen an Universitäten und Fachhochschulen einsetzen.

Für jede Einheit ist eine Bearbeitungszeit von ca. 1 bis $1\frac{1}{2}$ Stunden anzusetzen (zweistündige Lehrveranstaltung). In zahlreichen Aufgaben (von unterschiedlichem Schwierigkeitsgrad) wird anhand medizinischer, physiologischer und sozialwissenschaftlicher Daten die sachgemäße Anwendung statistischer Verfahren geübt. Die Lösungen der Aufgaben werden meistens in Bemerkungen (am Bildschirm) angegeben und diskutiert.

Eine wichtige Rolle spielen die Illustrationen der behandelten statistischen Untersuchungen durch rechnererzeugte Graphiken. Einerseits werden Simulationen (z.B. zu Konfidenzintervallen) graphisch dargestellt, andererseits kann durch einfache Eingabe von Parameterwerten eine Vielzahl von Computer-Graphiken (etwa Histogramme mit verschiedenen Klasseneinteilungen) erstellt werden. Insbesondere werden auch folgende Verteilungen von Zufallsvariablen jeweils durch die entsprechenden Stabdiagramme bzw. Dichten dargestellt: Binomialverteilungen, Poisson-Verteilungen, Geometrische Verteilungen, Hypergeometrische Verteilungen, Multinomialverteilungen, Normalverteilungen, Exponentialverteilungen, Weibull-Verteilungen, Cauchy-Verteilungen, t-Verteilungen, χ^2-Verteilungen sowie spezielle

Verteilungen von Testgrößen beim χ^2-Anpassungstest, Vorzeichentest, Zwei-Stichproben-Test von Wilcoxon-Mann-Whitney und Run-Test von Wald-Wolfowitz. Zusammenhänge zwischen den einzelnen Verteilungen aufgrund von Grenzwertsätzen werden durch gemeinsame Darstellung der Verteilungen illustriert. Dadurch kann die Güte der Näherungen für verschiedene Parameterwerte genau betrachtet werden. Dabei kann auch die schnelle Konvergenz der Verteilungen der standardisierten Summenvariablen (z.B. bei Rechteckverteilungen) gegen die Standard-Normalverteilung (Zentraler Grenzwertsatz) sehr gut deutlich gemacht werden.

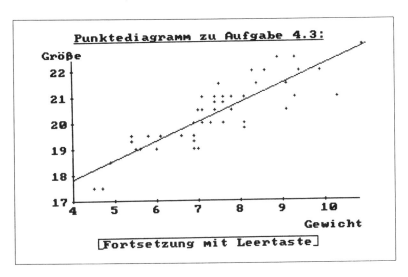

Bildschirmkopie: Regressionsgerade

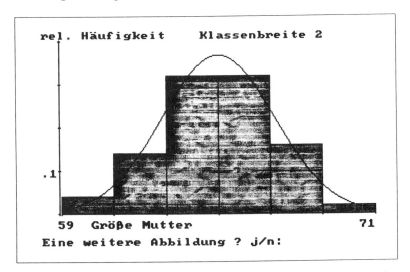

Bildschirmkopie: Histogramm und Dichte einer Normalverteilung

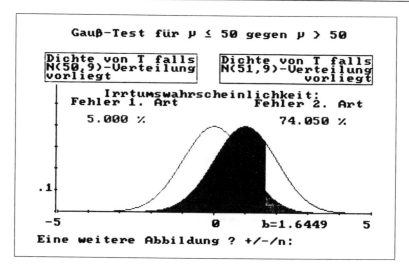

Bildschirmkopie: Fehler 1. Art, Fehler 2. Art beim Gauß-Test

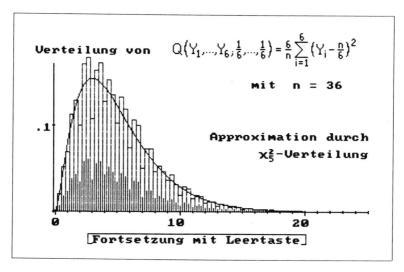

Bildschirmkopie: χ^2-Anpassungstest beim Würfelbeispiel

Diese wenigen Abbildungen können natürlich nur andeuten, welche Computer-Graphiken mit den Lernprogrammen des Statistik-Praktikums erstellt werden können. Mindestens ebenso wichtig wie die Computer-Graphiken sind die 131 aufeinander abgestimmten Aufgaben mit den in Bemerkungen diskutierten Lösungen. Die Mischung von einfachen Aufgaben, die spielerisch gelöst werden können, und tiefergehenden Fragestellungen ist sicherlich ein Grund für die relativ große Attraktivität des Statistik-Praktikums bei den Studenten. Ferner ist das gemeinsame Arbeiten von mehreren Studenten an einem PC recht vorteilhaft.

Die Lernprogramme sind selbsterklärend, d.h. es wird stets am Bildschirm ausführlich angegeben, was getan werden muß, um in der jeweiligen Einheit fortzufahren (z.B. einfache Eingabe von Werten oder *Leertaste drücken zur Fortsetzung*). Das Arbeiten mit den Lernprogrammen erfordert keine Programmiersprachenkenntnisse. Aufgrund der freundlichen Unterstützung durch den Fachbereich Lehre und Forschung der IBM Deutschland konnte das Statistik-Praktikum in relativ kurzer Zeit entstehen, da der Leih-PC ausschließlich für die Entwicklung der Programme zur Verfügung stand. Dies hat sicherlich dazu beigetragen, daß alle Programme eine einheitliche Formulierung und Gestaltung aufweisen.

Mit den Lernprogrammen übernimmt der Computer zu einem großen Teil die Betreuung der Praktikumsteilnehmer. Bei schwierigen Aufgaben gestatten die Programme auch ein Fortschreiten ohne auf einer Lösung der entsprechenden Aufgabe zu bestehen. Einfache Aufgaben müssen (als Mindestanforderung) gelöst werden, damit in den Programmen weitergegangen werden kann. Bei falschen Eingaben und beim Abbrechen einer Einheit ertönt ein Warnton. Es kann jederzeit in den Programmen mit **R** schrittweise zurückgegangen werden. Dadurch können Aufgabenstellungen, Computer-Graphiken und frühere Ergebnisse nochmals angesehen werden. Für die Betreuung des Praktikums ist nur noch ein sehr geringer Arbeitsaufwand nötig, da viele Bemerkungen zu den Lösungen der Aufgaben bereits in den Programmen enthalten sind. Ferner ist zu dem Praktikum ein Studienbuch (Afflerbach, 1987a) erschienen, in dem zu Beginn jeder Einheit die für die jeweiligen statistischen Untersuchungen benötigten Verfahren, Formeln, Sätze und Bezeichnungen kurz dargestellt sind. Neben den Aufgaben und entsprechenden Lösungsvorschlägen enthält das Buch auch viele Abbildungen von rechnererzeugten Graphiken.

Das Statistik-Praktikum ist für den IBM PC (XT, AT und Kompatible) mit CGA-, EGA-, VGA-Farbgraphikkarten sowie IBM PS/2 mit Farb- oder Monochrom-Bildschirm entwickelt. Ferner gibt es für Herkules-Graphikkarten eine Anpassung, bei der die verschiedenen Farben weitgehend anderweitig dargestellt werden (bei Pool-Lizenzen). Ab DOS 2.0 Betriebssystem und einer Mindest-RAM-Größe von 256 KB läuft das Statistik-Praktikum mit einem Menüsystem, bei dem die 13 Einheiten durch Eingabe der entsprechenden Zahlen gestartet werden. Durch die Betätigung der **Escape**-Taste kann eine Einheit abgebrochen und zum Menüsystem zurückgesprungen werden.

4. Der Einsatz des Statistik-Praktikums

Zunächst war das Statistik-Praktikum nur für die Mathematik-Studenten an der Technischen Hochschule Darmstadt gedacht, wie im zweiten Abschnitt bereits ausgeführt wurde. Dann kamen auch Informatik-Studenten und Studenten anderer Fachrichtungen hinzu. Bei der Präsentation des Statistik-Praktikums am IBM Hochschulkongreß '87 im ICC Berlin fand das Statistik-Praktikum erfreulicherweise bei vielen Hochschullehrern ein recht großes Interesse. Dadurch, daß der Preis für die Campus-/Pool-Lizenzen (s. Afflerbach, 1987b) lediglich als Schutzgebühr gedacht ist und weit unter dem angemessenen Betrag liegt, wurde der Einsatz des Statistik-Praktikums für viele andere Hochschulen ermöglicht. Inzwischen ist das Statistik-Praktikum auch bereits an verschiedenen Fachbereichen von Universitäten und Fachhochschulen in Deutschland und Österreich eingesetzt worden.

In erster Linie dient das Statistik-Praktikum als Ergänzung von Statistik-Grundvorlesungen (vorlesungsbegleitend). Wie bereits oben erwähnt, ist das gemeinsame Arbeiten von mehreren Studenten an einem PC recht vorteilhaft. Mit 2 - 3 Personen pro PC und Gruppen von ca. 20 - 30 Personen wurden gute Erfahrungen gemacht. Das Statistik-Praktikum hat sich aber auch als Blockveranstaltung (etwa unmittelbar vor einem Anwendungspraktikum oder vor einer weiterführenden Vorlesung) zur Auffrischung von statistischen Grundkenntnissen bewährt. Bei Seminaren des Zentrums für Graphische Datenverarbeitung Darmstadt (ZGDV) wurden die Programme des Statistik-Praktikums auch recht erfolgreich eingesetzt.

Literatur/Software:

Afflerbach, L. (1987a): *Statistik-Praktikum mit dem PC.* Teubner Studienbuch, B.G. Teubner Stuttgart.

Afflerbach, L. (1987b): *Programmdisketten zum Statistik-Praktikum mit dem PC.* Teubner-Software; Programmpaket zur Individualnutzung auf nur einem PC vom Teubner-Verlag über den Buchhandel. – Campus-/Pool-Lizenzen für 2 und mehr PC von: Dr. Lothar Afflerbach, Auf den Weiherhöfen 23, 5928 Bad Laasphe 2.

Hodges, J.L., Krech, D., Crutchfield, R.S. (1975): *StatLab, An Empirical Introduction to Statistics.* McGraw-Hill New York.

F. Faulbaum, R. Haux und K.-H. Jöckel (Hrsg.) (1990). SoftStat '89
Fortschritte der Statistik-Software 2. Stuttgart: Gustav Fischer, 575 - 583

Software Tools for Statistical Data Analysis in Education and Teacher Training?

R. Biehler and W. Rach

Summary

This paper presents results and methods of a project situated in the frame of research into perspectives for an innovative education in probability and statistics at the secondary level of schools providing general education. Statistical software tools including PC–ISP, S, STATVIEW and DATADESK are compared and analyzed. Constitutive elements of design are reconceptualised in order to develop a model of data analysis tools which could guide the development and application of statistics tools in the classroom.

1. The background of the study

The background of the project forms a potential line of innovation which is to integrate statistical graphics, multivariate real data and simulation into teaching. This integration is to be considered with various general objectives in mind. New modes of working and knowing belonging to statistics are to be made accessible for teaching. The new technologies are to be used to encourage an interactive–flexible mode of working with data and methods, and a systemic holistic approach to problems instead of applying isolated individual methods. Besides, the new technological achievements are to be used to attain a better understanding of statistics and a richer, more motivating and application-oriented teaching: for instance graphics and simulation can be used to illustrate and visualize, multivariate real data shall be used to link theory and practice and to treat more interesting 'real life' applications. With regard to existing curricular subject matter, this would imply, among other things, to develop descriptive statistics further towards Exploratory Data Analysis (EDA), that is to place more emphasis on an exploration of data from various points of view, and on statistical graphics as well as on the interpretation of data. A second potential line of growth is to transform inference statistics towards a more comprehensive understanding of statistical modelling which includes the developing and checking of models with data and to interpret and discuss results in the broader context of the data. By developing competencies and attitudes concerning the use of graphics, concerning data bases, simulation, and modelling, an innovative stochastics education could make a more important contribution to the educational goals in schools providing general education.

Two projects realized at the Institut für Didaktik der Mathematik (IDM) in close cooperation are oriented towards elaborating a perspective of innovation. The project GRAPHDAS (Graphische Darstellungen zur Datenanalyse im Stochastikunterricht) studies, in cooperation with a group of mathematics teachers, how ideas and techniques of Exploratory Data Analysis may be used to enrich mathematics instruction at the secondary levels I and II (cf. Biehler 1988, Biehler/Steinbring 1989). Along with this project, statistics software is used to allow for complex data analyses with elementary means of representation and operation. The fairly simple representations used are boxplots, scatter plots, histograms, stem-and-leaf - displays, enhanced scatter plots with numerical summaries such as lines or median curves. These are applied together with operations like identifying and localizing points and subsets, splitting the data into groups, reduction to subsets, zooming and overlaying graphics, definition of new variables.

In a second project SOMA (Software im Mathematikunterricht), we analyze and compare mathematical and statistical software tools. The SOMA project was more concerned with basic research into the design and use of software in various applicational contexts, and rather less concerned with direct recommendations of certain data analysis tools for the classroom. Our objective was to reconstruct constitutive elements and concepts of design and to reconceptualize them in order to develop a model of data analysis tools which could guide the development and application of statistics tools in the classroom.

Taking in account our intended educational applications, we placed the emphasis on tools which support an interactive graphical data analysis, and which, at first sight, seemed to represent certain design conceptions in a prototypical way. Within the "MacIntosh line", these were mainly the systems STATVIEW and DATADESK, besides MACSPIN and ELASTIC. For the systems aligned to command language resp. on interactive languages of statistics, we focussed on PC−ISP and S, but made allowance for GAUSS as well.

2. Models and dimensions for evaluating statistics software
2.1. Tools for data analysis in the conflict between user orientation and intended application

Statistics tools are influenced, among other things, by two factors: by the way the user is conceived of, and by the conception of the intended applications which are represented in the statistical methods available, in the problem types to be treated, and in the conception of statistics and of statistical activity. There is, as a rule, a relationship of conflict between an alignment to the user, and an alignment to applications.

From the point of view of intended applications, systems with well−designed extensible command languages (e.g. PC−ISP, S, GAUSS) are preferrable. To quote some of the advantages of these systems: locally and globally, they offer greater freedom of activity, a fact which makes for a more supple adaptation to different methodologies or individual styles of statistical work. After a protracted stage of learning, they convey an impression of economy and efficiency within the paths of familiar use. Without further ado, they permit extensions of language which can be used by the developer of methods, but also during exploratory data analyses for a redefinition, modification, refinement of methods. This usage conforms to the philosophy of EDA and to pedagogical concerns with regard to developing(!) statistical methods in the classroom. Another advantage are the possibilities for "record keeping" ("script" or "monitor files" in ISP, "Audit files" in S). "Monitoring" one's work or that of others through using the system to record user commands (and software responses) is important in educational settings but, of course, with indubitable profit to any kind work pertaining to data analysis, in particular for EDA.

However, in case students use statistical working environments, these
- have to be simple enough and clearly arranged as a model and mental representation of the working environment;
- should remain transparent and consistent both mathematically and as a model of the working environment;
- should be easily learnt and offer itself to be handled intuitively according to the paradigm of the incidental user.

These requirements can be more easily met by visual languages than by command languages. Implementations based on the MacIntosh user interface like DATADESK, ELASTIC, STATVIEW show that it is this kind of user orientation which makes computer-aided flexible interactive data analysis accessible for school. With regard to application orientation, however, they are inferior to the above command language systems.

2.2. Reference model for data analysis tools

For a comparative analysis and evaluation of software, our starting point is the following model of reference, within we distinguish between "low level" and "high level" functions of statistical software. The high level funtctions are intimately related to the design of the user interface.

Reference model for data analysis tools

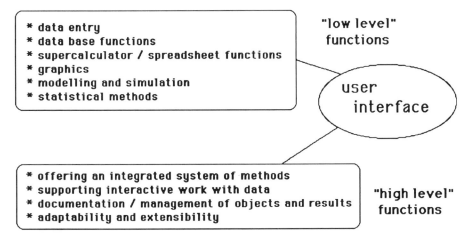

Fig. 1

We assume an intuitive understanding of these functions and should like to begin by discussing two functions which are both didactically relevant and related to our perspective of innovation. More detailed descriptions and comparative evaluations for the other software functions can be found in Biehler/Rach (1989).

The functional domain "**modelling and simulation**" designates the possibility of generating and processing random numbers for the most various probability distributions in order to simulate probability models, as well as the possibilities of handling deterministic and mixed models in relative independence of particular statistical methods. This, for instance, subsumes possibilities of defining mathematical functions and of comparing them to data without requiring that these emerge from a particular statistical procedure, e.g. the possiblity of overlaying straight lines by rule of thumb or eye into a set of data, or the possibility of graphically representing and comparing various binomial distributions. Such opportunities are important for developing new methods, for theoretical studies in statistics, and for those applications of data analysis, where the intention is to compare models and data in an unconventional way. In this area, there are many points of contact with traditional subject matter of mathematics education. Here, the opportunities offered by systems like DATA-DESK, STATVIEW and ELASTIC are limited by comparison.

By "**supercalculator/spreadsheet function**", we understand the possibilities of carrying out general mathematical operations with data (vectors), for instance applying basic arithmetical operations to pairs of data vectors, and also the applicability of mathematical functions to transformation of data, up to the possibility of calculating with matrices. Besides transforming data and defining new variables (on the basis of old ones), this functional domain permits to execute procedures which are not yet contained in the ready made library of "statistical methods".

While professional statistics software is mainly judged according to the extent of its **library of statistical methods,** the requirements for secondary education are somewhat different. A great variety in the field of **elementary** statistical methods is required, enriched by opportunities to extend, modify and elaborate these methods, and a skilled integration of these statistical methods into a graphical, algebraic-numerical and data base environment. These featues are important for increasing the efficiency of a statistical working environment for elementary applications.

Now we shall treat conceptions of statistical graphics in more detail.

2.3. Conceptions of statistical graphics

We distinguish between the following aspects:
- (exploratory) working graphics
- multiple representation
- direct interaction

- multiple, linked representation
- presentation graphics

If graphs are to be used as a means of insight, the graphical functions of statistics software must meet several requirements. The basic idea is to obtain a working graph as directly as possible which then can be modified and enriched further.

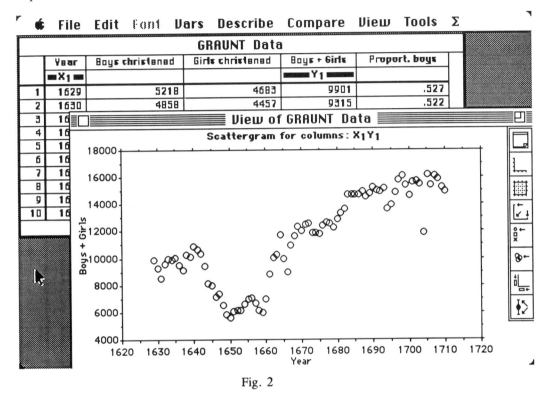

Fig. 2

Figure 2 shows a screendump from STATVIEW 512+. The working graph shown is created by selecting two variables and choosing the command *scatterplot*. A plot menu represented by icons offers various possibilities to vary and enrich the graph, for instance by rescaling, different plot symbols, new labeling, plotting "error bars" around the individual points, etc. The graph can also be quickly varied by selecting different variables from the table, or by confining the presentation to a certain subset of data. These modifications are immediately actualized in the graphics window. Other tools such as PC-ISP or S offer far broader opportunities for subsequent statistical analysis: plots already generated for instance, can be overlaid (with automatical adaption of the coordinate systems). It is also possible to add straight lines or curves to a plot, mark subsets with a special plot symbol, or use as plot symbols, instead of a simple point or asterisk, symbols with complex information (e.g. representation of further variables). Such a conception of **enrichment** or **overlay** can be helpful for elementary applications in school.

Multiple representations on the screen are very useful in educational and statistical respects. It is an important means of Exploratory Data Analysis which intends to explore a set of data from different points of view. The possibility of not only immediately actualizing graphics, but to put them into intermediate storage devices and to recall them for comparison with others is essential to counteract the volatility of screen graphics. Besides, there is the aspect that learning new representations is enhanced by relating them to familiar ones, as in relating a scatterplot of two variables to the respective histograms. Tables should be considered as semi−graphical means of representation. If tables can be flexibly manipulated, they have a considerable exploratory function. The possibility of multiple representation also includes that of presenting graphs and tables as well as texts containing numerical output (e.g. results of statistical tests) side by side on the screen and to relate them to one another. From an educational point of view it is important that students are able to handle tabular and graphical representation and their relationships competently and that graphics should be integrated into the treatment of other statistical methods.

Many novel ideas of ***direct interaction*** with statistical graphs as an important means to achieve insight, in particular in case of multivariate data, have emerged in connection with the PRIM concept, as it is implemented as in MACSPIN, PC-ISP and DATADESK 2.0. Besides interacting with rotating point clouds as in the PRIM conception, direct interaction is also used for other spatial transformations of data, and for brushing scatter plot matrices. Direct interaction with data graphs, similar to paper and pencil work avoids an intermediate complex symbolics. This feature constitutes an important advance for the use of data analysis tools in the classroom, and this not only for the analysis of multivariate data. Specific educational uses of direct interaction would be helpful, for instance, to create opportunities of adding summarizing lines to a scatter plot which then would not only serve to "embellish" the picture, but which permits a next step in data analysis, for instance, calculating residuals from the added line. If direct interaction with graphics is supplemented by ***multiple, linked representation,*** the chances of orientation in multivariate situations are considerable improved. Besides, multiple linked representations permit, from a educational point of view, new ways of supporting students in their flexible use of various modes of representation of mathematics and statistics (cf. Kaput 1986). Under the very requirement that data shall not remain abstract signs on the monitor for the students, it is important to be able to see which points in various diagrams (e.g. boxplot, table, histogram) "belong" to the same objects.

Presentation graphics as that form of graphics which serves to transmit the information at the analyzers disposal as poignantly as possible is a necessary supplement to (exploratory) working graphics. For presentation graphics, there are manifold software solutions: interaction on the pixel level combined with a set of geometrical primitives like in painting and drawing programs, configuration of graphics by parameters, icon−based graphics construction sets or special graphics programming languages. With regard to presentation graphics, there is justified criticism of the general level of quality, but there are hardly any consistent conceptions which might systematically guide the design of computer tools (cf., however, Cleveland 1985). A pertinent learning objective for school would be, for instance, to be able to reconstruct, criticize or improve graphics present in mass media, for instance by means of a "graphics construction set", and to acquire elements of good graphical representation by application.

There are interesting approaches in the data analysis tools examined, but no convincing conception. DATADESK is the closest approximation to the requirement of an extended working graphics with multiple representation and direct interaction. STATVIEW offers much more possibilities for presentation and overlay graphics. Against that, the possibilities of modification, extension, graphics programming and documentation are far more developed in PC-ISP, and even more in S. It seems to be a difficult task to link working and presentation graphics.

2.4. High–level functions in user interfaces

Hitherto applying methods in isolation is practiced in statistical education. This reductionistic treatment is also reflected in the widely available, merely additive collections of statistical algorithms. In view of this, it is important to stress the value of a software tool which *integrates* the various aspects of statistical activity and statistical methods *into a unified system*. It is essential for multiple and iterative analyses that the output of one procedure can be used again as input for others — be it graphical or numerical methods. This aspect has been most consistently realized in PC–ISP and S. This is attractive for classroom application, for the very reason that its openess permits combinations and local "micro-worlds" of methods which are useful under the specific conditions of learning in school, but do not necessarily correspond to the conventions and requirements of statistical practice. But with systems like S and PC–ISP, there is still the problem that the user himself must (mentally) organize such modules of statistical activity, an activity for which the students may fall back on prestructurizations provided by the teacher, and orientate themselves according to these.

Menu–supported systems, by contrast, reflect structures and sequences of possible statistical activities. A sensible requirement of menu systems is to not only give access to a collection of procedures, but to use them to structure the statistical activity and the "image of statistics". This seems to be most successfully solved in DATADESK. Nevertheless, for classroom applications a possibility for configuration and designing specific working environments for students with regard to certain statistical fields of application and users' previous knowledge were most desirable. Specifical educational software tools like ELASTIC provide a **closed** working environment that was designed from an eduational point of view, but, however, they are apt to be criticized if their basic pedagogical assumptions and points of emphasis are not accepted.

Statistics tools offer different ways of *documenting and administrating* (tentative) results (plots, textual-numerical summaries, transformed data), objects (new variables and functions, macros) and processes of data analysis as the sequence of the commands given to the system (scriptfiles in PC-ISP, Audit files in S). This is crucial for organizing work with a system if interactive work is being done. This is all the more true if different persons are to work on the same problem and in teamwork. Such is the situation in a classroom where the teacher prepares certain aspects of the data and of the graphics, and where certain problems are evolved across several lessons and under participation of different groups of learners. An essential basic idea for that seems to be a flexible conception of the *workspace* as implemented in slightly different versions in DATADESK, PC-ISP and S. The workspace possibilities in STATVIEW are rather limited, as only data tables can be stored as objects internal to the system.

Possibilities of "record keeping" play an important role in the frame of professional discussions about data analysis tools (cf. Huber/Huber—Buser 1988). Scriptfiles as in PC-ISP can take on different functions in a classroom context: preparing demonstrations by the teacher or by learner groups as well as documenting problem solving in order to reflect on the activity or to diagnose learning difficulties. Nevertheless, it must be stressed that this basic idea has not been realized in the present systems in a way which would make them easy to handle for teachers and students.

Possibilities of **adaptation and extension** have been frequently mentioned. We should like to summarize their significance within a classroom context in that they support the
— opportunity to configurate student working environments
— developing new methods in the classroom
— use of a statistics tool as a means of visualisation

Beyond that, we consider configurating and extending given systems according to individual needs to be an important learning experience with regard to new technologies. Adaptibility and extensibility is, as a rule, available only at a high cost in terms of user qualification. In the case of the command-oriented interactive languages, we consider opportunities for user-defined functions as realized in the new S-system an essential simplification. Until adaptibility and extensibility, however, can be actually used by average students, some important advances into the direction of iconic programming are still to be made.

3. Perspectives

The perspective of innovation noted at the outset requires a reorientation of teacher education and training in the field of probability and statistics. The educational offers for teachers must include experience with statistical data analysis tools, both with interactive command languages like PC-ISP, S, GAUSS, and with data analysis tools based on visual languages like DATADESK and STATVIEW.

The latter would seem to be preferable for secondary education as their user interfaces are better adapted to a student user. The "MacIntosh"—like approach to user interfaces seems to be flexible enough to be able to integrate conceptions from other data analysis tools which have been proved fruitful, as e.g. DATADESK shows in its successive versions. Classroom tests still have to be waited for before comparative statements can be made about the uses of DATADESK, STATVIEW or ELASTIC in school.

Such pilot tests in school can serve to initiate the necessary research into the effectivity of conceptions for data analysis tools which have been recognized to be educationally pertinent. Generally speaking, however, an independent development of a data analysis tool better suited to the user groups and application concerns in school must be taken into consideration if professional data analysis tools fail to meet these requirements still better.

4. References

Becker, R.A./Chambers, J.M./Wilks, A.R. (1988). The New S Language. Pacific Grove, CAL: Wadsworth & Brooks.

Biehler, R. (1988). Changing Conceptions of Statistics: A Problem Area for Teacher Training. IDM Occational Paper 114. Bielefeld. To be published in: Proceedings of the ISI Round Table Conference, Törökbalint, Ungarn, July.

Biehler, R./Rach, W. (1989). Softwaretools zur Statistik und Datenanalyse aus software-ergonomischer und didaktischer Sicht. Projektabschlußbericht. Bielefeld/Soest. To be published in: Landesinstitut für Schule und Weiterbildung (Hrsg.): Neue Medien im Unterricht: Mathematik 1989/90. Soest: Soester Verlagskontor.

Biehler, R./Steinbring, H. (1989). Graphische Darstellungen zur Datenanalyse im Stochastikunterricht. Materialien aus dem GRAPHDAS – Projekt. Universität Bielefeld: IDM.

Cleveland, W.S. (1985). The Elements of Graphing Data. Monterey, CAL: Wadsworth.

Huber, P.J./Huber – Buser, E.H. (1988). ISP: Why a Command Language? In: Faulbaul, F./Mehlinger, H. – M. (Hrsg.): Fortschritte der Statistik – Software 1. Stuttgart – New York: Gustav Fischer, S. 349 – 360.

Kaput, J. (1986). Information Technology and Mathematics: Opening New Representational Windows. In: Journal of Mathematical Behavior, 5, p. 187 – 207.

5. Software

DATADESK: 1986. Data Description, Inc., P.O. Box 4555, Ithaca, N.Y. 14852.

DATADESK Professional 2.0: 1988. Odesta Corporation, Inc., 4084 Commercial Avenue, Northbrook, Ill. 60062.

ELASTIC: 1988. Pre – release version. BBN Laboratories, 10 Moulton Street, Cambridge, MA 02238.

GAUSS: 1984, 1985, 1986, 1987. Aptech Systems, Inc., P.O. Box 6487, Kent, WA 98064.

MACSPIN: 1986. D 2 Software, Inc., 3001 North Lamar Boulevard, Suite 110. Austin TX 78705.

PC – ISP: 1988. Artemis Systems, Inc., 125 Berry Corner Lane, Arlisle, MA 01741.

S (see Becker/Chambers/Wilks 1988)

STATVIEW 512+: 1986. BrainPower, Inc., 24009 Ventura Boulevard, Calabasas, CA 91302.

STATVIEW SE+ Graphics: 1988. Abacus Concepts, Inc., 1984 Bonita Avenue, Berkeley, CA 94704.

On the Statistical Package GSTAT

F. Böker

Summary:

GSTAT is a statistical package to assist teaching in first courses of Statistics. In this paper the author of GSTAT reports on the aims of GSTAT, their realization and first experience with GSTAT.

1. Introduction, aims of GSTAT

GSTAT is a statistical package developed at the Institute of Statistics and Econometrics of the University of Göttingen to assist teaching in first courses of Statistics to students with limited mathematical background. Thus in contrast to other statistical packages it is not the principal aim of GSTAT to analyse data. In our opinion it is important to give students a feeling for Statistics before they start to analyse data. They have to learn what randomness means. For students in first introductory courses it is difficult to understand why a few numbers, given on a sheet of paper, can be regarded as realizations of random variables. "What is random in these numbers which are fixed on my sheet of paper?". What does it mean that statistical statements and decisions are not necessarily correct? In which way are they then correct at all?

Here a computer can help. Within seconds you may simulate and repeat a statistical experiment and the students can see at once that the results are different from realization to realization, they can see what randomness is. Another advantage in teaching Statistics with the aid of computers is the possibility of graphical displays. You may illustrate such complicated matters as the law of large numbers and the central limit theorem, which you are not able to prove in your course, by simulation and graphical representation of the results. Even if you have time to prove these theorems your students will be better able to understand them.

In our programs we often take a sample from a population which is known. We do this only for the purpose of illustration. In this way one may see whether the conclusions drawn from the data are correct or not.

It is always a problem, even for advanced students, to see the relation between empirics and the mathematical theory of probability. On the one hand you have the data, compute relative frequencies, means and standard deviations, draw histograms etc., on the other hand you have probability theory with probabilities, expected values and standard deviations, distribution functions, density functions etc.. It is one of the aims of GSTAT to show the relationship between these two spheres.

Apart from the material mentioned so far GSTAT contains programs for simple analysis and graphical representation of continuous and discrete data, for calculations and graphical representation of the Normal-, Exponential-, Binomial- and Poisson-distribution and for illustration of the concept of confidence intervals.

2. Realization of the aims

The first program 'ALTER' draws a sample out of the known age distibution of the inhabitants of the Federal Republic of Germany in the year 1974. This is to show what one usually does in Statistics. One observes only a part of the population and wants to make conclusions which are true for the whole population. How can one make conclusions for the whole community observing only a part of it? The first one can do is to calculate some statistics based on the data in the sample. These statistics should characterize the sample and should be related in some way to corresponding quantities in the whole population. The program 'ALTER' calculates two such statistics, the mean and the standard deviation. One may observe that both statistics vary from sample to sample, i.e. that they are random variables. Perhaps one may also observe by taking samples of the same size several times and then changing to another size, that the variation of these statistics decreases with increasing sample size. This last point is a very fundamental one in Statistics.

Another possibility to get an impression of how the whole population looks like is to make a picture of the data in the sample, i.e. to draw a histogram. In doing this one is confronted with the problem of how many classes should be chosen to get a realistic image of the population. One will learn at once that the answer for this question depends on the sample size. From the histogram you draw conclusions such as "there are fewer people in the age group 55-60 than in the group 60-65." Of course this conclusion could be wrong, you will soon see that every histogram differs from the preceding one, i.e. that histograms are random. Repeating the same experiment several times you will learn how often your conclusions are wrong. You will learn that you have to be careful in making such statements especially if the sample size is small.

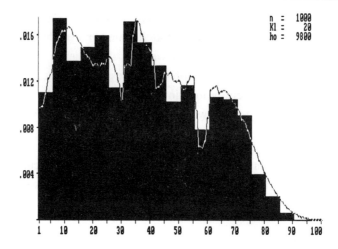

Figure 1: Histogram of a sample of size 1000 with known age distribution

In 'ALTER' the known distribution may be printed in the same figure together with the histogram (see figure 1). This offers the possibility to observe that histograms tend to a final form if one chooses bigger and bigger sample sizes and at the same time makes the partition into subintervals finer and finer and that this final form coincides with the known age distribution. Such a final form of the histograms corresponds to what is called a density function in the theory of probability. Now we have the first link between empirics and mathematical theory.

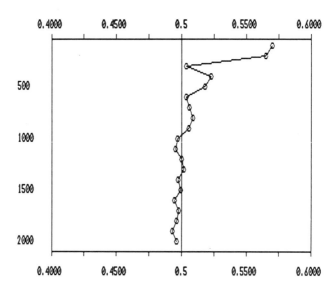

Figure 2: Path of relative frequencies in a cointossing experiment

The second connection between empirics and mathematical theory emerges by the program 'MUENZE' in which a cointossing experiment is simulated and a path of the relative frequencies of the number of heads is drawn (see figure 2). It is shown that the sequence of relative frequencies converges to the value 1/2, which even in common sense is accepted as the "chance" or "probability" of winning if a decision is made by tossing a coin. Thus it is easy to explain that in general relative frequencies converge to final values, which in the mathematical theory are called probabilities.

In a histogram the area of a rectangle is proportional to the relative frequency of the number of values falling into the corresponding interval. Starting with this one can deduce that the area under a density function between two points of the real line represents the probability that a corresponding random variable takes a value in this interval, because histograms converge to density functions and relative frequencies to probabalities, i.e. areas under a histogram to areas under a density function. Mathematically the area under a density function may be calculated by an integral over the density function. This shows why it is important to have density functions in the theory, but it remains an open question how to find the most appropriate density function for a given set of data.

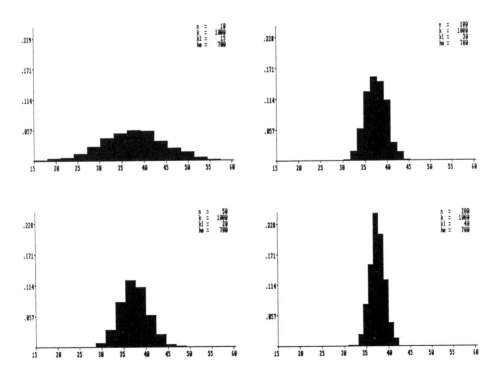

Figure 3: Histograms of 1000 means in samples of size 10, 50, 100 and 200

The program 'ALMIPFAD' is analoguous to 'MUENZE', but it draws the path of the means in a successively enlarged sample from the age distribution showing that the sequence of means converges to a final value, which the mathematical theory calls the expected value. Using all what was learned so far, it is easy to explain how this expected value has to be calculated (see Böker (1989), page 85).

We have already seen in the program 'ALTER' that the mean in the sample is a random variable and that its variability depends on the sample size. But until now we do not yet know how the values of the means in samples of the same size are distributed on the age scale and how the variability depends on the sample size and how we can measure it.

The program 'ALTMIHI' gives histograms of means in samples of the same size from the age distribution. As one may see from figure 3 all histograms have a characteristic shape. This leads to the normal distribution and the central limit theorem. The central limit theorem is further illustrated by the program 'STALMIHI' which allows one to draw the density function of the standard normal distribution into the same figure as the histograms for the standardized means in samples from the age distribution (see figure 4).

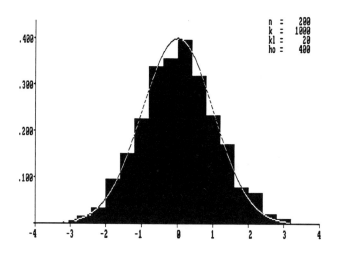

Figure 4: Histogram of 1000 standardized means in samples of size 200

As we may see from figure 3 the width of the histograms decreases with increasing sample size. At the same time the histograms become higher and higher, the values in the sample are closer to the known mean in the population, the expected value. From this one may deduce again that in estimating the unknown expected value by the mean in a sample the estimate will become better with increasing sample size. How can one measure the goodness or quality of the estimate?

As we may already have learnt the standard deviation is a quantity to measure the variability of a random variable and we know that the variability decreases with increasing sample size. But how does it decrease? The program 'SAWO' draws 10, 20, ..., 50 means in samples from the age distribution versus the sample size (50, 100, 200, ..., 1000).

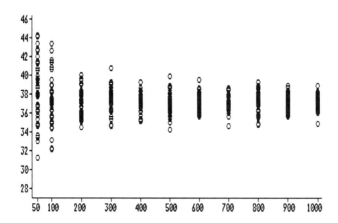

Figure 5: Means (50 each) versus sample size

As one may see from figure 5 the variation decreases slower than one would expect. The picture looks like a funnel. We usually put it as an exercise to measure several times the width of the variation for the sample sizes 100, 400, 900 by a ruler on the screen and to calculate the ratio of the mean width to the reciprocal of the square root of the sample sizes. The result is that these ratios are nearly the same showing that the width as a measure for the variation decreases proportionally to $1/\sqrt{n}$.

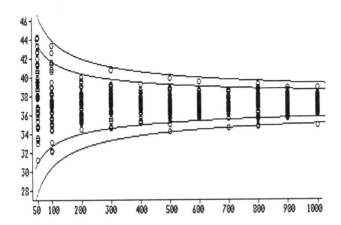

Figure 6: Means (50 each) versus sample size with 2- and 3σ-bounds

The mathematical theory provides indeed the result that the standard deviation of a mean in a sample of size n is $\sigma/\sqrt{n}$, where σ is the standard deviation in the population. The program 'SAWO' draws the curves $\mu \pm c\sigma/\sqrt{n}$ for c= 1, 2, 3 (see figure 6), where μ is the known mean in the age distribution. We see that most of the points lie between the two inner curves, that only a few exceed the 2σ-bounds and that a point outside the 3σ-curves is an extremely rare event. The reason for all this is, of course, the approximate normality of the distributions of the means.

The last program we want to mention is 'ALMI' which draws paths of the means of successively enlarged samples from the age distibrution. The crucial point is here that the horizontal axis has a logarithmic scale (see figure 7). So one may observe that all paths converge to a final point, namely the expected value. The mathematical theory calls this phenomenon the law of large numbers.

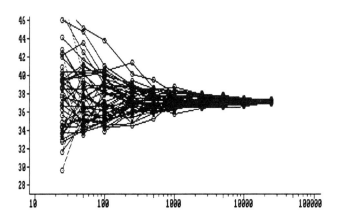

Figure 7: Paths of means in 50 samples from the age distribution

3. Experience with GSTAT

GSTAT is planned to supplement the usual tutorials in our first courses of Statistics, where we have about 800 students. Until now not enough rooms with computers were available and it was therefore only possible to use GSTAT twice or three times during a semester. The whole tutorial period was used for demonstrations with GSTAT. About half of the students were in favour of these tutorials, some were indifferent and some against, mainly because they thougt that the tutorials were not directly relevant for the examination. In the course starting next semester it is planned to use GSTAT in every tutorial, but not for the whole period, only to supplement the usual exercises. In each tutorial one must decide where GSTAT fits

So far most of the experience with GSTAT was obtained in small classes on a voluntary basis. In these courses we were very satisfied with GSTAT. We got reactions such as "Now I understand what Statistics really is", "now I understand the lectures in Statistics", "now Statistics makes fun" or "I am a fan of the normal distribution". We observed that students were working at their problems with great perseverance often hardly noticing that time was over. Often students experimented on their own. Often pictures on their screen did not make sense in my opinion. When I told them this they usually answered "we wanted to see what happens if we do this". So I learned that they had their own questions and if they get the answers through their own experiences this is also a kind of success.

Students also asked very many questions during such tutorials and in this way they contributed considerably to the development of GSTAT. One of these questions was "how can we visualize the standard deviation?" Now there are some exercises concerning this. A further experience in working with GSTAT is that Statistics becomes alive. You are always also concerned with some other topics not only with the isolated problem with which you wanted to deal. You do not only get nice data, matters become more realistic.

Recently I read the sentence "Let the learner learn before the teacher teaches" (see Bastow (1986)) and it is my hope that GSTAT is a step in this direction.

4. Availibility of GSTAT

Necesssary is an IBM-compatible PC with at least 512 KB RAM and DOS-version 3.0 or higher with CGA- or Hercules graphics card. The necessary text in the programs of GSTAT is written in German. GSTAT is published by Vandenhoeck and Ruprecht in Göttingen. It is available through book sellers at a price of DM 98 for the disks and a single licence. Pool licences can be obtained from the author.

Reference:

Bastow, B. (1986): The Place of Computers in the Learning of Statistics, in: Teaching of Statistics in the Computer Age, Editor L. Rade and T.Speed, International Statistical Institute, Studentlitteratur, Bratt Institut für Neues Lernen, Chartwell-Bratt Ltd.

Böker, Fred (1989): Statistik lernen am PC, Programmbeschreibungen, Übungen und Lernziele zum Statistikprogrammpaket GSTAT, Vandenhoeck und Ruprecht, Göttingen.

Erfahrungen im Einsatz von Statistiksoftware in der Statistikausbildung

W.-D. Heller und R. Rupprecht

Summary

Over years statistical programs running on mainframes have been the only help for analysing data in a computer-aided way. With effective statistical programs coming up on the PC new perspectives in statistical education at university are shown. Several experiences with the use of following programs in PC courses are introduced: SAS, ISP, NCSS, STATPRAK, EXPLO, and STATPAL. These statistical packages are differentiated with regard to their various possibilities of application in statistical education.

Einleitung

Nachdem jahrelang der Großrechner das unentbehrliche Hilfsmittel des in der Datenanalyse tätigen Statistikers war, haben sich mit der Verbreitung der PCs gravierende Verschiebungen ergeben.

- Die Bereitschaft, sich mit Statistik-Software zu beschäftigen, ist beim Zugang über den PC deutlich größer.
- Statistiksoftware ist verfügbar, in einem extrem weiten Preis- und Leistungsbereich.
- Der Hard- und Softwarezugang wird durch didaktisch aufbereitete Programme gefördert.
- Pflege und Auswertung von Datensätzen werden sowohl auf Großrechnern, Workstations und PCs durchgeführt, wobei bei der Aufgabenteilung die jeweilige Stärke des Arbeitsmittels im Vordergrund steht. Dies gilt um so mehr wie die Vernetzung und somit die Austauschbarkeit der Daten und Ergebnisse immer weiter voranschreitet.

Beschäftigen wollen wir uns nur mit einem kleinen Ausschnitt dieser Auflistung, der sich mit der Eignung des PCs als Lehr- und Lernmedium für Statistik befaßt. Dabei werden wir uns nicht auf Universalpakete beschränken, sondern auch die Eignung von mehr didaktisch orientierten Paketen mit einbeziehen.

Praktika und Produkte

Verschiedene Praktika wurden seit Frühjahr 1988 unter Verwendung unterschiedlicher Produkte am PC durchgeführt. In diesem Abschnitt sollen die verwendeten Produkte und die Zielsetzungen der Praktika beschrieben werden.

Die vorliegenden Erfahrungen wurden u.a. gewonnen aus folgenden Praktika und Tests:

Praktika	-	Grundkurs SAS
	-	Statistik mit SAS am PC
	-	Explorative Statistik mit ISP
	-	Einsatz von STATPRAK, STATPAL und EXPLO im Statistikpraktikum
Test	-	NCSS oder ISP zum Einsatz in Übungen zur Vorlesung Statistik I

Detailiertere Angaben zu den oben aufgeführten Praktika sind in der Tabelle auf der folgenden Seite zusammengefaßt.

Zusätzlich zu den Praktika wurde ein Paket gesucht, das sich in den Übungen zur Grundvorlesung "Statistik I" einsetzen ließe. Bedingt durch den hohen Teilnehmerkreis von ca. 400 Studenten war die Hauptanforderung, daß ohne großen Aufwand durch Betreuung bestimmte Methoden dem Benutzer (Student) gezielt angeboten werden können. Es sollte ein unkontrolliertes "Spielen" vermieden werden, das zu Lasten der Stoffvermittlung in begrenzter Zeit geht. Dabei standen die Pakete ISP (steht im Rahmen einer Campuslizenz zur Verfügung) und NCSS (in Erwägung gezogen aufgrund seines sehr guten Preis-Leistungsverhältnisses) zur Auswahl. Prinzipiell hätte auch die Möglichkeit bestanden, über SAS (Version 6.03 auf dem PC) die Übungen durchzuführen, jedoch sind u.a. die Hardwareanforderungen dieses Paketes zu groß, so daß es bei diesem Vergleich nicht berücksichtigt wurde. Der Test wurde von bis dahin in diesen Paketen unerfahrenen Statistiktutoren durchgeführt.

Veranstaltung:	SAS-Kurs	SAS-PC Praktikum	ISP-Praktikum	Statistik-Praktikum am PC ([4])
Software	SAS Version 6.03 ([9])	SAS Version 6.03 ([9])	ISP 2.10 ([6])	STATPRAK ([1]) STATPAL ([2]) EXPLO ([3])
Zeitdauer	5 Tage (ganztags)	5 Tage (vormittags)	4 Tage	5 Tage
Organisation	vormittags: Frontalunterricht mit Onlinedemonstrat. nachmittags: Übungen am PC mit Betreuung	Übungen mit Betreuung; eingeschobener Frontalunterricht	Übungen mit Betreuung; eingeschobener Frontalunterricht	Übungen mit Betreuung (3,5 h); Zeit zum Experimentieren (2 h)
Teilnehmerkreis	40 Teilnehmer; Studenten, Diplomanden, Doktoranden der verschiedenen Fachrichtungen	16 Studenten nach dem Vordiplom	14 Studenten; Teilnehmer der Vorlesung Explorative Statistik	14 Studenten nach dem Vordiplom
Inhalt	Einführung in SAS, Schwerpunkte: Datenmanagement und Funktionsumfang	Einführung in SAS, Schwerpunkte bei den Prozeduren zur Regression und Varianzanalyse	Einführung in ISP, Schwerpunkte bei dynamischen Graphiken, Medianpolieren, Zeitreihenanalyse	Deskriptive Statistik, Verteilungen, Grenzwertsätze, Regressions- und Varianzanalyse
Zielsetzung	SAS für statistisch/graphische Auswertungen, Funktionsumfang	Erfahrungen mit SAS am PC, Aufbau eines Universalpaketes	Erfahrungen mit ISP, Vertiefung von Methoden der EDA	Vertiefung des Vordiplomstoffes mittels didaktischer Pakete

Erfahrungen aus den Lehrveranstaltungen

Die nachfolgenden Ergebnisse rekrutieren sich aus den Beobachtungen der Dozenten während des Praktikums und aus den Umfragen unter den Teilnehmern, die am Ende der Praktika durchgeführt wurden.

Wie bereits erwartet wurde, erwies sich der PC als Lehrmedium als sehr geeignet. Beim SAS - Kurs, der bislang auf dem Großrechner durchgeführt wurde, zeigte sich ein deutlicher Anstieg des Umfangs der in gleicher Zeit über das Paket zu vermittelnden Kenntnisse. Während bei den Praktika mit typischer PC-Software die Teilnehmer generell die Eignung des Großrechners für vergleichbare Veranstaltungen verneinten, war bei den Teilnehmern der SAS Veranstaltungen bei etwa 20 % die Meinung zu finden, daß auch der Großrechner geeignet sei. Der Grund dafür ist primär in der Tatsache zu sehen, daß diese Teilnehmer bereits mit dem Großrechner vertraut sind und gewisse Projektabläufe in ihren Instituten stark großrechnerorientiert sind.

Die Arbeit am PC wurde fast ausschließlich in Zweiergruppen durchgeführt. Es zeigte sich, daß die Teilnehmer damit sehr zufrieden waren. Dies insbesondere, wenn mit der eingesetzten Software mehr oder weniger detaillierte datenanalytische Fragestellungen bearbeitet wurden. Stand etwa das Erlernen einer Programmiersprache (SAS) im Vordergrund, so versprachen sich auch etwa ein Drittel der Teilnehmer von Einzelarbeit guten Erfolg. Diese Aussage korrelierte mit den Gründen für die Kursteilnahme dieser Personen: Es stand ein "Institutszwang" (etwa das Anfertigen einer Projektarbeit) im Vordergrund.
Überraschenderweise war das Ziel eine Teilnahmebestätigung zu erreichen, wenig ausgeprägt, am deutlichsten noch bei den Teilnehmern des SAS-Kurses. Komplementäre Tendenzen zeigten die Gründe für die Teilnahme bezüglich Kennenlernen eines Produktes und Erweitern der Statistikkenntnisse auf: Während bei den SAS - Veranstaltungen, bei denen die Teilnehmer aus allen Fachbereichen der Universität kamen, das Kennenlernen/Erlernen des Produktes im Vordergrund stand, war dies bei den Teilnehmern der übrigen Praktika eher das Erweitern der eigenen Statistikkenntnisse, was allerdings z.T. aus dem Teilnehmerkreis zu erklären ist.

Ein vergleichendes Resumee der Praktika zeigt, daß eine Vermittlung bzw. Vertiefung von statistischer Methodik über Pakete wie ISP oder STATPRAK bei entsprechender

Aufbereitung und Begleitung sehr gut möglich ist. Teilnehmeraussagen in den SAS-Kursen zeigten ein Defizit in dieser Hinsicht. Dies gilt verstärkt für das Statistikpraktikum mit SAS, das ja die Vertiefung von Lehrstoff zum Inhalt hatte. Die Mächtigkeit und Universalität dieses Paketes machen es dem unerfahrenen, statistikinteressierten Teilnehmer schwer, sich um seine Interessen zu kümmern, da sehr viele dateiverwaltende- und modifizierende Elemente dieser Sprache gelernt werden müssen.

Da es sich bei SAS um ein relativ weit verbreitetes Paket handelt, das jetzt auch den PC und Workstationsmarkt erobert, wurden in den SAS-Kursen zusätzliche Fragen gestellt, deren Ergebnisse hier kurz dargestellt werden. Gefragt wurde nach der vermutlichen Benutzungshäufigkeit der einzelnen Komponenten. Naturgemäß glauben alle Praktikumsteilnehmer, das sie die Basiskomponente BASICS benutzen werden. Das gleiche gilt für die Graphikkomponente, die in der Nennung die gleiche Häufigkeit und Intensität wie BASICS erhält. Es stellt sich die Frage, ob das auslösende Moment, sich mit SAS zu beschäftigen, für die Vielzahl der Praktikumsteilnehmer in der Möglichkeit zu suchen ist, Daten graphisch darzustellen. Mit deutlichen Abstand - der aus Häufigkeit und Intensität gebildete Score erreicht nur etwa 75% des Scores für BASICS und GRAPHICS - folgt die Anwendung von Prozeduren aus STATISTICS. Alle weiteren erfragten Module (FSP, AF, IML, OR, ETS, "Macros" und SUGI Suppl. Lib.) lagen in ihrem Scoring deutlich unter 50% des maximal erreichbaren Wertes.

Bei der Frage nach den Interessensschwerpunkten in Anschlußkursen spiegeln sich die soeben geschilderten Ergebnisse wider. Das größte Interesse findet die Weiterbildung im Graphikbereich, gefolgt von der in der Anwendung der Statistikprozeduren. Kurse in anderen Bereichen werden gering (wahrscheinlich auch anwendungsspezifisch) nachgefragt.

Als "Erfolgskontrolle" für die in der vorangegangenen Tabelle formulierten Zielsetzungen der Praktika wurden die Teilnehmer nach Kursende zu bestimmten Leistungsmerkmalen befragt, die sie sich nun, nach dem Praktikum zutrauen:

> Gefragt wurde nach der Fähigkeit, das jeweilige Programmpaket generell zu beurteilen, was den Teilnehmern am SAS-Kurs und am Statistikpraktikum im großen und ganzen möglich war. Weniger glauben dieses die Teilnehmer am SAS-PC- sowie am ISP-Praktikum. Nur den Teilnehmern des Statistik-Praktikums gelang es, den abgedeckten Methodenumfang der dort behandelten nicht so umfangreichen Software zu beurteilen. Neben der bereits diskutierten "Graphikgläubig-

keit" der Teilnehmer im SAS-Kurs, die sich in hohem Maße zutrauen, diese Methoden auch einsetzen zu können, ist es interessant, daß auch im ISP-Praktikum dieser Erfolg erzielt wurde. Die Teilnehmer des ISP-Praktikums glaubten am Kursende in der Lage zu sein, auch komplexere Datenstrukturen bearbeiten zu können. Als Erfolg des SAS-Kurses ist es zu bezeichnen, daß die Teilnehmer nötige Informationen den umfangreichen Handbüchern entnehmen können. Die Teilnehmer aller Kurse trauten sich nach den Veranstaltungen das Arbeiten mit den entsprechenden Paketen zu.

Die Entscheidung für ein Softwaresystem, das in einem Begleitpraktikum für eine große Grundvorlesung eingesetzt werden kann, fiel zugunsten von ISP aus. Als Nachteile der beiden Pakete im Vergleich wären aufzuzählen:
- NCSS zeigt in vielen Masken der einzelnen Statitstikprozeduren eine große Anzahl von Maskenfelder, die speziell in Anfängerveranstaltungen große Verständnisschwierigkeiten bereiten können. Dies hat zum Grunde, daß das unkontrollierte Verändern der Felderinhalte zu beachtlichen Problemen in der Homogenität, wie ein vorgegebenes Aufgabengerüst innerhalb der Praktikumsgruppe gelöst werden soll, führen kann.
- Die Übungseinheiten bei ISP müssen mit Makros intensiv vorbereitet werden.
- Die Benutzeroberfläche von ISP entspricht nicht der Erwartungshaltung der Studenten (Menüorientierung etc.).
- In vergleichbaren Zeiteinheiten kann mit ISP weniger Lehrstoff erarbeitet werden, als im Vergleich dazu mit NCSS.

Die Vorteile der Pakete sind nach unserer Erfahrung:
- NCSS hat einen sehr guten "Spreadsheet-Editor", der im Anfängerpraktikum vorteilhaft einzusetzen wäre.
- Die Graphikeigenschaften des NCSS sind als überdurchschnittlich zu bezeichnen (z.B. Dynamische Graphiken).
- ISP erlaubt die Erstellung von Makros.
- Die interaktive Arbeitsweise und die flexible Graphikgestaltung von ISP ermöglichen ein gezieltes Hinführen zu Problemlösungen.
- Die Bewegungsgraphiken von ISP sind als (didaktische) Datenanalysetechnik sehr vielseitig verwendbar.

Der primäre Grund, NCSS in diesem Praktikum nicht einzusetzen, basiert auf der Vielzahl von Menüfeldern, mit denen ein Eingriff auf die statistische Prozedur möglich ist. So wünschenswert diese Eigenschaft für Anwender oder ein Fortgeschrittenenpraktikum ist, so nachteilig kann sich dies in einem Anfängerpraktikum auswirken.

Zusammenfassende Wertung

Die Erfahrungen aus den durchgeführten Praktika wurden in der folgenden Graphik zusammengefaßt:

	SAS	ISP	NCSS	Statprak	Statpal	Explore
Statistik in Grundausbildung	● A A	●● A	●	●●●	●	●
Statistik in Fortgeschrittenen- ausbildung und spezielleren Methodenvorlesungen	P ●●●	P ●●●	●●●	P ●	P ●	P ●
Statistik im Anwendungsbereich	P ●●●	●	●●	○	-----	-----

Die in dieser Graphik unterlegten Felder wurden durch PC-Praktika (P) abgedeckt. Die Punkte geben den Grad der Eignung für den jeweiligen Teilnehmerkreis an, wobei diese Eignung in 5 Stufen dargestellt ist:

---- nicht geeignet, O bedingt geeignet, ● geeignet, ●● gut geeignet,
●●● sehr gut geeignet; Das Ersetzen der Punkte durch "A" bedeutet, daß eine entsprechende Eignungsstufe durch Vorbereitungsaufwand (Makros, Menüführungen, Tutorials, etc.) erreicht werden kann.

Daraus ergeben sich die folgenden Konsequenzen:

- Die Auswahl der Software für einen Kurs (bzw. Praktikum) muß sich am Teilnehmerkreis orientieren. Universalpakete werden in allen Bereichen angewendet und sollten somit auch in der allgemeinen Ausbildung eingesetzt werden, während Kurse für einen definierten Teilnehmerkreis an der Zielsetzung orientiert sein sollten.
- Didaktische Pakete sind in aller Regel nicht zu Analysen einsetzbar, sondern eignen sich zum Vertiefen (oder auch zum Selbststudium) von entsprechenden statistischen Sachverhalten.
- Das Ausbildungsmedium PC hat sich bewährt. Interaktive Arbeitstechniken, die insbesonderer das flexible Einbinden graphischer Darstellungen in den Lehreinheiten ermöglichen, dürften als ein wesentlicher Vorteil gegenüber der Ausbildung am Großrechner gelten.
- Unterschiedliche Betriebssystemkenntnisse bereiten zu Beginn der Kurse z.T. große Probleme. Das Vorschalten einer entsprechenden Einführung in DOS (bzw. ein anderes Betriebssystem, wenn ein Kurs nicht am PC durchgeführt werden kann) empfiehlt sich.

Literatur

[1] Afflerbach, L. (1987). Statistik-Praktikum mit dem PC. Teubner, Stuttgart.
[2] Chalmer, B.J. (1987). Understanding Statistics. M. Dekker, New York/Basel.
[3] Doane, D.P. (1985). Exploring Statistics with the IBM PC. Addison-Wesley, Reading.
[4] Enenkiel, A.;Heller, W.-D. (1988). Erfahrungsbericht zum Statistik-Praktikum auf dem PC vom 22.2.88 bis 26.2.88. Interner Bericht, Lehrstuhl für Statistik und Ökonometrie (Prof. Rutsch), Universität Karlsruhe.
[5] NCSS 5.1 - Statistik & Graphik (1988). Unisoft, Augsburg.
[6] PC-ISP, Interaktive Scientific Processor (User's Guide and Command Description, Supplementary Manual (DGS), Macro Library) (1988). Artemis Systems, Carlisle.
[7] Rutsch, M. (1987). Statistik 1 - Mit Daten umgehen. Birkhäuser, Basel.
[8] SAS - Script des Rechenzentrums (1989). Universität Karlsruhe, Rechenzentrum.
[9] SAS User's Guides - Version 6 Edition (1988). SAS Institute, Cary.

Software-Ausbildung am Fachbereich Statistik der Universität Dortmund

J. Kübler

Summary

This paper discusses how recent developments of modern computational statistics have influenced the teaching of statistics at the department of statistics in Dortmund. This department is the only one of its kind in West-Germany. Thus the teaching of omputational statistics rather than the use of computers in teaching statistics is of primary interest here. Focus is on adding methods of computational statistics to the current program in training statisticians. Therefore emphasis is given on the use of different kinds of statistical software packages and of hardware configurations, especially mainframes, workstations and personal computers.

Among our students we observe a broad interest in these aspects of statistics. Moreover a tendency to more flexible software and hardware systems can be noticed.

Einleitung

Die Notwendigkeit einer intensiven Software-Ausbildung für Diplom-Statistiker scheint heute unstrittig zu sein. Die stürmische Entwicklung speziell auf dem PC-Hardware und Software-Sektor hat die Arbeit der Statistikers in einem so starken Maße beeinflußt, daß in der Lehre auf diese Entwicklung in angemessener Weise reagiert werden muß. Eine ausführliche Darstellung dieser Entwicklung und ihrer Konsequenzen für Forschung und Lehre findet man bei Schach (1987).

An dieser Stelle soll nur kurz auf einige Einsatzmöglichkeiten von Software für die statistische Forschung eingegangen werden. Große Bedeutung haben in den vergangenen Jahren computergraphische diagnostische Verfahren gewonnen. Hierbei steht nicht mehr der Aspekt der Präsentation im Vordergrund; vielmehr sollen die Methoden der explorativen Datenanalyse z.B. der visuellen Überprüfung von Modellansätzen, dem Auffinden von Ausreißern etc. oder nur der Darstellung der Beobachtungen dienen. Eine Reihe von Vorschlägen zu diesem Gebiet findet man z.B. bei Tukey (1977) und

Chambers, Cleveland, Kleiner und Tukey (1983). Daneben gewinnen graphische Darstellungen mathematischer Sachverhalte wie z.B. Höhenlinien bei Likelihoodfunktionen, um grobe Fehlschätzungen zu vermeiden, und das Aufsuchen von optimalen Lösungen z.B. in der Versuchsplanung zunehmend an Bedeutung. Einige statistische Verfahren sind aufgrund des hohen Rechenaufwands erst durch den Einsatz von Rechnern praktisch einsetzbar geworden. In diesem Zusammenhang sei an Permutationstests, Bootstrap- und Jackknife-Verfahren u.a. erinnert. Daneben finden Simulationen in höherem Maße an Beachtung. Zum einen wird dieses Verfahren nach wie vor eingesetzt, um z.B. über statistische Methoden Aussagen bzgl. ihres Verhaltens für kleine und mittlere Stichprobenumfänge zu gewinnen, wenn theoretische Resultate nur bzgl. ihrer asymptotischen Eigenschaften vorliegen. Daneben werden Simulationen immer häufiger auch als Hilfsmittel bei Beweisen eingesetzt, um eine mathematische Vermutung empirisch zu überprüfen oder gar um zu einer mathematischen Vermutung zu gelangen. In neuerer Zeit gewinnen darüberhinaus der Informationsaustausch über Computernetze und der Zugriff auf statistische Datenbanken eine vermehrte Bedeutung in der Forschung. Weiterhin sind noch statistische Experten-, Assistenten bzw. Beratungssysteme erwähnenswert, die mit großen Interesse kontrovers diskutiert werden.

Im weiteren Verlauf werden zunächst die möglicherweise unterschiedlichen Ansprüche der Industrie und des Fachbereichs Statistik der Universität Dortmund an eine Software-Ausbildung diskutiert. Anschließend wird erläutert, in welcher Form eine Software-Ausbildung in den bestehenden Studiengang integriert werden kann. Dabei wird insbesondere untersucht, wie auf der einen Seite eine möglichst breit angelegte Grundausbildung verwirklicht und auf der anderen Seite ein schwerpunktmäßige Vertiefung im Bereich 'Computational Statistics' angeboten werden kann. Abschließend wird die, den Studierenden zur Verfügung stehende, Soft- und Hardware-Ausstattung dargestellt und mögliche Ausbauformen erläutert.

Anforderungen an die Software-Ausbildung

Beschäftigt man sich mit den Anforderungen an die Software-Ausbildung, so lassen sich hier zwei verschiedene Bereiche erkennen. Einerseits existieren Anforderungen von Seiten der Industrie, bei der ein hoher Anteil der Diplom-Statistiker beschäftigt ist, andererseits lassen sich auch von

Seiten der Hochschule einige Ansprüche klar definieren, die nicht notwendig als Gegensätze betrachtet werden müssen. Als Beispiel für die industrielle Seite sei hier auf die chemisch-pharmazeutische Industrie verwiesen, die bisher am deutlichsten ihre Anforderungen an statistische Software und damit indirekt auch an eine Software-Ausbildung beschrieben hat.

Die Anforderungen der chemisch-pharmazeutischen Industrie an eine Software-Ausbildung wird durch die Entwicklung der Anforderungsprofile an die Software, die von den Zulassungsbehörden gestellt werden, stark beeinflußt. An dieser Stelle sei auf Passing (1987) sowie insbesondere auf Unkelbach und Passing (1988) hingewiesen. Diese Arbeiten machen deutlich, daß gerade von der FDA (Food and Drug Administration) heute nur noch Analysen akzeptiert werden, die unter Verwendung einer nach den Anforderungen des Software-Engineerings entwickelten Software erstellt wurden. Darüberhinaus werden weiterhin Systeme anerkannt, die schon seit langer Zeit im Einsatz sind und somit als gut ausgetestet gelten können. Aus diesem Grund muß die Industrie daran interessiert sein, daß gerade solche Systeme bereits in der Ausbildung von Biometrikern eingesetzt werden und das Konzept des Software-Engineerings mit eingebracht wird.

In der Ausbildung von Biometrikern scheint jedoch die Beschränkung auf die großen bekannten Programmpakete nicht sinnvoll zu sein. Vielmehr sollte das Ziel der Ausbildung in einer Anleitung zum flexiblen Einsatz unterschiedlicher Systeme bestehen. Die Verwendung von wenigen genau spezifizierten Methoden, die in ihrer Implementierung als ausreichend valide angesehen werden können, führt zu einer Einschränkung der Forschung, durch die viele Erkenntnisse verborgen blieben. Für einen Biometriker ist also auch die Fähigkeit zum Umgang mit einem System wichtig, das ihm nur Bausteine zur Programmierung statistischer Verfahren zur Verfügung stellt. Diese Arbeit hat durch die Entwicklungen der letzten Jahre zu einem Einsatz interaktiver Systeme und zu einer Aufwertung explorativer Verfahren geführt, deren Philosophie letztendlich den Grundzügen des Software-Engineerings widerspricht. Dennoch sollte aus den oben genannten Gründe auf den Einsatz solcher Systeme oder Systemkomponenten nicht verzichtet werden.

Die oben dargestellten Überlegungen betreffen allerdings im wesentlichen die allgemeine Software-Ausbildung und die dabei erworbenen Kenntnisse können als normales Handwerkszeug für einen praktisch arbeitenden Statistiker angesehen werden.

Aufgrund des zunehmenden Einsatzes von Rechnern und statistischer Software ist es allerdings auch notwendig, einen zusätzlichen Studienschwerpunkt anzubieten, der grob mit 'Computational Statistics' umschrieben werden kann. Ziel dieses Schwerpunktes ist die Vermittlung vertiefter Kenntnisse an der Schnittstelle zwischen Datenverarbeitung und Statistik. Besonders interessant ist diese Vertiefung innerhalb des Studiengangs Statistik insbesondere für Studierende mit Nebenfach Informatik und könnte, unter enger Zusammenarbeit mit Informatikern, zu einer verstärkten Beteiligung von Statistikern an der Entwicklung von statistischer Software führen.

Einbindung der Software-Ausbildung in den Studiengang

Bei der Einbindung der Software-Ausbildung in den Studiengang muß zwischen zwei verschiedenen Richtungen unterschieden werden. Für kurzfristige Änderungen im Ausbildungskonzept besteht nur die Möglichkeit der Integration neuer Ausbildungsinhalte innerhalb des bestehenden Studienverlaufsplans oder in einer Novellierung, die die Prüfungsordnung nicht betrifft. Mittels der hierbei gewonnenen Erfahrungen muß dann entschieden werden, ob für eine langfristige Konzeption auch grundlegendere Veränderungen des Studienverlaufs notwendig werden. In der momentanen Phase werden die kurzfristigen Lösungsansätze für die allgemeine und die vertiefende Software-Ausbildung untersucht.

Es zeigt sich allerdings, daß die Vorstellungen über die Ausgestaltung der Software-Ausbildung zum Teil recht unterschiedlich sind. So wird zum Beispiel die Frage nach dem Zeitpunkt des Einsatzes leistungsstarker Standardprogrammpakete kontrovers diskutiert. In der sehr frühen Einbeziehung dieser Systeme wird die Gefahr gesehen, daß Studenten nach dem 'Black-Box'-Verfahren Methoden anwenden, ohne mit den notwendigen theoretischen Grundlagen vertraut zu sein. Andererseits bietet sich hier der Vorteil, daß die Studenten langsam mit einem solchen System vertraut gemacht werden und somit zu einem späteren Zeitpunkt des Studiums langwierige Einarbeitungsphasen entfallen. Insgesamt scheint sich die Überzeugung durchzusetzen, solche System bereits im Grundstudium einzuführen, dabei aber gleichzeitig auf einen verantwortungsbewußten Umgang zu drängen.

Daneben muß unter den existierenden Programmsystemen eine Auswahl getroffen werden. Auch auf diesem Gebiet scheinen unterschiedliche

Vorgehensweisen möglich. So verwendet beispielsweise das 'Department of Probability and Statistics' der Universität Sheffield mit MINITAB nur ein einziges System für die Ausbildung, zum dem alle Studenten die gleichen Zugangsmöglichkeiten besitzen. Auf diesem Weg können zum einen für alle Studenten die gleichen Voraussetzungen geschaffen und zum anderen an alle die gleichen Anforderungen gestellt werden. Dagegen bietet die Verwendung unterschiedlicher Programme die Möglichkeit, flexibel mit mehreren Systemen umgehen und einen Einblick in die besonderen Stärken und Schwächen der Systeme gewinnen zu können.

Der Studienverlauf ist zum jetzigen Zeitpunkt im Grundstudium im wesentlichen durch die mathematischen und wahrscheinlichkeitstheoretischen Grundvorlesungen geprägt (Analysis I und II, Lineare Algebra I, Höhere Mathematik III und IV, Wahrscheinlichkeitsrechnung und mathematische Statistik I und II und Lineare Modelle). Diese Vorlesungen erscheinen für eine Software-Ausbildung wenig geeignet. Lediglich im Rahmen der Übungen für die Vorlesung 'Lineare Modelle' ist der Einsatz statistischer Software denkbar. Besser geeignet sind die Vorlesungen 'Statistische Schlußweise', 'Elementare Stichprobenverfahren', 'Anfängerpraktikum' und in besonderem Maße 'Deskriptive Statistik', die als Einführungsveranstaltungen für elementare statistische Methoden angesehen werden können.

Im Hauptstudium liegt der Ausbildungsschwerpunkt auf der statistischen Modellbildung und der Vermittlung spezieller statistischer Methoden. Möglichkeiten zum Einsatz statistischer Software bieten sich hier in den Seminaren, im Rahmen der Veranstaltungsformen 'Spezialgebiete der Statistik', 'Quantitative Methoden im Nebenfach' und insbesondere in den statistischen Fortgeschrittenenpraktika, in denen schon traditionell Einführungen in die Anwendung statistischer Software gegeben werden. Dabei liegt das Hauptgewicht für die allgemeine Software-Ausbildung bei den statistischen Fortgeschrittenenpraktika I und II, die von allen Studierenden des praktischen Studiengangs erfolgreich absolviert werden müssen. Zu Beginn eines solchen Praktikums findet i.a. eine kurze Einführung in ein Programmpaket statt. Im weiteren Verlauf müssen innerhalb der einzelnen Praktikumsgruppen für verschiedenen Projekte statistische Analysen mit Hilfe der zur Verfügung stehenden Soft- und Hardware erstellt werden.

Da aus den anderen Veranstaltungsbereichen nur in einem bestimmten Zeitumfang Veranstaltungen belegt werden müssen, eignen sich diese weniger für eine allgemeine Software-Ausbildung, obgleich auch hier in einigen Fällen rechnerbezogene Aspekte behandelt werden können. Darüberhinaus haben auch Seminare und Spezialvorlesungen bereits in der Vergangenheit Gelegenheit gegeben, spezielle computergestützte Methoden zu behandeln wie z.B. Monte-Carlo Methoden, Kernschätzung u.a., aber auch anhand von Beispielen Software-Vergleiche durchzuführen. Damit können diese Veranstaltungen zu dem Studienschwerpunkt 'Computational Statistics' gezählt werden.

Neben der Einbindung der Software-Ausbildung in bestimmte Veranstaltungsformen werden zusätzlich Software-Kurse angeboten. Obligatorisch ist dabei die Teilnahme an einem Programmierkurs, z.B. FORTRAN, der vom Hochschulrechenzentrum der Universität Dortmund angeboten wird. Der Fachbereich Statistik bietet allerdings ebenfalls in unregelmäßigen Abständen ein- oder mehrwöchige Kurse in beispielsweise APL, ISP, S und SAS an. Diese Veranstaltungen, die i.a. als Einführungen in bestimmte Systeme betrachtet werden können, haben dabei jeweils ein reges Interesse gefunden.

Software- und Hardware-Ausstattung

Obgleich im Bereich der Forschung eine verhältnismäßig gute Ausstattung zur Verfügung steht, kann im Bereich der Lehre nur eine recht beschränkte Anzahl für die ca. 600 Studierenden eingesetzt werden. Dazu gehört ein CIP[1]-Pool mit vier unvernetzten IBM-AT Personal Computern und ein weiterer, vernetzter, CIP-Pool mit drei Apollo DN 3000 und je einer SUN 3/50 bzw. 3/60 Workstation. Beide Pools enthalten noch jeweils einen Matrixdrucker. Von den Workstations ist darüberhinaus noch ein Laserdrucker ansprechbar. Innerhalb des Gebäudes können noch zehn Atari 1040 ST Rechner als Terminals zum Großrechner des Hochschulrechenzentrums der Universität Dortmund benutzt werden. Tabelle 1 zeigt, daß im Bereich der Software ein relativ breites Angebot zur Verfügung gestellt werden kann. Neben den angegebenen Systemen können auf dem Großrechner noch einige Software-Libraries eingesetzt werden.

---

[1] Computer Investitions Programm

Tabelle 1: Software-Ausstattung im Bereich der Lehre

PC (Dos)	Workstation (Unix)	Großrechner (CMS)
SAS	S-Language	SAS
ISP	ISP	SPSS
APL	P-Stat	BMPD
IAS		IAS

Wünschenswert wäre für die Zukunft ein weiterer Ausbau und eine zunehmende Vernetzung der CIP-Pools. Darüberhinaus ist z.B. auch zusätzlich die Bereitstellung von Apple-Rechnern anzustreben, da speziell für den MacIntosh in den letzten Jahren interessante neue Entwicklungen im Bereich der statistischen Software zu beobachten sind.

Schlußbemerkungen

Am Fachbereich Statistik der Universität Dortmund haben die rasanten Entwicklungen der letzten Jahren auf dem Soft- und Hardware-Bereich ihre Spuren auch in der Lehre hinterlassen. Dabei wird konsequent versucht, ein möglichst breites Soft- und Hardware-Angebot bereitzustellen, wobei die Tendenz eindeutig zu Systemen auf PC's oder Workstations mit steigender Anzahl interaktiver Komponenten verläuft. Im Gegensatz zu anderen Entwicklungen steht am Fachbereich Statistik der Universität Dortmund im Bereich der Software-Ausbildung der Umgang mit statistischer Software im Vordergrund. Der Einsatz von Software zur Motivation der mathematischen Statistik spielt dagegen bisher eine eher untergeordnete Rolle. Eine Reihe von Vorschlägen zu diesem Bereich findet man z.B. bei Afflerbach (1987) Böker (1989) und Bowman und Robinson (1989).

Trotz der wachsenden Bedeutung des Einsatzes von Computern in der Statistik besteht jedoch Konsenz darüber, daß eine fundierte theoretische Ausbildung und eine Anleitung zum kritischen Umgang mit statistischen Methoden von vorrangiger Bedeutung ist.

Literatur

Afferbach L. (1987). Statistik Praktikum mit dem PC, Teubner, Stuttgart.

Bowman A.W. Robinson D.R. (1989). Teaching Statistics: Microcomputer Graphics and Computer Illustrated Texts, SoftStat '89, Heidelberg.

Böker F. (1989). About the Statistical Package GStat: The Concept of "Teaching Packages", SoftStat '89, Heidelberg.

Chambers S.M., Cleveland W.S., Kleiner B., Tukey P.A. (1983). Graphical Methods for Data Analysis, Wadsworth, Delmont, California.

Passing H. (1987). Was bedeuten Software-Qualitätssicherung und -Validierung für den Biometriker? EDV in Medizin und Biologie, 18, 84-89.

Schach S. (1987). Auswirkung der EDV-Entwicklung auf Forschung und Lehre im Bereich der Statistik in der Bundesrepublik Deutschland. Statistical Software Newsletter, 13, 62-65.

Tukey J.W. (1977). Exploratory Data Analysis, Addison-Wesley, Massachusetts.

Unkelbach H.-D., Passing H. (1988). Software-Qualitätssicherung: Steuernde und prüfende Maßnahmen, Vortragsmanuskript, Arbeitsgruppe Computational Statistics der Internationalen Biometrischen Gesellschaft, Deutsche Region.

The Concept of Teaching Packages

T. Maröy

Summary

The Norwegian Social Science Data Services (NSD) has for several years been engaged in the development of computer-based teaching material for the political and social science classroom. The approach has been based on the idea of "teaching packages", comprising a well-documented dataset from a specific research area accompanied by a workbook with outlines of possible procedures of analysis.

The actual applications have until lately been based on SPSS, but in order to reduce the barriers between the user and the computer, we felt the need to develop a more user friendly and non-expert-oriented tool for data confrontation. The resulting software, NSDstat is designed with this requirement in mind, and is today widely used at both high-school and university level in Norway. Around this tool we are currently building several applications dedicated to different levels and areas of teaching.

The Norwegian Social Science Data Services (NSD)

The Norwegian Social Science Data Services is a nation-wide organization formally established in 1971 by the Norwegian Research Council for Science and the Humanities. NSD is a federally structured organization with offices at each of the universities in Norway and with close working arrangements with the regional colleges, and its main function is to maximise the accessibility of data to the social science community. NSD has put much work into making its data holdings easily accessible, and has established a wide variety of on-line resources across all fields of the social sciences.

The teaching package approach

The teaching package approach is a legitimate child of the international data archive movement. The improvements in information technology along with the proliferation of data archives accumulating and exchanging machine readable data, raised new challenges for the education of students and training of researchers. On the one hand it became momentous to encourage students to do empirical research and to develop the necessary analytical skills to confront collections of empirical information. On the other hand the new instruments and data resources could be applied to improve existing courses in research methodology or in broader areas of comparative politics or political sociology.

At the international level the efforts to meet these challenges followed two closely connected routes: International summer schools for graduate students and staff members and development of computer-based teaching material for local use. The Standing Committee on Comparative Research of the International Social Science Council (ISSC) played a leading role in both these efforts by initiating a special training program in research methodology as well as a project directed towards the production of workbooks or teaching packages based on data materials for two or more countries. The intention of these teaching packages was to stimulate and encourage comparative cross-cultural and cross-national research.

This project was a joint venture carried out by the ISSC in close cooperation with several data-archives, including NSD. Four packages were produced, each addressing a specific research area:

- Political Participation
- Time Budget Research
- Social Mobility
- Centre-Periphery Structures in Europe

From 1978 onwards NSD gave high priority to the development of similar teaching packages directed towards norwegian and nordic universities and regional colleges. Three packages are completed:

- Comparative Analysis of Regional Data from the Nordic Countries
- Analysis of Political Elites
- Analysis of Communal Accounts

The data material in these packages is extracted from three of NSD's larger data holdings: The Norwegian Commune Data-Base, The Nordic Data-Archive for Regional Time-Series and The Norwegian Archive of Political Elites.

All of these packages, both the international and the norwegian, have a similar design.

- Each package is based on a carefully selected and thoroughly documented machine-readable data set adapted to the specific needs of the teaching situation.
- The data material is accompanied by a workbook which introduces the addressed research area and presents outlines of possible procedures of analyses. The student is guided trough the complete process of empirical analysis, including the choice of appropriate statistical techniques and testing, all the way around to the evaluation and interpretation of the results.

The intention of these workbooks is not to empty the possibilities offered by the data material, but to inspire and encourage the student's own analytical curiosity through an active confrontation between theory and empirical information.

Even the most excellent introductory textbooks in research methodology seldom passes beyond the point of describing the rules and procedures of this activity, but a teaching package encourages the students to develop their analytical skills by integrating different aspects of political science.

Methodology: We believe that most lecturers giving introductory courses in methodology have felt the difficulty of integrating methods with other parts of the students' curriculum. The repertoire of techniques, examples and exercises of standard textbooks are often unsuited to the needs and profile of a particular discipline. Consequently, at an obligatory course in statistics for students in social science, they are lacking a very important motivating factor.

Theory: Data analysis can move beyond research methods and statistics into subject matter courses. There are reasons to believe that the students' understanding of the theories and models of a discipline grow when they are given the opportunity to test their validity and relevance on a concrete data material.

Technique: Most people will say that the mastering of modern information technology is the least important aspect of the three. While this may well be true, there is no doubt that the computer is indispensable in modern social science as a tool for statistical analysis. An essential quality of the teaching package approach is that the technological skills are acquired as a part of a data confronting activity.

To succeed in these efforts it is essential that the technological barriers of the teaching packages is kept as low as possible. Unnecessary technological problems breed "keyboard anxiety" and may overshadow the content of the lesson. The students' attention and creative resources must be directed towards the two first elements, theory and methodology, and not be strangled in frustration over the computers lacking ability to "keep up a conversation".

The idea of the teaching packages was conceived prior to the advent of modern micro technology. Most of the packages are consequently adapted to an old technological environment, SPSS on mainframes. The command-driven SPSS is an excellent and effective tool for the experienced and frequent user, i.e. the professional researcher. For the novice and infrequent user its rigid and cumbersome control language is not so easy to get familiar with. In addition the operating environment of the mainframe is not well adopted to the needs of the teaching situation. It requires some knowledge of the operating system as well as familiarity with an external editor for typing of SPSS commands. All experience goes to show that it takes a lot of hard work to penetrate this jungle.

If the purpose of the course is the development of the students' analytical skills, and not to teach them how to handle a particular professional statistical package, this is not an adequate solution. Too much time and energy will be wasted on travelling through technical matters before the students reach a stage where they realize what the journey was all about. The distance between the students creative mind and the data material is too great. This is a problem which it is absolutely necessary to find a solution to.

The technological challenge: First solution

In order to bridge this gap, and to adapt the teaching package approach to a new technological environment, NSD has adopted two different lines of action. The first solution was to download the existing packages to microcomputers and utilize the PC version of SPSS.

The SPSS/PC software has several features which have turned it into a much better tool for educational purposes than its mainframe forerunners. Its user friendly internal editor makes it much easier to type and submit commands and can even be used to inspect and edit the output. The major implication of this progress is that the student has to cope with only one piece of software. The student stays inside SPSS/PC all the way through the analysis and does not have to alternate between the operating system, an external editor and the statistical package.

Two drawbacks should however be mentioned:

First, the command language of SPSS/PC is still rather rigid and unnecessarily complicated. Second, when a large number of cases are involved, SPSS on a PC is very slow. Since time is always scarce in classroom situations, this is a major drawback.

The technological challenge: Second solution

In 1985, we launched our own development project, with the intention of creating a statistical package that could meet our demands in a classroom situation. In fact our first target was to create an easy-to-use statistical package, not directed towards university courses, but aimed at lower levels of the norwegian educational system. The project was partly financed by the Ministry of Education as a part of a national program for the development of norwegian educational software.

Several limitations had to be taken into consideration, like the restricted capacity of the commonly used school computers, and the target group's lack of prior knowledge about data analysis and social science methodology. What was needed at this level was not sophisticated analysis, but presentational techniques which maximised the communication between the student and the data. The challenge was to create a piece of software which made the data tell its story without too much technical effort from the student.

This special point of departure has influenced the end product in several ways. The technical limitations forced us to develop compact data storage and efficient algorithms, the intellectual limitations to concentrate on user-friendliness and effective presentation, both numerical and graphical.

The resulting software, called NSDstat, has now been in use in norwegian highschools for about two years as an integrated part of a teaching package specially adapted to this educational level. The package, called **Political Attitudes**, is based on selected questions from two national sample surveys, the Election Studies from 1981 and 1985.

Since then, the teaching packages have been significantly developed. The high-school version of the **Political Attitudes** package has also been applied in introductory courses in methodology at regional colleges and universities. Due to its simplicity and ease-of-use lecturers found it an effective instrument in familiarizing the students to the basic ideas of data-analysis. The repertoire of techniques was however too limited to meet the requirements of more advanced courses, and we decided to continue the development of NSDstat and adapt it to the specific needs of university teaching. What we aimed at was a piece of software which combined the simplicity of the high-school version with the more sophisticated requirements of the social and political science classroom.

The first stage of this development is now completed. The new version of NSDstat is a powerful tool which we believe will give the non-expert an easy access to the excitements of data analysis. The features of this program are based on our own demands to a program of this kind:

Ease of use:
NSDstat is so easy to use that an average student is capable of operating it efficiently after one hour. The system is completely controlled by menus. In addition several facilities connected to the function keys can be activated anywhere in the program. An interactive help routine gives instant context senistive help. These instructions are not limited to technical help: even methodological hints are given.

Efficiency and speed:
The program is truly interactive. The different menus are interconnected in an efficient manner, which makes it easy to move from one procedure to another. The result of the user's choice is shown on the screen immediately.

Power:
NSDstat is able to handle large datasets. Datasets containing 10.000 cases, or even more, do not cause any trouble. With only categorical data more than 30.0000 cases can be handled on a computer with about 500K of free memory. The number of variables is only restricted by external storage capacity.

Graphics:
Visual presentation goes along with the presentation of numbers. A variety of bar charts and pie charts can illustrate the significance of numerical results, together with box-whisker plot, scatterplot and cartography.

Documentation:
>In a teaching situation, and elsewhere, the documentation of data is crucial. While the possibilities for documentation in most statistical packages is limited to short variable and value labels, NSDstat allows as much as a screenfull of text to be connected to each variable in the dataset. This can be used to store the exact formulation of questions for survey data or definitions, or sources or comments for other kinds of data. The documentation for a particular variable is always available on the screen by a couple of keystrokes. When a new variable is recoded or computed, the coding scheme or the computing formula is automatically transferred to the documentation file. This implies that the user never will forget how a variable was constructed.

Easy data entry:
>NSDstat has an integrated data entry facility which makes it easy to enter and edit new data and documentation or to import data from (or export to) other programs, including automatic export/import of SPSS portable files.

Output facilities:
>Tables and other results from the analysis can be sent to a connected printer or transferred to a text-file.

NSDstat is, at this stage, not a full-fledged statistical package. The sofware's functionality as a teaching tool has been more important than the repertoire of sophisticated statistical techniques. How far we want to proceed by adding new statistical procedures is to a large extent dependent upon how this version will be welcomed. However, we have no intention to compete with programs like SPSS or SAS. There is always beauty in simplicity. The reason for adding new statistical techniques will always be that it can improve the way we teach our students these techniques.

This stress on pedagogy has, partly to our surprise, also been appreciated outside the educational system. Business and administration do in fact face problems comparable to the classroom situation: a lot of unexperienced users needing easy-to-learn tools to be able to carry out not too sophisticated data analysis.

Other teaching packages

Currently we are working with several teaching packages based on NSDstat:

- We have just finished a package called **Young in Europe**, with data collected from the European Value Studies. This is a major cross-national survey of moral, social and political values carried out in about 25 countries world-wide, and the teaching package contains data from 11 European countries. It is also, as the title suggests, limited to young people, i.e. the age group 18-24. This cohort was supplied with an additional booster quota sample of 200 persons, which give an average national sample of about 350 youths. The material resides on three diskettes each covering a separate theme; 1) political attitudes and values, 2) moral and religious values and 3) social conditions and quality of life. The three diskettes are accompanied by the usual workbook which this time also include a thematic atlas giving background information about the selected countries.

- A teaching package based on data about all the nations of the world is also completed. This package is prepared by the International Peace Research Institute in Oslo.

- Two datasets with data from the commune database are presently being prepared, one on demography and the other on political behaviour.

- We are also planning two historical teaching packages, about the agricultural society in the nineteenth century, and on the emigration to America.

We hope to continue to "package" data for educational purposes in NSDstat. We do also hope that other institutions will find our concept a suited vehicle for this purpose.

References

Asher, Richardson, Weisberg: Political Participation. Campus Verlag, 1984. ISBN 3-593-33383-X.

Harvey, Szalai, Elliot, Stone, Clarc: Time Budget Research. Campus Verlag, 1984. ISBN 3-593-33384-8.

Hertz: Social Mobility. Campus Verlag, 1986. ISBN3-593-33643-X

Rokkan, Urwin, Aarebrot, Malaba, Sande: Centre-Periphery Structures in Europe. Campus Verlag, 1987. ISBN 3-593-33436-4

Hansen, Roshauw, Sørensen: Analyse av kommunal økonomi, Universitetsforlaget, Oslo 1988. ISBN 82-00-18470-6

Wagtskjold (Ed.): Komparative analyser av regionale data for de nordiske land. Universitetsforlaget, Oslo 1984. ISBN 82-00-07120-0

Eliassen, Ryssevik: Analyse av politiske eliter. Universitetsforlaget, Oslo 1986. ISBN 82-00-07722-5.

Hult, Ryssevik: Politiske hodninger. NSD 1989. ISBN 82-7170-109-6.

Ryssevik: Demografi & næringsstruktur. NSD 1989. ISBN 82-7170-106-1.

Ryssevik: Politisk geografi. NSD 1989. ISBN 82-7170-104-5.

Ryssevik: Ung i Europa. NSD 1989. ISBN 82-7170-099-5.

F. Faulbaum, R. Haux und K.-H. Jöckel (Hrsg.) (1990). SoftStat '89
Fortschritte der Statistik-Software 2. Stuttgart: Gustav Fischer, 615 - 622

Der Einsatz von Statistik-Software in der einführenden Methodenausbildung

R. Wittenberg

Summary

Quantity and quality of computer assisted research training of sociology students in the FRG could be better. Reasons and conditions are discussed which make it necessary to prefer secondary analyses in the basic training courses. It is illustrated how the ALLBUS - the General Social Survey of the FRG - can be used as a reasonable data base and SPSS as statistic software product for these purposes.

1. Allgemeine Probleme der Methodenausbildung in den Sozialwissenschaften

Die Situation der Ausbildung sozialwissenschaftlicher Forschungsmethoden an vielen wissenschaftlichen Hochschulen der BRD ist noch immer nicht zum besten bestellt. So belegt eine empirische Untersuchung aus dem Jahr 1986 (Hofmann, 1986), daß das zahlenmäßige Dozenten-Studenten-Verhältnis, das quantitative Methodenveranstaltungsangebot in Grund-und Hauptstudium sowie das Ausmaß computerunterstützter Forschungsausbildung im bundesweiten Schnitt nicht ausreichend ist. Hofmann (1986:50) kommt anhand dieser Befunde zu dem Schluß, daß der Anteil an "in Methoden potentiell gut ausgebildeten Studenten" unter 2% liegen dürfte.

Für die Beurteilung der gegenwärtigen Methodenausbildung sind aber nicht nur solche quantitativen Faktoren bedeutend, sondern auch solche von Form und Inhalt der Ausbildung. Es ist demnach auch zu erwägen, welche Methoden empirischer Sozialforschung optimal wie vermittelt werden können: Wenn nämlich die Ausbildung in den grundlegenden Methoden der empirischen Sozialforschung prüfungsrelevanter Bestandteil des sozialwissenschaftlichen Studiums ist, dann stellt sich die Aufgabe, auch solche angehenden Sozialwissenschaftler für die Sache erfahrungswissenschaftlich ausgerichteter Sozialforschung zu gewinnen, die wenig Interesse an mathematisch-statistischen Kalkülen oder modelltheoretischen Konzepten entwickeln, sondern die Sozialwissenschaft eher als Geisteswissenschaft alter Prägung, also als Lehnstuhlwissenschaft präferieren.

Eine besonders gut geeignete Form der Ausbildung in Methoden der empirischen Sozialforschung dürfte die sein, wenn "learning by doing" betrieben werden könnte, wenn also Studenten die Gelegenheit gegeben werden könnte, sich an der Durchführung empirischer Forschungsprojekte verantwortungsvoll zu beteiligen; in der Regel kämen dafür wohl eigens eingerichtete Lehrforschungsprojekte in Betracht. Der Durchführung von Lehrforschungsprojekten sind allerdings an vielen Hochschulen durch die jeweiligen Prüfungs- und Studienordnungen institutionelle Grenzen gesetzt. Diese Ordnungen weisen der sozialwissenschaftlichen Methodenausbildung einen stark variierenden Stellenwert im Kanon diverser Fächerkombinationen zu. Infolgedessen ist der quantitative und qualitative Stellenwert der Methodenausbildung im Zeitbudget von Studenten oft mehr oder minder zwangsläufig äußerst gering. Die Chancen zur Ausbildung etwa in Form von Lehrforschung als didaktisch optimalem Ausbildungsinstrument tendieren - besonders im Grundstudium - daher gegen Null. Es muß somit ein möglichst adäquater Ersatz geschaffen werden. Dieser Ersatz kann allerdings keinesfalls im didaktisch anderen Extrem denkbarer Methodenausbildung, nämlich dem "Trockenkurs", gefunden werden, weil mittels dieses Instruments Studenten profunde eigene Erfahrungen mit den Eigenheiten von Methoden in der Konfrontation mit der Wirklichkeit nicht zu vermitteln sind. Es bleibt als Ausweg aus diesem Dilemma nur der Einsatz der Sekundäranalyse.

2. Sekundäranalyse in der Methodenausbildung

Generell lassen sich für den vermehrten Einsatz der Sekundäranalyse im Rahmen der empirischen Sozialforschung eine Reihe guter Gründe nennen. Nur einer davon interessiert in unserem Zusammenhang, nämlich die Eignung der Sekundäranalyse als Instrument anschaulicher Lehre, und zwar einerseits für Zwecke effektiver Theoriekritik (vgl. **Klingemann & Mochmann**, 1975:189; **Sahner**, 1982:226), wie auch andererseits "für die Demonstration und das Einüben der Techniken der empirischen Sozialforschung" (Klingemann & Mochmann, 1975:-189). Als Facit wird dort festgehalten: "Wohl kaum eine andere Verfahrensweise der Lehre ist so geeignet, Standards für die Qualität weiterer empirischer Arbeiten zu setzen" (ebenda).

Wenn man sieht, daß die Sekundäranalyse sowohl Möglichkeiten zur Einübung von Methoden als auch Möglichkeiten zu systematischer Theoriekritik an die Hand gibt, kann man fragen, warum die Ausbildung in empirischer Sozialforschung nicht ausschließlich mittels Sekundäranalyse betrieben wird. Den Vorteilen der Sekundäranalyse stehen jedoch im Kontext der Methodenausbildung auch Nachteile gegenüber: Als besonders gravierend erweisen sich **erstens** die wohl erforderliche Beschränkung auf die Erhebungsmethode "Befragung", **zweitens** der Verzicht auf Kreativität, die zu entwickeln bei der Konstruktion eines eigenen Erhebungs- und Auswahlinstrumentes nötig wäre, und **drittens** das ausbleibende Erlebnis all jener kleinen und großen Überraschungen, die einem das "Feld" mit Sicherheit bereiten würde. Diese Nachteile lassen es geraten erscheinen, Sekundäranalyse nicht als alleiniges Ausbildungsmittel einzusetzen, sondern nur dann, wenn die institutionellen Bedingungen die Durchführung von Lehrforschung nicht erlauben, oder wenn inhaltliche Gesichtspunkte es erforderlich erscheinen lassen.

Wenn sich allerdings die Sekundäranalyse als optimales Instrument für gehaltvolle Methodenausbildung erweist, stellt sich die Frage, welche Studie oder Studien denn tunlichst zur Reanalyse herangezogen werden soll oder sollen. Zwei Anforderungen müssen sie erfüllen: Sie sollten es einerseits erlauben, die Umsetzung theoretischer Konstrukte in handhabbare Erhebungsinstrumente exemplarisch und kritisch nachzuvollziehen; sie sollten weiters erlauben, jene zentralen mathematisch-statistischen Voraussetzungen auf einen konkreten Problembereich angewandt kennenzulernen und zu problematisieren, die Daten, sollen sie über rein deskriptive und univariate Zwecke hinaus verwendet werden, aufweisen müssen, um der Gefahr von Forschungsartefakten entgehen zu können. Dazu weiter unten mehr.

Klingemann & Mochmann (1975:189) verweisen im Zusammenhang mit der Theoriekritik auf "klassische" Studien. Man selbst denkt nahezu zwangsläufig zunächst an eigene Untersuchungen. Obwohl gute Gründe für die Wahl einer dieser zwei Alternativen sprechen mögen - bei der "klassischen Studie" könnte man etwa exemplarisch herausarbeiten (sofern sie befriedigend dokumentiert ist), wie eine bestimmte inhaltliche Fragestellung methodisch umgesetzt werden muß, damit wissenschaftliche Qualität entsteht; bei der eigenen Studie wüßte man genau um all die kleinen und manchmal großen, z.T. unausweichlichen Abweichungen vom Forschungsplan im Verlauf einer Untersuchung -, ist aus verschiedenen Gründen einer dritten Variante der Zuschlag zu erteilen, und zwar dem Programm der **A**llgemeinen **B**evölkerungs**u**mfrage der **S**ozialwissenschaften (**ALLBUS**), das von ZUMA verantwortlich betreut wird. Seit 1980 sind im zweijährigen Turnus bisher fünf repräsentative Bevölkerungsumfragen mit jeweils rd. 3000 Befragten im Bundesgebiet und West-Berlin durchgeführt worden. Mit dem ALLBUS werden vor allem drei Ziele verfolgt: erstens die Untersuchung des sozialen Wandels, zweitens die Bereitstellung von Daten für Sekundäranalysen zur Prüfung von Hypothesen über die Sozialstruktur der Bundesrepublik, über Wertorientierungen, Einstellungen und Verhalten ihrer Bevölkerung sowie drittens die kontinuierliche Sozialberichterstattung auf der Basis von Individualdaten (vgl. ZA & ZUMA, 1982:5). Dabei erlauben die ausgewählten Variablen die Bearbeitung sowohl von konfirmatorischen (Beispiel: verbalisierte Ausländerdiskriminierung 1980, 1984, 1988) als auch von exploratorischen Fragestellungen (Beispiele: Einstellungen und Verhaltensweisen im Rahmen von AIDS; Umweltbelastungen 1988). Ein solcher Anspruch, wie er für das ALLBUS-Programm erhoben wird, ist - zumindest im deutschsprachigen Raum - für kein anderes Untersuchungsprogramm proklamiert worden; weder eine "klassische", geschweige denn eine "eigene" Untersuchung dürfte dazu in aussichtsreiche Konkurrenz treten können.

Ist also der Anspruch des ALLBUS-Programms schon Anreiz genug, von der Sekundäranalyse eigener oder "klassischer" Studien Abstand zu nehmen, so wird diese Entscheidung noch begünstigt durch zwei weitere Vorzüge des ALLBUS-Programms, denen wiederum auch eine zusätzliche didaktische Wendung gegeben werden kann. Der erste Vorzug liegt in der sozialwissenschaftlich bedeutsamen Themenvielfalt dieses Programms begründet. Diese Themenvielfalt erlaubt es, die u.U. zunächst ungeliebte Methodenausbildung dadurch schmackhafter machen zu können, daß die inhaltlichen Gegenstandsbereiche der Ausbildung auch vom Interesse der beteiligten Studenten abhängig gemacht werden kann. Der zweite Vorzug ist von unmittelbarem methodischen Interesse und liegt in der beispielhaften Dokumentation des Erhebungs-und Auswahlverfahrens der Umfragen begründet, die z.B. auch die bewußte Offenlegung von Stichproben- und Meßfehlern umfaßt (vgl. Mayer, 1984:13). Diese exemplarische Offenheit, verbunden mit einigen über das eigentliche Fragenprogramm des ALLBUS hinausgehenden methodischen Zusatzerhebungen, erleichtert die Methodenausbildung erheblich, und zwar gerade dort, wo man "aufklärerisch" gegen den auch unter Studenten weit verbreiteten, naiven Glauben an Zuverlässigkeit und Gültigkeit von Meßinstrumenten und veröffentlichter Umfrageergebnisse arbeiten will.

3. Einsatz von Statistik-Software in der Methodenlehre

An der Wirtschafts- und Sozialwissenschaftlichen Fakultät der Universität Erlangen-Nürnberg findet die einführende Methodenausbildung im dritten und vierten Studiensemester statt. Im Grundstudium ist diese einjährige vierstündige Vorlesung und Übung eine von vier zentralen Veranstaltungen des Studiengangs für Diplom-Sozialwirte. Ihr voraus geht eine ebenfalls einjährige Statistikausbildung für alle Studenten der WiSo-Fakultät. Grob unterteilt, werden in der Methodenveranstaltung des Lehrstuhls für Soziologie im **Wintersemester** zentrale wissenschaftstheoretische Grundlagen und wichtige Methoden und Techniken von Auswahlen in der empirischen Sozialforschung vorgestellt sowie, ausführlicher, die grundlegenden Methoden der Datenerhebung behandelt. In der **vorlesungsfreien Zeit** zwischen den Semestern wird ein einwöchiger, ganztägiger Blockkurs zur Einführung in SPSS^x durchgeführt. Dem SPSS^x-Kurs voraus geht ein dreitägiger Kurs zur Einführung in das Arbeiten mit dem Großrechner und einem darauf abgestimmten "Full Screen Editor". Den Studenten werden hier die notwendigen Kenntnisse des Umgangs mit Rechnern und Datenanalysesystemen vermittelt, bevor im **Sommersemester** praktische Datenanalyse betrieben wird.

Im Veranstaltungsablauf im Sommersemester sind Schwerpunkte zunächst die Erarbeitung eines theoretischen Bezugsrahmens für die jeweils von den Studenten ausgewählten Themenbereiche, danach die Überprüfung der für diese Themenbereiche im ALLBUS enthaltenen einschlägigen Variablen auf ihre Verwendbarkeit für das Auswertungsprogramm. Wenn schließlich statistische Hypothesen ausformuliert vorliegen, wird geprüft, ob die Operationalisierungen der involvierten Indikatoren, das Skalenniveau und die Verteilungsform der betroffenen Variablen und, unter Umständen, Reliabilität und Homogenität von Skalen geplante Hypothesentests zulassen, oder ob daran vorab noch Modifikationen anzubringen sind. An diesem Punkt beginnt die eigentliche Datenanalysephase, und man kann anfangen, sich der Hilfe von statistischen Datenanalysesystemen (vgl. einführend hierzu Küffner & Wittenberg 1985), in unserem Fall überwiegend SPSS^x, zu bedienen.

3.1 Überprüfung der Verteilungsparameter von Variablen und Skalen als Voraussetzung für die Auswahl angemessener statistischer Testverfahren

Am ALLBUS 1980 sei kursorisch eine mögliche Vorgehensweise mit Variablen zur verbalisierten Ausländerfeindlichkeit demonstriert (vgl. dazu auch Porst, 1985).

Die zentrale **Forschungshypothese** (eine Zusammenhangshypothese) lautet wie folgt:

"In je mehr Lebensbereichen Inländer Kontakt mit Ausländern haben, desto geringer ist die verbal geäußerte Ausländerdiskriminierung."

Daraus läßt sich eine **einseitige unspezifische statistische Hypothese** formulieren (zur Unterscheidung verschiedener Hypothesenarten vgl. **Bortz, 1984**):

"Die Korrelation zwischen dem Ausmaß an verbal geäußerter Ausländerfeindlichkeit und der Kontaktfelder mit Ausländern ist kleiner als Null, also negativ".

Die zu prüfende Nullhypothese lautet infolgedessen:

"Es besteht kein oder ein positiver Zusammenhang zwischen den genannten Variablen, die Korrelation ist also größer gleich Null".

Bevor diese statistische Hypothese überprüft werden kann, müssen einige Voraussetzungen erfüllt sein. Die Studenten müssen überprüfen, welche **Indikatoren** (Variablen) aus unserem Datensatz die beiden **Dimensionen Ausländerfeindlichkeit und Kontakte zu Ausländern** repräsentieren, wie diese Dimensionen also operationalisiert sind. Weiterhin sollten sie versuchen, diese Indikatoren zu **Indices** zu konzentrieren, um so die Auswertung zu vereinfachen und zu verdichten. Wichtig ist das **Skalenniveau** der dann verwendeten Variablen und, falls sie metrisch skaliert sind, ihre **Verteilungsparameter,** da die sinnvolle Anwendung vieler Analyseverfahren davon abhängig ist. Außerdem müssen die verwendeten Skalen daraufhin überprüft werden, ob sie **homogen** sind, d. h., wirklich nur eine Dimension messen, und ob sie **reliabel** sind, d. h., als Meßinstrument so zuverlässig sind, daß die gemessenen Werte keine inneren Widersprüche aufweisen.

3.1.1 Operationalisierung der Indikatoren

Als erklärende Variablen stehen im ALLBUS 1980 vier Variablen zur Verfügung. Es handelt sich um dichotome Variablen, die für vier Lebensbereiche angeben, ob die befragte Person dort Kontakt zu Ausländern hat oder nicht: Kontakte in der eigenen Familie oder der näheren Verwandtschaft, Kontakte am Arbeitsplatz, Kontakte in der Nachbarschaft, Kontakte im sonstigen Freundes- und Bekanntenkreis.

Die abhängigen oder zu erklärenden Variablen, die Verbalisierung von Ausländerfeindlichkeit, sind in vier weiteren Variablen als siebenstufige Likert-Skalen operationalisiert: "Gastarbeiter sollten ihren Lebensstil ein bißchen besser an den der Deutschen anpassen", "Wenn Arbeitsplätze knapp werden, sollte man die Gastarbeiter wieder in ihre Heimat zurückschicken", "Man sollte Gastarbeitern jede politische Betätigung in Deutschland untersagen", "Gastarbeiter sollten sich ihre Ehepartner unter ihren eigenen Landsleuten auswählen". Nach den bisherigen Untersuchungen scheint diese Operationalisierung einen zuverlässigen Indikator für Ausländerfeindlichkeit zu ergeben (vgl. **Zuma-Skalenhandbuch, 1983**).

3.1.2 Skalenniveau und Verteilungsform der Variablen

Die Variablen zu den Kontaktbereichen mit Ausländern haben als dichotome Variablen **nominales** Niveau. Die Variablen zur verbalisierten Ausländerfeindlichkeit sind im strengen Sinne **ordinal**, können jedoch unter bestimmten Voraussetzungen als metrisch skaliert behandelt werden. Bei diesen Skalenniveaus sind zunächst die **Randverteilungen,** also Häufigkeitsauszählungen.

3.1.3 Bildung von Indices

Um die Auswertung zu vereinfachen und die Komplexität zu reduzieren, sollten den Studenten nahegelegt werden, aus den Indikatorvariablen Indices zu berechnen und diese dann auf ihre Zuverlässigkeit hin zu überprüfen. Für unser Ausländerfeindlichkeitsbeispiel bietet es sich an, einen Index für verbale Diskriminierung und einen Index für Kontakte zu Ausländern aus den genannten jeweils vier Variablen zu bilden. Dies kann durch einfache Addition der Ausprägungen in den Variablen erfolgen. Es werden also Summenscores berechnet. Diese Indices können durch Korrelationen mit ihren Ursprungsvariablen daraufhin überprüft werden, welche der Quellvariablen am stärksten in ihnen zum Ausdruck kommt. Die Quellvariablen und diese beiden Indices bilden dann die Basis für die eigentliche Auswertung, sofern Homogenitäts- und Reliabilitätsgesichtspunkte nicht dagegen sprechen.

3.1.4 Reliabilität und Homogenität

Die Variablen und Indices sollen der Messung der theoretischen Konstrukte "Ausländerfeindlichkeit" und "Kontakthäufigkeit mit Ausländern" dienen. Um eine valide statistische Überprüfung von Hypothesen auf der Basis dieser Variablen durchführen zu können, muß vorher sichergestellt sein, daß sie **reliabel** sind, also zuverlässig ohne allzu große Schwankungen die theoretischen Konstrukte widerspiegeln, und **homogen** sind, also jeweils nur eine Dimension oder, anders ausgedrückt, einen Faktor beinhalten und nicht auch allzu starke Effekte von anderen Faktoren, die wir nicht berücksichtigt haben, aufweisen.

3.1.4.1 Überprüfung auf Reliabilität

Zur Überprüfung der Reliabilität werden die skalenbildenden Variablen auf innere Widersprüche statistisch überprüft. Von den drei Möglichkeiten der Reliabilitätsinterpretation - durch Wiederholung, durch Kontrollgruppen und durch interne Konsistenz -, kommt für uns nur die dritte in Betracht. Diese Möglichkeit arbeitet mit der Berechnung eines Reliabilitätskoeffizienten **Cronbach's** Alpha. Ein Wert von $\alpha = .76$ deutet auf eine zufriedenstellende Reliabilität hin.

3.1.4.2 Überprüfung auf Homogenität

Die Überprüfung auf Homogenität ist Bestandteil der Überprüfung von Variablen auf ihre **formale Validität**. Eine Skala ist dann formal gültig, wenn sie nur eine Dimension mißt, anders ausgedrückt, wenn sie homogen ist.

Diese Überprüfung auf Homogenität einer Skala, also die Sicherstellung, daß durch die Variation der Variablen die Variation von nur einer Dimension gemessen ist, kann mittels einer **exploratorischen Faktorenanalyse** erfolgen. Sie analysiert die Variation einer Reihe von beobachteten (manifesten) Variablen, die die gleiche Dimension messen sollen, auf dahinter verborgene (latente) Dimensionen oder Faktoren. Sind die zu überprüfenden Variablen homogen, dann wird auch nur ein Faktor extrahiert. Werden dagegen mehrere deutlich ausgeprägte Faktoren extrahiert (Eigenvalue > 1), so sind diese Variablen nicht als homogen zu betrachten. In unserem Beispiel wird nur ein Faktor ausgewiesen; die Skala zur verbalisierten Ausländerfeindlichkeit ist demnach als formal validiert zu verwenden.

3.2 Überprüfung von Zusammenhangs- und Unterschiedshypothesen mittels angemessener statistischer Testverfahren

Nachdem die für die Hypothesenüberprüfung herangezogenen Variablen auf ihre Eignung überprüft sind, können nun konkrete, mit diesen Variablen oder mit aus ihnen erzeugten Indices gebildete, statistische Hypothesen überprüft werden. Wichtig ist, daß diese Variablen bereits auf ihre Eigenschaften untersucht sind, d. h. besonders, daß ihr jeweiliges **Skalenniveau** bekannt ist und, bei metrischem Niveau, daß geklärt ist, ob die Variable **annähernd normalverteilt** ist. Auch spielen Anzahl und Art der Stichproben eine Rolle. Danach muß bei der Auswahl der Prozeduren zuerst berücksichtigt werden, ob es sich um eine Zusammenhangshypothese, eine Unterschiedshypothese oder eine Veränderungshypothese handelt. $SPSS^X$ wie auch andere Datenanalysesysteme stellen eine Reihe von Signifikanztests für die Überprüfung von statistischen Hypothesen zur Verfügung.

3.2.1 Signifikanztests bei Zusammenhangshypothesen

Für die Überprüfung der Hypothese, daß ein negativer Zusammenhang zwischen der Stärke der Kontakte zu Ausländern und der Bereitschaft zu Äußerungen, die Ausländer diskriminieren, besteht, ziehen wir aus dem ALLBUS 1980 die oben gebildeten Summenscores heran.

Den Studenten kann veranschaulicht werden, daß grundsätzlich mehrere Möglichkeiten bestehen, Zusammenhangshypothesen zu testen, u.z. mittels **korrelations-, tabellen-** oder **regressionsanalytischer** Verfahrensweisen. Begründungen sowie Vor- und Nachteile der gewählten Strategien sowie mögliche alternative Rechenverfahren können erörtert und anhand des Datensatzes demonstriert werden.

3.2.2 Signifikanztests bei Unterschiedshypothesen

Eine Unterschiedshypothese kann man für unsere Auswertung wie folgt formulieren: Personen mit Gastarbeiterkontakt äußern sich signifikant weniger diskriminierend über Ausländer als Personen ohne Kontakt. Auch hier müssen Skalenniveau und Verteilung der verwendeten Variablen berücksichtigt werden, bevor entschieden werden kann, ob Signifikanztests auf Mittelwertsunterschiede mittels **parametrischer** (t-Test, Varianzanalyse) oder **verteilungsfreier Verfahren** (U-Test, H-Test) angemessen greifen können.

3.2.3 Signifikanztests bei Veränderungshypothesen

Der Test von Veränderungshypothesen erfordert einen vergleichsweise größeren statistischen Aufwand. In der Regel sollten Studenten im Grundstudium, wenn sie nicht Soziologie im Hauptfach studieren, damit nicht konfrontiert werden.

4. Diskussion und Probleme

Die didaktische Vorgehensweise kann so gestaltet werden, daß zunächst vom Veranstalter im Plenum die Funktion eines Analyseverfahrens sowie seine mathematisch-statistischen Grundlagen und Voraussetzungen erläutert werden. Danach kann an einem Beispiel aus dem ALLBUS vorgeführt werden, wie man z.B. mittels einer $SPSS^X$-Prozedur das Analyseproblem "programmiert" und löst. Den Abschluß eines jeden Analyseschrittes hat dann die entsprechende Interpretation des Analyseergebnisses zu bilden. Sofern dies nach Abwägung inhaltlicher und methodischer Aspekte möglich ist, können Studenten die demonstrierten Analyseschritte auf ihre Fragestellungen übertragen und sie einzeln oder in Kleingruppen durchführen. Die zwangsläufig auftretenden Schwierigkeiten sowie die inhaltlichen und methodischen Ergebnisse dieser studentischen Arbeit können jeweils zu Beginn der Nachfolgeveranstaltung und im Tutorium behandelt und besprochen werden.

Die Vorzüge dieser Vorgehensweise liegen auf der Hand: **Zum einen** kann in Vorlesungsform der erforderliche "Stoff" einer Methodenveranstaltung zur Datenanalyse jeweils an solchen ausgewählten Variablen aus der Vielzahl und Vielfalt von ALLBUS-Variablen behandelt werden, die die Studenten interessieren und die sich in theoretisch sinn- und mehr oder minder anspruchsvolle Zusammenhangs- oder Unterschiedshypothesen integrieren lassen, die darüber hinaus den mathematisch-statistischen Anforderungen solcher Analyseverfahren Rechnung tragen, die den Studenten zumindest grob bereits bekannt sind. Auch ist es möglich, alternative Auswertungsverfahren zu demonstrieren. **Zum anderen** müssen die Studenten selbst aktiv werden und die für ihr spezielles Thema geeigneten Auswertungsstrategien entwickeln, diese in die entsprechenden $SPSS^x$-Programme umsetzen, die Computeroutputs statistisch und inhaltlich interpretieren und die Arbeitsergebnisse im Plenum vortragen. Die Studenten werden dadurch Teil zur eigenständigen kritischen Datenanalyse motiviert. Sie erhalten ein Fundament, auf dem im Hauptstudium vertiefend Seminare zur Datenanalyse oder Lehrforschungsprojekte aufbauen können.

5. Literatur

Bortz, J. (1984). Lehrbuch der empirischen Forschung für Sozialwissenschaftler. Unter Mitarbeit von D. Bongers. Berlin, Springer

Hofmann, G. (1986). Die methodologische Ausbildung von Soziologen. Soziologie. Mitteilungsblatt der Deutschen Gesellschaft für Soziologie, I, 37-51

Klingemann, H.-D. & E. Mochmann (1975). Sekundäranalyse. In: Koolwijk, J. v. & M. Wieken-Mayser (Hg.), Techniken der empirischen Sozialforschung, Bd. 2. München, Oldenbourg

Küffner, H. & R. Wittenberg (1985). Datenanalysesysteme für statistische Auswertungen. Eine Einführung in SPSS, BMDP und SAS. Stuttgart, G. Fischer

Mayer, K. U. (1984). Zur Einführung: Die Allgemeine Bevölkerungsumfrage der Sozialwissenschaften als eine Mehrthemen-Wiederholungsbefragung. In: Mayer & Schmidt (Hg.)

Mayer, K. U. & P. Schmidt (Hg.) (1984). Allgemeine Bevölkerungsumfrage der Sozialwissenschaften. Beiträge zu methodischen Problemen des ALLBUS 1980. Frankfurt a. M., Campus

Porst, R. (1985). Praxis der Umfrageforschung. Erhebung und Auswertung sozialwissenschaftlicher Umfragedaten. Stuttgart, Teubner

Sahner, H. (1982). Theorie und Forschung. Zur paradigmatischen Struktur der westdeutschen Soziologie und zu ihrem Einfluß auf die Forschung. Opladen, Westdeutscher Verlag

ZA (Hg.) (1980). Maschinenlesbares Codebuch - ZA Studie 1000 - Nationaler Sozialer Survey 1980. Köln, Zentralarchiv

ZA & ZUMA (Hg.) (1982). Allgemeine Bevölkerungsumfrage der Sozialwissenschaften - ALLBUS 1980. Codebuch mit Methodenbericht und Vergleichsdaten ZA-Nr. 1000. Köln, Zentralarchiv

ZA & ZUMA (Hg.) (1982). Maschinenlesbares Codebuch - ZA Studie 1160 - Allgemeine Bevölkerungsumfrage der Sozialwissenschaf-ten (ALLBUS 1982). Köln, Zentralarchiv

ZA & ZUMA (Hg.) (1983). Allgemeine Bevölkerungsumfrage der Sozialwissenschaften 1982. Codebuch mit Methodenbericht und Vergleichsdaten zum ALLBUS von 1982. Köln, Zentralarchiv

ZA & ZUMA (Hg.) (1984). Allgemeine Bevölkerungsumfrage der Sozialwissenschaften (ALLBUS 1984). Codebuch ZA-Nr. 1340. Köln, Zentralarchiv

ZA & ZUMA (Hg.) (1986). Allgemeine Bevölkerungsumfrage der Sozialwissenschaften (ALLBUS 1986). Codebuch ZA-Nr. 1500. Köln, Zentralarchiv

ZA & ZUMA (Hg.), (1988). Allgemeine Bevölkerungsumfrage der Sozialwissenschaften (ALLBUS 1988). Codebuch ZA-Nr. 1670. Köln, Zentralarchiv

ZUMA & IZ Sozialwissenschaften (Hg.) (1983). ZUMA-Handbuch Sozialwissenschaftlicher Skalen. Mannheim und Bonn, ZUMA & IZ

Teaching Computational Statistics in APL

M. Zaus

Abstract. This paper is directed to first-semester courses regarding computational statistics in psychology. Unlike common courses, whereby students learn first statistics and subsequently the usage of a statistical software package, we encourage a quite different approach with emphasis on tailored computing by teaching simultaneously statistics and APL. Due to the limitations in space we delimit the scope of this paper to a brief outlook on computer-based courses in modern psychology, the interactive work with APL and the teaching of computational probability in APL. An extensive treatment of the subject matter in APL*PLUS II is currently in progress for conceptual and statistical modeling in fields like neural networks, genetic algorithms and cognitive science.

Introduction. Modern psychology is just as dependent on computer hard- & software as are, for instance, biology, physics, or economics. Its standard courses with emphasis on methodological foundations and practical methods can be structured effectively by a network as shown in figure 1. The outer ring of this network constitutes the obligatory coursework which a student will experience in about 10 or 12 semesters. The coursework of the first four semesters is shaded and covers essentially probability theory and statistics, algebraic measurement theory and scaling, and finally experimental design techniques, followed by at least two practice courses for laboratory experiments and field observations. The coursework from the fifth semester on is contained in the remaining cells of figure 1. These subject areas are both conceptually and methodologically dependent on each other. This is indicated by the thinned bidirectional arrows in figure 1.

The kernel of this network is a particularly chosen hard- and software environment which provides computer-based interactions and supports for all of the courses, from the first semester on. The choice of hard- & software differs of course in various departments. In what follows, we will consider the choice of STSC's APL*PLUS and STATGRAPHICS as the central software environment, while a cluster of PC's including printers and plotters constitutes the hardware environment.

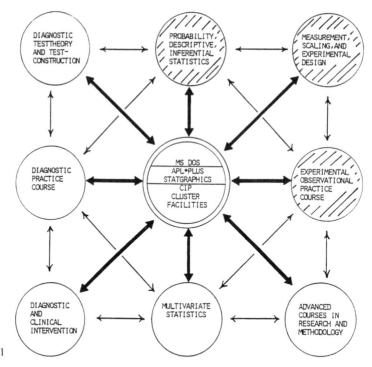

Fig. 1

There are many reasons for choosing APL*PLUS, though only few can be pointed out here. First of all, APL*PLUS is not a plain programming package, but an application system for creating mathematical and statistical tool boxes in no time. This makes the student independent from canned and rigid software, because it allows tailored computing for specific and often unexpected problems for which canned software packages do not offer any procedure. Take the simple case of nominal scaled data and ask the student to compute the corresponding measures of central tendency and dispersion, i.e. the mode and the variation ratio. Which statistical package offers a "procedure" for the variation ratio $((1-f_{mod})/N)$? Or take the case of symmetrically trimmed means, winsorized means, and convex means. In APL, these means are faster programmed than finding the right page in a statistical package's manual. The list of often necessary statistical procedures *not contained* in standard packages is virtually endless such that tailored computing must be considered as an every day activity rather than an occasional enterprise. The main advantage of APL is its versatility and computational power. It supports the student not only in his or her regular coursework, but also in writing efficient modular programs and in the creation of tools from fields like logic, settheory, linear algebra, and calculus.

A second major advantage of APL is the fact that the statistical package STATGRAPHICS is written in APL*PLUS. STATGRAPHICS offers at least 250 procedures including 50 powerful graphics procedures. Whenever this package serves the purpose, the student is adviced to take advantage of it. Otherwise he or she may write an own procedure in APL and link it with STATGRAPHICS, thereby extending it over the time. As a point in fact, this author and his students have extended STATGRAPHICS in the meanwhile by almost 250 procedures for special problems in statistics, scaling, psychophysics, cognitive psychology, and psychological test theory. For readers unfamiliar with APL and STATGRAPHICS it may be helpful to decribe briefly how students work with APL in general.

APL-dialogue. As illustrated in figure 2, the interactive work with APL offers basically two major modes. In the

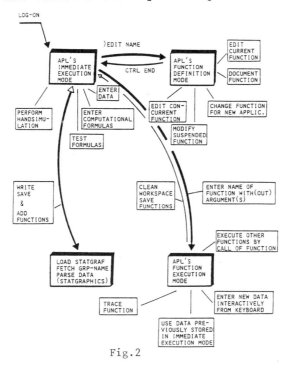

Fig.2

immediate execution mode, students may enter their data directly from the keyboard or they create systematic or randomized data sets with special operators. Computational formulas are entered from textbooks or developed within a given context. The immediate execution mode allows testing such formulas as well as performing hand-simulations. This mode can be used as an efficient desk calculator, but its main purpose is to prepare the building blocks of programs which are called *defined functions* in APL.

After sufficient familiarity with APL, the students start using the function definition mode by entering the full screen editor. Here they edit, document, change, modify and improve a particular function or several functions in a concurrent manner. When the programming job is done, they leave the function definition mode and return to the immediate execution mode.

This immediate execution mode serves also as the function execution mode. By entering the name of a niladic, monadic or dyadic function, i.e. one without any or one with one or two arguments, the function and any other contained in it becomes executed. For testing a function, either new data are entered interactively from the keyboard or previously stored data are used for this purpose. In cases where it remains unclear how a function works, the student may trace that function to find out what's going on line by line. Before functions are saved, the active workspace should be cleaned out by erasing undesired functions and variables. Excellent textbooks with different topics for applying APL help students in this respect. We mention, in particular, Ramsay & Musgrave (1981), Gilman & Rose (1984), Polivka & Pakin (1975), Peelle (1986), and Turner (1987).

Advanced students with sufficient familiarity in APL use, in addition, STATGRAPHICS. Either to borrow a procedure from STATGRAPHICS or to write new functions as addenda to this package. In any way, the dialogue with APL is just as easy to learn as the language itself, in spite of the fairy tales about this language. In the sequel, we will exemplify this for the case of distributional models in statistics.

Computational probability. The field of distributional models is virtually the limbo of statistics for beginning students unless orientation is provided repeatedly during the course. Escaping the limbo means learning the lingo. Although many psychologists seem to believe that there is no model other than the normal distribution, it is perhaps best to make the landscape of distributional models visible from a birds'view. Figure 3, which has been adopted from Graf et al.(1987), illustrates one way of doing this. Consider the left part regarding discrete distributions. What is actually necessary for a computation and how can this be made explicit ? By "lowering the altitude", details become recognizable such that we can pinpoint essential ingredients of particular models without loosing the sight towards neighboring models.

In this admittedly general setting the student learns to appreciate Polya's problem solving maxime : What is the unknown and what are the conditions ? In other words, they learn about the meaning of parameters *inside* a model and about the *impact of changing* specific parameters under limiting conditions. Monotonically changing parameters means approximating the neighboring target model by the source model until the target model becomes the adequate candidate model for a required computation. This line of approach is accompanied by emphasizing prototypical fields of applications, i.e. where the hypergeometric, the binomial or the Poisson model is applied or where special cases of the negative binomial distribution are used in psychology. Once general aspects for orientation are clarified, one moves to a particular model, say, the binomial distribution. There are *six stages* for treating such a model. These are:

Concept   Explanation   Mathematical Formulation
Computability   Programmability   Final Program

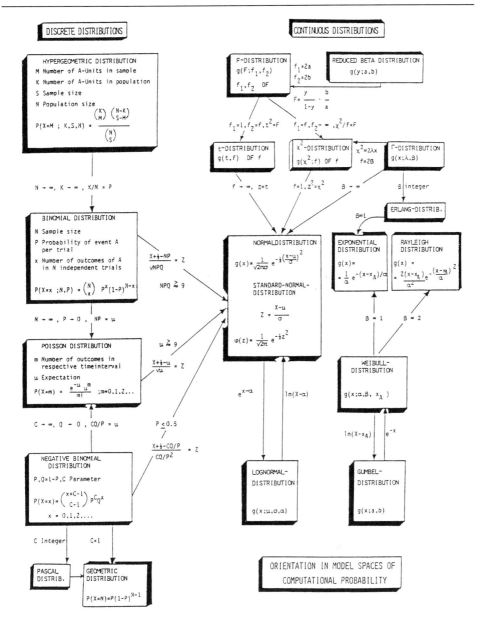

Fig. 3

In the lecture preceeding the computer session, the student becomes familiar with fundamental concepts about discrete random variables, induced probability spaces and discrete probability distributions. In addition, explanations of the notions of Bernoulli processes and experiments are given. Finally, when the equation of the binomial distribution is reached, i.e. its mathematical formulation, a step-by-step translation into APL is demonstrated. Figure 4 illustrates these steps alltogether. There is obviously no mystery in applying the operators of APL, it's a straight translation of the formula. Having translated the formula, the student enters the function definition mode and writes an explicit dyadic function named BINOM.

$$f(x;N,P) = \binom{N}{x} P^x (1-P)^{N-x}$$

$$= (x!N) P^x (1-P)^{N-x}$$

$$= (x!N) \times P^x \times (1-P)^{N-x}$$

$$= (x!N) \times (P*x) \times (1-P)* N-x$$

$$f(x;N,P) = (x!N) \times (P*x) \times (1-P)* N-x \leftarrow 0, \iota N$$

! Binomial
× Times
* Power
- Minus
← Assign
, Catenate
ι Index Generator

```
▽ BP←N BINOM P;x
[1]   ʀ x=0,1,2,...,N
[2]   BP←(x!N)×(P*x)×(1-P)*N-x←0,ιN
▽
```

Fig.4

The first argument of BINOM is the number of independent trials, while the second argument refers to the probability of the interesting event. The range of the random variable has been localized and the comment in line 1 tells us that it ranges from Zero to N.

This little program is then the point of departure for the students' computer-session. Here they extend the program, write selfcontained new programs with additional features, they include semigraphics, and they transfer the achieved skills to related problems such as computing the Poisson distribution, the geometric distribution, and still others. Figure 5 illustrates the payoff on the students' side for a 90-minutes session. On the right-hand side of figure 5, the landscape of figure 3 is recaptured, while the main part of figure 5 shows the programs and the output for the binomial, the Poisson, and the geometric distributions (the hypergeometric and the negative binomial distributions have been omitted due to limitations in space). The model equations of these distributions are contained in lines 2, 1 and 1, respectively. Again, these translations into APL are straightforward and to the point. In the remaining part of the computer-session, these distributions are then explored by manipulating specific parameters, in particular with respect to varying shapes or with respect to limiting conditions for the purpose of approximations.

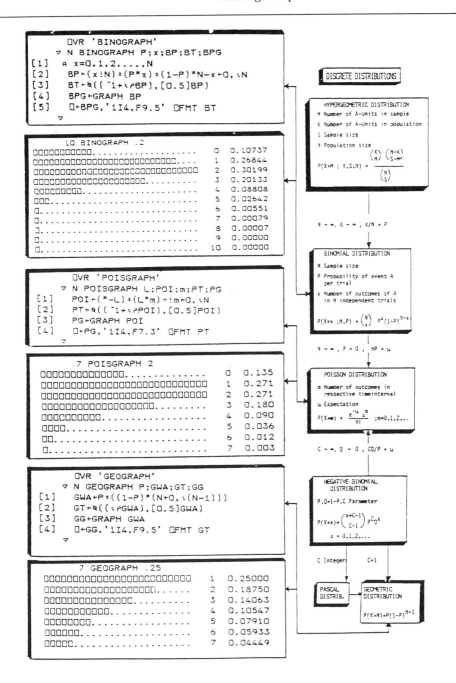

Fig. 5

The distribution of homework assignments serve finally to deepen the knowledge of the corresponding computersession.

Conclusion. Most students become interested in statistics primarily if the subject promises to do useful things for them. APL proved to be ideal for tailored computing, since students may use this language for mathematical problem solving and for creating highly efficient tools for tasks arising in statistics, measurement, scaling, test theory and test construction, experimental design, simulation methods, and advanced issues in empirical model building. The only problem with APL is the mode of how to convince potential users of its power. It's very much like trying to win someone for parachuting or skydiving : You have to jump from 12.500 ft. to find out how beautiful and relaxing it is.

References

Gilchrist, W. 1984 Statistical Modeling. John Wiley & Sons New York
Gilman, L. & Rose, A. 1984 APL : An Interactive Approach. John Wiley & Sons, New York
Graf, U., Henning, H.J., Stange,, K. & Wilfrich, P.T. 1987 Formeln und Tabellen der angewandten mathematischen Statistik. 3.Aufl. Wilfrich, P.T. & Henning, H.J., Springer Verlag, Berlin
Peelle, H. 1986 APL : An Introduction. Holt, Rinehart and Winston, New York
Polivka, R.P. & Pakin, S. 1975 APL : The Language and Its Use. Prentice-Hall, Inc., Englewood Cliffs, New Jersey
Ramsay, J.B. & Musgrave, G.L. APL-STAT : A Do-it-Yourself Guide to Computational Statistics Using APL. Lifetime Learning Publications, Belmont, California
Scientific Time Sharing Company (STSC) 1988 APL*PLUS & STATGRAPHICS, 2115 East Jefferson Street, Rockville, Maryland 20852
Turner, J.R. 1987 APL IS EASY. John Wiley & Sons, Inc. New York
Zaus, M. 1988 Konzeptionen einer rechnernahen und rechnergestützten Methodenausbildung. Berichte aus dem Institut für Kognitionsforschung, Universität Oldenburg
Zaus, M. 1989 Werkzeugfunktionen zur interaktiven Modell- und Datenanalyse in APL. In Fertigstellung.

Rechnernetze in der Statistik

Die Workstation des Statistikers in den 90er Jahren

H.-J. Lenz

SUMMARY

We try to sketch the 5-years future in statistical computation. Attention is paid to what statisticians really need and what they should get. However, often enough the statsticians have to use inferior tools, because they are just available, only. It's the author's intention to compare the statisticians profile carefully the profiles of the up to date machines.

1. Typisierung

Es ist zweckmäßig, von den folgenden beiden Statistikerprofilen auszugehen:

Typische Statistiker

- Methodiker / Theoretiker
- Anwender / Empiriker

Sieht man von der Wahrscheinlichkeitstheorie ab, so lassen sich die Hauptarbeitsgebiete eines Statistikers wie folgt zusammenfassen, wobei berücksichtigt werden sollte, daß der Theoretiker bzw. Empiriker verschiedenen Zugang dazu hat:

Statistikgebiete

- Stichprobenplanung
- Versuchsplanung
- Datenvalidierung
- Explorative Datenanalyse
- Konfirmatorische Datenanalyse

Getrennt nach den beiden Profilen des Statistikers lassen sich die folgenden Anforderungsprofile herleiten, die Arbeitsschwerpunkte in den Mittelpunkt der Betrachtung stellen:

Anforderungsprofil
Methodiker / Theoretiker

- 2D/3D - Farbgrafik zur Modellierung und Visualisierung
- M.C.-Simulation zum Schätzen von Dichte- und Verteilungsfunktionen, Momenten und Prozentpunkten usw.
- Kenngrößenberechnung von Gütefunktionen, Influenzkurven, Eigenwerten usw.
- Berechnung von Verteilungs- und Dichtefunktionen und von Statistiken
- Berechnung von Versuchs- und Stichprobenplänen
- Wissenschaftliche Textverarbeitung
- Präsentationsgraphik erstellen

HJL 1989

Anforderungsprofil
Anwender / Empiriker

- 2D/3D-Farbgrafik zur Modellierung und Visualisierung
- Information Retrieval mittels SQL-Datenbanken als de-facto-Standard
- Komplexe Datenanalysen von experimentellen, Zeitreihen-, Querschnitts- sowie Längs-und Querschnittsdaten
- Wissenschaftliche Textverarbeitung
- Präsentationsgraphik

2. Ausstattungsprofile

Den ermittelten Anforderungsprofilen typischer Statistiker lassen sich nun Ausstattungsprofile aufgrund von Erfahrungen gegenüberstellen. Dabei wird von vernetzten Workstations ausgegangen. Die Ausstattungsunterschiede liegen im Bereich der Prozessorleistung bzw. der IO-Leistung und der Entwicklungswerkzeuge bzw. des Datenbankzugangs. Dadurch wird das Konzept einer einheitlichen Grundausstattung mit individueller Anpassung möglich.

Ausstattung
Methodiker/Theoretiker

Hardware
Workstation

- CPU › 0.6 MFLOPS
- Math.-Koprozessor
- RAM › 6 MB
- DASD› 300 MB
- Screen › 1000*1000 pixel incl. Maus
- Proprinter mit Letter quality

Kommunikation
- WAN
  - EARN/BITNET/UUCP
  - X.400 (?)
- LAN
  - Token Ring/Ethernet
  - Novell
- BTX

Software
Betriebsystem, Benutzeroberfläche

- DOS 4.x/OS-2/UNIX,...
- FDO/ ISPF /Window-Manager

Kommunikation
- SNA,SDLC/BSC,TCP/IP,...
- LAN-Protokolle
- BTX,...

Werkzeuge

- 3GL-Compiler/Interpreter
- Interactive Debugger
- Window-Manager
- Math.-stat.Bibliothek
- Statistikpaket
- Grafiksystem
- Textsystem

HJL 1989

Ausstattung
Anwender/Empiriker

Hardware
Workstation

- CPU › 0.3 MFLOPS
- I/O-Prozessor
- RAM › 6 MB
- DASD› 500 MB
- Screen › 1000*1000 pixel incl. Maus
- Proprinter mit Letter quality

Kommunikation
- WAN
  - EARN/BITNET/UUCP
  - X.400 (?)
- LAN
  - Token Ring/Ethernet
  - Novell
- BTX

Software
Betriebsystem, Benutzeroberfläche

- DOS 4.x/OS-2/UNIX,...
- FDO/ ISPF /Window-Manager

Kommunikation
- SNA,SDLC/BSC,...
- LAN-Protokolle
- BTX,...

Werkzeuge

- rel. Datenbank
- Statistikpaket
- Grafiksystem
- Textsystem

HJL 1989

Die Einbettung derartiger Workstations in eine abgestufte Rechnerlandschaft zeigt das folgende Diagramm:

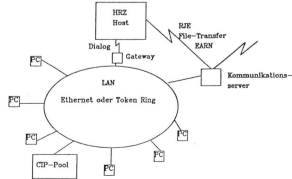

3. Werkzeuge

Zu den klassischen Werkzeugen des Methodikers unter den Statistikern gehören die 3GL-Sprachen und die Bibliotheksprogramme incl. Grafiksysteme wie z.B. GKS. Sie werden durch Statistikpakete und Spezialsysteme ergänzt. Letztere haben im Gegensatz zu den Statistikpaketen eine eingeschränkte Funktionalität. So ist TSP kompetent für die Zeitreihenanalyse, GLIM für verallgemeinerte lineare Modelle usw. Eine besondere Rolle spielen Systeme, die eine sehr komfortable Benutzerführung auszeichnet. Sie haben im allgemeinen eine reduzierte Funktionalität im Vergleich zu den Statistikpaketen, ermöglichen dafür aber einen schnellen Problemlösungsprozeß. Sie stellen sich dem Anwender als "Quickies" dar und werden hier -spaßeshalber- als 8GL-Sprachen bezeichnet. Die folgenden beiden Abbildungen geben einen Überblick über diese genannten Werkzeuge.

Werkzeuge des Statistikers I

3 GL - Sprachen	Bibliotheken	Statistikpakete
APL*plus	IMSL	BMDP
GAUSS	NAG	PSTAT
S	IBM SSP	SAS
FORTRAN 77 / 88	HARWELL	SIR
.	.	SPSS
.	.	.
.	.	.

HJL 1989

Werkzeuge des Statistikers II

8 GL - Sprachen	Spezialsysteme
ISP	TSP
NCSS	GLIM
STATGRAPHICS	GLAMOUR
MINITAB	LISREL
.	CLUSTAN
.	CHART

HJL 1989

KI-Werkzeuge wie PROLOG, LISP, XPS-SHELLS usw., aber auch Fenstersysteme ergänzen die genannten Tools. Die folgende Abbildung soll einen Eindruck von Benutzeroberflächen der Klasse "Quickies" vermitteln. Als Problem dient die Berechnung des Fraktils P(x a) bzw. P(x a). Abschließend sollen Hinweise auf Weiterentwicklungen der Werkzeuge für Methodiker und Empiriker gegeben werden.

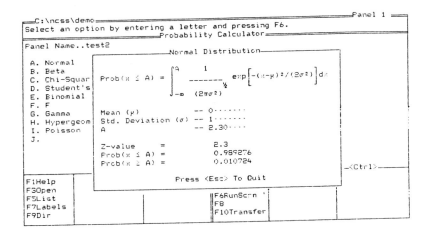

Benutzerfreundliche Werkzeuge
des Statistikers als *Entwickler*

- **Prinzipien:**
  - standardisierte Software-Schnittstellen
    vgl. SAA - Konzept der IBM, UNIX - Konzept
  - Front-Ends, Back-Ends
  - Precompiler
  - Graphische Editoren in Verbindung mit Codegeneratoren

- **Beispiele:**
  - Statt Graphik-Programmierung →
    graphischer Editor zur interaktiven Layout-Gestaltung aller graphischen Objekte und Attribute.
    Anschließend *automatische Codegenerierung*.
  - *Datenerfassung* mit SPSS-DATA_ENTRY auf PC's,
    Modellierung objekt-, matrix- oder Panel-orientiert auf dem PC-Front-End-System,
    File-Transfer PC/WS ←→ Host zum number crunching. *Postanalyse* unter APL+ auf PC/WS,...

HJL 1989

4. Notational Tools

Ein besonderes Problem stellt die Bereitstellung von Statistik-spezifischen Operatoren, Funktionen und Datenstrukturen dar, die vor allem für den Methodiker von Interesse sind. Insbesondere erzwingen Maschinenerfordernisse eine Notation, die für den Statistiker "unnatürlich" erscheint. Die Berechnung des arithmetischen Mittels einer Meßfolge x sei dafür ein Beispiel:

Notational Tool

Problem: $\quad x = 1/n \sum_i x$

GAUSS
$$\text{SUMC X / ROWS X}$$

LISP
$$\text{(DIV (SUM X) (LENGTH X))}$$

APL
$$+ / X / (\varrho X)$$

FORTRAN 77
```
xqu=0.0
for i=1,n
   xqu=xqu+x(i)
endfor
```

HJL 1989

5. Kostenabschätzung

Die Bereitstellung von vernetzten Arbeitsplatzrechnern eröffnet mit Funktionalität, Komfort und Flexibilität neue Anwendungsmöglichkeiten des statistical computing. Dies erfordert aber auch hohe Investitionen und Folgekosten. Einen Eindruck davon vermitteln folgende Fakten über den Fachbereich Wirtschaftswissenschaft der FU Berlin. Aufgrund des Kooperationsprojekts "Der wissenschaftliche Arbeitsplatz am Fachbereich Wirtschaftswissenschaft (WAP)" zwischen der IBM Deutschland und der FU Berlin wurde dieser Fachbereich "computerisiert". Die folgende Abbildung zeigt die DV-Ausstattung:

EDV - Ausstattung
FB WiWiss der FU Berlin

- Zentrale Ressourcen
  - 1 Fachbereichsrechner IBM 4361-4 mit Vorrechner IBM 3705
  - 1 Kommunikationsrechner IBM 9370-30
- Dezentrale Ressourcen
  - 40 PC's IBM AT-02/03, PS-2 in der Lehre
  - 39 PC's IBM AT-02/03, PS-2,RT's in der Forschung
  - 13 PC's in der Institutsverwaltung und FB-Verwaltung
- Vernetzung
  - 3 Glasfaserleitungen
  - 3 Wählleitungen incl. BTX-Anschluß
  - 10 Standleitungen nach FUB,TUB,ZIB
  - 7 PC's als Server (Drucker,Netz)
  - 1 Glasfaserumsetzer
  - 1 Token-Ring Anschluß IBM 3174

Die nächsten beiden Abbildungen geben einen Überblick über die Investitionen und die Jahresbetriebskosten. Die periodisch anfallenden Investitionen und die Personalkosten fallen dabei ins Auge. Der letzten Kostenart ist mehr Aufmerksamkeit zu widmen als bisher, da die installierte Rechen- und Netzleistung nur bei nur bei entsprechendem Personaleinsatz zu erzielen ist.

Investitions (DM/PC)- und Jahresbetriebskosten (DM/Jahr∗PC) im FB WiWiss der FU Berlin

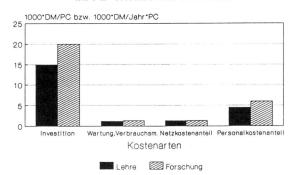

Jahresbetriebskosten-Verteilung (ohne Personalkosten) in DM/Jahr

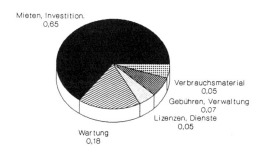

HJL 1989

6. Zusammenfassung und Perspektiven

Die bisherigen Ausführungen lassen sich wie folgt zusammenfassen:

Highlights
Die Workstation des Statistikers 1990...

- statt Terminals ⇒ *vernetzte Workstations*
- statt Adidas-Service ⇒ *Kommunikation*
- statt Hard- und Software-Hortung ⇒ *Server*
- statt Host-Kommandos bzw. -Menüsteuerung ⇒ aufgabenspezifische *Benutzer-Oberflächen* für die statistischen Tätigkeiten
- statt isolierter Softwaresysteme ⇒ *offene, standardisierte Subsysteme*
- statt Einzelplatzarbeit ⇒ *distributed computational statistics*

Blickt man in die 90er Jahre, so kann man folgendes prophezeien:

Quo vadis
Comp_Stat ?

- *Vereinheitlichte Systemschnittstellen* unter UNIX, SNA/SAA...?
- *Entwicklungssprachen* in 3GL, 4GL, ...?
- *Standardbetriebssystem(e)* wie DOS 4.x, OS-2, UNIX,...?
- Objekt-, matrix- oder wissensbasierte *Benutzeroberflächen...?*
- *Notational Tool* ist ...?

HJL 1989

Literatur:

G. Krüger (1987). Arbeitsplatzrechner in der akademischen Lehre. Informationstechnik it, 350-360.

H.-J. Lenz, G Haese, N. Apostolopoulos (1988). Der wissenschaftliche Arbeitsplatz. Arbeitsplatzrechner und deren Integration in ein abgestuftes DV-Versorgungskonzept. IBM Nachrichten special, 14-19.

Adressen

Afflerbach, Lothar, Dr., Technische Hochschule Darmstadt, Fachbereich Mathematik, Schloßgartenstraße 7, 6100 Darmstadt
Alt, Christian, Deutsches Jugendinstitut e.V., Freibadstraße 30, 8000 München 90
Altenburg, Hans-Peter, Dr., Fakultät für Klinische Medizin Mannheim der Universität Heidelberg, Theodor-Kutzer-Ufer, 6800 Mannheim 1
Andreß, Hans-Jürgen, Prof. Dr., Fakultät für Soziologie, Universität Bielefeld, Postfach 8640, 4800 Bielefeld 1
Arminger, Gerhard, Prof. Dr., Bergische Universität GHS Wuppertal, Postfach 100127, 5600 Wuppertal
Aufhauser, Elisabeth, Institut für Höhere Studien, Stumpergasse 56, A-1060 Wien
Becher, Heiko, Dr., Deutsches Krebsforschungszentrum, Postfach 101949, 6900 Heidelberg
Becker, Sylke, M.A., Forschungsgruppe Wahlen, Mannheim, N 7, 13 - 15, 6800 Mannheim 1
Bender, Donald, Deutsches Jugendinstitut e.V., Freibadstraße 30, 8000 München 90
Bentler, Peter M., Prof., University of California, Department of Psychology, Los Angeles, CA 90024-1563, USA
Biehler, Rolf, Dr., Universität Bielefeld, Institut für Didaktik der Mathematik, Postfach 8640, 4800 Bielefeld 1
Bien, Walter, Dr., Deutsches Jugendinstitut e.V., Freibadstraße 30, 8000 München 90
Blettner, Maria, University of Liverpool, Department of Community Health, P.O.Box 146, Liverpool L69 3BX, GB
Boucelham, J., University of Helsinki, Department of Statistics, Alaksanterinkatu 7, SF-00100 Helsinki
Bowman, Adrian W., Dr., University of Glasgow, Statistics Department, Glasgow G12 8QW GB
Böker, Fred, Prof. Dr. Dr., Institut für Statistik und Ökonometrie der Universität Göttingen, Platz der Göttinger Sieben 5, 3400 Göttingen
Buhler, Roald, P-STAT, Inc., P.O.Box AH, Princeton, New Jersey, USA
Cassidy, Carol, Zentrum für Umfragen, Methoden und Analysen (ZUMA) e.V., Postfach 122155, 6800 Mannheim 1
Craig, P., University of Dublin, Trinity College, Dublin 2/Irland
Dose, Bettina, Boehringer Mannheim GmbH, Abt. Biometrie und Medizinische Informatik, Sandhoferstraße 116, 6800 Mannheim 68
Eicker, F., Prof. Dr., Universität Dortmund, Fachbereich Statistik, Postfach 500 500, 4600 Dortmund 50
Engel, Bernhard, Dr., Zweites Deutsches Fernsehen, Postfach 4040, 6500 Mainz
Eymann, Angelika, Universität Konstanz, Fakultät für Wirtschaftswissenschaften und Statistik, Universitätsstraße 10, 7750 Konstanz
Fahrmeir, L., Prof. Dr., Universität Regensburg, Institut für Statistik, Universitätsstraße 31, 8400 Regensburg
Faulbaum, Frank, Dr., Zentrum für Umfragen, Methoden und Analysen (ZUMA) e.V., Postfach 122155, 6800 Mannheim 1
Fehres, Karin, Freie Universität Berlin, Institut für Sportwissenschaft, Königin-Luise-Str. 47, 1000 Berlin 33
Flache, Andreas, Im Winkel 17, 3155 Abbensen
Fröschl, Karl Anton, Dr., Universität Wien, Institut für Statistik und Informatik, Universitätsstraße 5/9, A-1010 Wien

Frost, H., Universität Regensburg, Institut für Statistik, Universitätsstraße 31, 8400 Regensburg
Gabler, Siegfried, Prof. Dr., Universität Mannheim, Seminar für Statistik, A 5, 6800 Mannheim 1
Geis, Alfons, Zentrum für Umfragen, Methoden und Analysen (ZUMA) e.V., Postfach 122155, 6800 Mannheim 1
Giegler, Helmut, PD Dr., Universität Bremen, Postfach 330 440, 2800 Bremen 33
Glas, Reinhold, Dr., Universität Dortmund, Fachbereich 15 - Institut für deutsche Sprache und Literatur, Postfach 500 500, 4600 Dortmund 50
Guiard, V., Forschungszentrum für Tierproduktion der AdL der DDR, DDR-2551 Dummerstorf-Rostock
Hartmann, Wolfgang M., Dr., SAS Institute Inc., P.O.Box 8000, Cary, NC 27512, USA
Haslett, J., University of Dublin, Trinity College, Dublin 2/Irland
Haux, Reinhold, Prof. Dr., Universität Heidelberg, Institut für Medizinische Biometrie und Medizinische Informatik, Im Neuenheimer Feld 400, 6900 Heidelberg
Held, Gerhard, SAS Institute GmbH, Postfach 10 53 07, 6900 Heidelberg 1
Heller, Wolf-Dieter, Dr., Institut für Statistik und Mathematische Wirtschaftstheorie, Postfach 6980, 7500 Karlsruhe 1
Hellwig, Otto, Dr., Universität Augsburg, Lehrstuhl für Volkswirtschaftslehre, Memminger Straße 14, 8900 Augsburg
Hennevogl, W., Universität Regensburg, Institut für Statistik, Universitätsstraße 31, 8400 Regensburg
Herold, Marcus, Technische Universität Berlin, Fachbereich 20 - Sekr. FR 6-9, Franklinstr. 28/29, 1000 Berlin 10
Hill, MaryAnn, Ph.D., University of Michigan, Department of Statistics, 419 South State Street, Ann Arbor, Michigan 48109-1027, USA
Hippler, Hans-J., Dr., Zentrum für Umfragen, Methoden und Analysen (ZUMA) e.V., Postfach 122155, 6800 Mannheim 1
Hörmann, Allmut, Gesellschaft für Strahlen- und Umweltforschung mbH (GSF), Ingolstädter Landstraße 1, 8042 Neuherberg
Hoffmeyer-Zlotnik, Jürgen H.-P., Dr., Zentrum für Umfragen, Methoden und Analysen (ZUMA) e.V., Postfach 122155, 6800 Mannheim 1
Holtbrügge, Werner, Dr., Boehringer Mannheim GmbH, Abt. Biometrie und Medizinische Informatik, Sandhoferstraße 116, 6800 Mannheim 68
Jöckel, Karl-Heinz, PD Dr., Bremer Institut für Präventionsforschung und Sozialmedizin (BIPS), St. Jürgen-Straße 1, 2800 Bremen 1
Jöreskog, Karl G., Prof. Dr., Uppsala University, Department of Statistics, P. O. Box 513, S-75120 Uppsala
Karczewski, Stephan, Sozialwissenschaftliche Informatik - EWH Koblenz -, Rheinau 3 - 4, 5400 Koblenz
Klein, Harald, M.A., Soester Str. 1, 4400 Münster
Klösgen, W., Dr., Gesellschaft für Mathematik und Datenverarbeitung mbH, Schloß Birlinghoven, 5205 Sankt Augustin 1
Knüsel, L., Prof. Dr., Universität München, Institut für Statistik, Geschwister-Scholl-Platz 1, 8000 München 22
Korn, Michael, Dr., Universität Münster, Institut für Ökonometrie und Wirtschaftsstatistik, Am Stadtgraben 9, 4400 Münster/W.
Kosfeld, Reinhold, Dr., Gesamthochschule Kassel, Fachbereich 7, Postfach 101380, 3500 Kassel
Kranert, T., Universität Regensburg, Institut für Statistik, Universitätsstraße 31, 8400 Regensburg
Kreibich, Volker, Prof. Dr., Universität Dortmund, Fachbereich Raumplanung, Postfach 500500, 4600 Dortmund 50

Kremser, Peter, Dr., Weissenburger Straße 30, 8000 München 80

Kuckartz, Udo, Dr., Freie Universität Berlin, Fachbereich Erziehungswissenschaft, Arnimallee 12, 1000 Berlin 33

Kübler, Jürgen, Universität Dortmund, Fachbereich Statistik, Postfach 500 500, 4600 Dortmund 50

Küsters, Ulrich, Dr., Scientific Center IBM, Via S. Maria, 67, I-56100 Pisa

Kukuk, Martin, Universität Konstanz, Fakultät für Wirtschaftswissenschaften und Statistik, Universitätsstraße 10, 7750 Konstanz

Lamers, Andreas, Dr., Universität Münster, Institut für Ökonometrie und Wirtschaftsstatistik, Am Stadtgraben 9, 4400 Münster/W.

Lehmacher, Walter, PD Dr., Gesellschaft für Strahlen- und Umweltforschung mbH (GSF), Ingolstädter Landstraße 1, 8042 Neuherberg

Lehmann, Ann, SAS Institute Inc., SAS Circle, Post Box 8000, Cary, NC 27512-8000, USA

Lenz, Hans-J., Prof. Dr., Freie Universität Berlin, Fachbereich Wirtschaftswissenschaft, Corrensplatz 2, 1000 Berlin 33

Lina, M. C. J., iec ProGamma, Kraneweg 8, NL-9718 JP Groningen

Lorenz, E., Deutsches Jugendinstitut e.V., Freibadstraße 30, 8000 München 90

Ludäscher, Peter, Dr., Institut für Geographie und Geoökologie II, Kaiserstraße 12, 7500 Karlsruhe

Marøy, Terje, NSD, Hans Holmboesgt. 22, N-5007 Bergen

Marschall, Franz, Universität des Saarlandes, Sportwissenschaftliches Institut, Im Stadtwald, 6600 Saarbrücken

Mathes, Rainer, Dr., Zentrum für Umfragen, Methoden und Analysen (ZUMA) e.V., Postfach 122155, 6800 Mannheim 1

Meier, Friedhelm, PD Dr., Forschungsgruppe IBIS, Hülsbergstraße 77a, 4630 Bochum

Mergenthaler, Erhard, Dr., Universität Ulm - Klinikum, Sektion Informatik in der Psychotherapie, Am Hochsträß 8, 7900 Ulm

Möhring, Michael, Ravensteynstraße 32, 5400 Koblenz

Mohler, Peter Ph., PD Dr., Zentrum für Umfragen, Methoden und Analysen (ZUMA) e.V., Postfach 122155, 6800 Mannheim

Molenaar, Ivo W., Prof. Dr., Rijksuniversiteit Groningen, Vakgroep Statistiek en Meettheorie, Oude Boteringestraat 23, NL-9712 GC Groningen

Mustonen, Seppo, Prof. Dr., University of Helsinki, Department of Statistics, Aleksanterinkatu 7, SF-00100 Helsinki

Naeve, Peter, Prof. Dr., Universität Bielefeld, Fakultät für Wirtschaftswissenschaften, Statistik und Informatik, Postfach 8640, 4800 Bielefeld 1

Nagel, Matthias, Dr., Forschungsinstitut für Hygiene und Mikrobiologie Bad Elster, Heinrich-Heine-Str. 12, DDR-9930 Bad Elster

Nürnberg, G., Forschungszentrum für Tierproduktion der AdL der DDR, DDR - 2551 Dummerstorf-Rostock

O'Brien, Carl M., Dr., Imperial College of Science, Technology and Medicine, Department of Mathematics, Huxley Building, 180 Queen's Gate, London SW7 2BZ, GB

Oldervoll, Jan, ISV, University of Tromsø, Boks 1040 Breivika, N-9000 Tromsø

Pokorny, Dan, Dr., Universität Ulm - Klinikum, Sektion Informatik in der Psychotherapie, Am Hochsträß 8, 7900 Ulm

Popping, R., Department of Behavioral Studies and Informatics, University of Groningen, NL-9712 Groningen

Rach, Wolfram, Universität Bielefeld, Institut für Didaktik der Mathematik, Postfach 8640, 4800 Bielefeld 1

Rasch, Dieter, Prof. Dr., Forschungszentrum für Tierproduktion der AdL der DDR, DDR-2551 Dummerstorf-Rostock

Ritter, Heinrich, Zentrum für Umfragen, Methoden und Analysen (ZUMA) e.V., Postfach 122155, 6800 Mannheim 1

Robinson, Derek R., School of Mathematical and Physical Sciences, University of Sussex, Falmer, Brighton, BN1 9QH, GB

Rosenkranz, Gerd, Dr., Hoechst AG, Pharma Forschung Informatik, H 790, 6230 Frankfurt am Main 80

Rost, Jürgen, PD Dr., Universität Kiel, Institut für die Pädagogik der Naturwissenschaften, Olshausenstraße 62, 2300 Kiel 1

Rudas, Tamas, Dr., TARKI, Frankel Leo U. 11, H-1027 Budapest

Rupprecht, R., Universität Karlsruhe, Rechenzentrum, Postfach 6980, 7500 Karlsruhe 1

Sawitzki, Günther, Dr., Universität Heidelberg, Institut für Angewandte Mathematik, Im Neuenheimer Feld 294, 6900 Heidelberg

Schach, Elisabeth, Universität Dortmund, Hochschulrechenzentrum, Postfach 500500, 4600 Dortmund 50

Schechtner, Oswald, ADIP-GRAZ, St. Veiter Anger 18, A-8046 Graz

Schepers, Andreas, Bergische Universität Gesamthochschule Wuppertal, Gauss-Straße 20, 5600 Wuppertal 1

Schimek, Michael G., Dr. Dr., Universitäts-Kinderklinik Graz, Auenbrugger Platz 30, A-8036 Graz

Schmidt, Vera, Hamelerer Weg 32, 5000 Köln 91

Schoenberg, Ronald J., Aptech Systems, Inc., 26250, 196th South East Place, Kent, WA 98042, USA

Schwarz, Norbert, PD Dr., Zentrum für Umfragen, Methoden und Analysen (ZUMA) e.V., Postfach 122155, 6800 Mannheim 1

Tettweiler, Manfred, Tettweiler GmbH Datenverarbeitung, Brahmsstraße 12, 8033 Krailling

Tettweiler, Wilfried, Tettweiler GmbH Datenverarbeitung, Brahmsstraße 12, 8033 Krailling

Troitzsch, Klaus G., Prof. Dr., EWH Koblenz, Sozialwissenschaftliche Informatik, Rheinau 3 - 4, 5400 Koblenz

Uehlinger, Hans-Martin, Dr., Schmiedgasse 15, CH-9000 St. Gallen

Unwin, A., University of Dublin, Trinity College, Dublin 2/Irland

Wackerow, Joachim, Zentrum für Umfragen, Methoden und Analysen (ZUMA) e.V., Postfach 122155, 6800 Mannheim 1

Wicke, Günter A., Dr. Bundesanstalt für Straßenwesen (BASt), Brüderstraße 53, 5060 Bergisch Gladbach 1

Wills, Graham, University of Dublin, Trinity College, Dublin 2/Irland

Wittenberg, Reinhard, Dr., Universität Erlangen-Nürnberg, Lehrstuhl für Soziologie, Findelgasse 7-9, 8500 Nürnberg 1

Zaus, Michael, Dr., Universität Oldenburg, Institut für Kognitionsforschung, Ammerländer Heerstr. 114-118, 2900 Oldenburg

Zelle, Karl, Dr., ADIP-GRAZ, St. Veiter Anger 18, A-8046 Graz

Zimmermann, E. J., VGSPS Vertriebsgesellschaft mbH, Goetheallee 19, 5300 Bonn 3

Statistik-Software

Fortschritte der Statistik-Software 1
4. Konferenz über die wissenschaftliche Anwendung von Statistik-Software, Heidelberg, 1987

Herausgegeben von Dr. Frank Faulbaum und lic. phil. Hans-Martin Uehlinger, Zentrum für Umfragen, Methoden und Analysen (ZUMA), Mannheim

1988. X, 595 S., 106 Abb., 30 Tab., kt. DM 76,–

Inhaltsübersicht: Statistik-Programme zur Datenanalyse, Datenerhebung und zum Datenmanagement: Anwendungen, Vergleiche und Bewertungen · Statistik-Pakete im PC-Bereich · Expertensysteme · Individuelle Modellierung mit Statistik-Software · Exploratorische Datenanalyse · Skalierung und Klassifikation · Simulation · Spezialsoftware für besondere Anwendungsgebiete · Kartographie und geographische Informationssysteme · Statistische und DV-Aspekte linguistischer Datenverarbeitung

Die 4. Konferenz über die wissenschaftliche Anwendung von Statistik-Software fand unter internationaler Beteiligung im März 1987 in Heidelberg statt. Das wissenschaftliche Programm, der interdisziplinär orientierten Konferenz fand bei der an innovativen Entwicklungen auf dem Gebiet der Statistik-Software interessierten Öffentlichkeit großen Zuspruch. Die in den 60 Beiträgen dieses Konferenzbandes angesprochenen Themen spiegeln die gegenwärtige Situation der wissenschaftlichen Anwendung von Statistik-Software wider und informieren über sich andeutende zukünftige Entwicklungen auf diesem Gebiet.

Bitte fordern Sie vom Verlag, Postfach 72 01 43, D-7000 Stuttgart 70, das kostenlose Gesamtverzeichnis „Datenverarbeitung und Statistik" an.

Preisänderungen vorbehalten.

Statistik-Software
3. Konferenz über die wissenschaftliche Anwendung von Statistik-Software, 1985

Herausgegeben von Dr. Walter Lehmacher und Allmut Hörmann, Gesellschaft für Strahlen- und Umweltforschung (GSF)/Institut für Medizinische Informatik und Systemforschung (Medis), Neuherberg

1986. XIV, 399 S., kt. DM 58,–

Inhaltsübersicht: Vergleich von Programmsystemen · GLIM-Generalized Linear Models · Pfadmodelle mit latenten Variablen · Software für die Analyse von Verweildauern · Software für Biologisch-Medizinische Anwendungen in APL · Software für Textanalyse · Verschiedenes · Neuere Entwicklungen allgemeiner Statistiksoftwarepakete · Kurzinformationen der Hersteller

Dieses Buch bietet Beiträge über die Anwendung von Statistik-Software in denen verschiedene wissenschaftliche Bereiche berücksichtigt werden, besonders Programmvergleiche und -bewertungen, Übersichtsreferate zu Software für spezielle statistische Fragestellungen sowie die Darstellung von Neuerungen bei den eingeführten Softwaresystemen. Das Spektrum reicht von allgemeinen Übersichten zu speziellen Themen, geordnet nach größeren Themenkreisen.
Ergänzend bietet das Buch Berichte seitens der Software Hersteller über Produktneuerungen sowie Kurzinformationen zum Stand der verfügbaren Produkte.
Das Buch beweist erneut, daß Statistiker aus verschiedenen Anwendungsgebieten ein breites gemeinsames Spektrum an Methoden haben und entsprechende Software benötigen, und daß außerdem die verschiedenen Disziplinen sich gegenseitig anregen und viel voneinander lernen können.

GUSTAV FISCHER VERLAG   Stuttgart New York

Aktuelle Literatur für EDV-Anwender

Schuemer/Ströhlein/Gogolok
Datenverarbeitung und statistische Auswertung mit SAS
SAS-Versionen 5 (Großrechner) und 6 (PC)
Band I · Einführung in das Programmsystem, Datenmanagement und Auswertung
1990. Etwa 450 S., kt. etwa DM 58,–
Band II · Komplexe statistische Analyseverfahren
1990. Etwa 440 S., kt. etwa DM 58,–

Frenzel/Hermann
Statistik mit SPSS^x
Eine Einführung nach M. J. Norušis
1989. X, 259 S., zahlr. Abb. u. Tab., kt. DM 54,–

Schubö/Uehlinger
SPSS^x
Handbuch der Programmversion 2.2
Autorisierte deutsche Bearbeitung des SPSS^x User's Guide. 1986. XVI, 659 S., kt. DM 58,–

Uehlinger
SPSS/PC+
Benutzerhandbuch Band 1
2. Aufl. 1990. Etwa 380 S., kt. etwa DM 52,–

Küffner/Wittenberg
Datenanalysesysteme für statistische Auswertungen
Eine Einführung in SPSS, BMDP und SAS
1985. VIII, 289 S., zahlr. Tab. u. graph. Darst, kt. DM 36,–

Küsters/Arminger
Programmieren in GAUSS
Eine Einführung in das Programmieren statistischer und numerischer Algorithmen
1989. VIII, 315 S., 25 Abb., kt. DM 68,–

Pfeifer
Statistik-Auswertungen mit SPSS^x und BMDP
Ein Einstieg in die beiden Programmpakete
1988. VIII, 216 S., kt. DM 29,80
(UTB 1497)

Zöfel
Statistik in der Praxis
2. Aufl. 1988. XII, 426 S., 48 Abb., 118 Tab., 22 Taf., kt. DM 32,80

Hübler
Ökonometrie
1989. XII, 342 S., 15 Abb., kt. DM 39,80
(UTB 1538)

v. d. Lippe
Wirtschaftsstatistik
3. Aufl. 1985. XII, 324 S., 74 Übersichten, 5 Tab., 4 Abb., kt. DM 23,80
(UTB 209)

Meier
Prozeßforschung in den Sozialwissenschaften
Anwendung zeitreihenanalytischer Methoden
1988. XII, 174 S., zahlr. Abb., kt. DM 58,–

Preisänderungen vorbehalten

GUSTAV FISCHER VERLAG   Stuttgart New York

TEXTPACK PC

Das System für die computerunterstützte Inhaltsanalyse

- Automatische Vercodung nach Benutzerspezifikationen

- Umfangreiche Optionen zur Textbeschreibung
    - Worthäufigkeiten
    - Index
    - KWIC
    - Vokabularvergleich

- Verbindungen zu den gängigen Statistik- und Textverarbeitungssystemen

- Vollständig Menü-gesteuert

Nähere Informationen zu TEXTPACK PC erhalten Sie bei:
ZUMA
Cornelia Züll oder Peter Mohler
Postfach 12 21 55
D-6800 Mannheim 1
Telefon: 0621/180040

P-STAT Statistisches Informationsanalyse-System

Die erste Programmversion des P-STAT Systems wurde bereits Anfang der sechziger Jahre am Rechenzentrum der Universität Princeton entwickelt. Umfang und Leistungsfähigkeit der P-STAT Software ließen Anfang 1979 den Vertrieb und die Weiterentwicklung des Systems durch ein kommerzielles Unternehmen erfolgversprechend erscheinen. So wurde die P-STAT Inc., Princeton, N.J., ins Leben gerufen. P-STAT wird heute weltweit von kommerziellen Unternehmen jeder Art, Universitäten und anderen Bildungseinrichtungen sowie Behörden und Agenturen benutzt. Die VGSPS mbH ist die Repräsentanz der P-STAT Inc. für die Länder Deutschland, Österreich und die Schweiz.

Der Erfolg des P-STAT Systems liegt sicherlich auch begründet in seiner Benutzerfreundlichkeit. Die P-STAT Steuersprache ist leicht zu behalten und anzuwenden, da sie viele Züge einer natürlichen Sprache besitzt. Ein weiterer Vorteil von P-STAT ist, daß es auf rund 70 verschiedenen Rechnertypen vom Großrechner bis zum PC mit absolut identischer Sprachsyntax und mit selben Funktionsumfang läuft. Natürlich können auf dem Großrechner mehr Variablen pro Datei (3000) verwaltet werden als auf dem PC (300).

P-STAT – Leistungs- und Funktionsumfang

P-STAT verfügt über folgende statistische Verfahren:
- deskriptive Statistik und Semi-Grafik
- t-Test
- nicht-parametrische Verfahren
- Korrelation
- nicht-lineare Regression
- Varianzanalyse
- Clusteranalyse
- Faktorenanalyse
- Diskriminanzanalyse
- explorative Datenanalyse
- statistische Qualitätskontrolle
- Trendanalyse
- ARIMA-Zeitreihenanalyse
- präsentationsfähige Tabellen
- Überlebensraten (SURVIVAL)
- kanonische Korrelation
- Stichprobenbalancierung

P-STAT enthält fernerhin eine sehr umfassende Prozedur zur Erstellung von Berichtslisten, eine eigene sehr mächtige Programmiersprache mit Möglichkeiten der Matrixverknüpfung sowie ein Dateimanagementsystem, das es erlaubt Daten aus einer Vielzahl von Dateien auch unterschiedlicher Datenstruktur zu lesen und gemeinsam zu verarbeiten. **Für PC's- und UNIX-Systeme ist eine Menü-Oberfläche verfügbar.**
Zusätzlich zum Dateimanagement-System gibt es die Zusatzoption P-RADE, ein P-STAT-eigenes Datenbanksystem, das speziell auf die Belange der statistischen Datenverarbeitung zugeschnitten ist.

Schnittstellen zu anderen Anwendungsprogrammen

Eine spezielle Schnittstelle zu Mikrocomputerprogrammen – das DIF-Interface – erlaubt es Daten und auch Variablenbezeichnungen zwischen P-STAT und Programmen, die ebenfalls ein DIF-Interface besitzen, in einfacher Weise zu transferieren. Ferner kann P-STAT BMDP-, SAS und SPSS-Dateien lesen und schreiben. Selbstverständlich kann P-STAT auch mit jeder Software kommunizieren, die Daten in ASCII- bzw. EBCDIC-Format liest und schreibt. Datenbankschnittstellen sind vorhanden zu dBASE, Informix, Oracle. Ferner können verschiedenste Grafik-Syteme durch P-STAT angesteuert werden.

P-STAT für Großrechner, Mini- und Mikrocomputer

P-STAT läuft auf rund 70 verschieden Computersystemen, darunter Apollo, Areta, AT&T, Compaq, CDC, Convergent Technologies, Cromemco, Data General, DEC, GOULD, Harris, HP, IBM, ICL, NCR, PCS Cadmus, Perkin Elmer, Plexus, Prime, Pyramid, SIEMENS, Sperry, SUN, Zenith u. a.

Das P-STAT Angebot: Bestellen Sie P-STAT zur Probe!

Sie können P-STAT jederzeit testen. Für PC- und verschiedene UNIX-Systeme gibt es ein Echtzeit-Demosystem. Für Großrechner- und Minisysteme wird eine 3-monatige Testinstallation angeboten. Die Gebühren hierfür überschreiten nicht die Bereitstellungskosten.

Service und Wartung

Selbstverständlich steht allen P-STAT Anwendern bei Fragen oder Anwenderproblemen das VGSPS-Servicebüro in Bonn jederzeit zur Verfügung. In den meisten Fällen aber können sich P-STAT Anwender leicht selbst helfen, denn das P-STAT System verfügt über eine sehr ausführliche on-line Hilfsfunktion. Außerdem gelangt mit dem Programm ein umfangreicher Satz an Handbüchern zum ausführlichen Nachlesen sowie ein knapp gefaßtes kleines Handbuch zum schnellen Nachschlagen zur Auslieferung. Ferner werden alle registrierten P-STAT Anwender ständig mit Updates versorgt und erhalten die P-STAT Benutzerzeitschrift P-STATUS und P-statE.

Servicebüro: Pützchens Chaussee 60, 5300 Bonn 3
☏ 02 28/46 00 38/39, Fax 02 28/46 38 04

Vertriebsbüro:
Martin-Luther-Str. 22, 5650 Solingen 1